CONFRONTING DISCRIMINATION AND INEQUALITY IN
CHINA

Edited by Errol P. Mendes and Sakunthala Srighanthan

CONFRONTING DISCRIMINATION AND INEQUALITY IN
CHINA

Chinese and **Canadian** Perspectives

University of Ottawa Press

LIBRARY AND ARCHIVES CANADA
CATALOGUING IN PUBLICATION

Confronting discrimination and inequality in
China : Chinese and Canadian perspectives / edited by
Errol Mendes and Sakanthula Srighanthan.

(Actexpress, 1480-4743)
ISBN 978-0-7766-0709-2

1. Discrimination—China. 2. Equality—China.
3. Human rights—China. 4. Human rights advocacy—China.
5. China—Social policy. 6. China—Social conditions—2000-.
7. China—Social conditions—1976-2000. I. Mendes, Errol
II. Srighanthan, Sakanthula, 1950- III. Series: Actexpress

HN733.5.C66 2009   305.0951   C2009-900463-1

The University of Ottawa Press
542 King Edward Avenue
Ottawa, Ontario K1N 6N5
www.press.uottawa.ca

uOttawa

The University of Ottawa Press acknowledges with gratitude the support extended to its publishing list by Heritage Canada through its Book Publishing Industry Development Program, by the Canada Council for the Arts, by the Canadian Federation for the Humanities and Social Sciences through its Aid to Scholarly Publications Program, by the Social Sciences and Humanities Research Council, and by the University of Ottawa.

The University of Ottawa Press also acknowledges with gratitude the support extended to this publication by the Canadian International Development Agency (CIDA).

Table of Contents

List of Contributors...viii

Editors' Note.. xv

Acknowledgements.. xvi

Introduction
ERROL P. MENDES 1

PART ONE
DISCRIMINATION AGAINST RURAL AND MIGRANT WORKERS

Chapter One
Prosperity at the Expense of Equality: Migrant Workers are Falling Behind
in Urban China's Rise
WENRAN JIANG...16

Chapter Two
The Historical Causes of China's Dual Social Structure
GONG RENREN 30

Chapter Three
Restoring Private Ownership of Rural Lands to Safeguard
the Basic Rights of Farmers
WANG KEQIN 70

Chapter Four
Changing the Policy Paradigm on Chinese Migrant Workers
CUI CHUANYI AND CUI XIAOLI...99

Chapter Five
Chinese Farmers' Right of Access to Judicial Relief: An Investigative Report
into Forest Land Expropriation Claims by Hebei Farmer Wen Shengcun
WANG XINAN 129

Chapter Six
China's War on its Environment and Farmers' Rights: A Study of Shanxi Province
ZHANG YULIN...149

PART TWO
DISCRIMINATION AGAINST WOMEN

Chapter Seven
The Gendered Reality of Migrant Workers in Globalizing China
CHEN LANYAN (LANYAN CHEN) 186

Chapter Eight
An Analysis of Rural Women's Entitlements to Land and Other Property
LIANG JIANGUO AND XU WEIHUA..208

Chapter Nine
Systemic Discrimination and Gender Inequality: A Life Cycle Approach
to Girls' and Women's Rights
COLLEEN SHEPPARD 232

PART THREE
DISCRIMINATION AGAINST THE DISABLED

Chapter Ten
A Study of the Legislative Inhibition of Discrimination on the Basis of Disability
WANG ZHIJIANG..246

PART FOUR
DISCRIMINATION AGAINST THOSE LIVING WITH HIV/AIDS

Chapter Eleven
The Application of International and Regional Instruments to
HIV-Related Discrimination in China and Southeast Asia
DAVID PATTERSON 276

Chapter Twelve
Gender and HIV/AIDS: Understanding and Addressing Stigma and
Discrimination Among Women and Girls
BARBARA CLOW AND LINDA SNYDER 292

Chapter Thirteen
Promoting the Right to Education for AIDS Orphans and
Vulnerable Children (OVC): A Study on Anti-Discrimination
MA YINGHUA, DING SUQIN, WANG CHAO, AND YUAN MENGYAO 312

Chapter Fourteen
The State of Life and Survival Strategies of AIDS-Infected Rural Women:
An Analysis Based on Field Investigations in Selected Areas of Henan
    Qin Mingrui and Lai Xiaole 362

PART FIVE
DISCRIMINATION AGAINST MINORITIES

Chapter Fifteen
The Canadian Constitution and Charter of Rights and Freedoms:
A Global Template for Minority Rights?
    Errol P. Mendes 396

Chapter Sixteen
Indigenous Peoples and Hunting Rights
    Scott Simon 405

List of Contributors

CANADIAN CONTRIBUTORS

BARBARA CLOW:

Barbara Clow is Executive Director of the Atlantic Centre of Excellence for Women's Health and Associate Professor Research in the Faculty of Health Professions at Dalhousie University, Halifax. In the past ten years, Dr. Clow has pursued a program of research, publication and policy work on diverse aspects of women's health, such as the gendered dimensions of health care reform in Canada; health implications for low income, immigrant, homeless, rural and African Canadian women; the role of gender in the HIV/AIDS pandemic; issues related to reproductive health; and the impact of women's unpaid caregiving work. She has a Ph.D. in the history of medicine from the University of Toronto.

WENRAN JIANG:

Wenran Jiang is Associate Professor of Political Science and the founding Director of the China Institute at the University of Alberta. He is a Senior Fellow at the Asia Pacific Foundation of Canada and a Working Group member of the Canadian International Council's Canada-China relations program. He has organized a number of major conferences on Canada-China relations. Dr. Jiang has written extensively on Chinese politics and foreign relations and his op-ed articles and comments appear regularly in Canadian and international newspapers.

ERROL P. MENDES:

Errol P. Mendes is a lawyer, author, professor and has been an advisor to corporations, governments, civil society groups and the United Nations. His teaching, research and consulting interests include public and private sector governance, conflict resolution, global governance, international business and trade law, constitutional law, international law (including anti-terrorism laws and policies) and human rights law and policy. He has been a project leader for conflict resolution, governance and justice projects in China, Thailand, Indonesia, Brazil, El Salvador and Sri Lanka. Since 1979 Professor Mendes has taught at law faculties across the country, including at the University of Alberta, the University of Western Ontario, and, since 1992, at the University of Ottawa.

DAVID PATTERSON:

David Patterson is a legal consultant, based in Montreal. He holds an LL.M. degree (human rights) from McGill University and a M.Sc. (public policy and management) from the University of London School of Oriental and African Studies. In 1993 he was a founding member of the Canadian HIV/AIDS Legal Network. Since 1994 he has specialized in legal and policy responses to HIV in developing countries, working with the UNDP, UNAIDS and other agencies. He was the Director of the Legal Network's International Program in 2001-2003 and initiated and managed programs to support legal responses to HIV in East Africa and the Caribbean. From 2004-2008 he was Team Leader for Policy for the Canada South East Asia Regional HIV/AIDS Programme, focusing on HIV and migration in Cambodia, Laos, Thailand and Vietnam. His first visit to China was in 1982, when he taught English for several months at the Hangzhou Electronic Engineering Institute. In 2007 he returned to Kunming at the invitation of the International Development Law Organization for the first workshop in China on HIV for practicing lawyers, law teachers and law students.

COLLEEN SHEPPARD:
Colleen Sheppard teaches at the Faculty of Law of McGill University. She is also the Research Director for the McGill Centre for Human Rights and Legal Pluralism. Her teaching and research focus on Canadian and comparative constitutional law, equality rights and feminist legal theory. Professor Sheppard completed her Honours B.A. and LL.B. degrees at the University of Toronto and her LL.M. at Harvard Law School. Prior to commencing her teaching career, she worked as a law clerk with former Chief Justice Brian Dickson of the Supreme Court of Canada. Colleen Sheppard has also been active in public interest work. She served as a Commissioner on the Quebec Human Rights and Youth Rights Commission from 1991-1996 and has been a consultant with the federal Department of Justice, the National Judicial Institute, the Canadian Human Rights Commission, the Ontario Métis Aboriginal Association and the International Labour Organization.

SCOTT SIMON:
Scott Simon is Associate Professor in the Department of Sociology and Anthropology at the University of Ottawa. He has been working on the Canada-China International Human Rights Implementation Project of the University of Ottawa and Peking University since 2005, with a focus on minority rights. A specialist in the anthropology of development, he is author of *Sweet and Sour: Life Worlds of Taipei Women Entrepreneurs* (2003) and *Tanners of Taiwan: Life Strategies and National Culture* (2005), as well as numerous book chapters and articles. Since 2004, he has been conducting research on development and human rights for the indigenous peoples of Taiwan, where he works with the hunters of the Taroko Nation. He is currently writing a book on that subject.

LINDA SNYDER:
Linda Snyder is the Knowledge Exchange Manager at the Atlantic Centre of Excellence for Women's Health (ACEWH). She has coordinated projects related to social and

economic inclusion and exclusion, lone mothers and farm family health and a range of research and policy projects that focus on knowledge brokering, social justice and women's health and well-being. Linda has more than 25 years of experience with international non-governmental organizations, both overseas and in Canada.

CHINESE CONTRIBUTORS

CHEN LANYAN (LANYAN CHEN):

Lanyan Chen was the Gender Advisor for Northeast Asia appointed by the United Nations Development Fund for Women (UNIFEM) from 1998-2003. She holds a Ph.D. in Sociology (with an emphasis on political economy) from the University of British Columbia. She taught gender and international development and gender in family and organizations at the University of Victoria for many years before joining UNIFEM. She has published research on poverty alleviation and women's cooperatives in China. Her research on healthcare policy reforms and HIV/AIDS in China has been published by the journal *Feminist Economics* in two special issues: one on Gender, China and the WTO in July 2007 and another on Sexuality, HIV/AIDS and Economic Development in September 2008. Her recent book, *Gender and Chinese Development: Towards an Equitable Society,* has been included in the book series of the International Association for Feminist Economics. She is now a Professor and Foreign Expert at the Institute of Gender and Social Development at the Tianjin Normal University of China.

CUI CHUANYI:

Cui Chuanyi received his Bachelor's in International Politics from Fudan University, Shanghai. Cui worked for eleven years in Chu County, Anhui Province, participating in agricultural reforms, after which he worked in the General Office of Anhui Province and at the Country Policy Research Centre of the Chinese Communist Party. Presently, he is a researcher in the Country Economy Department of the Development Research Centre of the State Council and an Associate Secretary-General at the Institute for Country Labour Force Development. His research focuses on the areas of agricultural management systems, wholesale markets, agricultural protectionism and revolutions in agricultural technology. Since 1993, he has devoted himself to researching the movement of the rural labour force. Cui has published dozens of papers and a book, *The Migration of Chinese Peasants: Institutional Innovation for Farmer's Employment and Citizenry.* He is also the co-author of *Reforms of Chinese Counties and Cities, Employment of Peasants and China's Modernization, Out of Duality: Research on Peasants' Employment and Business Starting,* as well as numerous other chapters and articles. Cui has been awarded the National Award for Development Research as well as the National Award for Technology Advancement in recognition of his outstanding research.

CUI XIAOLI:

Cui Xiaoli received his undergraduate education at the Beijing Foreign Language Institute in English. Following graduation, he worked at the Beijing Capital Airport until 1980, following which he studied at the Beijing Agriculture University (now the China Agriculture University) for three years and obtained a Master's. He then worked as an editor at the Agricultural Public House for six months, after which he was appointed Secretary in the Ministry of Agriculture of the People's Republic of China, a position he held for more than a year and a half. From 1985-1990, he worked in the Rural Development Research Centre of the State Council as a research member; he then went to the Development Research Centre of the State Council to be a Division Director until 1998. In 1997, Cui became a Senior Researcher. The main focus of his research is the relationship between rural and urban development. Over the last fifteen years he has published no fewer than 50 reports and essays.

DING SUQIN:

Ding Suqin holds a Bachelor's in preventive medicine from the Soochow University (2005) and a Master's in child and adolescent health from Peking University (2008). Her research interests are focused on child and adolescent development and health education on HIV/AIDS in schools.

GONG RENREN:

Gong Renren has been Director of the Research Centre for Human Rights at Peking University Law School since 1997. He holds a Doctorate of Laws from Hokkaido University in Japan. He has taught at the Peking University Law School since 1988, becoming a Professor in 1993. He was a Visiting Scholar at Columbia University Law School in 1995, a Visiting Professor at Kyoto University Law Faculty in 1997, and a Visiting Professor at the Kyushu University Law Faculty from 2005-2006. His publications include *Perspective of Japanese Judicial System* (1993) and *A Comparative Study of State Immunity* (1994). He has contributed to numerous publications concerned with human rights.

LAI XIAOLE:

Lai Xiaole is a Lecturer in Sociology at the College of Shenzhen.

LIANG JIANGUO:

Liang Jianguo is a Senior Researcher in the Department of Rights and Interests of the All-China Women's Federation. Liang's experience working for the All-China Women's Federation include successive posts at the General Office, the National Working Committee on Children and Women under the State Council, and the Department of Rights and Interests. During her tenure with the Federation, she participated in the drafting, publishing, and implementation of the National Program for Women's

Development. She has served as a coordinator between the central leadership of the Communist Party of China and various departments of the State Council. For the past thirteen years she has dedicated herself to protecting women's rights through the revision of several laws and policies.

MA YINGHUA:

Ma Yinghua is Deputy Director at the Institute of Child and Adolescent Health at the Peking University. In addition, she is an Associate Professor, a part-time consultant for the UNICEF Office for China on life skills and education, a Councilor for the Ministry of Education's National Teacher Training Centre for AIDS Education, the National Program Consultant for the Children and Youth Science Centre, a member of the Experts Committee of the China Children's and Teenagers' Safety-Health Growth Plan, and a Councilor for the Association of Smoke and Health. Ma's research focuses on health education in school, with a particular focus on education for AIDS prevention and life skills development. As a core research member, she has participated in developing the *Thematic Education Guidelines for HIV/AIDS Prevention Education for Primary and Secondary School Students* of the Ministry of Education and has conducted research for the Thematic Education Wall Map for HIV/AIDS Prevention Education. She is also the chief editor for several teaching materials on AIDS prevention, and has published several academic papers about school health education on AIDS prevention and life skill education in national journals.

QIN MINGRUI:

Qin Mingrui obtained his Ph.D. in 1992 from the University of Tübingen, Germany. He is currently a Professor in the Department of Sociology at Peking University.

WANG CHAO:

Wang Chao graduated from the Department of Public Health, Peking University in 1981 with a Doctor of Medicine degree. Her major research focus has been on HIV/AIDS and health education in schools.

WANG KEQIN:

Wang Keqin is Chief Reporter for the *China Economic Times*. He is also a Visiting Scholar at Hong Kong University and supervisor of graduate studies at the China Youth University for Political Sciences.

WANG XINAN:

Wang Xinan graduated from the Law School of Peking University in 2005 with a Master's of International Law. Wang has substantial working experience in local court and government. He is presently the managing partner of the Guangda Law Firm in Beijing.

WANG ZHIJIANG:

Wang Zhijiang holds a Master of Laws and is a Director at the Association for Research on Social Law of the China Law Society. He is currently serving in the Laws and Regulations Section under the Department of Rights Protection of the China's Disabled Persons' Association. Wang has devoted his research efforts to bankruptcy law, law of procedures and legal protection of disabled persons. He has participated in the formulation and passage of several laws. Through his work in the formulation and revision of laws, including the *Law on the Protection of Disabled Persons* and the *Civil Servant Law*, he has actively contributed towards safeguarding the rights and interests of disabled persons. Wang was a member of the Chinese delegation to the United Nations Ad Hoc Committee on the Convention on Persons with Disabilities, participating in the discussions and negotiations that led to the Committee's recommendations. He has also translated several books on topics including bankruptcy, the rights of disabled persons and the economics of civil procedures.

XU WEIHUA:

Xu Weihua was formerly Senior Research Coordinator at the Department of Rights and Interests of the All-China Women's Federation. She is currently serving as Vice-President of the Centre for Public Policy Studies and Legal Services at the University of Science and Technology, Beijing. For more than twenty years she has committed herself to safeguarding the rights and interests of women and children. She has participated in the drafting, formulation and revision of several laws, regulations and related policies in order to protect the rights of women, and handled hundreds of cases involving the violations of the rights of women and children. Xu has also served with several professional organizations, including as Secretary-General of the Sorority of Chinese Lawyers, Director of the Association of Women Lawyers, Standing Director of the Association for Research on Marriage Law, Counselor at the Beijing Association of Mental Health, as well as an elected Deputy to the People's Congress of Dongcheng District, Beijing. In 2003, Xu became Vice-President of the Anti-Domestic Violence Network. In early 2005, she was retained as Vice-President of the Centre for Women's Law and Legal Services of Peking University. In addition to performing her other duties, Xu has handled several high profile cases, through which she has gained invaluable insight for her theoretical research on legal and social issues.

YUAN MENGYAO:

Yuan Mengyao holds a Bachelor's in Chemical and Biomolecular Engineering from the Hong Kong University of Science and Technology. Her research interests are focused on health development of school adolescents. In 2006 she was nominated to be the "Unite for Children, Unite against AIDS" Youth Ambassador for UNICEF and the Youth League.

ZHANG YULIN:

Zhang Yulin holds a Doctorate in Agricultural Economics from the Graduate School of Agriculture at Kyoto University. She is currently a Professor in the Department of Sociology at Nanjing University. Zhang has also worked as a journalist for the Chinese *Xinhua Daily* from 1985-1992.

Editors' Note

The essays by Chinese authors in this book are significant for demonstrating the diversity of thinking and independence of thought displayed by some academics in China today; they are consequently of great importance in fostering intercultural dialogue and supportive engagement with the leading members of Chinese civil society. They are also important for providing a lens through which an English-speaking readership – academic or otherwise – may learn about the tremendous challenges occurring alongside the process of China's modernization through the voices of those closest to the frontiers of human rights violations and systemic discrimination occurring there today.

Translation of these essays into English and subsequent editing, however, were difficult. Readers should also note that the Chinese academic writing style differs from the North American academic writing style in numerous respects. The editors decided not to substantially alter this style while still attempting to generate some uniformity between the contributions and accessible texts. We hope that the published versions do justice to the quality of the original Chinese essays and we apologize in advance for any discrepancies that may have occurred in the process of translating them into English and preparing them for publication by the University of Ottawa Press.

Acknowledgements

This publication is a result of extensive grassroots research conducted as part of a Canadian International Development Agency (CIDA) funded project, implemented by a joint partnership of the University of Ottawa's Faculty of Law, and the Peking University's Research Centre for Human Rights. The editors would like to acknowledge with gratitude the funding provided by the CIDA which made this publication possible.

This could not have been accomplished without the commitment, cooperation and hard work of our Chinese colleagues and friends at Peking University in Beijing. In particular, our deepest thanks and admiration as always go to Gong Renren and Bai Guimei, the courageous leaders of the Research Centre for Human Rights and champions in promoting human rights and equality in China today. The editors would also like to thank the many researchers in China who made valuable contributions to this book.

The editors would like to express their sincere thanks to Yingliang Huang for his invaluable and tireless assistance in proofreading, translating and formatting the manuscript. Appreciation is also due to Sarah Reisler and Yu Mai for their assistance with editing, which helped us a great deal in finalizing the manuscript. We are also grateful to the Canadian contributors who shared their time, knowledge and expertise for the benefit of promoting anti-discrimination against vulnerable groups of people.

Sakunthala Srighanthan would like to thank Errol P. Mendes for his leadership, guidance, encouragement and expertise, without which the project or this publication could not have been a success.

Errol P. Mendes also acknowledges the great contribution, dedication, and collegiality that Sakunthala Srighanthan has made to the entire project that has resulted in this book. Without her patience and attention to detail this book would not have been possible.

Introduction

Errol P. Mendes

This book is the result of three years of research and dialogue between leading intellectuals from China and Canada, organized by the Research Centre for Human Rights of Peking University and the Faculty of Law of the University of Ottawa. The results of this research and dialogue, contained in this book, focus on the overwhelming social challenges and the discrimination against certain sectors of the population that face China, the planet's most populous country. The project was funded by the Canadian International Development Agency (CIDA).

The research that resulted in the chapters of this book focuses on the following four areas: (1) the social challenges and discrimination facing the vast number of migrant workers moving to the urban centres, including the discriminatory impact of environmental degradation on rural inhabitants by industry as well as the corrupt, improper and often illegal expropriations of rural inhabitants' land; (2) the particular challenges and discrimination facing women often left behind in rural areas, including their struggle to gain equality with their male counterparts in the cities; (3) discrimination against the tens of millions of Chinese who are disabled and until recently did not have legislative protection; and (4) the challenges and discrimination facing the growing numbers of persons afflicted with HIV/AIDS in a society that still has many taboos related to the infection.

In addition, this book contains one paper on the social challenges and discrimination facing ethnic minorities and aboriginal peoples in Taiwan. While the Chinese participants were also eager to discuss the challenges facing minorities on the mainland, the written output of the research by Chinese participants had to be limited given the immense sensitivity of the subject. Even in this context, however, the chapters from each of the targeted areas of research show a remarkable level of independence of thought and, indeed, courage, and combined offer a blistering critique of the way in which the Chinese government is attempting to deal with new social challenges and accompanying forms of discrimination.

The purpose of the chapters by Canadian researchers is that of offering international perspectives on some of major social challenges facing China today. The hope of the dialogue and its written products is that of provoking a sustainable debate, at least in academic circles, on what key issues are to be tackled if progress is to be made on the four areas of social challenge outlined above, and their accompanying forms of discrimination.

This introduction briefly describes the research in each of the four areas, and attempts to sketch some preliminary conclusions.

A. THE SOCIAL CHALLENGES AND ACCOMPANYING ISSUES OF DISCRIMINATION AGAINST RURAL AND MIGRANT WORKERS AND INHABITANTS.

The greatest migration of people in human history has gone on relatively unnoticed by the world through the second half of the 20th century and into the first decade of the 21st. It is that of the estimated 130 to 200 million migrant workers from the rural areas of China who have been moving to the industrialized urban centres in search of jobs, and, for those who bring their families with them, better education and prospects for their children. No country in the world could cope with such vast numbers flooding into cities that are unprepared for them. Other countries such as Brazil and Kenya have also faced immense challenges when tens of thousands of rural workers have flooded into the cities. The result can be burgeoning slums where the majority live in desperate poverty with little social or physical infrastructure; these slums can in turn become breeding grounds for crime and drugs.

In China, however, we are seeing a variation of the desperate situation that such migrants face. Wenran Jiang, Acting Director of the China Institute at the University of Alberta, lays out in his chapter, "Prosperity at the Expense of Equality: Migrant Workers are Falling Behind in Urban China's Rise," what he considers the fundamental reason for the social challenges facing the vast number of migrant workers moving into the Chinese cities. He argues that the price that China is paying for the first world conditions and upwardly mobile populations in its urban centres is a concomitant impoverishment of the lives of migrant workers, with low wages, long working hours, desperate conditions, little social welfare support, and often subject to discrimination and unjust treatment. He claims that the potential for social crisis and unrest is significant if the plight of migrant workers is not addressed. Professor Jiang also claims that that, with the ongoing modernization of China, migrant workers will play a crucial role in determining how socially stable China will be in the coming decades. He points out that there is a growing mountain of evidence that migrant workers are being exploited, mistreated, discriminated against and marginalized despite numerous proposals and government policies established on paper to improve their conditions and to combat discrimination against them. According to this leading China expert in Canada, none of these has so far made any qualitative change in the position of migrant workers in the Chinese economy and social life. Professor Jiang argues that in order to successfully confront this enormous social challenge, China must go through a paradigm shift in its overall development strategies. This must include moving from the traditional development model of capital-intensive, resource-intensive, labour-intensive, pollution-intensive and low value-added manufacturing-intensive industrialization based on China's abundant cheap labour. For China to narrow the social and economic gaps between the majority of its population that still live in the rural areas and the urban populations strategic adjustments will have to be made. This includes moving to a more value-added economic development model that is less concentrated on heavy industries in favour of more environmentally friendly sectors, as well as closing the income gap between migrant workers and their urban peers. He concludes with an ominous warning: "China cannot fundamentally change the status of its 200 million migrant and farm workers, therefore, unless it makes a paradigm shift in its strategic thinking. [...] And if China fails to do so, China will remain an unequal society, an unjust society and potentially an explosive society."

Professor Gong Renren, one of China's most independent intellectuals and a member of the Faculty of Law of Peking University, substantially agrees with the general diagnosis of Professor Jiang in his chapter, "The Historical Causes of China's Dual Social Structure"; however, he offers a further analysis of what is really at the root of the social challenges and accompanying discrimination facing migrant and rural workers. Professor Gong argues that it is the legacy of the Soviet model of governance in the industrial and agricultural sectors. According to Professor Gong, this legacy still today hangs like a noose around China even though it appears from the outside to have cast off the Soviet style of governance in favour of the free market and capitalism, particularly in the industrial sector. The Soviet model involves a dual social structure, with a privileged emphasis on heavy industries that characterized the Soviet economy to the detriment of the social, political and economic standing of agricultural workers. According to Professor Gong, this model remains the backbone of the current Chinese dual social structure of governance between rural and migrant workers and their urban counterparts. It is also the institutional foundation for the longstanding discrimination against farmers, and the key reason behind the widening gap between the urban and rural areas and the rich and poor. Professor Gong gives a unique historical account of how the incorporation of the Soviet model became an immense obstacle to China's modernization process and remains the cause of discrimination against agricultural and migrant workers in China today. In a shining example of intellectual courage, Professor Gong suggests that the only way to finally shake off the legacy of the Soviet model is for China to walk the talk on its more recent accession to international human rights treaties, and to insert human rights provisions in its own Constitution and legislation. This, however, would require China to move from the "rule by law" by Party officials to a rule of law overseen by an independent judiciary and ultimately a move to a democratic form of governance. Such intellectual courage is much to be treasured and nurtured.

One of China's leading social activists and one of its most independent journalists, Wang Keqin offers a very western solution to the protection of farmers' and other rural inhabitants' rights to land in his chapter, "Restoring Private Ownership of Rural Land to Protect the Basic Rights of Farmers." The author has traveled to many parts of China to record the countless number of improper and often illegal or corrupt land requisitioning or land enclosures driven by developers and village and government officials and often involving corrupt activities. After seeing first hand the size of the problem, the author suggests there is an urgency to restoring private ownership of land at the village level. The author suggests that such restoration of private ownership could have spin-off effects in terms of less land disputes, greater social stability, and more environmental and sustainable development. These benefits would in turn facilitate the establishment of modern agricultural systems and development.

Two leading Chinese researchers at the Chinese Government's State Council, Cui Chuanyi and Cui Xiaoli, offer interesting suggestions for confronting the major social crisis facing China in their article "Changing the Policy Paradigm for Migrant Workers." This article is particularly interesting as it shows how those around official circles are aiming to confront the issues related to migrant labourers. Like Professors Gong and Wenran, they also highlight the dual social structure between rural and urban Chinese as a major part of the problems associated with the migration of rural labour. But they also emphasize that at the highest levels of the governing Communist Party there has been a focus on a scientific approach to development and that this approach has led to the implementation of migrant worker-related policies that have the interests of the workers themselves at their core and that promote fair treatment. The authors suggest forcefully that policies alone do not result in effective solutions; they urge rather that it is the whole "social management system," including policy adjustment and improvement, that must be engaged in order to create an institutional environment that both protects the legitimate rights of migrant workers and also offers them a stable urban citizenship with full participation in the social administration of their urban communities.

Wang Xinan, a prominent Chinese lawyer, reinforces the powerful message of Professor Gong in his chapter, "Chinese Farmers' Right of Access to Judicial Relief." In it, he argues that combating discrimination and unlawful activities towards rural inhabitants and migrant workers will depend on the rule of law with an independent judiciary overseeing the adjudication of disputes over land and other rights. Mr. Wang offers the reader a troubling case study on the coercive expropriation of farmer's land in Bazhou, Hebei Province; in this case, the farmer was left without a properly qualified and independent judiciary to whom to appeal, local political influences trumped justice and corruption was rampant. Finally, he also points out that appropriate legal services, even with all the defects in the system, are still beyond the reach of rural inhabitants. The author focused on the land expropriation case study because, while land is the most important source of livelihood for generations of Chinese rural inhabitants, the frequent infringement of farmers' rights over land and the corrupt nature of land expropriations constitute the most serious infringement of the rights of rural inhabitants and threaten social stability.

Professor Zhang Yulin of Nanjing University presents a disturbing chapter titled "China's War on its Environment and Farmers' Rights," describing how the environmental degradation caused by the rapid industrialization of China, not only in the cities but also increasingly in the rural areas, has given rise to a new form of discrimination – environmental discrimination. The author goes on to describe how industrialization-induced environmental discrimination is proving disastrous for rural communities and farmers, especially following the widespread contamination of the food and water supplies of entire communities. Such environmental discrimination arises because factories and mines are becoming concentrated in rural areas while urban centres demand more environmental protections. The result is that ecological destruction and pollution is moving from larger urban centres to small towns and rural villages. The differential impact of environmental degradation on rural communities is far more significant as livelihoods from land are more vulnerable to the effects of environmental degradation. The author states that the condition of the environment in parts of China demonstrates nothing less than a generalized war against nature and that environmental degradation has reached crisis proportions. His chapter focuses on research conducted in Shanxi Province, a region of intense environmental degradation home of the now infamous "cancer villages" and "strange disease villages" mine disasters, severe water scarcity and collapsing villages due to coal excavation practices. The war against nature in this part of China – caused by extensive coal-mining, coking and related industries – has resulted in a crisis of governance in which local residents cannot rely on late and limited relief provided by the government, but must instead cope with their own resources with what is an ecological disaster area. Local residents are in some danger of becoming China's "environmental refugees." The most vulnerable of China's population at the bottom of the social strata are so affected by this war against nature that their very right to life has been compromised. The author suggests that nothing less than a profound social revolution that takes the environment as its central priority is needed to turn back the war against nature. These are warnings and research that should reach the highest levels of the Chinese government.

B. THE SOCIAL CHALLENGES AND ACCOMPANYING DISCRIMINATION FACING RURAL WOMEN AND MIGRANT WOMEN WORKERS

Chen Lanyan, a Chinese feminist scholar and professor at the Tianjin Normal University, aims in her chapter, "The Gendered Reality of Migrant Workers in Globalizing China," to broaden the context of the social challenges and accompanying discrimination facing rural and migrant women workers. Her chapter adopts a feminist political economy framework by integrating internationally agreed human rights treaties and rights-based advocacy with a gender relational perspective to discuss the changing faces of the working class in China during the recent industrialization drive beginning in the early 1980s. The author claims that, unlike the situation in the 1950s, the current industrialization is propelled by international capital drawn in by Chinese government policies and also fuelled by the mass migration of rural labourers who are incorporated into the changing faces of the urban working class, many of whom are women. According to Professor Chen, these workers do not have job security or enjoy the Labour Insurance Scheme that was extended to all workers, including those who came from the countryside in the 1950s. The chapter claims that migrant workers, especially women, are employed by international capital and are producing manufactured goods for international markets. The author claims that such women migrants work under harsh conditions and have no more rights than forced and bonded labourers. The chapter also claims that many other women migrant workers work in the growing service sector as clerks, waitresses, cleaners, nannies, maids and sex workers. The quality of life of those employed in service industries is no better than their sisters in manufacturing. However, the author goes on to claim that even these migrant women workers' awareness of their rights is growing as they increasingly organize locally and regionally to defend and assert their rights. Professor Chen continues to develop a gender sensitive and rights-based framework to examine the gender impacts of Chinese government policies that can promote economic growth with the proper labour market involvement of women migrant workers. Her examination of such gender impacts in a historical context reveals critical tensions and contradictions that pervade existing policies. She concludes by suggesting how such tensions and contradictions can be resolved including the identification of priority areas for future policy research and initiatives.

Xu Weihua, a lawyer and legal aid clinic leader at the Peking University, and Liang Jianguo, of the powerful All-China Women's Federation, provide a case study of the social challenges facing rural women in their chapter, "An Analysis on Rural Women's Entitlements to Land and Other Property." In their research, the authors focus on how to use gender perspectives and legal frameworks to analyze rural women's entitlement to land and related property in Hebei Province and Zhejiang Province. The authors sent detailed questionnaires to women in these provinces and organized panel discussions to follow up on research findings. Through the research they were able to uncover how the Chinese *Law on Rural Land Contracting* and other laws, regulations and policies are implemented, including in what ways rural women's right to land is impacted and an analysis of the reasons behind infringements of such rights and entitlements. The authors also focus on how village committees handle relevant conflicts and the attitude of relevant government officials. The findings from the case study were not encouraging. Violations of women's right to land have increased steadily in recent years. Growing numbers of women are being forced to sign agreements that on their face show they are willingly giving up rights to land and other benefits upon marriage. Married, divorced and widowed women are being forcibly deprived of their rights to land. Inadequate judicial and administrative remedies exacerbate the situation as do loopholes in relevant legislation and regulation. These findings are very serious in part because international experience has demonstrated that women's access to land is critical to sustainable development of rural communities, and that chronic infringements can impact heavily on entire families. This is especially true in the case of China where, according to some estimates, women comprise 60 percent of the agricultural workforce and are critical to the economic growth of rural communities.

Colleen Sheppard, Professor of Law at McGill University and one of Canada's most distinguished feminist legal scholars, in her chapter, "Systemic Discrimination and Gender Inequality: A Life Cycle Approach to Girl's and Women's Rights," offers a unique perspective to both China and Canada regarding the proper approach to combating discrimination on the basis of gender (and indeed discrimination on other bases as well). Professor Sheppard urges an examination of the connections between the various spheres of diverse women's activities across different periods in their lives, from girlhood to old age. She argues that focusing only on specific acts of inequality in time ignores the broad array of historical, social and economic sources of inequality and exclusion that are often systemic and embedded in societal structures. She argues that all societies should instead connect individual instances of exclusion and discrimination to a larger systemic pattern of inequality over time and across both the public and private spheres of citizens' lives. This approach, which Professor Sheppard calls a "life cycle" approach, would necessitate connecting how treatment of the girl child impacts upon her life chances as a woman, and how the reproduction of the human family operates as an ever-present source of joy and constraint in women's lives. The foundation of such an approach is the focus on systemic discrimination. Professor Sheppard points out how many countries have moved from focusing on instances of overt and intentional discrimination to a greater focus on examining the systems, structures, institutional policies and practices contributing towards such systemic discrimination; further, these forms of systemic discrimination may well be found not only in the public sphere but also in the private spheres of the family and the household. While Professor Sheppard focuses her life cycle and systemic discrimination analysis on the evolution of Canadian law in this area, her thesis has enormous significance for China. The girl child faces huge systemic inequalities in both the public and private spheres in Chinese society, and these impact on the entire range of social challenges and accompanying discrimination against adult women in the workplace and in the home. As the Chinese writers in this part of the book have pointed out, the systemic discrimination against women agricultural workers and farmers and urban women migrant workers is deeply embedded in Chinese economic, social and political systems. In a society that has deeply rooted cultural preferences for sons, such systemic discrimination may well begin with the prejudice against the girl child right from and even before birth. The social dysfunctions that arises from this cultural preference, located in the private sphere but from there transferred into the public sphere, include discrimination against the girl child in education, health and access to land rights. Increasing gender imbalances in the population, if unreversed, could potentially culminate in a serious national economic and social crisis.

C. THE SOCIAL CHALLENGES AND ACCOMPANYING DISCRIMINATION FACING DISABLED PERSONS IN CHINA

The chapter by Professor Sheppard connecting the life cycle to systemic discrimination on the grounds of gender can be equally applicable to any effective legal, social and economic framework regarding the rights of disabled persons in any society. In the chapter, "A Study on the Legislative Inhibition of Discrimination against the Disabled," Wang Zhijiang, the Head of the Legal Section of China's Disabled Persons' Federation, reinforces the need for such a life cycle and systemic approach to combat the enormous social challenges and discrimination facing disabled persons in China today. Much of the focus of his chapter is on the international, comparative and Chinese legislative frameworks and on the definition and categories of discrimination facing an estimated 60 to 83 million disabled persons in China. The author, like Professor Sheppard in her analysis of gender discrimination, points out the need to tackle the systemic foundations of such discrimination in both the public and private spheres of the family, workplaces, schools, health care facilities, government, recreational facilities and in sports, as well as in many other societal contexts. Mr. Wang provides a sketch of national and international legal regimes on protection of the disabled to stress the necessity and importance of establishing comprehensive and efficient legal institutions to respond to the social challenges and discrimination. The author examines the various definitions of discrimination against disabled persons and proceeds to analyze causes and characters of such discrimination in various national contexts including those of the U.S., China and Hong Kong. The author concludes that further reforms are still needed in China, and perhaps other national contexts, including the development of a more inclusive concept of discrimination and a special agency for the legal protection of, and elimination of discrimination against the disabled.

D. THE SOCIAL CHALLENGES AND ACCOMPANYING DISCRIMINATION AGAINST THOSE LIVING WITH OR AFFECTED BY HIV/AIDS

There is a morass of conflicting statistics on HIV/AIDS in China. The government claims that there is an estimated one million Chinese citizens who may be infected with HIV/AIDS. Many independent experts, however, discount these official figures and claim that they do not accurately reflect the actual number. The disagreement about the numbers of affected persons is in part due to the lack of extensive resources for information gathering, especially in the vast rural regions of China. Furthermore, some surveillance and measuring protocols by the Chinese government may focus primarily on high risk groups. As a result of these deficiencies in resources and methodologies, it may be that only five percent of HIV/AIDS cases are counted. UN and WHO experts estimate that the real figure may well be up to two million, while the UNAIDS agency has estimated that there could well be between ten and fifteen million HIV/AIDS affected persons by 2010 in China. While this still represents a small percentage of China's population of 1.2 billion people, the figures in comparative terms make the situation deadly serious not only for China, but, given the increased mobility of China's population both within and outside the country, a cause for grave concern for the rest of the world as well.

Two Canadian researchers start the international and comparative discussion in this part of the book.

David Patterson, an HIV/AIDS researcher and legal consultant, in his chapter, "The Application of International and Regional Instruments to HIV-related Discrimination in China and Southeast Asia," focuses on selected international and regional instruments endorsed by China and ASEAN member countries relating to HIV/AIDS related discrimination in order to determine how effective they are and how to strengthen them to effectively combat such discrimination. The author claims that HIV-related discrimination is a central obstacle to the success of prevention, treatment, care and support programs. For that reason Mr. Patterson argues that international scrutiny and the sharing of experiences and best practices is essential; he further argues that by encouraging compliance with relevant instruments, scrutiny and experience sharing contribute to national and global responses to this global pandemic. His chapter therefore addresses two questions: (1) what has been the contribution of international and regional instruments to national responses to HIV-related discrimination, as evidenced by law and policy reform?; and (2) how can the role of international and regional instruments be strengthened in support of national responses to HIV-related discrimination? His answers to these questions indicate that an adequate monitoring and reporting process along with financial and technical assistance is critical for effective implementation of these relevant international and regional instruments, as opposed to the creation of a new commitment or declaration. China, like the member countries of the ASEAN group, needs to take the results of such research in order to help it fulfill its commitments under the relevant international and regional instruments. In addition, as with the suggestions in the Chinese chapters on land rights, environmental and gender discrimination, there is a critical need for both law and policy reform at the national, provincial and local levels as well as education and training of legislators, policy makers, the judiciary, police, legal service providers and paralegals at all levels in the purpose and application of the law. The author suggests that there is a critical role for Chinese NGOs and youth to play in combating discrimination in the context of HIV/AIDS, as discrimination against those suffering from the condition discourages the most vulnerable from accessing prevention education and care, treatment and support services. Finally, the author suggests that China should use international and regional forums to share its initiatives with other countries as examples of best practices in order to help others consider, adapt and apply.

Two other Canadian researchers from the Atlantic Centre of Excellence for Women's Health in Halifax – Barbara Clow, the Executive Director, and Linda Snyder, the Knowledge Exchange Manager – focus on what is perhaps the most vulnerable HIV/AIDS affected group in the world in their chapter, "Gender and HIV/AIDS: Understanding and Addressing Stigma and Discrimination Among Women and Girls." The authors start with an overview of the ways in which sex and gender work together to put women and girls at risk of HIV/AIDS infection in many countries around the world. The authors assert that gender inequity throughout the world is deepening the suffering of women and girls afflicted with the virus as well as contributing to the spread of HIV/AIDS. Supporting the analysis of Professor Sheppard on the life cycle and systemic gender discrimination in both the public and private sphere, the authors demonstrate how gender roles and expectations contribute to the stigmatization of women and girls, particularly those from marginalized populations. The second part of their chapter provides a gender-based analysis of the epidemic in Canada and a comparative look at the South African experience. They discover that despite vast differences in infrastructure, culture and history, the trajectory of the pandemic is disturbingly similar – at least with respect to the vulnerability of women and girls and especially disadvantaged groups of women and girls – in both Canada and South Africa. Finally, the authors address specific international recommendations for responding to the pandemic; this includes an analysis of the gender based deficiencies of UN and WHO guidelines which may contribute to the spread of HIV/AIDS and deepen the stigma associated with it, and thus may encourage discrimination and marginalization of women and girls infected and affected by HIV/AIDS. The authors hope that low incidence countries, including Canada and China, may be in a position to learn from their analysis and to fashion more effective responses to the pandemic.

The two Chinese contributions in this part of the book reinforce the conclusions of the Canadian authors in the context of Chinese law and society.

Ma Yinghua, Professor at the School of Public Health at the Peking University, and a co-authoring research team focus on the plight of children and HIV/AIDS orphans in their chapter, "Promoting the Right to Education for AIDS Orphans and Vulnerable Children (OVC): A Study on Anti-Discrimination." Their study focuses on three categories of AIDS-afflicted children: HIV-infected children, children orphaned by AIDS (children under the age of 18 who have lost one or both parents due to AIDS), and children made vulnerable by AIDS (children with one or both parents infected with

AIDS, and living in a household with one or more chronically ill adult). The research and study was conducted between March 2006 and March 2008 to determine if these most vulnerable children are denied access to education due to discrimination, as well as the causes of such discrimination. Not unsurprisingly, they find that these categories of some of the most vulnerable in China have experienced discrimination in education. Sadly, again supporting the thesis of Professor Sheppard that discrimination is as much rampant in the private sphere as in the public, the researchers found that discrimination against these children has its origins not only in institutional discrimination originating in laws and governmental policies, but also in social and cultural factors resulting in public discrimination (some might term this private discrimination), including by parents and existing students. Finally, the authors suggest solutions to ensure non discriminatory access to education. To address what they term public discrimination, the authors also suggest steps to create a caring and non-discriminatory education environment, and to promote anti-discrimination in China for these most vulnerable members of Chinese society.

Turning to another of the most vulnerable sectors of Chinese society affected by HIV/AIDS, Qin Mingrui and Lai Xiaole, professors in the Department of Sociology at the Peking University, focus on a case study of HIV/AIDS affected rural women in their chapter, "The State of Life and Survival Strategies of AIDS-infected Rural Women: An Analysis Based on Field Investigations in Selected Areas of Henan." The tragedy of the people in this study became known globally when news filtered out of China that desperately poor farmers and their families in Henan Province had contracted AIDS by selling blood, often with the complicity of corrupt local officials. Within this group, the authors found that females who contracted the virus were in an even more desperate situation than their male counterparts, spouses and relatives. The authors focused on the basic survival tactics of these women, living in what became essentially an HIV/AIDS village, and, once again, how both the public and private spheres affected their choices of methods of survival. In this unique case study the researchers found that even the motives for selling blood differed between male and female afflicted persons. The lesson of this sad case study is that gender discrimination is pervasive in even the most tragic of human conditions.

E. THE SOCIAL CHALLENGES AND ACCOMPANYING DISCRIMINATION AGAINST ABORIGINAL AND ETHNIC MINORITIES

Given the recent unrest by China's national minorities in Tibet and in Xingjian Province in the lead-up to the 2008 Olympics in Beijing, this part of the dialogue between Chinese and Canadian partners was the most sensitive. In oral discussions, there was an unfettered and rich discussion of the relevant issues demonstrating intellectual depth and freedom of thought and expression. The written format, however, is a different matter

and resulted in only Canadian contributions to this section of the book, including one
by the project director and the author of this introduction, Professor Errol P. Mendes of
the Faculty of Law, University of Ottawa.

In my contribution, "The Canadian Constitution and Charter of Rights and
Freedoms: A Global Template for Minority Rights?", I aim to open up a possible new
approach to dealing with national minorities, even in China. The article argues that
multi-ethnic societies, whether federations like Canada or unitary states like China,
can only ensure social stability if the governance model offers substantive equality
within the notion of collective rights to its minorities. This is especially important
where historically settled national minorities not only form the majority in a part of the
territory of a federal state, but also where their communities are dispersed across the
geographic boundaries of the multi-ethnic state. Canada could provide an emerging
global template for states with multinational and multi-ethnic populations; the Canadian
minority rights model can help in developing substantive equality frameworks in order
to help prevent social and ethnic conflict and the breakdown of multi-ethnic states.
Canada's judicial and socio-political experience under the Constitution and Charter
of Rights and Freedoms provides the principles and frameworks of distributive justice
to balance the collective rights of minorities and individual rights, while protecting
and enhancing the multicultural heritage of Canada. Principled parameters for dealing
with unilateral secessionist attempts by a minority group are also being set down by the
Supreme Court of Canada.

The article then offers a few thoughts on how Canada's experience with national
minorities could offer some new approaches to China's relatively small (in percentage
terms), but growing, national minorities and asserts that China's territorial integrity will
in large measure depend of how the PRC government enhances ethnic relations and
minority rights. The author points out three critical weaknesses in the provisions for
limited autonomy and self rule in China's Constitution as a key source of the continuing
discontent of China's national minorities. I suggest that offering genuine autonomy
and substantive equality to national minorities can become a unifying force and a
competitive advantage in a globalized economy, pointing to the example of Canada.
Finally I suggest that with globalization making non-minority areas of China, such as
the Special Economic Zones (SEZs), more autonomous than the official Autonomous
Regions, it may be time to contemplate offering the minority Autonomous Regions the
status of Special Cultural Zones (SCZs), in which there could be permissible divergence
from the unified leadership of the Party. This could, in time, be the solution not only to
the problem of separatist movements, but could also generate a competitive advantage
to China in the global economy.

In the final paper of the book, a spotlight is thrown on one part of what the PRC
claims as its own – namely Taiwan – where indigenous rights are recognized, even as
mainland China refuses to accept that there are any indigenous peoples within its own
boundaries. Professor Scott Simon of the Department of Sociology at the University of

Ottawa in his chapter, "Indigenous Peoples and Hunting Rights," focuses on the hunting rights of Taiwanese indigenous groups within an international and comparative context. His research is the products of three years of field research in Taiwan on the issue of the rights of indigenous peoples, in particular their hunting rights. His discussion focuses on four themes: (1) hunting as a specifically indigenous right; (2) environmental aspects of indigenous hunting practices; (3) struggles for hunting rights in Quebec and Taiwan; and (4) the relationship between hunting rights and other indigenous rights. While it may seem strange to some to have such a focused chapter in a book on overwhelming social challenges and accompanying discrimination, the chapter outlines an important example of a predominantly Chinese society attempting to reconcile its own traditions and civilization with a minority that is particularly vulnerable to the dominant society and that faces major social challenges and discrimination. How such a small indigenous society fares could well portent the outcome of the larger struggles of the much larger national minorities in mainland China.

CONCLUSION

There are consistent threads that run through most of the chapters by both Chinese and Canadian authors. Wenran Jiang, Gong Renren and Lanyan Chen point to the priority given to the rapid economic rise and industrialization over the social, economic and political rights of rural inhabitants and migrant workers of both genders, and indicate how this lopsided priority has resulted in the overwhelming social challenges and accompanying discrimination issues facing China today. Professor Gong lays the blame on the legacy of the agricultural and industrial framework of the Soviet model that still is in play in China. Even the chapter from researchers from the Chinese State Council – Cui Chuanyi and Cui Xiaoli – seems to urge that any government policies and other attempts to alleviate the situation of these Chinese citizens, who constitute the majority of the population, need a much more effective social management system and institutional environment in order to offer equal and stable citizenship to the migrant workers. One assumes that this would require a rebalancing of economic and industrial priorities in favour of social development of the poorer parts of the Chinese population.

As the chapters by Wang Xinan, Wang Keqin, Zhang Yulin and Xu Weihua make clear, what is needed in China today is a move from the rule by law controlled by the Party to the rule of law overseen by both central and local governments and a much more independent judiciary that are not corrupt; only a separation of the legal apparatus and judiciary in this way would put in place the conditions needed to prevent the unlawful expropriation of agricultural land, protect the land rights of women in rural areas and protect the environment against the "war against nature" waged by industry and mining at the peril of the health and safety of local communities.

Professor Sheppard presents the thesis that what is needed to effectively fight gender and other forms of discrimination is an extensive life cycle and systemic discrimination framework that goes beyond laws and a reactive, complaints-driven process. Wang Zhijiang confirms the correctness of this thesis as far as the treaty, legislative and other frameworks needed to alleviate the condition of the estimated 60 to 83 million disabled in China. Canadian researchers David Patterson, Barbara Clow and Linda Snyder concur as well with respect to the growing numbers of HIV/AIDS affected persons in China and around the world. This thesis is of particular importance in regard to women and girls affected by the pandemic.

The case study of the plight of children and HIV/AIDS orphans by Ma Yingua and her team of researchers, together with the case study by Qin Mingrui and Lai Xiaole of the Henan women who contracted HIV/AIDS through donating blood, show that discrimination against the most vulnerable is pervasive even in the most tragic of human conditions, and that this follows from systemic discrimination in both the public and private sectors.

The final section focusing on social challenges and accompanying discrimination of national and indigenous minorities in China demonstrates which of the targeted areas has the greatest degree of political sensitivity by the absence of acceptable written contributions by the Chinese partners. In my chapter I attempt to make up for this lack by proposing that the offer of genuine autonomy and substantive equality to national minorities can become an asset not a danger to the unity of China, as it emerges into a global superpower and takes its rightful place as a leader of the global community. My colleague Scott Simon aims to suggest that there are both benefits and challenges accompanying the acceptance by a majority Chinese society that indigenous cultures and traditions, with their own ancient and modern traditions and values, can exist and thrive along with the dominant society.

It is to be hoped that this unique dialogue between scholars, practitioners and activists from opposite ends of the planet can demonstrate that bridges can be built across global divides; and that inter-cultural dialogue can help us all confront overwhelming challenges and accompanying forms of discrimination.

PART ONE

Discrimination against Rural and Migrant Workers

CHAPTER ONE

Prosperity at the Expense of Equality
Migrant Workers are Falling Behind in Urban China's Rise[1]

Wenran Jiang

In rapidly modernizing China, one of the major population groups that is not getting ahead is the huge army of 130 million migrant workers. China's booming cities are very impressive: new skyscrapers, new apartment high rises, new roads, and ever-improving services and marketplaces. But without migrant workers, none of these are possible. Yet, migrant workers get low wages, work long hours, live in inferior conditions, receive little social welfare support, and are often subject to discrimination and unjust treatment. Since President Hu Jintao and Premier Wen Jiabao came to power, they have put more emphasis on building a harmonious society. Premier Wen has personally intervened in the treatment of migrant workers. Thus, in recent years, the state of migrant workers has begun to receive substantial attention and to become an object of research.

In this paper, I approach the state of migrant workers and the discriminations they suffer from the following angles. First, I look at the potential for a social crisis in China. This part does not address the migrant workers in particular; rather, it addresses the overall situation of China's modernization process and its impact and how social tensions may or may not increase. With high mobility, high expectations and large numbers, migrant workers will play a crucial role in shaping China's social stability in the coming decades.

Second, I put the status of migrant workers in the broad context of the economy of China and its urban life. There are a lot of available materials, surveys and statistics available. I argue that there is enough evidence to show that migrant workers are being exploited, mistreated, discriminated against and marginalized. There are also a lot of proposals for how to improve the situation of the migrant workers. There are even policies and measures taken by the central and local governments to change the situation, address many of the grievances of migrant workers and implement some pilot projects to further improve their social and economic conditions. But none of these has so far made any qualitative change in the position of migrant workers in the Chinese economy and society.

Third, I argue that in order to win in the fight for migrant workers' rights and to accord migrant workers the treatment they deserve, more profound changes are needed. It is not only in some concrete policy areas that more efforts shall have to be made; rather, China must go through a paradigm shift in its overall development strategies. In the past three decades, the Chinese government, for the purposes of rapid modernization and "catching-up" with the West, has pursued a traditional development paradigm involving capital-intensive, resource-intensive, labour-intensive, pollution-intensive and low value-added manufacturing-intensive industrialization based on China's abundant supply of cheap labour. For China to narrow the growing income gaps between the urban centres and the countryside, between urban residents and migrant workers, Beijing should make strategic adjustment in all the above areas, as it is only by so doing that China can finally solve its "migrant workers problem."

I. The Dynamics of China's Social Crisis

China continues to impress the world with its high GDP growth, staggering trade volumes and surging appetite for consumption. Most figures out of Beijing are remarkable, indicating that the Middle Kingdom is reclaiming its great power status at a speed faster than most had previously forecast. Yet evidence is mounting that its development paradigm focused on high GDP growth shall be too costly to sustain indefinitely: rural, urban and environment-related protest movements are coalescing from local and isolated events into a more widespread and serious social crisis.

1. What do statistics, or the lack of them, indicate?

Some may point to Beijing's high-ranking GDP figures as proof of China's successful modernization: its national economy is about to overtake that of Germany to become the third largest in the world,[2] and it is projected to overtake that of Japan in the coming years; its economic structure seems to be more balanced than it had been previously with a larger service sector; and China's foreign trade grew by double-digits in recent years and its foreign reserves are now the largest in the world. Yet other recently released numbers, which have received less coverage, indicate another, more troublesome trend.

As revealed by the *China Human Development Report 2005*, regional disparities are threatening the country's overall growth potential, and the widening gap between urban and rural wealth and well-being has reached a dangerous level. Compiled by a group of Chinese researchers for the United Nations Development Program (UNDP), the report demonstrates that in all major categories of the human development index (HDI) – from per capita income to life expectancy to literacy rate – regional imbalances are severe and growing. It concludes that China's Gini coefficient, a measurement of a country's income inequality, has increased by more than 50 percent in the past 20 years, with urban dwellers earning nearly four times that of rural residents. At 0.46, "China's Gini coefficient is lower than in some Latin American and African countries, but its urban-rural income inequality is perhaps the highest in the world."[3]

The higher GDP numbers only make inequality worse, and when systemic factors biased against the rural population are included, China's city to countryside income ratio is as high as 6:1.[4] The result is that a person in richer cities enjoys a life expectancy of close to 80 years, the level of a middle-income country and ten to fifteen years longer than a farmer's life span in Tibet or other remote provinces. The UNDP report also shows that the inland regions lag behind in education, especially among the female population.[5]

Only two decades ago, China was one of the most equitable societies on earth. Today, it ranks 90th in the UNDP's 131-nation HDI. It is ironic that while 250 million people have been lifted out of poverty in record time – a proud achievement that no one denies – China is also leading the world in creating one of the most unequal societies in history.

2. How to measure social stability, or the lack of it?
The Chinese government has repeatedly told the world that it needs social stability to develop its economy, and Beijing claims to value economic and social rights more than political rights. The question is thus whether China's traditional political control can be accepted as a model of development by the very people who are now excluded from China's growing prosperity.

The last report the Chinese government released regarding social protest cited 87,000 incidents of "public order disturbances" in 2005, up 6.6 percent from the 74,000 figure in 2004; the number of events that "interfered with government functions" jumped 19 percent while protests seen as "disturbing social order" grew by 13 percent in 2005.[6] Some say this is an alarming acknowledgement of the looming crisis in Chinese society that may soon tear China apart, with unthinkable consequences. Others contend that the figure is not surprising and that it may not even be a new development, and that it reflects only the fact that Beijing now allows more reporting of these protests that have long existed. The Chinese government even puts this spin on reports of social disorder, claiming that China is now more democratic by allowing the protests to occur and then informing the public about them.

Despite the differences in assessment, the emerging consensus is that various grassroots protests are increasing in numbers, are becoming better organized, and often turn violent when local officials are no longer seen to be working to resolve ordinary peoples' legitimate grievances. Such protest movements are gaining wider social acceptance. Again, the UNDP *Report*'s survey of the Chinese public's perception of income distribution gaps reveals a popular appetite for social justice and potential support for radical actions: more than 80 percent of those surveyed believe that China's current income distribution is either "not so equitable" or "very inequitable."

Meanwhile, a recent global study by the Pew Global Attitude Project seems to contradict such pessimism. It shows that the Chinese in recent years are the happiest that they have been due to their improved standards of living, and that they are now more optimistic about their future than they have been in recent years. Seventy-two percent of Chinese, the highest among sixteen countries polled, expressed satisfaction with national conditions. Although the survey acknowledges that the "sample is disproportionately urban and is not representative of the entire country," its results convey one important message not recognized in the data analysis of the pollsters: the people of China have extremely high expectations about benefiting from the country's ongoing economic expansion; if these high expectations are not met in the near future, however, their frustration with inequitable income distribution may turn to demands for equity and social justice.

From the 1950s to the 1970s most Chinese were very poor but relatively equal; social protests were rare and the Chinese Communist Party (CCP) asserted control with little concern regarding large scale grassroots unrest. Today's China, after more than two decades of reform, is much more prosperous but at the same time a very unequal society. Historical experiences show that when a country is embarking on rapid economic growth, social mobility accelerates and people's expectations for their own share of the prosperity increase. Yet, at the same time, income distribution gaps widen and, with few exceptions, only a small portion of the population enjoys the benefits of the country's modernization drive. Such a paradoxical process often results in rising resentment among the populous and leads to large scale protests for a more equitable distribution of wealth. China today is at such a crossroads characterize by unprecedented prosperity, high and unmet expectations, and growing frustration with perceived social injustice.

3. When will the "tipping point" come, if ever?

The current Chinese leadership, headed by President Hu Jintao and Premier Wen Jiabao, is keenly aware of the growing disparity and its serious consequences. After years of promoting Deng Xiaoping's famous call "to get rich is glorious," now it is the "harmonious society" that seems to have become the central pillar of the Hu-Wen approach to easing China's social tensions. Despite a number of measures – ranging from investment in remote regions to elimination of agricultural taxes to "hard strikes" against corruption – social unrest is on the rise. With some of the recent bloody confrontations between peasants and local authorities, many wonder if some kind of a "tipping point" for a social crisis will arrive soon – a potentially explosive situation in which large scale upheavals could shake the entire Chinese political, economic, and social establishment.

Revolutions, for example the Russian Revolution of 1917, tend to be precipitated by three conditions: first, the masses can no longer be governed; second, the ruling elite can no longer govern; and third, the social forces are fully mobilized under the leadership of a revolutionary party to overthrow the existing regime. According to these conditions, China is nowhere close to a revolutionary "tipping point."

Yet it would be a profound mistake to take comfort from such abstract conclusions. The state of the first two conditions has been progressively deteriorating in recent years: widespread social protests are increasing and the corruption of government and CCP officials together with the plight of ordinary citizens have combined to weaken the governance structure. A deadly combination of these two elements could lead to a widespread belief that the majority of the population is left behind because of corrupt officials and the privileged few who have enriched themselves through exploitation at the expense of the masses. This perception may foster pressures that fundamentally reconfigure the existing social, economic, and political order.

This process may well be accelerated if the inevitable economic slowdown in the coming years occurs simultaneously with natural, environmental and other human-generated ecological disasters. An externally-imposed, alternative political mechanism is unlikely, if possible at all, given China's tightly controlled conditions. Yet a governance crisis of such magnitude is likely to trigger an internal split within the CCP ruling elite, with reform-oriented forces openly confronting hardliners who advocate total control by force. If history tells us anything about large scale social turmoil, it is that a total breakdown of society may not help in solving China's pressing problems. Thus, the great challenge for China, and by extension the world, is that of how to avoid such a dangerous internal "showdown" with reforms that effectively address the issue of income inequality, social injustice and lack of democratization.

II. THE STATUS OF CHINA'S MIGRANT WORKERS

It is in such a broader context that I shall examine the status and the treatment of China's migrant workers, and explore how continuous discrimination against such a large social group will risk China's political, economic and social stability in the long term. Premier Wen Jiabo specifically instructed in-depth research on migrant workers and related issues in February 2005, and since then the State Council has done some extensive studies.

1. China's migrant workers 101

According to the *Report on the Problems of Chinese Farm-turned Workers* by the Chinese Farm Workers Research Group of the State Council, farm workers are a special concept in China's economic and social transitional period. They are peasants in their household identity, have designated land rights in their home village, but work in the non-agricultural sector and have their main income from wages. The narrowly defined farm workers are those who leave home and enter urban areas to work. The broadly defined farm workers include not only those who go to the cities to work, but also those agrarian workers who work in the manufacturing and service industries in the counties near their homes. Currently, there are about 130 million migrant workers in the narrowly defined category and about 200 million nationwide if using the broadly defined standards.[7]

I agree with the *Report*'s conclusion that the development of China's migrant workers has gone through three historical phases. The first phase marks a transition from free movement to strong control, and lasts from the early 1950s to early 1980s. It is essential to understand that the origin of the division between the urban and rural regions began in 1958, when the government issued the household registration system. This system strictly controlled the movement of the rural population to the cities, and it thus marked the beginning of the "dual system" that has lasted until this day. The second phase is that of a transition that can be characterized as one from "leaving the land but not leaving the home" to "leaving both the land and the home," and it lasted throughout much of the 1980s and the early 1990s. The third phase is characterized by a policy shift from "negative constraints" on migration to "positive guidance," and has lasted thus far since the mid-1990s.

According to the State Council *Report*, migrant workers have the following characteristics:

First, China's rural migrant workers, usually young, have junior high school education on average. As suggested by statistics, among the migrant workers, 61 percent are between 16 and 30 years old, 23 percent between 31 and 40, and 16 percent between 31 and 40. The average age of the migrant workers is 28.6. 66 percent of them do not receive education after junior high school and 24 percent of them have received skill training of various kinds.

Second, 88 percent of migrant workers are introduced to their urban jobs through social networks formed either by relatives or other people from their hometowns. Only twelve percent of them go to the cities through organized channels. This phenomenon may be explained by the fact that most migrant workers have a general lack of information about the labour markets and thus show less confidence at job agencies than their urban peers. In recent years, there has been an increase in the number of migrant workers finding employment through government or job agencies, though these have not yet become the principal channel for job-seeking.

Third, most migrant workers come from central and western China. In 2004, 47.28 million migrant workers came from central China, accounting for 40 percent of the total, and 31.61 million came from western China, representing 26.7 percent of the total. Trans-provincial migrant workers from provinces and cities like Anhui, Jiangxi, Henan, Hubei, Hunan, Guangxi, Chongqing, Sichuan and Guizhou account for 60 percent of the total number of migrant workers in each respective province, and 81 percent of the total trans-provincial migrant workers in the whole country. The number of migrant workers from Sichuan and Henan exceeds ten million. In Anhui, Jiangxi, Hubei, Chongqing and Sichuan, migrant workers account for more than 30 percent of the total labour force.

Fourth, the majority of migrant workers work in sectors such as manufacturing, construction and service. In 2004, 30 percent of migrant workers worked in the manufacturing sector, 22.9 percent in construction and 10.4 percent in the service industry, 6.7 percent in hotel and restaurants, and 4.6 percent worked in wholesale or retail. The situation differs in different regions. In eastern China where manufacturing is developed, 37.9 percent of migrant workers work in this sector. The construction sector in central and western China accounts for 30.1 percent and 37 percent of those regions' respective migrant workers.

Fifth, most migrant workers prefer to go to eastern China or large and medium-sized cities where the rate of employment and the average income are high. In 2004, Beijing, Tianjin, Shanghai, Zhejiang, Jiangsu, Guangdong and Fujian received 82 percent of the migrant workers. More than 60 percent of migrant workers chose to work in large or medium-sized cities.

Sixth, many migrant workers are temporary migrants and have "dual occupations." While they work in the fields during planting and harvest seasons, they take up jobs in the cities as restaurant employees, factory workers, construction workers or housemaids during the slack agricultural seasons. In 2004, this category of migrant workers accounted for twenty percent of the total population of migrant workers. Other migrant workers switch between cities and villages on a yearly basis.[8]

2. Discrimination against migrant workers

Despite the contributions of the migrant workers to China's successful modernization, there are serious problems with how they are treated:

Employment. The household registration system (HRS) is the fundamental reason for unequal treatment of rural migrant workers, contributing to a series of related problems in fields such as social security, children's education, health care, and employment security.

Without urban household registration, the rural migrants cannot enter the official employment system in the city. But a substantial number of migrant workers move across several administrative areas in a given period searching for suitable jobs, thus depriving them of the chance to enter into long-term local residential registration system, and many workers do not actively ensure that they are registered in the local system. Furthermore, the instability and short-term nature of the work available to migrant workers exacerbates this problem.[9]

The majority of rural migrants are engaged in the most painstaking, exhausting, dirty and dangerous work, work which urban residents are reluctant to do. One of the most important reasons causing insecure employment for rural migrants is that they do not, or are not able to, establish stable contractual relationship with the enterprises that employ them. The overwhelming majority of rural migrants do not sign work contracts with these enterprises, and the regulation of labour law in China has so far failed to effectively protect rural migrants' employment rights and interests. Many enterprises use the abundant supply of rural labour as a means to only employ rural migrants for the short-term, and thereby to reduce their labour costs.[10]

Payment. Despite the legal protection set out by the *Labour Law* respecting the minimum wage, many workers receive less. It is common for migrant workers to receive only half or less than half of the pay received by their urban peer workers.[11]

As surveys conducted in Hunan, Sichuan, and Henan show, migrant workers' work time is twice that of their urban counterparts. But at the same time, they only receive 60 percent of urban workers' average salary. In other words, the actual hourly wage of migrant worker is only one fourth of that of urban workers.[12] And, according to another similar survey, in certain coastal areas, migrant workers' salary has only increased by RMB 10 for the past decade. If discounting the commodity inflation factor, those migrant workers in effect receive less income than a decade ago.[13]

According to the Guangdong Labour and Social Security Bureau, many employers deduct costs for accommodation and meals from employees' wages. In some cases more than RMB 300 was deducted from a monthly wage of less than RMB 700. In other cases, employers would make payment of the minimum wage contingent on employees fulfilling a wide range of onerous requirements, such as never taking time off. Workers paid on a piece-rate basis often had to work day and night in order to earn wages that could still be lower than the minimum wage.[14]

Data published by the National Statistics Bureau in 2004 show that the average monthly wage was only RMB 539 for rural migrants while it was RMB 1339 for urban workers.[15] Another problem associated with the underpayment issue is that of defaulted or even denied payments to the migrant workers. According to the All-China Federation of Trade Unions, delayed salary payment to migrant workers reached RMB 100 billion (US\$ 12 billion) by the end of 2003, and 72.5 percent of rural migrants encountered some delay in the payment of their salaries. As indicated by the statistics released by the National Statistics Bureau in 2004, more than ten percent of the migrant workers were unable to collect their due payment for a period of at least seven months.[16] Payment delays in the construction industry are the most serious, as it accounts for more than 70 percent of the total delay salary payment in all sectors.[17] Factory management often uses delayed payments as a means of retaining workers who might otherwise leave. In one construction project alone, the wages in arrears amounted to about RMB 3.3 million.[18]

As a common practice in the construction sector, property developers do not hire workers directly; rather, they work through building contractors who negotiate salary terms, supervise the work and distribute wages. In this hierarchical payment system of a debt-ridden industry, wages may not reach contractors, much less making their way into workers' hands. Unqualified contractors also contribute to wage disputes. According to a recent survey by the Beijing Legal Aid Office for Migrant Workers, about 80 percent of the wage arrears cases were linked to illegal contractors who disappeared with the money. This survey was carried out using over 1,000 cases with which the Legal Aid Office dealt dating from September 2005 to September 2006.[19]

To make matters worse, out of ill-advised trust or desperation, some workers never sign a contract with their employers at the commencement of the employment. As a result, they lose any legal basis for claiming unpaid wages. Such unprotected workers make up 13 percent of all migrant workers.[20] Moreover, some migrant workers may not even know the identity and contact information of the contractors, as was the case for 46 percent of workers surveyed in Xian recently. The few lucky ones who successfully get a court warrant to enforce their wage claims may in the end find that the contractor has run off with the funds.[21]

The central government has recognized the magnitude of the problem and made the payment of workers' wages a key policy priority. In January 2004, Prime Minister Wen Jiabao ordered eight ministries and committees to ensure that wages be paid. The tide of exploitation, however, has showed no signs of ebbing.

Why has all of this administrative marshaling failed?[22] While central government policies set off in the right direction, their local implementation seems only to stall workers with grievances. Requirements in labour law for written contracts, proper payment and compensation are often ignored by both sides in practice. While there are numerous government agencies that workers may approach for assistance, overlapping responsibilities, conflicting central and provincial regulations, procedural hassles, and high recovery costs often bar even the most determined from successfully claiming their wages.[23]

Under the PRC *Labour Law*, all labour disputes must first go through mandatory arbitration before being brought to the courts. But the current labour dispute regulations impose a 60-day limitation period, barring many aggrieved workers from bringing their claims to court after 60 days have expired since the date when the alleged dispute occurred. Their legal rights are further curtailed by the lengthy arbitration and litigation process, which exceeds more than one year in most cases.[24] Frustrated workers often resort to extreme but less costly measures such as blockades, demonstrations, and even suicide to claim their wages.[25] The root of all the problems facing migrant workers is deeply engrained in the loopholes that have existed in the social and legal system during China's rapid urbanization of the past three decades. Absence of employment contracts is the most obvious flaw, along with illegal or unauthorized contractors, insufficient labour supervision, and poor law enforcement.

Social security. Most rural migrants are not covered by unemployment insurance or health insurance provided by the government. According to government surveys, only 12.9 percent of migrant workers are covered by disability insurance, while 10 percent have medical insurance and 15 percent pension fund insurance.[26] One of the chief reasons for low coverage rates is the non-transferability of many basic insurance packages. In Dongguan, Guangdong Province for example, 400,000 migrant workers withdrew from pension funds every year, with the average participation period being of only 7 months.[27]

Living condition. To settle down in cities, migrant workers have to pay various required fees accompanying necessary certificates, such as temporary residency, work permits, health checks, etc. The total costs associated with obtaining these certificates vary in different cities. They were about RMB 500 in Beijing, RMB 600 in Shanghai and RMB 1000 in Shenzhen, while the average monthly wage of migrants is only RMB 539.[28]

Working condition. Another cause of labour disputes is the debilitating working conditions endured by migrant workers, including low pay, seven day work weeks, 15-hour work days, mandatory overtime, poor working environments and coercive factory regulations. Migrant workers are typically employed in labour-intensive sectors with poor working environments and must engage in high risk activities on the job. These sectors include construction, mining, restaurant service, and cleaning maintenance, all of which expose migrant workers to numerous hazardous substances. According to statistics from the State Administration of Work Safety, migrant workers account for the majority of the 700,000 workers disabled in workplace accidents every year. Mining is considered the most dangerous industry, with more than 6,000 work-related deaths every year.[29]

Children's Education. By the end of 2004, more than 6.4 million rural children of the age of compulsory education were living in cities with their migrant parents. It is difficult for migrant workers' accompanying children to enter the education system of a city unless the family has urban residential status or a good economic condition. This is the case even for the nine year compulsory education system.[30] Children who were brought to cities by their migrant parents are often charged school fees that are much higher than the ones in rural areas. To make matters worse, schools in the cities charge these migrant children a "transferring surcharge," with amounts ranging from RMB 600 to 1,000 per semester.[31]

III. Paradigm Shifts in Dealing with China's Migrant Workers

As we have analyzed, the migrant workers are indeed a vulnerable social group, suffering many kinds of discrimination. But the most important point is the fact that, despite all the policies, measures, legal challenges, protests and even unrests of recent years, the economic, social and political statuses of migrant workers have not changed that much in three decades. They remain a marginalized group in a society now building its prosperity upon a foundation of economic disparity and inequality.

There are a number of popular and prevailing explanations regarding the causes of the current problems, but these do not withstand scrutiny. The first claims that the dual system of urban and rural household registration (*hukou*) is the source of all the ills. Advocates of this view argue that once this system is reformed and its duality eliminated, migrant workers will get their share of the prosperity of the urbanization process. However, simply reforming the household registration system cannot substantially change the economic and social structure that is still adversely oriented towards rural migrants.

The second theory treats the entire "migrant workers problem" as an issue of economic transition. According to advocates of this view, the current discriminations endured by migrant workers are due to the fact that China is going through a rapid process of industrialization and urbanization. Once China reaches a higher stage of economic development and national income level, then migrant workers will come to receive a better income and higher social, political and economic statuses. This is known as the reverse-U model of income distribution. The problem with this view, however, is that there are many developing economies, especially those in Latin America, which have not followed that pattern of income distribution following economic growth. For these countries, the income gap began to grow in the so-called "take-off" stage and then never again narrowed, leaving the rich richer and the poor poorer. Based on the experience of these countries, China cannot assume that the pure logic of the market will take care of the migrant workers.

The third theory puts a heavy emphasis on democratization of China's political system and/or developing a better legal framework. This school of thought believes that if China were to have a better legal system that could provide better protection to migrant workers, then their rights would be secured and they would no longer be subject to discrimination. Even better, according to this view, would be China becoming a democracy; the ultimate solution would then be achieved by granting democratic representation to the migrant workers. But the reality is far from being so rosy. Many democratic societies have not been able to solve similar issues even today. The treatment of Mexican migrant workers in the United States is an example, and many Latin American societies are democracies but have not been able to confront their urban slums successfully over the past decades.

There is another school of thought that, while acknowledgeing all these problems, nevertheless argues that the migrant workers are happier in their current position than they would be with what they would otherwise have to do to make a living. According to an extensive survey by Li Piling and Li Wei, migrant workers are not only making contributions to the Chinese economy, enriching themselves, but they are also very satisfied with their economic and social status. They also tend to be more moderate on a range of social and political issues. And they are overall much more optimistic than urban workers. Thus, these authors conclude that their data indicates that all of the concerns about the role of migrant workers in China's stability – displayed especially by foreign observers – are misplaced.[32] The problem of arriving at such a conclusion without questioning the data collected is that it tends to lead to policy recommendations based on the presupposition that if not much is done to ameliorate the state of migrant workers, while there may be growing inequality and injustice, there will not be much danger to China's social stability. This is a dangerous conclusion because it is based on the workers' own perceptions of optimism or pessimism, and these are subject to change and they will change in the future. Not to take active measures to tackle the problems facing migrant workers, based on the assumption that things are fine as they are, risks negative long-term consequences if the growing inequalities are exacerbated and the workers optimism about the future declines.

Thus, we must turn to examine what the structural issues are involved in maintaining the status of migrant workers where it is. And these structural issues all relate to the policy choices China has made in the past 30 years of its modernization program. First, the globalization process has produced a "race to the bottom" effect on developing countries. In order to attract foreign investment, China has given many incentives to foreign capital, including low taxes, low wages, and low standards for environmental protection. In other words, the Chinese leadership made the decision that China should "catch up" with the West at the expense of the exploitation of Chinese labourers. Second, China has focused on basic manufacturing and heavy industry that are capital-intensive, labour-intensive, consume large amounts of resources and energy and are environmentally unfriendly. Such an industrial development model requires a low-cost labour force, and China's seemingly endless migrant workers have fit the bill – but at a heavy cost.

China cannot fundamentally change the status of its 200 million migrant and farm workers, therefore, unless it makes a paradigm shift in its strategic thinking. It must move to a more value-added economic development model, reduce its heavy industry in favor of less energy-intensive and more environmentally friendly industries, raise wages for migrant workers to close the income gap, and raise the value of its currency. And if China fails to take these steps, China will remain an unequal society, an unjust society and potentially an explosive society.

ENDNOTES

[1]   The author would like to thank Hong Nong and Yu Simin for their research and translation assistance.

[2]   "China's national power is expected to exceed that of Germany and rank third in the world" ("*yu ji nian nei jing ji zong liang zhong guo jiang chao yue de guo pai xing quan qiu di san*"), *Wall Street Journal*, 17 July 2007, quoted in *China Daily*, http://news.sina.com.cn/o/2007-07-17/143812221086s.shtml.

[3]   *China Human Development Report 2005: Towards Human Development with Equity*, Human
      Development Reports, United Nations Development Program, at http://hdr.undp.org/en/
      reports/nationalreports/asiathepacific/china/china_2005_en.pdf.
[4]   See the national survey conducted by Institute of Economic Chinese Academy of
      Social Sciences, at http://news.bbc.co.uk/chinese/simp/hi/newsid_3480000/newsid_
      3488300/3488372.stm.
[5]   For more statistics and analysis on the social and economic cost of China's modernization
      drive, see "The Cost of China's Modernization," Jamestown Foundation, China Brief,
      6 December 2005, at http://www.jamestown.org/publications_details.php?volume_
      id=408&issue_id=3549&article_id=2370556.
[6]   "Ministry of Public Security Holds Press Conference to Announce Public Security and Fire
      Situation for 2005," Ministry of Public Security, 20 January 2006, at http://www.mps.gov.
      cn/n16/n1237/n1432/n1522/96178.html.
[7]   See "Report on the Problems of Chinese Farm-turned Workers," Chinese Farm Workers
      Research Group of the State Council, *Reform (Gai Ge)*, No. 5, 2006, at http://www.chain.
      net.cn/document/20070606174745781189.pdf.
[8]   *Ibid.*
[9]   *Ibid.*
[10] Yan Wei, "Rural-Urban Migrant Workers in China: The Vulnerable Group in Cities,"
      School of Management, Xi'an University of Finance and Economics, 2007, at http://www.
      irmgard-coninx-stiftung.de/fileadmin/user_upload/pdf/roundtable07/Wei.pdf,.
[11] X. Dong and P. Bowles, "Segmentation and Discrimination in China's Emerging Industrial
      Labour Market," *China Economic Review*, 13(2-3), 2002, p.170-96.
[12] See "Report on the Problems of Chinese Farm-turned Workers," Chinese Farm Workers
      Research Group of the State Council, *op. cit.*
[13] *Ibid.*
[14] "Latest adjustment of minimum wage in Guangdong would exceed the standards in
      Beijing and Shanghai," *People's Daily*, 13 July 2006, at http://finance.people.com.cn/
      GB/1037/4588116.html, .
[15] See note 9 above.
[16] See "Report on the Problems of Chinese Farm-turned Workers," Chinese Farm Workers
      Research Group of the State Council, *op. cit.*
[17] See note 9 above.
[18] "The 3 million wage in arrears has exposed the 'latent rules' of the subcontract system of
      the construction industry," *Economic Daily*, 25 January 2008, retrieved from http://house.
      people.com.cn/BIG5/98374/101031/6822843.html.
[19] "China's Migrant Worker Wage Battle," *Xinhua News Agency*, 10 February 2007.
[20] Anastasia Liu, "China's Migrant Worker Pool Dries Up," *Asia Times*, 10 November 2005, at
      http://www.atimes.com/atimes/China_Business/GK10Cb01.html.
[21] *Ibid.*
[22] *Ibid.*
[23] *Ibid.*
[24] See "Report on the Problems of Chinese Farm-turned Workers," Chinese Farm Workers
      Research Group of the State Council, *op. cit.*
[25] "Man Under Pressure by Low Wages Survived Attempted Suicide," China News Network,
      27 December 2007, at http://big5.chinanews.com.cn:89/sh/news/2007/12-27/1117020.
      shtml.

26 See "Report on the Problems of Chinese Farm-turned Workers," Chinese Farm Workers Research Group of the State Council, *op. cit.*

27 *Ibid.*

28 Zhou Min, "How Long will Certificates of Temporary Residency Last?," at http://news.sohu.com/20060831/n245101088.shtml.

29 See "Report on the Problems of Chinese Farm-turned Workers," Chinese Farm Workers Research Group of the State Council, *op. cit.*.

30 See note 9 above.

31 See "Report on the Problems of Chinese Farm-turned Workers," Chinese Farm Workers Research Group of the State Council, *op. cit.*

32 Li Peilin and Li Wei, "*Nongmin gong zhai zhongguo zhuanxing zhong de jingji diwei he shehui taidu*" ("The Economic Status and Social Attitude of Migrant Workers in China's Transition"), Shehui xue yanju (*Research in Sociology*), No. 3, 2007. at http://www.sociology.cass.cn.

CHAPTER TWO

The Historical Causes of China's Dual Social Structure

Gong Renren

After the end of the Cold War, western countries shifted their focus to the human rights situation in China. Despite this scrutiny, discrimination against the majority of the country's population – farmers – failed to elicit widespread concern. Discrimination against farmers continues to constitute one of the most fundamental social issues in China. In fact, China's unique dual social structure provides the institutional foundation for the longstanding discrimination against farmers, and is the key reason behind the widening gap between the urban and rural areas, and the rich and poor. It is also an immense obstacle in China's modernization process.

I. INTRODUCTION

(I) Prerequisite for Respect of Human Rights: The Principle of Non-Discrimination

After the Second World War, when human rights found voice in international legislation, the international community established non-discrimination as the first principle of human rights. For example, Article 1(3) of the 1945 *Charter of the United Nations* states that it aims at "promoting and encouraging respect for human rights and for fundamental freedoms for all without distinction as to race, sex, language, or religion." Of the treaties making up the International Bill of Rights, Article 2 of the 1948 *Universal Declaration of Human Rights*, Article 2 of the 1966 *International Covenant on Civil and Political Rights*, and the 1966 *International Covenant on Economic Social and Cultural Rights* all prescribe to the non-discrimination principle. Other human rights conventions of the UN, such as the 1965 *International Convention on the Elimination of All Forms of Racial Discrimination* and the 1979 *Convention on the Elimination of All Forms of Discrimination against Women* are special instruments devoted to anti-discrimination.

The earliest explanation of discrimination in international legal documents appeared in the *Discrimination (Employment and Occupation) Convention, 1958* (No. 111).[1] Article 1.1 (a) of the *Convention* defines discrimination in the following terms:

> Any distinction, exclusion or preference made on the basis of race, colour, sex, religion, political opinion, national extraction or social origin, which has the effect of nullifying or impairing equality of opportunity or treatment in employment or occupation.

Therefore, "discrimination" refers to any distinction, exclusion, restriction or preference made on the basis of race, colour, sex, religion, political or other opinion, national extraction or social origin, property, physical condition, age, origin or other identity, which has the aim or effect of nullifying or impairing equality of rights and interests or freedom in politics, economy, society, culture or public life. Discrimination has different forms, and can be divided into official and unofficial discrimination. The former refers to discrimination in state policies and legal institutions while the latter includes discrimination in employment enterprises, social and cultural issues and customs. The non-discrimination principle encompasses many aspects. Some of the important elements, such as the prohibition of racial and gender discrimination in state policies, have already become principles of customary international law and *jus cogens*.[2]

Although non-discrimination and equality can be regarded as two aspects of the same principle,[3] there remain subtle differences. Some equality in form still reflects discrimination, as evidenced by the "separate but equal" doctrine determined in the case of *Plessy v. Ferguson* by the Supreme Court of the United States in 1896 in defence of racial segregation.[4] The Supreme Court in the case of *Brown v. Board of Education* struck down the doctrine only in 1954. Chief Justice Warren delivered the opinion of the court and concluded that, in the field of public education, the doctrine of "separate but equal" has no place. Separate educational facilities are inherently unequal.[5] Hence, certain forms of superficial or formal equality actually disguise real inequality. Another example is preferential measures or affirmative action adopted by some countries as public policies that favour vulnerable or minority groups. Some of these measures are compensation to historically discriminated groups. Despite being ostensibly inequitable in form and content to some, the policies embody the principles of anti-discrimination so long as they stay within reasonable timeframes and limitations. Greater social civilization and tolerance beget respect for individual dignity and choice. Many countries are driven by anti-discrimination principles and have formulated special laws to protect certain vulnerable minority groups. Therefore, the equality emphasized by the principle of anti-discrimination refers mainly to truly equal opportunities, as well as equitable outcomes in some cases.

Although the concept of equality has been discussed by philosophers and legalists for a long time, the principle of non-discrimination appeared on the scene quite late and was first cited in international human rights documents. This principle is a modern approach to correct historical inequality by bestowing special privileges. It is therefore an important means to achieving equality. By proposing that the basic requisites for respect of human rights must stem from the subject's perspective, the non-discrimination principle clearly demonstrates the universality of respect for human rights. In other words, because we respect human dignity, state laws and policies should not discriminate against or insult any person under any circumstances. Neither cultural relativism nor the so-called Asian values are grounds for objection under the principles of non-discrimination.

(II) Basic Characteristics of Discrimination against Chinese Farmers

Farmers have long suffered discrimination in modern China. According to the research report "Social Structure Changes in Contemporary China," written by a team from the Institute of Sociology in the Chinese Academy of Social Sciences, China is divided into ten social strata, with farmers forming the lowest stratum.[6] Discrimination against farmers in China presents four characteristics, which I shall discuss in turn.

First, the so-called farmers (literally "agricultural persons") in China are not defined by occupation but by China's unique *hukou* (household registration) system. A person who holds an agricultural *hukou* remains a farmer in identity even after working in non-agricultural sectors in the city for a long time. Therefore, discrimination against farmers in China is discrimination based on identity rather than on occupation.

Second, farmers in China are mainly discriminated against by policies and legal institutions rather than by the general public. In a report released at the International Seminar on the Rights-Based Approach to Development in 2003, I discussed several aspects of discrimination by legal institutions against Chinese farmers.[7] These include: (1) farmers do not enjoy the same right to vote as urban residents (when electing deputies to the National People's Congress, one urban resident's vote is equivalent to four farmers' votes[8]); (2) farmers have no right of association; (3) farmers are not entitled to the same labour rights as provided under the *Labour Law*; (4) farmers are not entitled to the same social security rights; (5) farmers' children are not entitled to the same right to compulsory education[9]; (6) farmers are not entitled to the same right to property and land use; and (7) farmers are not entitled to the same right of compensation for death in accidents as are urban citizens due to the *hukou* system.[10]

Third, discrimination in most countries is targeted at minority groups. However, in China, discrimination is targeted at the majority since the country's rural population totals approximately 870 million, or 68 percent of the entire population.[11] Despite constituting the majority, China's rural population has long suffered from all kinds of discrimination. In this sense, the issue of farmers' rights is the biggest and most fundamental issue in China.

Fourth, as can be seen in the histories of many countries, government and social discrimination against certain groups, classes and strata is based mainly on prejudices, including prejudices stemming from gender, racism, religion and ideology. However, discrimination against farmers in China arises from the needs of the country's economic development strategy during a specific period.[12]

(III) Issues for Deliberation

When studying the rights and interests of Chinese farmers, we have to first consider the following questions:

(1) Before 1949, the military struggle led by the Communist Party of China (CPC) started in the rural areas before moving on to and capturing the cities. This struggle relied mainly on the huge population of poor farmers for its success. How then after the CPC came to power did farmers become "inferior citizens" deprived of the same treatment as nationals that urban dwellers enjoy?

(2) China's economic reform in 1978 started with the rural areas. Why are farmers unable to share the benefits of rapid economic growth equally with urban residents after the reform and opening-up?

(3) For more than half a century, farmers have made great contributions to and sacrifices for China's early days of industrialization and the current rapid economic development. Then why do farmers suffer from perpetual discrimination and why have they become the largest disadvantaged group?

Preliminary answers to the above questions lie with China's dual social structure. This dual structure provides not only the institutional foundation for the longstanding discrimination against farmers, but also the fundamental reason behind the widening gap between the urban and the rural areas, as well as between the rich and poor. It is also a major obstacle in China's path to modernization. The focus of this article is on the reasons behind the formation of China's dual social structure.

II. CHARACTERISTICS OF A DUAL SOCIAL STRUCTURE

(I) Proposal of the Concept of Dual Social Structure

The Rural Industrialization and Urbanization Project Group of the Policy Research Centre from the Ministry of Agriculture first proposed the concept of a dual social structure in 1988. Based on two reports submitted by the Group in 1988 and 1989, the dual social structure comprises a series of institutions separating urban and rural areas or differentiating urban residents from farmers. The fourteen specific institutions that divide society and gave birth to the dual social structure are policies in household registration, housing, food supply, non-staple food supply, fuel supply, education, health care, employment, insurance, labour insurance, marriage, enlistment, supply of factors of production, pension insurance, human resources and child-bearing. According to the

Project Group, "China is divided into two distinct sectors, which together make up a Chinese social model that characterise the structure of developing countries."[13]

The dual social structure is the root of contemporary China's biggest social issue – the *sannong* issue, issues of the "countryside, agriculture and farmers" – and reveals the most fundamental peculiarities of contemporary Chinese society.

(II) Differences between the Dual Social Structure and the Dual Economy

The concept of a "dual economy" was first proposed in foreign economic theories. W. A. Lewis, a Nobel laureate in economics, released a series of papers after 1954 that analyzed the "dual economy" between the traditional agricultural sector and the modern industrial sector in some developing countries. He also put forward the "Dual Sector Model."[14]

There is a certain connection between the theories of the dual economy and the dual social structure because both touch on the relationship between agriculture and industry, and on the relocation of the rural labour force. A dual economy exists in many developing countries, including China, to varying degrees. As a result, most Chinese scholars have erred in the relationship between Lewis's dual economy theory and China's dual social structure. In fact, the two concepts differ in at least the following three respects.

First, the dual economy theory mainly refers to the economic relations among different economic sectors while the dual social structure includes politics, law and society as well as the economy. The dual social structure also emphasizes the identity, treatment and rights of people. The key weakness of the dual social structure is its discrimination against farmers.

Second, while the dual economy is the natural outcome of economic development in many developing countries, the dual social structure is an artificial social institution constructed by the policies and measures of a state's ruling party. It is, therefore, a phenomenon not shared by all developing countries. China's dual social structure is in fact relatively rare in today's world.[15]

Third, in a dual economy, the rural labour force is freely relocated to the urban industrial sector, while such movement is subject to strict restrictions within the dual social structure. Restriction or even prohibition of freedom of movement and residence by farmers is an important characteristic of the dual social structure.

(III) General Characteristics of the Dual Social Structure

The dual social structure is not found only in China; after the 1930s, the same phenomenon was experienced in the Soviet Union.[16] Viewed from a broad perspective, the dual social structure does exhibit certain general characteristics. The author proposes the following three general characteristics:

(1) First, the law strictly restricts farmers' freedom of movement and residence.

(2) Second, farmers and urban residents have completely different, relatively fixed and inherited identity and status, with unequal rights and treatments. Farmers clearly suffer from discrimination based on their identity.

(3) Third, urban and rural areas implement different and relatively segregated economic and social management systems.

Therefore, the dual social structure is a social state and a social institution that is built upon discrimination on the basis of the identity of farmer.

III. The Beginning of China's Dual Social Structure

(I) When it Started

1. Before 1949, the dual social structure did not exist in China.
The dual social structure appeared quite late in China. Although China's *hukou* system of population registration has, since China's many earlier dynasties, long been the spatially defined status hierarchy to some extent, it did allow a certain degree of spatial and social status mobility.[17] The urban-rural relationship in ancient China was more mobile than in Europe during the Middle Ages. Farmers who were subjects of feudal lords in certain autonomous European states could only find freedom by fleeing to the city. European cities and the countryside were also segregated from each other in history.[18] However, instead of being conflicting, the historical urban-rural relationship in China was a dynamic two-way flow and the two groups complemented one another. The rural population could move relatively freely.[19]

After the 1911 Revolution, China was under the influence of western law, and recognized the freedom of movement and residence under the law. For example, Article 6(6) of the *Provisional Constitution of the Republic of China* of 1912 states that "[c]itizens shall have the liberty of residence and removal." Although the *Household Registration Law* enacted by the Kuomintang government in 1931 contains detailed provisions on household registration, it did not restrict freedom of movement.[20] Therefore, despite the huge urban-rural disparity in China before 1949, a clearly defined dual social structure was absent.

2. 1953: Major Turning Point
1953 is a major turning point in the history of the People's Republic of China. That year saw the CPC Central Party Committee and its government enact several key measures, all of which are important precursors to the subsequent dual social structure.

The first measure was enacted on 15 June 1953, when Mao Zedong proposed "the General Line of the CPC for the Transition Period" (*dang zai guo du shi qi de zong lu xian*) at a session of the Political Bureau of the CPC Central Party Committee on industrialization and the transformation of private ownership to public ownership. According to Mao:

The general line and task of the CPC during the transition period is to complete the socialist transformation of agriculture, handicrafts and capitalist industry and commerce within ten to fifteen years, or over a longer period.[21]

This marked the CPC leaders' early termination of the "new democracy period," and entry into the Soviet-style "socialist" period. The second measure was carried out in 1953, the first year of China's first five-year plan (1953-1957), which charted China's planned economy. The third major measure was introduced on 10 October 1953, when Chen Yun, then Vice Premier and Chairman of the Central Finance and Economics Committee, was confronted with the food procurement crisis. He proposed the countermeasure of centralized procurement and distribution of food at the National Food Conference.[22]

Finally, on 16 December 1953, the CPC Central Party Committee adopted the *Resolution on Developing Agricultural Production Cooperatives*,[23] which expedited the process of agricultural collectivization (*nongye jitihua*).

We can conclude that 1953 is a benchmark year that marked the beginning of the formation of China's dual social structure.

IV. CHOOSING THE SOVIET MODEL

(I) Complete Sovietization

In June 1949, Mao stated that "the Communist Party of the Soviet Union is our best teacher. We must learn from them."[24] Prior to 1953, the CPC Central Party Committee had followed the ideals of a new democracy with Chinese characteristics that would differ from the Soviet model in some areas. The original model allowed for a multi-party coalition government led by the CPC, and recognized private ownership of land by farmers, the employment of national capital in industry and commerce, and the coexistence of multiple ownership modes (*duozhong jingji suoyouzhi*).[25]

However, soon after the CPC took the reins of government, Mao changed his stance about the new democracy being a lengthy phase, and was eager to establish Soviet-style socialism in China as soon as possible. On 24 September 1952, Mao proposed the immediate transition to socialism at a meeting of the Secretariat of the CPC Central Party Committee.[26] Later, Mao entrusted Liu Shaoqi, who was going to Moscow for the Nineteenth National Congress of the Soviet Communist Party, to solicit Stalin's comments on the issue. On October 20, Stalin gave a positive analysis of China's plan for industrialization and agricultural collectivization.[27]

On 15 June 1953 Mao announced at a Political Bureau session the General Line for the Transition Period, which gave equal emphasis to industrialization and socialist transformation.[28] Mao's move implied more than the abandonment of the policies of new democracy. It also foretold an accelerated process of Soviet-style socialization. In fact, the CPC's conception and proposal of the General Line was the direct outcome of the Soviet model.[29]

Thus, starting in the 1950s China followed the Soviet Union in political, judicial, economic and cultural institutions. The country was entirely sovietized: the political system was changed so that the CPC became the State's single ruling party; the constitutional system was reformed to adopt the People's Congress system, which is similar to the Soviet system; a localized judicial system that comprised courts elected by the various levels of People's Congresses was implemented; the economic system became a public ownership system controlled by the State and a highly centralized planned economy; and cultural institutions were implemented top-down, with strict supervision by the Party and government.

(II) Historical Reasons for Choosing the Soviet Model

After the Opium War, China was influenced by foreign institutions and cultures. Ideas and debates on "using western methods in the Chinese system" (*zhong ti xi yong*) and "complete westernization" (*quan pan xi hua*) mushroomed. It was unlikely that anyone expected "complete sovietization" after the founding of the People's Republic of China. The following historical reasons explain its emergence.

First, this was a natural political and ideological outcome. The CPC was born under the immediate guidance of the Soviet Communist Party's Third International (Communist International). Marxist ideology was also "processed" and introduced to the CPC by the Soviet Union. The CPC was already "bolshevized" before gaining power. Therefore, imitation of the Soviet model by the CPC, especially after it became the single ruling party after the founding of the People's Republic, was an inevitable outcome of its relation to the Third International.

Second, Russia and China have similar historical traditions in that both underwent long periods of despotic monarchy and had long histories of centralized bureaucracy subservient to the monarchy. Therefore, the highly centralized Soviet model could be transplanted to Chinese soil relatively easily.

Third, both countries were industrializing in economically backward agricultural settings. In 1917, Russia was also an agricultural country with a mainly rural population, and lagged behind the western powers economically and culturally. The rural population accounted for 83.2 percent of its entire population.[30] Both Russia and China faced the same problem of having to industrialize in a backward agricultural setting.

Fourth, both countries were confronted with similar international problems after their revolutions. Western capitalist countries greeted Communist governments in Russia and China with hostility, interventionist policies and economic embargoes. When the PRC was founded, it was forced to "lean one-sided" towards the Soviet Union in terms of foreign policy, economy and trade because of the embargo and blockade against the PRC by US-led western countries.[31]

Fifth, since the Soviet Union was the first "successful" socialist country in the eyes of CPC leaders, it was a natural decision for the newly founded PRC to reproduce the Soviet Union's political, economic and legal systems.[32]

Sixth, after the founding of the PRC, the Soviet Union had provided important assistance in many areas. This assistance includes formulating economic plans, building and upgrading large industrial enterprises, and reforming the health, legal and education systems. Based on Soviet documents, the USSR dispatched 10,000 advisors to China and trained 20,000 Chinese in the Soviet Union between 1950 and 1959. During the same period, China received a low-interest loan of US $300 million, one third of which was for military use, to build 300 industrial enterprises and other facilities.[33] Another contributing factor that should not be overlooked is that most of the early leaders of the CPC had worked or studied in the USSR at some point in their lives.[34]

To summarize, the PRC was clearly influenced by the USSR in every aspect after its founding. China's priority on heavy industry, its planned economy, agricultural collectivization and the establishment of various types of dual institutions discussed in the following sections all occurred under the influence of the Soviet Union.

V. Heavy Industry – the Priority

(I) Establishment of Guidelines on the Priority of Developing Heavy Industry

The USSR's policy of giving priority to developing heavy industry was first adopted during the resolution of the Fourteenth National Congress of the Soviet Communist Party in December 1925, after the demise of Lenin.[35] Stalin's 1926 proposal that "socialism should first be established in one country" laid down the theoretical foundation for the USSR's priority in heavy industry.[36] In 1927, the *Instructions on the Formulation of National Economic Plan* adopted by the Fifteenth National Congress of the Soviet Communist Party emphasized that "production of factors of production should first be strengthened, based on the State's industrialization policy."[37] Stalin also stressed that "industrialization is not the development of any industry. The centre and foundation of industrialization is the development of the heavy industry."[38]

The aim of the CPC's "General Line for the Transition Period" was thus mainly to achieve industrialization with a priority on the development of heavy industry, based on the experience of the USSR. On 7 February 1953, Mao said at the National Congress of the Chinese People's Political Consultative Conference (CPPCC) that the CPC was not sufficiently experienced at the extensive building of a country; therefore, it must learn from the USSR wholeheartedly. Mao called upon the whole nation to learn from the Soviet Union.[39] In June 1953, Mao announced officially that the priority of the "CPC's General Line for the Transition Period" was to "basically industrialize the country." For this, his explanation was:

What is basic industrialization of the country? Industries should contribute at least 51 percent to the national economy, or even up to 60 percent. Based on the Soviet experience, industrialization means that industries contribute at least 70 percent to the national economy. We still lag by 42 percent. China's industrialization should also achieve the target of 70 percent contribution.[40]

It is clear that Mao wanted to stress the Soviet experience. After eleven years, at an enlarged working meeting of the CPC Central Party Committee on 30 January 1962, Mao admitted, "the situation did exist at that time. Because we had no experience, we had to emulate the USSR's economic development, especially in heavy industry. Nearly everything was a duplication of the Soviet Union's. We created little."[41]

During the first five-year plan between 1953 and 1957, China's general guideline in industrial development was to give priority to heavy industry. 88 percent of industrial investment was allocated for the development of heavy industries, and focused on 156 Soviet-assisted projects. All of the 156 projects were heavy industrial projects. During this period, only 6.4 percent of the country's investment in capital construction went to light industry, and 7.1 percent was allocated for agriculture.[42] During the planned economy era, except for the first five-year plan period and the adaptation period between 1963 and 1965, China's investment in heavy industries was more than 50 percent of the entire investment budget, even higher than that of the Soviet Union (at its peak, the USSR's investment in heavy industry was no more than 40 percent).[43]

(II) Priority on the Development of Heavy Industry and the Emergence of the Dual Social Structure

1. Farmers' "tribute" (gong shui) provided funds for industrialization.
Funding was the first problem if heavy industry was to be the priority of development. Heavy industry is different from light industry in that it involves huge investments, long production cycles, and difficult internal accumulation of funds. The Soviet experience had relied on the exploitation of the peasantry. On 9 July 1928, Stalin delivered a speech at the Plenary Session of the Soviet Communist Party Central Party Committee, entitled *On Industrialization and the Food Issue*. This was the first time he proposed his "tribute" theory:

> This is an additional tax levied on the peasantry for the sake of promoting industry, which caters for the whole country, the peasantry included. It is something in the nature of a "tribute," a supertax, which we are compelled to levy for the time being in order to preserve and accelerate our present rate of industrial development, in order to ensure an industry for the whole country.[44]

In order for the USSR to promote its heavy industry, its government had to export food for foreign technologies and machinery. Therefore, farmers were forced to turn over a large proportion of food produce. For example, in 1931, 60 percent of food in some regions was seized by the government. As a result, many did not have enough food for the following spring and summer.[45]

During China's foray into industrialization, much capital had to be secured to promote heavy industry. Despite receiving loans from the USSR and Eastern European countries, the amount was limited. During the period of the first five-year plan, the country's fiscal revenues stood at RMB 135.4 billion, of which foreign loans accounted for only 2.7 percent.[46] China had to turn to internal accumulation for funds. Industry, still in its infancy, was unable to raise large amounts of capital. The large agricultural sector stood in stark contrast to industry in this regard.[47] The structure of the national economy meant the agricultural sector had to be the contributor of funds for industrialization. In his July 1955 report, "On the Issue of Agricultural Cooperation," Mao clearly admitted that according to the Soviet experience, "in order to meet the huge capital requirements of the country's industrialization and upgrading of agricultural technology, a substantial portion of capital must come from the agricultural sector."[48]

Capital accumulation from agriculture was derived mainly from centralized procurement and distribution of food, levying agricultural tax and using the "price scissors" (*jiandao cha*) to artificially keep down prices of agricultural products. Estimates for 1953 to 1981 indicate that farmers provided more than RMB 700 billion to the state in farm products or cash through price redistribution and tax payment, while the state's total investment in agriculture only amounted to RMB 80 billion during the same period.[49]

2. The priority on heavy industry directly restricted farmers' ability to change occupation.

According to the norms in many countries, industrialization runs in tandem with massive relocation of the rural labour force from farming to non-agricultural sectors; in other words, with farmers' change of occupation from agriculture to industry. However, due to China's priority in developing heavy industry, absorption of the rural labour force was relatively low. As a result, the size of the industrial labour force did not increase with greater industrialization.

To cite an example, the percentage of China's total industrial output as a proportion of its total industrial and agricultural output rose from 47 percent in 1953 to 72 percent in 1978.[50] Meanwhile, employment in the secondary industries (industry and construction) only accounted for 17.3 percent of total employment in 1978.[51] Thus, promoting heavy industry has excluded a large labour force from the industrial sector and stymied their transfer from the agricultural sector. This has also seriously impeded the latter's productivity.[52]

Under normal circumstances, industrialization runs parallel to urbanization. However, urbanization in China lags far behind the industrialization process. For example, in 1952 China's respective industrialization and urbanization rates were 17.6 percent and 12.6, while the figures for 1978 were 44.3 percent and 17.9 percent.[53]

VI. HIGHLY CENTRALIZED PLANNED ECONOMY

(I) Creating a Planned Economy in China

The USSR was the first country to adopt the planned economy. This adoption was driven partly by ideology and partly by the USSR's policy of "military communism" between 1918 and 1921.[54] The latter included the nationalization of industry and commerce, and the highly centralized control of economic activities.[55] In addition, Russia's lack of private capitalist enterprises made it easy to implement State socialism and a planned economy.[56] In 1926, the USSR began setting annual control targets for the national economy. In May 1929, the fifth Soviet Congress of the USSR adopted the first five-year plan.[57] The Soviet economic model incorporated a highly centralized and directive-driven planned economy and excluded private ownership and the market mechanism.[58]

The USSR played an important role in China's establishment of a planned economy. China formulated its first five-year plan with the assistance of the USSR.[59] The USSR also provided important financial assistance towards China's achievement of the plan.[60]

1953 thus marks the beginning of the creation of China's planned economy. Investment allocation for the first five-year plan focused on industrialization, and emphasized development of heavy industry.[61] And, following the Soviet Union, the strategy of China's nascent planned economy intended heavy industry to be the key development priority.[62]

(II) The Planned Economy in the Countryside: "Centralized Procurement and Distribution of Food" Policy

Between 1927 and 1928, the USSR experienced a "food procurement crisis." This occurred before it implemented agricultural collectivization. To mitigate the crisis, the government took compulsory measures similar to the "surplus food" collection system during the civil war.[63] Thus, the crisis offered an opportunity for the USSR's implementation of compulsory agricultural collectivization.

In 1953, China also faced food supply difficulties.[64] The crisis was a harsh revelation of the incompatibilities between China's focus on heavy industry and on the lagging agriculture sector.[65] The state could have employed economic measures to address the crisis; increased food prices will encourage greater sale of food produce to the State, allowing it to mitigate mismatched demand and supply. However, as the State will have to sell food to urban residents at old prices, higher fiscal subsidies would deplete investment for heavy industry.[66] After much consideration, the Central Finance and Economics Committee decided that the only feasible way to address the problems with food supply was through administrative means; in other words, by means of "centralized procurement and distribution of food."[67] On October 16, the enlarged meeting of the Political Bureau of the CPC Central Party Committee adopted the *Resolution on Implementing Planned Purchase and Planned Supply of Food.*[68]

The essence of centralized procurement and distribution of food is the State's monopolistic operations of major agro-products. Also called "planned purchase," centralized procurement refers to food requisitioning in the countryside. Centralized distribution, also known as "planned supply," refers to rationing in cities.[69] Besides food, the CPC Central Party Committee and the government also passed other decisions to extend the policy to include edible oils and cotton.[70] Although the policy was implemented to alleviate food supply shortages in the cities and to stabilize the society, its primary objective was to support industrialization by channelling agricultural surplus to national construction, military expenditure and the urban-based heavy industry development. Thus, the state controlled the trading of food produce.[71] At the same time, the policy also extended the directive-driven planned regulation of industrial production to include agricultural production.[72]

(III) Influence of a Planned Economy on the Emergence of the Dual Social Structure

1. Direct Impact on the Movement of Labour

The fundamentals of a planned economy are the exclusion of the mechanisms of a market economy and control on the movement of labour. We can discern the impact of the planned economy on the formation of the dual social structure simply by observing how the labour force flows.

First, a planned economy restricts production, distribution and sales; it eliminates market forces in the financial sector; and it throttles private enterprises and sole proprietors. This means that the development of tertiary industry – the best absorber of the labour force – was choked for a long time in China. In 1978, there were 48.9 million people employed in the tertiary industry, accounting for only 12.2 percent of the entire labour force.[73]

Second, a planned economy wipes out the labour market because the government masterminds labour movement. Thus, individuals are deprived of the right of choice of occupation. This produced a direct impact on the dual social structure. Since people had no freedom to choose their means of livelihood, farmers were deprived of the ability to move freely to cities to earn a living.

In addition, due to the planned economy's control of labour movement, several "anti-urbanization movements" were planned during the 1960s and 1970s. By reducing the number of workers in enterprises, and by deploying educated youth (*zhishi qingnian*: senior or junior high school graduates from the cities) to work in the countryside and mountain regions, China's urban population was reduced by more than 50 million.[74] Rural areas became a "super reservoir" for surplus labour.[75]

2. Impact of "Centralized Procurement and Distribution of Food" on the Dual Urban-Rural System

Centralized procurement and distribution of food not only enabled the state to extract farmers' funds for industrialization, it also led to urban-rural segregation in many ways.

First, the food market was closed after the introduction of centralized food procurement, and after the State Council issued the *Regulation on the Prohibition of Entry into the Free Market of State Centralized Purchased or Planned Purchased or Centralized Purchase of Agro-Products and Other Goods.*[76] Thus, centralized procurement and distribution of food, an embodiment of the planned economy in rural areas, eradicated the market economy through administrative measures, and isolated farmers from the market. As a result, all direct commercial linkages between farmers and urban consumers were severed.

Second, under centralized procurement and distribution of food, the State fixed the prices and allocated purchase quotas among various regions as planned. Thus, farmers grew crops based on the quotas as prescribed to them. Industrial development was restricted to the cities, and agricultural production confined to the countryside. This led to urban-rural segregation, even opposition.[77]

Centralized procurement and distribution of food also required the state to adopt different policies for cities and the countryside for food and non-staple food products. As a result, a coupon system for food, oil and cotton cloth was established at the central and local levels. Urban residents and farmers were treated differently. In the planned economy era, the food and oil supply system and the *hukou* system, which differentiated farmers from urban residents, were the main components of the dual social structure.

VII. Agricultural Collectivization

(I) China's Agricultural Collectivization Movement was Modelled after the USSR's Collective Farms

Besides giving priority to heavy industry, Mao's "CPC General Line for the Transition Period," introduced in 1953, also emphasized "the socialist transformation of agriculture, handicrafts and capitalist industry and commerce."[78] "Socialist transformation" referred to the nationalization of all major sectors including industry, commerce, finance and enterprises, as well as agricultural collectivization in the countryside.

The USSR's agricultural collectivization was initiated by Stalin in late autumn of 1929. Through "top-down revolution," agricultural production was carried out in collective farms across the country. Hundreds of millions of Soviet peasants were drafted into the system controlled directly by the ruling party and the government. By implementing agricultural collectivization, the USSR set up a new system led by the Soviet Communist Party Central Committee under Stalin's dictatorship. The new economic policy proposed by Lenin in his last days was abandoned, and the USSR took the path to industrialization that focused on heavy industry, bound farmers to their land, and prejudiced peasantry interests.[79] This was how the dual social structure took shape in the Soviet Union.

After the founding of the new PRC, land reform was conducted to distribute land equally among farmers. The reform also recognized the private ownership of land. Farmers were free to manage, trade or lease their lands. This was different from the Soviet system, under which all land was state-owned. Even before the collectivization of agriculture, Soviet peasants were granted only the right to use land. The land ownership system for Chinese farmers was even more flexible than that of Japanese farmers after the farmland reform in post-Second World War Japan.[80] China almost completed its nationwide land reform in 1953. In the same year, however, the CPC Central Party Committee abandoned its new democracy line to adopt the General Line for the Party during the Transition Period. This new roadmap included the "socialist reform" of agriculture. And, fortuitously perhaps, the Soviet model established after agricultural collectivization was precisely the same goal as stated by the CPC.[81]

Before that, the CPC Central Party Committee had already implemented agricultural cooperativization (nongye hezuohua yundong) in many parts of the country. However, it mainly took the form of mutual help groups and primary agricultural production cooperatives (primary cooperatives), leaving private ownership of land intact. After 1953, the CPC Central Party Committee refocused agriculture cooperativization on advanced agricultural production cooperatives (advanced cooperatives). Advanced cooperatives required that land be turned over for cooperative membership, the elimination of land remuneration, centralized management, and pure "allocation by labour." Advanced cooperatives thus caused a fundamental change in land ownership; previously privately owned land, farm animals and farming tools were put under public ownership. As ownership arrangements were the same as for the Soviet collective farms, advanced cooperatives in China used to be called collective farms, in their early days, before "advanced cooperatives" became the official name. The CPC Central Party Committee's Decision of 16 December 1953 on Developing Agricultural Production Cooperatives provided that "agricultural production cooperative in its current form may become an appropriate means to guide farmers to joining the more advanced and fully socialist agricultural production cooperatives (collective farms)."[82]

On 31 July 1955 Mao Zedong said in a meeting with provincial, municipal and autonomous region party secretaries that "the Soviet path is our right example"[83] for socialist agricultural reform. Mao criticized the Agriculture Department of the CPC Central Party Committee for making a right-leaning mistake, when the Department took a prudent position on the agriculture cooperativization movement.[84] In October 1955, the Sixth Plenary Session of the Seventh CPC Central Party Committee passed a Resolution on Matters Regarding Agriculture Cooperativization, stating that "the criticism against right-leaning opportunism was absolutely correct and necessary."[85] As a result, the CPC Central Party Committee's political pressure against being "right-leaning" prompted party leaderships at various levels to revise and increase their targets to artificially hype up agricultural collectivization. As a result, the formation of primary agriculture cooperatives was completed across the country in just months, in the second half of 1955.[86] One year later, in late November 1956, the CPC succeeded at establishing advanced cooperatives or collective farms across the country.[87]

China's agricultural cooperativization was modelled after Soviet collective farms, and both models were in essence the same. Ideologically, both models of agricultural collectivization highlighted public ownership as the bedrock of socialism. Both initiated agricultural collectivization as the linchpin for an industrialization strategy that focused on developing heavy industry, and used "class struggle" and anti-"right-leaning" as the means to drive to agricultural collectivization. Both countries showed little respect for the will of farmers, who were deprived of the ownership of and right to use their land and other factors of production without compensation.

There are also dissimilarities between Chinese and Soviet agricultural collectivization. First, in terms of ownership, land was state-owned in the Soviet Union while agricultural collectivization only dispossessed peasants of their private right to use the land. In China, agricultural collectivization deprived farmers of their private land ownership without giving them compensation, and their lands became collectivized. The other difference lies in the way in which agricultural collectivization was achieved. The Soviet Union used massive suppression and state violence to brutally "liquidate rich peasants" (*kulaks*), especially through execution by shooting, exile and imprisonment, as the major means to impose agricultural collectivization.[88] Although China carried out many enforced actions when it implemented collectivization, "liquidating rich farmers" was never a policy option. Furthermore, the CPC's strong grassroots leadership in rural areas prevented any possible unrest.[89] Compared to the Soviet Union, China had a larger population, less arable land and a lower degree of agricultural mechanization. These factors later contributed to different urbanization outcomes in China and the Soviet Union.

China's agriculture cooperativization did not draw upon the successes of western countries in developing agriculture cooperatives, nor was it derived from the theories of Engels and Lenin.[90] Instead, it duplicated the collective agriculture imposed by the Stalin regime. In a similar fashion to the tragic famine caused by heavy procurement that killed millions in the collectivized Soviet Union between 1932 and 1933,[91] China's agricultural collectivization, aggravated by the Great Leap Forward starting in 1958, also brought about a devastating famine that starved tens of millions of people to death between 1959 and 1961.[92] Like the Soviet Union, which suffered longstanding agricultural stagnation after collectivization, China's agriculture was generally unstable and relatively stagnant for more than two decades following agricultural collectivization to 1978.[93] An overwhelming majority of farmers had difficulty staying self-sufficient. Foreign scholars believe that the lives of Chinese farmers before *gaige kaifang* ("reform and opening-up") were worse than during the 1930s.[94]

(II) Implications of Rural Collectivization for the Dual Social Structure

1. Providing organizational framework for industrial capital accumulation

Both China and the Soviet Union had an unequivocal motivation for agricultural collectivization – to solve their food procurement crisis and power rapid industrialization by controlling and extracting agricultural surpluses.[95] On 31 July 1955, Mao Zedong explicitly pointed out at a meeting with provincial, municipal and autonomous region party secretaries that for socialist industrialization to become a reality, "the Soviet Union had resolved its problems by providing directions based on well thought-through plans and by systematically developing agricultural cooperativization. We could only follow the same approach."[96]

The CPC Central Party Committee had difficulty enforcing and operating its centralized procurement and distribution policy proposed in 1953. Rural collectivization was not in place, and hundreds of millions of farmers were widely scattered across the countryside.[97] In the Soviet experience, agricultural collectivization provided the organizational framework that made possible the use of "price scissors" to squeeze peasantry production.[98] On 6 October 1956 the State Council promulgated the *Regulations on Centralized Food Purchase and Distribution through Agricultural Production Cooperatives*, which provided that "the unit for centrally purchased and distributed quantities of the food production of agriculture cooperatives will generally be based on a single cooperative."[99] Thus, a centralized purchase and distribution system was put in place after collectivization. The State no longer had to deal directly with individual farmers scattered across the country; instead, it collaborated with hundreds of thousands of cooperatives. This provided greater convenience for accelerating food procurement, simplifying procurement and distribution procedures, and introducing a centralized procurement-and-sale system.[100]

As agriculture became increasingly collectivized, the State was able to secure more capital from the agricultural sector through "price scissors." Capital increased from RMB 3.621 billion in 1953 to RMB 5.132 billion in 1956 after the formation of advanced cooperatives (collectivized farms), and further to RMB 9.166 billion in 1958 after the introduction of the People's Commune. Except for selected years, the figures continued to climb. Between 1956 and 1978, farmers had contributed to RMB 325.4 billion worth of capital accumulation for industrialization; the per annum average was nearly RMB 14.1 billion, higher than the total infrastructure spending by the State on heavy industry during the same period.[101]

2. Further widening economic divide between urban and rural areas

The collectivization of agriculture in China has caused a lasting negative impact on the urban-rural relationship. A non-commodity exchange between urban and rural areas controlled by the State's administrative measures was established during collectivization. In other words, the State used administrative orders to acquire agricultural products from farmers at low prices. Accordingly, administrative restraints were imposed on farmers' production activities. Besides establishing collective agricultural organizations, the State also limited farmers' activities to agricultural production, and banned all non-agricultural production activities on the grounds that they were "pro-capitalist" in nature.

3. The Constraining "Unit System"

Along with the spread of public ownership in China, a special "unit" system came into being. By integrating political, economic and social functions, this "unit system" was introduced in 1949 as an organizational structure to manage people within a public ownership regime. This unit system was usually positioned in the cities for public servants (including government employees and workers).[102] This highly stifling and inward-looking unit system remains an important characteristic of Chinese society till today.

After collectivization, agricultural production cooperatives in effect became "units" that limited and constrained farmers. As the American scholar M. Selden has observed, there never was a tradition of voluntary participation and democracy throughout China's collectivized agriculture. The control of land, labour and harvests was transferred from individual households to collective units controlled by the State. State officials had absolute power over the lives and livelihood of villagers shackled to collectivized land.[103] In times of agricultural collectivization, farmers nearly became subject to labour under surveillance (*guanzhi laodong*).[104] After the introduction of People's Communes, organizations became military-like, activities were aggressive, and living was communal ("*Sanhua,*" or the *three changes*).[105] This bound farmers closely to collectivized land and collective agricultural production units.

In summary, agricultural collectivization caused farmers to turn over to the State (collective units) their land newly privatized from land reform. They lost economic leverage, having relinquished their right to rent or trade land, and even freedom of movement.[106] Farmers' freedom of movement and residence became increasingly restricted by the rural collective economic management regime.

VIII. DUAL *HUKOU* AND SUPPORT SYSTEMS FOR RURAL AND URBAN AREAS

As previously mentioned, the historical cause of the urban-rural dual social structure in China is multifold. Arguably, it is a result of an interplay of factors, such as the priority on heavy industry, the planned economy and agricultural collectivization. The dual social structure was further consolidated and manifested through a series of related systems.

(I) Legal Restrictions on Farmers' Freedom of Movement and Residence

1. From the Soviet Residence ID to China's Dual Hukou

After the October Revolution, especially during the time of New Economic Policy, Soviet peasants enjoyed freedom of movement. However, after agricultural collectivization, peasants were bound to the collective farm land. Their freedom of movement was in effect restricted. A real ban on peasants' freedom of movement under Soviet law was the domestic ID system introduced during the Great Famine of 1932. Heavy food procurement after agricultural collectivization and a host of other factors led to a massive human-induced famine. Driven by starvation, large groups of peasants tried to flee the countryside. To keep faminished villagers away from the cities, the Soviet Communist Party Central Party Committee and government adopted various restrictive measures, including mobilizing police, armies and internal affairs officers to set up posts on major roads and entrances to cities and towns.[107] Escaped peasants were forcefully deported.[108] On 27 December 1932 the government enacted the *Regulations on Resident IDs* (or the *Citizenship Law*), under which resident IDs were granted to city dwellers and workers over 16 years of age, but not to peasants. Therefore, there was no possibility that peasants could leave the countryside to live in the cities. For over 40 years until the new ID system was introduced in 1974,[109] Soviet peasants had completely lost their freedom of movement and residence. Soviet peasants had long been second-class citizens in the country. They were confined to the land, the ownership of which they were deprived of. Western observers argued that agricultural collectivization was the renaissance of the system of serfdom under the Czars.[110]

At the beginning of the new People's Republic of China, farmers also enjoyed freedom of movement and residence, and this freedom was reaffirmed by the Constitution. Pursuant to Article 5 of the *Common Program of the Chinese People's Political Consultative Conference* of 1949, essentially a temporary Constitution, the people of the People's Republic of China enjoy the freedom of movement and residence. Article 90.2 of the first Constitution of the PRC also clearly stipulates, "The citizens of the People's Republic of China enjoy the freedom of movement and residence."

In the run-up to 1957, the Chinese government had instituted policies to limit farmers' migration to cities. The *hukou* system that was initially developed solely for cities had set apart the urban household registration system from that of rural areas.

The law that limited farmers' freedom of movement and residence was the *Household Registration Regulations* passed at the Ninety-first session of the First Standing Committee of the National People's Congress on 9 January 1958.

2. *The direct cause for the introduction of the* Household Registration Regulations *of 1958*

With the adoption of the Party's General Line for the Transitional Period after 1953, farmers' freedom of movement and residence was subject to greater policy constraints.[111] Prior to advanced agricultural collectivization, however, farmers could be self-sufficient, and they could improve their lives with the land they owned; after collectivization in 1955, on the other hand, massive migration driven by starvation to the cities became much more evident.[112]

1956 and 1957 saw the exodus of farmers to the cities, after agricultural collectivization. Farmers' incomes were substantially shaved after the establishment of advanced cooperatives. According to a survey on 564 cooperatives in 20 provinces and autonomous regions, farmer households that suffered from an overall reduced income in 1956 accounted for a quarter to a third of total household numbers.[113] To make matters worse, greater empowerment for the management of advanced cooperatives translated into a higher frequency of verbal and physical abuse as well as torture against the farmers.[114] As a result of the extremes of collectivization, exacerbated by natural disasters, many provinces suffered a dramatically lower output in the fall of 1956. Farmers had difficulty filling their stomachs. Driven by desperation, many farmers fled their homes to seek a livelihood and opportunities in the cities.[115]

In response, the government issued several specific documents and directives starting in late 1956 to prevent the unregulated migration of rural population into the cities.[116] On 18 December 1957, the CPC Central Party Committee and the State Council jointly issued the *Instructions on Curbing Unregulated Outflow of Rural Population*, setting the stage for the promulgation of the *Household Registration Regulations* one year later.

The centrepiece of the *Household Registration Regulations* of 1958 was Article 10.2, which limits migration of farmers to cities. The Article reads as follows:

> To migrate from the countryside to a city, a citizen must possess the employment certificate of an urban labour department, the enrolment certificate of a school, or the certificate of migration acceptance issued by the city household registration authority, and shall apply for release with the rural household registration authority located at such citizen's place of domicile.[117]

Evidently, the immediate cause of the promulgation of the *Household Registration Regulations* of 1958 was the massive migration of farmers to the cities, which was driven by collective agriculture and the subsequent deprivation of their freedom of movement and residence. Article 10.2, which limits the mobility of farmers, was deemed the "true motive" for formulating the *Household Registration Regulations*.[118]

3. The expansion and completion of the dual household registration system that delineating the urban and rural populations

Restriction of farmers' freedom of movement and residence by law started with the implementation of the *Household Registration Regulations* of 1958. The *Regulations* imposed a set of review and approval procedures at the immigration destination and approval authority. Although it provided an institutional reference to restrict migration, the *Regulations* alone did not provide for strict differentiation between an urban and a rural *hukou*, or stringent restriction on the transfer and shift of *hukou*.[119] A dual household registration system that segregates rural and urban households was enacted by a set of policies and rules implemented in stages. For example, after 1963, the Ministry of Public Security started to draw clear distinctions between an "agricultural *hukou*" and a "non-agricultural *hukou*" in its demographic study.[120] In August 1964, the State Council circulated the draft *Regulations of the Ministry of Public Security on Handling* Hukou *Transfer*, which set forth very strict rules on the transfer of *hukou* from rural areas to cities and townships, and from townships to cities.[121] In December 1977, the State Council endorsed the official version of the *Regulations*, and further clarified the strict controls on *hukou* transfer from the countryside to big cities. By then, the dual *hukou* system that distinguishes between a city or township *hukou* and a rural *hukou*, and between a non-agriculture *hukou* and an agriculture *hukou*, had taken root.[122]

Furthermore, urban household administration involves more than the registration of residents and migrants. It also undertakes many other social functions. *Hukou* became a special instrument for political penalty, especially after 1958, the year that the dual household registration system was established. For example, as a result of the "cleansing of anti-revolutionists" and the crackdown of the "rightists" in the 1950s, many "anti-revolutionists" and "rightists" were revoked of their city *hukous* and were exiled to the countryside. After this came the Cultural Revolution, during which more people were denounced and criticized; they were released from their official duties, their city *hukous* were revoked and they were driven to the countryside. For urban and township dwellers in China, revocation of their city *hukous* was "punishment almost amounting to imprisonment."[123]

(II) Other Related Systems that Reinforced the Dual Social Structure

The Soviet resident ID system of 1932 not only limited the movement of peasants, but enforcement of the relevant institutions also deprived peasants of their right to live in the cities. The Soviet resident ID is by nature an "urban residence permit." In other words, the ID must be presented not only for residing in the city, but also for securing access to jobs, food, housing, children's education, healthcare, social security and domestic travel. It was also the only piece of personal identification.[124] Thus, no improvement was seen in the social status of farmers after agricultural collectivization; in fact, the second-class status of Soviet peasants had worsened.

The same applied to China. The household registration system was a major representation of the urban-rural dual social structure. However, without other support institutions, this system alone could do little except limit farmers' movement and residence. As identified at the beginning of this paper, the Industrialization and Urbanization of the Countryside Project Group of the Policy Research Centre, Ministry of Agriculture, recognized fourteen systems associated with the dual social structure in its two separate findings of 1988 and 1989.[125] The following is a further analysis of these systems.

First, these fourteen systems are intrinsically segregating by nature. They present China's dual social structure in different ways, in that they divide the urban and rural areas and distinguish between city dwellers and farmers. With the exception of the birth control system, thirteen of these fourteen systems favour urban residents as the "superior" breed.[126]

Second, to comprehend the entire picture of the dual social structure, we have to link the household registration system with the other systems in China. Many systems, such as the labour insurance system[127] and the grain and edible oil supply system, were in fact present long before the household registration system came on the scene.[128] Therefore, the unfair treatment of and discrimination against Chinese farmers did not start with the household registration system. The household registration system works in conjunction with several other systems.

Third, of all the fourteen systems, the labour insurance and welfare systems seem to be given greater weight. The greater labour insurance and welfare benefits enjoyed by urban residents are the direct result of a low wage system and a high rate of employment.[129] A low wage system compels the government to pay out higher fiscal subsidies every year to support urban and town residents. These subsidies, which translate into fiscal pressures on the government, were among the main reasons for maintaining curbs on farmers' emigration to the cities. This is also the reason why, till today, the dual household registration system cannot be abolished. A low wage system is thus part of a larger force that comprises the welfare and household registration systems.[130]

Fourth, one of the characteristics of China's household registration system can be seen from the "dual" marriage system; i.e. urban-rural relationships are based on the individual rather than on the household. This makes it difficult for young men and women who hold different *hukous* to marry each other. It also causes members of the same family to have different *hukous*. In other words, based on *hukou*, a family may consist of "urban residents" and "farmers" living under the same roof.

IX. Chinese Farmers' Rights after Reform and Opening-up

(I) Increasing Urban-Rural Disparity

Since China's reform and opening-up in 1978, the country's dual social structure has remained intact. Urban-rural disparity has become more pronounced despite the Chinese economy's sustained and rapid development. According to the *China Statistical Yearbook 2006*, the per capita disposal income of urban and township residents was RMB 1,374 in 1989, 2.29 times the rural resident's average net income of RMB 602. By 2005, the per capita disposal income of urban and township residents rose to RMB 10,493 and net income for a rural resident to RMB 3,255. The difference in their incomes has increased to 3.23 times.[131] Furthermore, according to the *Government Work Report* submitted to the 5th session of the 10th NPC on 5 March 2007, the per capita disposal income of urban and township residents was RMB 11,759 in 2006, 3.28 times higher than the RMB 3,587 per capita net income of rural residents. There are signs that this income gap will continue to widen. If other differential treatments in social security, welfare and education were factored in, the actual income gap would be much greater.

(II) Two Distinct Forms of Discrimination against Farmers after China's Reform and Opening-up

1. Land expropriation generated wealth for officials and businesses and deprived "sanwu" farmers of land

As China entered the 1990s, there was a countrywide scramble to build development zones and real estate projects. People rushed to acquire land. Under China's land policy, rural land cannot be traded in tier-one markets. Rural land for building development zones and real estate projects must be first expropriated by the government before it could be sold in tier-one markets. Rural lands were normally expropriated at a low cost and sold to developers with a high margin, creating a new type of "price scissors." These "price scissors" were far greater than those of the planned economy. As early as October 2002, Chen Xiwen, Deputy Head of the State Council Development Study Centre, already pointed out that "low cost land expropriation since the reform and opening-up has cost farmers at least RMB 2 trillion."[132]

According to the *People's Daily*, the official newspaper of the CPC Central Party Committee, a survey in Zhejiang province indicated that if the cost of land requisition is calculated as 100 percent, then the revenues from land sales are distributed as follows: 20-30 percent for local governments, 40-50 percent to business enterprises, nearly 30 percent to rural organizations and only 5-10 percent to farmers. A large part of the substantial returns generated from the huge margin was mostly taken by developers or local governments.[133] With most of the gains finding their way into the pockets of developers and governments or officials, farmers who had lost land received little in return. It is a well-known fact that many billionaires in China made their fortunes from land development and real estate speculation, and the second largest source of revenue for governments of various levels is land acquisition and sales.

Meanwhile, the *sanwu* farmers ("no farmland, no job, and no social insurance") have been deprived of land and have become a newly marginalized population.[134] The exact number of land-deprived farmers due to expropriation is unknown. As Han Jun, head of the Countryside Department of the State Council Development Study Centre, wrote in the preface to the *Survey on Landless Farmers* in May 2006, "the cumulative number of landless farmer might be around 40 to 50 million, already a huge population in society."[135] Land-deprived farmers have become a new vulnerable group.

The most fundamental cause of the plight of the *sanwu* landless farmers is the absence of real title to their properties. In other words, they have no right to own, use, profit from and dispose of their own properties. The historical cause of this problem is agricultural collectivization. When advanced cooperatives were formed in 1956, farmers were deprived of their land ownership without any compensation. And in its place was a collective land ownership system with ill-defined title. Such title was further obscured when People's Communes were set up in 1958. After the reform and opening-up, People's Communes were dissolved, and villages (towns) were formed. The former collective economic organizations disintegrated, and the household contract system was introduced in rural areas. Under the household contract system, individual farmers or households are only given the right to use the land for a specific term and purpose.[136] Whether as an individual or as a member of the rural collective ownership, a farmer does not really own his land. Thus, the cause of this problem still lies with the dual social structure.

2. Identity discrimination against migrant workers

After reform and opening-up, accelerated urban infrastructure construction and relaxed rules governing the outflow of rural labour resulted in the largest exodus of city-bound rural labour. Massive inter-regional rural labour migration started in the late 1980s. By the 1990s, migration numbers increased dramatically. According to an estimate by the National Office of Rural Fixed Watch Points, between 1995 and 2005, the outflow of rural labour had gone up from 50.66 million to 112 million people, and the percentage of the total rural labour population had risen from 11.2 percent to 22.2 percent.[137]

However, the fact is that farmers cannot alter their identities by simply taking jobs or running businesses in the cities. This is a unique attribute of the Chinese dual social structure. Since the beginning of the reform and opening-up, hundreds of millions of farmers have left the countryside to work in the cities. They live in the cities only "temporarily," because they cannot obtain city *hukou*s. Thus, the term "migrant worker" is unique to China.[138]

According to the 5th National Census, migrant workers represent 58 percent of the workforce in secondary industry, 52 percent in tertiary industry, 68 percent in processing and manufacturing, and 80 percent in the construction sector. Migrant workers are already a major component of the industrial workforce in China. Notwithstanding the vast numbers, migrant workers continue to be discriminated against in many ways in the cities. For example, they are generally underpaid, and the delay in salary disbursement is still a problem. They work long hours and under poor safety and sanitary conditions. They have no access to minimum labour protection, social security and public services provided by municipal governments.[139] A different identity also implies that migrant workers do not receive the same pay and treatment as urban residents for the same type of work. In addition, city employees enjoy many benefits, such as housing or a house provident fund, as well as health care and pensions; migrant workers are not entitled to any of these benefits.[140] Another study indicates that the actual monthly working hours of migrant workers are 50 percent longer than those of their city counterparts, but their monthly income is more than 40 percent lower. This means that a migrant worker's actual wage per working hour is only one quarter that of a city employee.[141]

X. CONCLUSION

In summary, guided by the General Line of the CPC for the Transition Period in 1953, the dual social structure in China has taken shape over time. It is the result of developing heavy industries as a priority, a planned economy, agricultural collectivization and other systems that segregate urban and rural areas. The Soviet model was the central influence behind these phenomena. It is, therefore, safe to conclude that the Soviet model was the principal hand behind the dual social structure in China.

As mentioned earlier, the Soviet Union was the first to create a dual social structure in the 20th century. The CPC followed the Soviet model after assuming power, and created a similar dual social structure. The commonality between the two models lies in the emphasis of the lofty goal of sacrificing farmers' interests for a strong socialist industrialized nation. Put otherwise, the so-called "long-term interest" of the nation was the goal, and for this it was necessary to sacrifice the immediate interests of farmers. A method of governance evolved where so long as the "ultimate end" is achieved, any cost is acceptable. However, history has proven that when the ruling party and its government accept any price or means to achieve the "ultimate end," any policy or measure will become an institution. Often, the "ultimate end" is not attained, while the evolved systems of injustice will become fixed, and their eradication impossible. The "immediate interests" of farmers or other social classes are sacrificed for this purpose, and they, and their many subsequent generations, are discriminated against. No remedy is adequate for their seriously eroded rights as citizens, and the high prices they have paid. Gu Zhun, a person who had long suffered political persecution but had remained steadfast in his opinions, made the following insightful observation on the relationship between the "ultimate goal" and democracy:

> A revolutionist per se is first a democrat. However, when he establishes an ultimate goal and finds it in his heart to believe in this goal, he will have no reservation in sacrificing democracy and imposing dictatorship to attain this goal. Stalin was indeed brutal, but perhaps his brutality was not 100 percent for amassing personal powers. Instead he believed it was for the public good, and that was the way it had to be to achieve the ultimate goal. It is lamentable that someone with good intention had actually committed depravity.[142]

History has attested that an illegitimate means often negates a justifiable end. Underhanded means employed after an extreme revolution often lead to totalitarianism and social tragedies. Under the Soviet regime, many government practices often required unscrupulous methods, or achievement of the end at any price. This was because of the concentration of power within the ruling party and its government. These powers were not governed by law. The party and government were not separate. There was no independent judiciary. In effect, the party and government officials appointed top-down were only accountable to their superiors. Their superiors, on the other hand, assumed no political or judicial liability for any consequence that resulted from serious prejudices of the individual or collective rights of citizens. Opinions and speeches were under stringent control. Thus, a critical deficiency in the Soviet model is the absence of democracy and the rule of law. This author believes that this is what determined the failure of the Soviet system.

Since the reform and opening-up in 1978, China has experienced sustained and rapid economic growth, as well as profound societal changes. Within three decades after 1978, China has also implemented reforms in politics, legislation, administration and justice, with notable progress. For example, the lifelong tenure of state and party leaders was eliminated. The birth of many laws, including the *Administrative Procedure Law*, the *State Compensation Law*, the *Criminal Procedure Law*, the *Labour Law* and the *Law on the Protection of Women's Rights*, ended an under-legislated and disorderly era. Also as a result of reform, the attorney system, which was abandoned in 1957, was resumed. As an important step in juridical reform, a nationally centralized annual bar examination was instituted in 2002. Previously taboo human rights issues are now fervently debated. Many universities even opened human rights research centres and organized human rights courses.[143] In 2004, Article 32 of the NPC-amended Constitution had its first human rights-related insertion, stating: "[t]he State respects and protects human rights." So far, China has ratified over 22 international human rights treaties. In February 2008, the Chinese government published a *White Paper on Building the Rule of Law in China*, which stated that "[t]he rule of law is a hallmark of political civilization arriving at a certain historical phase. It incorporates human wisdom and is aspired to and sought after by people of all countries."

That being said, China's political reform has only made partial and limited progress. For example, despite the inscription of the human rights clause, China's Constitution continues to bear resemblance to a political agenda or manifesto.[144] China has no judicial review system, meaning that the human rights and citizens' rights clauses provided for in the Constitution cannot be readily applied in courts as a general rule. As a matter of fact, under the highly ideological and politically charged constitutional framework, the author doubts whether a judicial review system for the Constitution, if it exists, would actually achieve its purpose. No human right treaty ratified by China is readily applicable at domestic courts.[145] Although the idea of human rights is no longer taboo, the topic is still very sensitive. Literature with shrewd and penetrating criticisms against the political system usually remains unpublished.

In a separate instance, although the Chinese government has recognized the rule of law as a mark of political civilization ("*zhengzhi wenmin*"), the CPC central government, the official media and even most legal experts have nonetheless confused the "rule of law" with "rule by law." Their understanding of the former principle still deviates considerably from international consensus. Historically, the rule of law was derived chiefly from the Magna Carta of 1215 in England. After the Glorious Revolution in 1688, England was the first country in the world to have established the systems and theories on the rule of law. The intrinsic qualities of the rule of law were further enriched by the experience and lessons of the US and other countries. The rule of law, as understood by the international community, should generally include, among other things, limiting the supreme power of a state and all powers of public officials, protecting individual freedom and fundamental rights in strict accordance with the due process of law, and observing judicial independence, with the independence of judges being central.[146] This is the rule of law set forth in the preamble to the 1948 *Universal Declaration of Human Rights*. China's political reform should start by instituting the rule of law and fulfilling its basic requisites. More specifically, it should take institutional measures to effectively restrict the powers of all state organs, parties, groups and organizations controlling public powers, and to protect individual rights through independent justice. On this, we may find corresponding provisions under the current version of the Chinese Constitution of 1982.[147] Promoting democracy on the premise of an established rule of law will also create a stable social environment, because the rule of law can prevent top-down autocracy and bottom-up unrest.[148] A sustainable Chinese economy also requires the protection provided by the rule of law.

The recent *sannong* problems and discrimination against migrant workers in cities have captured widespread attention, even that of the government. China has abolished the agriculture tax since 2006. The Chinese government has also substantially increased its investment in rural development and agriculture. Aggregate State spending on addressing the *sannong* problems amounted to RMB 1.6 trillion over a five year period.[149] However, Chinese farmers continue to face discrimination in terms of social and economic rights, as well as citizen and political rights. For example, as farmers have no freedom of association to this day, they are deprived of a central vehicle to ensure that their voices are heard. China offers incomplete freedom of publication. Some works that depicted the real life of farmers were banned. For instance, the *Survey on Chinese Farmers* (*Zhong Guo Nong Min Diao Cha*) authored by the husband and wife team of Chen Guidi and Chun Tao in 2004, was banned soon after it became a bestseller, despite the availability of its English and Japanese versions. Another example is the quasi-Soviet People's Congress system in China. This system not only has minimal direct elections, but also contains no election system to reflect voters' will.[150] Without the freedom of association and of expression, elections often become a system without teeth. Of all the delegates represented at the National People's Congress, even without indirect election, farmers are few and far between, and there are even fewer representatives who have farmers' interests in mind. At the Tenth NPC meeting in 2003, only 56 out of a total of 2,984 delegates, or 1.9 percent, were farmers (not to mention many of them were rural entrepreneurs), despite the fact that farmers account for over 70 percent of the entire population of China. By contrast, county-level and above party and government officials amounted to 1,240, a staggering 42 percent of the total number of representatives.[151] China currently has a migrant worker population of 220 million, yet these people have no right to vote in the cities.[152] At the Eleventh NPC in March 2008, only three migrant workers were represented out of a total number of 2,987. In addition, locally staffed and financially dependent Chinese courts[153] make it difficult for farmers to seek judicial relief through the justice system when local governments infringe on their rights. Farmers, therefore, have to rely on the more tedious channel of *shangfang* (direct appeal to the authorities). At the same time, some instances of group violence and conflicts in rural areas have occurred in recent years. The fact is that civil, political, and socio-economic rights are inseparable and interrelated. As set forth under Paragraph 5, Part I of the *Vienna Declaration and Program of Action* passed by the Second UN World Conference on Human Rights of 1993, "All human rights are universal, indivisible and interdependent and interrelated." The lack of adequate and equal legal protection for the civil and political rights of Chinese farmers is also a major factor leading to the continued discrimination against them.

Understandably, despotic traditions and the Soviet model remain the two critical elements in the politics of contemporary China.[154] The Soviet model left its imprint not only on China's economic structure, but also on its political, legal, ideological and cultural regime. Since reform and opening-up, China's economy has developed beyond the Soviet stereotype. However, its political system and many aspects of its justice system continue to operate under the ex-Soviet structure due to relatively slow political reform. Therefore, together with China's transformation from a planned economy to a market economy with Chinese characteristics, there is greater leeway for abuse of power by party and government officials. This trend of deteriorating circumstances is well exemplified by the different levels of government profiting from the expropriation of farmers' land; by the government's disregard of the basic rights of migrant workers for the sake of further investment; by the many land-deprived farmers and migrant workers resorting to *shangfang* because they have no access to fair judicial remedies; by the involvement of businesses and government agencies in corrupt "crony capitalism"; and by the rampant operation of sweat shops and black kilns that have complete disregard for human rights, among other ills.[155]

To this day, the Soviet economic model has been the main target of China's reform; for example, transforming from collective agricultural production to a household contract system, from a planned economy to a market economy, from solely public ownership to the coexistence of diversified ownerships, and so on. However, China's economic reform is still ongoing – such as reform of the state-owned enterprises (SOEs), the SOEs' industrial monopoly and the financial sector – and the dual social structure continues to prevail. Many new social challenges have emerged, such as the widening of the income gap, urban-rural disparity, the stripping of state-owned assets, the destruction of the natural environment, and rampant corruption and embezzlement. These challenges cannot be addressed by simply restructuring the economy. There must be political reform. It is about time that casting off and rising above the Soviet model become the central items on China's political agenda.

ENDNOTES

1   M. Banton, *Discrimination*, Buckingham of Philadelphia: Open University Press, 1994, p. 7.
2   *Restatement of the Law Third, Foreign Relations Law of United States*, §702, Comment, l gender discrimination, Vol. 2, St. Paul, Minn.: American Law Institute Publishers, 1987, p. 166.
3   B.G. Ramcharan, "Equality and Nondiscrimination," *The International Bill of Rights: the Covenant on Civil and Political Rights*, ed. L. Henkin, New York: Columbia University Press, 1981, p. 252.
4   163 U.S. 537 (1896). Although the US abolished slavery in 1865, racial segregation existed as a legal institution for the better part of a century thereafter.
5   347 U.S. 483 , 495. (1954).
6   From top to bottom the ten social strata include: (1) State and social management; (2) Managers of large and medium-sized enterprises; (3) Owners of small and medium-sized businesses; (4) Special technicians; (5) Clerks – middle and low-level civil servants in government and party agencies; (6) Sole business proprietors; (7) Employees in commerce and service sector; (7) Industrial workers; (9) *Farmers*; (10) Urban and rural jobless, unemployed and semi-employed people. Therefore, *farmers* and the jobless and unemployed people all belong to the bottom strata of the society. *Research Report on Contemporary Chinese Social Strata (Dang Dai Zhong Guo She Hui Jie Ceng Yan Jiu Bao Gao)*, ed. Lu Xueyi, Social Sciences Academic Press, 2002, p. 10-23.

7   The 2003 Seminar was co-organized by the Research Centre for Human Rights of the Law School of Peking University, OHCHR, UNDP and DFID China Office. This report was published on p.1-39 of No. 2, Volume 3 of the *Peking University International and Comparative Law Review (Bei Da Guo Ji Fa Yu Bi Jiao Fa Ping Lun)* in 2005.

8   For example, Article 16 of *Electoral Law of the National People's Congress and Local People's Congress* (Amended in 1995) provides that the number of deputies to the National People's Congress to be elected by the provinces, autonomous regions, and municipalities directly under the Central Government shall be allocated by the Standing Committee of the National People's Congress in accordance with the principle that the number of people represented by each rural deputy is four times the number of people represented by each urban deputy.

9   In the earthquake in Sichuan, China on 12 May 2008, many rural primary and middle schools were destroyed, causing many student casualties. One of the major reasons is the long-term inadequacy of rural education funds, which leads to the poor quality of school buildings. Yang Dongping, *Offering Education Responsible for Children (Ju Ban Dui De Qi Hai Zi De Jiao Yu), The Beijing News*, 24 May 2008. Of course, there are other reasons including the issue of "jelly" projects due to corruption in local governments and construction departments.

10 According to the *Interpretation Relating to Certain Questions Concerning the Application of Law to the Hearing of Person Damage Compensation Cases (Guan Yu Shen Li Ren Shen Sun Hai Pei Chang An Jian Shi Yong Fa Lv Ruo Gan Wen Ti De Jie Shi)*, issued by the People's Supreme Court in 2003, damages for death should be calculated according to the per capita disposal income of urban residents or per capita net income of farmer in the previous year in the hearing court's locality by twenty years (Article 29). Since there is a four to six fold difference between the incomes of urban and rural residents, the damages for death will also correspond to such a gap. *Gazette of the Supreme People's Court of the People's Republic of China (Zhong Hua Ren Min Gong He Guo Zui Gao Ren Min Fa Yuan Gong Bao)*, Issue 2, 2004, p. 3-7.

11 *China Population Yearbook (Zhong Guo Ren Kou Nian Jian)*, 2006, p. 449.

12 Of course, there are some ideological factors. According to the guiding principles of the CPC and Article 1 of China's incumbent Constitution, the working class are the leaders while the peasants are their allies under the leadership of the working class.

13 Urbanization and Industrialization of the Countryside Project Group, Policy Research Centre, Ministry of Agriculture, *Dual Social Structure: The Urban-Rural Relationship, Industrialization and Urbanization (Er Yuan She Hui Jie Gou: Cheng Xiang Guan Xi: Gong Ye Hua·Cheng Shi Hua), Economic Research Reference (Jing Ji Yan Jiu Can Kao Zi Liao)*, 1988, Issue 90, p. 17-19. Industrialization and Urbanization of the Countryside and Agricultural Modernization Project Group, written by Liu Bin, *Dual Social Structure: One Way to Analyze Industrialization and Urbanization of China's Countryside (Er Yuan She Hui Jie Gou: Fen Xi Zhong Guo Nong Cun Gong Ye Hua Cheng Shi Hua De Yi Tiao Si Lu), Economic Research Reference (Jing Ji Yan Jiu Can Kao Zi Liao)*, 1989, Issue 170/171, p. 10-11. In 1990, key members of the two groups, Guo Shutian and Liu Chunbin, published a book entitled *Imbalanced China (Shi Heng De Zhong Guo)*, elaborating the dual social structure of China.

14 Part III. Dual Economies in *Selected Economic Writings of W. Arthur Lewis*, ed. M. Gerosvitz, New York: New York University Press, 1983, p. 329-339; p. 461-478.

15 Zhang Yinghong and Qi Zuliang, *The Chinese Farmer and Contemporary Politics (Zhong Guo Nong Min Yu Dang Dai Zheng Zhi)*, China Literature and History Press, 2005, p. 2; *Breaking the Dual Social Structure: Rural Migrant Workers, Urbanization and the Building of a New Countryside (Zou Chu Er Yuan Jie Gou Nong Min Gong, Cheng Zhen Hua Yu Xin Nong*

Cun Jian She), ed. Chinese Association of Rural Labour Force Resources Development, China Development Press, 2006, p. 107.

16   See Part V.

17   Wang Weihai, *China's Household Registration System: Historical and Political Analyses* (*Zhong Guo Hu Ji Zhi Du Li Shi Yu Zheng Zhi De Fen Xi*), Shanghai Culture Publishing House, 2006, p. 258-260.

18   Henri Pirenne, *Cities in the Middle Ages* (*Zhong Shi Ji De Cheng Shi*) (*Les villes du moyen âge*), trans. Chen Guoliang, The Commercial Press, 2006, p. 107-108.

19   Zhao Gang, Chen Zhongyi, *A History of China's Economic Systems* (*Zhong Guo Jing Ji Zhi Du Shi*), New Star Press, 2006, p. 339, 363; Zhao Gang, *Thesis Collection on China's Urban Development* (*Zhong Guo Cheng Shi Fa Zhan Lun Ji*), New Star Press, 2006, p. 12-22.

20   Compiled by the Bureau of Household Administration, the Ministry of Public Security, *Household Administration Laws and Regulations from the End of Qing Dynasty to the Republic of China* (*Qing Chao Mo Qi Zhi Zhong Hua Min Guo Hu Ji Guan Li Fa Gui*), Beijing: Mass Publishing House, 1996, p. 29-53. Although the Kuomintang government also used the *bao-jia* system to restrict people's freedom, the system was limited to designated anti-CPC areas with no purpose to restrict urban-rural population movement. See *Regulations for Compiling and Investigating Bao-Jia and Hukou in Counties within Suppression Area X* by the General Headquarters of Yu-E-Wan Suppression Area X, and the *Bao-Jia Regulations* of 1937. See above 209, p. 227.

21   The full text of the speech was first published in the *CPC's Literature* (*Dang De Wen Xian*), Issue 4, 2003, p. 20-24.

22   *Selected Works of Chen Yun* (*Chen Yun Wen Xuan*) (*1949-1956*), People's Publishing House, 1984, p. 207-214, 216.

23   *Compilation of Important Documents on Agricultural Collectivization* (*Nong Ye Ji Ti Hua Zhong Yao Wen Jian Hui Bian*), Vol. I, Publishing House of the Central Communist Party School, 1981, p. 215-227.

24   *Selected Works of Mao Zedong* (*Mao Zedong Xuan Ji*), (Four Volumes in One), p. 1418.

25   For example, Mao Zedong pointed out in his report at the 2nd Plenary Session of the 7th CPC Central Party Committee on 5 March 1949, "For a long period of time in the future, China's agriculture and handicrafts will still be scattered and individual in terms of mode." With regard to industry, "we should capitalize on the initiative of urban and rural private capital as much as possible." In the period of new democracy, the economy of various ownerships including private ownership should be maintained in the long-term. *Selected Works of Mao Zedong* (*Mao Zedong Xuan Ji*), (Four Volumes in One), p. 633-639.

26   Mao Zedong believed that the PRC began to transfer to socialism from its establishment. It would take ten to fifteen years to complete the transition, instead of preparing for the transition. Such an observation "changed the opinion of the CPC in essence" because it clarified that the period of new democracy was the "transition period." Bo Yibo, *Retrospection on a Few Major Decisions and Events* (*Ruo Gan Zhong Da Jue Ce Yu Shi Jian De Hui Gu*), Vol. I, Publishing House of the Central Communist Party School, 1991, p. 228-229.

27   Lu Zhenxiang, Yang Maorong and Wang Chaoxiang, "On the Proposal of the General Line for the Transition Period: A Brief Introduction of Relevant Publications" (*Guan Yu Guo Du Shi Qi Zong Lu Xian De Ti Chu: Wen Xian Fa Biao Qing Kuang Jian Shu*), *The CPC's Literature* (*Dang De Wen Xian*), Issue 4, 2003, p. 28, 34.

28   *The CPC's Literature* (*Dang De Wen Xian*), Issue 4, 2003, p. 20. The Constitution adopted at the 1st Session of the 1st NPC in September 1954 included the CPC's General Line for the Transition Period in its General Outline as the central task of the country in the transition period.

29 Xing Heming, *The Soviet Model in the CPC's Eye* (*Zhong Gong Yan Li De Su Lian Mo Shi*), Fujian People's Press, 2006, p. 45-66.

30 *USSR Population in 70 Years* (*Su Lian Ren Kou Qi Shi Nian*) (Население СССР за 70 лет Рыбаковский 70 Л.Л.), compiled by Рыбаковский, Л.Л., trans. Guo Liqun, Beijing: the Commercial Press, 1994, p. 16.

31 In December 1947, in his report *The Current Situation and Our Task* at a session of the CPC Central Party Committee, Mao accepted the concept of "two camps" and began to criticize the middle route. *On People's Democratic Despotism*, published on 30 June 1949, explicitly expressed the one-sided policy. *Selected Works of Mao Zedong* (*Mao Zedong Xuan Ji*), (Four Volumes in One), p. 1202-1204, 1296-1299, 1410. See also Xu Xiaotian, Li Chunlong and Xu Zhenze, *High-level Exchanges between the New China and the USSR* (*Xin Zhong Guo Yu Su Lian De Gao Ceng Wang Lai*), Vol. I, Changchun: Jilin People's Press, 2001, p. 43-44.

32 The CPC leaders represented by Mao Zedong always thought that the Soviet model was the only socialist model. Although they tried to surpass the Soviet model in theoretical and practical explorations with Chinese characteristics, they never discarded the model's guiding principles. Instead, they tried to improve it. See *Comments on The Cambridge History of China* (*Ping Jian Qiao Zhong Hua Ren Min Gong He Guo Shi*), ed. Jin Mingchun, Shijiazhuang: Hebei People's Press, 2001, p. 143.

33 In return, China provided mineral and agricultural products and huge amount of foreign exchange to the USSR. Dieter Heinzig, *The Soviet Union and Communist China 1945-1950* (*Zhong Su Zou Xiang Lian Meng De Jian Nan Li Cheng*) (*Die Sowjetunion und das kommunistische China 1945-1950*), trans. Zhang Wenwu, Li Danlin *et al.*, Beijing: Xinhua Press, 2001, p. 671.

34 Among the early leaders of the CPC, and with the notable exception of Mao, most of the others had studied in the USSR, including Liu Shaoqi, Zhang Wentian, Kang Sheng, Deng Xiaoping, Dong Biwu, Yang Shangkun, Chen Yun, Li Lisan, Zhu De, Chen Boda and Ye Jianying. See Xu Xiaotian, Li Chunlong and Xu Zhenze, *High-level Exchanges between the New China and the USSR* (*Xin Zhong Guo Yu Su Lian De Gao Ceng Wang Lai*), Vol. I, p. 57.

35 *Compilation of Resolutions of Soviet Communist Party Congress Sessions, Representative Meetings and Plenary Sessions of the Central Party Committee* (*Su Lian Gong Chan Dang Dai Biao Da Hui Dai Biao Hui Yi He Zhong Yang Quan Hui Jue Yi Hui Bian*) (КПСС в резолюциях и решениях), Compilation and Translation Bureau of Works by Marx, Engels, Lenin and Stalin of the CPC Central Party Committee, Book 3, People's Publishing House, 1964, p. 77-79.

36 *Complete Works of Stalin* (*Si Da Lin Quan Ji*), Vol. 8, p. 64-65.

37 The resolution approving the 1st five-year plan at the 5th Soviet Congress in May 1929 also pointed out, "investment in industry is mainly for means of production (accounting for 78 percent of the total investment in industry)." *Compilation of USSR National Economic Plan Documents: the First Five-Year Plan* (*Su Lian Guo Min Jing Ji Jian She Wen Jian Hui Bian: Di Yi Ge Wu Nian Ji Hua*), People's Publishing House, 1955, 11, p. 86.

38 *Complete Works of Stalin* (*Si Da Lin Quan Ji*), Vol. 8, p. 112-113.

39 Cited by Xing Heming, *The Soviet Model in the CPC's Eye* (*Zhong Gong Yan Li De Su Lian Mo Shi*), p. 45-66.

40 Mao Zedong particularly criticized the views of "establishing new democracy social order," "moving from new democracy to socialism" and "ensuring private property," deeming these ideas as right-leaning and divergent from the General Line. *Selected Works of Mao Zedong* (*Mao Zedong Xuan Ji*), Vol. 5, p. 81-82.

[41] *An Anthology of Mao Zedong's Works* (*Mao Ze Dong Zhu Zuo Xuan Du*), Vol. II, People's Publishing House, 1986, p. 831.

[42] *Economic History of the People's Republic of China* (*Zhong Hua Ren Min Gong He Guo Jing Ji Shi*), Vol. I, ed. Dong Fureng, Economic Science Press, 1999, p. 268-269, 300-301.

[43] Xiao Donglian, "A Historical Examination of China's Dual Social Structure" (*Zhong Guo Er Yuan She Hui Jie Gou De Li Shi Kao Cha*), Research on CPC History (*Zhong Gong Dang Shi yan Jiu*), Issue 1, 2005, p. 25-26.

[44] *Complete Works of Stalin* (*Si Da Lin Quan Ji*), Vol. 11, p. 138-140.

[45] Zhores Medvedev, *Soviet Agriculture*, New York: W.W. Norton & Company, 1987, p. 87-88.

[46] *A Brief History of China's Socialist Economy* (*Zhong Guo She Hui Zhu Yi Jing Ji Jian Shi*), ed. Liu Suinian and Wu Ganqun, Heilongjiang People's Press, 1985, p. 110.

[47] On average, from 1949 to 1951, China's agricultural output accounted for over 55 percent of total social output and took up more than 65 percent in industrial and agricultural output. Net output of agriculture accounted for over 65 percent of the national income and took up more than 80 percent in industrial and agricultural net output. The rural labour force accounted for more than 85 percent of the total and the rural population accounted for more than 89 percent of the total. Chen Wenhui, Feng Haifa and Shi Tongqing, *The Farmer and Industrialization* (*Nong Min Yu Gong Ye Hua*), Guizhou People's Press, 1994, p. 26, p. 68-69.

[48] *Selected Works of Mao Zedong* (*Mao Zedong Xuan Ji*), Vol. 5, p. 182.

[49] Compiled by Liu Guoguang, *Studies of Strategic Issues in China's Economic Development* (*Zhong Guo Jing Ji Fa Zhan Zhan Lue Wen Ti Yan Jiu*), Shanghai People's Press, 1984, p. 409.

[50] *China Statistical Yearbook* (*Zhong Guo Tong Ji Nian Jian*), 1983, p. 16.

[51] *China Labour Statistical Yearbook* (*Zhong Guo Lao Dong Tong Ji Nian Jian*), 2006, p. 7-8.

[52] *China's Dual Social Structure: Conflicts and Strategic Choice of Industrialization* (*Wo Guo Er Yuan Jie Gou Mao Dun Yu Gong Ye Hua Zhan Lue Xuan Ze*), ed. Wang Jiye and Wang Jianye, China Planning Press, 1996, p. 38.

[53] *China Statistical Yearbook* (*Zhong Guo Tong Ji Nian Jian*), 2006, p. 99.

[54] Soon after Russia's October Revolution, due to foreign military intervention and the months-old civil war, the Soviet government began to implement the policy of "military communism" (the policy or "war communism") in the summer of 1918. Apart from temporary measures to meet the needs at wartime, "military communism" also included transition measures towards "communism." Wang Shutong and Qian Yajun, "Comments on Communism at Wartime and Direct Transition Path" (*Ping Zhan Shi Gong Chan Zhu Yi Yu Zhi Jie Guo Du De Dao Lu*), Collection of Papers on the Modern History of the USSR (*Su Lian Xian Dai Shi Lun Wen Ji*), p. 48-49.

[55] *Compilation of Resolutions of Soviet Communist Party Congress Sessions, Representative Meetings and Plenary Sessions of the Central Party Committee* (*Su Lian Gong Chan Dang Dai Biao Da Hui Dai Biao Hui Yi He Zhong Yang Quan Hui Jue Yi Hui Bian*), Book 1, p. 541, 546-547.

[56] Edward Hallett Carr, *The Bolshevik Revolution 1917-1923*, London: Macmillan, 1952, Vol. 2, p. 364.

[57] *Compilation of Documents on the USSR's Economic Construction Plans: the First Five-Year Plan* (*Su Lian Guo Min Jing Ji Jian She Ji Hua Wen Jian Hui Bian Di Yi Ge Wu Nian Ji Hua*), People's Press, 1955.

58   Chen Huashan, "Tentative Review of National Monopolistic Socialism: Discussion of the Economic Mode of Stalin" (*Shi Lun Guo Jia Long Duan She Hui Zhu Yi Dui Si Da Lin Jing Ji Mo Shi De Tan Tao*), *Historical Issues of the USSR* (*Su Lian Li Shi Wen Ti*), 1993, p. 3-4, 12.

59   *Economic History of the People's Republic of China* (*Zhong Hua Ren Min Gong He Guo Jing Ji Shi*), Vol. I, ed. Dong Fureng, p. 130.

60   It did so in the following ways: first, it helped design 156 (154 were finalized) industrial construction projects, carrying out a series of work ranging from inspection, location, collection of basic design material, design and construction. Second, it provided complete sets of equipment and key single unit equipment for these projects. Personnel were dispatched to instruct installation and operation as well as provide technical material for new products. Third, experts were sent to provide technical and material experience and managerial expertise. In addition, in October 1954, the USSR provided long-term loans to China of 520 million roubles (US$ 580 million). Li Zhining: *Big Industry and China to the 1950s* (*Da Gong Ye Yu Zhong Guo Zhi Er Shi Shi Ji Wu Shi Nian Dai*), Jiangxi People's Press, 1997, p. 217-218.

61   *Rural Economic Affairs of the New China* (*Xin Zhong Guo Nong Cun Ji Shi*), p. 111.

62   Xiao Donglian, "A Historical Examination of China's Dual Social Structure" (*Zhong Guo Er Yuan She Hui Jie Gou De Li Shi Kao Cha*), *Research on CPC History* (*Zhong Gong Dang Shi yan Jiu*), Issue 1, 2005, p. 25-26.

63   In January 1928, the Political Bureau of the Soviet Communist Party Central Party Committee secretly ordered unusual measures to purchase food, in order to acquire farmer's food by force under Article 107 of the *Criminal Law*, which punished speculation. In addition, in spring 1929, Ural-Siberian style compulsory requisitioning of food by purchase was implemented throughout the nation. Taniuchi Yuzuru, *The Establishment of the Stalinist Political System* (in Japanese), Vol. 1 and 4, Tokyo: Yiwanami Press, 1970; 1986, p. 363, 484. R. Conquest, *The Harvest of Sorrow: Soviet Collectivization and the Terror-Famine*, London: Hutchinson, 1986, p. 94.

64   *Selected Works of Chen Yun* (*Chen Yun Wen Xuan*) (*1949-1956*), People's Publishing House, 1984, p. 202-203.

65   Lin Yunhui and Gu Xunzhong, *A Rhapsody on People's Commune* (*Ren Min Gong She Kuang Xiang Qu*), Henan People's Press, 1995, p. 127.

66   *The Cambridge History of China: The People's Republic; Part I: The Emergence of Revolutionary China: 1949-1965*, ed. R. MacFarquhar and J.K. Fairbank, trans. Xie Liangsheng *et al.*, China Social Sciences Press, 1990, p. 171.

67   *The Memoir of Xue Muqiao* (*Xue Mu Qiao Hui Yi Lu*), p. 217.

68   *Compilation of Important Documents on Agricultural Collectivization* (*Nong Ye Ji Ti Hua Zhong Yao Wen jian Hui bian*), Vol. I, p. 212.

69   *Selected Works of Chen Yun* (*Chen Yun Wen Xuan*) (*1949-1956*), p. 207-214, 216.

70   On 15 November 1953, the CPC Central Party Committee made the *Decision on Implementing Planned Purchase of Oil Bearing Materials Nationwide* (*Guan Yu Zai Quan Guo Shi Xing Ji Hua Shou Gou You Liao De Jue Ding*). On 9 September 1954, the State Council of the central government issued the *Order on Implementing Planned Purchase and Planned Supply of Cotton Cloth* (*Guan Yu Shi Xing Mian Bu Shou Gou He Ji Hua Gong Ying De Ming Ling*) and the *Order on Planned Purchase of Cotton* (*Guan Yu Mian Hua Ji Hua Shou Gou De Ming Ling*).

71   Edward Friedman, Paul G. Pickowicz and Mark Selden: *Chinese Village, Socialist State*, trans. Tao Heshan, China Social Sciences Press, 2002, p. 15.

72   *Economic History of the People's Republic of China* (*Zhong Hua Ren Min Gong He Guo Jing Ji Shi*), Vol. I, ed. Dong Fureng, p. 257.

73   *China Labour Statistical Yearbook* (*Zhong Guo Lao Dong Tong Ji Nian Jian*), 2006, p. 7-8.

74   Gao Peiyi, *Comparative Studies of Urbanization in China and Foreign Countries* (*Zhong Wai Cheng Shi Hua Bi jiao Yan Jiu*), Nankai University Press, 1991, p. 91.

75   Li Ai, *Government Behaviour in the Relocation of the Rural Labour Force* (*Nong Cun Lao Dong Li Zhuan Yi De Zheng Fu Xing Wei*), Shandong People's Press, 2006, p. 70, 78.

76   *Agriculture in Contemporary China* (*Dang Dai Zhong Guo De Nong Ye*), ed. Zhu Rong, Contemporary China Publishing House, 1992, p. 119-120.

77   Du Runsheng, *Institutional Changes in China's Countryside* (*Zhong Guo Nong Cun Zhi Du Bian Qian*), Sichuan People's Press, 2003, p. 65, 85.

78   The full text of the speech was first published in the *CPC's Literature* (*Dang De Wen Xian*), Issue 4, 2003, p. 20-24.

79   Robert Conquest, *The Harvest of Sorrow: Soviet Collectivization and the Terror-Famine*, p. 47; Taniuchi Yuzuru, *op. cit.*, Vol. 1, p. 364.

80   Fukushima Masao, *Study on the People's Commune* (in Japanese), Tokyo: Ochanomizu Press, 1960, p. 217.

81   Well before the CPC took power, Mao had argued in 1943 that the collectivization of agriculture is necessary for realizing socialism, while the only means to collective agriculture is to institute the Soviet models of collective farms or agricultural production cooperatives. See "Organize Up" (*Zu Zhi Qi Lai*), in *Selected Works of Mao Zedong, op. cit.*, p. 885.

82   *Compilation of Important Dossiers on the Collectivization of Agriculture* (*Nong Ye Ji Ti Hua Zhong Yao Wen Jian Hui Bian*), Vol. I, p. 215-227.

83   *Selected Works of Mao Zedong*, vol. V, p. 174-175, 181-182 and 186.

84   *Selected Works of Mao Zedong*, vol. V, p. 168.

85   *Compilation of Important Dossiers on the Collectivization of Agriculture* (*Nong Ye Ji Ti Hua Zhong Yao Wen Jian Hui Bian*), Vol. I, p. 450.

86   *Compilation of Important Dossiers on the Collectivization of Agriculture*, Vol. 1, p. 449, 528; *Historical Facts on China's Agriculture Cooperativization Movement*, Vol. II, SUP Press, 1957, p. 857.

87   *Milestones in the Economy of the People's Republic of China: Oct.1949-Sept.1984* (*Zhong Hua Ren Min Gong He Guo Jing Ji Da Shi Ji*), Beijing Press, 1985, p. 136.

88   Taniuchi Yuzuru, *op.cit.*, Vol. 4, p. 142. Moshe Lewin, *Russian Peasants and Soviet Power*, trans. Irene Nove, London: Allen & Unwin, 1968, p. 508-509. Ray Medvedev, *Let History Judge: the Origin and Consequences of Stalinism*, trans. Li Yuanchao, Jilin People's Press, 1983, p. 85. In January 1932, Stalin was told by the head of the Soviet National Political Security Bureau that 1.4 million farmers were exiled and relocated. Sheila Fitzpatrick, *Stalin's Peasants: Resistance and Survival in the Russian Village after Collectivization*, New York: Oxford University Press, 1994, p. 83.

89   Kobayashi Kouji, *Peasant Revolutions and Communist Movements in the 20th Century: The Rise and Fall of China's Policy on Agricultural Collectivization* (in Japanese), Tokyo, Keisou Press, 1997, p. 275.

90   V. I. Lenin, "On Cooperatives," in *Selected Works of Lenin* (Chinese trans.), 2nd Edition, Vol. 4, p. 681-687.

91   Robert Conquest., *The Harvest of Sorrow: Soviet Collectivization and the Terror-Famine*, London: Hutchinson, 1986, p. 307; Sheila Fitzpatrick, *Stalin's Peasants: Resistance and Survival in the Russian Village after Collectivization*, New York and Oxford: Oxford University Press, 1994, p. 72-75.

92   The author devoted a paper in 2003 to the Great Leap Forward and the causes of the Great Famine. For the English version, please refer to Gong Renren, "Freedom of Expression and

Social Development: An Empirical Analysis of the Great Leap Forward," in *Bridging the Global Divide on Human Rights: A Canada-China Dialogue*, ed. Errol P. Mendes and Anik Lalonde-Roussy, Ashgate, 2003, p. 243-267. The English version has a mistake on p. 256: "Unofficial estimates published by foreign scholars range from 200 to 300 million"; the numbers here should read "from 20 to 30 million."

93   Li Debin, *Chronicles of the Rural Economy in the New China (Xin Zhong Guo Nong Cun Jing Ji Ji Shi) (1949.10-1984.9)*, Peking University Press, 1989, p. 3-10.

94   Michael Ellman, *Socialist Planning*, Cambridge: Cambridge University Press, 1989, p. 105.

95   Yang Junshi, *Modernization and Chinese Communism (Xian Dai Hua Yu Zhong Guo Yong Chan Zhu Yi)*, Hong Kong, Chinese University Press, 1987, p. 80.

96   Shi Jingtang, *Historical Facts on Agriculture Cooperativization in China (Zhong Guo Nong Ye He Zuo Hua Shi Liao)*, Vol. I, p. 38.

97   The state of dispersed individual farmers in rural China after the land reform would not only cause a decrease in commodity grains available on market terms, but also difficulties for centralized food procurement on non-market terms, because farmers as private property owners were also fully independent economic entities, hence reluctant to hand in their harvests at lowered prices. Zhu Rong *et al.*, *Agriculture in Contemporary China (Zhong Guo Dang Nai Nong Ye)*, p. 117-118.

98   Chen Wenhui, Feng Haifa and Shi Tongqing, *The Farmer and Industrialization, op. cit.*, p. 74.

99   *Factual Records of the People's Republic of China (Zhong Hua Ren Min Gong He Guo Shi Lu)* (1953-1956), p. 1498.

100 Dong Fureng, *The Economic History of the People's Republic of China (Zhong Hua Ren Min Gong He Guo Jing Ji Shi)*, Vol. I, Economics and Science Press, 1999, p. 256.

101 Chen Wenhui, Feng Haifa and Shi Tongqing, *The Farmer and Industrialization, op. cit.*, p. 83.

102 Zhou Yihu and Yang Xiaomin, *The Unit System in China (Zhong Guo Dan Wei Zhi Du)*, China Economic Press, 1999, p. 3.

103 Mark Selden, "Household, Cooperative, and State in the Remaking of China's Countryside," *Cooperative and Collective in China's Rural Development*, ed. Vermeer, E.B. *et al.*, Publisher Armonk, New York: M.E. Sharpe, 1998, p. 24.

104 *Compilation of Important Dossiers on the Collectivization of Agriculture*, Vol. I, p. 641-642.

105 Du Runsheng, *Collective Agriculture in Contemporary China (Dang Dai Zhong Guo De Nong Ye He Zuo Zhi)*, China Contemporary Press, 2002, p. 525.

106 It was under the guidelines of the CPC Central Committee and the government and under the pressure of Mao Zedong's incessant criticism of "right-leaning" that advanced cooperatives or collective farms were able to be instituted by the end of November 1956. *Milestones in the Economy of the People's Republic of China (Oct.1949-Sept.1984)*, Beijing Press, 1985, p. 136.

107 Жорес Медведев, *Let History Be the Judge (К суду истории)*, Vol. I, trans. He Hongjiang, Eastern Press, 2005, p. 260.

108 Sheila Fitzpatrick, *op. cit.*, p. 95.

109 The Soviet Union did not introduce a new domestic passport law until 1974. Only by 1980 did farmers all have their own domestic passports and the old passport or urban dweller ID system was removed. Niimi Jiichi, *The Freedom to Live and Move Where One Pleases* and *The Domestic Passport System, Socialism and Freedom* (in Japanese), ed. Fujita Yisamu, Kyoto, Legal Culture Press, 1984, p. 394-396.

110 Robert C. Tucker, "Stalinism as Revolution from Above," in *Stalinism: Essays in Historical Interpretation*, ed. R.C. Tucker, New York: Norton, 1977, p. 96.

[111] On 2 March 1954 the *Instructions on Continuing to Persuade Farmers out of Unregulated Flows into the Cities* (*Quan Zu Nong Min Mang Mu Liu Ru Cheng Shi De Zhi Shi*), issued by the Interior Ministry and the Ministry of Labour, stipulated that "for the farmers who have migrated into cities, civil affairs and labour authorities may join other departments in persuading them to return to the countryside, the travel expenses of which should, as a general rule, be borne by the farmer themselves." *Compilation of Central Government Legal Instruments* (*Zhong Yang Ren Min Zheng Fu Fa Ling Hui Bian*) *1954*, Legal Press, 1955, p. 148.

[112] The Research Group on Industrialization and Urbanization in the Countryside and Agriculture Modernization (actual writing by Liu Chunbin), *Dual Social Structure: Thoughts on Industrialization and Urbanization of China's Countryside* (*Er Yuan She Hui Jie Gou: Fen Xi Zhong Guo Nong Cun Gong Ye Hua Cheng Shi Hua De Yi Tiao Si Lu*), Economic Study Reference, Issue 171/172, 1989, p. 5. In addition, job losses were severe in cities in the early 1950s. Difficulties in job creation also contributed to a suspension of the farmers' migration. Yuan Yayu, *Social Movement of Farmer in China* (*zhong guo nong min de she hui liu dong*), Sichuan University Press, 1994, p. 73.

[113] Also according to a brief update from 6 December 1956 by the CPC Rural Work Department, there was a 10 percent to 20 percent income reduction among cooperative members in all provinces. *Compilation of Important Dossiers on the Collectivisation of Agriculture*, vol. I, p. 655.

[114] *Compilation of Important Dossiers on the Collectivization of Agriculture*, Vol. I, p. 687, 695.

[115] Yu Depeng, *Urban and Rural Society: From Isolation to Openness. A Study on China's Household Registration System and Law* (*cheng xiang she hui: cong ge li zou xiang kai fang --- zhong guo hu ji zhi du yu hu ji fa yan jiu*), Shandong People's Press, 2002, p. 17.

[116] Pursuant to the State Council Instructions on Preventing the Unregulated Outflow of Rural Population on 30 December 1956, the State Council Supplementary Instructions on 2 March 1957 and the State Council Notice on Preventing the Unregulated Flow of Farmer into Cities on 14 September 1957.

[117] State Council Laws and Regulations Bureau, *Compilation of Regulations of the People's Republic of China (January through June, 1958)*, Legal Press, 1958, p. 206.

[118] Yu Depeng, *Urban and Rural Society: From Isolation to Openness. A Study on China's Household Registration System and Law*, Shandong People's Press, p. 23.

[119] Lu Yilong, *The Household Registration System-Control and Social Distinction* (*hu ji zhi du – kong zhi yu she hui cha bie*), The Commercial Press, 2003, p. 124-126.

[120] Yao Xiulan, *Household Registration, Identity and Social Evolution: A Study on China's Household Administration Laws* (*hu ji shen fen yu she hui bian qian: zhong guo hu ji fa lv shi yan jiu*), The Legal Press, 2004, p. 176.

[121] Yuan Yayu, *The Social Movement of Farmers in China* (*zhong guo nong min de she hui liu dong*), p. 88.

[122] Yin Zhijing and Yu Qihong, *Household Administration System Reform in China*, p. 7; Ban Maosheng and Zhu Chengsheng, "Current Status of the Study and Actual Progress on the Household Administration System Reform" (*hu ji gai ge de yan jiu zhuang kuang ji shi ji jin zhan*), *Population and Economy*, 2000, Issue 1, p. 47.

[123] Guo Shutian and Liu Chunbin, *China out of Balance* (*shi heng de zhong guo*), p. 31.

[124] Niimi Jiichi, *The Freedom to Live and Move Where One Pleases* and *The Domestic Passport System, Socialism and Freedom* (in Japanese), ed. Fujita Yisamu, *op. cit.*, p. 380, 385-386, 390.

[125] *Economic Study Reference*, Issue 90, 1988, p. 17-19; *Economic Study Reference*, Issue 171/172, 1989, p. 14-36.

126   *Economic Study Reference,* Issue 171/172, 1989, p. 35.
127   On 23 February 1951, the Department of Political Affairs published the Labour Insurance Provisions, which stipulated that labour insurance was only applicable to city-based companies reaching a certain size. *Compilation of Central Government Legal Instruments (1951),* People's Press, 1953, p. 397. The Labour Insurance Provisions as amended by the Department of Political Affairs in 1953 marginally enlarged the scope of application to only city-based business units. *Compilation of Central Government Legal Instruments (1953),* Legal Press, 1955, p. 249.
128   In 1953, the CPC Central Committee and government decided to adopt a centralized procurement and distribution policy. On 5 and 25 August 1955, the State Council issued respectively the *Provisional Measures on Food Rationing in Cities and Townships and the Provisional Measures on Centralized Food Procurement and Distribution in Rural Areas.* They stipulated that "a universal food rationing system shall be introduced among the non-agriculture population" while farmers "travelling to and from townships may carry food on their own." *State Council Regulations 1949-2001,* China Democratic and Legal Press, 2001, p. 340-348.
129   On 31 August 1955, the employees of state organs began to receive cash salaries, as opposed to material supplies as in the past.
130   Zhou Yihu and Yang Xiaomin, *The Unit System in China,* China Economic Press, 1999, p. 53.
131   *China Statistical Yearbook 2006,* p. 345.
132   *China Economic Times,* 7 October 2002.
133   *People's Daily,* 11 August 2004.
134   Research Group, *Promoting the Transfer of Excessive Rural Labour in the Urban-rural Harmonized Development, Out of the Dual Structure: Migrant Workers, Urbanization and the New Countryside,* p. 108.
135   Wang Guolin, *A Survey of Farmers Losing their Land (shi di nong min diao cha),* Beijing: Xinhua Publishing House, 2006, p. 1. Scholars estimate the actual number of farmers who have lost their land has already gone beyond 60 million. Liao Xiaojun, *A Study on Land-losing Farmers (shi di nong min yan jiu),* Beijing: Social and Science Literatures Press, 2005, p. 98-99.
136   Article 14 of the *Land Administration Law* prescribes a 30-year term for the contract. Article 17.1 of the *Law on Land Contract in Rural Areas* of 2002 states that the agricultural purpose of the land and prohibits the use of land for non-agricultural construction.
137   National Office of Rural Fixed Watch Points, *The Employment Status and Features of Rural Migrant Workers (Nong Cun Lao Dong Li Wai Chu Jiu Ye Zhuang Kuang Ji Te Dian),* China Population Yearbook, 2006, p. 310.
138   The term "migrant worker" first appeared in the Sociology Journal of the Chinese Academy of Social Sciences in 1984, before it became widely used. *Master Report on Migrant Worker Issues in China,* Reform, Issue 5, 2006, p. 6. The *Provisions on Recruiting Farmers as Contracted Workers by Publicly-owned Enterprises (Quan Min Suo You Zhi Qi Ye Zhao Yong Nong Min He Tong Zhi Gong Ren De Gui Ding),* promulgated by the State Council on 25 July 1991, was reportedly the first official document that brought forward the idea of "migrant worker." Qi Yanping, ed., *Rights Protection for Vulnerable Groups in the Society (She Hui Ruo Shi Qun Ti De Quan Li Bao Hu),* Jinan, Shandong People's Press, 2006, p. 304.
139   Drafting Group for the Master Report on Migrant Worker Issues in China, "Master Report on Migrant Worker Issues in China," *Reform,* Issue 5, 2006, p. 9-11.
140   Research Group, *Promoting the Movement of Excess Rural Labour during the Integrated Development of Urban and Rural Areas (Zai Cheng Xiang Yi Ti Hua Fa Zhan Zhong Tui*

Jin Nong Cun Fu Yu Lao Dong Li Zhuan Yi); *Out of the Dual Structure: Migrant Workers, Urbanization and the New Countryside (Zou Chu Er Yuan Jie Gou: Nong Min Gong, Cheng Zhen Hua Yu Xin Nong Cun Jian She)*, p. 108.

[141] Drafting Group for the Master Report on Migrant Worker Issues in China, "Master Report on Migrant Worker Issues in China," *Reform*, Issue 5, 2006, p. 9.

[142] *Works of Gu Zhun (Gu Zhun Wen Ji)*, Guizhou People's Press, 1994, p. 375. Gu Zhun (1915-1974) was a self-made scholar and thinker. He joined the CPC in 1935 and once served as the Director General of the Shanghai Financial Bureau and Taxation Bureau after the CPC came to power in 1949. He was released from his duties in 1952. In 1956, Gu became a research fellow with the Economic Research Institute. He was caught in the "rightist" oppression movement in 1957 and died in 1974. Despite being under long political persecution, Gu managed to think independently under harsh conditions. He had insightful thoughts on Chinese and foreign politics, philosophy, history and economic issues.

[143] For example, the Research Centre for Human Rights of Peking University founded in 1997 not only conducted academic exchanges and joint researches with foreign research facilities and UN agencies, including the University of Ottawa Law School in Canada, but also opened the first postgraduate program on human rights in the mainland, in partnership with the Raoul Wallenberg Institute of Human Rights and Humanitarian Law of Lund University, Sweden.

[144] L. Henkin, "The Human Rights Idea in Contemporary China: A Comparative Perspective," *Human Rights in Contemporary China*, by R.R. Edwards, L. Henkin, A.J. Nathan, New York: Columbia University Press, 1986, p. 26-27.

[145] Gong Renren, "Implementing International Human Rights Treaties in China," *Bridging the Global Divide on Human Rights, op.cit.,* p. 102-106.

[146] *The Rule of Law in a Free Society: A Report on the International Congress of Jurists*, New Delhi, India, 1959, Geneva: International Commission of Jurists, p. 2-14; UN Doc. E/CN.4/Sub.2/2002/36, p. 6, para. 22; The World Justice Project: http://www.abnet.org/wjp/.

[147] For example, Article 5 of the Constitution stipulates, "No law or administrative or local rules and regulations shall contravene the Constitution. All state organs, the armed forces, all political parties and public organizations and all enterprises and undertakings must abide by the Constitution and the law. All acts in violation of the Constitution and the law must be investigated. No organization or individual may enjoy the privilege of being above the Constitution and the law." Article 126 reads, "The people's courts shall, in accordance with the law, exercise judicial power independently and are not subject to interference by administrative organs, public organizations or individuals."

[148] The 1948 *Universal Declaration of Human Rights* points out in its preamble that it is essential, if man is not to be compelled to have recourse, as a last resort, to rebellion against tyranny and oppression, that human rights should be protected by the rule of law.

[149] Government Work Report delivered by Wen Jiabao, Premier of the State Council, at the first meeting of the 11th NPC on 5 March 2008, http://gov.people.com.cn/GB/46733/46842/7020650/html/.

[150] China adopts a National People's Congress (NPC) system, but direct elections are only limited to below the county (or a district of a large city) level. Provincial people's congress deputies are elected by county-level people's congresses and NPC deputies by provincial people's congresses.

[151] Farms are counted by the resident councils of where they live and work. Apart from 1,240 leadership officials, there were also 37 grassroots (village and township) officials. See Cai Dingjian, *China's National People's Congress System,* 4th ed., Legal Press, 2003, p. 220-221.

152   Pursuant to Article 16 of the *Electoral Law of the PRC* on drawing a clear distinction between rural and urban populations; in practice, citizens can only elect and be elected in the areas where their household information is registered.

153   Pursuant to Article 128 of the Chinese Constitution and Article 35 of the *Organic Law of the People's Courts*, local people's courts at different levels are established by election of local people's congresses and their standing committees; therefore, local courts are overpowered by local party committees and governments of the same level in terms of staffing and finance.

154   Gong Renren, "International Human Rights, Comparative Constitutionalism and Features of China's Constitution," *Human Rights: Chinese and Canadian Perspective*, ed. E.P. Mendes and A.-M. Traeholt, The Human Rights Research and Education Centre, 1997, p. 87-89.

155   As exposed by many media sources after May 2007, some private-run brick kilns in Shanxi province had been using farmers from outside the province, minors and disabled people in forced and slave-like labouring conditions with the tacit consent of the local governments.

CHAPTER THREE

Restoring Private Ownership of Rural Lands to Safeguard the Basic Rights of Farmers

Wang Keqin

The reform of the system of land ownership in China's rural areas is one of the most controversial topics at present. Among other things, the debate focuses on the issue of who owns the land, with a view to promoting and enhancing productivity in rural areas; maintaining the security of the agricultural economy; avoiding political risks and protecting social stability; etc. However, both sides of the debate address this issue from a government perspective with pragmatic arguments, in order to maximize their respective interests in the decision-making process (of course, the distribution of interests under the table contributes to the complexity of the public debate). In consequence, the debate has become an endless and meaningless controversy in which one side always raises challenges and the other side keeps rebutting them. It is not uncommon for both sides to become so overwhelmed by this kind of debate that real reform is delayed and disrupted. Such complexity and confusion largely derive from the fact that, in addressing this issue, parties are over-attentive to the empirical distribution of interests rather than natural rights.

Land ownership has already become the most outrageous issue in China's rural areas and even the whole Chinese society; the issue of the "enclosure movement" is already gravely serious; and farmers' rights to land are being comprehensively violated and are barely surviving. Under these circumstances, some farmers become aware of the real issue, and after plenty of appealing to authorities, consciously raise claims of land ownership. This movement also illustrates that the development of the society entails reform of the system of land ownership.

The farmer's predicament is an institutional outcome. It is the public ownership of land that disregards the farmers' basic rights. Under the emerging rule of law and democracy, so-called "owned by all" under the collective ownership regime has effectively nullified "everybody's" ownership. On the basis of the extensive surveys conducted, it is concluded that, at least in the current phase when the development of rural democracy and the rule of law remain premature, collective ownership is virtually government ownership, and government ownership is virtually ownership by government officials.

Thus, the system of "public ownership" is virtually "public lack of ownership," which may easily transform into some kind of "private ownership" backed by administrative powers. This kind of transformation is the outcome of institutional discrimination against farmers. Therefore, such vague "public ownership" has to be changed to a kind of equitable and clear "private ownership"; that is, to a system of private land ownership under which farmers' rights are fully recognized.

In this context, it is necessary to compare alternative systems regarding the reform of land ownership. From the perspective of citizens' rights, the current disadvantageous status of farmers has well illustrated that the system of public ownership is not the best choice; in contrast, private ownership may be the least bad one. This chapter will analyze and compare the disadvantages of public ownership and the advantages of private ownership from the perspective of the protection of farmers' rights, taking into account the regular rules of socio-economic development as well as the implications of the development of land ownership in China. It will be concluded that private ownership of land is the fundamental safeguard for farmers' rights; one of the necessary requirements for the establishment of a modern agricultural system and the development of a social economy; one of the essential prerequisites for sustainable development; and the ultimate direction for reform, justified by both history and reason.

In the present China, the infringement of farmers' civil rights often manifests itself through the infringement of their land rights, the protection of which is, therefore, an important "bottom-line" for protecting farmers' civil rights.

1. RURAL LAND DISPUTES: SERIOUS INJUSTICE IN CHINESE RURAL AREAS

During the last three or four years, the Chinese government has received a massive number of cases of *shangfang* (direct appeals to authorities). According to media reports, most of the appellants were from the rural areas, among which most were victims whose land rights had been infringed. Having continued for more than ten years, land dispute claims have become the most serious issue not only for rural areas, but also for the entire Chinese society.

Shangfang cases have flooded not only the various levels of government, but also the media (particularly the Beijing media), which could provide truthful reporting.

The project team of the Chinese Academy of Social Sciences conducted a special statistical analysis by telephone and voice recordings, targeting the media audience of the central government. Between 1 January 2004 and 30 June 2004, 62,446 phone calls or voicemails were received, and leading the ranks were calls relating to the *sannong* issue (issue about "agriculture, farmers and rural areas") with 22,304 or 35.7 percent of the calls and recordings. Among those referring to the *sannong* issue, 15,312 or 68.7 percent were regarding rural land problems, representing 24.5 percent of all of the feedback received for the study.

Since 2003, the author, as a journalist, has been receiving an average of two to three complaint calls or calls for help per day from various parts of China. Approximately 60 percent were calls for help or complaints from the rural areas, among which 60 percent were complaints about land disputes.

The author has carried out investigations in most of the provinces and regions in the eastern, central and western parts of China. Studies and analyses were conducted for 52 typical cases of land disputes in 22 provincial regions (and municipalities); they were conducted after also contacting and communicating with a large number of land-deprived farmers, and the local governments and the relevant departments. The current rural land disputes and intensified land enclosure movement point to the fact that, given the scope and number of people involved, rural land disputes have become the most serious social injustice facing present-day China.

Of the 52 cases studied by the author, 20 (39 percent) involved land expropriations of more than 1,000 *mu* (1 *mu* equals approximately 666.7 square metres). Wuhan city accounted for most of the expropriated areas: 100,000 *mu* expropriated in 1992 for building the Wuhan Economic Development Zone; and 32 were cases of expropriation of less than 1,000 *mu*, representing 61 percent of the total. Among these cases, the key complaints of farmers whose lands were expropriated were: (1) illegal expropriation; (2) use of violence; (3) lack of compensation; (4) low compensation; (5) retention of compensation; (6) chaotic resettlement arrangements; (7) greater poverty; (8) deception; and others. Expropriators were generally county and township governments expropriating the land for economic development, construction of enterprises and urban development. Many land expropriation exercises were opposed by farmers. Land expropriation cases inducing violence totalled 13, or 25 percent of the total. For example, the tarsus of Xiong Quangen, the farmers' representative of Banchangbei Farm at Shajingjie, Honggutan Xinqu, Nanchang City, Jiangxi Province, was broken by gangsters threatening that "whoever dares *shangfang*, their family shall be slaughtered." This must have been provoked by their repeated *shangfang*. In 2007, the government of Shafu Town in Qinnan District, Guangxi, forced villagers of several villages in Dashigu to lease land to the government at a rate of RMB 580 per *mu* per year. The farmers refused to comply. To achieve their end, the government had their newly planted rice paddy and tree seedlings flooded. When the villagers tried to prevent the sabotage, the government deployed nearly 200 policemen to beat them. Many were bleeding and seriously injured and had to be hospitalized.

Of these 52 cases, nearly all land-deprived farmers opted for *shangfang* and complained to higher authorities as a means of relief. Villagers from Yongquan Village of Longfeng Town in Longfeng District, Daqing City, Heilongjiang Province, reported the highest *shangfang* frequency of 1,359 times within three years or so. Retaliation against *shangfang* amounted to 23, or 45 percent of the total. The most serious retaliation was seen in three cases, in which more than 20 villagers who were *shangfang* representatives were prosecuted and convicted for criminal offences, such as "disruption of social order due to illegal gathering" and "obstruction of public administration."

1.1 The Land "Enclosure Movement" Driven by Governments and Developers

To farmers, land is the basic guarantee of their livelihood, and the only capital on which they depend to build wealth. After the implementation of the Household Contract System in 1979, various levels of local governments subcontracted rural lands for agricultural production to agricultural households, during which time the farmers enjoyed a period of stability.

By the 1990s, industrialization and urbanization were in full steam. When state-owned urban land was comparatively scarce, rural lands located just at the outskirts of the urban areas became the top choice for factory construction and city development.

From the political perspective, government officials were evaluated on the basis of their economic contributions during this period, the government therefore focused on economic performance and growth figures; building development zones and industrial parks became the key mission of local governments. Most of the places that the author visited had large industrial parks built. During a visit to Jinjiang city in Fujian Province in 2005, the author saw that the originally scarce basic farmland had been replaced by development zones, and several towns and townships were occupied by industrial parks. The parks were connected to one another, but few arable lands were seen. Visit any large province or small county-level township, and local officials will proudly show you the local industrial districts and development zones. Even administrative villages, in some cases, were occupied by industrials parks. Every place has been waving in investment capital. The truth is that Chinese rural areas had already seen a wave of campaigns for building township enterprises during the mid 1980s, prior to the current frenzy for "industrialization and urbanization." At that time, the slogan was "every village shall see smoke oozing from industrial chimneys, and every hamlet shall build factories." Yet, each of these "political campaigns" is actually premised on the expropriation of rural land.

From an economic perspective, high profits are sought by both government and enterprise. As a non-renewable resource, land is the most important resource for economic development, and an asset whose value growth is the fastest and greatest. While gains in the primary and secondary industries stabilize and thus become thinner, land value has been appreciating rapidly. The room for the appreciation of land value has been expanding. Land and housing have become everybody's core assets, as well as important bequests for the next generation. In recent decades, suburban lands and urban housing properties in developed cities have seen their value double every seven to eight years. The same trend is experienced in other Chinese cities. Seeing the general economic pattern, many cash-rich enterprises concentrate on land investments; that is, the "enclosure" and sale of land. The rapid growth of the real estate market is a case in point. While enterprises are engaged in the land-rush, the larger players – governments – refuse to be left behind. Governments intervened in the entire process of national economic development, by monopolizing the primary market in which rural land is converted to urban development. Low land requisition costs became the engine for rapid urbanization and industrialization. Revenue from land concession became the major source of fiscal income and future public investments by local governments. And land mortgages became the main financing instrument for urban infrastructure and real estate investments. According to public sources, as early as 2003, income earned from land concession in Yiwu city was RMB 1.5 billion, or 60 percent of its extra-budget income. Liu Shouying, a researcher at the Agricultural Department of Development Research Centre of the State Council, discovered during an investigation in 2005 that,

> in Shaoxing, Jinhua and Yiwu in Zhejiang Province, the income obtained after deducting the difficult-to-estimate land charges, direct land taxes and indirect taxes from city expansion accounts for 40 percent of the budgeted income. Net income from land concession accounts for around 60 percent of the extra-budget income. After adding up all the items, income generated from land accounts for more than half the local fiscal revenue.

Land finance has become the largest moneybag for many local governments.
Whether driven by political or economic motives, the strong demand and desire for land by governments and developers have themselves been driving *quandi* activities. Land encroachment and land enclosure activities in support of grand development plans have been widespread, taking place in every city and village, big or small, in China.

The present problem of Chinese farmers losing their lands and jobs has become a matter of immense gravity. Acute reduction of arable land combined with a sharp population increase has led to the continued decrease in area per capita of arable land. According to statistics from the Ministry of Agriculture, the total area of arable land in China is 1.951 billion *mu*; however, arable land resources per capita is only half that of the world's average.

Non-agricultural constructions are concentrated mainly in suburbs and economic development zones where the population is dense and land scarce. Most people living in these areas have less than 0.7 *mu* per capita, and every one *mu* of arable land taken will result in 1.4 persons losing their land. According to statistics, within the agricultural population, approximately 150 million people have lost the lands on which they depend for their livelihood.

1.2 The Major Forms of Infringement and Deprivation of Farmers' Land Rights

Infringement and exploitation of farmers' land rights may be divided into several forms. The most common are the infringement and exploitation of land contract management rights in the rural areas, and more serious is the infringement and deprivation of farmers' title to their land.

1.2.1 Infringement and Deprivation of Farmers' Land Contract Management Rights

By investigating the actual circumstances of farmers' land contract management rights, the author discovered that the so-called "permanence" of policies and regulatory provisions on contract rights does not prevent the frequent and wilful deprivation or infringement of the land contract rights and other relevant lawful rights enjoyed by farmers. The forms of such deprivation or infringement are as follows.

The most common is retracting and trading farmers' land contract rights by means of administrative powers, and non-implementation of the "second round of the lease," thus directly depriving farmers of the right to contract land. Take the Sumabao Village of Wuxing Town in Dengta City, Liaoning Province, as an example. A local grassroots organization recovered contracted land from farmers by force, and triggered a group *shangfang* action by several hundred villagers. Villagers involved in *shangfang* were detained and finally imprisoned.

Another common form is interference with farmers' independent right of production and management through the use of administrative powers, such as forced purchase and sale, as well as through restriction of lawful land transfers, the deduction of gains from land transfer, and other actions.

Many localities refuse to implement the "second round of the lease" policy. Arable lands suitable for the application of the household contract were not granted an extension of their land contracts for thirty years as provided by the policy, and land contract agreements were not signed with farming households.

Other cases involved village management taking advantage of their powers of office by altering or canceling the land contract agreements with farmers, illegally repossessing contracted lands, and forcibly repossessing land belonging to farmers working or doing business in other cities. Most such actions are taken under the pretext that the farmers owed payments in arrears.

In other cases, the contracting party would be forced to transfer his land contract right, such as through mandatory repossession of the contracted land of farmers to effect a land transfer; or the town/township government or village-level organization would take on the lease of farmers' contracted land before they could transfer the lease or contract out the land. These were the problems in the aforesaid Liaoning case, whereby villagers were imprisoned due to *shangfang* or *qunti shijian* ("mass incident" – a Chinese euphemism for a large protest, riot, demonstration, or mass petition).

Illegal contracting-out of rural land includes contracting to entities or individuals who do not belong to the collective economic organization without the consent of more than either two-thirds of the members of the economic organization or two-thirds of the village representatives.

Discrimination against the contract management rights of women is rife; they are the vulnerable among the vulnerable. To cite an extreme example, a woman from Village A marries a man in Village B. She cannot take with her the contracted land in Village A; on the other hand, Village B does not allocate her any contracted land. She divorces with her husband after giving birth to two children, with each of them taking custody of one child. She no longer has land from her parents' family, and receives no land from her husband's family. Under this land regime, women and their children have no land to make a livelihood. Many who work in the rural areas are aware that such cases truly exist.

Some local governments confiscate farmers' land at will under the pretexts of building scale and centralized management, and redistribute the acquired land to those which they regard as major farming households.

Omission by the administrative and judicial authorities, and the village-level organization also causes deprivation of rights; for example, the refusal by primary courts to accept cases on land contract disputes and the refusal by the rural land contract arbitration and management authorities to accept arbitration petitions for rural land contract disputes.

1.2.2. Infringement of and Deprivation of Farmers' Land Title
Article 10 of the Constitution provides that "[r]ural and suburban lands shall be collectively-owned, save if otherwise provided under the law that such lands shall be State-owned. Rural housing land, and 'private plots' (*ziliudi* and *ziliushan* for villagers) are collectively-owned." As such, rural lands are collectively-owned.

The villagers understand that being collectively-owned equals ownership by all villagers. Under the provisions of the *Villagers' Organization Law*, action for major matters and major economic interests concerning the village shall be carried out only upon obtaining two-thirds affirmative votes from the villagers' assemblies and village representatives' meetings.

That being the case, how do local governments and developers infringe upon and deprive villagers of their land rights?

1. After deliberation and resolution of the expropriation at the village assembly or villagers' meeting, some governments and developers will infringe upon farmers' land rights as follows:
    i.   Requisition before approval, i.e. "enclosure" before submitting for approval. Local governments call it "board the ship then buy the ticket."
    ii. Submit less than the actual quantity of land requisitioned for approval. Due to strict State policies, the amount of land local governments may submit for approval is limited. However, as actual demand is high, the amount submitted for approval is less than the actual quantity "enclosed."

iii. Report good land requisitioned as wasteland. Officials report land as wasteland in the submission for approval, but in fact the "enclosed" land is either arable land or basic farmland.

The aforesaid is infringement on and deprivation of farmers' land rights with "observance" of land expropriation procedures. In reality, most land expropriations and encroachments are carried out with a blind eye to the laws and regulations.

2. Illegal Land Expropriation:
    i.   Illegal land sales by village functionaries.
    ii.   Illegal land sales by village committees and village branches.
    iii. Lease in place of expropriation: enters into a long-term lease agreement with the village committee, where it does not appear that land title has been transferred, but yet in fact the village committee has taken full possession of the land.
    iv.   Mandatory (*zhilingxing*) requisition by county governments: to build large industrial parks and development zones, city and town governments would take forced possession of land from villages directly upon the issuance of orders by local governments, to fulfil their political missions. In 2003, the government of Baogai Town in Shishi City, Fujian Province, issued an order for the construction of a Baogai Footwear Industrial Park. As the villagers of Xueshang Village refused to accept the expropriation of their land by the town, village functionaries refused to give their stamp of approval on the document. The town secretary said, "punishment shall be issued if the approval stamp is not given."

The most common land expropriation, enclosure and requisition practice across the country is to bypass the resolution phase of villagers' assemblies and village representative meetings, while the higher level government and developer arrive at an agreement directly with the village functionaries. This practice is frequent and widespread. As said by Chen Xiwen, Deputy Director of the Office for the Central Financial and Economic Leading Group, CPC, in 2003, 6015 or 70 percent of the various levels and types of development zones (industrial parks) were built at will, and in violation of the law.

3. Infringement and Deprivation of Farmers' Rights in Compensation and Resettlement Arrangements:
    i.   Reduced compensation: while State compensation standards are already very low, certain local governments continue to depress compensation standards.

ii.   Delayed payment of compensation.

iii. Retention of compensation.

iv.   Deduction of compensation when passing through different levels of
      governments: depending on the nature of the land expropriation and source
      of compensation funds, some compensation is released to the provincial
      governments, other compensation to the municipal governments. These
      governments will transfer the funds to the county-level governments,
      which will then transfer to the tier-one town/township governments,
      and then through the village committee to the villagers whose lands have
      been expropriated. While passing through many hands, a part of the
      compensation disappears at each level. The many places that the author
      has visited seem to tell the same story. And the reason is because there is
      a lack of effective supervision of the administrative behaviour of public
      institutions.

The author found that most farmers would not have pursued the legitimacy of a
land expropriation if the local governments and developers had been reasonable in their
actions and compensations, ensuring that farmers are provided with another possibility
of livelihood. However, deprived of a transparent process and the title to their lands,
without compensation, farmers had to take action to protect their rights.

Lives of Land-Deprived Farmers

Most farmers have become social refugees, having been rendered landless and jobless,
and without social security, as a result of the low compensation for land expropriation
and the absence of equitable resettlement arrangements and a social security system.

Indeed, more than 100 million Chinese farmers have been estimated to have lost
their lands, and several million are added to the pool each year. In 2004, Sun Shengwen,
Minister of Land and Resources disclosed at a periodic joint-inspection meeting for
land and market order governance and reorganization, that a preliminary finding on
compensation and resettlement payments owed to farmers across the country amounted
to RMB 9.88 billion, of which only RMB 5.99 billion had been paid. Farmers who rely
on their land for a living, and whose lands have been substituted by a blank note, fall
into greater destitution. According to the forecast, another 270 million *mu* of land will
be converted to urban land within the next 20 years. This will translate into a more
acute problem, as more farmers will become landless refugees. A study conducted by
the 93 Society in 2003 indicated that 60 percent of the land-deprived farmers were
living under extreme poverty; those who had a stable income and whose basic living
conditions were not affected by the loss of land only accounted for 30 percent.

According to media reports, millions of young university graduates are unemployed
under the harsh employment situation in China at present. Finding a job would be

more difficult for the land-deprived farmers, who have an absolute disadvantage in age, skill and education level.

Farmers lose their basic guarantee of livelihood as soon as their lands are taken away. Many farmers who are left with no land to farm, no job and no minimum insurance live at city fringes and do not enjoy any policy protection for employment, schooling of children or social security. Land-deprived farmers therefore are confronted with a crisis of survival, as their basic rights are trampled on and prejudiced.

For centuries, Chinese farmers have been living under the "land and family protection" model, whereby they rely only on themselves and their families for all their necessities of life, from birth until demise. However, with large parcels of collective rural lands being expropriated due to urbanization and industrialization, farmers are losing their only guarantee of livelihood. Combined with the inadequate social system in the rural areas and the currently meagre compensation and poor resettlement arrangements – not to mention that even minimum resettlement is not seen through – many land-deprived farmers have been reduced to urban poor.

Perpetual acquisition of land by the government and business enterprises – and without the minimum compensation – has led to the loss of the basic guarantee of a livelihood for many farmers. Land-deprived farmers were hence driven to appeal to the authorities (*shangfang*) for justice.

Land disputes in Chinese rural areas have now become organized and collective warfare. Many bloody conflicts arising from farmers protecting their land rights have occurred across China, the most renowned of which was the "Dingzhou murder" in Dingzhou City, Hebei, on 11 June 2005. A developer joined hands with the head of the local party committee to plan a deadly attack carried out by nearly 300 "gangsters" on farmers guarding their "expropriated land." More than 100 villagers in Shengyou Village were injured, and six were killed.

According to the statistics provided by the Chinese Academy of Social Sciences project team, between January and June 2004, 87 conflicts between the police and farmers occurred during those six months alone. 48 or 55.2 percent of the conflicts arose because farmers tried to prevent construction from being carried out on expropriated or requisited land; 31 or 35.6 percent were due to local policemen preventing farmers from *shangfang*; 8 or 9.2 percent arose from sitting petitions by farmers at municipal governments' offices, railroads, highways or major communication routes. And of the 87 cases, hundreds of farmers were injured, three died, more than 160 were detained, and some were even tied up and paraded through the streets as a public warning. Twelve had to be suppressed by special police or riot police, and seven by the military police. As many as several hundred policemen had to be deployed for certain instances. Crimes of which the farmers were convicted were mainly illegal gathering, disruption of social order and obstruction of public administration. Some even took enforcement actions against farmers' groups for *shangfang* to Beijing or the provincial capitals, using the pretext of Falungong affiliation.

Methods Employed and Embarrassment Encountered by Farmers in Protecting their Own Rights

The author has discovered through frequent contact with land-deprived farmers that they are generally very passive even when their land rights have been infringed upon or deprived. Some take action to protect their rights, but there are few successful cases.

When their rights were infringed or deprived, Chinese farmers often responded in the following ways:

1. Tolerate it and keep silent. An absolute majority of farmers would choose to tolerate or give in as much as possible. There is a Chinese saying that "ordinary folks will not fight with government officials." Historical incidents have proven that there have been few cases of ordinary citizens winning a case against the official courts. Hence, most Chinese farmers whose rights were infringed chose to tolerate the injustice and remain silent.

2. Seek out an upright official. Cases of farmers defending their rights are rare. Most choose the most traditional method in China which is that of seeking out one upright official after another, through the whole official hierarchy. However, most find their efforts to be of no avail.

3. Appeal (shangfang) *from one level to another.* When land rights have been exploited and infringed upon, some farmers' representatives have sought out governments of various levels for resolution. This generally leads to a cyclical process: appeal to the township government, the township government passes the buck; appeal to the county-level government, the county-level government passes the buck; appeal to the municipal government, the municipal government passes the buck; appeal to the provincial government, the provincial government passes the buck; finally appeal to the central government, and then get referred back down to the local level by a *Xinfang* ("letters and visits": complaining by writing letters and paying personal visits to the authorities) Transfer Advice. The farmers will then have to begin the entire process again, by appeal from one level to the next. Many *shangfang* farmers told the author that the passing-the-buck tactic used by the various levels and departments often dragged out the confidence of even the most determined and resilient. Many ended up mentally ill. In the worst cases, some *Xinfang* Transfer Advice may fall directly in the hands of those who violated the farmers' rights, so that many farmers often become the target of retaliation and revenge. Many such evil deeds have occurred over the years. And successes due to *shangfang* are rare.

4. Take legal action. Few dare to sue. And those who could afford to do so and knew how were even fewer. Most importantly, many local courts refuse to accept cases of legal action taken by farmers in defence of their land rights.

Among the many cases on the defence of land rights which the author has investigated, about 80 percent or more of the farmers' representatives had been arrested at some time or another due to *shangfang*, and approximately one fifth of the farmers' representatives were sentenced to imprisonment due to "extreme behaviour" during *shangfang*.

Farmers' Own Choices

Farmers employed various methods to protect their rights when title to their land – their basic right – was deprived or infringed upon; nonetheless, most failed.

Farmers realized that the fundamental cause to the repeated infringements on their rights, and their awkward and helpless efforts at protecting their rights, was the institutional deficiency in land right protection. In fact, it is the current system of collective-ownership of rural land that has led to the displacement of farmers' land rights.

As with what happened during the 1970s, farmers in Fengyang County of Anhui Province boldly "divided the fields among the households" (*fentian daohu*), many farmers across the country were courageous enough to propose the declaration of the "return of land rights to farmers" (*di-quan gui-nong*). The bold move of Anhui farmers succeeded in bringing about the household contract system, whereby the management right of rural lands was returned to farmers. Today, farmers are demanding the return of land titles.

- In November 2007, 40,000 farmers from 72 villages, including Dongnangang Village, in Fujin City, Heilongjiang Province, officially announced their possession of land title, and published an announcement to that effect across the country. This was the famous Fujin Declaration from China's rural areas. Thereafter, farmers from different locations started issuing the same declarations;
- More than 8,000 farmers in Qingwu District, Tianjin, took to protecting the title to their land of nearly 10,000 *mu*;
- 250 rural households in Shengzhuang Village in Yixing City, Jiangsu Province demanded that "dwellers shall own";
- Approximately 70,000 farmers in the Sanmenxiaku District of the Yellow River at Shanxi Province made a nationwide announcement that they will be taking back their land titles;
- A group of villagers in Suzhou City of Jiangsu Province submitted a Proposal on Land Privatization to the National People's Congress.

This leads to the questions: why do farmers choose a private land-ownership system? Why do they not recognize the original land regime?

2. FUNDAMENTAL CAUSES FOR THE ABSENCE OF A GUARANTEE OF FARMERS' LAND RIGHTS

2.1 Unreasonable Institutions that Lead to the Hollowing of Farmers' Land Rights

Article 10 of the Constitution of the People's Republic of China provides that "[r]ural and suburban lands shall be collectively-owned, save if otherwise provided under the law that such lands shall be State-owned. Rural housing land, and 'private plots' (*ziliudi* and *ziliushan* for villagers) are also collectively-owned."

The Constitution also provides that China's economic system is a public-ownership system. As such, China's State-owned lands and collectively-owned lands are publicly-owned. Rural lands are collectively-owned, hence also publicly-owned, lands.

Although Chinese farmers abolished the People's Commune system (under which land-ownership rights and management rights were consolidated under collective units) in order to implement the collective ownership of farmland and a "separation of the two rights" whereby the household holds the management right, the rural land regime has remained essentially a public-ownership system from the perspective of property rights.

After investigating the final right of disposal over rural land in many cases, the author has discovered that "collective" ownership amounts in fact to "organizational" ownership. And "organizational" ownership is in fact ownership by the power-holders of the organization.

Hence, the reality is, rural land ownership is not equally distributed among every farmer; nor is it ascribed to the farmers' collective group formed by every farmer. It is assigned to a "group" alienated from them except for a select handful of spokespersons.

How does this situation come about?

Fundamentally, inconsequential legislation has led to the displacement of the rights of farmers in collectively-owned land. Administrative powers prevail over legislated statutory rights as a result.

Current law provides that rural lands are collectively owned by the rural population, and the definition of collective ownership includes: collective ownership by village farmers; collective ownership by town/township farmers; and by farmers' groups within a same village comprising two or more collective economic groups.

But, in the real world, "rural collectives" and "farmers' collectives" are intangible collectives that differ from farmers' collective organizations. Without any legal entity, they are neither legal persons nor natural persons. Hence, local governments and the relevant departments deliberately confuse "farmers' collectives" with "farmers' collective organizations," and endow non-economic groups such as villagers' assemblies or villagers' groups with legal personality. In doing so, they give them actual land title to control the will of all "farmers' collectives." On the other hand, each member of a "farmers' collective" loses the direct right to participate and decide. In some places, such rights are even concentrated in the hands of the village branches.

According to current legal provisions, the village committee is a "self-managed, self-educated and self-serviced autonomous organization and autonomous group of the grassroots masses." It is not a collective economic organization. Hence, the village committee does not possess the basic legal standing of a title-holder. Rural land title-holders that are currently the law enforcers, i.e. the legal personality of the village committees, are in fact illegal. This implies that the villagers' collective rights are displaced. Village committees may appear to hold title, but based on the present laws, village committees lack the standing to hold title. The result is that rural land title is disconnected from the specific farmers concerned.

On the one hand, the village committee has no standing to hold title; on the other hand, other collective economic organizations in the village, such as township enterprises, demand to exercise their land titles. They could go as far as dividing and distributing rural land at will, without consent from the village collectives. Farmers' interests are prejudiced as a result, and so they encourage and prompt administrative intervention by township governments or village committees. Therefore, township enterprises or township governments could be possible infringers of farmers' land rights. Having diverse and dubious title-holders of rural land inevitably leads to ill-defined lines of responsibility, rights and interests, and thereby dampens the motivation of farmers to invest for the long term in their land; encourages the wilful expropriation of rural lands by the various governments at low costs; affects farmers' forecasts on land returns and risk uncertainties; and eventually drives the many actors to exploit the farmers.

Consequently, farmers' individual rights have been completely displaced by an abstract "collective" and controlled by administrative powers. In fact, the additional provision on land title in the Amendment to the Constitution adumbrates or, should we say, gives silent consent to this natural outcome. The Amendment to the Constitution states: "No organization or individual shall buy, sell or transfer collectively-owned land, and shall not lease or mortgage it. The State, however, may expropriate collectively-owned land."

The true implication of the provision is therefore: the "owner" does not have the right of disposition to his own property, and administrative authorities may dispose of property belonging to a few people (collective) in the name of the public. Having gone full circle, we now realize that the owner, as provided under the Constitution, does not truly "own," because the final right to decide does not lie with him. And administrative powers, which should rightfully be restricted by the Constitution, nonetheless receive powers above and beyond the basic property rights of individuals and collectives granted under the Constitution. This means that legislation has put administrative powers at a higher level than itself; yet, legislative powers must be higher than administrative powers under "the rule of law." Hence, finding that the Constitution is self-contradictory with respect to its purpose, it becomes clear that implicit in the mechanism of the Amendment to the Constitution there lies a serious paradox.

2.2 The Drawbacks of Rural Democracy
If, based on the system proposed by institutional designers, villagers are granted autonomy within their platforms for democracy, and also administrative powers can effectively represent the interests of each individual within the scope of its governance, then the assumption that "village collectives" and "each villager" are separate and opposed cannot stand. This would mean that even if there were legislative flaws, the aforesaid scenario would not come to pass. However, the current democratic state-of-affairs negates this perfect conception.

Based on the current *Village Organization Law*, important matters concerning the disposal of collectively-owned land must be carried out after resolution by the villagers' assemblies and villagers' representatives meetings. But what exactly is the true picture?

First, villagers' assemblies. This is the highest authority in the village. All major matters of the village must be finally decided by the villagers' assembly. As a "collective," this is the authority which best represents the interests of all villagers from a jurisprudential standpoint. Unfortunately, it appears pitiful when exercising its powers. After visiting many Chinese villagers across the country, the author discovered that many villages almost never organized a villagers' assembly after the division of fields among households (*fentian daohu*); the same applied to Shengyou Village at Dingzhou City in Hebei Province, the place where the "Dingzhou murder" was committed. Also, the younger farmers in most villagers are working in other places throughout the year, making it impossible to convene a villagers' assembly for major matters such as land expropriation. Thirdly, residents of many villages are very scattered; this makes the calling of meetings very difficult. More importantly, as time goes by, and as villagers discover that their opinions have often been vetoed by the "organization" representative deployed by the higher authority, their enthusiasm dampens. Therefore, in reality, there were few villages which were able to convene villagers' assemblies to deliberate on issues of land disposal.

Villagers' representatives meetings. At present, the convening of villagers' assemblies at places which somehow respect farmers' rights is still possible. But, in reality, the villagers' representative is usually designated by the village chief or the village secretary; at times, the township government will make the appointment directly. When the several dozen villagers' representatives of Shengyou Village in Dingzhou City refused to comply with the city's illegal land expropriation request, a deputy secretary from the city went and "dismissed" all the villagers' representatives. He later appointed a new villagers' representative.

Finally, there is the village committee. Although the village head should be elected by the villagers' assembly, election is usually directly controlled by the township. This seriously affects the village's autonomy. There are worse cases. The township government may directly organize and intervene in the elections or designate a particular person to act as the village head. In worse cases still, a village Party branch is set up in all villages, and the major powers in the villages are held by the secretary. Under the principle of "the party governs all," the village head, village committee, head villagers' sub-group and villagers' representatives are governed by the secretary. At the same time, the village secretary is usually designated and his election arranged by the township Party committee; the township's secretary is usually appointed by the township organization. As such, the village "organization" must submit to the orders of the township "organization," and the township "organization" will fully obey the county "organization." Many village functionaries told the author that they have in fact no jurisdiction over land because those with such jurisdiction are the land management departments of the tier-one county-level governments. This means that land rights are in fact far removed from the farmers and the small farmers' collectives, and have become highly concentrated. This explains why many decisions taken at villagers' representatives meetings are opposed by most villagers, resulting in a bizarre situation whereby "our collective" opposes "our collective."

Some pointed out that, although there remain many problems in the village democracy whereby villagers exercise their own powers and the village functionary often has the final say, there are some villages that did well in protecting the rights of farmers, and farmers do live quite happily. The author has witnessed the same. Under the current institutional framework whereby a specific functionary represents everybody's powers and interests, the greatest wish of the people is to see an upright and good government official; that is, to see a good person govern. However, this is not an eager anticipation of democracy. It puts its hopes in the most undependable probabilities, and reveals that Chinese villages are still lacking in normal democratic qualities and have stayed put in the days of chiefdom. Farmers, who account for the majority in the villages, thus remain in a disadvantageous position.

3. The Importance and Urgency of Restoring Private Land Ownership

3.1 Restoring Rights to the People and Transforming the Virtual Non-Existence of Public-Ownership to Ownership by Every Family to Guarantee the Fundamental Rights of Farmers.

Based on the previous section, we know that public ownership is a risky system of ownership. Farmers do not hold the most fundamental rights; instead, such rights are "centrally controlled" under the organization. Before the democratic regime matures, these important powers often concentrate in the hands of the organization managers. Such managers are not only entities with their own independent intentions and personal identities, they are also removed from farmers and their specific interests. Hence, farmers' land rights run the perpetual risk of being exploited and infringed upon by the power-holders.

Under such circumstances, between public ownership and private ownership, private ownership is, at the very least, the least bad option. Firstly, the original intent of "public ownership" was the sublimation of "private ownership." It was founded on the recognition that everyone has these basic rights of ownership, and is thus a hybrid form of ownership which aimed to better realize the fundamental interests of the general public and to promote equality.

Based on this original intent, a 100-person collective in a village owning the land in the village is intrinsically the same as a 100-shareholder company. But why then should the former example be described as "collective ownership" under "public ownership," and the latter "shareholding" under "private ownership"? It appears that "public ownership" and "private ownership" have little to do with the number of people. The real difference lies in the fact that if the 100 shareholders' collective truly benefits everybody, then the company, as a standard entity, will have a sound and democratic management system that allows every shareholder to benefit. Therefore, the shareholders will, on the premise of interest maximization, assign part of their interests to the company's administrative system, and arrive at some compromises to allow the company to continue its operations. If some shareholders feel this is unfair, or if they are not optimistic about the company's future, such that their personal interests may be prejudiced, then they may withdraw their personal shares from this collective at any time. However, on the contrary, under public ownership's collective ownership system, although land belongs to everyone, the plot of land of every villager is part of the large collective and cannot be taken out at the will of every villager. Whether or not the administrative management system of this piece of land is reasonable and effective, the villagers are unable to withdraw or assign their own share. This, in fact, has gone against the original intent of "public ownership." "Public ownership" in this case is none other than a reckless venture from the standpoint of utility; it does not demonstrate any superiority of collectivism, or any value preference.

To guarantee the fundamental rights and personal interests of farmers, collective ownership should have an "exit mechanism," i.e. a mechanism to endow farmers with the basic freedom to choose if they wish to hand over their own land to the current administrative management system for centralized management of its title. At the same time, in order to ensure that any specific plot of land can make its exit effectively, land should carry specific dimensions and be registered under the name of its farmer. That way, each small plot of land will have a specific owner. If modern agricultural development, especially certain types of agriculture, demands collective efforts; and if the administrative management system which farmers may choose or establish at their own will is able to manage and ensure that the individual gains exceed the losses and guarantee the fundamental rights of every farmer; then farmers will make their choice based on personal benefits and they will assign part of their interests to the organization and join this collective. In essence, this right to choose is a basic civil right.

This in fact differs little from private ownership's shareholding system. Thus, differentiating public ownership from private ownership becomes meaningless. Restoring land title to every farmer is as good as land privatization. At present, certain locations in Guangdong Province have abolished the traditional "land expropriation" during urbanization. Instead, a compromise of "buy shares of land title" (*diquan rugu*) – converting the collective land resources in the original village into shares and giving these shares to the farmers – was struck with the farmers. To a certain extent, this is a silent acknowledgement of farmers' title to the land; more specifically, it is a respect of the basic property rights of farmers, as land owners, and their civil rights, as equal individuals. Compared to land expropriation and compensation, there is a fairly large difference in its degree of civilization and in outcome.

3.2 Clear Property Rights to Facilitate the Establishment of a Modern Agricultural System and Agricultural Development

The first premise when establishing a modern enterprise system is "clear property rights." On such a premise, explicit rights and duties, and a separation of government administration and enterprise management, will allow enterprises to develop on a healthy and free platform. This is the experience derived from China's development of its secondary and tertiary industries.

Building a modern agricultural system and developing modern agriculture rely on the same principles. Land is the core production factor and most important capital in agricultural production. Privatization of land title is the most important condition for creating an advanced agricultural market economy. According to Coase's theorem,[1] so long as there are clear property rights in a market under the rule of law, and where freedom to trade is permitted and where the cost of exchange is zero or sufficiently low, resource allocation will be optimized. Even though the initial distribution of property rights was unequal, a fair and even market mechanism will facilitate automatic adjustments.

During this adjustment process, the property rights must specify every interested entity participating in the game. Otherwise, any deficiency in rights will lead to injustice. In reality, the vulnerable party will often be compelled to accept unreasonable actions; and dubious right ascription will prevent accurate valuation, and result in the failure of value leverage.

Efficiency will only emerge with clear property rights. All market actors will arrive at compromises or establish cooperation based on plans that guarantee their interest maximization. In developed countries, especially countries and regions which have achieved success in agricultural modernization, land is circulated and its allocation optimized among farmers, giving rise to professional family farms of scale. On this premise, different capital and forms of ownership systems find their way into production, warehousing, transportation and processing, etc., giving rise to a detailed division of labour and the effects of collectivization. In the various transportation segments, farmers generally join in the different cooperatives. In deep processing, different companies join in, such that the entire agricultural production chain is freely and efficiently formed by a rich diversity of ownerships, and costs are reduced and efficiency enhanced. But the prerequisite is clear property rights. And the preliminary and central starting point to these is that every family owns title to its land. One who has perpetual property will have determination.

For China, where the population is enormous and land scarce, low agricultural productivity is a very serious problem. The population is ever-increasing, and urbanization is picking up speed. Hence, for the material assurance of the people's livelihood and the long-term benefits of urbanization, establishing a highly efficient and modern agricultural system is a necessary course that must be followed. Privatization of property rights is the beginning.

3.3 Property Rights Protect the Environment and Render Development Sustainable

When land becomes private property, and when the mechanism for value-preservation and value-adding is in place, everyone will treasure their "own" land. They will not allow their land to be left idle, deteriorate or depreciate; nor will they over-cultivate "public" farmland, or engage in unrestrained deforestation or over-grazing. This will effectively mitigate problems such as reduction in fertility of land and desertification. These are the most pronounced forestry problems in present-day China.

On 17 June 2006, Zhu Lieke, Deputy Director of the State Forestry Bureau, said that desertification is seriously threatening the living spaces of China, and severely restricting its socio-economic development. Every year, direct economic losses incurred due to land desertification amount to more than RMB 54 billion. 889 counties and districts in 30 provinces across the country were found with sanded land, occupying 1,739,700 square kilometres, or 18.12 percent of the national land area.

When the author was researching in the major prevention and control areas for wind and sandstorms in Beijing and Tianjin, many villagers reported that it was the unrestrained logging of "collective forest lands" by grassroots functionaries that appeared to be the more serious cause. At the same time, because of the specificities of the forestry business, contract and management both utilize wood timber forests. As it takes many years to groom seedlings to fully-grown trees ready for logging, and even so, trees cannot be completely logged all at one go, continued operations must be carried out as required under regulations. At this time, having only the "right to contract" will send a strong signal that "perhaps they might just change it anytime. No one knows to whom this plot of land ultimately belongs." Illegal activities often happen, and "fewer approvals, more logging" is a commonly reported phenomenon. Also, many forest farmers are unwilling to invest in nurturing forests, because they do not have title to the specific plot of land. Their sons and grandsons have no succession rights. Thus, they have neither the patience nor confidence for long-term operations, and lack the "fair-mindedness" needed to preserve the land for better valorization into the future.

Under these circumstances, if land were privatized, with clear property rights, not only would the collective forest lands not be destroyed by power-holders under the name of the collectives, but farmers would also be able to better manage a piece of forest land for the future and for later generations. They would be more driven to plant trees and nurture forests, and the perplexing desertification problem in China would be resolved over time.

The same goes for crop-farming and animal husbandry. Land, by itself, is an extremely precious and non-renewable resource. Management-by-plundering will result in irreversible destruction.

3.4 Privatization of Land Title has Important Significance in Reducing Social Disputes, Ensuring Social Stability, and Stabilizing Local Fiscal Revenue

Friedrich A. Hayek once said that "without property rights, no other rights are possible."

There have been many controversies in Chinese rural areas; one of the most important is the unfair distribution of wealth. Wealth is distributed unfairly because it belongs to the collective, the controller of which – i.e., the cadre leader – is responsible for the distribution of goods to the members of the collective. To allow one individual to distribute collective wealth is, in fact, endowing this individual with a lot of power. Without sound supervision and the rule of law, such distribution is usually unfair.

However, when land title becomes privatized, the distribution of the land's value and all added-value will be carried out by the title-holder. The "organization" shall have no right to interfere. The legal relationship of wealth distribution is very clear, which means that social controversies due to wealth distribution and possession will be substantially reduced.

Also, after land privatization, the market price of land will increase, and so likewise will land transactions and local fiscal revenues. This enables institutionalization of the local fiscal measures, infrastructure, effects between land prices, and elevates the income and efficiency of local government officials. Local governments of western countries rely very much on land taxes and real estate transaction taxes, which are founded on private land title and the free market.

Yang Xiaokai has said:

Some say that the demise of many Chinese dynasties was due to land annexation by local despotic powers, and that privatization of land ownership may lead to social problems. In fact, land annexation by despotic powers had resulted from the lack of legal protection of land title. According to the Qing dynasty's records on court disputes, the right to repurchase sold land at the original price restricted the free transaction of land, and became the cause of many cases of homicide and social unrest. Many current land disputes in Guangdong are also the result of inadequate protection of the private land title.[2]

4. EVOLUTION OF CHINA'S LAND REGIME AND HISTORICAL CHOICES

China is an agricultural country whose lands are principally located in inland areas, whose people are highly dependent on land, and who have always had a great admiration and love for the land. The Chinese compare the sky and the earth to the emperor and empress or to their mother and father, and Chinese mythology has it that their ancestors were made from yellow soil by Nü Wa, a mythological character. For thousands of years, people have obtained food and wealth from the land, and have planted the roots of their lives in the land. Land is their family heirloom and provides the source and meaning of their lives. In Chinese history, the loyalty of court officials, the rise and fall of dynasties, and other such events, were nearly always closely interwoven with changes to the land system.

Since 1949, Chinese rural land has witnessed four phases of change, and the difficulties encountered during this period fully attest to the natural flow of history.

4.1 Private Ownership and Private Operation
Around 1949, the Chinese government confiscated all of the lands of landlords and distributed it equally among the farmers. This reform saw the implementation of the policy of "the grower shall own his land." Land title and management rights belonged to the farmer, who owned and managed his own land. Land title was freely transferrable and circulated, bought and sold, leased, pawned, and bestowed. The State managed land through land registration, the issuance of permits, the collection of deeds, taxes, and so on.

Ownership of land provided a huge motivation for the farmers to produce. By 1952, and within only three years, national food production in China grew by 42.8 percent, cotton by 193.7 percent, total agricultural output rose by 41.4 percent and the buying power of farmers doubled. Under free competition, land was transferred and circulated, its allocation optimized, and the percentage of middle income and rich farmers increased every year. The formation of a class of "middle income farmers" at that time, i.e. of a spindle-shaped social structure, told of an increasingly healthy economy.

4.2 Private Ownership and Collective Operation

Farmers working independently by household often encountered the problem of insufficient production tools and capacity. Hence, some began combining production and operation, without altering ownership on their lands. Cooperation teams of different forms were organized to fill each other's needs. Called "Agricultural Cooperatives" (*nongye hezuohua*) or "Primary Agricultural Cooperatives" (*chuji nongye hezuoshe*), this model was widely promoted by the Chinese government.

The government's choice of this model was largely inspired by the Soviet Collective Farms. To avert the economic risks of a small and independent farmer and to achieve economies of scale, agricultural cooperatives mushroomed across the country.

The setup of a primary agricultural cooperative is as follows. Except for a small private plot, members hand over their land to the cooperative. The cooperative becomes the central coordinator for the use of land, and members of the cooperative receive returns according to the quantity and quality of land contributed. Primary agricultural cooperatives recognize that land is the personal property of the farmers, and that only the right to its use is transferred from the individual to the collective.

In fact, starting with private ownership, agricultural modernization and commercialization driving private ownership and generating diversified modes of shareholding and cooperation is a natural and normal process of agricultural development. Although China's agricultural cooperatives were still immature at the time, they had their strengths. Nonetheless, this immature model soon became a "communist" venture.

4.3 Public Ownership and Collective Operation

As of around 1957, the country was swept by a wave of "communism" and many still immature primary cooperatives started on even more radical socialist reform. Farmers handed over not only the management rights of their land to the collective, but also their title to the land. They wanted to "run towards communism." The Advanced Agricultural Cooperative (*gaoji nongye hezuoshe*) was thus born. Within just one year, the agricultural cooperatives quickly became People's Communes (*renmin gongshe*). By early November 1958, there were 26,572 People's Communes, with 99.1 percent of total farmers joining their memberships.

By forming People's Communes, farmers contributed to the commune all their lands under the various agricultural cooperatives; private plots; graveyards and housing land belonging to members of the cooperatives; their production resources, such as farm animals and agricultural tools; and all public property. The commune took over the central planning, production and management of land, and distributed the returns equally. Rural land was collectively owned and managed. With increased public ownership, land use and management rights were completely under the command of the commune, effectively a fusion of the government and the collective. By keeping control and management of land production and operation through highly centralized planning, the transfer or lease of any right associated with the land was absolutely prohibited. In fact, after the reform, what had originally been the personal property of farmers became the property of the government.[3]

Collectivization of land rights, in essence, caused farmers to lose all their personal land. They became general workers who perform collective tasks based on uniform orders, and rewards were calculated based on a work point system. Collective operations differed in nature from flexible cooperation among farmers. Passive working attitudes and aggressive eating from the public rice pot became the norm. Agricultural productivity deteriorated drastically. China's agricultural sector suffered a disastrous setback; not only did productivity decline, many people suffered and died from starvation. Certainly, this disastrous outcome may have partially resulted from many natural calamities. But farmers who lost their land lost the opportunity for independent management, their last chip. They could do nothing but bear hunger.

4.4 Public Ownership and Private Operation

At the end of 1978, a touching episode took place at Xiaogang Village in Fengyang County, Anhui Province. Eighteen farmers, who refused to starve and beg any longer, took the chance of being "arrested" by defying the system. They affixed their red ink-stained handprints on a piece of paper, and announced that they would implement "contracting of work to households" (*baogan daohu* or the "Baogan System") for their collectively owned land. It was fortuitous that the reform and opening-up was underway, and their insight did not turn them into "policy rebels" or "capitalist factions"; instead, they became heroes who initiated rural land reform in China. That year, the Third Plenary Session of the Eleventh Central Committee of the Communist Party of China decided to implement rural land reform. By 1983, *shuangbao daohu* ("household double guarantee" - *dabaogan* and *baochan daohu* combined) was implemented in more than 95 percent of the production brigades (*sheng-chan-dui*).

The Household Responsibility Contract System represents the abolition of the consolidation of land titles and management rights under the People's Communes. The system allows land management rights to be contracted out to farmers, and the contracting units are individual households. This is a change from the previous highly centralized land ownership and land use rights, and the malpractice of the single manager mode. The relationship between farmers and land went through a material change, such that the benefits to farmers were pegged to their land output; this was a change welcomed by the farmers.

In 1993, the Chinese government initiated a second round of the land contracting exercise. Relevant documents and laws were promulgated, providing that the term for contracting land may be extended for another 30 years upon the expiration of the 15-year rights mandated by the earlier document under the same terms. Farmers were also permitted to subcontract, transfer, acquire shares or lease among them.

The new land regime was encouraging, and farmers' readiness to produce was a stabilizing force for the society and an impetus for agricultural and rural economic development. Also, the massive exodus of the labour force to the cities brought a fresh energy boost for the rapid development of the secondary and tertiary industries. However, the loss of ownership remains a shackle to farmers' confidence and remains a true lack of fundamental protection. Even today, such missed ownership is a drag on agricultural development that continues to harm farmers' interests, and many other problems as earlier described.

A glimpse at human history will tell us that rural public-ownership has been rare. And looking at the land histories of each country, we will discover that private ownership of rural land is a very stable regime, and the one most used in China's traditional society.

During the Liberation War, the Chinese Communist Party (CPC) relied on the simple slogan of "Down with the Haves, share among the Have-Nots" (*da tuhao, fen tiandi* – literally "fight the local despots and redistribute their land") to win the fervent support of Chinese farmers. When the CPC assumed power, land was immediately distributed to the farmers, by which rapid restoration and development of the agricultural economy during the early days of governance was achieved. Cooperatives were established subsequently, and land originally belonging to farmers then became collectively-owned land during the advanced cooperatives era. Therefore, in essence, the lawfulness of farmers having the eventual title to these lands was not extinguished.

Looking back at history, it is clear to us that returning the land to the farmers is fundamental to protecting their interests, and the best route to facilitating agricultural and social development.

5. Analysis of Several "Concerns"

There have been many opposing voices in recent years on the restoration of private land ownership. The following sets forth the author's views toward some of these reservations:

5.1 "Privatization Will Affect the Essential Qualities of Socialism"

The essential spirit of socialism is to liberate and develop productivity and to eradicate exploitation and social polarization. Based on what has already been said, the privatization of land is the most pressing road to take for the maximization and development of productivity, and a demonstration of the spirit of socialism.

If land originally belongs to the people, its distribution to everybody would merely be the government's decentralization of management to give the people true power. This is also the original object of socialism.

Thus, privatization of land title is a requisite of socialism.

5.2 "Privatization Will Lead to Farmers' Massive Loss of Land and Further Social Instability"

First, the massive "loss" of land by farmers is a natural consequence in history. In the history of mankind, many developed countries have evolved from being agricultural and rural countries into industrialized and urban states. Large rural populations were released from lands and entered the cities to carry out different types of occupations. Cities of all sizes began to enlarge as their populations multiplied. Through market transactions, rural land was transferred into the hands of major growers, which became a family farm holding many lands. In the US alone, the agricultural population was reduced from a level in the 1860s of 81.23 percent to 60.23 percent in the 1900s. Its agricultural population is even smaller now, at only two percent. Within 150 years, the US has transformed from a major agricultural country to a modern industrialized nation, and from a country which is rural-based to one that is urban-based.

China's strategy of transforming the country into an industrialized city during the past years is no doubt a correct direction. Large rural populations are migrating to the cities through different channels. Any observant person would notice the mushrooming of large numbers of "villages with empty nests." At the same time, cities of various sizes have been expanding, and many new cities, towns, and satellite cities have come into existence. The population of many new cities is basically made up of people who have migrated from the rural areas during the last thirty years.

Thus, the author judges that the process of large numbers of farmers selling their lands is a necessary component of urbanization.

Second, the way in which farmers "lose" their lands should guarantee their best interests. The question is whether farmers should be free to sell and transact their own land, or whether the government should represent "farmers' interests" to assist in such endeavours. To "lose" a massive amount of land is an irreversible and natural consequence of history. But the key lies in "losing" it justly and reasonably, and the critical issue is whether social problems will arise as a result.

If farmers are forever without actual ownership, losing land will naturally cause them to become true "proletarians" or refugees. For compensation is still income obtained from the restricted trading of property, and what the government gives the farmers is merely a token of compensation.

Third, establishing farmers' title to their land is the only way to maximize wealth and protection for farmers while they "lose" their lands. Establishing farmers' title to their land will give farmers huge leeway in the disposal of their land. Some worry that this may lead to an over acquisition of land, resulting in some farmers losing their homes, and therefore a bigger social disaster. But such a disaster could happen if farmers' land title is not established. On average, several million *mu* of land are converted to non-agricultural usage every year. An aggregate of more than one hundred million farmers can never return to their lands. With the figure growing, is this not devastating? If farmers have title to their lands, land transfer prices will be greatly elevated, the power strata will no longer make exorbitant profits, and this by itself is sufficient discouragement of over acquisition and infringement.

As more than a hundred million – or perhaps even a greater number – of farmers move into the cities, there is no proper solution to settlement of the lands under their management as farmers; the lands are either entrusted in the hands of other people, or left uncultivated. However, if the land titles were to belong to the farmers, those who chose to become urban dwellers could sell their land to major farmers, so that the land would be freely, naturally and legally transferred to these big farmers. Economies of scale and centralized management would be achieved and the land owners would obtain a sizeable sum to purchase housing or property in their new places of residence. Everybody's rights would be protected, unemployment would be under control, and farmers would become wealthier because of the freedom to trade their lands.

Some authorities have estimated that cumulative differential income from land sales since the reform and opening-up have amounted to more than two thousand billion RMB that has flowed from farmers to other social organizations. Who says that farmers' income cannot be increased? If this sum is left for farmers, farmers transferring land will become wealthier. The average land area given to each farmer in many urban-rural combination zones in eastern China is 0.7 *mu*. These developed areas usually pay farmers between a few thousand RMB to twenty or thirty thousand RMB per *mu*, and sell the land for a few million RMB in the market. This tells us that some local governments and developers have "legitimately" robbed that few million RMB originally belonging to the farmers.

Transactions between farmers are also very important. One farmer who is better at rearing ducks can concentrate on doing so, and the extra land he has could be productively sold to another who is better at cultivating. Another advantage is that after collectivization, land wastage due to ridges between the small fields will be greatly reduced, and more land will be released for productive use.

The problem of the huge population and scarce land in Chinese rural areas is currently pronounced, and industrialization and urbanization also imply that there will be a huge exodus of farmers from their lands. However, there is a huge difference between leaving by will and leaving by force. Thus, land privatization is necessary, and allows farmers to leave their lands voluntarily, and not otherwise. They would then maximize their interests based on their own circumstances. From the human rights perspective, farmers are thus given basic freedoms, and from a material perspective, land resources can become the true guarantee of farmers' livelihoods.

Fourth, restoration of land rights to farmers will give rise to a more stable society. The difference between a person who has property rights and one who does not is like that between a gentleman and a gangster. The former thinks first of his intrinsic interests, generates a sense of awareness of his social responsibilities to maintain the current order and will of the community, and opposes revolution. The latter, who has no private interests, fears neither the good nor the bad. He will choose the quickest route to making a fortune, and his greatest hope is to destroy the current order to find opportunities. The controllers of property rights under a public-ownership regime lie between these two categories. As soon as they discover that they might lose their power, they will want to do anything to take it back, even if this means destroying the social order. The earlier Hunan farmers' movement is a typical case in point. Although some holders of power and power resources will own land and receive personal gains, stability of a minority is not reliable stability. Converting dubious ownership structures into clear title in the hands of everyone, especially farmers, is the only avenue to permanent stability.

5.3 "Privatization Will Lead to a Food Crisis"

This problem will not arise under a market economy. Only inflexible administrative orders under a planned economy result in this problem. The invisible hand is more effective than a visible hand directing; an agricultural product will produce greater profits when supply fails to meet demand, because greater profits will produce a supply pull. Hundreds and thousands of products provide the market with diverse possibilities for market regulation, and no one will suffer from hunger simply because production of one type of food has decreased. The government will only have to ensure that the macro-level control measures are in place, that there is sufficient agricultural land not used for developing secondary and tertiary industries, and that they restrict land transactions that convert the land usage. Sufficient agricultural production will thus be secured.

This is not all. Land privatization sets the foundation for creating a modern agricultural regime, and provides the requisites for the swift building up of agricultural productivity. This way, under highly efficient collectivized production, food production quantity and quality per unit area can only increase.

5.4 "Privatization Will Lead to Further Wealth Disparity in the Rural Areas"

There is a fundamental principle here: wealth disparity arising as a result of free competition is more reasonable and fairer than disparity emerging from direct compulsion. Fair competition-created wealth disparity is harmless, while power-compelled wealth disparity is detrimental. In the process of building and developing a market economy, the existence of a certain level of wealth disparity is justifiable, and evidence of equity.

Based on Deng Xiaoping's principle of "let those who got rich first lead the way to universal riches," disparity is the beginning of universal progress. So long as the starting point is an equal footing, and no plundering or infringement exists, not only will unreasonable wealth disparities not develop, disparity will in fact be more effectively controlled.

On a macro perspective, for more than 50 years urban-rural disparity in Chain has been increasingly widening. This is embodied in the urban-rural inequality brought about by policy discrimination. Decision-makers cannot employ a bird's-eye view when developing the rural economy. Instead, they should respect farmers' autonomous right to choose, in the same way that they have with respect to the development of the urban economy. They should allow the agricultural economy's primary market to take shape freely and healthily, adjust itself, and play its rightful role.

Given the present circumstances, it is somewhat absurd to ask if "a new wealth disparity will occur after the privatization of land" from a theoretical standpoint; it is perhaps even a pseudo-issue. Wealth disparity brought forth by free competition cannot be any worse than the current wealth disparity caused by institutional discrimination because, fundamentally, the vulnerable are competing against an institutional upper-hand and are in a compromised position; put otherwise, people without their own rights in their hands are competing with those who are close to or holding power… and there is a huge difference between fate being held in one's own hand and being held in those of another.

6. Conclusion and Recommendation

To conclude, the privatization of land is not only a necessary resolution of the current social problems in China, but also in line with the law of historical development and essential for socio-economic growth. Most importantly, it is to be hoped that privatization will alleviate the deprived circumstances of Chinese farmers today, and, in so doing, build a harmonious society that is fair and free from discrimination.

From a legislative perspective, the recognition of the land rights of farmers equates to guaranteeing their fundamental and most important private property, and provides the foundation for the elimination of policy discrimination and the recognition of the economic status of farmers (to a certain extent). Farmers with title to their land will be able to determine their own fates. The right of disposition over their own land ensures their freedom of speech in various social relations through which they will enjoy social equality, and walk away from the shadow of discrimination.

Finally, privatization provides the tool to effectively delineate what is private from what is public. Economic status and political freedom provide a platform to progressively build a secure democratic regime and a rule of law by adversarial means and compromise. And equality and human rights will be thus further stabilized and reinforced.

Contemporary China has included the protection of the private property of its citizens in the Constitution, and formulated the *Real Rights Law*. This is a good start. To continue its reform process, China must take major steps to change the rural land regime. For this is a natural choice, due to our respect for farmers, for human rights, and for history.

The next steps should be:

1. The Chinese government must regard the protection of farmers' land rights as the fundamental policy for the protection of farmers;
2. The current land contract right must be further consolidated;
3. Reform of the land regime must be implemented as soon as possible, with the key task being to restore land title to farmers. Hence, revision of the provisions concerning the rural land regime under the Constitution and relevant laws and regulations must be completed as soon as possible in order to truly confer rights on farmers.

Restoration of the private ownership of land is thus the only way to lay the foundation for guaranteeing the fundamental and basic human rights of farmers.

Endnotes

1   Ronald Coase proposed that it is unimportant whether the initial distribution of statutory rights is efficient, so long as there is zero exchange cost.
2   Yang Xiaokai, "Underlying Problems Confronting China's Reform" (*zhong guo gai ge mian lin de shen ceng wen ti*), *Strategy and Management*, Issue 5, 2002.
3   Cheng Taolin, "An Analysis of the Evolution of China's Land Regime and Privatization Reform" (*wo guo nong di zhi du de yan bian ji si you hua gai ge shen xi*), http://www.nlj.suzhou.gov.cn/web/.

CHAPTER FOUR

Changing the Policy Paradigm on Chinese Migrant Workers

Towards Balanced Urban and Rural Development, People-Orientation, Equal Treatment and Consultative Management

Cui Chuanyi and Cui Xiaoli

The exodus of the rural labour force to work in the non-agricultural industries of cities and towns, part of China's process of reform and opening–up (*gaige kaifang*) and industrialization, has engendered a large new social group called the "migrant workers." The effects of the previous planned economy, its system of urban-rural segregation and ideologies that emphasized economic growth rather than social development and welfare improvement have all become prejudicial to the lives of migrant workers: migrant workers' legitimate rights have been infringed, their fair treatment as citizens denied, and their interests and needs forgotten in public policies. These increasingly pronounced problems have become obstacles to urban-rural development and social harmony. To adapt to a market economy and urbanization in the new century, China has proposed a scientific approach to development and has aggressively transformed migrant worker-related policies to make them more oriented to the people and to guarantee their fair treatment. But policies alone cannot be solutions. Public policy formulation and implementation are related to the social management system. Currently, what needs to be explored and addressed is the way to continue making policy adjustment and improvement, and how to reform the social management system, in order to create an institutional environment that protects the legitimate rights of migrant workers and offers them a stable urban citizenship.

I. Formation of the Migrant Worker Group and its Socio-Economic Implications

Before China's reform and opening-up, economic planning and urban-rural segregation led to national development based on heavy industry and restriction on the movement and migration of rural labour. Farmers, who account for 80 percent of the Chinese population, were confined to rural land with a low per capita average income to carry out a single activity: agricultural production. Added to that was the rural People's Commune system – under which the farmers were granted very few property and democratic rights – which further prolonged under-development and poverty within the rural community. Hence, the first target for recent reforms was the rural community. With implementation of the household contract system and progression of the market-oriented reforms from urban to rural areas, farmers were granted property rights as well as the freedom of surplus labour to change occupation. Motivated to reduce poverty and accumulate personal wealth, farmers began developing township enterprises and the private sector in the rural areas. However, many farmers in the vast central or western traditional agricultural regions were unable to do so because of multiple restraints. Hence, they chose to leave home to find employment in the cities. These are the two sources of migrant workers, who continue to retain their rural household registrations (farmer identity) while being employed in secondary or tertiary industries, receiving wages as their main source of income. The group has expanded along with ongoing industrialization, including the inflow of local and foreign capital. Migrant workers are now an integral component of the industrial workforce, and a major force in the labour-intensive secondary and tertiary industries. This strengthened force has facilitated industrialization, urbanization and reform. In nearly three decades of reform and opening-up, China has become the centre for global investment and labour-intensive manufacturing industries, and the creator of the miracle of sustained and rapid economic growth. It has also transitioned from a planned economy to a market economy, and has leapfrogged from merely meeting basic needs to becoming a complete *xiaokang* society ("society of modest means"). These achievements could not be accomplished without the contribution from the over 200 million Chinese migrant workers.

The massive influx of migrant workers affects the livelihood and development of millions, as well as China's overall development, reform and stability. As of 2006, the number of migrant workers employed in township enterprises was 146 million, having grown from 28 million at the start of the reform. The number that has migrated across regions and worked in cities has increased from about two million to 132 million. Excluding any duplication and the number of part-time workers whose main occupation is in farming, the total number is approximately 220 million. This implies that nearly half the rural labour force has moved into non-agricultural industries. More than 200 million of their family members and children were left behind in the rural areas, and approximately two million have followed them to the destination city. For these reasons, the overall situation for migrant workers has a direct impact on the survival and development of 400 to 500 million people.

Migrant workers account for 60 percent of the people employed in the commercial, food and beverage, and service sectors, 70 percent in processing and manufacturing, and 80 percent in construction. Their main contributions to China's socio-economic development are: (1) Facilitating China's industrialization, urbanization and internationalization, and the transformation of an agricultural power into an industrial, commercial and service power; (2) Opening up an avenue for farmers to assuage poverty and find wealth, and initiating a glorious chapter in Chinese history on the diversion of the rural labour force into industry, which has had a profound impact on the progress of modernization; (3) Enhancing corporate competitiveness, hastening capital accumulation, and creating mutual reinforcement between the development of enterprise and industry and the employment of migrant workers who are typically young, diligent and low-cost. Migrant workers are one of the key catalysts for China's rise to the most attractive country for foreign investment and a global manufacturing and trade power[1]; (4) The concentration of migrant workers in developed areas and cities has propelled the development of the industrial, commerce and service sector. Migrant workers have been hard at work, constructing skyscrapers and transportation networks that connect rural and urban areas, and contributing to the emergence of large number of new cities and towns, and the formation of the three urban clusters: the Pearl River Delta, the Yangtze River Delta and the Bohai Sea Rim regions; (5) Tearing down the urban-rural dualistic structure to enable reform of the traditional employment and hiring systems; enabling the nurture of a uniform labour market across the urban and rural areas, and extensive restructuring of vital resources to meet industrialization and restructuring needs; forging close socio-economic ties between the urban and rural communities, which in turn has contributed to the development of rural areas; (6) Promoting reform of the dual social management system. Although migrant workers' migration to cities is driven by economic objectives such as greater employment opportunities and income, migrant workers are also social beings and citizens who work and have social needs such as the needs to live, develop, dwell, seek medical treatment, learn and be trained, as well as requiring education for their children, social participation and urban permanent residences. However, the tradition of urban-rural segregation, the dual household registration system, and the associated public service and welfare systems have excluded migrant workers' needs. This has led to unequal status and prejudiced rights. Therefore, breaking the dual social structure and creating a system conducive to structural changes are imperative.

II. CHARACTERISTICS AND LIMITATIONS OF THE OLD POLICY PARADIGM ON MIGRANT WORKERS

The formation of the migrant worker population and the flow of surplus rural labour into non-agricultural industries and cities are indeed driven by the pursuit of self-interest, in the form of better employment and income. But desire is not all that makes things tick. The market behaviour of the workers is determined by labour demand, and this in turn is related to the need to progress from an agricultural society to a modern industrial society. But, for some time, reform was restricted to strictly economic aspects. Relative to the formation and expansion of the migrant worker population during the process of industrialization, there was a lag in the reshaping of the pertinent policies and the social management system, as there were many dimensions that were still based upon the planned economy and the urban-rural dual structure. These dated policies and systems needed to be brought into line with the new economic regime, and recalibrated to accommodate the flow of the rural labour force, the newly created labour market and the social demographic changes induced by the rural labour movement between urban and rural areas. The migrant worker policies were not fundamentally changed until the 21st century. For the purpose of this article, the author refers to the policies in force at the end of the 1980s and in the 1990s as old policies, to differentiate them from the new policies on migrant workers formulated in recent years, especially those relating to the migrant workers' employment in the cities.

On the issue of migrant worker policies of the 1990s, we can look broadly at two aspects: one aspect concerns policies that encouraged the development of diversified ownership enterprises, such as township enterprises and the private sector of the economy in rural areas, the transfer of surplus rural labour to the nearest available jobs, or the migration of workers to small towns below the county level for work or business.[2] The other aspect concerns policies on the movement of the rural labour force to the cities and migrant workers' employment in the cities that were not adapted to development and the situation of reform. Though there were occasional affirmative comments on migrant workers working in the cities,[3] the policies of the State were generally restrictive, usually in the name of providing systematic guidance.[4]

On policies in the 1990s relating to migrant workers: between 1989 and 1991, the policies in practice aimed to strictly control and "block" city-bound migrant workers. Thereafter, rural labour movement was administratively controlled and restricted, using economic, legal and administrative means. For example, the *Provisional Regulations on the Cross-Provincial Movement and Employment of Rural Labour* and *Opinions on Strengthening the Administration of Migrant Population* issued by State authorities in 1994 and 1995 adopted a standard employment and temporary residential permit system. Migrant workers were required to have valid temporary documents, the "Emigrant Employment Registration Card" (*waichu renyuan jiuye dengji ka*) and the "Emigrant Employment Permit" (*waichu renyuan jiuye zheng*), as well as the temporary residence permit (refer to Table 1). As of 1994, some local governments in the coastal areas formulated their own local policies for the migrant worker population in their regions and cities. These policies were aimed at controlling the overall size of the migrant worker population, as well as the industry and employment categories in which migrants can work. Migrant worker administration is undertaken by the municipal office for migrant population, which issues and inspects certificates – charging expensive fees – and identifies and even deports those without the "three certificates."

Table 1: Policies on Migrant Workers at the End of the 1980s and 1990s

Time of Issuance	Document	Policy Highlights
March 1989	*Urgent Notice Issued by the General Office of the State Council on the Strict Control of Outflow of Migrant Workers*	Local governments adopt effective measures to strictly control the outflow of local rural labour.
April 1989	*Notice by the Ministry of Civil Affairs and the Ministry of Public Security on Continuing Control over the Rush Outflow of Migrant Workers*	Strictly control the excessive outflow of local rural labour.
April 1990	*Notice by the State Council on Improving Labour Employment Administration*	Encourage surplus rural labour to "leave farming but not home." Develop forestry, husbandry, fishery and sideline industries, township enterprises, service industry and construction of the rural area to absorb and transfer surplus labour locally and prevent a large rural labout force from leaving for the cities indiscriminately to seek employment. Employ legal, administrative and economic means to exercise effective control and strict rule over migrant workers working in the cities. Formulate plans for the employment of the rural labour force in the cities within a specific period, for which it shall be reviewed and approved by the labour departments to ensure strict control. Establish temporary employment permit and employment registration system to tighten the monitoring and checks on employment operations. Hiring outside the existing plan definitions, particularly rural labour, shall cease as provided by State policy. Strict control of excessive increase in city-bound rural labour migration.

Key characteristics of the 1990s policy paradigm:

1. Planned economy-engendered administrative control and restriction.

Farmers' willingness to migrate and enterprises' willingness to hire were regarded as "blind movement" (*mang liu*), and the total migration number was capped by a planned "quota." This quota was redistributed downwards, and employment operations of enterprises were subject to review and approval by the administrative departments. Special permits and cards for outflow and inflow of the rural labour force were required, such that migrant workers were required to apply for an emigration employment permit at a home location as well as an immigration employment card at the destination. Review and issuance of such certifications were means employed by the government to exercise "control by quota" and restriction. Without the government's review and approval, enterprises' hiring was deemed "unapproved recruitment and employment," and without the necessary documents, migrant workers' employment was labelled "blind movement," both offences would be subject to punishment, and the employment revoked. Through such planned policies, the government tried to keep the control and decision-making for floating employment centralized at the administrative organs. The original intention was to eliminate indiscriminate labour movement. Unfortunately, without understanding the manpower requirements of different employers and the personal profiles and preferences of migrant workers, the government had interfered blindly, not having to be held accountable for the risks involved. Instead of keeping a disciplined labour movement, such intervention had prejudiced the independence of the farmers and the employers, and frustrated the market mechanism. In addition, migrant workers were required to apply for a temporary residence permit, employment card and certificate, health certificate and marriage certificate, for which they would be charged as high as RMB 400 to 700 every year. As well, permit application, charges, certificate verification and fines related to the administrative procedures impeded movement, and therefore employment, of migrant workers.

2. Urban-rural dualistic division and unequal identity and rights constituted discrimination.

The trans-regional movement of farmers for employment in the cities sloughed off regional isolation and urban-rural segregation instituted under the traditional system. Migrant workers provide labour for enterprises seeking to hire, participate in economic growth and receive income. However, certain policies remained restrictive, tending to keep the rural labour force within their local confines, and perpetuate the unequal rights as manifested under the agricultural and non-agricultural *hukous* (household registration). Employers recruiting were to observe the rules of "Three Firsts and Three Lasts" (*sanxian sanhou*), which means the recruitment of candidates in the following order of priority: local township *hukous*, local rural *hukous*, migrant workers from the same province, and migrant workers from other provinces. Special charges for processing permits for migrant workers were instituted as a means of control. Only urban residents were eligible to benefit from employment services provided in the urban areas for the general public and government-sponsored labour markets. Migrant workers did not qualify. Migrant workers without the necessary documents – in some cases, even those with the necessary documents – would be deported; certain cities required employers to pay administration fees for employing migrant workers. The list goes on. Founded on the dual household registration system and unequal rights, such policies were discriminatory.

The cities classify industries and jobs into three categories: those inaccessible to migrant workers, those with restricted access, and those with access. Migrant workers' employment opportunities were therefore extremely restricted; usually jobs that were available for them were dirty, tiring, tough and dangerous. Most industries and jobs were reserved for people with urban *hukous*. Under the pretext of protecting the urban unemployed and laid-off workers, the urban-rural divide in employment treatment was perpetuated, and institutional discrimination against farmers and stratification of the rural and urban residents exacerbated. Also, employed migrant workers in the city were not treated as fellow urbanites. They were instead marginalized and discriminated against and excluded from public services such as housing, children's education, medical care and social security. The dual system was extended into the city following the flow of migrant workers to the cities. Hence a social divide was created whereby unequal rights existed between city dwellers and migrant workers.

3. Prevention and Control.

Migrant workers were treated as a potential threat to social order and security. Social security is a common need of urban residents, enterprises and migrant workers. Many factors may hamper social safety, including emerging problems during social transformation and institutional reform, absence of proper coordination mechanism, and infringements upon the interest of migrant workers. However, although the wages of farmers migrating to work in the cities is lower than that of the urban average income, they are still higher than than the rural average income. As such, instead of destabilizing, migrant workers could contribute to stability and development. However, there was a belief that the rural labour movement was indiscriminate and disorganized, and that if left unchecked, it could cause instability. On this premise, the migrant worker policies were very much focused on the maintenance of public security. The fact that the administration offices for migrant population affairs were under the jurisdiction of public security departments attests to the official presumption that migrant workers were potentially dangerous to the urban society. Such a focus on the prevention of public disturbance resulted in the neglect of the interests and demands of the migrant workers themselves. Migrant workers became a target for increases in measures of social order, including mandatory background checks. Residential districts with a dense migrant worker population were often targets of inspection, verification, fines, repression, and expatriation. Together with local residents, migrant workers created wealth, and became owners of the society and direct or indirect taxpayers. The paradox was their inappropriate treatment, subject and targeted for purposes of regulation and control.

4. Multi-Department Policies Lacked in Consistency.

Development of the market economy and the migration of farmers to urban areas has integrated the urban and rural labour markets. Institutional regulations such as employment rights, personal freedom of citizens, and related administrative charges should have been governed by standard State policies and laws. Nevertheless, for some time, policies governing migrant workers were issued by many different authorities. Some municipal government departments enacted regulations that limited the industrial sectors or types of jobs in which migrant workers were eligible to work, with which they actually deprived them of the right to work in certain sectors. Also, the extradition of migrant workers to their homes was in violation of the laws. Our investigation of a city in August 2003 showed that different districts within the city applied different charges for migrant worker permits: nine for temporary residence permits, ten for employment permits, and six for health certificates. Different authorities making up different regulations unchecked by laws have led to chaos in policies and administrative operations, and serious prejudice of migrant workers' interests.

The incompatibility of migrant worker policies during this period with the market economy, with the movement of rural surplus labour to non-agricultural industries and cities, and with industrialization and urbanization came ultimately to determine their limitations and unsustainability.

First, in the context of China's development, the policies failed to capture the true implications of migrant workers being a new genre of labour force in China's industrialization and the social significance of the change in the rural-urban divide embodied by the migrant workers. The movement of Chinese farmers seeking employment to the cities is an economic behaviour. Migrant workers are not immigrants who stay idle or beg, or create a "crime wave" and therefore must be restrained and controlled. They are a surplus labour force that had been confined to meagre farmlands by the planned economy, the public commune system and urban-rural segregation. Their behaviour was the result of emancipation from the reform of the household contract system. As individuals, they were workers looking for jobs in the cities to earn money; as a group, they were a surplus labour force struggling to make a living by joining in the process of industrialization. This was also exactly the need of the developed regions and cities. Industrialization required us to capitalize on our labour resource advantage to improve our current lack of competitiveness, build up assets and develop businesses. By combining migrant workers' labour input and production factors, domestic and foreign industrial and commercial enterprises generated and developed new productive forces. Through hard work, migrant workers had driven industrialization; this went on to trigger the flow of the surplus agricultural labour forces. Migrant workers became an increasingly integral part of the non-agricultural labour sector, and a new genre of labour in China's industrialization process. An increasing rural labour force and rural population were moving into non-agricultural sectors and into the cities as a result of industrialization. This became a force of change for the urban-rural divide. Rural areas benefited from increased farmers' income as well as improved agricultural resource allocation in people and land. The result was less self-sufficiency and greater commercialization, giving impetus to agricultural and rural modernization.

Migrant worker policies continued to segregate rural from urban dwellers, and restricted farmers only to agricultural activities; even if they did otherwise, they could only do so in nearby areas, and were prohibited from moving around or going to the cities. Such restrictions ran against the patterns of change and the need to transfer the surplus labour force, and the needs for industrialization and urbanization. Regarding migrant workers as a threat to the employment opportunities of urbanites, and therefore restricting their movements and occupation choice, is an example of the old notion of urban-rural segregation and unequal employment rights for urban and rural populations. In truth, it was the demands of the industrial, commercial and service sectors that prescribed the entry of migrant workers. To allow jobs shunned by urbanites to be carried out by migrant workers was the filling of mutual needs and wants. The existence of competition for employment within the labour force benefits development, allowing labourers to give their best and receive what they deserve. The enlarging migrant worker population was not a result of snatching employment opportunities from urban residents. For, the huge employment opportunities were generated by the combination of local and foreign capital and other factors with the rural labour force driving industrialization. Migrant workers are integral to the era of the need for labour services and industrialization. They are a new breed of workers emanating from the surplus labour force in the rural areas, and they should be incorporated into the process of industrialization, of which cities are the main vehicles. This determines that the dated policy of urban-rural segregation cannot continue.

Secondly, migrant worker policies were not standardized according to the mechanisms of market economy reform and market-driven employment. Under the traditional planned economy, the government was responsible only for employment in urban non-agricultural activities, and in state-run and large collective enterprises. Such policies were highly centralized and planned, and farmers' movements were under strict control. The machinery for allowing farmers to migrate to cities to work was founded during reform, when farmers were granted freedom to distribute their labour and to migrate for work, and when enterprises were given the autonomy to hire. Farmers normally obtain from relatives, friends or fellow villagers information on urban employment opportunities. Migrant workers and enterprises are on the two sides of supply and demand in the labour market, which are granted free and bilateral choices to create jobs and hiring decisions. Such market-determined employment is fundamentally different from the system under the planned economy. For farmer households or farmers and enterprises exercise the power of independent decision, and the benefits of being employed and employing are directly related to migrant workers and employers. Under the planned economy, administrative orders planned and arranged employment. The policy continued to determine the size and quota of migrant worker movement using administrative orders, as well as restricted the movement of migrant workers and hiring by enterprises via review and approval procedures. Such administrative controls cannot accommodate the demands of workers and enterprises, and they fail to converge with requirements of the market economy and market-determined employment. Administrative departments were unable to curb the outflow of migrant workers in pursuit of poverty alleviation and wealth; neither could they deprive enterprises of the right to operate nor to hire as they deem fit. Market-driven employment may be curbed, but migrant worker employment could not be stopped. During the mid 1990s, although the higher authorities in the Pearl River Delta region were controlling the inflow of migrant workers and dictating the staff size and quota of enterprises, and distributing these targets downwards, eventually the enterprises came to have the final say. In order to stimulate economic development and attract foreign investment, local governments relaxed restrictions on foreign enterprises' right to hire. Subsequently, other enterprises were allowed to hire as many migrant workers as they needed, eventually exceeding the quota prescribed by the higher authorities. This was a *de facto* invalidation of the administrative controls. Administrative controls eventually consisted only of permit fees chargeable to migrant workers and migrant workers administrative fees chargeable to employers.

Thirdly, the policies caused government administrative dysfunction, "inversion" of the "official-citizen" relationship, unregulated administrative behaviour and public discontent. Government interference in certain issues related to migrant workers and their situation at the location of employment may be unnecessary. However, the government should provide services and governance, such as providing employment information, protecting labour rights and labour interests, setting up social security, and assistance in housing, medical care, children's education, and safety in the work and living environments. The old policies, while imposing excess restriction and regulation, lacked in service and protection. Protection of the migrant workers' legitimate rights was considered secondary. Such policies served two key priorities: first, they restricted the movement of migrant workers. This is a government dysfunction under market-driven employment. Migrant workers' movements are not subject to past economic constraints under the collective economy such as working collectively, earning "credits" based on the amount of work, and receiving food allocation based on work-points accumulated. Nor is there difficulty posed by the food-coupon system if they leave for the city. Administrative regulations were their only barriers. Under such regulations, approvals and permits were required, and administrative fees had to be paid. Further measures included shaking-down and extradition if the required certificates were incomplete. However, migrant workers were resistant to such restrictions, believing that they were making an honest living. Most migrant workers who were removed from their jobs did not leave the city unless they were forcibly deported. Even so, they often escaped during their journey home. The second priority was that of controlling the migrant workers. Although based on the premise of providing better public security, such controls in fact inverted the official-citizen relationship. Migrant workers are labour providers for developed regions and the development of the urban economy, they are the main force in the production front line, and they are direct or indirect taxpayers. Governments who depend on taxpayers to provide the funds for publicly financed operations should provide public services not only for urban residents but also for migrant workers. Instead, migrant workers were regarded as the cause of social disorder and instability, and the trigger for restrictive rule over them. In reality, most migrant workers are law-abiding citizens, but they are main target of infringement of rights. Migrant workers should be protected as they constitute a contributing force for societal safety. To generalize migrant workers as potential threats to public security and to regard them as persons to guard against and to be controlled is discrimination. Certain measures such as inspections, controls and deportation are infringements of their legitimate rights, and detrimental to social integration of migrant workers with existing urban residents. Together, these would manipulate the whole society, leading to high social administration costs and difficulty in the thorough renewal of social order and public security. Since administrative overheads for employment and security are derived from the administrative targets, government departments become interest-driven and their administrative behaviour unregulated. Other repercussions include multiple administrators and overcharging, which result in greater social chaos.

III. The Formation of New Migrant Worker Policies

Since the beginning of the 21st century, the Communist Party of China (CPC) and the State government have placed heavy emphasis on migrant worker-related issues. Fundamental policy changes have taken place. The various factors leading to such changes are: first, growth in the number of migrant workers during reform and development, increase in migrant workers' income, and change in public practices due to industrialization and urbanization. Second, China's adoption of a people-oriented scientific conception that proposes comprehensive, balanced and sustainable development. As part of the overall strategy to drive industrialization and urbanization, China is addressing issues related to *sannong* (issues of agriculture, farmers and the countryside), including giving due recognition to the status of migrant workers, and devising improved policies.

The commendable contributions to socio-economic development by migrant workers have facilitated public awareness and policy changes. During the 1990s, trans-regional migration to the cities was the main form of transfer of rural surplus labour. During this period, an additional 36 million were transferred to nearby township enterprises, migrant worker numbers increased by about 50 million, from 36 million to 83 million. Tens of millions of farmers left their lands and the countryside to work in towns and factories, driving industrialization and urbanization at a faster speed. Statistics of the fifth national census in 2000 show that migrant workers account for 58 percent of employees in secondary industry, 52 percent in tertiary industry, 68 percent in processing and manufacturing and 80 percent in construction. At one end of the employment spectrum, migrant workers serve as a vital workforce in cities and developed regions, strengthening industrial competitiveness, supporting industrial growth, and promoting urban development and prosperity. On the other end, having their roots in villages and under-developed regions, they have expanded job opportunities for farmers and provided a vital source of increased income. This has pushed optimal labour resource allocation between the urban and rural areas, and integrated the solutions for *sannong* issues with industrialization and urbanization. In doing so, they have charted a new path for the integrated development of rural and urban areas. As such, the contributions and status of migrant workers in socio-economic development were becoming apparent.

However, in spite of their huge contributions, migrant workers were still subject to difficult work and living conditions and were socially disadvantaged. This has now become a striking issue that has to be addressed at the policy level. Here are some of the problems they face: low and stagnant wages for many years; often delayed or defaulted wage payments; poor working conditions and serious lack of labour protection; often working overtime with excessive workload and no overtime pay; absence of social security and burdened by insurance issues throughout their lifetime; poor housing and difficulty providing education for their children; labour rights subject to frequent infringements and difficult access to relief; *hukou* restriction which prevents migrant workers with stable jobs from enjoying equal rights of a citizen. Many of these issues point to the severity of migrant worker-related problems that must be addressed urgently.

The CPC and the government are giving high priority to addressing the increasingly prominent migrant worker issues and the infringement of migrant worker rights during reform and industrialization. Some of the issues to be addressed are the comparatively low increase in farmers' income, the expanding urban-rural divide, the balance between urban and rural development, and addressing the *sannong* issues. Since 1997, annual per capita net income growth of farmers has been declining. As at 2003, the target of 5 percent annual increase rate proposed in the tenth five-year plan had not been reached. The income gap between the urban and rural residents rose to 3.23:1 and the real consumption gap exceeded 5:1. A basic limiting factor on rural income is under-employment. The solution would seem to be the promotion of the movement of rural labour to the cities, amid the drives for industrialization and urbanization. The CPC Central Committee holds that employment is the source of livelihood and therefore absorption of surplus rural labour through industrialization and urbanization is a strategy to resolving the *sannong* issues, thus gradually transforming the urban-rural dual structure. For that purpose, migrant worker policies should be adapted to accommodate increasing industrialization and urbanization. Also, the policies should be adapted to the market economy. Secondly, in 2001, at the CPC Central Committee Conference on Economic Affairs, it was pointed out that farmers' trans-regional migration to cities for employment meets the needs of urban-rural communication, economic development and the market economy and, therefore, that policies should not be restrictive or discriminatory. Thirdly, the government should reconstitute its functions and provide public services, address problems closely related to farmers' and migrant workers' interests, facilitate and provide services for migrant workers' employment in the cities and safeguard their legitimate rights and interests. This will increase urban and rural employment, raise public income and achieve universal affluence. To support this strategy, migrant worker policies should be adjusted to focus on the protection of rights and the creation of a favourable employment environment.

In the new century, the policies have been changed substantially: from being restrictive to encouraging, and focusing on the protection of rights and the creation of a favourable employment environment for migrant workers. Chinese public policies are reoriented to become people-centred, fair and aimed at achieving a balanced urban-rural development. In 2001, a review was conducted, and, except for the permit processing fee, all administrative charges were revoked. In 2002, the "Fair Treatment, Reasonable Guidance, Sound Rule, and Good Service" principle was proposed to eliminate institutions and policies obstructing urbanization, and provide guidance to the rural labour force for rational and orderly migration. In 2003, for the first time in history, the General Office of the State Council issued the *Notice Concerning Providing Administrative Services to Farmers Migrating to Towns for Employment*, a comprehensive document on facilitating the farmers' search for employment in towns. The *Notice* requested that local governments unshackle themselves from outmoded mindsets, remove unreasonable restrictions on migrant workers, resolve the problems of delays and default of wages, improve migrant workers' living and working conditions, and provide training services and expanded schooling provisions for migrant workers' children. The State Council's *Regulations on the Insurance of Employment Injuries* provided for insurance benefits for migrant workers for the first time. The *Measures on Providing Shelters for and Sending Back the Tramps and Beggars from Cities* was revoked. Other policies included the responsibilities of the local governments of the migration destinations to provide compulsory education – mainly in full-day public primary and middle school – for migrant workers' children; allocation of special funds by local financial departments to support the training of migrant workers; and the proposition

Table 2: Policies in the New Century

Time of Issuance	Document	Policy Highlights
March 2001	*The Tenth Five-Year Plan for National and Social Development PRC*	Increase the degree of urbanization; transfer the rural population; eradicate the urban-rural relationship through the market economy; reform the household registration system to establish a mechanism for the orderly flow of urban and rural population; remove unreasonable restrictions over the migration of rural labour to towns for employment and guide the inter-regional flow of surplus rural labour.
November 2001	*Circular of the Advices on Reforming the Household Registration Administration System in Small Towns* by the Ministry of Public Security, Approved by the State Council	Anyone who has permanent lawful residence, permanent employment or steady source of income in small towns and all immediate relatives living with such person may be granted urban permanent household registration.
November 2001	*Circular on Reviewing and Removing Charges for Migrant Workers,* jointly issued by the State Planning Commission, the Ministry of Finance, etc.	Except for the permit processing fee, all administrative charges, including charges for temporary residence, temporary (migration) population administration, family planning administration, urban capacity enhancement, labour regulation, emigrating business operators and workers administration, and foreign building (construction) enterprises administration.
January 2002	*Advice on Affairs Related to Agricultural and Rural Community in 2002* by the CPC Central Committee and the State Council	The principle for the rule of migrant workers is "fair treatment, reasonable guidance, sound rule and good service."

January 2003	*Notice Concerning Providing Administrative Services to Migrant Workers* by the General Office of the State Council	Local governments are urged to free themselves from outdated mindsets, remove unreasonable restrictions on migrant workers, address the problem of delayed and defaulted salary payment to migrant workers, improve their living and work conditions, provide training and expand channels to arrange for migrant workers' children to go to school.

of the integration of the urban and rural labour markets in phases to establish an equal-opportunity employment system for urban and rural workers. In 2004, the CPC Central Committee held that migrant workers have currently become an important constituent of the industrial workforce, and that their legitimate rights should be protected. In planning for their regular fiscal budgets, city governments were also urged to consider including expenditures for vocational training for migrant workers, their children's education, labour protection and other administration and services. In 2005, the CPC Central Committee and the State Council proposed that public employment service agencies should provide free employment services and one-off vocational training subsidies for migrant workers. In 2006, the State Council's *Advice on Resolving the Problems of Migrant Workers* stated that migrant workers interest-related issues should be addressed to embrace Chinese specificities and the principles of people-centredness and balanced urban-rural development. The *Advice* also provided that the administration of labour and employment shall be regulated according to law, to address the problems of low wages, and delayed or defaulted wage payments, provision of employment service and training, social security and public services, and to strengthen the protection of migrant worker rights. A series of policies were proposed to provide a foundation for the comprehensive resolution of migrant worker issues.

IV. KEY ASPECTS AND CHARACTERISTICS OF THE NEW POLICIES

(1) Key Aspects of the New Policies

1. Support migration of the rural population for employment, and aim to establish an equitable employment system and uniform labour market for the urban and rural areas. Discriminatory regulations and unreasonable restrictions against migrant workers are reviewed and removed; administrative approval and charges are simplified; it is now forbidden to dismiss or ostracize migrant workers under the pretext of facilitating employment of urban workers. Urban and rural employment systems are to be integrated and the divisive employment administration system reformed to establish a uniform labour market countrywide in order to encourage fair competition. Employment

mechanisms for the transfer of surplus rural labour under the market economy are to be progressively formed in steps to provide equal employment opportunities and services for urban and rural workers.

2. Address remuneration and labour rights issues, establish migrant workers wage payment guarantee system and standards for payment by employers in order to ensure that salaries are paid promptly and fully to the recipient every month, or as provided in the labour contract. Monitor the wage deposit systems established in order to eradicate payment delays and defaults. The labour protection departments are to pay special attention to the salary payment situation of companies that hire a large number of migrant workers. Severe penalties are to be imposed on companies that default on salaries. Other measures include upward adjustment of the exceptionally low salaries of migrant workers, and ensuring equal pay for equal positions. The new policies also provide for strict enforcement of minimum wages, establishment and modification of minimum wages, and formulation and implementation of hourly minimum wage rates. Enterprises are to strictly observe all State regulations on rest days and leave for employees; compensation is to be paid as provided by law where overtime work, work on off-days or on official holidays is required. A standard collective consultation system is to be established in order to facilitate due salary increases for migrant workers. Also, migrant workers' rights to a safe and healthy workplace are to be protected according to law. National procedures and standards on professional safety and labour protection are enforced. The enterprises must be equipped with facilities for safe production and the prevention of occupational diseases, and regular health checks must be conducted for workers who may be exposed to occupational hazards. Migrant workers working in high risk industries or special operations are to be specially trained and certified. The policies forbid the employment of child labour, and require the special interests of female workers to be protected.

3. Public services are to be applied equally to urban and rural residents, including migrant workers. Being a party to national development, migrant workers are to be included in the urban public service system to ensure that they are also entitled to the benefits. Migrant workers are under the jurisdiction of the local governments of the locations of their work, and are given rights to enjoy public services such as employment service, training, children's education, housing and the prevention and treatment of epidemic diseases. The needs of migrant workers residing and working in the urban areas are to be taken into account during the formulation of urban development plans and public policies and the construction of public facilities. Public fiscal expenditures will be increased to gradually improve the public service system, which includes migrant workers. Public employment service agencies will be opened to migrant workers, providing policy consultation, employment information, guidance and employment agency services. Migrant workers' children who reside with them will receive compulsory education, mainly for public primary and middle schools, for which

local governments of the emigration destination are responsible. Other responsibilities of the local governments include preparing educational development plans, budgets and allocating public funds to schools based on the student population. Public schools providing compulsory education shall accord equal treatment to migrant workers' children and local students in terms of charges and management. No "temporary-schooling fee" (*jiedu fei*) or any other fee against the state regulation shall be imposed on foreign students. Governments will provide support and guidance to private schools designated to provide compulsory education for migrant workers' children in the form of education funds and faculty training. Also, health education is to be conducted for migrant workers and disease monitoring for their residence. Other policies include free treatment of selected infectious diseases and inclusion of migrant workers' children in local vaccination plans. Local governments of emigration destinations shall include administration and services funds for family planning programs of migrant workers in their fiscal budgets. Migrant workers' living conditions shall be improved, with more stringent regulatory operations to ensure that their dwellings comply with the basic health and safety requirements. Under the new policies, there shall be improved planning, construction and management of the living communities at the urban-rural fringes, and expanded capacities for public infrastructures.

4. Accelerate training and professional education to enhance the occupational skills and quality of migrant workers and continue with the Sunshine Project (*yangguang gongcheng*) of training for the transfer of migrant workers. The new policies also include measures for improving the system for migrant worker training subsidies in order to provide due subsidies for migrant workers undergoing training and to encourage the wider use of direct subsidies such as "training coupons." Employers will be given support to set up permanent training bases and develop customized training programs. Local governments of the emigration destinations shall include migrant workers' skills enhancement programs in their vocational training plans. Since the duty of training migrant workers lies with the relevant governmental departments and employers, employers who fail to fulfil their obligations will be required to contribute employee training funds under State regulations, and such funds will be used for government-organized training. Education and training institutions, as well as women, youth and workers' organizations, are encouraged to play a role in the training of migrant workers. There will also be major focus on the development of vocational education for rural communities, and various vocational and technical colleges are encouraged to expand their recruitment in the rural areas. Rural middle school graduates will be given incentives to undergo formal vocational and technical education.

5. Social security for migrant workers shall be progressively established. The priority is on medical insurance for employment-related injuries and serious illnesses, and on the introduction of support for seniors in phases. All employers must ensure that migrant workers are promptly given insurance coverage for employment-related

injuries. In the event that migrant workers who are not covered suffer an injury at work, the employer will be responsible for the worker's medical expenses based on the benefits covered under insurance policies. The first priority is in-patient medical care during the period of stay in the cities, which shall be borne mainly by employers. Since migrant workers are highly mobile and their salaries comparatively low, their eligibility standards for pension should be transferable and renewable. This will protect migrant workers' rights to social security during floating employment. Where possible, migrant workers with long-term employment may be included directly in the urban workers' basic pension scheme.

6. The household registration system shall be further reformed to gradually accommodate migrant workers with long-term employment and residency in cities in order to enable them to become urban residents. Resolution of migrant workers' household registration problem will be carried out conditionally and in phases. Restrictions on household registration of migrant workers in small- and medium-sized cities or towns shall be relaxed; in large cities, migrant workers who meet the prescribed criteria shall be addressed positively and prudently; model workers, senior mechanics, technicians and outstanding performers shall be given priority in acceding to urban residency.

7. Protection mechanisms for migrant workers' rights and interests shall be reinforced. Migrant workers' democratic political rights, personal freedom, dignity and land rights shall be protected. There will also be greater law enforcement to defend their rights and interests, employers who infringe on migrant workers' rights shall be subject to severe punishment, and the institutions for receiving complaints shall be improved in order to enable migrant workers to better defend their rights. Labour dispute arbitration and mediation systems shall be improved with simplified procedures and shorter lead time to a hearing, and priority shall be given to cases involving labour remuneration and work-related injuries. As well, migrant workers will be entitled to legal aid. Trade unions shall focus on labour contracts, salaries, work conditions, occupational safety and health. Employers are urged to honour their obligations under laws and regulations and to protect the legitimate rights of migrant workers.

(2) Characteristics of the New Policies

The new policies stress the protection of rights and interests and the creation of favourable employment conditions for migrant workers. Policies and rules have been improved to establish an integrated labour market across urban and rural areas; to develop an employment system that encourages fair competition; to enact a policy regime and law enforcement surveillance mechanisms that protect migrant workers' rights; to promote public service institutions and systems that benefit migrant workers; to expand employment channels for the transfer of rural labour; and to promote urban and rural economic prosperity, social progress and the healthy development of industrialization, urbanization and modernization with Chinese characteristics. The main characteristics of the new policies are the following:

1. *Reflecting the current call for synergy between market-determined employment, people-orientation and balanced urban-rural development.* Policies are synchronized with the development of a market economy and urbanization, and aim to remove the last clutches of administrative planning and control of the flow of farmers and employment while moving towards market-regulated, government-facilitated and self-determined employment. They also liberate farmers from their confines of countryside-only employment and address *sannong* issues on the pace of the rural labour force transfer and urbanization; they thus reengineer the dual structure and affirm the nature, status and significance of migrant workers as a part of a new industrial labour force. This is a natural process for market-regulated employment, as well as for the industrialization and urbanization of this agricultural country to take place. Migrant workers are the subjects of social transformation and should not be treated as cheap labour, whose rights are subject to wilful infringements. Public interest is the core of these policies, for such policies integrate market-regulated employment, urbanization and people-orientation. They also seek to address issues related to the interests of migrant workers, to improve their livelihoods and to give equal rights to migrant workers who work and live in urban areas.

2. *Breaking the dual* hukou-*based divisive structure and providing fair treatment for all.* The policies are undertaken by municipal governments and are centred on the interests of all residents, including migrant workers. Hence, they accord equal treatment to migrant workers, who are an integral part of economic development and urban construction. The policies also respect and safeguard the legitimate rights of migrant workers, eliminate discriminatory regulations and institutional barriers, and grant equal rights and duties to migrant workers. The various policy dimensions, such as employment, government services and participation in enterprises and social administration all attest to the focus on equity.

3. *Embodying the public service spirit through improvements in government sevices and administration and the incorporation of government administration into services.* The policies transform government functions, shifting them from restriction and control of migrant workers to the provision of services to them and protection of their rights. For example, the construction of public facilities will incorporate the migrant workers' needs, education budgets will include the education funds for migrant workers' children, and other services such as disease prevention and treatment and vaccination of children will be provided. The policies also bolster public services and social administration for migrant workers from many aspects and provide directions for enterprises, social communities and intermediary organizations to play their part in creating favourable working environments and living conditions for migrant workers.

4. *Providing flexibility in the multiple channels for labour transfer and drive for location-specific institutional innovation.* The policies support the transfer of the

rural labour force to the cities, as well as the local absorption of surplus labour by developing township enterprises and county economies. The policies also support both the temporary floating employment in the cities and towns, as well as enable migrant workers with long term employment to assume local citizenship. Migrant workers are also encouraged to return home to start their own businesses. Thus the number of channels for the transfer of surplus labour is increased. The policies address problems through considering local conditions and exploring effective methods to protect migrant workers' interests and facilitate the systematic transfer of surplus rural labour, instead of adopting a one-size-fits-all model.

5. *Reflecting the operability of solutions and promoting goal-based institutional development.* The policies emphasize addressing the prevailing situations, promptly resolving major migrant worker issues, and strengthening the operability of policies and measures. Some universal problems are institutional and system-related. In addressing more deeply-rooted problems, fundamental systems and institutions to protect migrant workers are formed. For problems that cannot be resolved immediately, it proposes policy opinions which include the principles for resolution, directions and perspectives to provide room for further exploration and improvement.

V. DIFFICULTIES IN THE IMPLEMENTATION OF NEW POLICIES

In recent years, China has made extensive policy adjustments for migrant workers, and social administration is moving towards the protection of their rights and the provision of services to them. However, all of this is still undergoing changes. Although the policy proposals have identified the problems, they have not solved them. Despite huge progress by different locations in the implementation of State policies, many fail to effectively implement them, which proves that many problems cannot be immediately resolved in the short term. In implementing these policies, infringement of migrant workers' rights remains the most pronounced problem. Migrant workers who have long-term employment in the cities are still denied the rights enjoyed by permanent urban residents. The administration system has not been improved, and the interests and requirements of migrant workers are not included during the formulation of urban public policy. Some cities continue to employ restrictive rules.

(1) Existing problems during execution of new policies: Continued serious infringements of the socio-economic rights of migrant workers.

1. Migrant labour rights continue to be seriously infringed. According to research[5] conducted by the National Bureau of Statistics in August 2006, more than half of the migrant employees had not been given labour contracts, and 20 percent of those who had were not aware of their contract provisions. The infringement of their rights to rest days and holidays was severe: 47 percent had no rest days on Sundays; for those

who work overtime, 53 percent had monthly salaries under RMB 800, 20 percent did not receive timely payment of salaries, 20 percent were without full salaries, and 50 percent were denied overtime pay. Some enterprises reduced the wage rate to the minimum to force workers to work overtime for extra income. Migrant workers are also the main victims in the frequent occurrences of job-related injuries, mining disasters and occupational diseases.

2. Approximately 70 to 80 percent of migrant workers have no social security insurance, and those who are given social security have difficulty enjoying their rightful benefits. According to the 2006 investigation, the percentage of migrant workers not covered by pension, medical, employment-related injury benefits or unemployment insurance account for 73.8 percent, 73.8 percent, 67.5 percent and 84.7 percent respectively. Of those investigated, 6.6 percent, 7.2 percent, 4.6 percent and 2.6 percent paid for their own insurance. Excluding those who paid for their own insurance coverage, the number of workers not covered by insurance totals 80 percent. 57 percent of those who suffered job-related injuries did not benefit from insurance, nearly 80 percent of the female workers did not have paid maternity leave, and over 90 percent of migrant workers received no housing subsidies. Even those with insurance coverage have difficulty obtaining insurance claims. In the case of work-related injuries, professional knowledge is required to produce proof for obtaining certification by medical institutions and the labour departments. Even at dispute arbitration, migrant workers are disadvantaged because of their lack of the necessary knowledge, and it usually costs them several years and substantial amounts of money to submit complaints and claims. Even with the money and time spent, many still found it difficult to obtain reasonable reimbursements. Many injured or disabled migrant workers return home and become part of the poor rural population. Those who have been covered by pension insurance cannot renew their policies when they switch jobs. Also, only the portion contributed by the migrant workers is refundable when they surrender their policies; the portion relating to the employer's contribution is not. This is a prejudice to their rights. In many developed regions and cities, urban residents are covered by "urban insurance." Farmers who have entered non-agricultural sectors are covered by "urban insurance" or "township insurance" (housing subsidies included); those who remain in agriculture are covered by "rural insurance"; however, most migrant workers have no social insurance coverage at all. The dual-structured society is therefore reinforced by the urban-rural and inter-regional gaps.

3. There is unfair provisioning or lack of public services in housing, medical care and children's education for migrant workers. In 2006, more than half of migrant workers' children entering the age of compulsory education were required to pay a "temporary schooling fee" (*jiedu fei*) and sponsorship fee. The average amount payable was RMB 1,226 per entrant. Nearly 50 percent of migrant workers' children received education at private schools with poor study environments. Because such private schools did not

receive public funding, migrant workers have to pay tuition and other miscellaneous fees, as well as rental fees, teachers' salaries and administrative expenses. Due to their low income, few locations could accommodate their housing, medical and maternity care needs. When sick, migrant workers avoid medical care as much as possible. Most would visit cheap private clinics or self-administer medicine. Most babies are delivered privately, and few receive vaccination. Migrant workers live in poor housing. In many cities, the reconstruction of urban-rural fringes and "villages within cities" where most migrant workers live has improved the appearance of the cities. But for migrant workers, finding a place to stay has become a concern.

4. Migrant workers with long term employment in the cities are still not allowed to migrate permanently. About 40 percent of migrant workers have long term employment; more than 20 percent are living with their families in their location of employment; 55 percent wish to settle down for good; and some employers have also indicated their need for the steady supply of skilled workers. However, the reform of the household registration system has stagnated at the phase where migrants are required to meet a certain criteria for investment and technology. Even when some migrant workers have skills that are needed by employers, they are still not allowed urban household registration. For most small townships in the developed regions, household registration is available only to local rural residents. Even those migrant workers who meet the prerequisites are denied. One of the conditions for migrant workers to be eligible for urban household registration is "lawful residence," which provides that only people who own their residences can register. Those who live in legally leased residences are denied registration. This makes the criterion impossible for migrant workers. For example, household registration in small towns in southern Jiangsu Province is managed by the central cities. Migrant workers who apply for household registration in the central cities or small towns have to own local residences that measure between 70 and 100 square metres. Even civil servants can hardly own houses of that size without loans. The small towns in the Pearl Delta Region require migrant workers to not only own residences, but to pay RMB 12,000 as capacity expansion fees. In some cities, migrant workers are treated as low-class citizens of poor quality and are ostracized.

(2) Migrant workers have no right to participate in rural social administration; they have no channel to express their desire to promote their own welfare; and the balance between urban policy-making and other interwoven interests is disturbed.

In most developed regions and cities, voting rights hinge on the citizens' household registration status. Migrant workers have no right to vote or to stand for election in the cities where they live and work, and cannot participate in democratic elections, management and supervision. This leads to neglect of their needs or infringement of their interests when balancing policy-making and their interests. Recent regulations provide that migrant workers can vote if they register at their emigration destination, and if they possess a formal statement issued by the government of their hometown proving that they do not vote there. However, owing to hefty travel expenses and complex procedures, most migrant workers choose not to vote. In regions and cities with large numbers of migrant workers, mayors and other heads of local governments are only accountable to the electorate, which only includes residents with local household registration. Migrant workers do not have the same rights. It is therefore easy to explain why certain policies and regulations prejudice their interests, and why some administrative departments simply ignore their complaints about infringement of their rights.

Social organizations are immature, and urban grassroots communities are not open to diversification. Under the negative influence of household registration system, social organizations, activities and services of grassroots communities remain closed to migrant workers. At present, few migrant workers are members of trade unions, and no such organizations fulfil the role of protecting the legitimate rights of workers. For some private firms, the employers easily control the trade unions, and trade unions do not represent employee interests. The mechanism of inserting the government as a participant in negotiations in the interest of the workers, and between trade unions and employers, is still being tested. It is impossible to protect employees' legitimate rights in the absence of some such mechanism.

In some places, state policies with regard to prohibitive measures are not implemented. These include regulations by the State Council prohibiting the imposition of charges on migrant workers for urban employment or charges by employers for hiring migrant workers, and the imposition of a "temporary-schooling fee" (*jiedu fei*) for the education of migrant workers' children. Also, the regulations provide that public security expenses shall be covered by fiscal funds, and that migrant workers shall not be charged public security maintenance fees. However, some provincial and municipal government departments continue to prejudice the interest of migrant workers by imposing such fees.

(3) Some local governments continue to impose restrictions.

As important components of the urban industrial workforce and as permanent residents of the cities, migrant workers should be provided the same degree of security and protection as registered urban citizens. However, in some places, despite the policy regulations, public security is given higher priority than the protection of migrant workers' rights, and migrant workers are regarded as destabilizing factors and targets for social restriction. Although they should in fact be considered a key group eligible for protection and a force that contributes to public security, the existing system indiscriminately excludes them from social administration, including public security. Because there is little effort spent to explore the administrative methods that would incorporate services and protection to ensure migrant workers' civil rights are respected, there is no fundamental improvement in the security environment. Some local governments continue to exercise restrictive measures and even impose fees on migrant workers to cover their administrative costs. Yet, these are exactly the places where the security conditions are amongst the worst in China.

VI. Recommendations on Improving the Enforcement of New Policies

The present conditions show that enforceability of the new policies is a challenge as the socio-economic rights of migrant workers are still severely infringed. In some places, the system of administration and methodology has not been fundamentally transformed. The main reason is that there is a lack of awareness of the harm inflicted by the unfair treatment of migrant workers, and a lack of complete understanding of how the interests of the migrant workers are interwoven with those of the urban society. We have to look at the reality and renew our perspectives before we can implement new policy initiatives and progressively create a regulatory environment that protects migrant workers' rights and provides them urban citizenship and stable, safe employment.

(1) Raise awareness on the serious consequences that result from unfair treatment of migrant workers.

Unfair treatment of migrant workers and their poor living conditions demonstrate the institutional-driven depreciation of their labour, the deficiency of their rights, and the sacrifice migrant workers and rural interests have made to the industrialization and urban development of China. This hinders not only the resolution of *sannong* issues, but also socio-economic development and modernization. It curtails the farmer and migrant worker income and thereby growth in domestic consumption. This is a major cause for the mismatch between investment and consumption, and increases the risk of excess production capacity in industries, and deflation.

Discrimination against migrant workers also results in growth in the urban-rural gap, regional gap and wealth gap, and the large exodus of migrant workers has disadvantaged the central and western regions. It results in many enterprises relying solely on cheap labour to compete with low prices; thus, unfair treatment also obstructs technological progress and transformation of the mode of growth. The depreciation of the value of labour due to the low cost of the migrant workers results in export price wars, resulting in sanctions, anti-dumping and special safeguards against Chinese products. It also widens international trade imbalances and increases the pressure for appreciation of the renminbi. This also creates a negative profile of China in the international community, as some international media classify Chinese enterprises that accord differentiated treatment to migrant workers "sweat shops" and raise this as a human right issue.

People must be made aware of other negative results of discrimination against migrant workers. These include: a heavy burden on society with future social security responsibilities; it seriously obstructs the progress of industrialization, urbanization and transformation of China from an agricultural power to an industrialized, urbanized modern society; it damages equality, justice and the spirit of equal efforts and equal benefits, and exerts a negative impact on the building of a harmonious society; and it reduces the economic, political and social status of the Chinese working class. Low salaries of numerous migrant workers stifle the income of urban industrial workers; this in turn affects the relationship between the CPC and the government with farmers and workers, and may even discourage the next generation from taking up jobs as workers or farmers.[6]

(2) Understand the status of migrant workers in urban socio-economic development and the necessity of fair-treatment policies and consultative rule.

In line with industrialization and urbanization, it is natural that the dual social structure be ended and the status of migrant workers transformed, from being marginalized to being given ownership of the urban society. Millions of migrant workers joining the non-agricultural sector and city workforce are driving industrialization. This is a historic process, during which surplus rural labour is transferred to other sectors and the underdeveloped dual economy – the majority farming population – is transformed into a single, modern society. From an economic perspective, migrant workers are integral to the industrial, commercial and service sectors. Nonetheless, the policies and regulations did not recognize them as such. Instead, they could only live as labour service-providers, and not in a family unit. This contradicts reality and the rules of development. The fact that only elites are recognized and accepted while migrant workers are marginalized depreciates the value of migrant workers, and takes away the responsibilities of cities in driving rural development for this era. Urban enterprises require not only investors, managers and technical staff, but also a large number of workers. Industrialization and the market economy require that the free flow of migrant workers be tied to independent hiring by employers; that investors, technical talents, as well as migrant workers be welcomed to play their part; that the isolation and feudalism caused by self-sufficient small-time farming be substituted for the openness and tolerance of modern cities; that migrant workers be integrated into the urban society and be given the choice to become urban residents; and that a platform be provided for enterprises to have a stable workforce and improved corporate qualities.

Because migrant workers and the original urban residents are both owners and taxpayers of the economic society, it is necessary to correctly establish the relationship between urban governments and all residents, including migrant workers. Some migrant workers work in the cities most of the time, returning home only during busy farming seasons; the majority of them work in the cities year round. Some have even started businesses of their own. Just like the original urban residents, migrant workers are actors and labour providers in the market economy that drive urban economic development. They are also urban residents and social citizens. As taxpayers, they contribute directly or indirectly to urban tax income and public fiscal funds by participating in economic development, the creation of public wealth and daily consumption. The relationship between government public policies and urban residents, including migrant workers, should be approached from three aspects:

First, the relationship between the government and the public. The urban government's mandate is determined by the public needs of the citizens in the society. The right to rule is given by the public and the administration costs, including the salaries of administrative staff, are derived from taxpayers, of which migrant workers represent a substantial part. Therefore, the relationship between the government and the urban residents, including migrant workers, is one between public servants and owners.

Second, government policies should represent the interests of all urban residents, including migrant workers, and should ensure that the legitimate rights of all citizens are protected. Two types of relationships should be prudently handled. One is the employment relationship between investors and workers, including migrant workers. Corrective action should be carried out in order to reverse the overemphasis on the role and interests of investors, and the corresponding neglect of those of migrant workers. The government should regulate according to law, participate in a coordinated effort to address the infringements of migrant worker rights, and provide guidance to establish a legally equal and mutually beneficial relationship between employees and employers. The other relationship is that between migrant workers and native urban residents. The government should address the neglect of migrant worker needs and interests and provide them with equal public and administration services, create channels and platforms for two-way communication, help migrant workers adapt to the cities and to re-socialize, and facilitate cultural integration. The government should provide the regulatory framework to guarantee the basic rights of migrant workers in employment, economic benefits, housing, education, social insurance and participation in social administration.

Third, the relationship between government decisions, rule and the enforcement of policy, and public participation. We should dispel the old notion that government rules over the public. Government rule is not about forcing public compliance. It is a process of reflecting the interests and needs of the public, and providing public services. We should also correct the old notion that government is the natural representative of the general public and operates independent of public participation. Where migrant workers are denied necessary rights and are therefore unable to participate in social administration, government policies, unintentionally or intentionally, exclude or even prejudice migrant workers' interests and needs. In certain places, state policies favourable to migrant workers are not implemented. Migrant worker interests should be represented by the migrant workers, and expressed and protected through regular public administration channels. With social stratification, development of social organizations and diversification of interest relationships, it is necessary for governments, experts and the general public to participate together, to guarantee reasonable and democratic decisions and to ensure that the decisions are realistic and in the interest of the public. Meanwhile, governments should foster the capability of self-rule among the public, support their self-rule, provide support for the self-discipline of individuals and enterprises, the automatic adjustments of relationships, and the autonomous rule of communities. Governments should also encourage participation of the social forces and non-governmental organizations, to combine government rule with public participation, self-rule and social supervision. It is natural that consultative and collaborative rule will prevail.

(3) Adopt People-Oriented, Fair Treatment and Consultative Rule-Driven Measures and Policies

1. *Policies should be enforced, regulations improved and effective supervision by government agencies exercised to reverse the trend of rampant infringements of migrant workers' labour rights.* The *Several Opinions on Addressing Issues Related to Migrant Workers* by the State Council proposes to "enable migrant workers to enjoy equal rights and duties as urban workers in the principle of people-orientation and fair treatment" and to "create favourable environment and conditions for them to integrate into the cities and live in harmony with urban citizens." A series of policies were formulated. Policies must be specified in practice to improve legislation. At present, the priority is to enforce policies governing employment services and training, labour rights and basic public services. At a time when the market is still underdeveloped and when the rules of the game for the various interest groups within the market economy have not been formed, government should provide guidance, help coordinate and regulate according to law. In fact, the government should promote a mutually beneficial relationship between the employees and employers and improve labour standards to ensure that migrant worker salaries are paid fully and promptly. Minimum hourly wages should be established to eliminate uncompensated overtime, and to ensure the observance of production safety requirements. Trade union membership should be expanded to include migrant workers, grassroots trade union leaders should be elected by members, and trade unions should increase their responsibilities and rights to protect workers. The *Opinions* proposed that the State may designate a specific month within a year for annual negotiations between employees and employers on labour rights and labour interests such as salaries. It should be ensured that the provisions of the governing laws and regulations, such as the *Labour Law*, concerning workers' rights and labour standards are reasonable. Specific issues that are disputed should be promptly investigated to establish clear regulations, and enforcement procedures should be simplified.

2. Public service discrepancies should be addressed to establish a public service system that includes migrant workers' interests and meets the basic social needs of migrant workers. For example, housing, medical and health care, maternity care and children's compulsory education for low-income migrant workers should be incorporated into the urban social development plan for pragmatic regulatory arrangements. As it is not feasible to allow them to enjoy equal treatment as urban citizens in all aspects of social welfare, priority should be given to addressing their urgent needs so that they can be progressively covered by basic public services. Governments should make comprehensive plans and provide incentives for housing for industries serving middle- and low-income families. Preferential policies should be formulated for rural communities to build low-rent housing, apartments for migrant workers and residential areas at urban-rural fringes, and to provide support to maintain and develop the supply of water, electricity and gas facilities and schools, hospitals and communication facilities.

3. As the social security and household registration systems are intertwined with the long term development of migrant workers, substantial reform of these areas is necessary. After nearly two decades, second generation migrant workers have now moved to the cities. However, until now, migrant workers could only drift from job to job, and have been denied the stability of livelihood enjoyed by urban workers and dwellers. The failure to break free of unequal treatment endangers the stability of the urban economy and society. The urban-rural gap will widen if the young and able-bodied rural labour force is absorbed by the cities while the burden of raising the young and supporting the elderly is left to the rural community. Strategies and procedures should be specific, as it is now time to resolve the issue of the right of migrant workers who have worked and operated many years in the city to choose to stay or leave. According to the "strategies for population urbanization by category" as set forth under the eleventh five-year plan, some migrant workers and entrepreneurs with permanent employment should be selected to settle in the cities as urban residents. Migrant workers should be covered by employment injury insurance. As for medical insurance, coverage for major illnesses may be contributed by employers (or cooperative medical insurance currently under pilot study in Shenzhen, the premium of which is mainly contributed by employers), while supplementary contributions can be provided by migrant workers. Personal pension accounts should be established at a lower rate, with contributions mainly from employers, and supplementary contributions from individuals. All contributions should be paid into personal accounts and accepted – but not transferred – anywhere in the country. Settlement upon retirement will be standardized and carried out at a national level. As an alternative, an account may be transferred to another location when jobs are switched, and converted at the prevailing local insurance rate. The urban social insurance system should cover migrant workers with stable employment in the city for more than five years.

4. Integrate migrant workers into the urban community and encourage their participation in social administration at different levels. An open urban community should be established to facilitate social integration by granting membership to migrant workers, and incorporating migrant workers' rights in its development. By providing social services for migrant workers, they can be logically organized to participate in public activities related to culture, education, health and security. Migrant workers should also be encouraged to interact with urban citizens as equals to foster a community spirit of fraternity, trust, cooperation and coexistence. Migrant workers' right to participate in social administration at various levels should be respected. Qualified migrant workers should be entitled to register to vote and run for elections in cities where they live and work (for those who do not want to vote in cities, written proof should be provided to allow them to vote from home). This simple and convenient procedure can ensure their rights to vote and to run in elections their cities of residence so that that their interests and requests may be reflected during policy making and implementation.

ENDNOTES

[1]   Labour movement has caused the perpetual oversupply of labour in the coastal areas under rapid growth. According to an investigation in the Pearl Delta Region (PDR) in 1992 by Hong Kong scholars, in the first year, the labour efficiency of migrant workers was 60 percent that of Hong Kong workers; in the second year, the labour efficiency in both places were at par (Nanyang Commercial Bank, *China's Reform and Opening Up and the Economic Development in Pearl River Delta*, 1992, p. 75); however, labour costs in the PDR were lower. According to our statistics, in 1997 the average monthly salary in Shenzhen in the manufacturing and construction sectors was RNB 1120 (the monthly salary for migrant workers was even lower, generally at RMB 500-650). The figures provided by Handelsblatt on 6 January 1994 showed that if other factors are not considered and only the salary levels are compared, in 1997 in Shenzhen the average salary in the manufacturing and construction sectors was only 15.8 percent of that in Hong Kong (where monthly salary in 1995 was HK$ 7,087), 12 percent of that in Taiwan (1992), 24 percent of that in Mexico, 52 percent of that in Poland and 2.5 percent of that in West Germany (1992). In addition, Gong Sen, a researcher with the Development Research Centre of the State Council did an analysis based on studies by the International Labour Organization and Chinese statistics. He calculated that in 1999, the overall labour costs (including salary costs and non-salary costs) rose to US$ 0.756 per hour in China; Germany rose to US$ 26; approximately US$ 20 in the US and Japan; between US$ 7 and 9.5 in the Four Tigers, and US$ 2.12 in Mexico. China's relative labour cost is 3 percent to 4 percent that of Germany, Japan and the United States, 10 percent to 14 percent that of the Four Tigers and about one third that of Mexico. This is of special advantage to the coastal areas in attracting foreign investments and expanding exports.

[2]   In June 1997, a pilot program proposal by the State Council on the administration of household registration in small towns advocated that the administration of household registration should be reformed as appropriate, to permit rural labour with permanent employment, who are residing in small towns and meet certain criteria to apply for permanent household registration in such towns, in order to facilitate orderly migration of surplus rural labour to the nearest small towns. Migrant workers who have been granted household registration in small towns enjoy the same treatment as local residents.

Local governments, relevant departments and entities should treat migrant workers as local residents in education, employment, food and oil supply and social security. Local governments and the various departments should not charge extra fees or to the equivalent of capacity-enhancement fee.

[3]   In November 1993, *Decisions on Several Issues regarding the Establishment of the System of the Socialist Market Economy* by the Central Committee of the Communist Party of China (CPC) proposed the grooming of the labour market, and encouraged and guided surplus rural labour to move in an orderly fashion into non-agricultural industries and across regions. And the *Labour Law* promulgated in 1994 is also crucial on this issue. However, policies that could bring real benefit to migrant workers were absent. Rather, policies that were put in place did not encourage "orderly movement" and the *Labour Law* was not applicable to migrant workers.

[4]   See Jiang Wensheng, "Protection of Migrant Workers' Rights and Interests: Policy Shifts and Prospects," in *The Establishment of an Equal Employment System for Rural Labour*, compiled by Chen Xiaohua and Zhang Hongyu, China Financial and Economic Publishing House, September 2005, p. 161.

[5]   Research Centre on the Service Sector, *Research Report on Migrant Workers' Quality of Life*, National Bureau of Statistics, http://210.72.32.25/tjfx/fxbg/.

[6]   Gu Yikang, *Thoughts on Issues Related to Migrant Workers: A Research Report on Chinese Migrant Workers*, China Yanshi Publishing House, April 2006, p. 497- 498.

CHAPTER FIVE

Chinese Farmers' Right of Access to Judicial Relief

An Investigative Report into Forest Land Expropriation Claims by Hebei Farmer Wen Shengcun

Wang Xinan

INTRODUCTION

Having played an important role in the founding of New China, farmers are crowned with a noble and impressive political designation and hailed as the pivot of the current regime and a pillar of strength. In reality, however, the political rights accorded to farmers do not correspond with their nobility as portrayed in official ideology. To examine in detail the current state of the various rights of farmers would be an elaborate task, as political rights are broadly defined and their applicability varies. To know the tree by its fruit, the author shall use farmers' access to judicial relief to illustrate his case. Access to judicial relief under civil rights as provided by a constitution and the law is an important yardstick with which to measure the level of democracy in a country and society. Thus, a farmer's right to judicial relief may be read in conjunction with any of his political rights. The level of access to judicial relief is a measure of the basic political right given to farmers, and the legal protection accorded to farmers vis-à-vis people of different social strata.

I. BACKGROUND

Bazhou is located east of the central plains of Ji County in Hebei Province, and sits in the centre of a triangle formed by Beijing, Tianjin and Baoding. Its temperate continental climate and geographical conditions provides a good habitat for the fast-growing poplar tree, a perennial woody plant. Poplar trees offer commercial value, being used for construction and paper-making, as well as ecological value, being fully grown in one, three or five years. Encouraged by the State to convert plough land to forests, many farmers have sub-contracted wasteland in recent years to cultivate profitable forest trees, such as the fast-growing poplar. In early 2001, the State Planning Commission issued a basic document for planning, number (2001)1888, approving NCPG's (North China Power Group) construction of a 500 kV high-voltage power transmission and transformation project. By the end of 2002, construction commenced. This project spans across a huge forest long cultivated by farmers. Article 24 of the *Regulations on the Protection of Power Facilities* provides that

> Where any new construction, modification or expansion of power facilities are carried out, and where crops must be damaged, trees or bamboos felled, or buildings or other facilities demolished or moved, the power construction company shall offer a lump-sum compensation as provided by the relevant State regulations.

Furthermore, Paragraph 1, Article 16 of the *Implementation Measures of the Regulations on the Protection of Power Facilities* provides that

> Where any new construction or project on overhead power transmission lines requires such power lines to pass through forest areas, a ground transmission path shall be created in accordance with relevant power design regulations as provided by the State, and no tree shall be planted on such transmission path. Where trees are felled, the construction company of such power transmission lines shall complete the relevant procedures in accordance with State regulations, provide lump-sum compensation for owners of such felled trees, and enter into agreement with such owners that no trees shall be planted on such transmission path.

In this case, a substantial number of trees planted by local farmers were felled.

The compensation criteria for trees to be felled are set out in the following instruments: Article 4 of the *Notice on the Relevant Issues on the Collection of the Four Charges for the Expropriation and Encroachment of Forest Land under the Laws, Rules and Regulations* issued by the Ministry of Forestry, under document *Lin Ce Zi* (1991) No. 177; Article 12 of the *Measures on the Implementation of the Forest Law of the People's Republic of China in Hebei Province* of the Hebei Forestry Department; and Paragraph 1, Article 4 of the *Regulations on the Collection of the Four Charges for the Expropriation and Encroachment of Forest Land* issued by the Forestry Department, Finance Department, Price Bureau and the Land Administration Bureau of Hebei Province, under document (1992) *Ji Lin Ji Zi* No. 111. The compensation criterion is that regardless of the level of maturity of the forest, compensation shall be based on the actual harvest value during the final clearing. In other words, compensation is paid based on the timber value, regardless of whether the matured trees are available for cutting. Based on this criterion, the compensation paid for every fast-growing poplar tree should be approximately RMB 1,000.

However, NCPG did not pay the required compensation. Instead, it chose the following traditional administrative methods:

Step 1: NCPG paid a lump sum to and entered into an agreement with the Bazhou municipal government. The agreement stated that the government shall be responsible for felling all the trees involved in the case. Both parties have not disclosed the amount paid by NCPG.

Step 2: The government will forward the compensation to farmers and supervise the prompt logging of trees. However, in reality, the government's military forces forcibly felled most trees, and no compensation has been paid.

Five years have gone by. Most farmers have been busy with *shangfang* and in seeking relief but have found no resolution. After much encouragement by various judge friends, Wen Shengcun, who was formerly military personnel and had better education and social experience than most farmers, decided to seek judicial relief.

II. *WEN SHENGCUN V. NORTH CHINA POWER GROUP AND BEIJING POWER TRANSMISSION AND TRANSFORMATION COMPANY*: A CASE OF DISPUTE OVER FOREST TREES[1]

In October 2004, Wen Shengcun, a local farmer, decided to prevent protectionism from pervading the local justice system by taking action against the defendant at the place of the defendant's principal place of business. Legal suits were instituted at competent courts in Beijing. The case was first registered at the Xuanwu District People's Court, Beijing Municipality (place of the first defendant's domicile) and the Fangshan District People's Court, Beijing Municipality (place of the second defendant's domicile). In both instances, the courts refused to accept the case either on the grounds that it did not fall within the scope of a civil litigation case, or that the competent court should be located at the place where the subject of litigation is located. Finally, the plaintiff had no choice but to increase the claim amount in order to have the case registered with the First Intermediate People's Court of Beijing Municipality.[2] Shortly after registering the case, the court consulted with the plaintiff and advised him to drop charges in order to avoid affecting the court's performance appraisal with an increased number of unconcluded cases. The plaintiff had to comply with the court's request, and re-lodged legal proceedings one month later, at the end of December 2004.

During the first instance proceedings, the defendant's attorney spoke of the importance of constructing power plants, and the duty of farmers to comply with the State's construction requirements. However, he avoided mentioning the duty of compensation for the trees, and advocated that the court should not have accepted the case, and that the government should resolve it. There was no further hearing after the first one, and the court did not make a decision. Finally, Wen indicated to the chief judge that he would have to resort to *shangfang* by lying at the doorstep of the Supreme People's Court if no decision was made soon. This was clearly a case of overdue hearing; a hasty first instance decision was made on 22 July 2005. In its written judgment, the court ruled that, even though it was of the opinion that Wen's legitimate right should be protected, it dismissed Wen's motion on the grounds that the case is outside the scope of a civil litigation case. The court went further to deliberately distort the implication of a regulation in order to render judgment against Wen.

The regulation that was deliberately distorted by the First Intermediate People's Court of Beijing Municipality was the *Design and Technical Regulations for 110-500 kV Overhead High-Voltage Power Transmission Lines*. The court of first instance pointed out that, "Upon separate investigation, the *Design and Technical Regulations for 110-500 kV Overhead High-Voltage Power Transmission Lines* provides that the perpendicular distance between the transmission line and the trees shall be 7 metres" (refer to page 5 of the first instance written judgment). In fact, this provision is not set forth under the *Regulations*. The relevant provision under the *Regulations* provides as follows:

16.0.7: Where the power transmission lines pass through a forest, a transmission path must be created. The net width of this transmission path shall not be less than twice the sum of the width of the transmission line and the height of the principal trees in the forest. Individual trees in the vicinity of the transmission path exceeding the height of the principal trees shall be removed.

Under the following circumstances, no transmission path may be created if there is no obstruction to the construction, operation, inspection and repair and maintenance of the power transmission lines:

1. Where the natural height does not exceed 2 metres.
2. Where the perpendicular distance between trees (taking into consideration the natural height) is not more than the value as listed under Table 16.0.7.1.

The court of first instance dismissed the plaintiff's claim on the grounds that "the fast-growing poplar trees planted by Wen Shengcun have not exceeded the perpendicular distance between the power transmission lines and the trees as provided by the relevant State regulations." Clearly, this was a misinterpretation of the *Design and Technical Regulations for 110-500 kV Overhead High-Voltage Power Transmission Lines*. The perpendicular distance stated under Article 16.0.7 of the *Regulations* refers to the distance between the transmission lines and the height of the trees after natural

Table 1: Perpendicular distance between the transmission line and the trees

Standard Voltage (kV)	110	220	330	500
Perpendicular Distance (m)	4.0	4.5	5.5	7.0

growth, and not the actual distance between the transmission lines and the fast-growing poplar trees as interpreted by the court of first instance. The *Explanation of the Provisions under the Design and Technical Regulations for 110-500 kV Overhead High-Voltage Power Transmission Lines*, issued by the State Economic and Trade Commission, provides an explicit and authoritative interpretation: the smallest perpendicular distance between the 500 kV transmission lines and the trees refers to the distance between such transmission lines and the trees after natural growth. The *Explanation* went further to illustrate that the natural height of Poplar trees in the north-east region should be calculated based on 20 metres. Furthermore, the natural height of the fast-growing, Zhonglin-46 poplar trees in this case was greater than 25 metres, and perpendicular distances between these trees and the transmission lines were far less than seven metres. Even if we were to compute using the largest perpendicular distance of 27 metres between the overhead lines from the ground, the perpendicular distance between the transmission lines and the trees was still less than two metres, which meant that these trees had to be cut. Hence, the first instance court's ruling that, "the trees concerned have not met the statutory requirements for mandatory felling; therefore, they are not trees that must be cut," was defective.

The fact that the perpendicular distance between the transmission lines and the trees, according to the *Regulations*, refers to the height of the trees after natural growth instead of the actual height is apparent. Power operation and personal safety would be seriously threatened if felling were only carried out according to the perpendicular distance between the trees' actual height and the transmission lines. This is because when the distance between the high-voltage power lines and the trees reaches or exceeds the safe distance as set forth under the *Implementation Measures of the Regulations on the Protection of Power Facilities*, electricity will be conducted from the high-voltage cable to the trees. On days of rain or high humidity, trees will become conductors under high voltage, and will pose serious hazards to buildings, equipment, people and underground lines in the vicinity. In particular, when the lines are under a high voltage of 500 kV, there could be casualties and other grave consequences. Therefore, the court of first instance's interpretation that cutting should be carried out only when the actual height of the trees reaches the statutory height limit is faulty.

In view of the apparent defect in the first instance ruling, on 8 August 2005 Wen Shengcun appealed to the Supreme People's Court of the Beijing Municipality. On 19 December 2005 the court made an inconceivable decision to reject Wen's appeal and to uphold the original decision. It was inconceivable because the written judgment did not comply with the norm. There was no mention of the reason for the plaintiff's appeal, and the reason for the decision was an exact duplication of the first instance judgment. Why was there no mention of the plaintiff's grounds of appeal? The reason was clear: the court of second instance could not provide an explanation of this apparent mistake.

Based on the principle that the judgment of the second instance is final, the plaintiff should have lost all confidence in seeking relief through judicial channels after the second ruling. However, a friend who is also a judge in Hebei persuaded Wen to try re-registering the case at a local court. On 29 December 2005, Wen instituted legal proceedings at the Bazhou People's Court in Hebei Province, demanding that the construction company compensate him for his trees. During the proceedings, the president of the court sought the opinion of a higher court, the Langfang Intermediate People's Court. After much effort by the various parties, the city's intermediate court agreed to Wen's claim in principle. The collegial panel heard the case several times, and conducted on-site investigations and a judicial audit. The court ruled in favour of Wen, and prepared a written judgment signed by the president in charge. However, just before the written judgment was delivered, the president of the court became aware of the case and instructed that the court cannot rule in favour of Wen. The president of the court feared that other farmers would follow Wen's example and take legal action. The written judgment, which was signed and sealed by the court, was discarded. As instructed by the president, the collegial panel dismissed the plaintiff's claim on the grounds that the case was out of the scope of civil action. The court gave the following decision:

> This court is of the opinion that the "Wuba" 500 kV power transmission and transformation construction project by the defendant, the North China Power Group for the Beijing Power Transmission And Transformation Company, is a construction project approved by the State Development Planning Commission. Hence, land expropriation and encroachment, as well as forest tree compensation involved in the construction thereof is not a case relating to a legal relationship between civil subjects with equal status; therefore, the civil law does not regulate this matter. The court rules that the Plaintiff's motion be dismissed under the provisions of Article 108 of the *Civil Procedure Law of the People's Republic of China*.

Subsequently, Wen appealed to the Langfang Intermediate People's Court. Wen believed that his case had been affirmed by the rulings of the First Intermediate People's Court of Beijing Municipality (2005) *Zhong Min Chu Zi* No. 402 Civil Judgment, and the Supreme People's Court of Beijing Municipality (2005) *Gao Min Zhong Zi* No. 1244 Civil Judgment. During hearings by the aforesaid Beijing courts, the defendant claimed that this case was not governed under civil procedures. However, both levels of courts in the Beijing Municipality had studied the case, and were of the following opinion:

> Civil procedure refers to property or personal disputes between civil subjects with equal status. These disputes occur between citizens, legal persons or other organizations. Legal action is instituted with the People's Court for resolution

by trial to protect legitimate personal rights. Wen proposed that the power transmission and transformation company and NCPG had not complied with the relevant laws, regulations and rules when the high-voltage power lines passed through his forest during construction. The companies had failed to discuss and enter into an indemnity agreement with Wen, or indemnify Wen. Therefore, they had infringed on his legitimate rights. Demanding compensation under the law is for disputes that arise between subjects of equal status as a result of a property relationship. Wen Shengcun's action meets the criteria for instituting legal proceeding under the *Civil Procedure Law*; therefore, the suit is within the scope of acceptance for civil lawsuits.

Thus, the case is within the scope of acceptance for civil lawsuits as determined by the judgment. The first instance decision of the Bazhou People's Court was in open disregard and violation of the rule of *res judicata*, and was therefore defective.

After much effort, the Langfang Intermediate People's Court expressed support for Wen in extremely ambiguous language. The court held that the trees planted by Wen, the appellant, had indeed been felled. However, the defendant answered that the compensation criteria and the indemnifying Party were unclear. Thus, the court ruled in accordance with the provisions under Article 108 of the *Civil Procedure Law of the People's Republic of China* to quash the ruling under the Bazhou People's Court (92006) *Ba Min Chu Zi* No. 159 Civil Judgment, and remand for retrial by the Bazhou People's Court. At that time, Wen was optimistic and glimpsed hope. To him, the Bazhou Intermediate People's Court was still the higher level court, and it was not possible that a superior court's instruction would be ignored. However, he could not have imagined that the true leader of a primary court is not the court of a higher level, but the Party commission and government at the same level. After the case was remanded for retrial, the Bazhou court again dismissed the motion when it could no longer delay judgment. The court held that

> The construction process had not caused the plaintiff to suffer any injury. The plaintiff's trees are felled by the municipal government department according to instructions from a superior level to clear obstructing trees within the protection zone of the overhead power transmission lines; hence, it is not within the scope of acceptance for civil lawsuits. The court had worked with the relevant government departments during the court proceedings. However, complete resolution was not possible. Therefore, the plaintiff's motion is dismissed.

Wen appealed, believing that the first instance court's findings had no legal grounds, nor were they based on facts. In reality, the duty of compensation for trees is required by law, and is not transferred based on whether or not the trees have been felled, or who performed the felling. The reasons are as follows: according to the provisions under Article 24 of the *Regulations on the Protection of Power Facilities*, and Paragraph 1, Article 16 of the *Implementation Measures of the Regulations on the Protection of Power Facilities*, first, the indemnifying subject responsible for compensating for the trees is the construction company of the power transmission lines. Hence, NCPG is under the duty to indemnify. Second, the claimant of the compensation is the owner of the forest trees. Hence, Wen is entitled to demand indemnity from the defendant. Third, the conditions precedent for tree compensation are: (1) timing of indemnity: "…when the new overhead power transmission lines construction or project must pass through the forest area," should refer to the period during construction; (2) scope of indemnity: "trees that have to be felled," means that compensation has to be paid for trees within the power transmission lines protection zone that have to be cut, and not payment after the actual felling of the trees. During the previous hearings, NCPG recognized that the 1951 fast-growing Zhonglin-46 poplar trees located within the overhead transmission line protection zone were endangering the power facilities and power-supply and should be removed. Hence, NCPG should discharge its duty of indemnity before the actual felling of trees. The performance of this duty has no connection with when the trees are felled and who fells the trees. Furious with this reasoning, Wen said,

> The court has pointed out that trees are chopped by the government under the orders of a higher authority. However, there was no mention of government of which level or on what basis. A hasty decision was made without making clear the most fundamental facts. Where is judicial justice and authority? Furthermore, can the so-called instructions be the basis on which the People's court applies laws?

Despite the evident facts, the Langfang Intermediate People's Court refused to deliver judgment even up to the day this article was written. Four years have passed, and the case is still being tried.

III. KEY ISSUES PREVENTING FARMERS' ACCESS TO JUDICIAL RELIEF

The difficulties which Wen Shengcun encountered when he attempted to seek judicial relief for his legitimate personal rights exemplify the many country-specific problems faced by farmers seeking judicial relief:

(1) *The lack of a qualified and independent court, and the strong government powers behind the justice system.* A truly qualified and independent court is the prerequisite that guarantees the right to judicial relief. Wen's unsuccessful suits with the four courts in Beijing and Bazhou are testimonies to the dominance of administrative powers over the courts, and of the courts' lack of capacity in independent decision-making. As a large state-owned company with quasi-government powers, the defendant had a huge

influence over the proceedings in both the Beijing people's courts, as opposed to a small-time farmer. According to unwritten rules, and in an era where judicial supervision is ineffective, it is normal that the powerful defendant was able to exert influence over the judge. When the case was tried in Hebei, the government's influence was even more apparent. To avoid government intervention, the plaintiff sent representatives and personally met with the deputy mayor in charge. The deputy mayor indicated that he would not interfere with the case. After this the superior court demanded that the trial court render a fair hearing; the chief judge and the deputy president in charge had even completed preparation of the written judgment. However, a single telephone call from a government official had caused the court's president to order withdrawal of the prepared judgment. The president even voluntarily initiated discussions within the judicial committee on how to implement the municipal government's opinions, and rule against the plaintiff. Evidently, the local Party committees and governments exert a far greater influence over the local courts than courts of a higher level.

(2) *Farmers' fear of lawsuits and lack of confidence in the justice system.* There were at least a dozen households in Bazhou's Xinzhang Village, the place where Wen resides, that were in the same predicament. Imagine the number of trees owned by farmers all along the 200 kilometre stretch of 500 kV high-voltage power transmission lines which were felled! However, Wen was the only one to institute legal proceedings. Most of the other farmers were either ignorant of the compensation criteria for felling trees, or were otherwise unaware of the means for resolution. Farmers would immediately think of their low social status that makes them powerless to bargain with the government. Farmers cannot differentiate between the judicial system and the government. They do not expect to claim their rights, thinking that both are in fact one entity.

Another reason is that even though judicial relief is sought, the preference is for resolution by the authorities. Traditional, folk theatrical writings and drama stories have formed the deep-rooted perception that the administration and judiciary are one and the same. Thus, farmers would not resort to judicial means to seek relief under normal circumstances. On the contrary, they would have abnormal expectations: they would hope for a fair official to come along and carry out justice. *Shangfang* becomes a preferred avenue as a result. Hearsay on and personal experiences in judicial practices have also gradually eroded people's confidence in the justice system. Most conclude that "no one uses the judicial system." The People's Supreme Court's recent proposal of gradual withdrawal of the people's courts from towns and townships will distance justice from farmers even more. Farmers will no longer meet judges at the marketplace, and judges who have become more distant may seem even more mysterious and terrifying to farmers. Eventually, farmers will find it difficult to establish necessary trust and expectation in the justice system.

(3) *Despite seeking judicial relief, farmers prefer* shangfang. *Shangfang* has always

been the preferred and natural choice of farmers when seeking support for their rights. This is because of a desire for "clean and upright officials." Another reason is the continued dominance of the system of the "rule of man" (*renzhi*) versus the "rule of law" (*fazhi*). In recent years, collective *shangfang* was employed in nearly all cases concerning farmers' rights. In this case, Wen also used *shangfang*, having visited the various government and power departments, as well as the construction company of the high-voltage power transmission lines. Because the departments shirked responsibility and refused to accept Wen's petition, he had no alternative but to eventually turn to judicial channels. This exemplifies the phenomenon that judicial relief is often the last resort for the agricultural community, after exhausting all other avenues. What is worth noting is that most farmers taking legal action do not look directly to the justice department for an ideal judgment. Rather, the judicial process is a means which they use to compel the relevant government department to grant them an audience in order to resolve their problems. While they distrust the judicial system, they do not believe entirely in *shangfang*; aggrieved persons will usually grab any resolution method that comes their way. Nonetheless, *shangfang* lacks the explicit regulations set forth under the procedure law. Furthermore, *shangfang* is a more arduous process, as it necessitates a struggle to avoid detention for obstruction of social safety and requires the toleration of an extended wait and the repeated avoidance of responsibilities by the authorities. Wen has been busy running about between the municipal government, the provincial government, and the State Council's complaint offices, but his efforts have thus far yet to yield any encouraging results.

(4) *High litigation costs and deficient legal services in towns and townships*. Total litigation and verification costs chalked by the four court trials in Wen's case exceeded RMB 50,000. This can only be afforded by a "farmer" like Wen, who also runs a business. Farmers without savings, or those who rely on loans from friends and relatives, cannot afford to sue. Rules like payment postponement, reduction and exemption as provided under the *Regulations on Litigation Charges of the People's Courts* seem unlikely to ever benefit farmers. One of the reasons for these rules is that courts derive their major source of income from collecting litigation charges, and are reluctant to run a money-losing business. The other reason is the idea that if the court offers reduction or exemption of litigation charges for farmers who "make trouble with the government," they would then be encouraging more trouble. Hence, litigation cost is a major obstacle for cases involving farmers' suits against governments or quasi-governmental authorities. To these farmers, justice is expensive.

Let us look at the legal services market in the rural areas. The level of education within the agricultural community is generally low; in other words, the agricultural community should rely even more than average on assistance by the legal professionals during litigation. However, what we see in reality is otherwise: it is rare to see a farmer accompanied by a lawyer. At present, legal services in rural areas are mainly offered by town and township legal service offices under the justice bureau. Personnel who lack professional expertise staff these offices, and a substantial proportion of personnel are civil servants who are afraid to speak up for the farmers. Although it is difficult to find lawyers in towns and townships, finding a lawyer in a county city is not difficult. The difficulty, however, lies with the meagre number of farmers who can afford legal fees. Perhaps a couple of thousand yuan to hire a lawyer may seem unimaginably cheap to us. Imagine, however, how many kilograms of grain a farmer would have to sell to raise that money!

IV. Three Main Causes Affecting Farmers' Access to Judicial Relief

(1) A Justice System Driven by Political Correctness

After having seen and experienced Chinese judicial practice for more than a decade, the author believes that there are fundamentals that must be understood in order to have an accurate view of China's judicial system. Some important questions include: what is the primary objective of China's justice system? After receiving a case, what are a judge's goals and priorities?

This is a question that most have taken for granted and neglected. Anyone will say that the primary goal of a judicial system is to uphold justice, because it is a fundamental good. However, locals might give the answer that it is to be politically correct. There is an enduring institutional context and theoretical foundation behind this answer. The author provides the following empirical analysis.

Firstly, Chinese judicial organs are set up in exactly the same manner as administrative regions. The only exceptions are the railway transportation court, maritime court and military court. There is the Supreme People's Court at the national level, provincial people's high courts, and prefecture or city intermediate people's courts. the courts and administrative organs of the same level have exactly the same jurisdiction in the region; both are the highest authority at the Party level, have the same political goals and missions, and need to adjudicate based on the local Party committee's central task. In other words, they must fulfil their role as effective instruments for achieving the goals of the local Party committee. What then is the goal of the local Party committee? Since the Third Plenary Session of the eleventh Central Committee of the Communist Party of China in 1978, the key objectives of the various levels of Party committees may be divided into two categories: (1) the maintenance of social stability to ensure the CPC's continued rule; and (2) the aggressive development of the economy. For a long time, the protection of civil rights, especially political rights, has not been on the agenda. In fact, the concept of human rights has not been acknowledged. Despite talk of human rights protection at the CPC's highest levels, it remains a means of political mobilization and propaganda, devoid of concrete protection measures. This is because the criteria for performance appraisal of government and Party officials remain social stability and economic development. Human rights protection is not evaluated. In fact, many official actions sacrifice civil rights for social development and stability. One of the most striking and extreme phenomena is the forced removal and deprivation of farmers' land rights. Under these circumstances, instead of providing real judicial relief for civil rights, the main duties of judicial organs is to maintain local social stability and economic development.

Secondly, the leadership system for Chinese judicial organs is organized such that external affairs are led by the Party committee of the same level, whereas internal affairs are governed by the respective court's Party leadership group. The Party commission demonstrates its leadership by having the power to appoint and release (*renmianquan*) personnel. Application of the *Organic Law of the National People's Congress* or the *Organic Law of the People's Courts* is not as simple as might seem. Within the courts, the Party committee's decision prevails. To begin with, the president and vice president of the court are recommended by the Party committee of the same level. This recommendation is reviewed by the Party committee's organizing department and submitted to the People's Congress of the same level, or its standing committee, for consideration. An important issue here is that the appointment of the highest leadership within the court system is not governed by the *Judges Law*. Many presidents of provincial-level or higher courts were heads of the Party committee or administrative departments prior to their transfer; they knew little about the law, despite trying very hard to learn the ropes after their appointment. They have many years of political experience in the Party committee or administrative organ, and have cultivated political acumen. Additionally, courts appointing personnel who are judges or a higher level must first report to the Party committee's organizing department at the same level. The Party's organizing department must approve of the candidate before submission for appointment by the People's Congress or its standing committee of the same level. This way, a judge whose performance is found unsatisfactory by the Party's relevant department will find it difficult to get a promotion. Internally, the court is still run by the Party leadership group. Under normal circumstances, the president of a court is the secretary of the Party leadership group of the Court. In fact, the Party leadership group ranks high in the hierarchy. The full name of the Party leadership group is the Party Leadership Group of the People's Court of XX (or city, county) of the Communist Party of China XX Provincial (or city, county) Committee. Within the CPC, it must be governed by the provincial (or city, county) Party committee. Within the court, the Party leadership group ranks higher than the president, vice president and the judicial committee. Any appointment or dismissal of any judge must be first approved by the court's Party leadership group. Any vice president who is not a member of the Party leadership group (for example, a vice president who is either a member of the Democratic Party or not Party-affiliated) will have the lowest status within the court's hierarchy; perhaps, even lower than the head of the political department or office administrator who is a member of the Party leadership group.

Thirdly, the Chinese justice system is not independent of Party politics; this relates to ideology education in the judicial system. On the contrary, there is a strong emphasis on educating Party spirit. Within every court of every level, there is a Political Department (or "Political Work Section" for primary courts), which is not stated under the *Organic Law of the People's Courts*. The department conducts political education for existing judges, monitors their orientations, and gives out reward or punishments based on their political performance. Each year, the court system devotes a lengthy period to conducting political education. The goals are to enable learning of the prevailing Party policies, and to enhance education of Party spirit through politically driven activities, such as restructuring practices and disciplines. Diligent participation in these activities by every judge is mandatory, whether or not he or she is a member of the CPC. They must also report their political stance and state their political opinions. Most judges are CPC members. Those who are not will still be obliged to obey the orders of the Party leaders during adjudication, and to carry out the Party's instructions. In this respect, the presidents of the courts of various levels were candid during reporting at the People's Congress, admitting that adjudication must be based on the Party's central tasks. Most judges, especially those in leadership positions in the courts, view being politically correct as more advantageous than being legally correct. Many technicalities are involved in the administration of justice. A legal mistake is at worst a matter of deficient knowledge or inadequate professional performance; a political mistake involves a judge's standing, and directly affects his future in politics and in his career. Having undergone perpetual political brainwashing, judges are extremely careful with maintaining their political correctness during adjudication. Another serious outcome of unceasing political education is judges' failure to recognize the importance of an independent judicial system, and its value in democratic rule. Instead, they emphasize their political mission. Many young judges who worked in the court system for a period after graduation experience the same thing. The damage to China's justice system is subtle and far-reaching. We must decide if the courts should intensify political education like Party organs.

We can see that China's unique political structure puts courts in an inferior position to Party leaders. Since achievement of political goals ranks above all else, political correctness will shape the adjudication process of judges. The key is to understand the definition of "political correctness" at work here. The measurement of "political correctness" is broad and ambiguous; it generally means staying consistent with the Party's policies. If all policies at every level of the Party committees were to respect farmers' rights, then political correctness as a criterion for justice would not disadvantage judicial relief for farmers. The problem is that a court or judge usually complies with the policies of the Party committee immediately above it. Yet, policies respecting farmers' rights are often inconsistent with the central policies of the CPC; these policies focus more on ensuring local stability and economic development, and delivering quick political performance during the local leader's short term in office. For a long time, the best way to deliver swift performance was to initiate major construction projects, such as large development zones of various titles, without considering local practicalities. These kinds of construction projects inevitably involve the expropriation of farmers' lands and infringement of their land rights. What will judges do when farmers seek judicial relief? No doubt, the primary consideration is political correctness – which means: look at the big picture and serve the bosses' interests. Judges will leverage every means and measure in procedure law, as exemplified in the case of *Wen v. NCPG*; or they will refuse to accept the case; or they will drag the case on for several years under the pretext of insufficient standing in order to consume the plaintiff's energy and confidence in the action. When judges can no longer delay the case, they would rather commit a legal violation and miscarriage of justice than make a political mistake. Of course, we could say that the judges have their hands tied to a certain extent. Chinese judges are not protected under any employment policy. Where the local government dictates personnel movements and financial support, the future of the court president or judge who does not cooperate in his judicial practice will be endangered. When a party to an action is an ordinary farmer and his counterparty represents the government's interests, the court will usually take the government's side. Apart from the personnel and financial reasons mentioned previously, judges subconsciously put themselves in the same rank as government officials. They believe that they belong to the same bureaucratic level. They also have to take into consideration that certain government officials may become the key leaders of their court, or the immediate superiors of their relatives. Protecting or siding with the government may be beneficial for judges. In addition, where judges must first consider political demands, taking the initiative to safeguard the government's interest, or to resolve the government's difficulties and minimize trouble are important measures of a judge's political reliability. Therefore, any rational judge will know which choice is most beneficial. Farmers will almost always be put in an extremely unfavourable position during an action.

The fact that political correctness is the primary consideration in the justice system seriously prejudices farmers' rights. The root of this problem lies fundamentally with the absence of political rights for farmers. Where the courts are completely politicized locally, the governing Party, the government, and the judiciary share the same political mission despite a division of powers. As a result, a single group or individual may rule over the court. Thus, when a farmer seeks justice against the government to safeguard his legitimate rights, the role of the justice system may not be one that protects farmers' rights. Instead, the common political mission is the guiding tenet, and under the leadership of a group or an individual, judges work with the administrative departments to stabilize the situation. Farmers' interests and the principles of equity and justice intrinsic to an independent judicial system are sacrificed. Hence, the key to resolving injustice in China's judicial system does not lie with the reform of the technical rules of operation in the justice system, or the improvement or revision of the procedure law. It is about the power structure and division between the central and local governments, the administrative and judicial organs, and the governing Party. In recent years, many legal academicians and judicial practitioners have taken actions to mitigate injustice in the judicial system. Major amendments have been carried out in the various procedure laws. Yet little improvement has been seen in judicial reform after more than a decade. Corruption in the judicial system is still prevalent. The only apparent change is the increasingly modern, luxurious and imposing offices of the judicial organs. This is mainly because no one places any hopes on constitutional reform; there is a lack of passion and diligence in this regard. It is true that constitutional reform may require the efforts of a few generations. However, China's academics and policy and legal practitioners should look further, for the benefit of the country and the nation, by undertaking this mission and responsibility that could beget generations of peace, and work to eradicate these fundamental constitutional problems. If the judiciary can be free from local politics by changing the constitutional structure so that justice can be truly independent, then farmers' rights will have found a real linchpin – the law. When farmers' rights are effectively protected under the law, farmers will no longer need to form agricultural associations as proposed by many scholars. In a truly democratic country, the custodian of rights is none other than just laws and fair courts.

(2) Corrupt and Imperious Justice System

The other reason why farmers are deprived of access to judicial relief is because of general depravity within the judiciary. The seriousness of corruption far exceeds imagination; it must be experienced to be believed. Judges who take advantage of their powers of office to serve their own self-interest deliver fatal blows to farmers' judicial relief. There are two aspects to judges' self-interest: material benefits, and favours. General poverty and low social status prevent farmers from bribing or exchanging favours. Accused parties in cases involving farmers' rights are either governments or large corporations with material wealth or social influence that farmers cannot match. Even Wen, the plaintiff of the case previously mentioned, is no match for the municipal government, the power supply bureau and large state-owned monopolies like the NCPG. Judges' pursuit of self-interest through their powers of office is inevitable where the Chinese bureaucracy is generally corrupt. Most cases of judicial corruption do not involve the acceptance of monetary or material gains, but involve relationships instead. Many see the basis of this problem on the use of relationships as a Chinese social tradition. However, to say that this social tradition interferes with judges' actions is inaccurate. Relationships and social dealings exist in any society, and decisions are usually taken with relationships in mind. Why then do Chinese judges put a greater emphasis on relationships? It is not because they are more sentimental; rather, the motive for favour in any case is self-interest and benefits. When a judge takes into account personal relationships in a case he is not driven by pure friendship, but by an expectation of the exchange of favours, for advancement of his political career, or for the sake of his relatives. This begs the question of why judges are exceptionally benevolent to authority and especially heartless to farmers? The answer is because the judge cannot expect any exchange of favours if he bestows kindness on farmers. Any "relationship" is, therefore, intrinsically selfish. Never-ending personal desires must be curbed by an external system because the self-discipline of judges is unreliable.

What are the supervision mechanisms for Chinese judges? First, there is opposition by the People's Procuratorate and adjudication supervision by it or by a superior People's Court; second, disciplinary supervision by the ruling Party is available; and third, there is the "leading case review and approval system" within the various segments of the court's internal process. Despite numerous supervision mechanisms, they provide little value in reality because they are, by nature, intra-system mechanisms that fail to offer real supervision. Where the police, the Procuratorate and the court are integrated, the Procuratorate and the court are essentially partners, not adversaries, that serve a common goal. The Party's discipline supervision, the court's internal Party leadership group, or the Party's discipline supervision department of a higher level, are but supervisors of their own compatriots within a bureaucracy. The same applies to supervision within the court system. The system is further stymied by complex private relationships within specific administrative regions; the supervisors and the supervised being either former classmates or friends.

What China lacks is a truly effective external supervision mechanism – public watchdogs. Public opinion can only become a watchdog with the freedom of the press. Freedom of the press guarantees freedom of speech, which in turn provides an effective channel for the expression of public grievances. Cases involving the protection of farmers' rights usually involve complex power and personal relationships that affect or even influence justice. The supervisor and the supervised in a court, which is almost completely shaped by local politics, usually stand on the same platform in terms of their interests; both are players within the local bureaucracy. Where the nature of the case is a battle between farmers and the local bureaucracy, we cannot expect the multiple judicial supervisory mechanisms to be of any benefit. That being said, most farmers tend to choose *shangfang*; bypassing immediate leadership to go to a higher authority and hoping to bring their problem to the notice of a higher level within the bureaucracy. Nonetheless, the Letters and Visits system ("*Xinfang*") is increasingly ineffective. Local governments are cautious of any complainant, striking back or retaliating against petitioners, as well as the corrupt and inefficient *Xinfang* system. The higher-level leaders cannot hear the cries of farmers. Therefore, we can only rely on public opinion; yet, to rely on public opinion entails a long process under the current political system. We do not see much hope for farmers with existing concerns.

Another important reason that contributes to the general fear of litigation among farmers is the imperious justice system. As an avenue to resolve social conflicts, justice should be a platform for civilized dialogue. Yet the contrary is true; the judicial system in China is imbued with a perplexing air of tyranny, which is far worse than the government's dominance. One wonders how a genteel graduate from law school could metamorphose into an unreasonable judge within a few years. The author believes that the key lies in the exceptional powers of judges and their lack of supervision. A sense of superiority will invariably emerge when judges meet litigants who are frustrated farmers and who have no power or influence. The judge could openly choose to reject an application for action, or deny a person's right to speak in court, or even mock, ridicule or berate anyone in court. When the author was working at the primary courts ten years ago, the court system had placed "Difficult Entry, Unfriendly Face" (*Men Nanjin, Lian Nankan*) as the priority for reform. This issue was discussed in many meetings. More than a decade later, when the author encountered judges as a lawyer, the same feeling persists. No change has occurred, in spite of the courts being at a higher level or the fact that judges are well educated. The unpleasant attitude of judges cannot be corrected by a supervisory mechanism. Bad attitude does not constitute any violation of the law. Hence, it is a question of improving the cultivation of judges. Besides being constrained by the living and work environment, personal cultivation is also indicative of general social humanity. With low pay, stress from a heavy workload and malpractice, many judges feel a sense of defeat. This could contribute to their unreasonable attitude at work. Most farmers in China have been living in small and confined regions for generations. Poor education and insulation from the outside world make them extremely fearful of the external world. Imperious judges erode farmers' confidence in the judicial system, and instil fear. This prevents farmers from coping with a legal suit, and some may even go as far as withdrawing legal action or resorting to extreme means to fight back at the justice system or the government. Thus, insignificant as it may seem, the attitude of judges has considerable impact on farmers' access to judicial relief.

(3) Legal Services Are Beyond Farmers' Reach

Farmers are generally poorly educated, and many have no legal knowledge. On the other hand, justice is a highly professional sector, and farmers seeking judicial relief will require professional legal services more than anything else. Lawyers are the providers of this service. As of the end of 2007, there are more than 200,000 in China, a sizable team indeed. However, farmers' cases involving litigation seldom receive effective legal assistance.

There are two main reasons why lawyers are reluctant to provide legal help to farmers: one reason is the difficulty in collecting fees; and the other reason is the apprehension of government retaliation. Farmers are poor and are unable to afford high legal costs. Therefore, able lawyers who have good client sources will not want to represent farmers. This is not surprising since we live in a market economy; lawyers are legal service providers who are driven by profit and are not protectors of justice. This should have little impact on farmers, however, as cases involving farmers' rights do not entail a complex application of the law. Lawyers with average ability would suffice. In many cities, there are many new lawyers who pass the annual bar examination and are just entering the profession; they have little income and do not have a steady clientele. These lawyers are ideal candidates to take on cases involving the protection of human rights. However, even these lawyers generally refrain from accepting such cases because they fear government retaliation. New lawyers who have little experience work within a restricted region, usually in the city in which they reside. Thus, they may be placed under undue pressure by the local judicial administrative department. They may face retaliation by the relevant government department if they represent farmers in a suit against the government. In China, it may appear that the lawyers' association regulates the practice of lawyers; in truth, the association is an agent of the judicial administrative department and must carry out the orders of the department. Furthermore, the judicial administrative department is part of the same level of government. These are the practical circumstances that prevent farmers from appointing local attorneys. Therefore, in many high-profile cases involving the protection of farmers' rights, many attorneys are from a different city, especially from major cities like Beijing, Shanghai, Guangzhou and Wuhan. This problem is resolved to some extent by the fact that lawyers are regulated by the judicial administrative department at the location where they are registered, and the fact that there is no restriction as to where lawyers practice. However, recent events have shown that the judicial administrative department of a lawyer's place of registration has restricted him or her from representing farmers' rights in other cities. The judicial administrative department is now given the important responsibility of maintaining social stability. To fulfil its political mission, the judicial administrative department disregards any violation of the *Lawyers' Law*; the department openly interferes with lawful professional behaviour. In general, in cases where farmers' rights are involved, lawyers refrain from accepting these cases either for financial reasons, or for fear of retaliation.

In China's judicial practice, the subtle relationship between judges and lawyers does, to some extent, affect the legal help available to farmers. Although judges and lawyers clearly play different roles and have different duties, both are persons of the legal fraternity, and should maintain a spirit of mutual respect and professional cooperation. However, in most cases, the relationship between the judge and the lawyer is not of cooperation for personal interests, but of professional rivalry. In cases where the judge maintains an extremely close relationship with certain lawyers in private, these lawyers will become the agent and executor of bribery for the judge. Thus, how a case should be handled has been privately arranged in advanced. The lawyer representing the counterparty becomes an adversary to the judge, who would employ tyrannous means to restrict or deprive a party's rights. Hence, we cannot attribute the entire helpless situation to a corrupt judicial system. In fact, the entire legal profession, including lawyers, are depraved. For example, when most lawyers become aware that a specific judge is handling his case, his key tasks are not to gather evidence or to prepare the case from a legal perspective. Instead, he would mobilize all his resources to get in touch with the judge and bribe the judge with favours and material benefits. A case will not be given a fair trial if the relationship with the judge is not well-established in advance. Indeed, this seems to be an unspoken rule. Some say that great lawyers in China are more socialites than legal experts, whose social activities are mainly to build good relationships with judges and to promptly offer bribes to win cases. With the entire legal fraternity depraved, farmers will find difficulty obtaining legal assistance. On the one hand, farmers, being vulnerable parties in action, have no financial means to feed the corrupt party; on the other hand, the system does not encourage honourable and upright lawyers who work to protect farmers' rights.

CONCLUSION: THE PROPOSAL TO ESTABLISH NON-GOVERNMENTAL ANTI-CORRUPTION ORGANIZATIONS

For more than four years, Wen's case has been tried five times in four courts, in Beijing and Langfang, Hebei Province. We do not see any possibility of resolution by law. As this article was being written, there was news that the forest belonging to a farmer and adjoining Wen's land had been subject to forced felling by government-led police after a battle of many years. In the case illustrated here, judicial relief failed completely, whether the Beijing courts with sound professional knowledge, or Hebei judges, who are simple and kind, tried it. The grounds for dismissal may differ, but the outcome is identical. This illustrates that farmers receive basically no right to judicial relief in China today, especially when government's interests are involved. The State's fundamental political system, the way in which the CPC rules, the personnel and financial systems, the organizational structure of the People's courts, and the systems of education and official ideology are the reasons why the judicial system is shaped completely by local politics. The right to judicial relief is further prejudiced by rampant judicial corruption and tyranny and the lack of political rights and financial means of farmers. In order to change the situation, we need to first change the way that the CPC rules. Courts must be freed from absolute command over their personnel and the financial and material deployment of the court by the local Party commission. These changes are required so that the judicial system may disentangle itself from the control of the Party commission and government within the regions of its jurisdiction. Qualification and independence of the judicial system must be set in place in order to change the present situation.

Reform and eradication of abuse at the political level is a long, gradual and tedious process. However, a party who has suffered under a corrupt and unfair justice system requires expedient remedy. Therefore, we need to explore a "quick fix" under the current political system; one that exerts a force of influence over the judiciary in order to shape a just judicial system. The author calls for the formation of a non-governmental anti-corruption organization as soon as possible. This organization should have a membership comprised of academics, journalists, lawyers and other relevant persons who handle complaints. The justice system would, under such an organization, be subject to public scrutiny. The media could be used as a vehicle to censure the court or judge in the event that the judiciary is found to be corrupt or unjust. Because the Constitution provides citizens the right to criticize and provide recommendations to State organs or to its personnel, to complain of judicial injustice or judicial corruption does not constitute a violation of the law. This organization will allow academics to implement their proposals; journalists to represent the public voice; and lawyers to mediate, understand and handle cases. Supervision will be the objective. As a force formed of the general public, courts and judges handling cases will not be able to retaliate. With convenient and fast internet access, and with governments and courts being wary of their reputations, this organization will be an effective force that prohibits judicial tyranny, injustice and corruption. It will also increase the awareness of vulnerable groups, promote observation of the law by government departments, and promote the rule of law in general. Last year's "Nail Household" ("*Dingzi Hu*") case in Chongqing involving forced removal revealed that public watchdogs can play a significant role in promoting judicial justice. If this organization were to materialize, the public would be certain to line up behind it and support it.

ENDNOTES

1   The facts set forth here are based mainly on the various legal documents used during the proceedings. Some facts are as stated by the parties concerned. The author does not guarantee them to be absolutely true and objective.

2   The division of jurisdiction for civil cases among Chinese courts is based mainly on the amount claimed. Thus, if the plaintiff deliberately makes a larger claim amount, the case may be under the jurisdiction of the higher People's Court.

CHAPTER SIX

China's War on its Environment and Farmers' Rights
A Study of Shanxi Province

Zhang Yulin

Since the 1980s, rapid industrialization in China has given birth to two dramatic events. One is the double digit average annual economic growth rate that has lasted for more than twenty years, and which has transformed what was a predominantly agricultural society into the 21st century's "workshop of the world." The second is the unprecedented speed and scale of ecological destruction and environment pollution by far unmatched by any country, nor rivalled by any previous period of human history, including that of the Great Leap Forward in the 1950s.

In fact, if we could decipher the usually ambiguous language games[1] in the *Environmental Status Bulletins* published by the various levels of environment administration, supplemented by honest documentation by journalists and writers, we should be able to produce a close enough account of the environment's general deterioration: ecological destruction brought on by the Chinese mode of industrialization[2] has long passed the point of "crisis" (a designation the importance of which is dubious in any case); instead, it has now entered a phase in which a full-scale war is waged against nature on home ground.

This war has already gone on for more than two decades. Although the true gravity of its consequences has yet to emerge, some situations that have surfaced suffice to bring home its capacity to devastate, and to instil terror. Persistent outcries for humanitarian intervention by Chinese leaders concerned for the country's future have been, "let the people drink clean water, breathe clean air…".[3] Nevertheless, with globalization as the general backdrop, two formally incompatible institutions are joining forces. Together, they wield enough power to derail China's industrialization train. With the war engine ramming away, the war on nature will go on.

We cannot predict when we will see the end of this war on our environment. But the clearing up of calamities brought forth by this war – and they are not mere "losses" – is possible and necessary. In the next phase of our work,[4] we shall focus on the battlefield where fighting is most intense – the province of Shanxi[5]– a land filled with the legacy of ancient civilization, rich with coal, inhabited by 33.75 million people and spanning 156,000 square kilometres. We shall examine the degree of ecological destruction, the disasters inflicted and their distribution, as well as their destructive impacts on the farmers' livelihoods and the society of the countryside.

With most of China entrapped in a serious "ecological environment crisis," there are two reasons for selecting Shanxi as the object of study. The first relates to technique and considerations of methodology: studying the problem from the macro level may affect the depth of our study, given China's size. Superficial and general studies have been done by many local and foreign academics. For in-depth study, we must target a particular provincial area or river basin in order to obtain a "middle view." Second is Shanxi's representativeness: Shanxi typifies China in its abundance of resources, mode of economic growth, and the universality, degree and social outcomes of ecological destruction.

Most data used in this study are the results of the author's on-site investigation in certain areas in Shanxi. Extensive use has been made of media reports and official statistical bulletins on the state of Shanxi's environment. It also includes a small number of qualitative studies done by researchers.

I. The Expansion and Distribution of Wealth and its Ecological Price

Known as the "heaven of black gold," Shanxi is rich in coal deposits. It has coal buried under 70 percent of its land, and, with 264.5 billion tons in available reserves, it has 26 percent of the country's total proven coal reserves.[6] Since the early 1980s Shanxi has been declared a State "energy base" (*nengyuan jidi*) (assuming an even more important role in the 1990s as an "energy and heavy chemical industrial base"), and the policy of the central government has been to encourage coal mining activities wherever possible and by whatever means (*youshui kuailiu*). Intensive coal mining has been carried out on a large scale. For a long time, coal output in Shanxi accounted for approximately a quarter of national production. Especially since 2001, coal prices soared with the country's rapidly growing economy. Countless coal mines, legal and illegal, have contributed to the rush for black gold. Coal output in 2005 was 600 million tons, nearly the output for the entire decade of the 1970s. Reports also indicate that total output over the last twenty years was close to eight billion tons.[7] Coal-related industries, such as coking, electrical power, smelting, chemical engineering and building materials, have also developed swiftly.

The total economic wealth of Shanxi indeed multiplied quickly. Based on total output of the entire provincial region, annual output increased by 13.1 percent during the period of the tenth five-year plan, five percentage points higher than the 8.2 percent growth during the period of the ninth five-year plan and the original target. Output value during 2006 was RMB 474.7 billion, 2.9 times the 2000 level.[8] Shanxi leaders said, "the tenth five-year plan period is the time during which Shanxi grew fastest and grew best, and in which people benefited most substantially."[9]

Undoubtedly, the greatest beneficiaries from such new found weath are the "coal bosses" – *nouveaux riches* and the government – rather than the "masses of the people" (to embrace a highly political concept). Despite the unavailability of accurate statistics on the "coal bosses" and the amount of wealth they have amassed, an article from the *First Financial Daily* quoted the head of the Xinjiang Office of the Shanxi Provincial Government saying "there is at least RMB 400 billion in the hands of private coal bosses seeking out investment avenues." This amounts to 2.7 times the income of the province's entire urban population of 14.51 million in 2006 (RMB 145.54 billion), and

Table 1: Shanxi's Economic Growth and Wealth Distribution (1980–2006)

Year	Regional Output RMB 100m	Total Fiscal Income RMB 100m	General Budgeted Income RMB 100m	Urban Residents per Capita Disposable Income RMB	Farmers per Capita Income RMB
1980	108.8	–	21.0	380	156
1985	219.0	–	25.0	595	358
1990	429.3	–	51.8	1,291	604
1995	1,092.5	129.4	72.2	3,306	1,208
2000	1,640.1	194.5	114.4	4,724	1,906
2001	1,774.6	243.7	132.6	5,391	1,956
2002	2,001.8	292.4	156.7	6,234	2,150
2003	2,445.6	369.6	186.0	7,005	2,299
2004	3,042.4	533.5	255.2	7,903	2,590
2005	4,121.2	757.9	368.2	8,914	2,891
2006	47,46.5	1,048.0	583.1	10,028	3,181
2006/2000	2.9	5.4	5.1	2.1	1.7
2006/1980	43.6	–	27.8	26.4	20.4

Source: For 1980 to 1995 figures, refer to the National Bureau of Statistics of China's *Comprehensive Statistical Data and Materials on 50 Years of New China* (China Statistics Press, 1999). Per capita net income of farmers is computed based on current prices, and urban residents per capita disposable income is computed based on comparable prices; for 2000 to 2006 figures, see the Shanxi Bureau of Statistics' Statistical *Communiqué of Shanxi Province on the 2000-2006 National Economic and Social Development.*

6.5 times that of its 19.23 million rural population in 1923 (RMB 61.17 billion)[10] – a definite indication of the immense amount of their wealth. Official statistics provide a glimpse into the additional wealth accumulated by the government[11]: fiscal income has been growing faster than residents' income since the 1980s; and government income has experienced exponential growth in the new millennium. Total fiscal income in 2006 was 5.4 times more than the 2000 figure, 2.6 times that of urban residents and three times that of rural residents. This implies that even if we were to disregard the "unbudgeted income," the government is, compared to the urban and rural residents, the greatest beneficiary of economic growth.

Behind the rapid expansion in the weath of "coal bosses" and the government lie ecological destruction and grave environmental degradation. The 2001 *Shanxi Environmental Status Bulletin* reported that Shanxi's emission levels of key pollutants far exceed the environment's tolerance, and that all its cities, key regions and river basins are seriously polluted. The total per capita pollution load for every square kilometre is 3.7 times the national average; per capita pollution load for pollutants such as industrial smoke and ash, sulphur dioxide and dust is many times, even tens of times, higher than the national average.[12] In September 2002, a vice mayor of Shanxi made a public request in Beijing, asking the central government to include Shanxi as a "key province for national environmental protection." Thereafter, over the next three years, dozens of members of the National Committee of the Chinese People's Political Consultative Conference (CPPCC) would petition for "the nomination of Shanxi as a key province for national environmental protection at every National People's Congress (NPC) and CPPCC meeting in Beijing."[13] They would also request funding and policy support to prevent and treat the pollution of the Huai River, similar to the similar support given to Beijing. What is really behind this *repeated* call for help? We may look at it systematically from four perspectives:

1. A Different Kind of "Mine Accident"
The lack of protection for miners' safety is a well-known fact. The Shanxi public conjures the image of "blood-smeared" coal due to frequent mine accidents. However, what is here reduced to mere "mine accidents" is in fact more than the innumerable number of miners who have lost their lives to an unknown hand. Even more, they themselves tell of the devastation of the environment and the ecosystem.

Destruction of the ecosystem first manifests itself in the attenuation of water resources. Geological exploration indicates that Shanxi's coal and water systems are both located within the same geological structure; the mining of coal and the discharge of pit water thus destroys the natural equilibrium of groundwater. Water flows towards the pit, forming a cone of depression, with the shaft at the centre, and the water table falls when the original water-bearing layer becoming an impervious water bed. Based on calculation, 2.48 cubic metres of water will be affected, destroyed or lost for every ton of coal extracted in Shanxi. If we then calculate based on the amount of coal extracted in 2005, 600 million tons of coal extracted translates into 1.5 billion cubic metres of water wasted. This is equivalent to one fifth of the entire province's groundwater reserve.[14]

Intensive coal mining causes critical geological calamities. Studies by the Land Resource Administration Bureau of Shanxi Province discovered that, as of 2004, there were as many as 20,000 square kilometres or more of goaves left over from various mines in Shanxi, which means that more than one seventh of the total ground surface of the province consists of "suspended areas." Geological disasters affect more than 6,000 square kilometres, spanning more than 1,900 villages and affecting 2.2 million people. Sinking due to mining was found in 1,842 places, and mining-induced depression areas increase at a rate of 94 square kilometres per year.[15] Geological calamities include cave-ins, cracking and collapse of housing, damage to water and road facilities, and flows of mud and debris. Every ton of coal extracted will cause 1.07 persons in the province to be affected by cave-ins and destruction to housing and infrastructure. Also, coal mining is increasingly affecting surface waters. A study that ended in 2004 indicated that destruction to water resources due to coal mining covers as much as 20,352 square kilometres, or 13 percent of the total area of Shanxi. Six million people and tens of thousands of large animals suffer as a result from serious water deprivation.[16]

2. Shanxi's Sky

Public data shows that every year dust produced from coal mining, coking and power generation activities in Shanxi amounts to approximately 900,000 tons, or nearly six tons per square kilometre. Intensive discharge and unfavourable geographical conditions have resulted in the major cities in the province suffering under a perpetually envelope of "medium" or "heavily" polluted air. Air quality of eleven municipality cities and many county towns are often rated at Grade Three, or Grade Four, or even Grade Five and lower. These are levels which are "fairly" or "extremely" hazardous to human health. Among the country's 30 most polluted cities in 2001, thirteen were from Shanxi. And among the top ten polluted cities in China for 2004, Linfen, Yangquan and Datong were ranked top three, while Changzhi, once among "China's ten cities of charm," was ranked ninth. In 2005, during a nationwide city environment quality evaluation, air quality for nine prefecture cities, including Datong, Yangquan, Lüliang and Linfen, and seven county-level cities, including Gujiao, Jiexiu and Xiaoyi, were rated at Grade Four or lower, accounting for 37 percent of the country's "Grade Three inferior cities."[17]

The provincial capital, Taiyuan, and Linfen, capital of the ancient kingdom of the ruler Yao, are two representative cities. Since 1989, when assessments of overall environmental conditions for 32 major cities in the country were conducted, and for more than ten years thereafter, Taiyuan's air quality has always ranked dead last. The World Bank reported in 1997 that among the world's twenty most polluted cities, ten were in China, and Taiyuan ranked first. As we step into the 21st century, Taiyuan was overtaken by Linfen. During the 1980s, Linfen was a "city of flowers and fruits on the Loess Plateau," well-known in the country, whose fame attracted many foreign visitors. But after the 1990s, rapid development of coal mining, coking and iron industries gave it a new name: the city with the worst air pollution for 2004 and 2005. It was also propelled by such development to the ranks of the world's most polluted cities in 2006.[18] Environment experts once jested, "if you have an enemy, let him live permanently in Linfen!". In 2006, a Taiyuan reporter once described his experience in Linfen in the following terms:

> You walk into a grocery store to buy an ice cream. You leave the store and stand by the roadside, only to find that the naked ice cream is coated with a layer of black soot within minutes. You will not want to wear light-coloured clothes in summer, for you have hard time coping with one washing, or perhaps more, per day. You can only learn of the weather situation, whether sunny, cloudy or overcast, from the weather forecast, because a cloud of grey fog is forever billowed up in the city's sky, obsuring your vision. This is living, the way of life in Linfen.[19]

Needless to say, there is more than one place like this to send your "enemies." In Baode County of northwest Shanxi, three Xinhua Agency reporters recounted what they saw in the spring of 2004, during an on-site investigation with officials of the State Environment Protection Administration (SEPA):

> A troubled-faced old lady told the reporter: "20 years ago, the skies here were exceptionally blue and air particularly fresh. Now, we don't even want to go outdoors in broad daylight. I only long for the arrival of the Lunar New Year. Come New Year, they will go on holiday, and we won't have to cover our noses when we go out. We really have not seen the sun for 20 years!"[...] Many wear a mask when they leave the house; even when standing beside health equipment, some old folks were wearing masks and exercising. A middle-aged woman wheeling a pram told the reporter, "the kid insists on coming out, but the air is really toxic. I heard that our babies here have lungs as black as those smokers out there." [...] A Mr. Yuan told the reporters, "when production is on-going for these two factories, you won't see the sun before ten in the morning, and you cannot tell a sunny day from a cloudy day. On the most serious days, you can't see anything within a few metres. You go in the morning and return at noon, and your nostrils will be all black; even the phlegm which you cough out is black."[20]

Lüliang was a very beautiful city. But its air quality fell to the worst among the eleven major cities of Shanxi in 2006. A recent report described it in the following terms:

Coking industries and resident dwellings enveloping (embracing) development, and the entire Lüliang city seems to be enshrouded within a huge tank armoured with coal dust. Rarely do we see blue skies. The occasional sun was a jumbled sight, enwrapped in dark clouds. Coal dust found its way to every nook [...] inside and outside the house, at the foot of hills and on the treetops, even concealed within the laughing lines on the face [...] the coking plants that fill the city spaces makes the sun as precious as gold.[21]

Air pollution presents an even more breaktaking sight in the various counties and cities under Lüliang's jurisdiction. In January 2007, on their way to Jiaokou County, SEPA inspectors discovered a large quantity of mini-turbine boilers and coking furnaces, which were ordered to be discarded and closed down. "Smoke and soot was rumbling forth, flames were blazing into the sky, visibility was low and the stench was choking," was their description of the sight in Jiaocheng County, Fenyang County and Lishi District located along the freeway. "Fenyang and Xiaoyi are places where coking factories congregate; and the sky looks as if it is encapsulated by a 'grey screen'."[22] In a village called Tianjiagou in Xiaoyi City, a CCTV reporter once recorded her conversation with a six year-old and what she had seen:

"Have you seen stars?"
"No."
"Have you seen white clouds?"
"No."
"How does the air smell?"
"It stinks."
She fanned her hands in front of her nose.

This is the world in the eyes of Wang Hui, a six year-old Shanxi resident. The odour she smells is that of tar. But what is more dangerous is the odourless gas which she cannot smell. This is a highly carcinogenic substance known as benzopyrene, and emissions have exceeded the safety standard by a factor of nine. 50 metres from her classroom is a slope on which stands a coking plant with an annual production of 600,000 tons; opposite the plant, 100 metres away, are two chemical engineering factories. And she has to pass a coal washery on her way home from the classroom. But even at such proximity, she cannot see clearly these huge shops, for visibility is no more than 10 metres.[23]

3. Shanxi's Rivers and Well-Springs
Compared to its rich coal deposits, Shanxi's water resources are extremely scarce. Nonetheless, Shanxi has chosen to "capitalize on its coal abundance to make up for its water shortage" to grow and build wealth.

Annual rainfall in Shanxi ranges between 350 and 700 mm, decreasing from the southeastern to the northernwestern region. Rainfall in the northern region of the province usually fall short of 400 mm, with rainfall in the Sanggan River basin at less than 300 mm. Results of a water resource census carried out some years ago indicated that total water resources in the province amounted to approximately 12.38 billion cubic metres, translating to a per capita amount of 376 cubic metres, one fifth of the nation's average, and lower than the international "standard of severe water shortage" of 500 cubic metres per capita. Water resources available for arable land averaged 192 cubic metres per acreage (per *mu*, or 667 square metres), one ninth of the national average. According to the national water resource index ranking in the *China Sustainable Development Research Report 2000*, published by the Chinese Academy of Social Sciences, Shanxi was ranked 29th. Since the 1980s, Shanxi has been suffering from low rainfall, resulting in continued reduction in the province's total water resources. Between 1980 and 1999, average water resources stood at only 10.2 billion cubic metres, 28 percent lower than the previous 25 years. Calculations in 2006 indicated only 8.85 billion cubic metres of water resources available for the year,[24] or a per capita average of 262 cubic metres, losing another 30 percent from the census figure many years ago.

Reduction of water resources is due to reduction of net water volume in, and perhaps even the drying up of rivers. Between 1982 and 1992, 1993 and 1996, and 1997 and 2001, were three periods during which the instream flow of rivers in the entire province fell by 59.3 percent, 21 percent and 52 percent respectively. Looking at the situation of the three major rivers in the province, the Fenhe, Qinhe, and Sanggan rivers, as early as the late 1980s, a writer noted, "[b]etween 1949 and the 1980s, most of Fenhe River's tributaries have dried up; likewise water in more than half the springs." And in the most recent ten years, water volume in the three rivers fell by 44.8 percent, 48.9 percent and 13.4 percent, respectively, from their long-time averages; the Fenhe and Sanggan rivers actually dried up for as long as 270 to 320 days per year. And the Yuhe River, the largest in Datong, "had abundant water historically, but not a drop is seen even during flood periods in recent years, and downstream river courses are relegated to car parks or driving practice centres."[25]

The rivers are not alone, for the wells and springs too are attenuating and drying up. There are a total of nineteen karst springs in Shanxi. Actual volume measured during the period 1956 to 1984 was 2.93 billion cubic metres, and the volume fell to 1.95 billion cubic metres between 1985 and 1996. Three had completely dried up several years ago, two were near to drying up, and twelve had decreased instream flow.[26] As a result of coal mining and ground water extraction at the Xishan coal mine in Taiyuan, water flow from the renowned "Evergreen Spring" (*Nanlaoquan*) in the Jin Temple complex (*Jin Ci*) has been drastically reduced, plunging from 2 cubic metres per second during the 1950s to 0.54 cubic metres during the 1980s; by the 1990s, the figure was reduced to 0.26 cubic metres. And, in April 1994, the spring dried up completely. Water flow for Shentou Spring, an important water source for Shuozhou city, has also reduced from its peak of 9.28 cubic metres per second to 4.45, leading to the fall in the instream flow of the Sanggan River. The Sanggan River's water flow fell from ten cubic metres per second during the 1960s to five in the 1990s; its water flow fell further to three in the new millennium. Reduction in water flow has also resulted in the reduction of the river's irrigation area by more than 100,000 acres.[27]

There is something that lies behind this attenuation of the horde of well-springs, and it is the intensive extraction of groundwater leading to a fall in the water table. In 1971, groundwater consumption for the entire province totalled 1.1 billion cubic metres; by 2006, the figure had swelled to two billion cubic metres, accounting for 61.5 percent of the province's water consumption; of this figure, 700 cubic metres was attributed to over-extraction. As extraction volume far exceeds recharge volume, the water table falls at a rate of two to three metres per year. Since the 1980s, water tables within Shanxi have fallen by 40 to 300 metres. The five major basins - Datong, Xinding, Taiyuan, Linfen and Yuncheng - have all been subject to over-extraction of groundwater. In Yuncheng and Linfen, attainable well-drilling depth has gone down to 700 or 800 metres, attaining even a kilometre at times.[28]

Water pollution is even more rampant in the province than the reduction of water-bearing volume. Among more than 20 rivers and 100 sections in Shanxi that are subject to regular checks, 80 to 90 percent of the sections were polluted since 2001; among these, 60 to 70 percent have been classified as "Grade Five Inferior," having lost all functional capabilities. More than 80 percent of the province's 1,000 or more rivers are polluted, and 70 percent have lost their functional capabilities.[29] Shanxi now tops the list of Chinese cities in terms of the extent of its water pollution.

We will continue to use the Fenhe River as an example. The largest river and second largest tributary of the Yellow River, the 710 kilometre Fenhe traverses Shanxi in a north-south arc. However, since already the early 1980s, with the exception of the upstream section before the Lancun Reservoir, the river's mid- and downstream sections have been nearly catastrophic, while the Taiyuan and Jiexiu sections have literally become sewage drains. Examinations show that heavy metals such as cadmium, copper and mercury in the Taiyuan section exceed the maximum levels, and average annual level of volatile phenol exceeds the Grade Three standard for surface water by 313 times - thus the name "*Fen*" (phonetically the same as "phenol" in Chinese) for the river, coined by experts. It has been reported that the chief engineer of the Shanxi Environment Protection Bureau even told inspectors to "[f]orget it. What is there to test? It's all polluted water. What is the point of meddling with the alarming numbers? [...] Biologically, this is literally a dead river, with no animal or plant, not even the hardiest algae."[30] During the summer of 1999, a reporter from the China Environment Protection Foundation described the scene on the Fenhe River's mid- and downstream sections so: "[t]he river waters are black and exude a foul stench; either that, or they simply vanish, exposing the river bed...".[31]

By the 21st century, even the upstream sections have become polluted. Tests of 21 river sections carried out in 2003 indicated that only the section at Leimingsi of Xinzhou, located at the river source, met the national Grade Three quality standard for surface water; the other three sections, including the Fenhe Reservoir located in Taiyuan, were under Grade Five. Even worse, the 17 sections located downstream are all classified Inferior Grade Five. By calculating the average concentration of the main pollutants in the 21 sections, concentrations of chemical oxygen demand (COD), volatile phenol, ammonia nitrogen and petroleum exceeded the national Grade Three quality standard for surface water by 2.2 to 36.5 times.[32] And following large scale coking sewage discharge in the mid- and downstream sections, a new phenomenon is detectable: benzopyrene, a highly carcinogenic substance, grossly exceeded the maximum limit. Tests performed in 2005 showed that the substance's average concentration in Linfen exceeded the limit by 196 times, and the highest concentration of which exceeded the limit by 374 times.[33]

The reservoirs, groundwater and well water all suffer from pollution in general. The original intent of the Shanxi Wanjiazhai Yellow River Diversion Project was to resolve the gravity of Shanxi's water shortage problem. After ten years and more than RMB 10 billion, the project was completed in October 2003. However, an inspection conducted in 2005 discovered that Wanjiazhai Reservoir, responsible for delivering water to Taiyuan and even Beijing, contained Inferior Grade Five quality water.[34] And water quality tests conducted in recent years on the Fenhe Reservoir, another important water source in Taiyuan, and on the Cetian Reservoir in Datong (which delivers water via the Sanggan River downstream to the Gongting Reservoir in Beijing), have also discovered that their waters are of Grade Five, therefore, not advisable for human exposure. Penetration of polluted surface waters and coal mining have also led to the degradation of groundwater. For example, coal mining caused Datong's groundwater to increase in mineral concentration and hardness, to the extent that the maximum levels have been exceeded. In certain locations, the concentration of hazardous substances exceeds the limits by as much as 26 times.[35]

4. Shanxi's Lands

With smoke, gas and dust looming from above, irrigated with Inferior Grade Five polluted water for a long time, subject to the the unchecked use of chemical fertilizers and pesticides, Shanxi's lands could not have escaped unscathed by pollution. In fact, land and soil have eventually become the key substrate for different kinds of pollutants.

According to a report published on 14 October 2004 in the *Shanxi Daily*, information in the Shanxi Agricultural Environment Inspection Centre showed that total farmland in the province classified as "seriously polluted" amounted to 1.2 million acres, and that more than 10 million acres were in a "relatively serious" condition. Most of the polluted lands are located in major food and cotton production areas in Taiyuan,

Linfen and Yuncheng. And agricultural and livestock products from these regions have shown the most acute pollution by pesticides, chemical fertilizers and heavy metals. The report did not elaborate what was meant by "serious" or "relatively serious"; however, some inference may be drawn from other pieces of information. A report at the end of the 1980s provided the following: according to tests performed by the Agricultural Environment Inspection Centre, average cadmium and lead levels of all Taiyuan soil exceeds their natural background values by more than twenty times. Water quality tests conducted for seven irrigation ditches in the irrigation areas of the southern suburbs in Taiyuan discovered more than ten types of chemical substances, including phenol, cyanogen, mercury, chromium and fluorine; most heavy metal detection rates exceeded 90 percent, and detection rates of 100 percent were discovered for eight pollutants. For pollutants whose concentrations exceeded the National Standards for Irrigation Water Quality, the situation stood as follows: chromium, 4.8 times; zinc, 5.7 times; total salt, 8.2 times; sulphides, 13.4 times; lead, 28 times; phenol, 102 times; and, based on the highest concentration of mercury detected, 4,169 times.[36]

The safety of crops is naturally compromised if they are cultivated in an environment where the air, water and soil are hazardous. A test carried out at specific points within the polluted irrigation zone in Taiyuan during the 1980s indicated that key detected substances in grains and vegetables were toxic substances or heavy metals, such as phenol, cyanogens, arsenic, as well as chromium and mercury. The detection rate for chromium was 24 percent. "Jin Ci rice," produced in the Jin Ci irrigation zone, contains chromium level equivalent to 20 times that of the "chromium rice" prohibited for consumption in Japan. Detection rate for lead was 75 percent, the highest concentration of which exceeding the maximum limit in foreign countries by fourteen times; mercury was 41 percent and 45 percent in grains and vegetables, the concentration of which exceeds the national limit by several times, and up to more than ten times. Based on tests performed on twenty sample points within the Fenhe River irrigation zone at the southern suburbs of Taiyuan, and looking at grains, vegetables and fruits which contain pollutants exceeding the national food hygienic standards, more than one-quarter of the areas were found to contain excessive quantities of lead, half for mecury, and two-thirds for chromium. Among the different types of agricultural products, the concentrations of mercury in wheat, cucumber and Chinese cabbage; chromium in tomatoes, eggplant, Chinese cabbage and cabbage; and lead and chromium in paddy rice, are classified as "heavily polluting." Many vegetables are also polluted by arsenic, copper and zinc.[37]

The same article cited above from the *Shanxi Daily* reported some results from tests conducted in the new century. The Shanxi Agricultural Environment Inspection Centre conducted sampling tests for 99 samples taken from three types of vegetable sold in 33 markets in eleven cities within the province. The test results were as follows.

Vegetables from the different cities were polluted to different extents. Mercury was "seriously exceeding limits" for some types; heavy metal pollution seemed to be deteriorating. Based on two separate investigations carried out during April to June 2005 by the Shanxi Department of Agriculture and the Taiyuan Bureau of Agriculture, among the 76 samples picked at random at some of the vegetable wholesale markets, supermarkets and production bases in Taiyuan, 45 contained excessive pollutants, and these pollutants exceeded the limit by on average 59.2 percent. Among 28 samples selected from the vegetable production bases in Yanqu County and Qingxu County, eighteen exceeded limits, with an over-limit percentage of 64.3 percent.

The above study indicates that the ecosystem destruction and environmental pollution in Shanxi is systemic, complex and real. It is a systematic and thoroughgoing process. We can better understand the situation by looking from a few perspectives. The first is to see its status relative to the big picture. The China Sustainable Development Strategy Report published annually since 2000 by the CASS showed that Shanxi's ecosystem and environment support systems rank among the last three nationwide; the two systems were ranked last in 2004.[38] Second, we may use the more easily understood words of a leader in Shanxi to summarize the situation: "The mountains and rivers are destroyed. The sight is startling!"[39] Third, a judgment that encompasses these two conclusions, and which forewarns devastation: some areas no longer hold the possibility of life sustenance. A recent report disclosed that the ecological and natural environment of the Datong mining zone have been rated by environment authorities as "no longer possess[ing] basic conditions for the survival of human beings."[40]

II. DISASTER DISTRIBUTION: ANOTHER KIND OF INEQUALITY

Economic parameters such as "direct economic losses" and "green GDP" may be used to measure part of the consequences of the environmental challenges in Shanxi. Research organizations and researchers in Shanxi have already made some effective inroads. For example, the Shanxi Coal Industry Sustainable Development Policy Research Group calculated the losses incurred from coal mining. Between 1978 and 2003, total coal production in Shanxi was 6.53 billion tons; losses incurred as a result of environment pollution and ecological destruction amounted to RMB 398.8 billion.[41] Studies by the Shanxi Social Science Academy showed that, at present, financial losses due to environmental pollution account for approximately 15 percent of provincial GDP.[42] If we take the results of the latter study to derive the losses incurred in 2006 due to environmental pollution, the amount will be RMB 71.2 billion, or 116 percent of the aggregate income of the province's entire rural population. In other words, the losses are greater than the GDP growth of the province's entire rural population.

However, a substantial part of the consequences of such a war are immeasurable by economic standards, and cannot be translated into monetary terms. For example, non-economic parameters such as scars, disasters, adversities, or the pain, torture, struggle, fear, anger, and even hopelessness suffered every day. These are part of life, emotions and humanity, and symbolize the moral qualities of a society, system and civilization. These are qualities which can only be experienced and discerned, and cannot be "calculated."

It may be important to perceive the problem from this angle, but it hardly suffices. This should not be the focus of a sociologist. My focus is rather: the "losses" and "disasters" brought on by environment war and their distribution, and if such "distribution" or "allocation" is in line with the allocation of wealth.

Strictly speaking, even if all members of a society eventually share the fruits of long-term economic growth, they will also have to pay for the price of that growth, including the adverse consequences of long-term degradation of the ecological environment. A sandstorm will not bypass Zhongnanhai if it hits Beijing, and the government officials located there, including "Party and State leaders," may just become victims as well. However, what may seem to be an "objective and complete" understanding has not touched on the crux of the problem. As revealed by the many findings of environment studies in the west and in Japan, and as in the case where growth does not translate into equal distribution of income or wealth, the "allocation" of calamities brought forth by environmental degradation is not equal. Such allocation has a clear differentiation by the "level of fitness" biologically and sociologically; in it there are differences of class and even race at work.[43] Study of the local distribution of such disasters is important not only for the study of social justice in China, it also provides the key to comprehending the impetus necessary to overcoming the country's ecological crisis. This is because the distribution of environmental calamities necessarily determines the different levels of understanding, or the "sense of pain" on the general "eco-crisis," by different groups and classes; this understanding in turn influences their actions, eventually affecting the results of crisis management and the direction that the crisis will take; that is, whether it eases up, "maintains steady," or whether the situation continues to deteriorate.

Of course, it is difficult to measure the distribution of disasters the way we quantify the distribution of wealth and poverty; that is, disasters cannot be divided into "five equal portions," and neither can we use the "Gini coefficient" as a parameter[44] for their measurement. Part of the reason is because a "disaster" is subjective and social in nature, and therefore difficult to measure. The other reason is that there can be no complete and methodical investigation; or, if there were any investigation, it is difficult to obtain investigative results. The only possibility is to interpret and analyze fragmented results, to determine the geographical distribution of disaster zones, as well as the distribution of the key social groups.

1. Distribution of Disaster Zones

(1) Social and Geographical Characteristics of Serious Disaster Areas
The Shanxi Environmental Protection Bureau designed an "Environment Improvement Project Plan for Major Cities and Major Areas" in 2005, selecting eleven major city

planning zones and 51 counties (cities, districts) where there is "greater industrial concentration, more serious pollution and greater public concern" for environment improvement.[45] We may infer that the areas selected as "major" are regions where ecosystem destruction and environment pollution are serious, and, to a great extent, areas with a high concentration of disasters. This implies that a large area is affected: eleven major city planning zones means that all the urban areas of eleven prefecture cities are included; 51 county-level cities and districts represent 43 percent of the province's 119 counties and cities. If the fifteen or so "urban zones" (*chengqu*) under the major city planning zones are included, this percentage would be 55 percent instead. To take it one step further, if "greater industrial concentration" and "greater public concern" are the prerequisites for the major areas where improvements are to be made, then the area involved may be even bigger. Experience has shown that many areas heavily inflicted by disasters may not be areas where industries congregate, and where the polluting sources are located externally. The "public" who are not familiar with polluting sources may not show "concern" in a manner that sufficiently arouses the government's notice.

Aside from simply looking at the size of the disaster area, we should also be concerned with the distribution of such serious disaster areas based on their administrative and socio-geographical characteristics. The aforesaid "Plan" of the Shanxi Environment Protection Bureau may have listed two characteristics – "greater industrial concentration" and "greater public concern" – but they are ill-defined. My guess is that although "medium" or "heavy" pollution generally occurs in medium-sized and large cities, if we were to look at the entire province, from large or medium-sized cities, small towns and townships, to villages, we would find there is increasing eco-destruction and environmental pollution throughout.

This conclusion has two key bases, both of which are related to cities being the centres of power and their natural advantage. First of all, urban environment governance is the "most important priority" for environment departments of all levels. The fact that most "environment protection efforts" have yet to "go rural" means that rural areas become the dead nooks for pollution prevention and control efforts, and heavens for polluting industries. Secondly, urban areas are better equipped for disaster prevention and treatment than rural areas, which implies that rural areas are susceptible to harm. We shall look at the issue from three perspectives as follows:

Air pollution. For years, the air quality of eleven prefecture cities has been rated Grade Three or lower. Many cities have been in SEPA's pollution discharge rankings. However, this does not necessary imply that the situation in county cities and villages that have not been checked regularly is any better than that in the urban areas of prefecture-level cities. New reports have shown that the air quality of many county-level areas, especially villages, is worse. Take Yuncheng's Hejin city for example: in December 2002, air quality tests conducted over the 210 square kilometre area surrounding the operations of Daxing Group, a large coking enterprise, discovered that many pollutants were "seriously over limit." During the first half of 2003, there were more than nine weeks in Hejin during which the air quality was lower than Grade Five. If air quality is lower than Grade Five, "the area would be unfit for inhabitation by human beings. The public were extremely dissatisfied because of the poor environment quality. Thus, there has been no more publication of local air quality weekly reports since July."[46] Especially benzopyrene, recognized internationally as one of the most formidable carcinogens, is found to exceed the maximum limit by six to 55 times in all eleven surveillance sites, and so much so that the locals said that "one would rather stay in Xia County for one year, but not in Hejin for a day."[47] Villages with chemical factories and coking plants would experience "thick smoke rumbling," "sky-blazing flames" and "pungent and choking" odours, bespeaking not only the unsuitability for living, but even for a stay.

Water pollution. Seriously polluted areas are of course located at river sections where environment agencies have rated their water qualities as Inferior Grade Five. Generally, the situation is more serious on sections located along cities or industrial areas; downstream sections are worse than those upstream. Nonetheless, these are sections where "scientific tests" have been conducted. Many rivers in villages, especially small ponds and ditches, were not checked. The impression of "black and smelly" drawn merely from sight and smell, without using any scientific means, should suffice to conclude that they could be of "Inferior Grade Five." To take this one step further, sewage has a different relationship with rural and urban areas; as such, both areas fall victim to pollution differently. Urban residents may stay far away from sewage, as domestic water used is "tapwater" that has been treated to some extent. Rural residents, however, use the same water for irrigation and drinking. The use of polluted water is closely woven into their daily living. According to official data published by Shanxi, nearly half the rural population in Shanxi use "unsafe" drinking water.[48]

Mining-Induced Ecological Disasters. Mining-induced eco-disasters are mainly found in villages where underground mining is carried out. A small number of towns and townships may be involved, but medium-sized and large cities are excluded. This is because underground mining in larger cities is usually prohibited or subject to stringent controls. The same activities in villages are usually carried out in private and without control. As mentioned earlier, as at 2004, geological disasters caused by mining activities have afflicted more than 1,900 villages and 2.2 million people. Of course, mining-induced destruction of water resources does affect cities more. Reports have indicated that fourteen of Shanxi's 22 cities, and 42 of its 91 country-level cities, have been affected. Still, the most severely affected are rural areas, including as many as 8,503 villages and a rural population of 4.96 million people.[49] This number represents nearly 80 percent of the affected population size.

(2) Areas of High Disease Incidence

There is data indicating that there are at least three environmental pollution-related diseases for which Shanxi is a high incidence area, with perhaps the highest rate of incidence in the country.

The first is cancer. A report in 2005 revealed that, "Shanxi's cancer incidence is higher than the national average, and many 'strange diseases' appeared in major disaster areas."[50] An article printed on 22 April 2007 in the *Taiyuan Daily* reported that in recent years, the Shanxi Tumor Hospital alone has been receiving as many as 200,000 cancer patients,[51] among whom 20 percent suffered from lung cancer. Based on statistics published by the relevant departments, Shanxi's number one cancer has been lung cancer for the last ten years.

The second is pneumoconiosis. A report printed in the *China Youth Daily* in 2002 stated that "serious air pollution has put Shanxi in the number four ranking in the country, in terms of the number pneumoconiosis patients." This is in stark contrast to its population size (which ranks nineteenth in the country). And, according to investigations made by the Shanxi General Labour Union, between 1990 and 2002 the aggregate number of new pneumoconiosis patients diagnosed was more than 36,000, one one-thousandth of the province's population size, and the highest among all Chinese provinces. Aggregate deaths resulting from the illness were more than 8,000, and the mortality rate was 23 percent.[52]

The third is birth defects. The Ministry of Health implemented the "China Birth Defect Surveillance" program as part of the national science and technology project of the seventh five-year plan. Results of the project indicated that the national total birth defect incidence rate was 9.96 per thousand births, the highest in the world. The country was hence called the world's "Mount Everest" for birth defects. Yet, Shanxi's rate of birth defects is twice the national average. Its 18.99 per thousand rate of birth defect incidence makes it the highest in the country. Retrospective investigation carried out by the province in 1997 indicated that the total incidence rate for birth defects was 18.65 per thousand. This was a figure close to that found five years ago.[53] If we calculate based on approximately 500,000[54] new births per year in Shanxi during the 1990s, the number of newborns with birth defects would exceed 9,000.

Of course, any disease with a high incidence rate is not equally distributed within the province. Certain regions are more notable than others. Existing information mentioned the situations in the following counties and cities[55]:

- "Now, the incidence of cancer in Linshi is increasing multifold."
- "The incidence for cancer as well as its death rate in Yanquan is increasing every year. Cancer death rate is number two in China."
- "According to an investigation in 1997, 37 percent of the people in Taigu and Zuoquan suffer from respiratory diseases; rate of incidence of aesophageal cancer and lung cancer is three percent."
- "Hejin is a region of high incidence of respiratory diseases and pneumonia."
- "Lishi has a high incidence of respiratory and digestive diseases. Investigations discovered that this phenomenon is directly related to the congregation of coking factories, heavy air pollution and poor groundwater quality in the area."

There is some fairly detailed information concerning the concentration and distribution of birth defects. A report from the end of 1980 revealed that in nearly a hundred villages in five townships along the Fenhe River in Qingxu County, "the rate of deformed births in recent years averages between 45 and 50 per thousand." Among these, the rate in the village of Bokui is 408 per thousand. The most common deformity is *spina bifida*, a congenital defect in which the spinal column is imperfectly closed such that part of the meninges or spinal cord protrudes. The lower limbs are limp, and the patient is unable to stand erect. Also, the number of mentally impaired children is also increasing.[56] A report in 2002 said that in certain mining areas, the rate of birth defects is as high as 44 per thousand.[57] An epidemiological study carried out by the Beijing Pediatric Research Institute in Zhongyang County and Jiaokou County in the Lüliang mountain areas between 2000 and 2004 showed that birth defects in these two areas were as high as 71.8 per thousand and 91.7 per thousand,[58] i.e. between seven and nine newborns out of a hundred are defective births.

The results of an investigation by researchers at the Shanxi Medical University on the state of health of primary school students indicated the distribution for a few types of respiratory diseases: among 203 students near a Tufa Coking Zone, 137 or 67.8 percent suffered from rhinitis, 176 or 86.8 percent suffered from pharyngitis, and 174 or 85.7 percent had tonsillitis. The relative percentages of 208 students, a control group in a different area, are 4.9 percent, 24.1 percent and 1.1 percent. The white blood counts of the same students from the Tufa Coking Zone are also worse than those from the control group.[59]

Owing to a lack of clear information about relevant diseases in Taiyuan, the province's political and economic centre, and from the other ten prefecture cities, we are unable to obtain a clear picture of the distribution in the entire province. However, from the above information, we may roughly deduce that the distribution of the relevant diseases is skewed towards the rural areas in the county and county-level cities, and lower. Also, news reports from recent years about Shanxi's environment problems and the high incidence of diseases often mention specific villages (see references). These reports seem to verify the conclusions of this study. In fact, the exceptionally high incidence of certain special diseases in the rural areas, disasters resulting from the environmental war, is related to the fact that pollution in certain rural areas is more serious than in the urban areas as a whole, as explained above; it is also related to the fact that most rural residents are forgotten by effective medical security systems, and to their lack of the capacity and means of self-protection.

Reports on Shanxi Villages with High Incidence of Diseases

- Since 1980, 17 people in Nanyan Village, located in the southern suburbs of Taiyuan, have died of cancer. Ten deformed births, eight still births, and five abnormal births occured. (Mai Tianshu, 1989)

- Since 2001, when a refractory brick factory lit its first fire in Zhuang Village of Yuejia in Chakou Township, Pingding County, the villagers have been living among dust, noise and waste gases, and oftening choking and suffocating, and feeling giddy and nauseous. Many villagers suffer from gastrointestinal disorders, respiratory diseases, cerebrohaemorrhage, cerebral infarction, and other infliction. (*Xinhua Daily Telegraph*, 19 September 2005)
- In 1998, 190 goats in Wujunsi Village in Tongyu Township, Zuoquan County died as a result of drinking waste water discharged from the town's papermaking factory; ten people in the same village died due to water pollution within the same year. Due to heavy pollution of well water, most inhabitants in Shiluomen Village of Wugong Township in Taigu County have left their village to find a livelihood in another location. The village's farmland of 750 acreages has been left barren. (Jiao Ruilian *et al.*, 2000)
- In recent years, 60 villages in Linshi County had to drill 25 deep wells, driven by drinking water deprivation as a result of pollution in the Fenhe River. But tests have indicated that hardness of water in the wells was 519 times in excess of the standards, sulphides were thirteen times over limit [...] And cancer incidence rate in Linshi nowadays increase multifold. (Mai Tianshu, 1989)
- Affected by pollution from the Zhuozhang River, more than ten thousand inhabitants living in Xiangyuan, Pingshun and Licheng counties located along the river were found to have a significant increase of incidence rate of gastrointestinal diseases and cancer. (*China Water Resource News*, 28 July 2000)
- In Beilu Village of Liucun Town in Yaodu District, Linfen, abnormal illnesses continued to emerge, as a result of clusters of highly-polluting enterprises mushrooming in the vicinity. More than 200 people have suffered from such illnesses. More than twenty cancer patients have died during the recent years, the oldest being older than 50, the youngest only fourteen. (Zimin, 2005)
- At Xiakang Village in Duandian Township in Raodu District, many suffer from malignant illness, such as paralysis. This is how the name "The Village of the Cripples" came about. More than 50 people have suffered from paralysis due to cerebral thrombosis; nearly twenty have died in 2004. The little village streams and wells are polluted. The villagers said, "The water in the well tastes either salty or bitter. Drink it, and you suffer from diarrhea." (*Shanxi Youth Daily*, 15 June 2006)
- Around 1999, a huge congregation of coking plants congregated in Duizhu Town of Fenxi County. A strange phenomenon appeared on the scene, together with the coking plants: for many successive years, no one from the town joined the army. And the reason was because no young man of age managed to pass his physical examination. (*Shanxi Youth Daily*, 15 June 2006)
- Water in several wells in Chenguo Village of Chengguan Township, Xiangfen County was found to contain hexavalent chromium at levels nearly 100 times

higher than the maximum limit. The results are an annual progressive increase in incidence rates of diseases; health conditions deteriorating, aches in backs and legs, grey hair at a young age, skin diseases, and cancer. The taste and odour of well waters in the villages nearby were also found to have turned bad. (Gao Aizhi *et al.*, 2000)

- Near Taixing Group's coking plant in the city of Hejin stands Yin village. There, "Many little kids suffer from pneumonia and tracheitis." Dust discharged by the coking plants fall on the maize, wheat and padi rice. Crops are prevented from pollinating, and harvests are drastically reduced. (*Market News*, 22 June 2004)
- Many in Chenliuzhuang in the Gujiao Township of Xinjiang County suffer from aching legs in recent years. The village's air is often filled with the foul odour of the Fenhe River; villagers have to travel far to obtain drinking water. (CCTV, "Sannong Focus" (*jujiao Sannong*), 11 July 2005)
- Due to water pollution, the villagers in Niudu Village of Linyi County, Yuncheng City have been suffering from cerebral thrombosis, paralysis and cancer in recent years. The numbers are increasing every year, and most patients are between 40 and 60. In their complaint letters, the villagers said that, by June 2004, 42 have already died of abnormal diseases, and another 28 are suffering from abnormal diseases. (*Ban Yue Tan*, 28 June 2005)
- In recent years, an increasing number of people in Nanzhiguang Village in Meiyang Town of Liyi County are suffering from abnormal diseases. Some who are in their prime years have lost all capacity to work, and young people suffer from growth impairment. Many villagers in Dijiaying Village are inflicted with different types of cancer, and villagers generally do not live beyond the age of 50. Other villages suffering from a similar phenomenon include nearby villages as Qirenzhuang and Xizhiguang. In Xu Village, a seventh-level township in the county, no young man from the entire village could join the army because of failure to pass the physical examination. Many middle aged and older villagers suffer from abnormal diseases. Among the 79 households inhabiting Chengzilei Village of Kaizhang Town, Yongji City, just next to the downstream Sushui River, 72 suffered from diseases. Among them, many suffered from leukaemia and aesophageal cancer. (http//tangyuanhh. bokee.com/1866573.html; http://www.sxrtv.com, 12 May 2005; http://blog. sina.com.cn/hanzhenyuan)
- The existence of illegal enterprises and pollution has led to the successive deaths of persimmon trees in a certain village in Caochuan Town of Pinglu County. The village suffered from reduced or even no harvest. Some diseases continue to threaten the lives of the villages, the most prominent of which being myocardial infarction and cerebral thrombosis. (CCTV, "Half-Hour Economy" (*Jingji Ban Xiaoshi*), 14 April 2007)

2. Disaster Distribution by Groups and Social Strata

As a result of the lack of statistics from systematic investigations, there is a lot of difficulty detailing the distribution of ecological disasters in Shanxi among the different occupation groups and social strata. Here, we will combine deductions based on observations and case studies to illustrate the level at which disaster has befallen the main groups and strata, and to discover the overall distribution trend.

(1) Government Officials and Entrepreneurs: Geographical Differentiation Versus Level of Affliction.

Generally, the ecological destruction and environment degradation of the overall environment of Shanxi should affect all its inhabitants, from ordinary farmers and townspeople, to intellectuals, big and small entrepreneurs and senior officials. However, the probability of exposure to areas with degrading ecosystems differs among people located at different geographical locations, and among people with different occupational backgrounds and political, economic and social status; the types of pollutants inhaled are different, likewise the abilities to respond to and overcome the crises vary. Based on the ecological degradation and environmental destruction in Shanxi, we will explore the relevant conditions of a few major groups: 1) government officials; 2) entrepreneurs; and 3) farmers living in heavily polluted areas.

Government officials and entrepreneurs living in a city with polluted skies may breathe suffocating air; but power and financial resources enable them to live in staff residences, estates for senior officials or "high-class residences," as they are promoted by developers and advertisers. The air may not be fresh, but at least no apparent source of pollution is present. They do not have to be subject to irritating chemical odours throughout the day, as do residents living in the periphery of coking or chemical plants. Their mode of transportation is the car, instead of the bicycle or public transport. They do not need to wind down the window for ventilation if they do not wish to, and they do not need to cover their noses faced with the dust and waste gases outside the window. They move around mainly in spaces with air conditioning, such as offices, meeting rooms, restaurants, hotels, instead of having to stand beside blazing coking furnaces, around which dust is afloat, or in the wilderness and farmhouse courtyards where pungent smoke and gas fill the air. All this is rather different from life for the "coal bosses." All in all, the differentiation of their living space from that of "general society," and of moving and activity spaces from the "normal natural" spaces, enables them to stay far away from heavily polluted areas and avoid harm.

If the river is black and stinks, the government officials and entrepreneurs will be affected; at the very least, they lose aesthetic enjoyment, like that from scenic spots and swimming in its water. Nonetheless, they have enough substitutes: they can swim at a commercial swimming pool or relax and entertain themselves at a sauna club. Looking at a black river that exudes a foul stench does bring physical and mental discomfort.

However, these people are free to look away. And even the small minority who "must look" because of responsibilities are not perpetually faced with it all the time, as are residents living along the river. The river bank inhabitants face dramatically reduced or even zero harvests.

Furthermore, the victims of coal mining accidents were neither government officials nor entrepreneurs. Those who perished in mining accidents were always "migrant workers"; not-government cadres or coal bosses. Government officials and entrepreneurs are not confronted with the problems of having cracks in their houses, drying up rivers and wells, and caving-in of lands; they do not live in constant fear; and they do not become true-blue environment refugees (see below).

Of course, as mentioned earlier, this does not negate the fact that these two advantaged groups will not be able to completely escape unscathed. They will be affected, either directly or indirectly, if the air is bad, tap water of low quality, and if numerous "unknowns" exist in the quality and safety of agricultural products. However, this for them is only a necessary price which they pay for driving or inducing "development." The price they pay for the outstanding "political performance" and enormous financial returns is negligible. This implies that to government officials and entrepreneurs, the more generally defined eco-crisis means only temporary discomfort; at the very most, it is "trouble" that will be eventually resolved. In sum, they are positioned in the centre of the "circle of benefit" and at the periphery of the "circle of harm."[60] To the rest of the people, these same ill effects may be a perpetual torment, probably a disaster from which they have no idea how to escape, or in which they are trapped for the rest of their lives. Or perhaps, the next generation is ensnared into the same turmoil of pain emerging from biological or social processes. For the next section, we turn our attention to farmers, inhabitants of areas that are heavily polluted and where ecological destruction is serious. We shall examine the state of the lives of this group inhabiting the periphery of the "circle of benefit" and the centre of the "circle of harm."

(2) Victims of Depression Areas (Areas with Mining-Induced Subsistence)
It is difficult to draw a conclusion about the living conditions of farmers living in highly polluted and depression areas using social science terminology. What the author has done here is take cases from some recent news reports in order to try to provide an objective description of how they live:

> In the vicinity of the villages of Ganting and Li of Ganting Township, Hongdong County, the Shanxi Fenhe Bio-Chemical Company plant (one of the city of Linfen's "key protection enterprises") was constructed in 2000, and production commenced in 2002. There was no sewage discharge facility, and the sewage discharged into the Fenhe River via the drains carried an unbearably foul stench. Windows of every household are firmly closed even on warm nights, and the

floating dirt and soot are woven into a thick blanket of dust, covering crops that stretch over miles in radius. Finding it intolerable, the angry villagers organized a meeting with the plant, demanding that the pollution discharge be stopped. The company was compelled to install sewage treatment facilities; these however only operate during inspection tours by their superiors and the relevant authorities. Massive discharge of sewage is carried out in the night, and villagers live in constant torment of the revolting odour. (Zhang Hong *et al.*, 2005)

About 500 metres outside the compound of Li Aixian, a villager of the Ji village of Jingmao Township, Xiangfen County, thick yellow smoke is emitting from a coking plant and shooting skywards; thereafter, it dissipates into the surroundings. "It can choke you to death," Li lamented. The biting odour pays its visit to the Li family almost every day, and clothes that are left hanging to dry in the courtyard would be quickly coated with a layer of black soot. The water tank may be covered, but a layer of black powder on the water surface and at the bottom of the tank would still be discernible. For five years, since the coking plant commenced production, strange phenomena have appeared in the village: some villagers would suffer from occasional giddiness and nausea; jujube trees would only flower but would not bear fruits. Apples would be clothed in "black armour"; they would all be cut down, and their master could only squat at a side, lamenting, "Now they've chopped all my trees, and why are they not paying a cent as compensation?". (*Shanxi Youth Daily*, 15 June 2006)

Since four years ago, when a large coking facility of the Shanxi Zhonglü Coking Co. found a home in the village of Xiaogaojiagou, the nights that used to be crystal clear are now as inaccessible as their dreams to the 700 or so families in the village. The entire village is permeated with a barbed stinkiness, and people struggle with adversity amidst the stench. "You don't know how it bites, like rotten eggs. No one can breathe at all!", a 50 year-old women said, covering her nose with her hands, even when production is already semi-halted, yet she still seemed to be smelling the stench which she cannot evade and which gives her a splitting headache. "When the power fails, you can't see anything but a white expanse of smoke. The dust is formidable too. You go out wearing a white outfit, and it turns into a black outfit within an hour." (Zhao Xiaojian, 2007)

These three scenarios depict the situation of polluted villages located at the vicinity of coking and chemical plants. We are not sure how many such villages there are in Shanxi, and how many farmers live in them. In comparison, what is apparent is the condition of villagers and farmers located at "serious geological disaster areas": as at 2004, this accounted for more more than 1900 villages, with a farming population of 2.2 million. A recent issue of the *China Youth Daily* reported the details of the total caving-in of a village.[61] Called the Da'antou village, it is located on Kele Hill, approximately twenty kilometres northeast of Jincheng City. During the "Learn from Dazhai in agriculture"[62] campaign, the village was a national model for its high productivity of cotton. Li Yin, an ex-Party Branch Secretary, was twice received by Prime Minister Zhou Enlai. When the extraction machine of a mine drilled into Kele Hill in the spring of 2003 to dig beneath the village, it was also the beginning of its physical and social downfall. This is an exceptionally precious specimen of the ruins left in the wake of the environmental war. As the author has already given an in-depth account of the situation, the rest of this section consists of material already published; the original text is simply reorganized and certain parts deleted to avoid excessive interpretation and analysis.

As early as the summer in 2003, the villagers would start getting busy. Work stopped; no one bothered with work in the fields; few men drank or gambled; women no longer gossiped. People scurried around in the village with only one purpose in mind: find a house which they can make do, a shelter for the family living in constant terror. People are always moving in and out. Many pieces of luggage and packages are not even opened, as they are prepared to be move at any time. Some families are broken up and installed in different households, others don't eat and sleep at the same place. Those who really could not find shelter would simply leave the village. Since 2003, only twenty percent of the households in Da'antou village have never moved. More than a hundred houses in the the village are damaged; half are new homes, and 70 percent of them are not habitable.

Soon after, cracks appeared in the cave dwelling in which Wang Yuzhen's family made its home. Although courageous by nature, she started living in horror. "I was afraid when it rained. I was also afraid to sleep." When the rain was heavy, she would not dare even lie down; she would either sit up, or drag her husband along to find somebody else's house in which to stay, returning home only after the sun came out. Almost every night, she would tweak her ears to listen for any commotion in the house. Sometimes, she would suddenly sit up, and start checking around the house. "A few times, I dreamt that the house collapsed, and I was buried alive." She even hoped at times that the cave dwelling would quickly collapse. That way, she no longer needed to be bothered by its impending implosion [...] The three room cave dwelling which had been seizing Wang Yuzhen in terror finally collapsed in May 2004 during a rainstorm. Startled, her husband fell ill, and she had to take her husband along to look for shelter. She found one, after much effort, but it was also in imminent danger of falling after a while. She once again had to go house-hunting. Many turned her away, "fearing that it was inauspicious having an old man at home." Eventually, the head of the town came forward to mediate, and she moved into the village committee's old office. But her husband died only a few days afterwards. "The old man said he wanted to die at home before he gasped his last breath," she said. To treat him, she spent nearly all her savings. But when he died, "I couldn't find even a place to put his coffin," said Wang.

Wang Yuzhen's paranoia is not rare. Chen Xiao suffered from more severe symptoms. She always left the light switched on at night, and slept fully dressed, waiting for the moment when she would have to flee for her life. That September, when she was about to lie down, the sound of cracking glass left her panic stricken. She stood at the balcony, crying the entire night. One month or so later, she moved into her husband's elder brother's house. But she finally fell ill, after the many scares. She often felt dizzy and palpitations, and weak; sometimes she would faint. She spent between five and six thousand yuan in medical treatment, but saw little improvement. Chen Xiao's two-storey house was built in 2000. Today, the walls are filled with cracks, and the building is obviously slanted. The house's main door and courtyard are now completely overrun with weeds.

Li Xiaozhi, the village doctor, can no longer recall how many times he has changed homes. His two-storey house was only completed in 2002, but was no longer fit for habitation after one year. In April 2004, Li and his wife changed houses for the first time. Nine months later, even the temporary shelter became a dangerous structure. They had to move for the second time. Not long after, they had to move again. By then, all the houses in the village which had not become dangerous were filled with people. Some even had to accommodate three or four families, with more than ten members. The couple had no alternative but to scrounge around for shelter and food, drifting from one house to another, staying for as long as a month, and as briefly as a couple of days. They have slept on the floor, in sheds, and squeezed on brick beds, leading a life of destitution for three months. "This was horrifying guerrilla warfare!", Li said, standing in his desolate courtyard, "A perfect home is now ruined." A young wheat seedling was sprouting in the yard.

Like everyone in the village, Wang Yuzhen is confronted with a mind-boggling problem: the hills are dug empty, and all the water is pumped dry. Water used to run in unrestrained abundance in the mountain streams located at the eastern end of the village. Wang would always wash her clothes there, and the children would frolic there too Now, the river bed has run dry, and the well at the eastern end of the mountain stream no longer oozes water. The well platform is left abandoned, leaving behind only weeds, rubbish and rotten sewage. Only a tiny stream runs in a ravine at the village's west end. During the dry season, this would become the only source of water for the entire village. To fetch a pail of water would require between half and three quarters of an hour. When fetching water, every village family would take out their water containers and specially deploy someone to wait in line. Often, disputes would arise because someone had cut the queue, and a fight among those waiting in the line would ensue.

At this moment, this land is torn apart by deep-set crevices and overwhelmed by weeds. Due to water shortages, economic crops such as cotton and the broom cypress fruit (*saozhoumiao*) no longer thrive. Villagers had to give up their income of approximately RMB 3000 per acreage. As there had been incidents of plough machines being trapped in the crevices and their drivers thrown out, machines which cost more than RMB 4000 became mere display pieces, and farmers had to revert to hoes and spades. The hills are covered with these crevices, and many cracks are hidden among the rough tussocks and thistles; even goatherds who wander frequently on the hills have to stay vigilant, as goats often fall into the cracks.

The houses have become catalysts for more frequent quarrels between husbands and wives. Many have ended up in divorce. Different cliques are formed, and relationships between cliques are increasingly strained. "The general climate in the village has changed; people are increasingly plotting against each other. And hostility seems to come between certain people."

As this village gradually caved in, something else too slipped away. The village committee's old office in which Wang Yuzhen now lives has long been classified dangerous. She did not even have her reunion dinner during this year's spring festival, and no making of *jiaozhi* (a dumping prepared during new year). "With everyone's life now in such mess, who would have thought of making *jiaozhi*?" Outside the house stands a huge courtyard – profuse with weeds, and rubbish abounds – empty; and long gone are the days of song and dance.

For four or five years, no bride has married into Da'antou Village. "The village young men are going crazy, hoping to have a bride." There are almost 30 over-aged men of approximately 30 years of age. "A home does not resemble a home; neither does the village." It is now a lackadaisical village, completely lifeless.

III. WHERE BOTH LAND AND INSTITUTIONS ARE "HOLLOW"

From what has been said thus far, we know that damages and disasters emerging from the war on the environment can take different "directions" because of different degrees of environment degradation and socio-economic complexy. Many adverse consequence have been concentrated on farmers in many rural areas. These farmers, therefore, have become "ecological refugees" or "war refugees." What we shall next examine are the different responses and self-help capabilities of different social groups and strata during ecological crisis. People who are at the periphery of the circle of disasters escape more, while those located at the centre may be entrapped. Let us look at two major groups: the "coal bosses" and farmers in depression areas.

1. Different Migrant Groups
Since 2006, several local media have reported that different classes of "Shanxi house hunting groups" have been buying properties in other provinces.[63] After the Wenzhou house hunters, "Shanxi people" have become the second group going around the country buying housing properties. Some astute real estate property developers from other

provinces used "eco-friendly" as their selling point and set up sales offices at Taiyuan, the provincial capital, and other heavily polluted county-level cities. For example, in Xiaoyi city, a first-tier county-level city, alone, Yintan Real Estate Company from Rushan, Shandong, has set up six agencies. And in Linfen, a prefecture city where air pollution is very serious, agencies of twelve Shandong and Hainan real estate companies have been set up along an over 200 metre long lane lined with coal chemical industries; particularly eye-catching are advertisements such as "National AAA Grade Original Ecology Holiday Resort," "A City Most Suitable for Living," and "A Dream Garden, A Return to Nature, A Health Reservoir."

Most news reports stressed that the Shanxi people buy their houses for a different purpose than their Wenzhou counterparts. They are not speculators who are profit driven, as are the latter; but they instead are "eco-migrants." Reports focused on the *nouveau riches* coal bosses, who have already developed something of a preconceived image. In fact, "coal bosses" have gone extra-provincial house-hunting since a few years ago. The target cities of their migration are mainly major cities, such as Beijing, Shanghai, Guangzhou and Dalian. There was a report that a coal boss once bought all the sun-facing units of an entire block of luxurious flats. At the end of 2005, "a Shanxi group of coal boss house buyers first arrived at Shanghai. Within two days, sixteen units were bought up; after one week, 45 units of a development in Chongqing were purchased." In July 2006, another house hunting group made up of coal bosses with "net worth in excess of RMB 50 million" flew into Shanghai and "snapped up six developments within two days." "Even the youngest coal boss makes four to five million a year. The older ones earn tens of millions, even a hundred. That is why they buy properties as they wish; they buy to stock." Usually, the rest will follow suit when one buys. One of them, called Wei Dong, even said, "this is for the convenience of our mahjong games." Wei's family shifted from the mining district ten years ago. At first, they shifted to Xiaoyi; later, they moved to Taiyuan. He has not been to the mine back in the village for years. His manager manages his coal business, while he concentrates on public relations in Taiyuan. Wei Dong said that he is temporarily staying put in Taiyuan as his child is still young, and that he needs to look after his business in Shanxi. However, "he will want to migrate to Beijing eventually."

Many middle-class "ordinary citizens" echo the somehow exaggerated house-buying spree and migration of the "coal-bosses" by buying housing properties outside their own province. Data indicate that in February 2005, 82 people from Shanxi rushed to buy up four seaside apartment blocks in Rushan, a county governed by Weihai City, Shandong. This was the cause of the moves by the Shandong real estate companies. Business was truly good. A Linfen agent for the Yintan Real Estate Company revealed that weekends are the times where the agents set off to Rushan for house viewing. He said, "The coaches were always filled to the brim. We had to negotiate with clients to delay their viewing." The company sold three to four hundred units shortly after coming to Linfen. "House buyers included doctors, teachers and civil servants. Many purchases were group purchases." A state-owned power plant in Linfen which operates as a monopoly and in a highly polluting industry "just bought 50 units here," he added. According to the agent, at least 2,000 Linfen families have bought homes in Rushan. Reports said that "Linfen people with extra cash would go out and buy properties [...] Most of these people intend these new homes to be their retirement homes. Few buy for investment. A large proportion of the residents bought homes in Weihai, and the families will stay at these homes during festive seasons."

Intra-China and extra-China emigration for Shanxi inhabitants has just begun.[64] At this moment, no one can predict how much the exodus will increase, and if major "braindrain," "capital outflow" or some other unforeseeable outcome will result. Certainly, we need to be concerned. But something else demands concern: the nearly 2,000 villages and the rural population of 2.2 million located at the caved-in mines! If they are "refugees" who do not have the ability of escape from disaster, then what has happened to the Shanxi government's or society's "refugee relief" or "crisis response" mechanisms? Clearly, this is an issue of social justice that goes beyond being simply an ecological environment issues. It involves the minimum rescue capacity of a society when confronted with a large-scale humanitarian disaster.

2. Farmers in Depressed Areas: Walk Out or Wait

The general deterioration of the state of the environment prompted the Shanxi provincial government to launch the Green Water and Blue Sky Project (*bishui lantian gongcheng*) in 2006. The project was launched with a huge impetus and much determination. However, absent was the most critical and urgent element – a "comprehensive" relief package for the eco-environment refugees. Based on existing information, most victims living in the villages of the heavily polluted areas could only deal with the disaster by pushing their resilience. Actions taken through lawful means such as letter writing and visits (*shangfang*), or through extreme means such as barricading roads or blocking river flows or preventing factory production, were often abandoned. A typical case was the blocking of the flow of black water in the Sushui River by the villagers from Chengzilei village in Kaizhang Town of Yongji City.[65] As for economic damages and high incidence rates of diseases clearly attributable to pollution, a uniform mitigating policy is absent.

Shanxi had not enacted any prior policy to address the issue of the areas depressed by mining. However, investigations were carried out in the same year, and the investigation found that there was more than 1,000 square kilometres of coal mining-induced depression in nine major state-owned coal mines. Nearly 600,000 people in more than 170,000 households as well as 71 hospitals and 312 schools were affected. In 2005, the National Development and Reform Commission (NDRC) approved the treatment and rectification plan for the nine depression areas; RMB 6.87 billion was channelled to them; the plan was initiated in 2006 and to be completed within three years.[66]

Such treatment and rectification aim to resolve the housing problem of residents of depression areas. The plan does not include rectification for the destruction of water resources, ecological degradation or land desolation. Based on their level of damage, residences in the depressed areas were divided into four grades, A, B, C and D; reinforcement and reparation subsidies of RMB 67.5 and RMB 135 per square metre will be given to each owner of a Grade A and Grade B house. Urban residents of the latter two categories may move into new estates, whereas rural residents will be allocated RMB 450 per square metre as reconstruction costs. Although an additional compensation land area of 50 square metres per household is also given over and above the RMB 450 per square metre financial compensation, and although such rural housing land (*zhaijidi*) is provided by the government, the level of compensation falls far short of the amount required for the cost of reconstruction on another piece of land. Most importantly, the plan included only the "nine depression areas of major state-owned coal mines," which means that "local mines" were excluded from the plan. Based on the implementation of this policy, we shall explore the overall disaster relief mechanism by studying the following cases in four villages.[67]

The Da'antou Village of Yangcheng County

When the housing problem emerged, the villagers had repeatedly reported the problem to the cadre members of the village and township and to the Sihe Mine, hoping to find some means of mitigation. But the Sihe Mine maintained that compensation in excess of RMB 4 million had been paid to the village. The villagers then turned to the village cadres, approaching the village Party branch secretary for compensation. Some received financial compensation; some of those whose homes were basically undamaged but which were determined to be dangerous structures received compensation; while some others received nothing. "Those who received compensation were basically those who had a close relationship with the village Party branch secretary."

After the collapse of her cave-dwelling, Wang Yuzhen would find time to "work" in town. She went to the town government to speak to the official in charge, to find out what she should do in the future, and what the villagers should do, but to no avail. After the collapse of her house, the village committee and the mine had deployed personnel to inspect the site of the collapse, but no one told her what she should do in the future. She also did not receive any compensation. Wang said, "I have been running around for years, and I know that my efforts might be futile. But I cannot think of any other way out, except to seek audience with the government time and again." Some said that there were instances in which all the people of a village move as a group. But they were still moving within the depression areas. No one knows when another problem might emerge one day. Others said that new problems surface after moving out, such as the farmland issue that remains unresolved. "It's been so long. It's about time that the government comes up with a solution," she said.

Haojiazhai village, located in Xiaoyi city under the jurisdiction of Lüliang city
Haojiazhai village was originally called Goudi. In 1979 and 1986, the villagers were moving to the hills when sinking in Goudi village was getting serious. The original Goudi village became a place of ruins where weeds and long grass luxuriantly grew. Water in the Duizhenhe River, a river that flows past the village, is also getting black, and villagers call it "*heilongjiang*"("*hei*" means "black" in Chinese). For more than two years, the number of mines has been multiplying, and the amount of mining activities has been increasing. Now made up of "New Villages" (*xincun*) and "New New-Villages" (*xinxincun*), Haojiazhai is seeing a worsening of its sinking in recent years. Even the "*heilongjiang*" has dried up.

In early 2002, the villagers initiated an appraisal by the Mining Damage Technical Appraisal Committee of the China Coal Society, and the results of the appraisal showed that the damages to the houses were due to the surrounding mining activities. From then on, there had been unending conflicts between the villages and the private mine at the foot of the hill. Previously a collectively owned mine in Haojiazhai village, the mine was sold to a private owner by the village administrator. Thereafter, the villagers were subject to actions of reprisal whenever they sought out the mine or when they complained to the government. A villager called Hao Hualin reported to the provincial government's committee of the CCP during mid-September 2005. One month later, on 21 October, five to six strangers climbed over his garden wall and entered his house in the middle of the night. They forced open his bedroom door, and beat up Hao and his mother. Both suffered from bone fractures. Hao wanted to call for help from the villagers, but his phone line was cut, and the garden gate was sealed with iron wires. He did not know who the mastermind was, but the village administrator sent someone to deliver RMB 6,000 for him.

Now, Haojiazhai is preparing for another collective house-moving. A notice of "House Construction Agreement" newly posted by the village committee said that RMB 516.38 per square metre must be paid for newly constructed houses. The new village will be located at Yugou, a subsidence area two miles away. There are two closed down black coal mines; before they closed, mining activities were carried out day and night for five to six years. The land was long hollowed out. The village administrator decides where to move, without discussing it with the villagers. The village administrator operates coal mines in other places, and his family long ago moved to Xiaoyi. He would use a mobile phone to give instructions to the village committee. Only half the villagers remain. The younger ones who could work left; the remaining ones waiting to move are the old and the the weak. The village primary school shut down due to reduced enrolment, and this had expedited the villagers' exodus.

Villagers of Haojiazhai do not know if their village is part of a state-owned mining zone, and if it is under state governance. The village is located within the mining zone of the state-owned Shuiyu Coal Mine, yet the coal mine at the foot of the hill is privately owned, i.e. it is a typical "mine within a mine." An official at the Xiaoyi subsidence treatment office (*zhichenban*) said, "There is one way to determine if Haojiazhai is within the state-governed area. If the government sends someone to inspect the degree of damage in the village, it means you are within the area of the state-owned mine; otherwise, you are not." No one had inspected the Haojiazhai Village. And yet the villagers refuse to give up. They stubbornly believe that the state policies will have their interests at heart, and patiently wait amidst the sounds of blasting from the coal mountains.

Taoniu village at Linshi County

Situated on a mountain more than 1,000 metres in height, Taoniu village sits on a depression area of a major state-owned mine. Mining operations on the mines surrounding Taoniu village are carried on the Fujiatan Mining Zone, owned by the Fenxi Mining Group. Cracks were long found on the walls of the village homes. Some cave-dwellings started collapsing during the 1990s. Today, nearly all the walls in the homes of the 100-odd households are lined with cracks, and some cave-dwellings have subsided.

The wells dried up seven years ago. Villagers had to resort to pumping water from the foot of the mountain. Water is thus drawn from the Fujiatan Mining Zone, passing through two levels, and travelling five kilometres to reach Taoniu village. Everybody in the village depends on a single water pipe. Villagers could not bear to use the water that costs RMB 5.5 per ton, and that is barely adequate for their living needs, for watering the lands. They could depend only on the "sky" for harvest. Wheat production fell from its previous level of 500 katis to the current 200. Due to water shortages, fruits trees on the mountain have withered.

Of the 530 people living in the village, 300 have moved out. Some moved to nearby locations such as Fujiatan and Linshi County City; others moved as far as Taiyuan, or even out of the province. Yang Jianguo's family of four had also moved out. They rented a dilapidated cave dwelling at Fujiatan for RMB 100 a month. Compared to the three really good cave-dwellings in the village, Yang is very unhappy with his current home. Still, he had no alternative. People in the village who are slightly better-off have left, and fewer children are left behind to go to school. Taoniu's primary school had to shut down because of a shortage of students. With his daughter turning eight, Yang had to leave. But being unable to find any work in Fujiatan after moving out, Yang had to return to the village to farm. He planted wheat on ten acreages of land. But with a harvest of 2,000-plus katis, he would not have enough to even feed his own family.

In 2004, the local government sent someone to Taoniu Village to check on the geological disaster caused by coal mining-induced depression. A decision was made to move the entire village. The villages also heard that the government may provide some compensation for the subsidence area. But two years have passed, and there is still no news of the moving.

*Jiaozhong Village, also located at Linzhi County, and not far from the renowned Wang Courtyard (*wangjia dayuan*)*

Two years ago, the villagers heard the low blasting of cannon sounds under their homes, and cracks began appearing in their homes. Seventy percent of the homes of the hundred-odd households found their homes cracking, even the structures of the village committee and the village-run primary school. A dozen places on their farmland were found to contain crevices. There was also a long and deep cleft. Then there was the drying up of the water source, and then the withering of fruit trees that spanned nearly one thousand acreages. The withered fruit trees could only be chopped up and used as firewood. Disaster infected the villagers' lives with fear. Some villagers left. And the students of the village-run primary school, originally catering to student intake from other villages, transferred out.

Coal under the land of Jiaozhong village had long been completely extracted by the state-owned Hongqi Coal Mine. The villagers suspected that their problems were caused by the safety coal pillars left behind by Hongqi. In July 2005, they reported the matter to the State Land and Resources Bureau of Linshi County. Upon approval by the Land and Resources Department of Shanxi Province, an assessment team, made up of the State Land and Resources Bureaus of the relevant counties and cities, geological exploration agencies and the Jiaozhong Village Committee, was formed. However, when the actual in-well testing was to be conducted in early August, the staff of the Jiexiu State Land and Resources Bureau of Jiexiu surprisingly proposed that the Jiaozhong Village Committee members should not be allowed to enter the well. Technical personnel who entered the Houdangyu village border to conduct inspection of surface structures were stopped. When the Land and Resources Bureau of Jizhong city was about to continue the investigation, the Land and Resources Department of Shanxi Province ordered investigations to be stopped, giving as its reason that the province's office would take over the investigation. But more than one year has passed, and the province's land and resources office as well as its authorized technical assessment unit had never set foot on Jiaozhong Village.

Information thus shows that the our villages, which belong to three different counties and cities suffer from similar damage: houses cracking up, land subsidence, heavy pollution and shortage of water resources, as well as the impossibility of habitation on their existing lands, and the inability of villagers to produce and live normal lives. Some or a majority of the villagers moved away of their own accord; yet, not all were willing or able to move. Those who stayed put could only wait for the government to reach out a helping hand.

However, there were apparent distinctions among the four villages. Only Taoniu village really found its way under the government's relief spotlight; yet nothing happened two years after the government had investigated. The remaining three villages are still trapped in the government's blind spot. Among them, Haojiazhai was at the junction of "two possibilities," but because the government did not carry out any investigation, the villagers could not enjoy the reconstruction subsidy of RMB 450 per square metre. Instead, the address of the "new village" decided by the village administrator would still sit on top of a hollowed out mine.[68] Da'antou Village is not under the government's relief plan. Although the mine responsible had paid "more than RMB 4 million in compensation," only some villagers received their compensation. The villagers had "repeatedly sought out the government," but the government did not help them devise a "solution." As for the last example, Zhongjiao Village seemed to in the worst position: disaster had hit it, without doubt. But complex interests and relationships have prevented the villagers from even knowing the reasons for their plight.

Therefore, villagers and villages sitting on "hollowed" areas are also located in an institutionally "hollow" zone. The various scenarios in each village not only fully exposes the "crisis of governance" at the base level, and even the mid- and upper-level regimes, they also reflect the disunity and disharmony within the local societies. On the tumultuous eco-environment battlefield, we can truly feel the exact and intrinsic implications of the phrase "social disintegration."

CONCLUDING REMARKS: LOOKING TO THE FUTURE THROUGH A WINDOW ON THE PAST?

Since the end of the previous century, many intellectuals in non-mainstream circles have been discussing China's future. This is a topic which bears huge risks no matter which perspective is taken, and it is avoided by most "prudent" academics in China. However, when I began research on the agricultural areas of China and learned of the eco-environment, I became interested by the state of affairs in Shanxi. After years of groping and studying situations like those cited above as a "bystander," I have found myself having difficulty side-stepping something which I had been diligently avoiding.

If we examine the eco-environment crisis objectively and from a different angle, China is definitely approaching a dangerous zone. It is difficult to predict if this road will eventually lead the country to disintegration, or perhaps destruction. But if we shift the subject of our discussion from all of China to just a part of it, Shanxi villages, then the sociological or physical disintegration or destruction will no longer be just "scenarios" to be predicted, but rather realities to be discovered and recognized. The problem lies in the many influencing and blinding elements, so much so that the government and government officials, even academia and intellectual circles, have become accustomed to the circumstances – something they regard as a *state*, not an *event*. Perhaps we have lost the ability, or courage, to restore our sense of how a dramatic event should be perceived.

This could mean that China truly needs another "revolution" – a social revolution to fight for the right of survival – triggered by environmental problems, and aiming at their resolution. Of course, the possibilities, methodologies and outcomes still remain unknown. But the author has to stress that an unpolished version of "revolution" has occurred in Shanxi, the subject of our study. Because occasional flashes amidst the storm of revolution may leave behind petified memories that offer eternal value, the author attaches a brief explanatory postscript. I hope it can provide some insight.

POSTSCRIPT

When the Cultural Revolution was engulfing the lands of China, the "rebel party" that was first established in Lingshi County on the middle section of the Fenhe was neither "*Jinggangshan*" nor "*Wutaishan*," neither was it called the "Red X" nor the "Fight X." It was called the "Drink to Revolt Army" (*Chizshui Zaofan Bingtuan*). The Army's soldiers (mainly farmers residing along the river) rushed into the office of the county Party committee and county government, took a ladle and scooped the muddy waters from the Fenhe River, and put it on the desk of the committee's general secretary. They forced the "party in power" to drink up the water. They said, "we drink this everyday. Now we want you to have a taste of it!". The committee secretary was powerless, as it was indeed a polluted river. The "rebelling warriors" charged into the provincial capital and surrounded the county Party committee, sitting down in silence. They wanted a "clean Fenhe River" and "a mouthful of fresh water." From then on, the dozens of villages along the Fenhe River in Lingshi County had two cars, three tractors, and started a life of pulling drinking water (*la shui chi*) (Mai Tianshu, 1989).

ENDNOTES

1   A tactic used usually to "conceal problems." The language is usually ambiguous, the results seemingly apparent, and the problems always indistinct. For example, a frequently used term to describe the environmental condition is "maintained steady," the true implication of which could mean "irreversible" deterioration.

2   This article adopts this concept based on the two purports as follows: first, compared to normal market economies, China's ruling party and government clearly play a role in the promotion of and support for industry-driven economic development. Second, the lack of an effective checks and balances mechanism results in both the government's and enterprises' frequent disregard of the basic rights of workers and the protection of the environment. Consequently, growth had resulted in vicious competition – a race to the bottom, accompanied by huge economic, social and ecological costs.

3   See the *Government Work Report* of Premier Wen Jiabao at the Third Session of the Tenth National People's Congress, *People's Daily,* 6 March 2005.

4   The author has conducted macro studies on the overall impact on the *sannong* issues (those relating to agriculture, farmers and the countryside). Studies by region during the recent two years have focused on Henan, the Yangtze River Delta, and Zhejiang province. See Zhang Yulin, Gu Jintu, 2003; Zhang Yulin, 2006; 2007a; 2007b.

5   This conclusion is based on what an official of the Shanxi Environment Protection Bureau had said: Shanxi has always been called "one of the most heavily polluted provinces in

China"; but when the new governor knew of it, he removed the words "one of" during internal meetings. See the *Southern Metropolis Daily*, 24 September 2006.

6   *Economic Information Daily*, 20 June 2007.

7   *The Beijing News*, 10 January 2007.

8   Shanxi Bureau of Statistics, *Communiqué of Shanxi Province on the 2001-2006 National Economic and Social Development*. http://www.stats-sx.gov.cn/tjgb/default.htm.

9   See the *Government Work Report* of Yu Youjun, Acting Governor of Shanxi at the Fourth Session of the Tenth People's Congress of Shanxi held on 10 January 2006, *Shanxi Daily*, 11 January 2006.

10   That year, disposable income of the urban residents in Shanxi was RMB 10027.7; net rural income was RMB 3180.9. See Shanxi Bureau of Statistics, *Communiqué of Shanxi Province on the 2006 National Economic and Social Development*. http://www.stats-sx.gov.cn/tjgb/default.htm.

11   Based on logic, fiscal income should be "public income"; however, as China's fiscal institution lacks transparency and supervision, "public finance" often carries a strong flavour of "department finance," or even "personal finance." Here, we call it "government's wealth" in keeping with its actual behaviour.

12   *Economic Information Daily*, 21 March 2002.

13   Zhang Kejia in 2002, quoted in *First Financial Daily*, 10 March 2005.

14   Han Wen in 2007, quoted in *People's Daily*, 29 March 2007.

15   Chen Yanhui, 2006; Guo Jianguang, 2007.

16   *Shanxi Wan Bao*, 20 and 21 April 2005.

17   An environment expert in Shanxi said that there were only five prefecture cities which were included among the major surveillance areas by the State in 2004. If the rest of the eleven prefecture cities were included, then the province will take up the first nine positions among the top ten cities with the worst air pollution. For relevant information, please refer to *Economic Information Daily*, 21 March 2002; *Wen Wei Po* (Hong Kong), 15 July 2005; *Shanxi Daily*, 29 December 2006.

18   *Economic Information Daily*, 1 March 2002; Zhang Kejia, 2002; *Wen Wei Po* (Hong Kong), 15 July 2005.

19   *Shanxi Youth Daily*, 15 May 2006.

20   *Xinhua Net*, 29 March 2004.

21   Zhao Xiaojian, 2007.

22   *Outlook Weekly*, 30 January 2007.

23   *Southern Metropolis Daily*, 2 July 2007; CCTV News Probe (*Xinwen Diaocha*), 9 September 2007.

24   Lie Aizhen, 2004; *Shanxi Commercial Daily*, 10 May 2007.

25   *China Environmental News*, 9 October 2001; *Shanxi Commercial Daily*, 10 May 2007; *Market News*, 27 November 2006; Mai Tianshu, 1989; *Shanxi Wan Bao*, 21 April 2006. The three rivers flow through ten cities and 45 counties in Shanxi, with a river basin spanning 43.8 percent of the province, and accounting for 70 percent of the province's GDP in 2005.

26   *China Environmental News*, 9 October 2001; *Shanxi Wan Bao*, 20 April 2005.

27   Liu Aizhen, 2004; *Shanxi Wan Bao*, 21 April 2006; *Xinhua Net*, 23 November 2006.

28   *Xinhua Net*, 23 November 2006; Han Wen, 2007.

29   *Economic Information Daily*, 21 March 2002; *Shanxi Wan Bao*, 22 March 2005; *Shanxi Daily*, 5 June 2007.

30   Mai Tianshu, 1989.

31   *China Land and Resources News*, 13 July 1999.

32 *Shanxi Daily*, 1 March 2004.
33 http://info.water.hc360.com/2006/12/05082975642.shtml.
34 Han Wen, 2007; http://info.water.hc360.com/2006/12/05082975642.shtml.
35 Li Mingsan, 2006.
36 Mai Tianshu, 1989.
37 Mai Tianshu, 1989.
38 *Economic Information Daily*, 21 March 2002; *First Financial Daily*, 10 October 2005.
39 *The Economic Observer,* 6 November 2005.
40 Li Mingsan, 2006.
41 There were fifteen items included for damage computation, including permanent damage to water resources, soil erosion, water shortage, damages to building and housing structures, etc. *Shanxi Wan Bao*, 28 April 2005.
42 *China Land and Resources News*, 27 October 2004; *First Financial Daily*, 10 March 2005.
43 Nobuko Iijima *et al.*, 2001; Ulrich Beck, 2004.
44 The development of the "Misery Index" and the partial use thereof should be regarded as a kind of attempt. But some of the "indices" which we see nowadays do not seem to be able to truly reflect the level of "misery."
45 *Wen Wei Po* (Hong Kong), 15 July 2005.
46 *China Economic Times*, 6 February 2004.
47 Xia County is a poor county in Yuncheng.
48 *Shanxi Wan Bao*, 22 March 2005.
49 Han Wen, 2007.
50 *Wen Wei Po* (Hong Kong), 15 July 2005.
51 Which is equivalent to 5.93 per thousand of the entire population in Shanxi in 2006. If all patients were regarded as Shanxi residents, it implies that out of every 1000 Shanxi residents in that year, nearly 6 would have to go to the Shanxi Tumour Hospital for cancer treatment.
52 Zhang Kejia, 2002; Chen Hongai, 2006.
53 Beizi, 2001.
54 National Bureau of Statistics of China, *Comprehensive Statistical Data and Materials on 50 Years of New China*, China Statistics Press, 1999.
55 Mai Tianshu, 1989; Shi Jiumei, 1999; Jiao Ruilian *et al.*, 2000; *Market News*, 22 June 2004; Chen Aihong, 2006.
56 Mai Tishu, 1989.
57 Zhang Kejia, 2002.
58 He Yanwei *et al.*, 2006.
59 Chen Hongai, 2006. Date of investigation uncertain.
60 "Circle of benefit" and "circle of harm" are a pair of concepts used by Japan's environmental social science circle to analyze environment problems. See Nobuko Iijima *et al.*, 2001.
61 Guo Jianguang, 2007.
62 A campaign organized by Mao in the early 1960s encouraging peasants from all over China to follow the example of the village of Dazhai, in Shanxi province.
63 Li Yang, 2006; Chen Yanhui, 2006.
64 No detailed information on the extra-China emigrants is available, the same way we are ignorant of similar circumstances in the country. However, when many urban newspapers introduced a special section on "migration agents," we have to think: does this, to some extent, reflect the other facet of China's overall "eco-migration" problem?
65 *Shanxi Wan Bao*, 22 November 2006.

66   Li Yang, 2006; *The Beijing News*, 10 January 2007.
67   For information on the four villages, refer to Guo Jianguang, 2007; Li Yang, 2006; *The Beijing News*, 10 January 2007; *People's Daily*, 26 December 2006.
68   The subsidence treatment office (*zhichenban*) official of Xiaoyi City revealed the deceptiveness and awkwardness of the institution during his interview with the reporter. According to him, Xiaoyi City had planned a new district at the southern part of the city, occupying an area of more than 500 acreages. The intention was to move all the residents located at the caved-in areas. "However, this matter cannot be made known publicly, otherwise, the residents located at private mines will look them up, demanding why housing is given only to those living on state-owned mines," he said. Li Yang, 2006.

PART TWO

Discrimination against Women

CHAPTER SEVEN

The Gendered Reality of Migrant Workers in Globalizing China

Lanyan Chen

INTRODUCTION

According to a survey by the Development Research Centre of the State Council published in April 2006, there are 200 million rural migrants who are working and living in urban areas, 120 million of whom work in China's cities and another 80 million in smaller towns.[1] All of them have left low paying farm life, and they now make up 68 percent of the employees in the manufacturing sector and 80 percent in construction. Most of these workers not only face lower salaries and poorer working conditions than their city counterparts, but they also do not receive the social benefits such as pension plans, schooling for their children or health care which many of their counterparts in state-owned sectors enjoy. 68 percent of the rural migrant workers have monthly salaries of between RMB 300 to 800 (US$ 38 to 100). Seventy-six percent of rural migrant workers work on holidays and are not paid overtime. On average they work up to 11 hours a day and more than 26 days a month.

These findings depict the reality of the vast majority of rural migrants in urban China, who thus face discrimination and violation of their rights. Many of these migrants will ultimately find permanent residence in their adopted urban home but they will still not be entitled to the social benefits mentioned above. Admittedly, China is in an unprecedented process of urbanization that by some accounts will see its city population grow to include half the population by 2010.[2] These accounts indicate the huge challenge that faces Chinese policy-makers to both expand urban infrastructure to accommodate this rapid urbanization while also developing ways to improve the migrants' well-being and protect their rights as citizens and labourers.

Research on the migrant population has been incomplete and lacks some important details which would help guide future directions in policy-making. These details include two important aspects of the rural migration: on the one hand, informatiom about the effects globalization exerts throught its integration of China and its cheap migrant labour force into the world economy; and, on the other, information about the gender-specific effects of rural migration resulting from the feminization of the migrant labour force in export-oriented manufacturing sectors, services, and agriculture. The effects of globalization started in southern coastal cities where international capital was first introduced to the designated special economic zones (SEZs), and has recently moved interior and northward in search of even cheaper labour. The gender effects of rural migration occur across China's cities and range from domestic work to nurse-aid jobs and any commercialized services that are "dirty" and pay so little that most urban residents will not consider working in them. In the meantime, women in the countryside, who stay behind while their husbands have moved to urban areas to seek employment, shoulder most, if not all, the agricultural work and family care. Understanding these aspects of rural migration in China will help us to recognize the gendered nature of government policies and practices in economic reforms that increase inequality and are at the root cause of discrimination and of the violation of rights experienced by rural migrants. It will also help suggest priority areas for future policy research and action to protect rural migrants while promoting gender equality and justice.

This paper is the first of a series of research reports written in relation to the China-Canada collaborative research project on anti-discrimination, and aims to examine the extent to which government policies and practices are responsive to the expansion of rural migration. It seeks to adopt a feminist political economy framework, drawing on international rights-based advocacy and a gender relational perspective to help identify potential gender impacts of government policies on rural migrants. These policies, I claim, fail to adequately take into consideration the effects of globalization and existing gendered power relations, and are, in actuality, discriminative against rural migrants, especially women. Tensions and sometimes contradictions between the goals and methods of policies promoting foreign investment, trade and economic growth, and reducing labour market regulations; and policies adopting a conservative fiscal policy on the provision of social services, create discriminatory treatment of migrant workers in both industrial work and domestic work, especially in those areas dominated by women. This paper employs this gender sensitive and rights-based framework to analyze the gender impacts of current government policies on rural-to-urban migrants, and it does so in order to identify an alternative to the current government strategy for promoting economic growth and development. This alternative is in line with the Chinese government's current goal of building a harmonious "*xiao kang*" (literally in English, "well-off") society through balancing economic with social development and upholding principles of accountability and fairness for all, as well as with China's effort to realize the Millennium Development Goals (MDGs) agreed upon by the international community. It will also encourage rights-based policies to address the needs of women migrant workers and to promote equality and justice. Future papers will focus on the movements for women workers' rights on the part of women working in export-oriented industries and the services sector, as well as examine other issues relating to rural migration, including the abduction of and trafficking in migrant women and children for forced labour (sometimes for the sex trade), the schooling of children of migrant workers and children who are left behind by parents gone to work in cities, and the exercise of rights and participation by migrant workers in political and social processes.

This paper attempts, therefore, to advance policy and research related to migrant women workers and gender issues associated with the rural-to-urban migration based on a synthesis of the existing published literature in and outside of China. This published research includes Tan Shen (1998) and Arianne Gateno and Tamara Jacka (2004), which are largely about the experiences and activities of migrant women and the relationship between rural women's migration and socio-cultural changes in China, and the research of Anita Chan (2001) and Jin Yihong (2006), which examine the experiences of rural migrant women as workers under international capital and their plight due to China's industrial restructuring. This paper takes their findings further by using a conceptual framework to integrate international human rights standards with a gender relational perspective so as to identify gender gaps in Chinese policies and the impacts of these gaps on rural migrants, especially migrant women workers. The purpose of this study does not, however, end at the identification of gaps in policies, but it aims to search for ways to advance policy strategies to build a harmonious society within the context of a more stringent implementation of international goals and standards.

This paper begins with discussion of the conceptual framework, drawing upon international rights-based advocacy and research on gender inequalities and migration. This international research is in turn rejuvenated by the international provisions of equal rights in employment as they apply to migrant workers. Also, it is energized by the efforts of migrant workers to organize and demand just and favourable working conditions and equal protection under the law, as well as for the protection of women migrant workers specifically against exploitative terms of work.[3] The use of these provisions in an application of the gender relational perspective which embraces two interconnected approaches – the gender relational approach and the women's rights and men's involvement approach – will enable an analysis of the gender effects of policies on the creation of inequalities in migration. It will also help identify and focus policy interventions to address women's needs as a consequence of their biological and social differences from men and to protect their basic rights with the involvement of men.[4] The adoption of these focused policy interventions will be an important step towards harmonizing domestic legislation and government actions in meeting women's needs and protecting their rights with international standards that promote gender equality and justice in migration.

In this paper, this perspective is applied to evaluate China's strategy of economic growth at the expense of migrant workers. I argue that this strategy has been affected by traditional values and stereotypical expectations to the extent of failing to reflect fully the interests and needs of migrant workers, especially women. This paper agrees with recent recognition by Chinese officials and scholars and their counterparts abroad of the unfair treatment of rural migrants.[5] It points out that policies based on promoting economic growth through the increase of FDI (foreign direct investment) and trade marginalize rural women migrant workers and at the same time segregate them. The reduction of government spending on social services, moreover, left gaps in services, and these gaps are mostly filled by cheap labour from the countryside. Some examples of this are domestic services, nurse-aid and cleaning services. There is some expectation that the government is considering new policies which would grant rural migrants proper urban registration in order to build a harmonious *xiao kang* society that promotes economic growth as well as the rights of workers. It is also expected that the government will use legislation to promote equality and justice in accord with labour rights standards granting migrant workers social security and welfare. What I believe will be of particular value in this study is the identification of a gender sensitive, rights-based approach for future policy initiatives which recognize differences in gendered needs among migrant women, to which the Chinese strategy has failed to respond. Hopefully, the study will also generate new reflections on, and insights into, efforts to promote the adoption of international standards to help cope with the challenges associated with the migration in China.

In what follows, the paper will, first, develop a gender-sensitive and rights-based framework to examine the gender impacts of Chinese government policy to promote economic growth through the employment of rural migrant workers. This examination, cast in a historical perspective, will help to identify tensions and even contradictions existing in the current policies. Resolving the contradictions will be the topic of the last section, which contains a discussion of priority areas for future policy research and initiatives.

CONCEPTUALIZING GENDER EQUITY IN RURAL-TO-URBAN MIGRATION

Recognition of gender inequalities in world migrations has been an important part of international research efforts of the last decade.[6] This recognition has informed the international advocacy for women's rights and equitable participation of migrant women and men in economic and political processes, which has occurred through forums such as the Fourth World Conference on Women in Beijing in 1995 and international human rights treaties. This advocacy provides a basis for a gender-sensitive and rights-based conceptual framework useful not only for analysis of rural migration as a gender equity issue, but also for developing critical solutions to the issues of discrimination and violation of rights resulting from the interplay of gender roles, industrial restructuring and globalization. This expands upon the feminist political economy framework developed in a study published in July 2008[7] and is useful for the present study to evaluate the Chinese strategy of economic growth through the use of migrant workers, and especially to identify the gender impacts on rural migrant workers of Chinese policies to promote economic growth and participation in global markets. This evaluation suggests that there are tensions in the policies between promoting foreign investment and reducing labour market regulation, tensions which potentially give rise to discrimination and violation of the rights of rural migrant labourers in China. This section shall consider the conceptual framework with a discussion of the international standards and their integration with a gender relational perspective, in order to identify gaps in China's compliance with international standards.

The Conceptual Framework

The conceptual framework of this study expands on an interdisciplinary study of society as a totality which conceives of all aspects of human life – including the political, economic, social, and cultural, as well as sexual and gender – as mutually interdependent. This interdependent nexus forms, on the one hand, a basis upon which to understand how gender intersects with globalization, politics, and social and economic transformations. In this interdependent nexus, the production of wealth and social reproduction are part of one integrated process, and the government occupies both an overwhelmingly powerful position, subordinating women by its gender insensitive policies, and "a contested site," over which women have to exercise agency to influence its policies (Chen 2008). This recognition of the state as both a power and a contested site is of crucial relevance to an analysis of the impacts on women in China of globalization and economic and social transformation. It helps delineate how, within the historical and cultural processes of social organizations, women's experiences with discrimination and subordination have become widespread. It also helps show how the government, through its policies, has systematically treated social reproduction through childbirth, child rearing, and general care giving as the responsibility of women, and has often ignored and undervalued this sphere and demarcated it from that of the production of subsistence and wealth. It also helps investigate how the state can potentially adopt policies, establish structures and recognize alternative organizations in order to improve women's access to resources and the exercise of their rights (Chen 2008). Women's organized demands are, on the other hand, what we are able to perceive with the study of society as an interdependent nexus. The perception of women's organized demands as a basis of women's agency that can "advance analyses of progressive social change" for economic and social justice (Chen 2008) is essential to understanding women's initiatives and their demand to hold the government accountable to its commitments to achieving international goals and standards relevant to gender equality in migration.

This framework recognizes that globalization has ushered in an increase of migration of labour at the same time as it has resulted in decreasing regulation of the labour market, growth in the informal sector and the emergence of new forms of exploitation. It advocates international standards especially in areas of equal rights in employment, just and favourable working conditions and equal protection under the law as well as protection for women migrant workers against exploitative terms of work, and it takes these standards as they have been outlined in the four most relevant human rights treaties and international research on migration from a gender perspective in the recent years. These treaties are the *Convention on the Elimination of All Forms of Discrimination against Women* (CEDAW), the *International Covenant on Social, Economic and Cultural Rights* (ICESCR), the *International Covenant on Civil and Political Rights* (ICCPR), and the *International Convention on the Protection of the Rights of All Migrant Workers and Their Families* (MWC).[8] China is a signatory party to the CEDAW since 1981 and to the ICESCR since 1997. The National People's Congress, the Chinese legislature, considered signing the ICCPR in 1998 but so far has not signed it. China is not considering signing the MWC. The application of these human rights standards to the situations of migrants, as this paper suggests, requires the use of all of these treaties together as each one addresses some different aspect of the issues. Only with the application of these treaties can migrant women's interests and needs be considered in full. This application is aided by the gender relational perspective and the use of the women's rights and men's involvement approach to policy-making in order to discern gender differences and to meet the specific gendered needs of the disadvantaged, especially migrant women workers. The use of these two analytical approaches will strengthen efforts of recent international research to identify how major signifiers of inequality, such as gender, interact with economic restructuring and other adverse effects of policies on economic growth and labour regulation and how advocacy for gender equality advances women's participation in migration and access to services and decision-making.[9] This use of the women's rights and men's involvement approach is the basis for a gender-sensitive and rights-based framework in order to extend policy research so as to overcome inequalities, through the protection of migrant women's rights with the involvement of male decision-makers and their responsibility in future policy initiatives.

International Standards and China's Implementation

The "Platform for Action" (PfA) adopted at the Fourth World Conference on Women in Beijing in 1995 recognized in its account of the Global Framework (p. 21-30) that women form a majority of the poor in the world and that an important contributing factor in women's poverty is the gender disparities in economic power sharing. Many women migrate and enter the segmented labour market in under-remunerated and undervalued jobs, largely seeking to improve their household income and to get out of rural poverty. The above gender disparities continue to affect them in the labour market by limiting their choices to finding jobs often through informal arrangements and without the protection of a formal contract. The PfA also recognized that women's migration has profound consequences for family structures and well being and has unequal consequences for women and men, including in many cases the sexual exploitation of women. Additional barriers also exist for migrant women workers, especially those who provide for several dependents, as they may face an increased workload without any reduction in their household responsibilities.

The "Platform for Action" calls for rethinking and reformulating macroeconomic policies so as to expand from focusing exclusively on the formal sector to including the needs of women migrant workers in informal sectors as well (p. 38). It also demands the full realization of the human rights of all women migrants, including women migrant workers, and their protection against violence and exploitation and their full integration into the labour force through an improvement in their productive employment (p. 41). It affirms that social development is primarily the responsibility of governments and requests all parties involved in the development process, including academic institutions, non-governmental organizations and grassroots and women's groups, to improve the plight of the most disadvantaged groups of women, including migrant women (p. 43).

The *Convention on the Elimination of All Forms of Discrimination* (CEDAW) demands that all states ensure to women the same rights as to men and, in Article 11(1), that women's rights be guaranteed equal to men's in employment opportunities and remuneration, including equal benefits and treatment for work of equal value, and proclaims women's rights to social security and the right to paid leave.

The *International Convention on Economic, Social and Cultural Rights* (ICESCR) states in Article 2 that governments must ensure the enjoyment of all economic, social and cultural rights included in the Covenant without discrimination based on race, color, sex, language, religion, political or other opinion, national or social origin, property, birth or other status (most relevant to the present study are the prohibition of discrimination based on sex, social origin and birth). Article 3 further states the equal rights of women and men to the enjoyment of the rights in the Convention. Article 7(a) recognizes the equal right of women and men to just and favourable conditions of work, including fair wages, and, at a minimum, to be paid a decent living for the worker and her family. Article (b) guarantees workers' rights to safe and healthy working conditions, rest, leisure, reasonable limitations on working hours and periodic holidays with pay as well as remuneration for public holidays.

The *International Covenant on Civil and Political Rights* (ICCPR) provides in Article 8 that no one shall be held in servitude or required to perform forced or compulsory labour. It also states in Article 26 that all persons are equal before the law and are entitled without any discrimination to equal protection of the law. The law should guarantee to all persons the rights included in the Covenant without distinction of any kind, such as sex, national or social origin, birth or other status, and should prohibit discrimination by providing all persons equal and effective protection against discrimination on any grounds, including sex, national or social origin, birth or other status.

The *International Convention on the Protection of the Rights of All Migrant Workers and Their Families* (MWC) provides in Article 11 that no migrant workers shall be held in slavery or servitude or required to perform forced labour. Article 25 requires states to take all appropriate measures to ensure that migrant workers are not deprived of any rights concerning remuneration and other conditions of work on the basis of irregularities in their work or residence status. The same Article also guarantees equal treatment for migrant workers concerning terms of employment, including remuneration, overtime, paid holidays, hours of work, safety, health, and termination of employment. Article 54(2) provides that if a migrant worker claims that his or her employer has violated the terms of her or his work contract, he/she shall have the right to address his/her case to the competent authorities of the state of employment on the basis of equality with nationals of that state. This provision, though it is meant for migrant workers who have gone to a different country, is considered relevant for migrant workers in China going to a different province, for example, migrant workers from Hubei working in Guangdong and having to address their issues to the authorities in Guangdong.

China has signed on to, or is considering signing on to, all of the above treaties except the MWC, and is an active supporter of the PfA which was adopted at the Fourth World Conference on Women held in Beijing. To implement the CEDAW, China adopted the *Law to Protect the Interests and Rights of Women* in 1992; this was amended in 2006 to address some newly emerging issues and to make it more operational, given that it has not even once been used in legal proceedings in the previous fourteen years. In an effort to align domestic laws with international standards, such as the ICESCR, the Chinese government revised the *Marriage Law* (2001), the *Land Contract Law* (2001), and the *Labour Law* (2001), and has just adopted the *Property Law* (2007). The *Employment Promotion Law* and *Labour Contract Law* have also come into force as of the beginning of 2008. In the process of discussions prior to their adoption women's groups had been actively advocating on behalf of women's interests. Migrant women workers are one of the women's groups voicing their opinions on issues of minimum pay, lack of social security and violence at the workplace.

In the laws that have been adopted, there has been varying success in considering women's concerns and making a positive impact on women's lives. Women's access to land is an area where women are able to use the *Land Contract Law* to win their rights to land, whereas women's equitable employment opportunities continue to be an area where women feel unprotected as the enforcement of the *Labour Law* is very weak. Migrant women workers are finding more areas in which they are gaining employment, but they are not gaining rights as labourers in terms of access to benefits and entitlements.

Similarly, China has made moderate progress towards the goals of the Beijing PfA, though it has carried out a first national action plan from 1995 to 2000 and it is now implementing the second National Program for the Development of Chinese Women, extending from 2001 to 2010. Progress is even more insignificant with respect to migrant women workers. Considering the challenges Chinese rural women have had over the past decade, from the collapse of the collective economy and welfare in the countryside to the rise of vulnerability among migrant workers to industrial restructuring, any progress in rural women's advancement in a country that is in rapid transformation is a very difficult, but increasingly urgent task, and one which needs active, appropriate government support. To identify gaps in government policies, and the impacts of these gaps on women and especially migrant women workers, there is a need for a perspective which, discerning gender relations as key social institution and integrating a women's rights and men's involvement approach, helps recognize women's gendered needs, and the way these arise from the disadvantaged position of women in gendered power relations.

Gender Relational Perspective in Policy Research

The gender relational perspective is concerned with elucidating the role of gendered power relations in the rise of inequalities in migration in China in recent years. Although inequality generally occurs between rural migrant workers and local urban residents due to discriminatory policies and treatment, there is, more importantly, gendered inequality experienced by women migrant workers. Gendered inequality arises from the influences of cultural values on the existing unequal gender relationships and from the different needs and interests of women and men due largely to their different economic and social positions in society. These influences form a barrier to the realization of equality as traditional norms devalue women's work at home and segregate women into the lowest end of labour markets where low pay is combined with poor working conditions and low protection of labour rights. For instance, women's vulnerability to discrimination is increased by the widespread belief that it is appropriate for them to work in domestic service or as casual labour because their main responsibility is to be at home. Cultural expectations have encouraged women to be submissive and therefore they are less likely to be organized and are often excluded from labour unions. Women, especially in the countryside, are in a weaker position than men in owning property, have less access to productive resources and are, consequently, frequently dependent on men. This is connected to the fact that women resort to risky behaviour – selling blood and sex – when they experience disruption of their families and poverty, and when migrating from rural to urban areas in search of jobs. Women and girls are particularly susceptible to the growing trade in forced labour. Men's social and cultural superiority, furthermore, has enabled them more easily to move to other areas and does not encourage them to take on domestic tasks or provide care at home. This understanding of gendered power relations as obstacles to promoting equality in migration in China shall help identify priority-targeting areas in government strategy to addressing migration. It also enables recognition of vulnerabilities in relation to the infringement of the rights of women (and men) migrant workers to human dignity, to access to services and healthcare, and to participation in decision-making. This recognition is built on the integration of a women's rights and men's involvement approach and is helpful in capturing the gender impacts of policies, impacts of which we cannot acquire full recognition simply by looking at women and their interests and needs.

The women's rights and men's involvement approach highlights the specific needs of women and girls as a consequence of biological and social differences and, therefore, the need for focused interventions to protect their rights with men's involvement (Chen 2008). This analysis of women's gendered needs, in addition to their biological needs, from their involvement in gendered power relations helps to identify grey areas in policies and practices related to economic growth and labour regulation in China that are seemingly discriminatory and biased against women. For instance, in China, rural women (and men) who are attracted to work for international capital in transnational corporations are not organized and receive poor labour protection and benefits. Those rural women who came to urban areas for jobs often find it easier to be employed in domestic work and often receive low pay and are exposed to abuse as their work is in most cases arranged informally. Policies that may appear to be gender neutral but, in actuality, fail to take into account women's interests and needs, especially as they relate to domestic service and informal work, therefore, do not promote equality. Only strategies which address women's gendered needs and promote women's rights to labour protection and which increase men's involvement and awareness of their responsibility for promoting equality will be efficient in overcoming discrimination. Men's involvement and awareness is crucial because the elimination of discrimination needs men to be not only responsible citizens and corporate citizens but also because they are the "gatekeepers" of policy-making and as such need to be gender-responsive.[10]

This women's rights and men's involvement approach complements the gender relational perspective as the latter helps recognize gender discrimination in Chinese policies while the former pays attention to women's growing gendered needs in part as a consequence of gender differences and inequalities. To bring the recognition of gender inequalities and women's growing gendered needs into the mainstream of policy-making constitutes an important step forward for the rights-based approach to future policy initiatives because it promotes men's involvement and their increased awareness of their responsibilities. These policy initiatives aim to identify proactively, and then to respond adequately to, different gendered needs, and in so doing to overcome vulnerabilities and promote fairness. They will also help promote the equitable participation of women migrant workers in policy-making. Such policies will, moreover, help transform gendered power relations, encourage changes to stereotypical perceptions of roles and behaviour, and overcome discrimination.[11] Discussions on priority areas for future policy research and action in the last section are provisional but are derived from an analysis of gender gaps in government policies, especially those that promote economic growth at the expense of migrant workers, and that diminish social services and increase individuals' burden of their care and costs. What immediately follows is an examination of these gaps in Chinese policies under the light of the above analytical framework.

Gender Gaps in Chinese Economic and Migration Policies

At the Sixteenth Congress of the Chinese Communist Party in November 2002, the ideal of a *"xiao kang"* (literally, "well-off" in English) society was adopted as China's development goal and was written into the Constitution of the Party to orient every aspect of the government work in the next decades. With the goal of an annual per capita income of more than US$ 2,000 by 2020, this "well-off" society aims to further the development of a socialist market economy and also adjust socio-economic structures, including industrial, agricultural and social sectors. A "scientific course of development" emphasizes two fundamental elements for China's future development: people-centred governance, and a strategy to overcome the imbalances in economic and social processes in both rural and urban areas that have arisen from the single-minded pursuit of economic growth.[12] This course of development is not only meant to correct the past course of development oriented towards growth of the Gross Domestic Product (GDP), but also aims to shift China's future development towards a *xiao kang* society founded on the principles of fairness, justice, harmony and equality and the democratic principles of openness and participation. It is to understand the imbalance between economic and social developments in China that the following section examines gender gaps in government policies which have affected the lives of migrant workers, especially women.

Gendered Impacts of Economic Policies on Migration

At the start of economic reforms in the late 1970s, the Chinese government adopted the system of household responsibility for land contracts in the countryside; this allowed villages to distribute land use rights to individual farm households. This system entailed the collapse of the communes, the base of the previous collective rural economy, and released thousands of surplus labourers from the land. While the development of rural industries has been a government strategy to keep many of these labourers employed in rural areas, many others began to migrate to urban areas seeking employment. Men migrated to the cities first in order to work in construction and other heavy manual labour areas; this left the responsibility for farm work and running the household, including raising children and care for the elders, to their wives. Soon young women also left their rural homes to take advantage of the demand for labour created by the open-door policy of the early 1980s, which allowed international investments in labour-intensive manufacturing and factories. These young women subsequently found employment in newly opened economic zones created to encourage these investments.

In the beginning these zones were located in the south, especially Shenzhen and other areas of Guangdong province. By one estimate, women made up 80 percent of migrant workers in Guangdong in the 1990s.[13]

Both the land contract household responsibility system of the countryside and the open-door policy in urban areas seemed gender-neutral and oriented towards stimulating production and reviving an economy that was on the verge of bankruptcy. But, in actuality, these policies were one-sided and were filled with gender biases, especially against rural women. For instance, the land contract household responsibility system was, on the one hand, so economically focused that it did not devise social and gender-sensitive means to help relieve pressures on those who left their land and went into the cities to find employment. Without social organizations to help with the transition from rural to urban settings, migrant workers in the 1980s, especially women, were left unprotected from abuse by criminals profiting from the unregulated labour markets by selling trafficked women into forced labour or other dismal situations. Unlike their predecessors, who were absorbed into the industrialization process more systematically through the expansion of factories and cooperative movements in the 1950s in the period after the CCP took power in China, today's migrant workers are commonly classified as "floating population" (*liudong renkou*) by different levels of government to indicate their unofficial, temporary, de facto, and "non*hukou*" status. This term "floating population" refers to anyone who has moved, either temporarily or for the long term, from their registered place of residence without a corresponding transfer of official residence registration, or *hukou* (Jacka and Gaetano 2004, p. 1). The term suggests that migrants move blindly or unsystematically and that their non*hukou* status distinguishes them from local residents who have a household registration. Also different from their predecessors, who were brought under the coverage of the Labour Insurance system established in 1953 upon becoming workers in a factory or a cooperative (Kang 2003), today's migrant workers are unorganized, mostly rely on (informal) social networks for job opportunities and are excluded from any welfare programs.

The open-door policy, on the other hand, invited foreign capital to start factories in special economic zones (SEZs) such as Shenzhen and to form joint ventures with state-owned enterprises in government-designated industries. It favoured foreign capital while the Chinese government invested in buildings, roads and overall infrastructure. Though the government was concerned that some level of advanced technology was transferred to the SEZs, it did far less to assure that labour issues were dealt with in accordance with the *Labour Law*. Thus, when local governments implemented the open-door policy, employers and management were treated favourably, which included favourable tax rates and tax holidays, as well as reduced tariffs for imports and exports. However, because this capital investment inflow was attracted to China in order to take advantage of the abundant supply of cheap labour, local governments largely ignored the rights of the workers. The supply of cheap labour is largely composed of migrant workers. The international capital that first started locating factories in China's SEZs was predominantly based in nearby Korea, Taiwan and Hong Kong, and would take advantage of the supply of cheap Chinese labour by operating labour-intensive industries, such as manufacturing of footwear, textiles, toys and other lines of quick return consumer products. These factories and their private recruiters often targeted young rural women fresh from the countryside and imposed on them strict and intimidating rules, assuming that young rural women were cheaper, inexperienced and docile. Also, many parents of these young rural women were willing to send them away, based on the word of a friend or a fellow villager, in order to find work and to support their families back in the village. This almost inexhaustible pool of labour allows factories to maintain tough terms of employment because any employees who want to leave or complain about the sometimes unbearable working conditions are simply replaced by fresh, vulnerable batches of workers (Chan 2001, p. 10).

As Anita Chan (2001, p. 11-15), Tan Shen (1998), Gaetano and Jacka (2004) and others discuss, there are several reasons that migrant workers were under atrocious terms of employment in Shenzhen and other coastal cities. All suggest that the open-door policy failed to consider gendered power relations and the way in which discriminative practices by different levels of the government affect migrant workers, especially women. Firstly, the migrants are subject to tight "immigration" controls under China's household registration system. In order to leave their village, farmers have to apply for a permit from their local government. To stay in any city, they have to apply to the local police for a temporary residential permit. To work in the cities, they need to secure a contract with an employer, and then their stay needs to be approved by the local labour bureau, which issues a work permit. They are often trapped if the employer takes their temporary residential permit away from them. This residential status makes the character of their stay in the cities like that of foreign nationals living as guest workers. They are not entitled to any of the benefits enjoyed by the local residents such as social welfare, schooling, the right to own property, to bring their spouses or children with them, or even any right to residency. Once their labour is no longer required, they are supposed to go back to their place of origin. Periodically, the police carry out raids to round up those who do not possess a proper permit. Those caught are harassed, humiliated, and mistreated, thrown into detention centres where the conditions are sometimes worse than state prisons, and then sent back to their rural homes. The effect of this temporary residential permit system on migrant workers has been noted repeatedly at the Chinese legislature, the National People's Congress, in recent years, and some local governments, including that of Beijing, have been discussing reforming the system. To date, changes in this system have been inconsequential.

As the temporary residential permit is extremely important to migrant workers, it often provides the perfect tool with which to coerce them into forced and bonded labour. For example, when migrant workers are required to pay for this permit and the work permit in one lump sum, which is too much for the migrants to afford, the factory pays on behalf of the worker and then deducts a sum from each month's wages, trapping the worker in a bonded relationship and ensuring that they cannot easily move to another employer. Worse still, some factories collect these permits and identity papers from the migrant worker for "safekeeping." Though this practice is illegal, it is a common practice and the result is that the worker cannot go out in public (to search for other employment, for example) for fear of being caught by a police identity check, and, also, that if they find other work it can be difficult to retrieve the permit. This practice makes the worker vulnerable to dictation of the terms of employment by the factory, which include being forced to work long hours and to stay in regimented, poorly-built and often very crowded dormitories heavily guarded by private security guards.

Secondly, the use of private security guards in factories and dormitory compounds is very common. Companies that supply security guards are often connected to the police and sometimes police officers work as security guards in their spare time (Chan 2001, p. 10). This internal security system set up behind factory walls is extremely effective at intimidating and controlling workers, especially as it is often augmented by off duty police who simply switch uniform. Chan (2001, p. 9) comments that while "[t]he discrimination against migrant workers in the Chinese case is not racial, [nevertheless] the control mechanisms set in place in the so-called free labour market to regulate the supply of cheap labour [and] the underlying economic logic of the system and the abusive consequences suffered by the migrant workers, share many of the characteristics of the apartheid system."

Thirdly, the labour terms are dictated by the employer who charges "deposits" of between half a month and a month's wages, not only further bonding the workers to the employer but also forcing the workers to stay till the end of a year (when it is required that employers pay in full the wages owed to the workers, a requirement that is not always followed). For migrant workers, the labour market is not free, insofar as they are unable to appeal to the terms of the *Labour Law* that recognizes, for instance, a minimum wage standard and the maximum overtime hours a month. The non-application of the *Labour Law* for the protection of migrant workers is not just the government's oversight, but it is rather a selling point to attract international capital to take advantage of the cheap, docile labour in China. In the 1990s, the Chinese government introduced minimum wage standards for its urban workers and made paying minimum wages mandatory in the *Labour Law* in 1994 (Chan 2001, p. 11). In 1997, the legal work week was shortened to forty hours and the minimum monthly wage was set at RMB 420 (US$ 54 at the fixed exchange rate of US$ 1 to RMB 8.26 at that time) for the Shenzhen SEZ, RMB 290 (US$ 36) for Beijing, and RMB 315 (US$ 45) for Shanghai.[14] Despite the very low minimum monthly wage standards set for Shenzhen and other cities, migrant workers could seldom receive it except if they worked a large amount of (basically unpaid) overtime. For instance, Chan (2001,

p. 12) observed a Taiwanese-run footwear factory in Dongguan, Guangdong where 40,000 workers producing running shoes for Adidas, Nike, Reebok and other major brand names made RMB 600 to 700 a month, double the minimum month wage of 350 in Guangdong. This seemingly high wage is attained, however, by working about eighty hours of overtime a week, while the *Labour Law* then stipulated a maximum overtime of thirty-six hours per month. When averaged out, this pay rate is barely above the minimum wage. Moreover, when the forty hour work week was adopted for the entire country, Shenzhen city government appealed to the State Council to delay implementation under pressure from international investors. As Chan (2001, p. 15) learned, the State Council did not grant the request, but did compromise by allowing flexible overtime, so long as permission is granted by the local labour bureau and the workers agree. But the total amount of overtime per month should still be within the maximum limit of thirty-six hours, as stipulated by the *Labour Law*. In the end, the central government has allowed the law to be eroded because migrant workers have neither the power nor representation to negotiate with management (or government), due largely to the one-sided tilt of the open-door policy and local governments' partiality towards investors' interests as they fear that if they enforce the laws then this investment will move to other, more "flexible," regions.

Fourthly, local governments must compete to attract international investors as they rely on corporate taxes as revenue. Investors come to do business with local governments when there is a more relaxed enforcement of labour standards. Considering, moreover, that local governments and bureaucracies in many cases are partners of joint ventures and that they provide land, buildings and roads, they have a vested interest in ensuring the docility of the workers through the erosion of labour market regulations. It is not unheard of for local governments to stand together with management and against labour. Tan Shen (1998) has documented many cases in which migrant workers suffered from violence and local governments did nothing to help. The fact that the workers are migrants, not constituents of these local governments, makes them all the more vulnerable to exploitation.

This exploitation is particularly gendered as it deprives migrant women of their rights not only as labourers but also as women. As researchers (Chan; Tan) have documented, factories only recruit women up to 29 years of age and adopt strict rules against dating and pregnancy. Pregnant women faced immediate discharge. Migrant women workers have no chance to gain entitlement to reproductive healthcare and other women workers' benefits, which the government has granted workers in the state sector. Worse still, they are frequently exposed to sexual abuse and violation of their right to human dignity at the workshop. It is also documented that security guards conduct strip searches on the suspicion of theft.[15] Eighty women workers were burned to death in a factory fire because the building was locked to keep workers working and from leaving without permission.[16] These are all aspects of an exploitative labour regime emerging out of the economic reforms and the open-door policy, which not only represents worsening gender relations in the globalizing Chinese economy but also epitomizes the devastation of all past achievements to secure the rights of Chinese women workers.

Nowadays, this exploitative labour regime has extended from the southern coastal cities north and westward to the interior provinces as international capital continues to seek cheaper labour, and as migrant workers have refused to go down to Guangdong to endure the exploitative terms of employment (Jin 2006). This geographic spread in the exploitation of Chinese labour by international capital has become an urgent issue for the Chinese government in its adoption and enforcement of international standards to protect the rights of workers. The plight of these workers is linked to the decline of social policies in China.

Gendered Impacts of Social Policies on Migration

Since the economic reforms, the Chinese government cut social spending at the same time as the system of collective welfare in the countryside collapsed and there was a massive layoff of workers in light industry and manufacturing during industrial restructuring. By one account (*An Analysis Report of the National Health Services Survey in 2003*, 2004, p. 9, 178), for instance, the annual increase of per capita income between 1998 and 2003 was 8.9 percent in urban areas and 2.5 percent in rural areas. Annual expenditure on healthcare, however, had gone up at a rate of 13.5 percent for the urban population and 11.8 percent for the rural population. In 2003, a visit to the hospital cost RMB 219 on average in urban areas and RMB 91 in rural areas. Based on 1998 rates, this is an increase of 85 percent and 103 percent, respectively. On average, a person paid RMB 7,606 per year for hospitalization in urban areas and RMB 2,649 in rural areas (more than a year's income in many rural areas), up by 88 percent and 73 percent from 1998. Between 1978 and 2002, personal health expenditure rose 40-fold (Blumenthal and Hsiao, 2005). Also, between 1980 and 2004, while the economy grew by leaps and bounds, the total health expenditure increased from RMB 14.3 billion, which was 3.17 percent of the GDP in 1980, to RMB 568.5 billion, about 5.7 percent, in 2004 (Zhu 2005, p. 25). The government spending on health, however, went down from 36.4 percent of the total health expenditure in 1980 to 15.3 percent in 2003, leaving individuals to pick up an increased health expenditure of between 23.2 and 60.2 percent (Rao and Liu 2004, p. 36). Eighty percent of government spending on health, moreover, was concentrated in the big cities, and thirty percent of this was invested in the big hospitals of these cities, especially in purchasing high priced equipment (Zhu 2005, p. 25). This reduction, therefore, brought about a de facto privatization of the medical system as facilities turned to the sale of drugs and other health commodities to finance their operations and pay workers' salaries. While the government covers only 10 percent of hospital budgets, facilities are allowed to take a 15 percent increase on the price of drugs and use 10 to 15 percent of the hospitalization services for making profit (*ibid.*, p. 32). This government policy, in effect, encouraged facilities to increase revenue through promoting the use of high-tech equipments and selling expensive drugs, leaving actual care for patients or their families to pick up. This, thus, creates a market in patient-care workers, who are mostly migrant women workers of various ages and are hired on an individual basis by patients' families. This commercial behaviour of medical facilities greatly increases the costs for users, the majority of whom are uninsured and pay for care out of their pockets.

By and large, one central reason for the cutbacks on healthcare and other social spending is, as Diane Elson (1999) has argued, that governments' lost revenue through the reduction of tax levies on businesses with foreign investment. A consequence of the cutbacks is the rise of the cheap and extremely low-paid so-called "informal work force" in cities, which includes those who provide personal care to patients in hospitals and domestic services to the young, the old and the sick in private homes; those who do janitorial and cleaning work in public and private buildings and establishments; and the increased use of women's unpaid labour at home. While women's unpaid work is not the subject here, the "informal work force," which is made up of laid-off workers, an overwhelming majority of whom are women who have left a regular paid job and fallen out of the coverage of the Labour Insurance, is invariably under recognized. In this "informal work force" are also those migrant workers who have come from rural areas and are working in low-paid, heavy and dirty jobs which most city dwellers would not do and which are likewise excluded from the Labour Insurance coverage. One reason this work force is "informal" is that it is dominated by marginalized women who seldom hold proper contracts with employers and thus rarely fall within the protection of the law, including the rights to minimum wage and maximum overtime. Thus, social policies based on the reduction of spending on public goods and services are inherently biased against women, not only in terms of the poor, the majority of whom are women who are not able to to access services, especially in reproductive and preventive healthcare, but also in terms of generating an increased burden of care for women and discriminatory treatment of women who take up jobs in the services sector in "informal" arrangements.

Recognition of employment in the service sector based on "informal" arrangements started to appear in China in the 1990s. During this period, this sector expanded rapidly to include a growing number of migrant workers and laid off workers, a majority of whom are women, and who found self-employment, subcontracting, part time and casual labour as a way to make ends meet. The ability of this sector to absorb many of the retrenched workers during industrial restructuring, as "a shock absorber," has led Chinese policy-makers to advocate expanding community services but without taking away the "informal" arrangements.[17] Also, this sector has absorbed many of the migrant workers coming to the cities from the countryside. In 2003, more than 80 million of the 150 million surplus labourers in rural areas moved to the cities either as migrant workers or for business as a result of the lifted restrictions by government on the employment of rural people in cities.[18] Many of the migrant women workers are poorly educated and lack the skills to find stable jobs, and they end up working as casual or domestic labour in the informal sector. By one account, 15 million of these migrant workers work in domestic services. Even the Ministry of Labour and Social Security has taken note of this increase and adopted measures to regulate this labour market, through defining contractual relationships between the migrant worker, the employer and the recruiting agency and liability for compensation of work-related injuries.[19] Unfortunately, however, while the informal sector is still growing rapidly, most of the workers in this sector have slipped through the social safety net and experienced challenges to their security of income and livelihoods.[20] They have also experienced sexual abuse and violence by employers, deprivation of their rights to human dignity and security, and frequently have worked as forced labour. For instance, *yue sao* (literally, "new child sister-in-laws," namely, domestic workers who take care of new babies) are not allowed to go out of the house for months and live like forced labour with little freedom. The exploitative role of recruiting agencies in this sector has also been documented in recent events concerning foreign franchises in Guangdong Province, including MacDonald's and KFC, where cleaning women are used on a part time basis and paid below the minimum wage.[21]

The rise of vulnerability among those in the informal sector, especially migrant women workers, has highlighted the need for a more comprehensive approach to employment promotion and social security. Such a comprehensive approach would demand legal recognition and vigorous enforcement of contracts with minimum hourly wage standards and maximum overtime hours as well as entitlement to decent working conditions and social benefits. This approach, moreover, would reject the previous social security system based on employer liability mechanisms and endorse innovative contribution mechanisms, some of which have been incorporated in the recent Chinese experiments with social pooling for the eventual coverage of workers in all sectors, public and private (Chen 2008). A catch, however, is whether the Chinese experiments will take on a policy framework of protecting labour rights among migrant women workers while promoting "informal" employment.

A further issue with the gendered impact of social policy on migration is that of schooling for the children of migrant workers. Up until 2006, children of migrant workers in Beijing, Shanghai and Guangzhou have been invited to attend local schools. However, high school fees imposed on children without local household registration, long travel distances from remote suburban neighborhoods where migrant workers live and discriminatory treatment of these children by teachers and local students continued to intimidate them. In the end, after many appeals, these children still opted to go to the underfunded, segregated schools for migrants set up by volunteers and NGOs working to improve migrant workers' conditions, often in suburban areas.

Lihua Primary School in Tongzhou District, Beijing is an example; it was set up in 2005 by a migrant workers' organization called the Workers' Family.[22] This organization was established in 2002 as a non-profit enterprise by obtaining a license from the local Bureau of Industry and Commerce. It has conducted computer, skills and legal training among migrant workers and organized a song and dance troupe to perform in factories, construction sites and areas where migrant workers concentrate. Like several similar migrant workers' organizations I interviewed in Shenzhen in September 2007, this organization is concerned not so much with political rights but with migrant workers' economic rights as it aims to prepare migrant workers to become qualified members of the working class, who function knowledgably in an industrial setting and who use existing laws to protect their legitimate rights. One right of migrant workers the organization considered legitimate is the right of migrant workers' children to education. In 2006, when the Beijing Municipal Government threatened to close all schools like the Lihua Primary School set up only for children of migrant workers, the organization launched a public campaign in coalition with other civil society organizations. After much publicity, the Municipal Government gave up pressuring the school to close. At the time of my visit on 26 September 2007, the school had 400 students; each paid up to RMB 400 a term and RMB 100 extra for boarding costs, a fee much lower than that of a local school. When finishing at this primary school, one third of the students would join their parents looking for work in Beijing. Another third would try to find a vocational school somewhere to learn a trade; their fees would be paid by their parents who most likely would have saved enough money from operating small businesses to pay for their child's training. A final third, who had done well at school and demonstrated potential in learning, would be sent back to their native areas to attend senior level schooling and to prepare for higher education. This last group of students, when sent back without the company of their parents, would sooner or later develop what Chinese researchers have called the syndrome of "left behind children," one shared by many children who stayed behind with grandparents or other relatives in villages while their parents moved to the cities for work (Yang Juhua and Duan Chengrong 2008). Evidence suggests that this group of children is most vulnerable as they miss care and guidance and they develop a dislike for learning and other unhealthy attitudes.

CONCLUSION: PRIORITY AREAS FOR FUTURE RESEARCH

This paper is part of a research project that seeks to understand the impacts of gender gaps in policies on migrant workers in China, especially migrant women workers who have been subject to exploitation and the deprivation of legal protection of their rights in "informal" employment under the deregulation of the labour market. It has developed a feminist political economy framework, making use of a gender relational perspective with a women's rights and men's involvement approach, to analyze the economic policies of distributing land to individual households in agricultural and rural areas, and opening the door to international capital in industrial and urban areas. These policies contain gaps due largely to the fact that they failed to take into consideration gendered power relations and women's gender specific needs. These gaps exist especially in areas marked by an absence of government action, such as in facilitating and supporting equitably rural-to-urban migration, the erosion of labour market regulation creating oversupply of cheap labour, and lax enforcement of labour standards. The gaps affect migrant workers, especially migrant women workers who form the majority of the work force, in both the exploitative labour regime dominated by international capital and the exploitative "informal" labour regime dominating the services sector. Both regimes are exploitative and dangerous to inexperienced rural women who travel to urban areas in search of employment as they are exposed, from time to time, to the predation of abduction and trafficking and fall increasingly into forced commercial sex work as competition in the job markets intensifies. The analysis that is planned to follow shall be devoted to an examination of these two exploitative labour regimes in which migrant women workers experience violation of their rights to human dignity, freedom, and decent work conditions.

The identification of these above gaps supports the gender relational perspective, including the approach marked by recognition of women's rights and men's involvement, used in the conceptual framework of this study, and provides sufficient evidence for the need for a gender-responsive and rights-based strategy to balance development with the equitable use of migrant workers. The adoption of this strategy, which forms the subject matter of the last analysis of my forthcoming research project, will enhance the ability of the government to address differences in gendered needs between women and men. In addressing actual or probable gender inequities in rural-to-urban migration, I suggest that there are three priority areas which need attention from policy-makers and monitoring efforts by researchers and activists.

The first is the need for more systematic examination and monitoring of the impacts of exploitative labour regimes on migrant workers from a gender relational perspective, in order to inform policy and legislation towards a more equitable and harmonious *xiao kang* society.

The second urgent issue is that of identifying gender-based biases in government policies and legislation that have potential bearings on the lives and work of migrant workers. An important area to examine is the gendered impacts of contradicting goals of policies to promote economic development versus social services and social security, including labour benefits, healthcare, migrant children's schooling and the prevention and care of HIV/AIDS. One step to take is to harmonize these policies and remove gendered impacts by achieving compliance with international standards, including the MWC.

The third area for policy attention is the need for increased government action and institutional services to boost social support to migrant workers and to meet the different gendered needs of women. Civil society organizations and self-help groups can be established with the professional and technical assistance of government agencies and academia as well as the support of social institutions and service agencies. These organizations and groups may be formed voluntarily by migrant workers and operate with an agenda to eliminate discrimination against migrant workers, especially women. They likely provide a kind of social support that sometimes governments are unable to deliver due in part to gender blind policy making and uneven distribution of resources. Key to the adoption of gender sensitive policies towards migration is access to and participation in policy-making processes and social mobilization by migrant workers, especially migrant women workers themselves. China has been reminded by the international community of its obligation to its migrant workers and migrant women workers. The Chinese government will hopefully find a way, as it has already endeavored to do, to promote equality and justice towards the building of a harmonious *xiao kang* society.

ENDNOTES

[1]   Xinhua News; *Sun*, 30 April 2006.
[2]   See Sun Xiaohua, *China Daily*, 7 November 2006, p. 3, where it is stated that 40 percent of the population now live in urban areas in China.
[3]   See the UNIFEM report, "A UNIFEM Briefing Paper" (2003, p. 8).
[4]   According to Danforth (2003), "*Male involvement* seems to be the most comprehensive and useful term. Involvement can be of many kinds. *Male participation* is likewise quite broad, but implies participation in existing reproductive health activities, usually services for women. *Male responsibility* is less comprehensive than the first two terms. The term reflects the widespread belief that men have been 'irresponsible' and now should take their fair share of responsibility for birth control and STD use. Many men may well be irresponsible, but this cannot form the basis for a positive reproductive health programme that seeks to involve men and women in a transformative way." This paper employs the three expressions all in accordance with Danforth's delineation.
[5]   See Research Group of Rural Women Migrant Workers of the Sociology Institute of CASS (2000).
[6]   See Anita Chan (2001), Christa Wichterich (1998), Barbara Ehrenreich and Arlie Russell Hochschild (2002) and UNIFEM (2003).
[7]   See Lanyan Chen's *Gender and Chinese Development: Towards an Equitable Society* (Routledge, 2008). Further references to this work will appear in the text.
[8]   Though the *International Convention on the Elimination of All Forms of Racial Discrimination* (CERD) has been used in studies of migration in the world, it may have limited application here as China is not a party to the convention and has not considered different ethnic groups as races. The current study may have not had enough resources to expand the scope to include an examination of the gender issues encountered by migrant workers of ethnic minority origins.

9   For a discussion of an earlier version of the gender relational perspective, see Chen (2008).

10   For the notion of men as "gatekeepers," see Connell's paper on "The Role of Men and Boys in Achieving Gender Equality." The paper suggests that men still dominate the policy-making processes.

11   The absence of a legal definition of discrimination has been raised by the CEDAW Committee on China's sixth report on the implementation of the CEDAW as an issue that inhibits women's fight against discriminatory policies and practices.

12   The Chinese Premier confided on 21 February 2004 in a speech at a high-level seminar for provincial and ministerial officials at the Party School of the Central Committee of the Communist Party that building the "well-off" society would require the practice of a new "scientific concept of development." According to an official media discussion of the seminar, "The scientific concept of development proposed by the Chinese leadership featuring people-centred governance as well as comprehensive, coordinated and sustainable development of the economy and society will be crucial to the country's modernization drive in the future." See *Beijing Review*, vol. 47, no. 13, 2004, p. 22-23. Many believed that the unexpected SARS (severe acute respiratory syndrome) epidemic of 2003 sounded an alarm for China's leaders and prompted them to adopt the "scientific concept of development" (*ibid.*).

13   See Zai Liang and Yiu Por Chen (2003).

14   These numbers were first published by the *China Labour News* on 28 July 1997 and here they are taken from Chan (2001, p. 11). During my research trip to Shenzhen in September 2007, I learned from local informants that the minimum wage went up to RMB 800 per month.

15   For more, see Southern Weekend, 2002.

16   For more, see Southern Weekend, 2003.

17   According to Ren Yuan (2003) there were a total of 10 million people employed at the urban community level and the rate of job increase at this level is 40 percent. Seventy percent of the employed at the urban community level are made up of laid-off women.

18   See Tai Wei in *Beijing Review*, 18 March 2004, p. 22.

19   More from Li Minghui's presentation at the workshop organized by the Beijing Migrant Women Workers' Club in Beijing on 6 April 2007.

20   For a discussion of the social safety net in China, see Cook (2003) and ESCAP Study (2003).

21   See Guan Xiaofeng, "Fast-food Unions Taking Shape," *China Daily*, 6 April 2007, p. 3.

22   The following discussion is based on my field notes.

CHAPTER EIGHT

An Analysis of Rural Women's Entitlements to Land and Other Property

Liang Jianguo and Xu Weihua

I. An Overview of the Research

The research presented here is on rural women's entitlement to land and related properties. The target and goals of this research are: (1) to understand the real situation, to identify the major problems, and to discover the prevalence of and the reasons for these problems; (2) to understand how relevant laws and policies are implemented, and how effective they are at resolving the problems; (3) to understand rural women's needs for land and related property; and (4) to study how an effective system and legal framework can be established in order to protect rural women's entitlements by collecting, soliciting and submitting policy recommendations. To better understand the situation in some parts of China, the Task Team conducted targeted investigations and surveys.

Hebei Province and Zhejiang Province were chosen for this research. Questionnaires and panel discussions were organized. Through this research, we aim to find out how the People's Republic of China's (PRC) *Law on Rural Land Contracting*[1] and other laws, regulations and policies are carried out; how rural women's right and entitlement to land are realized; what the infringements of the laws are and the reasons behind them; how village committees handle relevant conflicts; what the government's attitude is toward this issue; and other connected issues.

II. Problems and their Manifestations Relating to Rural Women's Right and Entitlement to Land

1. Infringements of Rural Women's Right and Entitlement to Land Increase Year by Year

Infringements of rural women's right and entitlement to land have surfaced and evolved with the development of the local economy. During the reform establishing the household contract responsibility system in the countryside, and the reform to prolong the period of a land contract in 1998, infringements upon women's right to contract land and to use housing sites were typical. In recent years, there has been rampant expropriation of rural lands. Compensation for expropriated land has become a major source of revenue for rural collectives and an important part of income for local peasants. In this process, women were frequently deprived of their share of the compensation or given a smaller cut. In addition, some villages banned women from equal enjoyment of related property entitlements (derivatives of land entitlements such as land compensation fees, dividends on land shares, etc.) as well as related benefits. In some places, women were denied equal treatment during rural economic restructuring. In distributing lands or other quantified shares or year-end dividends, women are often given a smaller cut. Thus, their entitlements to land-related compensation are infringed upon. Our survey shows that in some villages, inequality between men and women is very obvious. For instance, women who married someone from a different village but kept their *hukou* (residence permit) unchanged are deprived of or banned from a full share of the compensation. Their children are only entitled to half their share.

2. More Women Fall Victim to Infringements

During the first round of land contract reform, the victims were primarily women who married outside of the village and their children; these women were discriminated against. In some places, single women's right to contract land was also restricted. Namely, they were entitled to no land or a lesser share of the land. During the second round of reform, the contracted tenure was prolonged. Many problems emerged concerning rural women's marital status. Namely, if a woman is married, either out of or into the village, or becomes divorced or widowed, her entitlement to land becomes vulnerable to local restrictions. Our survey shows that victims in the countryside have expanded to include not only women who are married out of the village, but also women who moved into the village after marriage, women who are married to urban citizens, divorced and widowed women, women whose *hukou* is still registered in their maiden home, children of those women, and uxorilocal sons-in-law. Women who married out of or married into the village, as well as divorced and widowed women are especially vulnerable. Our survey revealed that in both Zhejiang and Hebei provinces, village codes of conduct contain unequal requirements. For instance, some villages require that before marrying into the village, a woman would have to sign an agreement with the village committee to relinquish her entitlement to distributed land shares and related benefits.

3. More Forms of Infringement

In recent years, infringements of women's entitlement have taken the following forms:

A. Rural collectives take back a woman's land when she moves out of the village after marriage.

In China, rural land is distributed among registered households in the village. State policy on rural land is summarized as "(contracted tenure for land) remains valid for

30 years, with no major changes but small adjustments." Enforcement of this policy, however, varies in different parts of China. In our investigation, we found that rural women would usually re-register their *hukou* in their husband's village when they get married. In this process, it is easy for them to lose their original land. The local rural community would usually be taking back the women's contracted land at their maiden home. Since rural households instead of individuals contract land, and there is no clear delineation of individuals' rights within the family, the rights due to women are not well protected. Even with a 30-year tenure, if a woman gets married and leaves her maiden home, she effectively loses her right to use the contracted land and to enjoy its proceeds. She has to transfer these rights to her parents or brothers without compensation.

Rural women are likely to lose their land entitlements in their maiden village once they get married and move into their husband's village. On the other hand, it is hard for them to receive new land in their husband's village. Most Chinese villages do not keep enough reserve land for potential newcomers to contract. After re-registering their *hukou* in their husband's village, these women could only wait for a re-allocation of land by the local community. If the village does not re-allocate land for contracting, these women and their children could never have the chance to get their share of land.

B. Rural collectives take back land from divorced and widowed rural women.

In rural China, once married, a woman moves in with her husband's family. Our survey shows that when a couple gets divorced, the village of the divorced husband would often take back the wife's share of the land and force the wife to give up her *hukou* and return to her village. This is done regardless of whether the divorced wife could regain her share of land in her maiden village or whether she gets a share of land from her next husband's village if she remarries. Some divorced women find that after returning to their maiden villages, the village accepts only their *hukou* and gives land to them but not to the children they support. In panel discussions we found that in both provinces there are villages that adopt the policy of *one moves out before another moves in*; that is, if the divorced wife chooses to stay in her former husband's village, when her former husband remarries, all of her entitlements would be transferred to her former husband's new wife.

C. There is a lack of protection for the rights of men who move in with their wife's family after marriage.

In many rural villages, local codes and rules discriminate against men who move in with their wife's family. For instance, some codes say that uxorilocal sons-in-law are entitled to either less contracted land or none at all. Some villages require that in households with only daughters, no more than one live-in son-in-law be entitled to village land. In other villages, if a household has both sons and daughters, it cannot take in uxorilocal sons-in-law. If it does, the son-in-law has no entitlement to local land.

D. Rural women's land rights and entitlements are infringed upon in the process of transferring rural land rights.

With economic development, more and more rural surplus labourers leave villages for cities. Consequently, land-contracting rights began to change hands. In this process, the land entitlements of rural women who leave their village to work in the cities are often violated. Such violations often take two forms: a) when agriculture tax needs to be paid, the women's land is either counted as waste land or directly taken back by the village and given to others to till; b) if these women get married in cities, they are regarded as city dwellers, and the village then takes back the women's land and they are deprived of all their entitlements as members of the village.

E. Villages arbitrarily remove the hukou *of some rural women who marry urban citizens.*

During our investigation, we found that some villages arbitrarily require that if a woman marries an urban citizen, her *hukou* must be removed. Once the *hukou* is removed, the village deprives her of her land entitlements.

4. Lack of Effective Remedies

The reasons behind land disputes are multiple and complex. To solve the problems and conflicts related to this issue, land authority, local governments, village committees and courts all need to be involved. Lack of cooperation from any player would lead to the shifting of responsibility and deadlock. Grievances of this kind are not easily redressed by the courts; therefore, women have to repeatedly present their claims to government authorities and courts. For instance, compensation is often not paid immediately in the distribution of land. The court's verdict, if there is one, is only valid for one installment. Thus, even for one claim, women with these problems will have to file many court actions. Judges often find cases of this kind hard to deal with; some judges even shun such cases. Coordination among competent authorities is poor. Local offices of the Communist Party and local governments are not willing to interfere.

III. AN ANALYSIS OF THE REASONS BEHIND THIS PROBLEM

1. REASONS RELATED TO CHINA'S REALITY

A. Firstly, land is scarce in China. There is increasing tension between the expanding population and the shrinking land-related resources. Such tension is especially obvious in the periphery of cities where more and more land is expropriated and population concentration is high. In recent years, rapid urban expansion has created demand for land in peripheral rural areas. This has sharpened the tensions amongst people over land.

Secondly, thanks to high unemployment in cities, inadequate social security coverage in the countryside and other factors, land has become the main source of support for peasants. The fight for land and related entitlements becomes ever more fierce. Peasants are divided into different interest groups. In the struggle for economic gain, when the interests of one group have to be sacrificed, women are usually singled out, especially divorced and widowed women.

B. Land is immovable, but women traditionally move from their maiden home to live with their husband's family after marriage. Certain problems stem from the immovability of land and the mobility of women. Because land cannot be moved, most women can only keep nominal rights over their land located in their home villages. Currently, rural households contract land. There are no clear rules on the land rights of individual family members. Women, single or married, often cannot claim their land rights as individuals and, as a result, risk losing control over their land.

C. The *hukou* system and its effect. Rural women's *hukou* situation is quite complicated. There are women who are married to urban citizens but could not get re-registered for an urban *hukou*; their *hukou* is still in their home village. In prosperous villages, women often do not want to marry men from other villages. Even if they do marry outside of the village, these women often do not want to change their *hukou*. There are also women whose *hukou* is separated from their residence because of divorce, remarriage or widowhood. This is especially true for women who marry urban citizens but could not change their *hukou* into an urban one. These women suffer from inequality not only between the sexes but also between cities and the countryside.

2. Current Laws and Policies are Inadequate

A. Loopholes in the current legal framework.

Under the PRC Constitution, women enjoy equal rights to men in political, economical, cultural, social and family spheres. In China, a framework of laws that include the Constitution, the *Law on the Protection of Women's Rights and Interests*,[2] and supporting regulations has been put in place. The legal system upholds equality between men and women, stresses the protection of women's rights and interests, and contains provisions that are in the best interests of women. In terms of the legal constitution, China is quite sophisticated in the protection of women's rights and interests. However, some legal provisions are not practical in reality and cannot be enforced properly. As for violations of women's rights, sanctions are weak and remedies hard to access. The linkage among relevant laws is poor. Some legal provisions are general, abstract and hard to enforce. Last but not least, some provisions are not designed from the perspective of gender equality.

For instance, currently there is no clear legal definition for membership in rural economic collectives. A major part of rural collectives is made up of women. How to define their membership and how to protect their related interests, especially with changes brought about by marriage, are still legal challenges. Despite improvements in laws and policies to protect peasants' land entitlements over recent years, the crucial issue of the definition for membership has not been addressed.

Article 24 of the *Supreme People's Court (SPC) Interpretation*[3] provides that compensation for land shall be distributed among persons qualified as members of the rural economic collective, when the land expropriation compensation and settlement plan is set. However, it does not define the qualification for membership or for distribution. In reality, villagers directly or through rural collectives, and following different rules, distribute and redistribute the proceeds of land. So much so that within a village, among different production teams or at different periods, there are different ways and criteria for distribution. This situation leads to inequity and disputes. It also explains why there are a great deal of disputes between rural women or newcomers and rural economic collectives.

B. Poor Linkage Between Laws

Firstly, differences among laws provide loopholes that can be taken advantage of. The PRC Constitution grants women equal economic and political rights. The revised *Law on the Protection of Women's Rights and Interests* stipulates clearly equality between men and women. The *Marriage Law* gives men and women equal access to family property. The *Law on Rural Land Contracting* contains specific provisions on women's entitlement to land and related property. Nevertheless, the *Organic Law of Village Committees*[4] stipulates that village committees are elected by all villagers to represent them, and are self-administered. Villagers' meetings can be called as long as at least half of the villagers who are above 18-years-old are in attendance, or with representation from 2/3 of village households.[5] Decisions from the meeting are adopted by a majority. However, some village committees have abused these provisions in order to infringe on women's rights. In enforcing the *Organic Law of Village Committees*, many rural officials at the grassroots level misunderstand the intention and role of this law. Some of the problems include:

- Many rural officials believe that since the Standing Committee of the National People's Congress adopted this law, it should be the most authoritative law in governing the administration of village affairs in the countryside.
- This law is on how to organize self-administrative entities in the countryside. Once constructed, an administrative system would remain stable. Since issues in the countryside are complex, the principle of 2/3 quorum should be maintained.
- Many village committees only emphasize provisions that are conducive to their work, and downplay restrictive provisions.

Due to these factors, many decisions detrimental to women's interests are often made or agreed upon by village committees. Numerous victimized women choose to report their grievances to local governments, but often to little avail.

Secondly, there is a lack of supervision and monitoring of village rules, codes or decisions that contravene laws. The *Organization Law of Villagers' Committees* stipulates that codes of self-administration, rules or decisions made by villagers shall not contravene the Constitution, other laws and national policies, nor shall they infringe on the personal, democratic and property rights of members of the village. However, the *Organization Law* does not designate an entity to review the compliance of village codes, rules and decisions, or to supervise villages. The *Organization Law* also does not provide for sanctions on violations, or remedies for victims. Because of the lack of such provisions, it is hard to correct violations by village committees.

C. Gender equality is not considered when some laws and policies are made.

Legislation is a process in which opinions from all sides should be expressed and heard, in particular those from minority groups. All affected parties should be represented in the process of legislation. If men make up the majority of legislators or if legislators are not aware of gender equality, women's interests and needs cannot be properly reflected in the laws and male values would dominate legislation. For instance, under the rural household contract responsibility system, the contracting unit is the household. Even though heads of the household allocate land, each member's rights are not clarified, let alone are clear property relationships among members of the family. An individual's property entitlements and rights concerning land remain ambiguous. Land contracts often bear the husband's name only, which means that the law does not recognize the wife's land entitlements. Thus, when an individual's interests are infringed upon, it is hard to find support for a claim. During divorce, contracted land is often not regarded as the common property of the couple.

This phenomenon produces a ripple effect. At the grassroots level, women are often excluded from important discussions or development of village codes or rules. Frequently, women's voices are too low to be heard or to influence the decision-making process. As a result, these women's claims to land are often marginalized.

3. Inadequate Publicity of Laws

Equality between men and women is a basic national policy. It is also clearly stipulated in the Constitution, the *Law on the Protection of Women's Rights and Interests*, the *Marriage Law*,[6] the *Law on Rural Land Contracting*. The central and sub-national governments have issued decrees and policies to support the protection of rural women's land entitlements. Since 1985, China has been organizing national five year campaigns to popularize legal knowledge. So far, five campaigns have been organized successively, and many people have been educated about these laws. However, due to various reasons, efforts to popularize laws do not produce great results at the grassroots level, especially in remote areas of the countryside. In addition, after the government staff trained in these campaigns retires, the training of new staff at the grassroots level is not organized in a timely way. Without proper training, new staff is not very conscious of protecting women's entitlements. This in turn affects efforts to popularize laws. In some parts of China, there is limited knowledge of the laws relating to women's rights.

Through our investigation, we found that some local government officials are not very conscious of relevant laws or how to comply with them. In handling complaints concerning rural women's land entitlements, some officials over-emphasized respect for villagers' self-administration and the importance of village codes. In formulating local policies, some officials gave too much consideration to villagers' self-administration, which misled villagers and gave rise to conflicts in certain cases. After receiving complaints from women, some town/township officials would try to avoid these cases by urging the women to file their complaints with local courts, saying that the township government could not issue compulsory decisions on these disputes. Some local governments institute policies that require consent from 2/3 of the members of the rural collective's general meeting in order for rural women, who marry into city households but maintain a village *hukou*, and their children, to have a share in village land. In addition, some women are not aware of relevant laws and do not know how to use these laws to protect themselves. Many women do not make a claim on the right to contract land or waive the right in a divorce, which makes it hard to claim the right later on.

4. Lack of Effective Remedies

A. Administrative inaction. Some town/township governments do not exercise effective guidance on villagers' self-administration. Currently, town/township governments can guide, rather than directly lead, the work of village committees. Thus, they cannot use direct administrative orders to interfere in the internal affairs of villages. When facing land disputes, local governments usually do not want to offend the majority of villagers. Furthermore, they are passive in reaching out and educating villagers. When there is an individual complaint, the government would try to whitewash the problem; if the situation deteriorates into a group problem, the government would not know how to handle it.

B. Lack of Effective Judicial Remedies. Filing a case of a rural woman's land dispute remains an outstanding problem. With the *Law on Rural Land Contracting* and its interpretation going into effect, and the *Law on the Protection of Women's Rights and Interests* revised, rural women now have legal protection for their entitlements. However, there are still numerous impediments. In disputes involving rural women's land rights and rural economic collectives, it is still hard for victims to get effective legal remedy. There are still places where courts refuse to accept such cases. Since 2005, many grassroots level courts have ceased to take cases involving rural land and compensation disputes. The following reasons may explain the courts' action:

i) Ambiguity with litigation parties

Some argue that since village committees are not administrative organs, it is not suitable for courts to hear the cases as administrative disputes. On the other hand, village committees do exercise administrative functions, which means that these cases cannot be heard as civil disputes either. Some judges propose that these complaints should first be handled by local governments under central government policies and then be heard as administrative cases. However, due to apathy and resistance from local governments, it is difficult to channel such cases into the judicial system through administrative procedures.

ii) Legal provisions that land compensation should not be divided and distributed.

The Supreme People's Court's Judicial Interpretation provides that, in principle, courts should not accept disputes concerning land compensation distribution. In reality, even if this kind of dispute is accepted, the case would usually take a long time because of the difficulty in collecting evidence, and the court is concerned about resistance from local villagers. Nonetheless, there are judges conscious of gender equality who could ignore pressure and rule objectively. However, winning a case is far from a complete victory; enforcing the verdict is another hurdle. Fortunately, local courts in Jinhua, Shaoxing, Lishui and Taizhou in Zhejiang province have made experimental efforts in this regard. They bundled together cases in which women achieved a favourable ruling, and made concerted efforts in enforcement. For instance, a county court in Xingchang enforced 63 cases in a campaign. Shima village in Liuxia town, Hangzhou city, used mediation in handling compensation and house-site disputes involving 31 rural women.

The *Legal Interpretation on the Application of Laws in Handling Cases of Rural Land Contract Disputes* by the SPC went into effect in September 2005.[7] Items 2 and 3 of Article 1 provide that if members of rural economic entities file a civil action in court for their unfulfilled land contracting right, they shall be informed by the court that they should first file their complaints with competent administrative authorities; if members of rural economic entities file a civil action in court for disputes concerning land compensation distribution, the court can refuse to accept the case. At present, enforcement of these provisions varies in different courts. An action may be accepted by one court but refused by another, or the same court would handle similar cases differently at different times.

C. Lack of non-litigation channels to solve conflicts. Arbitration agencies and procedures that can handle disputes involving the right to land use are not widely established in China, and their roles are quite limited. The possibility of using mediation is still under discussion. Legal liability procedures for violations of farmers' land rights should be further improved.

D. *The current response is passive and not preventative.* Some regions are not forward-looking in carrying out national policies. For instance, they fail to consider the impact of population mobility caused by marriage and do not put in place counter-measures. That is why these kinds of disputes are so hard to resolve. Many villages do not put aside reserve land when allocating or reallocating land. Some villages distribute land compensation and land shares once and for all. Therefore, it is quite hard to call for re-collection and redistribution. Some rural economic entities do not even put aside reserve funds for their future development, let alone money to compensate women whose rights are violated. If land or compensation is already divided up among village households, even if the claims of women are supported by courts, it is very hard to enforce. Pushing for enforcement often means meeting strong local resistance.

E. *Women are often a disadvantaged group in village organizations.* Women are underrepresented in village decision-making organs. They are not active in the self-administration of villages. Heads of village women's committees are often not members of the highest decision-making organs in the village. Even if they are, they are not in key positions and do not have a strong voice. In some villages, all decision-makers are men. For this reason, when decisions against women's interests are made, there is little opposition. Even if women have different opinions, they are not able to initiate a review procedure in the village, or would meet strong opposition from the majority of villagers who could benefit from the decision.

5. Legacy of Traditional Concepts and Customs

In China, it is a long-established custom for women to move into the family of their husbands after marriage, particularly in the countryside. Daughters are treated like boarders, and women can only hope to get property and succession rights through their husband's household. Women are always seen as dependent, on father or brothers before marriage and on their husband after marriage. They cannot get land as independent individuals.

Against this cultural background, many regions adopted a policy of "not to increase the share of land of a household when the family has a new member; nor to reduce its share when it loses one." Women are disproportionately affected by these policies. In regions where land is scarce, in order to get a larger share of land, villagers often do not accept women who married into the village or divorced women as one their own. In economically prosperous villages, particularly suburban ones, villagers or village committees would often adopt decisions to the detriment of these women in distributing land and proceeds. This stems from the fear that women who are married to someone outside the village would not want to change their *hukou*, or would even want to move their husband's *hukou* into the village.

IV. POLICY RECOMMENDATIONS AND SUGGESTIONS

Conflicts and disputes concerning women's land entitlements reflect the disparity between men and women in terms of resource division, social status, and access to development. They reveal that there is still discrimination against women, a legacy from the feudal past. Even some law enforcement officers and government officials have misunderstandings like "village codes can surpass laws." This type of thinking shows problems in the legal framework. To remove discrimination, to protect the life of women and their children, and to facilitate the resolution of current problems, we make the following suggestions:

1. The Standing Committee of the National People's Congress should improve legislation.

From our investigation, we find that the current *Law on Rural Land Contracting* is rather general and hard to enforce. To facilitate enforcement of the law, we suggest that the Standing Committee of The National People's Congress put more effort into improving supporting legislation and in giving substance to provisions on rural women's land entitlements.

A. *Clarify membership of rural economic entities.* Membership of rural economic entities is an important right for citizens. Under the *Law on Legislation*, this right should be defined and regulated by laws instead of administrative regulations, local bylaws, government decrees or judicial interpretations. Therefore, we hope that the National People's Congress can clarify this issue through legislation, and in so doing provide institutional protection to women in land related conflicts.

B. *During marriage between two rural households, land contracting right should be adjusted according to changed status of family members and their hukou.* Firstly, there should be clear legal provisions on: the entitlements of rural women (including women who marry outside of the village) to land contracting; on their participation in bidding, contracting and managing non-economic activities of the rural collective that they belonged to before marriage; on partaking in the distribution of shares and dividends; and on the allocation of economic profits, welfare benefits and house sites.

Secondly, there should be clear legal principles governing the *hukou* status, the right to choose domicile, and other rights of rural women (including uxorilocal sons-in-law) after marriage or with any change to their marital status. Men who move in with their wife's family or women who move into their husband's household after marriage should receive land from local economic entities. If they do not change their *hukou* accordingly, they should be persuaded to do so. If a woman, after marriage, remains in her original home with her husband and does not change her *hukou*, she should be allowed to keep her contracted land. If her children are registered in the village, they should be given equal treatment to other villagers. As for divorced or widowed women and their children, if their *hukou* is not moved to another place, they should be allowed to keep their contracted land. If a divorced or widowed woman returns to her maiden village or gets remarried, her *hukou* should be changed accordingly, and she should be given the same land entitlements as others in the recipient village. As for households with only daughters, if their husbands move in with the family after marriage, these sons-in-law should be given the same land contracting rights as other villagers.

C. Individual rights should be protected separately from the rights of families. It should be added into the *Property Law* that for a married rural woman, both names of the couple shall appear on the written land contract. The wife and the husband shall hold separate copies of the contract that sets out the equal rights and obligations of both parties. The *Property Law* should clearly state that transferring or leasing of the land is only valid when both copies of the contract and both signatures of husband and wife are produced. This is to safeguard the rights of women to possess, use, benefit from and transfer their contracted lands. This will also protect rural women from the danger of losing their rights and interests on land without their knowledge, especially for women who are divorced, widowed or who have separated from their husbands.

D. The law should also provide for clear-cut regulations on the usage and distribution of compensation for land expropriation and corresponding mechanisms in case of disputes. These are necessary provisions that can fill in the loopholes of current legislations. They will also prevent further violations of women's legitimate rights and interests via abusive usage of compensation for land expropriation.

E. Property contracts on rural lands should be normalized. Normalizing all land contracts is very important for stabilizing the rural land contracting system and for better defining the rights and obligations of parties involved. It is also important for maintaining the stable development of the countryside. Local People's Congresses at different levels should make predictive policies to tackle problems that arise in the processes of land expropriation, transfer of contracting rights, and urbanization reforms. Implementation of the basic State policy of "gender equality" should be guaranteed to normalize and to guide the behaviors of collective economic organizations. In counties and villages where land contracts are performed properly, and where there are successful experiences of protecting rural women's rights to land against violators, these experiences should be noted down and disseminated. For example, Hebei Province, the Chang Li County of Qinghuadao and Yan Shan County of Changzhou are carrying out pilot projects involving the publishing of relevant policies that have witnessed good results in protecting women's entitlements to land. For instance, Chang Li County issued documents containing relevant land rights and interests of rural women on three occasions, in 1994, 2000 and 2004. These documents contain detailed safeguard measures relating to women's land contracting rights, which have provided strong policy support to local women. Currently, eight cities and counties (city districts) in Hebei Province, including Tang Shan, Langfang and Changli have published fourteen local policy documents. Altogether, 220 cases concerning women's right to land have been dealt with.

2. Adoption of Local Legislation to Protect Women's Rights should be Accelerated

State legislation on land management and contracting still contains many deficiencies in terms of protecting the land rights and interests of rural women. To ensure the integrity of the legal system, local legislations and supplements are necessary to enhance and particularize state legislation within the local context. Some districts and cities of Hebei Province are doing very well in this respect. A typical example is the case of Chang Li County. *Supplementary Regulations on Land Contracting* and *Opinions on Implementing Rural Land Contracting Law* and *Strengthening Administration of Rural Land Contracting* were issued based on a field investigation of selected villages. The county secretary of the Party Committee, the County Party Committee, as well as the county government carried out this investigation for one month. In addition, the various departments of the region, headed and coordinated by local authorities, reached a consensus on the *Announcement on Protecting Contracting Rights to Land of Divorced Rural Women*. These are all are guidelines for promptly and effectively resolving disputes concerning rural women's right to land, and for safeguarding these rights against improper influences from other local factors.

3. Dissemination of the State Policy of Gender Equality and Relevant Laws and Regulations should be Strengthened

Stipulations on the protection of women's rights and interests can be located in many laws and policies promulgated and issued by the State. These include the Constitution, the *Marriage Law*, the *Law on Protection of Women's Rights and Interests*, the *Law on Rural Land Contracting* and the *Law on Protection of Minors*.[8] However, people are not familiar with these regulations and polices in many places. Therefore, more effort should be made to spread the State policy of gender equality and related laws to the general public, and especially to the various levels of leading cadres. Government branches, the judiciary, and village cadres at the grassroots level should be targeted in order to increase awareness of the responsibility for protecting rural women's right to land among law enforcers. This will enable law enforcers to know and understand the law, and to behave as models in using and abiding by the law. It is also necessary to raise the legal consciousness among the general rural public about the protection of women's rights and interests, and especially among women themselves. This will equip women with the knowledge and capacity to protect their own rights and interests.

4. Local Governments' Responsibilities in Protecting Women's Right to Land should be Reinforced

Real cases have shown that in places where disputes about women's right to land were properly settled, it was always the local governments, as enforcers of the State land contracting system, who were playing the leading roles. Successful past experiences reveal the following:

First of all, an arbitration mechanism for land contracting disputes should be set up and perfected. Arbitration, as opposed to judicial remedies, has unique advantages. These advantages are evident where the woman in question has difficulty bringing an action in court, and where she wishes to solve the issue in a simple, fast and convenient way. Hence, arbitration can be a very effective means for solving land contracting issues in rural areas. Agricultural administrations at all levels should strengthen their petition reception desks, as well as their investigation and punitive mechanisms. They should also create arbitration committees dedicated to land contracting, and develop a whole institution of arbitration rules and procedures. These measures are to ensure that all land disputes can be handled appropriately, including those disputes concerning rural women, and to address all disputes at the local and grassroots level.

Secondly, administration of land contracting should be intensified and illegal village regulations or conventions should be invalidated. By way of making and implementing policy measures, government departments can intensify their control and supervision over the process of land contracting and the distribution of interests. This is to avoid the infringements of women's rights and interests related to their entitlements to land. At the same time, local codes of conduct, such as village self-rule charters, village regulations, folk conventions and rules of allocating interest in rural collective economic organizations, should be scrutinized. Laws and regulations that contradict the protection of women's rights and interests should be deleted or abandoned. Local regulations should be amended or even overhauled in accordance with State standards for the protection of women; local authorities should be urged to do this and their compliance verified. There should be certain penalties to correct misdeeds and to punish those who are guilty of violations.

Thirdly, channels for women to seek help should be expanded, and more remedies should be provided. Mediation should be expanded to play a role equivalent to its full potential. With their patience and experience in persuading others, the people's mediation committees would be ideal for resolving conflicts and misunderstandings. A variety of punitive measures should be taken against persons liable for infringements. Legal punishments as well as administrative disciplines should be adopted to prevent encroachments by the government.

5. Judicial Remedies to Women Victims should be Provided

A society with a fast growing legal system will not allow silence by law and law enforcers regarding the land rights issues. Courts, as the major law enforcer in society, should provide transparent and unimpeded proceedings to rural women against those who violate their right to land. No excuses by the judiciary for shunning their responsibility for providing remedies are acceptable. Now that the government is shifting from serving a judicial function, it seems that rural women will have to turn to the law for relief. Our suggestions for how to define and expand the role of courts in the protection of rural women's entitlement to the land include: first, courts should accept land cases filed by rural women as long as the conditions prescribed by the law are satisfied; secondly, while deciding these cases, courts should hear the cases as required by law, and apply the law appropriately; thirdly, the scales of legal judgments should sometimes be slightly tilted in favour of the underprivileged; fourthly, judgments should all be based on the idea of respecting individual rights and sustaining reasonable claims by women; finally, more research and field surveys should be carried out in order to further explore judicial remedies for violations of women's rights to land and property. Precedents should be established for courts to rely on in future cases.

6. The People's Congresses over the Implementation of Laws and Regulations should Intensify Supervision

Once a legal framework has been established, it is the implementation of these laws that really matters. As stated above, one of the first steps in implementing State laws is to supervise the making and enforcement of village codes of conduct. The People's Congress should, at this stage, perform its function as a supervisory body to defend the authority of law. The autonomy of villages shall not surpass the boundaries set by law. Specifically, no local codes of conduct shall contravene laws and regulations made by legislative bodies. In dealing with infringements committed by village assemblies or village representatives' conferences, People's Congresses at various levels should ask local governments or administrative organs to take certain measures to ensure the integrity of the law. It is worth considering the adoption of a report and review system of village codes and folk conventions by People's Congresses. This would means that all village codes would first be reported to and reviewed by the People's Congress at the township or county level before they could be put into force. This proceeding would facilitate the administration of village codes and folk conventions; and any nonconformity of local codes that might lead to violations of women's rights would be detected immediately and potential infringements prevented.

7. Legal Services should be Procured from Civil Organizations or Non-governmental Organizations (NGOs)

In recent years, civil society organizations and NGOs are becoming more and more active in carrying out experiments in rights advocating, such as research and legal actions. These actions have achieved exciting breakthroughs in the admissibility of cases filed by women on land disputes. The difficulties that rural women face in filing land dispute cases and in winning them have been lifted to some extent. These activities have not only opened the minds of relevant government departments, but also shed light on the judicature by opening a window through which a future with better protection of women's rights to the land can be seen.

While working in the Centre for Women's Law and Legal Service of Peking University, a member of our task group was deeply impressed by the Centre's commitment to the protection of rural women's entitlements to land. The Centre, by providing pro bono legal aid services, has made great progress in promoting rural women's legal actions defending their land rights. The following cases are chosen to demonstrate how the government can benefit from purchasing legal services provided by civil organizations. They are all typical and well-known cases in which the authors of this paper have been personally involved.

Case One
Nie Cuilian, Xu Donghai, Xu Shuange and another 25 married women v. Village Committee of Shang Liang Village, Inner Mongolia.[9]

Brief Description of Facts:
In December 1999 and November 2000, two meetings of village representatives were convened by the Village Committee of Shaliang Village, located in Bashan County, Saihan District of Hohhot, capital of the Inner Mongolia Autonomous Region. The meetings, moderated by local village cadres, reached the following decisions that were against the law:

- A previous decision that the village would not allocate land to women born in the village during the second round of land contracting was sustained.
- Each villager was entitled to two houses constructed by the village collective: a flat one for residence (about 75 square meters), and another one with street frontage for commercial use (about 75 square meters). This policy does not apply to everyone. Women who married outside of the village and their husbands were excluded from the list of beneficiaries, irrespective of whether they are still living in the village or not.

The philosophy behind this decision is that married women, whether they stay or leave the village, become "outsiders" after their marriage. Following this philosophy, 28 plaintiffs altogether were deprived of their entitlements to land for the second round of contracting. They were also deprived of their share of the houses and many other important economic interests (e.g., RMB 300 land compensation and food subsidies, etc.). Consequently, these 28 plaintiffs and 40 other women born in the same village and who suffered from the same kind of discrimination, embarked on a hard journey to seek remedies. Since April 1997, they filed several complaints to higher authorities, including the district government of Saihan, the municipal government of Huhhot, the CPC Commission of the Autonomous Region, the Provincial Government, the People's Congresses of various levels and the women's federations. They allege that the defendant has, in violation of the *Constitutional Law*, the *Law on Land Contracting*, the *Law on Protection of Women's Rights and Interests*, the *Organization Law of Villagers' Committee* and the *General Principles of Civil Law*,[10] infringed upon their rights and interests under the law.

In response to these pledges, some authorities issued orders requiring the village to correct its "misdeeds." However, the orders were resisted by village cadres and many ordinary villagers. On 7 June 2002, in order to come to terms with the village, the plaintiffs waived parts of their rights and reluctantly signed an agreement (referred to as the June 7 Agreement) that assigned them 1.7 *mu* (1 *mu* is equal to 0.0667 hectares) of land per person for the second round of contracting. This agreement did not last long. Two years later, the land assigned to the plaintiffs was taken back by the villagers committee again to build resident houses and commercial buildings. Due to some void clauses in the June 7 Agreement, the plaintiffs, who had just suffered from loss of land, were denied their rights to get houses either for residence or for commercial purposes. As a result, the 28 plaintiffs and their families were thrown into a predicament where they lacked adequate sources of income. It was against this background that a claim for the right to subsistence and equal treatment was made by the 28 plaintiffs. An action was lodged before the People's Intermediate Court of Huhhot, alleging that the *Constitutional Law*,[11] the *Law on Land Contracting*, the *Law on Protection of Women* and the *Organization Law of Villagers' Committees* were breached by Article 4, Paragraph 1 of the June 7 Agreement drafted by the Shaliang villagers committee. The plaintiffs then asked the court to rule against the defendant. They demanded that the defendant correct its wrongdoing and treat the plaintiffs the same way as the male villagers, and thus that it reallocate the villages' land and houses fairly and objectively. Specifically, the plaintiffs demanded that:

1. The court declare Article 4 of the Agreement signed on June 7, 2002 between the Shaliang Villagers' Committee and the village's married women on the second round of land contracting void.
2. The defendant assign all plaintiffs, as equals to the male villagers, with two houses: one for residence (about 75 square meters), and the other for commercial use (about 75 square meters). Alternatively, the defendant shall pay each plaintiff a lump-sum compensation of RMB 400,000, or RMB 9,999,999 in total.
3. The defendant bear the fees and costs arising out of litigation, including the litigation fees charged by the court, the costs for property preservation and the costs for executing the judgment, and any other such costs that may be incurred.

In their statement of facts, the 28 married women of the village described themselves in the following terms: "We, 28 married women, were all born in the Shaliang Village and are still residents of the village after we got married. Our *hukous* are still registered here. Over the years, we have been working on our contracted land and contributing to the development of the local collective economy."

The first hearing was held on 11 May 2006 by the court of competence. During the trial hearing, the plaintiffs presented evidence retelling the story of when and how the June 7 Agreement was formulated. The defendant did not deny the allegations, neither did it contest the evidence produced by the plaintiffs; instead, it argued that the June 7 Agreement was a result of group discussions by the entire village committee. The agreement found its legal basis in the *Organization Law of Villagers' Committees*, and it expressed the will of the majority of villagers; hence, the agreement should not be overruled. The plaintiffs denounced this line of defense. They called the court's attention to the fact that gender equality is provided by the Constitution as one of its basic principles. Furthermore, during the Fourth World Women's Conference held in Beijing in 1995, the Chinese government promised the world that China would incorporate gender equality into its decision-making process as a basic State policy. The plaintiffs argued that the Constitution and the law should circumscribe the autonomy enjoyed by villagers. The precondition for exercising village autonomy is that all laws, regulations, state policies and the whole legal system be respected. Nothing could justify an autonomy surpassing the boundaries of the Constitution and other laws; no organization or individual stands beyond the reach of the Constitution or other laws. Discriminatory and oppressive practices against a minority, under the pretence of majority rule, should not be allowed. This is especially true when the majority opinion is wrong or even illegal. Relying on the basic State policy of gender equality, the plaintiffs called upon the court to dismiss the defendant's argument and to make a judgment in favour of the plaintiffs according to law. In its last statement to the court, the defendant agreed to abide by the judgment.

The judgment of the first instance was made on 19 June 2006. The written judgment of the People's Intermediate Court of Huhhot defined the case as "a dispute on membership of village collective economy and fair distribution of properties within the village collective economy, which at the same time, touched upon rights and interests of women and was associated with the implementation of the basic State policy of gender equality."

The judgment reads as follows:

Pursuant to Paragraphs 3 and 5 of Article 52 of the *Contract Law*,[12] the court believes that Paragraph 1, Article 4 of the June 7 Agreement is void. Reasons for this ruling include:

1. The Shaliang village in which the plaintiffs were born and raised is a comparatively rich village with a fast growing economy. For that reason, women are unwilling to leave the village even after marriage. Instead, they and their husbands choose to abandon their entitlement to the second round of land contracting in their husbands' villages and to continue residing in Shaliang. As a matter of fact, this choice is not contrary to law; it is the natural result of the human instinct for a better life. The village of Shaliang and society as a whole should respect the couple's choice; this is part of democracy and the "rule of law" in the context of village life. Furthermore, this is also the prerequisite for constructing a harmonious society.

2. It has been clearly laid down in Article 2 of the *Law on the Protection of Women's Rights and Interests* that women shall enjoy equal rights to men in all aspects of political, economic, cultural, social and family life. It is a basic state policy to realize equality between men and women. The state shall take necessary measures to gradually improve various systems in order to protect the rights and interests of women and to eliminate all forms of discrimination against women. Even though all daughters-in-laws from outside Shaliang Village of Xi Bazha County are accepted without dispute, villagers are still unwilling to accept uxorilocal son-in-laws. According to villagers, married women are like spilled drops of water that no longer belong to the maiden family; thus, they think it unjustified for them to compete with members of their maiden village for a share of its interests. Though popular among Chinese farmers, this way of thinking is against the State Policy and the law.

3. Article 4, Paragraph 1 of the June 7 Agreement is not a manifestation of the plaintiffs' true consent. Instead, it was a compromise they had to make in order to win back their rights step-by-step. After they acquired the contracting rights to 1.7 *mu* of land, they did not quit striving for other due rights. It was when all the other efforts had turned out to be fruitless that they lodged the suit.

4. Article 5, Paragraph 3 of the *Organization Law of the Villagers' Committees* stipulates that the villagers' committee shall, in accordance with the provisions of the law, administer the affairs concerning land and other property owned collectively by the peasants of the village. Article 20, Paragraph 2 further requires that no charter of self-government, rules and regulations of the village, villagers' pledges or matters decided through discussion by a village assembly or by representatives of villagers, may contravene the Constitution, laws, regulations, or State policies, or contain contents that infringe upon villagers' rights of the person, their democratic rights or their lawful property rights. It is obvious according to the above stipulations that the village meeting's decision that "married women and

their husbands are not entitled to the two houses built by the collective economy, irrespective of whether they are still living in the village" is unlawful. As to the June 7 Agreement, even though it satisfied formal requirements for a contract, Article 4, Paragraph 1 of the Agreement violated compulsory regulations of law and constituted a so-called "illegitimate purpose concealed under the guise of legitimate acts." Based upon that reasoning, the court decided to declare Article 4, Paragraph 1 of the June 7 Agreement void, and to rule for the plaintiffs.

The second issue is whether the 28 plaintiffs are entitled to two houses like the male villagers. The nature of the dispute involves deciding who, as members of the collective economy, are entitled to jointly owned properties of the collective economic organization. Therefore, the first question to be settled is whether the plaintiffs can be qualified as full members of the village collective economy. No statutory standards for this qualification could be found. To take care of the issue, the court has decided to apply the principle of fairness and equity as provided by the *General Principles of Civil Law* and the theory of "analogous interpretation." In other words, if the plaintiffs are no different from other villagers in their status and in other comparable aspects, they should be entitled to two houses just like the male villagers. By hearing the case, the court has discovered that all male villagers who continue to live in the village after their marriage are entitled to two houses, and the only thing distinguishing these male villagers from the 28 plaintiffs is gender. Here, the principles of "gender equality," "fairness and equity" and "non-discrimination" come into play, giving all the female plaintiffs equal rights. However, while affirming the plaintiffs' rights to houses, the court noticed that the claim for RMB 9,999,999 compensation was based on inaccurate estimation and subsequently decided to dismiss the compensation claim.

The final issue is whether the contracted land of 1.7 *mu* per person has been taken back by the village committee. Since the defendant had expressly told the court that the plaintiffs could get back their lands whenever they want, the court felt that what the plaintiffs alleged was inaccurate and irrelevant. Based upon Article 2 and Article 48 of the *Law on Protection of Women's Rights and Interests*, Article 4 of the *General Principles of Civil Law*, Article 25 of the *Contract Law*, and Articles 5 and 20 of the *Organization Law of Villagers' Committees*, the People's intermediate court of Huhhot came to the following judgment regarding the dispute between the 28 women villagers against the Shiliang Village Committee:

1. Article 4, Paragraph 1 of the Agreement between the Shiliang Village Committee and the Village's Married Women on the second round of land contracting is invalid.

2. The defendant, the Shiliang Village Committee of Xi Bazha County in the Saihan District of Huhhot, is ordered to deliver two houses, one for a residence and one for commercial use, or equivalent compensation, to each plaintiff. The size and location of the houses assigned to the plaintiffs should be the same as those assigned to male villagers. The plaintiffs, in exchange, should pay necessary fees in the same amount as male villagers.

3. The defendant bears the burden of costs.

Even though the 28 female plaintiffs had won their case before the court, they had to wait before they could celebrate their victory. The defendant failed to fulfill its promise to the court. Instead, using the old excuse of majority disapproval, the village committee refused to perform its duties under the judgment.

After several months of trying to have the judgment executed, the plaintiffs became so disappointed and angry that they decided to take another course of action. On 5 August 2006, the plaintiffs submitted open letters to all relevant departments and authorities at different levels. After ten days or so, these open letters finally received replies. Some authorities realized that the case represented a serious infringement of the women's rights. Mediations were organized, and the court was finally pressed to take the mandatory measures necessary to execute the judgment.

The plaintiffs, with all their unremitting efforts, finally welcomed a satisfying, and hard won victory.

Case Two
Zhai v. Village Committee of X village, Beijing.

Plaintiff: Zhai, female, born on 19 June 1968, a farmer of X village in the suburbs of Beijing.
Defendant: Villagers' Committee of X village, represented by Xu, Chairman of the Committee.

The plaintiff asks the court to declare illegal the defendant's decision that the plaintiff was not entitled to a share of the compensation from the expropriation of land; and to order the defendant to pay the plaintiff her due land compensation in the amount of RMB 23,775.

Zhai is a villager from a village located in the suburbs of Beijing. She was married in December 1990. Subsequently, she moved to her husband's village, the X village, and has been residing there ever since. In 2000, Zhai divorced from her husband after suffering years of domestic violence. She did not leave the X village after her divorce, and her *hukou* was still registered in the village.

The land of the X village was expropriated. In 2005, the village decided to allocate compensation from land expropriation among the villagers. The rules for allocation were: (1) Any person who has his or her *hukou* registered in the village is qualified for the compensation; (2) The time span for calculating compensation is that between 1 January 1985 and 31 December 2004; (3) Villagers working outside the village are only entitled to an amount of compensation accounted from the date of their marriage.

The plaintiff got married in 1990. According to the rules of calculation made by the village, she was eligible to compensation for 15 years, that is, RMB 23,775 in total.

On 13 July 2005, the defendant convened a meeting of village representatives. A decision was made to deny the plaintiff her entitlement to the compensation for land expropriation. The reason provided was that she had never really worked in the village. The plaintiff then went to various authorities of the village, the township and the city district, seeking help from any "superior department." However, all she encountered was disappointment.

After we were engaged as lawyers for the plaintiff, we paid several visits to the chairman of the village committee. It was obvious that our presence was not pleasing to him. The first time we met with the chairman, we were told after a few words with him that he was leaving for a meeting on conscription that was too important to be interrupted; he asked us to return later. The second time he was again busy, this time with an educational activity among Party members in the village. The third time, we finally got a chance to discuss the case with the chairman. His reply was that "Zhai is divorced, she is no longer our villager. Besides, we are talking about compensation for land we inherited from our ancestors, which is by no means available to an outsider." The explanation was inadequate because of the fact that none of the villagers were natives to the village; they are all from families. In other words, they all have different ancestors who moved to the village from different corners of China. The land reform took place at the birth of the People's Republic of China, which made all farmland collectively owned. The chairman interpreted collective ownership as "collective ownership by males." As head of the village, he seemed convinced of the soundness of his own interpretation of the issue. While frustrated by the chairman's stubbornness, we also paid visits to several relevant administrations and organizations. From these visits, we learned that such discriminative practices against women are not uncommon in the larger suburbs of Beijing. Like us, people from other organizations also want to find a solution to this issue. After discussions with one of the government departments, we decided to cooperate with them. We combined information about all the problems we found and launched a motion at the People's Congress at the district level. We provided the data that we collected and submitted a proposal in the name of the government department to the local People's Congress. To our disappointment, the proposal was later sent back to our partners because the way that the District People's Congress deals with motions and proposals is to send them back to whoever proposed them to resolve the issue. Thus, all the proposals, including ours, were sent back to their starting points after going around in a big circle. Another door was slammed close before us.

After much deliberation, we chose to lodge a suit against the defendant. The court accepted the case and notified the defendant to prepare a defense within an appointed time limit. The defendant initially completely ignored the court's notification and assumed that the plaintiff was just bluffing. When the second notification came, the defendant became flustered. Feeling ashamed to go to court, the defendant proposed reconciliation with the plaintiff. We grasped this opportunity and advised our client to bargain with the defendant over the following items: first of all, the plaintiff wanted to be recognized as a villager with equal access to the same rights as other villagers. Secondly, the village committee should correct its decision and give the plaintiff her share of the compensation. Lastly, the plaintiff should be treated equally in all other aspects of village life and activities, such as economic affairs, security and social participation. Due to our precise analysis of the case and prompt interference, the parties successfully reached an agreement.

These two cases were both resolved through litigation. Looking back, we find that the major contribution to their resolution came from the judges. In both cases, judges were well equipped with knowledge and morality; they appreciated the importance of gender equity; and they applied and interpreted the law accurately. It is amazing to see how important judges are in realizing women's rights to equality. The success of these cases also reminds us that if the judiciary were to become more open and transparent, a shield of social justice could be constructed to protect the rights of the underprivileged from violations. This would in turn win the judges and the judiciary more trust and respect from the people.

Another contributing factor that is worth mentioning is the legal service provider in these cases, civil organizations. Compared to other sources of legal service, the advantage of civil organizations is that their benefits could enormously outweigh their costs. Additionally, recipients of their services are always those who are most in need. While serving their clients, civil organizations are also serving society by dissolving conflicts, reducing judicial costs, and maintaining social stability. At the same time, they do not do this for nothing; instead, they are repaid by having their services recognized and their reputation established. For these reasons, we believe it would be a good strategic choice for the government to establish a relationship with civil organizations by procuring the legal services they provide. This relationship would be beneficial to both sides. On one hand, the government would get what it wants, and on the other hand, civil organizations would be encouraged to develop and make more progress in helping the underprivileged.

ENDNOTES

1   *Law on Rural Land Contracting*, 9th National People's Congress, 29th Sess., Presidential Decree 73, 2002.
2   *Law on the Protection of Women's Rights and Interests*, 7th National People's Congress, 5th Sess., 1992, as am. by Standing Committee of 10th National People's Congress, 17th Sess., Presidential Decree 40, 2005.
3   *Supreme People's Court Interpretation on Application of Laws in Handling Cases of Rural Land Contracting Disputes*, Trial Committee, 1346th Sess., [2005] 6.
4   *Organization Law of Villagers' Committees*, 9th National People's Congress, 5th Sess., Presidential Decree 9, 1998, repealing the Provisional Regulation.
5   *Ibid.*, s. 17.
6   *Marriage Law*, 5th National People's Congress, 3rd Sess. 1980, as am. by Standing Committee of 9th National People's Congress, 2001.
7   *Supra* note 3.
8   *Law on Protection of Minors*, Standing Committee of 7th National People's Congress, 21st Sess., 1991, as am. by Standing Committee of 10th National People's Congress, Presidential Decree 60, 2006.
9   *Nie Cuilian et al. v. Village Committee of Shang Liang Village*, Huhhot Intermediate People's Court, Huhhot, Inner Mongolia, 19 June 2006.
10 *General Principles of Civil Law*, 6th People Congress, 4th Sess., Presidential Decree 37, 1986.
11 *Constitutional Law*, 5th National People's Congress, 5th Sess., 1982, as am. by 7th National People's Congress, 1st Sess., 1988; 8th National People's Congress, 1st Sess., 1993; 9th National People's Congress, 2nd Sess., 1999; 10th National People's Congress, 2nd Sess., 2004.
12 *Contract Law*, 9th National People's Congress, 2nd Sess., 1999. Article 52 provides that "A contract shall be null and void under any of the following circumstances: ... (3) An illegitimate purpose is concealed under the guise of legitimate acts... 5) Violating the compulsory provisions of the laws and administrative regulations."

CHAPTER NINE

Systemic Discrimination and Gender Inequality
A Life Cycle Approach to Girls' and Women's Rights

Colleen Sheppard

> Today's girl child is tomorrow's older woman worker, and it is her opportunities and experiences now that will shape her ability to obtain and maintain decent work throughout her adult life, and enjoy security and protection in her old age. If girls, compared to boys, face negative cultural attitudes and practices and discrimination from birth, they will grow up to be women with greater constraints and few choices and opportunities.[1]

I. INTRODUCTION

To understand gender inequality, it is important to be attentive to the connections between the various spheres of diverse women's activities across different periods in their lives – from girlhood to old age. Yet legal rights are usually framed to address specific moments in time and regard harms or exclusions experienced with respect to discrete places and acts.[2] Such a narrow approach to legal rights makes them less responsive to the broad array of historical, social, and economic sources of inequality and exclusion that are often systemic and embedded in societal structures. The challenge for those who seek to use a discourse of equality rights, therefore, is that of insisting on the necessity of linking individual instances of exclusion and harm to the larger patterns of inequality over time and across the public and private spheres of our lives.

In this article, I endeavour to broaden the lens through which we explore inequality in women's lives across an historical and spatial trajectory. I adopt a life cycle approach that examines how one's treatment as a girl impacts upon one's life chances as a woman, and how the reproduction of the human family operates as an ever-present source of joy and constraint in women's lives. This broader lens of inquiry across time and social structures is then applied back to law through the concept of systemic discrimination. I suggest that the kernels of a more expansive legal approach to inequality can be found in the concept of systemic discrimination.

Although early anti-discrimination laws in many countries focused on prohibiting overt, intentional, group-based differential treatment, the deeply embedded social and systemic dimensions of discrimination are being increasingly recognized. No longer is the mission of anti-discrimination law simply retroactive state-ordered redress for sexist, racist or other discriminatory conduct that is perpetrated by individuals and rooted in stereotypes about social groups; rather, systems, structures, institutional policies and practices have also come under legal scrutiny. Inequality and social exclusion are not discrete, individual problems; they are systemically reproduced over time and across generations. Moreover, inequality and exclusion are linked to the socio-structural interdependence of different spheres of human engagement, such as the family, the household and the workplace. Integral to the concept of systemic discrimination, therefore, is recognition of the relational and dynamic dimensions of inequality. This expansive approach to discrimination provides important insights into the nature and reproduction of inequality throughout girls' and women's lives. Thus, this article begins with a discussion of the emergence of the concept of systemic discrimination, focusing on its articulation in Canadian law. I then consider the insights to be derived from an expansive life cycle approach to gender inequality, drawing on work in the domain of international development. I conclude by highlighting a few of the strategic implications that flow from connecting the emerging legal concept of systemic discrimination to a life cycle approach to gender inequality.

II. Legal Recognition of Systemic Discrimination

The concept of systemic discrimination was recognized in Canadian equality law in the late 20th century. In a series of cases involving workplace discrimination, the courts steadily expanded the legal meaning of discrimination to embrace both intentional and effects-based discrimination, as well as to acknowledge the individual and collective, institutional and structural dimensions of discrimination. Early legal understandings of discrimination focused on the overt unfair treatment or exclusion of individuals because of their membership in a particular group. Legal discrimination occurred when individuals were accorded harmful differential treatment, based on their sex, race, national or ethnic origin, or religion. More recently, such direct discrimination based on mental or physical disability, sexual orientation, social condition or age has also been prohibited in anti-discrimination laws. This direct, unfair and disparate treatment of an individual based on stereotypes, prejudices, and ignorance about his or her group continues to be an important form of discrimination. The legal concept of discrimination, however, has been expanded beyond direct and intentional differential treatment.

(i) Adverse Effect Discrimination

Adverse effect discrimination or disparate impact discrimination recognizes that discrimination may occur when a rule, standard or policy that, while neutral on its face and applying equally to all individuals, has disproportionately harmful effects upon some groups in society. For example, a requirement that store clerks work on Saturdays was held to discriminate against Seventh Day Adventist employees who observe their religious day of rest and worship on Saturday.[3] Height and weight requirements for police officers were held to have discriminatory effects on women and certain ethnic minorities.[4] Standardized workplace testing has also been found to have discriminatory effects.[5] Adverse effect discrimination may also arise when a particular category or classification disproportionately affects particular groups. For example, migrant workers may be disproportionately made up of racial minorities; domestic workers may be disproportionately women and racial minorities.[6] Adverse effect discrimination is more difficult to prove because it requires courts and tribunals to assess quantitative dimensions, including statistical disparities, as well as qualitative inequities, based on experiential accounts of exclusion and marginalization.[7]

Legal recognition of adverse effect or disparate impact discrimination represents a major shift in anti-discrimination law and opens up the possibility of challenging the apparently neutral background norms of society. As Nitya Iyer notes, "The particular set of social characteristics of the dominant social identity and its ideology constitute the invisible background norm against which categorizations of difference are made."[8] Problems of discrimination are recognized as the result of institutional practices, policies and social norms, rather than acts of aberrant anti-social individuals. Moreover, the inequalities experienced by women, ethnic, racial and religious minorities, persons with disabilities, and the economically disadvantaged are recognized as being linked to social rather than biological factors. It is the social, not the biological significance of pregnancy, for example, that makes it a liability in the workplace or society. It is the social construction of difference, rather than the differences themselves, that leads to unfair exclusions and treatment.[9] Martha Minow suggests that "[f]ocusing on the relationship or matrix in which difference is created may offer people the chance to acknowledge difference and not locate it in another who then is unequal, but instead in the relationship used to define that 'difference'."[10] In other words, "there is no normal person or position which is itself free from being different."[11]

Developing a legal theory of equality that does not presume a world of abstractly similar individuals requires that group-based differences be taken into account.[12] These group-based differences are linked predominantly to social experiences and life circumstances – diversities that exist independently of particular institutional policies, practices or rules. For example, women seeking access to a particular job, workplace or opportunity, arrive with life experiences, biological differences, educational backgrounds, social constraints, household work responsibilities and future expectations shaped by gender, class, race, religion, and so on. Adverse effect discrimination requires that these differences not be a source of disadvantage in accessing jobs and opportunities. It prompts us to examine, therefore, the intersection between realities inside and outside specific institutional contexts. In the employment context, it broadens the lens of inquiry beyond the strict parameters of the workplace to the family, household, community, nation, and world – from the past, to the present, and into the future.

Of further significance in cases of adverse effect discrimination are the remedial consequences. In adverse effect discrimination cases, two remedial options exist. First, the apparently neutral rule or policy may be abolished or changed for everyone to eliminate the inequitable effects.[13] For example, a standardized test may be revised or abolished. It is important, as a first step towards remedying adverse effect discrimination, that the validity of the standards, rules or policies, be scrutinized and only left in place if they are necessary.[14] It is only after this scrutiny of the rule or policy itself that a second remedial option emerges – reasonable accommodation to secure the inclusion of those detrimentally affected by the adverse effects of apparently neutral practices and policies.

The doctrine of reasonable accommodation is of critical importance to modern legal conceptions of anti-discrimination. It requires that employers, educational institutions, service providers, and governments provide differential treatment to particular groups with specific needs and circumstances to secure equality of outcomes. It mandates, therefore, the accommodation of differences rather than equal treatment as a pathway to inclusion and fair results. Indeed, it has been widely acknowledged that, in a society characterized by significant diversity among individuals and groups, "the accommodation of differences... is the essence of true equality."[15] Rather than requiring that everyone assimilate and accept dominant norms, reasonable accommodation endorses inclusion even in the face of difference. In anti-discrimination law, accommodation is required to the point of undue hardship, determined by factors such as: "financial cost, disruption of a collective agreement, problems of morale of other employees, [and] interchangeability of work force and facilities."[16] In the Canadian context, it has been elaborated to include both substantive and procedural dimensions.[17]

(ii) Systemic Discrimination

The concept of systemic discrimination builds upon legal recognition of adverse effect or disparate impact discrimination but expands the analysis further by examining how specific policies, standards and practices, as well as attitudes and prejudices, combine to create institutionalized and even structural problems of inequality. Employing a systemic lens goes beyond a focus on discrete instances of discrimination to highlight the accumulated effects of institutional policies, social practices, and socio-structural realities in addition to the continued dynamics of prejudice, entrenched exclusion and marginalization over time. In a pathbreaking report on equality in employment, Justice Rosalie Abella recognized the phenomenon of systemic discrimination as a structural and institutional problem that combines direct and adverse effect discrimination. In a subsequent Supreme Court of Canada case involving systemic sex discrimination

against women seeking non-traditional jobs in the railway industry, Chief Justice
Dickson wrote:

> ...systemic discrimination in an employment context is discrimination that results
> from the simple operation of established procedures of recruitment, hiring and
> promotion, none of which is necessarily designed to promote discrimination.
> The discrimination is then reinforced by the very exclusion of the disadvantaged
> group because the exclusion fosters the belief, both within and outside the group,
> that the exclusion is the result of "natural" forces, for example, that women "just
> can't do the job."[...] To combat systemic discrimination, it is essential to create a
> climate in which both negative practices and negative attitudes can be challenged
> and discouraged.[18]

Systemic discrimination, therefore, creates a mutually reinforcing relationship
between direct and indirect (or adverse effect) discrimination; effects-based exclusions
reinforce the discriminatory attitudes and beliefs and thereby prompt continued
direct discrimination. The phenomenon is dynamic and relational, and inequality is
institutionally reproduced. It is self-perpetuating, and built upon overlapping layers of
exclusion and discrimination; exclusion at one level is connected to exclusion at a previous
level. Moreover, exclusion, discrimination and unfair treatment in the workplace are
intimately connected to group-based patterns of disadvantage, stereotyping, inequities
and marginalization outside of the workplace. Both reinforce and justify each other,
legitimating social and structural inequality as inevitable and natural.

In terms of remedies, Justice Abella perhaps put it best when she explained
that, "[s]ystemic discrimination requires systemic remedies."[19] From a law reform
perspective, legal recognition of systemic discrimination brings into question the
adequacy of traditional instrumental and retroactive forms of legal regulation that
focus on individual misconduct and discrete instances of discrimination. Early anti-
discrimination laws in Canada enumerated prohibited discriminatory conduct subject
to a retroactive complaints-based process. If an individual woman believed that she
had experienced discrimination in the hiring or promotion process, she could file a
complaint with a provincial or federal human rights commission. The human rights
commission would then investigate her complaint and pursue it on her behalf before
a human rights tribunal and the courts if necessary. The resulting remedy would be
to provide her access to the job or promotion, in addition to compensation for losses
incurred. Of note is the individual and retroactive character of the remedy.

In contrast, a systemic approach to remedies rejects the adequacy of retroactive
individual complaints and instead puts in place proactive and systemic remedies and
raises questions about broader macro-economic and socio-structural public policies. In
the Canadian context, efforts to develop proactive systemic approaches have included

legislated employment and pay equity schemes. At the federal level, for example, Canada introduced the *Employment Equity Act* in 1985.[20] The *Act* states that its purpose:

> ...is to correct conditions of disadvantage in employment experienced by women, aboriginal peoples, persons with disabilities and members of visible minorities by giving effect to the principle that employment equity means more than treating persons in the same way but also requires special measures and the accommodation of differences.[21]

The legislation requires all federally-regulated employers to do a proactive assessment of any systemic barriers to access in their workplaces for the four targeted groups – women, persons with disabilities, Aboriginal peoples and visible minorities. It also required the development of an action plan for remedying identified systemic problems, including a clear articulation of goals and a timetable for their accomplishment.[22] Legislated pay equity provides another important example of a shift in regulatory strategy away from a retroactive complaints-based model towards a proactive, systemic approach.[23]

Legal recognition of systemic discrimination, therefore, represents an important concept that broadens the legal inquiry beyond individual instances of discrimination to examine proactively and systematically the institutionalized dimensions of group-based patterns of discrimination. While it tends to focus on specific social contexts (e.g. workplaces, schools, universities), it also raises important questions about the ways in which institutional exclusions are linked to inequalities experienced in other spheres of life and past histories of exclusion or inequity. For example, workplace inequalities may be connected to inequities in family, household and community life or differential educational opportunities. Recognizing inter-sectoral factors that change over time makes it useful to consider how the concept of systemic discrimination might be linked to an emerging approach to international development that focuses on poverty and inequality across an individual's life cycle.

III. Gender Inequality across the Life Cycle: Expanding the Historical and Spatial Trajectories

In the domain of international development and human rights, there has been a growing interest in what has been called a "life cycle" or "life course" approach.[24] Such an approach highlights the importance of understanding "critical periods" during an individual's life cycle, given that such periods have impacts on other periods in the life cycle and even have intergenerational effects. This approach has been described as focusing "on the trajectories of individuals through life and on how key life events and transitions affect these trajectories."[25] Thus, a life cycle framework examines:

- The participation (and non-participation) of individuals in the institutions of society over their lives; and
- The interchanges of resources between the individual and those institutions. The institutions of society include market, family, community organizations, and government programs. Resources include stocks and flows of money, time, services, information and skills.[26]

In affirming the relevance of a life cycle approach to the International Labour Organization's efforts to eliminate poverty through decent work initiatives, Juan Somavia notes that a life cycle approach "helps us to connect directly with.... realities and the interconnectedness of people's needs. People experience life in an integrated way."[27] An approach that connects different spheres of activity in an individual's life also resonates with the longstanding concerns of feminist scholars of linking the public and the private domains.[28]

Three dimensions of this framework are of particular significance. First, it recognizes the importance of taking into account cumulative effects over time. Second, it highlights the intersections between different domains, social structures and contexts in an individual's life. Third, by highlighting the relational and systemic dimensions of inequality, it allows for attentiveness to diversity between women, and the intersectional effects of inequalities linked to race, national or ethnic origin, religion, sexual orientation, disability, language, and economic status.[29]

Both the historical and the intersectional dimensions of a life cycle approach are critical to our understanding of systemic gender inequality. Applying a life cycle approach to girls' and women's rights underscores, for example, the pivotal importance of the socio-cultural valuation of the girl child to the possibility of positive life prospects of any girl or woman in a given society, regardless of economic condition, and throughout her own lifetime.[30] As Lin Lean Lim notes, "[e]quality between women and men and the elimination of discrimination is a fundamental right throughout all stages of life – from childhood to old age."[31] The intergenerational effects of this early discrimination, deeply embedded in societal norms and values, make certain a recurrent cycle of gender inequality, as disempowered girls grow up into disempowered women. As noted in a recent UNICEF report, "[g]ender equality means that girls and boys have equal access to food, healthcare, education and opportunities."[32] The UNICEF Report also highlights what it calls the "double dividend" of gender equality. The affirmation of women's rights not only ameliorates women's lives; it is also critical to the promotion of children's rights, particularly girls' rights:

> By upholding women's rights, societies also protect girl children and female adolescents... Evidence has shown that women whose rights are fulfilled are more likely to ensure that girls have access to adequate nutrition, health care, education and protection from harm.[33]

Peering further ahead in a young girl's life cycle, we can see that if she is denied equal educational opportunities, it will no doubt have a significant impact on her employment opportunities later in life. In this regard, the United Nations Population Fund, in developing a life cycle approach aimed at empowerment throughout life, underlines a number of critical messages for specific stages of life, including encouraging "governments to promote universal and non-gender discriminatory education for girls and boys."[34] A fundamental strategy for advancing women's equality in employment has been that of securing equitable access to educational opportunities. Not only does this require full access to educational domains traditionally dominated by men, but it requires fair treatment, the elimination of gender-based stereotyping, and protections against sexual or other forms of harassment.

Gender-based employment discrimination (which reduces access to good jobs and equitable compensation) also has a critical impact on the risk of poverty in elderly women's lives. In their study *The Dynamics of Women's Poverty in Canada*, Clarence Lochhead and Katherine Scott confirm the heightened risk of poverty among elderly women and its connection to the quality and duration of women's working lives.[35] Many regions of the world are facing a rapidly aging population, and given that women consistently outlive men, the effects of discrimination throughout the life cycle will have a direct impact on the prevalence of poverty and exclusion among elderly women.[36]

Finally, a life cycle approach acknowledges that women's diverse life experiences in one domain have critical effects in other contexts. Thus, women's family and household responsibilities, for example, have a significant impact on their employment opportunities – the public and private lives of women are intricately interwoven. Another stage in the life cycle in which women face socio-structural barriers to true equality and inclusion, therefore, is the extended period in adulthood when commitments to family life and the workplace are in conflict. Enduring socio-cultural conceptions of gender roles with respect to child-bearing and rearing may shed light on why closing the gender gap has been a challenge worldwide. In Asia, for example, young women are outperforming their male counterparts in the education system, but are finding it harder to enter the labour market and compete successfully with men once they are working.[37] This experience can be common across social and economic strata, but poverty and economic exclusion render certain women more vulnerable to ongoing and future poverty at this crucial stage.

Thus, a life cycle approach compels us to focus on the relational nature of gender inequality and exclusion, both within a woman's lifetime, and across the spheres of her life. As noted in an important report by UNICEF that affirmed women's equality as a necessary condition for children's rights, "[w]omen need influence in decision-making in three spheres – household, workplace and political sphere."[38] Remaining cognizant of the implications of this approach will allow more effective responses in policy and law to the complex realities of inequality.

IV. CONCLUSION: RETHINKING LEGAL STRATEGIES

What is the significance of a life cycle approach to the development of strategies for securing effective gender equality? Does it assist us in developing creative and effective policies that will have a positive impact on securing girls' and women's rights in countries around the world? And what are the links between an expansive legal definition of discrimination – illustrated by the concept of systemic discrimination and the historical, structural, systemic and intersectoral dimensions of life cycle approaches? No doubt, the lessons to be learnt from combining a systemic discrimination analysis with a life cycle approach will vary depending on the specificity of the historical, political, cultural and economic contexts. Nevertheless, a few general conclusions may be advanced.

First, it is critically important to insist upon a broad and expansive definition of discrimination – one that embraces both direct, intentional discrimination as well as effects-based, indirect discrimination. Effective channels for investigating, adjudicating and redressing discrimination are also of utmost importance.

The lessons of systemic discrimination and a life cycle perspective on problems of exclusion and unfair treatment, however, teach us that grafting a retroactive discrimination complaints procedure onto complex, intersectoral and structural problems of systemic inequality will only address a small part of the problem. Too often legal regimes tend to presume the legitimacy and the fairness of the underlying institutional status quo – focusing exclusively on aberrant individual conduct, or discrete rules or policies that are discriminatory. Beyond individual remedies, a second conclusion is the need for broader systemic strategies to address problems of inequality that affect large numbers of women in particular industries, social institutions and workplaces. Some of these should be initiated at the institutional level – through a proactive assessment of barriers and obstacles to equality – and the initiation of new policies and changes in social practices. Of particular significance at the institutional level is attentiveness to the way in which obligations, responsibilities, and life chances in one sphere of life impact upon equitable treatment in other spheres of activity. Equal rights require the redesigning of institutional policies to take these factors into account, or the development of policies of reasonable accommodation to ensure inclusion in the face of difference. The development of systemic responses to systemic discrimination should also take into account diverse girls' and women's lives, recognizing how multiple and intersecting forms of discrimination and exclusion affect diverse communities in different ways.

A third conclusion is derived from the insights of life cycle approaches to social policy. Given the historical and spatial trajectories of systemic inequality, it is necessary to think about gender equality in more macro public policy terms that transcend specific institutions or discrete spheres of activity. A more expansive approach is necessary in the face of social realities of inequality that span generations, intersect both private and public spheres, and are embedded in law, political economy, institutional policies, customs and traditions. It also underscores the importance of pursuing multiple reform strategies – from the formal political channels of law reform to diverse forms of resistance to inequality in everyday life.

ENDNOTES

1 International Labour Organization, *Working out of Poverty*, Report of the Director General to the International Labour Conference 91st Session (Geneva: International Labour Office, 2003), p. 26; cited in Lin Lean Lim "Gender and Human Rights in the Life Cycle: Taking the Life-cycle Approach to the World of Work," in *Gender and Human Rights in the Commonwealth: Some Critical Issues for Action in the Decade 2005–2015* (London: The Commonwealth Secretariat, 2004) 83 at 86.

2 As Kim Lane Scheppele has noted, "the set of events giving rise to the lawsuit and the legal statement of facts usually focuses narrowly on what made those events happen" rather than exploring the larger context through "wide-angle descriptions." Kim Lane Scheppele, "Foreward: Telling Stories" (1989) 87 Michigan L. Rev. 2073 at 2094-2095 & 2096.

3 *Ontario (Human Rights Commission) and O'Malley v. Simpsons-Sears* (1985), 23 D.L.R. (4th) 321 (S.C.C.), [1985] 2 S.C.R. 536.

4 *Colfer v. Ottawa Police Commissioner* (12 January 1979) (Ontario Board of Inquiry) [unreported].

5 See *Griggs v. Duke Power Co.*, 401 U.S. 424 (1971) [*Griggs*].

6 See discussion in *Egan v. Canada*, [1995] 2 S.C.R. 513 at para. 78, L'Heureux-Dubé J, citing Anne F. Bayefsky, "A Case Comment on the First Three Equality Rights Cases Under the Canadian Charter of Rights and Freedoms: Andrews, Workers' Compensation Reference, Turpin" (1990) 1 Sup. Ct. L. Rev. (2d) 503 at 518-9.

7 See Dianne Pothier, "M'Aider, Mayday: Section 15 of the Charter in Distress" (1996) 6 N.J.C.L. 295.

8 Nitya Iyer, "Categorical Denials: Equality Rights and the Shaping of Social Identity" (1993) 19 Queen's L.J. 179.

9 Dianne Pothier, "Miles to Go: Some Personal Reflections on the Social Construction of Disability" (1992) 14 Dalhousie L.J. 526 at 526.

10 Martha Minow, "Learning to Live with the Dilemma of Difference: Bilingual and Special Education" (1985) 48 Law & Contemp. Problems 157. See also, Martha Minow, *Making All the Difference: Inclusion, Exclusion and American Law* (Ithaca: Cornell University Press, 1990).

11 *Ibid.*

12 Similar theoretical developments have occurred in Canadian constitutional equality jurisprudence in which courts have endorsed the concept of substantive equality, rejecting the more narrow conception of formal equality, that focused on the equal treatment of individuals regardless of the social reality of group-based differences: see *Law v. Canada (Minister of Employment and Immigration)*, [1999] 1 S.C.R. 497 at para. 88.

13 Some scholars suggest that this approach is required to dismantle discrimination systemically; see Gwen Brodsky & Shelagh Day, "The Duty to Accommodate: Who Will Benefit?" (1996) 75 Can. Bar. Rev. 433 at 462.

14 See, e.g., *Griggs, supra* note 4 at 431 where the United States Supreme Court outlines that the defendant must demonstrate the business necessity and job relatedness of an employment policy once the plaintiff has made out a *prima facie* case of disparate impact.

15 *Andrews v. Law Society of British Columbia*, [1989] 1 S.C.R. 143 at 169, McIntyre J.

16 *Central Alberta Dairy Pool v. Alberta (Human Rights Commission)*, [1990] 2 S.C.R. 489 at para. 62.

17 David M. Lepofsky, "The Duty to Accommodate: A Purposive Approach" (1993), 1 Can. Lab. L.J. 1.

18 *Canadian National Railway Co. v. Canada (Canadian Human Rights Commission) (Action travail des femmes)* (1987), 40 D.L.R. (4th) 193 (S.C.C.), [1987] 1 S.C.R. 1114 at para. 34.

19 Canada, Commission on Equality in Employment, *Equality in Employment: A Royal Commission Report* (Ottawa: Supply & Services Canada, 1984) (Chair: Judge Rosalie Abella), online: http://www.queensu.ca/ equity/disabilities/equity.php> at 9.

20 *Employment Equity Act*, S.C. 1995, c. 44.

21 *Ibid.*, s.2.

22 The Federal Contractors Program for Employment Equity was implemented 1 October 1986 and applies to provincially regulated employers with a workforce of 100 or more employees.

23 See *e.g. Pay Equity Act*, R.S.Q. c. E-12.001; *Pay Equity Act*, R.S.O. 1990, c. P.7; *Pay Equity Act*, R.S.N.S. 1989, c. 337. See generally, Final Report of Federal Task Force on Pay Equity, *Pay Equity – A New Approach to a Fundamental Right* (Ottawa, Canada: 2004). http://www.payequityreview.gc.ca.

24 See, e.g., "Life-cycle Approach: A Framework to Identify Vulnerabilities and Opportunities," online: World Bank http://www.worldbank.org/childrenandyouth .

25 Policy Research Initiative (PRI), *A Life-Course Approach to Social Policy Analysis: A Proposed Framework* (Discussion Paper) (Ottawa: PRI Project, Population Aging and Life-Course Flexibility, December 2004) at 5.

26 *Ibid.*

27 ILO, *Social Protection: A Life Cycle Continuum Investment for Social Justice, Poverty Reduction and Development* by A. Bonilla Garcia & J.V. Gruat (Geneva: ILO Social Protection Sector, November 2003) at 2 (in Preface by Juan Somavia).

28 See, for e.g. Susan B. Boyd, ed., *Challenging the Public/Private Divide: Feminism, Law, and Public Policy* (Toronto: University of Toronto Press, 1997). In the context of China, see Barbara Entwisle & Gail E. Henderson, eds. *Re-Drawing Boundaries: Work, Households, and Gender in China* (Berkeley: University of California Press, 2000).

29 See, for e.g., Kimberle Crenshaw, "Demarginalizing the Intersection of Race and Sex: A Black Feminist Critique of Antidiscrimination Doctrine, Feminist Theory and Antiracist Politics" (1989) Univ. of Chicago Leg. Forum 139; Joanne St. Lewis, "Beyond the Confinement of Gender: Locating Space of Legal Existence for Racialized Women" in Radha Jhappan , ed. *Women's Legal Strategies in Canada* (Toronto: University of Toronto Press, 2002), 295-332; Sherene Razack, *Looking White People in the Eye – Gender, Race and Culture in Courtrooms and Classrooms* (Toronto: University of Toronto Press, 2001), ch. 7; Linda Martin Alcoff, *Visible Identities – Race, Gender, and the Self* (Oxford: Oxford University Press, 2006).

30 See Lin Lean Lim, *supra*, note 1 at 83 & 87.

31 *Ibid* at 86.

32 UNICEF, State of the World's Children Report 2007, *Women and Children: The Double Dividend of Gender Equality* (New York: UNICEF, 2007) at 2.

33 *Ibid.*

34 "Population Issues: Promoting Gender Equality: Life Cycle Approach", online: United Nations Population Fund (UNFPA) http://www.unfpa.org/gender/empowerment4.htm

35   Clarence Lochhead & Katherine Scott, *The Dynamics of Women's Poverty in Canada* (Ottawa: Status of Women Canada, 2000). Some scholars have articulated concerns that a life cycle approach that focuses on labour force preparation and attachment does not resonate with the lives of women who are not active labour force participants. See, Orla O'Connor & Mary Murphy, "Developmental welfare state, the life cycle and gender" (Dublin: NDP Gender Equality Unit) (Draft report online at: http://www.ndpgenderequality.ie/newproj/newproj_17.html.)

36   ILO, *Realizing Decent Work in Asia: Report of the Director General*, Fourteenth Asian Regional Meeting; Busan, Republic of Korea, August-September 2006 (Geneva: International Labour Office, 2006), online: ILO, <http://www.ilo.org/public/english/ standards/relm/rgmeet/asia.htm> at 23.

37   *Ibid.* at 2.

38   UNICEF, *supra* note 32 at 12.

PART THREE

Discrimination Against the Disabled

CHAPTER TEN

A Study on Legislative Inhibition of Discrimination on the Basis of Disability

Wang Zhijiang

I. Discrimination on the Basis of Disability – An Overview

(I) Definition

Discrimination is usually defined as a person or group being treated differently (usually worse) than others. Chinese[1] and English[2] language interpretations of discrimination are basically similar.

Discrimination is a prejudice by its very nature. Although there may be different reasons for discriminatory behaviour, a commonality exists: the party who prejudices feels psychologically superior, so much so that it leads to a psychological imbalance that affects his behaviour and manifests itself in unfair treatment of other parties. Discrimination exists in many forms, including discrimination based on gender, race, ethnic group, disability, geography, religion, age and appearance.

Discrimination against disability is prevalent in human history and has been ongoing. It arises out of fear or incomplete knowledge of disability, resulting in differential treatment against the disabled and other people. The most direct expression of discrimination is the rejection, exclusion and ostracism of the disabled by non-disabled people. From a broader perspective, it also includes the neglect of the disabled in legislation or policies, and the failure to provide accessible facilities for the physically disabled.

The *United Nations Convention on the Rights of Persons with Disabilities* defines discrimination on the basis of disability as:

> any distinction, exclusion, or restriction on the basis of disability which has the purpose or effect of impairing or nullifying the recognition, enjoyment or exercise, on an equal basis with others, of human rights and fundamental freedoms in the political, economic, social, cultural, civil or any other field. It includes all forms of discrimination, including denial of reasonable accommodation.

(II) Causes of Discrimination on the Basis of Disability

Discrimination on the basis of disability has historical origins and practical causes. In early human society, when human beings were less able to change or conquer nature and when living conditions were poor, a healthy body was a prerequisite for survival. Discrimination against disability was a natural reaction to this condition.

With social progress and greater civilization, society has evolved from rejection of the disabled to being accepting and accommodating. There are at least four reasons that can be attributed to this change:

First, human beings are now better able to deal with and change the environment, society has lower expectations of human health conditions, and human labour is able to satisfy the basic requirements of all members of society. This implies that any forced displacement of the disabled is unnecessary.

Second, acceptance of the disabled is integral to social progress. Civilization is the major element that differentiates human beings from animals. Disabled persons, being a part of human society, should enjoy the basic right to live. This is a concept that is gradually recognized and accepted by society.

Third, acceptance of the disabled is the result of technological progress. For example, the invention and use of wheelchairs, hearing aids and other aids compensate for the inadequacies of the disabled to different degrees. This gradually eliminated any obstacles in communication between disabled persons and other people, so that disabled persons are able to integrate and become part of society.

Finally, society's standard of judgment of a person's ability is no longer based on physique; rather, it has evolved into multiple standards, whereby intelligence becomes increasingly important. People who have disabilities in their appendages, hearing or sight show the ability to contribute to overall social well-being. Together, these reasons enable the disabled to be progressively recognized and accepted by society.

However, discrimination on the basis of disabilities has not been eradicated from modern society. There are a few major reasons for this. First, because people are still dependent on a healthy body to some extent, the original causes for discrimination against the disabled continue to exist. Second, non-disabled people do not have a complete understanding of disability, as well as the necessary means and techniques to communicate and interact with the disabled. "Able-bodied members of our society often feel discomfort and embarrassment around people with disabilities and do not know how to react toward them."[3] Such discomfort and embarrassment result in the exclusion of the disabled by the healthy, and the unwillingness of the disabled to integrate into society, and finally, to their estrangement. The third reason is the failure of the healthy to translate their will into action, despite being ready to help the disabled. Hence, although there is no emotional negligence as far as the disabled are concerned, discrimination does occur in practice. Many help the disabled out of sympathy, but often without respect and lack observance of their dignity. This is referred to as "benevolent paternalism." In the case of *Alexander v. Choate* (US 1985), the Supreme

Court observed that discrimination on the basis of handicap is "most often the product of…benign neglect," and that "federal agencies and commentators on the plight of people with disabilities… have found that discrimination against people with disabilities is primarily the result of apathetic attitudes rather than affirmative animus."[4] The fourth reason is misunderstanding and worry about certain handicap attributes. "Many people are afraid of persons with disabilities, especially people who have mental disabilities."[5] The fifth reason is the neglect of the disabled. Some countries have failed to consider the special needs of the disabled in their legislation and formulation of policies. Laws and policies not only do not protect the rights of the disabled, but become the basis for discriminatory conduct.

(III) CLASSIFICATION OF FORMS OF DISCRIMINATION ON THE BASIS OF DISABILITY

1. Direct Discrimination and Indirect Discrimination

Based on the different makeup of discriminatory behaviour, discrimination may be divided into direct discrimination and indirect discrimination.

Direct discrimination refers to less favourable treatment received by the disabled compared to the non-disabled under similar circumstances. Generally, direct discrimination must fulfil the following three criteria: (1) treatment received by the disabled is less favourable than the non-disabled; (2) disability is the only cause of such differential treatment; and (3) the discriminating person cannot provide a justifiable reason for his behaviour.

Indirect discrimination refers to additional requirements or conditions imposed on the disabled, without doing the same to the non-disabled, and these requirements or conditions are unjustifiable. Generally, indirect discrimination must fulfil the following three criteria: (1) the percentage of disabled persons who can fulfil these requirements or conditions is far smaller than that of non-disabled persons; (2) the requirement or condition seem unjustifiable from a practical standpoint; and (3) disabled persons are prejudiced by virtue of their failure to fulfil these requirements or conditions. In comparison, indirect discrimination is more latent, often discriminating disabled persons under the guise of fair play, and making the identification of discrimination against disability difficult.

2. Discrimination in Politics, Education, Employment, Culture, Sports and Consumption

Based on the different sectors in which discrimination against disability occurs discrimination may be classified into political, educational, employment, cultural and sports, and consumption discrimination.

Political discrimination refers mainly to the restriction of the right to vote and seek election, and the right to participate in and manage national affairs. Educational discrimination refers mainly to the refusal to allow disabled persons to go to school or the imposition of addition conditions on disabled persons in the management of school affairs, thereby resulting in the restriction or obstruction of the exercise of the right to education by disabled persons. A common discrimination against disability, employment discrimination is usually seen in the refusal to employ disabled persons or unfair treatment to such persons in training, promotion, salary and remuneration, and work conditions. Cultural and sports discrimination is discrimination against the disabled in the cultural, sports or recreational and leisure sectors. Consumption discrimination refers to discrimination against the disabled in the sale of commodities and the provision of services. Such discriminatory behaviour occurs everyday. According to a survey of 1,000 disabled persons submitted by the United States Congress when it conducted legislative hearing on the *Americans with Disabilities Act*, two-thirds of those surveyed are of employment age but were unemployed, and, of those seeking employment, two-thirds were not offered jobs due to employers' attitudes. The survey also showed that in the one year before the public hearing, two-thirds of those surveyed had not watched a movie, three-quarters had not attended a theatre performance or concert, two-thirds had not watched a sports event, seventeen percent had not eaten at a restaurant, and 30 percent had never shopped in a shopping centre.[6]

3. Personal Discrimination, Organizational Discrimination and State Discrimination

Based on the different discriminating entities, discrimination against disability may be classified into personal discrimination, organizational discrimination and State discrimination.

Personal discrimination refers to discrimination against disabled persons on an interpersonal basis. Examples include an employer refusing to employ a handicapped person seeking employment, or a retailer refusing to sell its merchandise to a disabled person. Organizational discrimination refers to discrimination by a company or organization, such as schools refusing to allow disabled persons to attend, or an academic institution refusing the membership of a disabled person. State discrimination refers to the discrimination or neglect of a disabled person by his or her country. State discrimination usually manifests itself in legislation and policies. Some countries deny disabled persons the right to vote or seek elected office, or exclude disabled persons from participating in the formulation of policies closely related to them.

4. Discrimination against Disabled Persons and Discrimination against Related Persons

Based on the different victims, discrimination against disability may be classified into discrimination against disabled persons and discrimination against associates.

Discrimination against persons with a disability is discrimination against disabled persons on the basis on their handicap. Discrimination against associates refers to the discrimination against persons associated with disabled persons on the basis of the handicap of disabled persons. The *Disability Discrimination Act 1992* of Australia provides that an "associate," in relation to another person, refers to a spouse, someone who is living with the person on a genuine domestic basis, a relative, a caregiver, or someone who is in a business, sporting or recreational relationship with the person. The term "associate," used in the *Disability Discrimination Ordinance* of the Hong Kong Special Administrative Region, also has the same definition as its Australian counterpart. To cite an example, a Hong Kong SAR resident complained to the Hong Kong Equal Opportunities Commission when his application to become a relief worker was rejected. The answering party acknowledged that the application was rejected on the grounds that the resident's father was a mental patient, and that, due to the highly dangerous nature of relief work, pressure may induce mental illness in its workers, all of which could be detrimental to relief work and public safety. Eventually, the parties arrived at a settlement. The answering party agreed to employ the resident and pay HKD$ 275,000 in compensation and interest for emotional damage and loss of income.[7]

II. INHIBITING DISCRIMINATION AGAINST PERSONS WITH DISABILITIES

(I) Reasons for Prohibition

1. Discrimination on the Basis of Disability is a Common Phenomenon
Discrimination against persons with a disability is a common phenomenon. Disabled persons from every part of the world are discriminated against in different ways:

> They are denied jobs, excluded from schools, are considered unworthy of marriage or partnership, and are even barred from certain religious practices. Millions of persons with disabilities around the world do not have access to the resources necessary to fulfil their basic needs, nor do they have influence over the policy decisions that affect their daily struggle for survival. Discrimination occurs in a range of arenas, including the workplace, schools, health care facilities, government, recreational facilities, as well as many more societal contexts. Moreover, as a result of discrimination, segregation from society, economic marginalization, and a broad range of other human rights violations, persons with disabilities have consistently been excluded from the decision-making fora where positive changes in law and policy can be developed and implemented.[8]

Whether it is in developed or developing countries, or in the political, economic, social or cultural sectors, there are different levels of discrimination against disabled persons.

Under most circumstances, these are discriminations by non-disabled people against the disabled; the more serious discrimination is the neglect of disabled people by the State. The result is a misguidance of society, such that discrimination against disabled persons becomes the norm. Children, women, or elderly people who are handicapped, or people with disabilities in movement, hearing, vision, mental state or mental ability, have invariably suffered discrimination during their lifetime. Many countries have adopted legislative, administrative or outreach measures to eliminate discrimination, and have seen some results in preventing and mitigating discrimination against people with disabilities. However, unless the fundamental cause of discrimination against disability is eradicated, disabled persons will continue to face prejudice.

2. Discrimination against Disability Leads to Serious Consequences

The state of human rights of disabled persons due to discrimination against them is astonishing. Leandro Despouy, the United Nation's Special Rapporteur on Disability, observed in 1991, "[people with disabilities] frequently live in deplorable condition... As a result, millions of children and adults throughout the world are segregated and deprived of virtually all their rights and lead a wretched marginal life."[9] Disabled persons are prevented from integrating into mainstream society, and are living in segregation, exclusion and neglect. At the same time, discrimination against disability often results in the abilities of disabled persons being neglected: "[a]ll of these factors contribute to the second-class citizenship status of Americans with disabilities"[10]; "[p]ersons with disabilities are often thought of as worthless members of society or as helpless people who cannot have a job or otherwise contribute in a meaningful way...".[11] Such negation of persons with disabilities based on their handicap will become a vicious cycle that affects the behaviour and decisions of persons with disabilities:

> "[o]ppressed groups who have been systematically denied power and influence in the society in which they live internalize negative messages about their abilities and so often come to accept them as their "truth." Internalized oppression works in combination with economic and social contexts and serves to restrict options that people perceive as open to them and legitimate for them.[12]

What happens is that people with disabilities grow accustomed to living in isolated environments. The healthy, on the other hand, will take discrimination for granted over time, and begin to ignore, neglect and forget about disabled persons. Discrimination against disability thus results in serious consequences.

3. Discrimination against Disability will not Disappear Naturally

Facts have proven that civility and the protection of human rights are not natural outcomes of technological advancement and wealth accumulation.[13] The same applies to discrimination against disability – rights must be fought for. Even the voting rights of disabled people living in the United States have been fundamentally infringed upon: "[i]n the 2000 elections in the United States, in at least 18 states, disabled voters found inaccessible polling places, confusing ballots and a lack of privacy and independence in voting."[14] These occurrences did not arise because of technical or financial problems; instead, they happened because of the neglect of and indifference toward persons with disabilities by the State and society at large. Congress also stated that society had historically isolated and segregated

> individuals with disabilities and discrimination persisted in critical areas such as employment, housing, public accommodations, transportation, communication, education, recreation, institutionalisation, health services, voting and access to public services, etc. The discrimination occurs in various forms including outright intentional exclusion.[15]

Hence, socio-economic progress and technological advancement do not necessarily imply the elimination of discrimination against disabilities, especially when under many circumstances the discrimination results from deliberate exclusion. Passive waiting will not therefore eliminate discrimination against disabilities. Aggressive and effective inhibitive methods and measures are the answer.

4. Discrimination against Disability is an Abnormal Social Phenomenon
Jean-Jacques Rousseau proposed during the mid-18th century that all human beings are free and equal, and everybody has "natural rights," which are an innate part of being a human being and cannot be denied by society. Any form of discrimination is scorn and impropriety against human liberty and equality. Article 7 of the United Nations *Universal Declaration of Human Rights* states that "[a]ll are equal before the law and are entitled without any discrimination to equal protection of the law. All are entitled to equal protection against any discrimination in violation of this *Declaration* and against any incitement to such discrimination." Discrimination against disabilities is an abnormal social phenomenon that shows deep-rooted human flaws. Any discrimination against persons with disabilities is infringement of their basic human rights. Elimination of such discrimination not only demonstrates the progress of human civilization, it is also a requisite for the protection of the rights and fundamental freedom of disabled persons. Many countries have gradually realized the socially detrimental discrimination against disabilities, and have imposed strict prohibitions on such discriminatory behaviour via various avenues, and have appealed and encouraged society to combat any discrimination against disabled persons.

(II) Legislative Inhibition of Discrimination against Disabled Persons

Legislation is an effective means that the State may use to prohibit and eliminate discrimination against disabled persons. The legislative 'reforms of many countries aim to provide equal opportunities for disabled persons and eliminate discrimination against them, in order to resolve the problem of ostracism and exclusion that often co-occur with disabilities. At present, approximately 40 countries have passed laws against discrimination on the basis of disability.

Human society experienced three phases of change of attitude towards disability and persons with disabilities. During the first phase, disabled persons were regarded as passive, sickly, dependent, and needing medical treatment and relief. This traditional perception was usually known as the "medical model of disability." This model classifies social activities into those carried out by "normal persons" and those carried out by "persons living with disability." It proffered that material wealth and spiritual wealth in society is created by social activities carried out by "normal persons." Persons living with disability were "abnormal persons" who were social baggage and troublemakers, and who only consume but do not create material and spiritual wealth. Thus, education, employment, cultural and transportation facilities and services were designed for normal people, and disabled persons were not to be part of them. In this phase, some countries established progressive legislation targeted at helping those living with disability; however, legislation alone could not fundamentally change their status. The value of persons living with disability continued to be neglected, and even negated.

In the second phase, along with social progress and improvements in civilization came peoples' gradual realization that the exclusion and ostracism of people living with disabilities by society is not the result of the handicap, but rather of the decision to exclude the handicapped. Consequently, the belief was that removal of these obstacles would allow such persons to create material culture and life just like other people, and thus that a more conducive environment must be created for the disabled, rather than expecting them to adapt to society. This is called the "social model of disability." During this phase, society not only accepted people living with disability, but believed as well that they could be creators of material and spiritual wealth, and, therefore, that those with disabilities should be able to participate in social activities without discrimination. The nature of the relevant legislation during this phase is mainly social law, and partly civil law.

In the third phase, society came to believe that persons living with disability should enjoy basic innate rights, being social actors, and that they are not only regular participants in society, but should also be entitled to different rights. People living with disability are thus conceived as subjects with rights which the State should provide, such as those to education, employment, voting, transportation and cultural rights, including relief and measures in the event of infringement of such rights. Also, it is believed that persons living with disability should participate in the legislative process

Historical Phases	Attitude Toward Disability	Status of the Disabled	Nature of Legislation
Phase 1	*Medical Model of Disability*	Object of Relief	Welfare Law
Phase 2	*Social Model of Disability*	Social Actor	Social Law
Phase 3	*Rights Model of Disability*	Subject with Rights	Human Rights Law

and in making policies related to them, rather than leaving such decisions in the hands of other people. This is known as the "rights model of disability." In this phase, people living with disability are entitled to rights, while the State takes measures to ensure that such rights are exercised. The legislative nature is under the human rights law or constitution, focusing on the protection of the equality of rights for people living with disability. Of course, such legislation does not exclude provisions for social, welfare and civil considerations.[16]

Along with the paradigm shift from one model to another is the change of the social status of people living with disability, from being "object of relief" to "social actor" to "right-owner." The same process of change was seen in the nature of legislation for disability, from "welfare legislation" to "social legislation" to "human rights legislation." Although the nature of the present legislation for disability is human rights-based, it contains multi-dimensional aspects, including welfare and social legislation, thereby providing comprehensive and complete protection for people living with disability.

III. UNITED NATIONS' LEGISLATIVE INHIBITION OF DISCRIMINATION AGAINST DISABILITY

(I) United Nations Efforts

Since its inception, the United Nations (UN) has been seeking to elevate the status of people living with disability, to improve their lives, and to eliminate discrimination against persons living with disability. The UN's concern with the issue of people living with disability originates from its recognition that disabled persons often suffer from discrimination, because of prejudice or ignorance, and may also lack access to essential services. This is a "silent crisis" which affects not only disabled persons and their families, but also the economic and social development of entire societies, where a significant reservoir of human potential often goes untapped. Considering that disabilities are frequently caused by human activities, or simply by lack of care, assistance from the entire international community is needed to put this "silent emergency" to an end.[17] Founded to promote human rights, basic freedom and peace initiatives, the UN should ensure that persons living with disabilities can exercise their civic, political, social and cultural rights on an equal basis. It was because of this belief that the United Nations Assembly, the United Nations Educational, Scientific and Cultural Organization (UNESCO), the World Health Organization (WHO), the United Nations Children's Fund (UNICEF), the International Labour Organization (ILO) and other special agencies have driven to create the conditions for the equal and effective protection for the rights of persons living with disability.

The UN's work for people living with disability shifted from being simple to multi-dimensional, and from being welfare to human rights-driven. During the 1950s, the UN's efforts in this respect were mainly on rehabilitation plans and programmes. During the 1960s, issues concerning disabled people were viewed as social welfare problems; the UN employed a social model in its operations, encouraging full social participation of people living with disability. The 1970s marked a new era for efforts towards building up people with disabilities. On 20 December 1971, the United Nations General Assembly adopted the *Declaration on the Rights of Mentally Retarded Persons*, and the concept of rights for persons living with disability became generally accepted internationally.

The UN legislative inhibition against discrimination on the basis of disability took time to evolve. On 9 December 1975, discrimination against persons living with disability was first mentioned in the *Declaration on the Rights of Disabled Persons*. There were several propositions in the *United Nations World Programme of Action Concerning Disabled Persons* adopted on December 3, 1982 relating to the inhibition of discrimination against persons living with disability. On 17 December 1991, the UN General Assembly passed a resolution against discrimination on the grounds of mental illness under the *Principles for the Protection of Persons with Mental Illness and the Improvement of Mental Health Care*, and defined the meaning of "discrimination." The *Standard Rules on the Equalization of Opportunities for Persons with Disabilities*, adopted by the UN General Assembly on 20 December 1993, also provided for the inhibition of discrimination on the basis of disability. The *Convention on the Rights of Persons with Disabilities* adopted by the UN General Assembly is a comprehensive instrument that specified not only the relevant concepts of discrimination against disability, but also provided for many measures and means to prohibit such discrimination in its main provisions.

(II) Legislative Inhibition of Discrimination on the Basis of Disability under the *UN Convention on the Rights of Persons with Disabilities*

The *Convention on the Rights of Persons with Disabilities* is a legislative inhibition by the UN of discrimination against persons living with disabilities as well as an instrument of authority. The key aspects of the *Convention* are as follows. First, the *Convention* embodies non-discrimination and equal protection of persons living with disabilities in both its basic principles and its main provisions. Other conventions do not provide for anti-discrimination for disabled persons in the same depth and breadth. Second, the

Convention is a legally binding international treaty formulated by the members of the UN. Upon signing and ratification by State Parties, signatories must drive the work for persons living with disability according to the provisions of the *Convention*. This means employing all resources to ensure that disabled persons enjoy and exercise their rights. Any violation of the *Convention* will be subject to serious consequences.

1. Inhibitive Legislative Institution Provided under the Convention

The relevant provisions concerning the legislative inhibition of discrimination against persons with disability under the *Convention on the Rights of Persons with Disabilities* includes the following aspects. First, "non-discrimination" is the basic principle of the *Convention*. Article 3 of the *Convention* provided for eight general principles and "non-discrimination" is one of them with high priority. Second, the purpose of the *Convention* is to eliminate discrimination, in order to provide equal protection for persons living with disability. Article 1 of the *Convention* sets forth the purpose of the *Convention* in the following terms: "to promote, protect and ensure the full and equal enjoyment of all human rights and fundamental freedoms by all persons with disabilities, and to promote respect for their inherent dignity." Thus, the *Convention*'s purpose is to eliminate discrimination against persons living with disability and to ensure equal protection for such persons. Third, the *Convention* provided a definition for discrimination on the basis of disability. Under Article 2, "discrimination on the basis of disability" was clearly defined. Fourth, the *Convention* clearly provided under its "General Obligations" that "States Parties undertake to ensure and promote the full realization of all human rights and fundamental freedoms for all persons with disabilities without discrimination of any kind on the basis of disability." Fifth, the *Convention* contains special provisions for non-discrimination. Article 5 of the *Convention* specially provided for "equality and non-discrimination," under which States Parties shall prohibit all discrimination on the basis of disability and guarantee to persons with disabilities equal and effective legal protection against discrimination on all grounds. Finally, all provisions under the *Convention* have directly or indirectly provided for the inhibition of discrimination on the basis of disability.

2. Means of Legislative Prohibition Provided under the Convention

Typical measures and methods of legislative inhibition provided in the *Convention on the Rights of Persons with Disabilities* include the following:

> *Participation in Political and Public Life:* to guarantee to persons with disabilities political rights and the opportunity to enjoy them on an equal basis with others, State Parties shall (1) ensure that voting procedures, facilities and materials are appropriate, accessible and easy to understand and use; (2) ensure persons with disabilities may vote by secret ballot in elections and public referendums without intimidation, and to stand for elections, to effectively hold office and perform all

public functions at all levels of government, facilitating the use of assistive and new technologies where appropriate; (3) guarantee the free expression of the will of persons with disabilities as electors and to this end, where necessary, and at the request of such persons, allow assistance in voting by a person of their own choice; (4) encourage the participation of persons with disabilities in non-governmental organizations and associations concerned with the public and political life of the country, and in the activities and administration of political parties; (5) encourage persons with disabilities to form and join organizations, so as to ensure their representation at international, national, regional and local levels.

Education: for the purpose of realizing the right of persons with disabilities to education without discrimination and on the basis of equal opportunity, States Parties shall: (1) ensure an inclusive education system at all levels and life-long learning directed to the development by persons with disabilities of their personality, talents and creativity, as well as their mental and physical abilities, to their fullest potential; (2) ensure persons with disabilities are not excluded from the general education system on the basis of disability, and that children with disabilities are not excluded from free and compulsory primary education, or from secondary education, on the basis of disability; (3) ensure persons with disabilities can access an inclusive, quality and free primary and secondary education on an equal basis with others in the communities in which they live; (4) provide reasonable access for persons living with disability to fulfil their personal requirements, and enable persons with disabilities to access general tertiary education, vocational training, adult education and lifelong learning without discrimination and on an equal basis with others; (5) enable persons with disabilities to receive the support required, within the general education system, to facilitate their effective education; (6) provide persons with disability environments which maximize academic and social development, which in fact is a provision for special education; (7) facilitate learning by persons with disability, use of alternative communication methods, such as Braille and sign language.

Work and Employment: To ensure the right of persons with disabilities to work, on an equal basis with others, the *Convention* provides that States Parties shall take appropriate steps, including through legislation, to, *inter alia* (1) prohibit discrimination on the basis of disability with regard to all matters concerning all forms of employment, including conditions of recruitment, hiring and employment, continuance of employment, career advancement and safe and healthy working conditions; (2) protect the rights of persons with disabilities, on an equal basis with others, to just and favourable conditions of work, including equal opportunities and equal remuneration for work of equal value, safe and healthy working conditions, including protection from harassment, and the redress of grievances; (3) ensure that persons with disabilities are able to exercise their labour and trade union rights on an equal basis with others;

(4) enable persons with disabilities to have effective access to general technical and vocational guidance programs, placement services and vocational and continuing training; (5) promote employment opportunities and career advancement for persons with disabilities in the labour market, as well as assistance in finding, obtaining, maintaining and returning to employment; (6) promote opportunities for self-employment, entrepreneurship, the development of cooperatives and starting one's own business; (7) employ persons with disabilities in the public sector; (8) promote the employment of persons with disabilities in the private sector through appropriate policies and measures, which may include affirmative action programmes, incentives and other measures; (9) ensure that reasonable accommodation is provided to persons with disabilities in the workplace; (10) promote the acquisition by persons with disabilities of work experience in the open labour market; (11) promote vocational and professional rehabilitation, job retention and return-to-work programs for persons with disabilities. (12) ensure that persons with disabilities are not held in slavery or in servitude, and are protected from forced or compulsory labour.

Health: to ensure that that persons with disabilities have the right to the enjoyment of the highest attainable standard of health, States Parties shall: (1) provide persons with disabilities with the same range, quality and standard of free or affordable health care and programmes as provided to other persons, including in the area of sexual and reproductive health and population-based public health programmes; (2) provide those health services needed by persons with disabilities specifically because of their disabilities, including early identification and intervention as appropriate, and services designed to minimize and prevent further disabilities; (3) provide these health services as close as possible to people's own communities; (4) provide care of the same quality to persons with disabilities as to others; (5) prohibit discrimination against persons with disabilities in the provision of health insurance, and life insurance ; (6) prevent discriminatory denial of health care or health services on the basis of disability.

Social Protection: to ensure that persons with disabilities have an adequate standard of living and social protection for themselves and their families, State Parties shall: (1) take appropriate steps to safeguard the right of persons with disabilities to have adequate food, clothing and housing, and to the continuous improvement of living conditions; (2) ensure equal access by persons with disabilities to clean water services, and to ensure access to appropriate and affordable services, devices and other assistance for disability-related needs; (3) ensure access by persons with disabilities to social protection programmes and poverty reduction programmes; (4) ensure access by persons with disabilities and their families living in situations of poverty to assistance from the State with disability-related expenses, including adequate training, counselling, financial assistance and respite care; (5) ensure access by persons with disabilities to public housing programmes; (6) ensure equal access by persons with disabilities to retirement benefits and programmes.

Family: to eliminate discrimination against persons with disabilities in all matters relating to marriage, family, parenthood and relationships, on an equal basis with others, States Parties shall take effective and appropriate measures to ensure that: (1) the right of all persons with disabilities who are of marriageable age to marry and to found a family on the basis of free and full consent of the intending spouses is recognized; (2) the rights of persons with disabilities to decide freely and responsibly on the number and spacing of their children and to have access to age-appropriate information, reproductive and family planning education are recognized, and the means necessary to enable them to exercise these rights are provided; (3) persons with disabilities, including children, retain their fertility on an equal basis with others; (4) render appropriate assistance to persons with disabilities in the performance of their child-rearing responsibilities; (5) children with disabilities have equal rights with respect to family life. State Parties shall provide early and comprehensive information, services and support to children with disabilities and their families; (6) a child shall not be separated from parents on the basis of a disability; (7) where the immediate family is unable to care for a child with disability, provide alternative care within the wider family.

3. Monitoring of the Convention's Implementation

The *Convention on the Rights of Persons with Disabilities* provides that State Parties, in accordance with their system of organization, shall designate one or more focal points within government for matters relating to the implementation of the *Convention*. Also, to facilitate related action in different sectors and at different levels, State Parties shall give due consideration to the establishment or designation of a coordination mechanism within government to facilitate implementation of the *Convention*. At the same time, the *Convention* also requires a State-level implementation mechanism and a UN implementation mechanism. These are to ensure that the *Convention* follows through in its implementation, in order to eliminate discrimination against persons with disability, and to render equal protection for those persons.

IV. Legislative Prohibition on the Discrimination against Disability in the United States

During the 1960s and 1970s, the US Congress enacted a series of disability rights laws to cope with the rising disability movement. The most famous were the *Rehabilitation Act* of 1973, the *Individual with Disabilities Education Act* (IDEA) and the *Architectural Barriers Act* (ABA). The *Rehabilitation Act* of 1973 prohibits discrimination on the basis of disability in programs conducted by Federal agencies, in programs receiving Federal financial assistance, in Federal employment, and in the employment practices of Federal contractors. The *Individual with Disabilities Education Act* (IDEA) requires the State to provide early intervention, special education, and related services to children with disabilities. The *Architectural Barriers Act* requires that facilities designed, built, altered, or leased with funds supplied by the US Federal Government be accessible to the public. Subsequently, the US Congress further enacted a series of laws to eliminate unequal treatment to persons living with disability, including the *Air Carrier Access Act* of 1986, prohibiting discrimination against persons with disabilities by air carriers; the *Fair Housing Amendments Act* of 1988, which extended the scope of application of the *Fair Housing Act*, which prohibits discrimination on the basis of disability in all types of housing transactions; the *Child Abuse Amendments* of 1984, which prevents the refusal of medical treatment for children with disabilities. According to a recent study, its full effectiveness is still ambiguous:

The *Americans with a Disability Act* (ADA) was enacted in 1990 to assist in

> remedying the problems related to access by persons with disabilities to public
> facilities, employment and transportation services. While the full effects of the
> ADA are still being worked out over a decade after its passage, it is still widely
> hoped that the law will live up to its potential and assist in alleviating much of the
> discrimination against people with disabilities.[18]

The ADA is a wide-ranging civil rights law that prohibits discrimination based on disability under various areas. Key areas include employment, public services, public accessibility accommodations and services operated by private entities, and telecommunications. Title I, Section 102 of the *Act* includes a detailed provision strictly prohibiting discrimination against a qualified individual with a disability because of the disability of such individual in regard to job application procedures, the hiring, advancement, or discharge of employees, employee compensation, job training, and other terms, conditions, and privileges of employment. To prevent discrimination against persons with disability, the said Article prohibits employers from conducting a medical examination or making inquiries of a job applicant as to whether the applicant has a disability or as to the nature or severity of such disability. An employer may require a medical examination after an offer of employment has been made to a job applicant and prior to the commencement of the employment duties of the applicant; however, the results of the medication examination shall be kept confidential. Section 202 under Title II of the *Act* provides that no individual with a disability shall be excluded from participation in or be denied the benefits of services, programs, or activities of a public entity. The section provided for accessible service in bus, rail, and intercity or commuter rail transportation in great detail, including ensuring accessible dining in single-level and double-level cars. Title III provides for the inhibition of discrimination against people with disability in public accommodations and services operated by private entities, under which, the definition of discrimination is divided into general and specific prohibitions. General prohibition is classified into activities, integrated settings, opportunity to participate, administrative methods and association. Activities are further divided into denial of participation, participation in unequal benefit, separate benefit, etc., or which detail explanations are provided. In setting forth the specific prohibitions, the provisions explain the five specific discriminatory behaviours, as well as discriminatory behaviours in a fixed route system, demand responsive system and over-the-road buses. Title IV provides for accessible telecommunication services for hearing-impaired and speech-impaired individuals. Title V contains miscellaneous provisions, including amendments to the *Rehabilitation Act* of 1973, litigation costs and technical assistance.

The *Americans with a Disability Act* has provided for relevant legal relief proceedings for any violation thereof. Take Public Accommodations and Services operated by Private Entities under Title III for example. (1) Persons who have been discriminated against or have reasonable cause to believe that they will be discriminated against as provided hereunder may apply the relief and procedures as set forth under the *Civil Rights Act* of 1964. Injunctive relief is available for certain discriminatory behaviour. (2) The attorney general shall investigate alleged violations of the subchapter. The attorney general may, if he has reasonable cause to believe that there has been discrimination practice, commence a civil action in any appropriate United States district court. A court may grant any equitable relief, including granting temporary, preliminary, or permanent relief; providing an auxiliary aid or service, modification of policy, practice, or procedure, or alternative method; and making facilities readily accessible to and usable by individuals with disabilities. The court may award such other relief as the court considers appropriate, including monetary damages to persons aggrieved when requested by the attorney general. To vindicate the public interest, the court may assess a civil penalty against the violating entity in an amount not exceeding US$ 50,000 for a first violation, and not exceeding US$ 100,000 for any subsequent violation. Article 513 of the said *Act* provided that where appropriate and to the extent authorized by law, the use of alternative means of dispute resolution, including settlement negotiations, conciliation, facilitation, mediation, fact-finding, mini-trials, and arbitration, is encouraged to resolve disputes arising under the chapter. The Equal Employment Opportunity Commission in the US helps an individual decide if a complaint should be raised. After raising a complaint, the Commission will notify the employer that a complaint has been lodged against him. Under the law, the Commission will recommend mediation as a means of dispute settlement between the parties. Of course, mediation is voluntary, free of charge and confidential. If no mediation is carried out or where mediation fails, the Commission will deem no infringement has been committed, and the complaint will be overruled, and the complainant may be free to commence legal action. On the other hand, if the Commission believes that discrimination exists, non-official resolution methods will be proposed. If, however, such resolution fails, the Commission will decide if legal action should be instituted, or may recommend that the complainant commences legal action as an individual.

V. THE LEGISLATIVE INHIBITION OF DISCRIMINATION ON THE BASIS OF DISABILITY IN HONG KONG

The *Basic Law of the Hong Kong Special Administrative Region of the People's Republic of China* is the main law applicable to persons with a disability in Hong Kong, China. Under its provisions, all permanent residents and non-permanent residents of Hong Kong are equal before the law, and enjoy the basic rights and freedom under the protection of the law. The *Disability Discrimination Ordinance* prohibits the discrimination and harassment of persons with disability, guarantees equal opportunities for persons with a disability, and facilitates their integration into the society as much as possible. Under the *Inland Revenue Ordinance*, taxpayers who take care of family members with a disability may apply for a corresponding tax exemption. The *Crimes Ordinance, Criminal Procedure Ordinance, Enduring Powers of Attorney Ordinance, Legislative Council Ordinance, Mental Health Ordinance* and *High Court Ordinance* provide legal protection for persons who are mentally ill or mentally handicapped and for their caregivers. The *Buildings Ordinance* provided for the relevant design standards to ensure that buildings are accessible to persons with disabilities. The *Cross-Harbour Tunnel (Passage Tax) Ordinance, Dutiable Commodities Ordinance, Motor Vehicles (First Registration Tax) Ordinance* and the *Road Traffic Ordinance* provided for the various tax exemptions during the use of motor vehicles by persons with a disability. Although the *Education Ordinance, Employment Ordinance, Employees' Compensation Ordinance, Guardianship of Minors Ordinance, Legal Aid Ordinance, Occupational Safety and Health Ordinance* and the *Protection of Children and Juveniles Ordinance* have no special provisions for persons with disabilities, the provisions specify their applicability to all persons, which includes disabled persons.

The *Disability Discrimination Ordinance* is the main legal basis for the elimination and inhibition of discrimination on the basis of disability. The *Ordinance* provides that any discrimination, harassment or vilification of persons with a disability or the associate of this person are unlawful. "Discrimination" is defined as any person: (1) who, on the ground of that other person's disability, treats such person less favourably than he treats or would treat a person without a disability; (2) who applies to that other person a requirement or condition which he applies or would apply equally to a person without a disability but which is such that the proportion of persons with a disability who can comply with it is considerably smaller than the proportion of persons without a disability who can comply with it; and which he cannot show to be justifiable irrespective of the disability or absence of the disability of the person to whom it is applied; and which is to that person's detriment because he cannot comply with it; (3) who, on the ground of the disability of an associate of that other person, treats such person less favourably than he treats or would treat a person without such a disability. The interpretation of discrimination on the basis of disability includes direct discrimination, indirect discrimination and discrimination against associates. Harassment is any unwelcome conduct towards a person or an associate of the person on account of that person's disability, where it can be reasonably anticipated by a reasonable person who has considered all circumstances that such conduct could cause the said disabled person or his associate to feel offended, humiliated or intimidated. Simply put, harassment is unwelcome behaviour towards persons with disabilities or their associates. It is unlawful for a person, by any activity in public, to incite hatred towards, serious contempt for, or severe ridicule of, another person with a disability or members of a class of persons with a disability. The *Disability Discrimination Ordinance* ensures that persons with disability or their associates are free from discrimination in the following areas: (1) employment, including partnerships, trade union memberships, qualifying bodies, vocational training, employment agencies and commission agents, etc.; (2) education; (3) access to, and disposal and management of premises; (4) goods, services and facilities; (5) the practice of barristers; and (6) clubs and sports.

The Equal Opportunities Commission is a statutory body established under the Sex Discrimination Ordinance, responsible for enforcing Hong Kong's *Sex Discrimination Ordinance, Family Status Discrimination Ordinance* and the *Disability Discrimination Ordinance*. According to the provisions under the *Disability Discrimination Ordinance,* the Commission focuses on eliminating discrimination, promoting equal opportunities between persons with and without disabilities, eliminating harassment and vilification, and encouraging conciliation of parties to any unlawful behaviour through mediation. The Commission also carries out continued monitoring of the state of observance of the ordinances, prepares proposals for amendments to the ordinances for submission to the chief executive, and executes duties of the Commission as prescribed by ordinances or other statutes. After submission of written complaints to the Commission by persons with disabilities who are subject to discrimination or harassment, the Commission conducts investigations, and attempts to seek resolution via mediation, unless the Commission exercises its discretionary powers to terminate the investigation. The Commission may terminate its investigation under the provisions of the ordinances, by ensuring prudent exercise of its powers in terminating the investigation and balancing the complainant and respondent's rights. The Commission shall exercise independence and fairness during its investigation and mediation to ensure equal treatment for both parties. The Commission is not an advocate for any party in a complaint, nor does it deliver judgment in any specific complaint. Delivery of a judgment is the function of the court. Mediation allows the parties concerned to find a way to settle their dispute together. Through mediation, the parties can find a satisfactory common ground on which to resolve their disputes. Mediation allows the parties to air their views, and enables them to better understand each other's standpoint; for example, the parties can clear up misunderstanding arising from wrong inferences or inaccurate data. Mediation can fundamentally change the attitudes of the parties. Data presented during mediation is strictly confidential, and will not be presented in court during legal action. Mediation is free and saves time with respect to going to court. It is also carried out in a less formal environment, and the parties are not exposed to the media. Because of its voluntary nature, the parties to a mediation process will sign a legally-binding mediation agreement upon arriving at an agreement. Conciliation conditions could involve an apology, a change of policy or operating methods, a review of procedures, a reinstatement or monetary compensation, etc. If mediation fails, the complainant may institute civil proceedings, or apply to the Commission for legal aid, including providing opinions, and arranging for advocates or barristers to render opinion or help.

VI. THE CHINESE LEGISLATIVE MECHANISM PROHIBITING DISCRIMINATION ON THE BASIS OF DISABILITY

(I) The Chinese Legislative Framework on the Inhibition of Discrimination against Persons with a Disability

A second sampling survey on disabled persons in China conducted in 2006 discovered that the total number of persons with various disabilities in the country stood at 82.96 million or 6.34 percent of the population. With protection of the rights of persons with disabilities high on its agenda, China has tried to eliminate discrimination on the basis of disability through legislation and policy enactment so that such persons may be fully integrated into society. At present, China has established a sound constitution-based legal system that protects the rights of persons with disability and that facilitates equalization of opportunities and full participation of disabled persons. Developed from criminal, civil and administrative laws and focusing on the protection of persons with disabilities, its legal system consists of administrative regulations governing the education and employment of disabled persons and supplemented by local legislation that provides for privileges and assistance for persons with disability. As elimination and inhibition of discrimination against persons with disabilities is one of the key objectives of Chinese legislation, more than 60 laws in the country contain provisions directly relating to the protection of disabled persons' rights.

1. The Constitution of the People's Republic of China

The Constitution of the People's Republic of China is the fundamental and paramount law of the nation. Article 33 of the Constitution provides that "the citizens of the People's Republic of China are equal before the law" and that "the State respects and protects human rights." Persons living with disabilities enjoy the same rights as others, as well as the equal protection by State laws. The Constitution also provides for the basic rights and freedom of Chinese citizens, including the right to vote and seek election, freedom of speech, the press, assembly, association, procession, demonstration and religion; the non-infringement of personal freedom, dignity and residence; the freedom of communication and confidentiality in communication; the right to criticize, propose, complain, sue, report and compensation; as well as labour rights, the right to rest and right to education, etc. Persons with disabilities enjoy all of these rights on an equal basis with others citizens, and no other person may infringe upon them.

Of particular note is Article 45 of the Constitution of the People's Republic of China, which provides that "the citizens of the People's Republic of China shall have the right to receive material assistance from the State and the society during old age, when they suffer from illness, or when they lose their capacity to work. The State shall develop the social insurance, social relief as well as medical and health benefits to be enjoyed by its citizens." The Constitution also provides that "the State and the society shall provide guarantees for the lives of military personnel suffering from disability, and shall support family members of martyrs and provide privileges for family members of military officers"; and that "the State and the society shall help with the labour, livelihood and education arrangements of citizens who are blind, deaf, mute or are handicapped in other manners." According to those provisions, persons living with disabilities shall receive labour, livelihood and education assistance from the State, and shall be entitled to receive material aid from the State and the society. Also, military officers who are disabled will be protected by the State and society. Few constitutions in the world contain special provisions for the protection of the rights of disabled persons.

2. Law on the Protection of Persons with Disabilities

China is one of the earliest countries to enact special legislation for persons with disability. The *Law of the People's Republic of China on the Protection of Persons with Disabilities* was adopted on 28 December 1990, the amended *Law of the People's Republic of China on the Protection of Persons with Disabilities* was adopted on 24 April 2008 and effective as of 1 July 2008. The *Law of the People's Republic of China on the Protection of Persons with Disabilities* provides comprehensive protection of the rights of disabled persons in China; it plays an important role in facilitating the equalization of opportunities and the full participation of disabled persons in society, as well as in the elimination of discrimination on the basis of disability.

Article 3 of the *Law of the People's Republic of China on the Protection of Persons with Disabilities* provides that "Persons with disabilities shall enjoy equal rights with other citizens in political, economic, cultural and social respects and in family life as well"; and that "Discrimination on the basis of disability shall be prohibited. Insult of and disservice to persons with disabilities shall be prohibited. Disparagement of and infringement upon the dignity of persons with disabilities by means of mass media or any other means shall be prohibited." Article 38 of the *Law of the People's Republic of China on the Protection of Persons with Disabilities* provides that "No discrimination shall be practiced against persons with disabilities in recruitment, employment, obtainment of permanent status, promotion, determining technical or professional titles, payment, welfare, holidays and vacations, social insurance or in other aspects."

The *Law of the People's Republic of China on the Protection of Persons with Disabilities* has developed many specific measures to protect the rights of people with disabilities. For instance, the *Law of the People's Republic of China on the Protection of Persons with Disabilities* provides for compulsory measures and incentive measures that address different issues relating to the employment of disabled persons. Article 33 is an example of a compulsory measure. The provisions are as follows:

> Government agencies, social organizations, enterprises, public institutions, and private-run non-enterprise entities shall, in accordance with the quota stipulated in relevant regulations, arrange job opportunities for persons with disabilities, and offer them appropriate work and positions. Those who cannot reach the quota as prescribed in relevant regulations shall fulfil their obligation to guarantee job opportunities for persons with disabilities in accordance with relevant state regulations. The State encourages employers to over fulfil their obligation to employ more persons with disabilities.

Article 36, which exemplifies incentive measures, provides that:

> The State shall implement preferential tax treatment, according to law, for enterprises and employers who have fulfilled or over fulfilled their quota obligations to employ workers with disabilities, welfare institutions that have a significant staff of persons with disabilities, and self-employed disabled workers, and shall provide them with assistance in production, management, technology, capital, materials and workplace, etc. [...] The State shall exempt administrative fees for self-employed disabled workers. [...] Local people's governments and departments above county level shall identify certain products and businesses suitable for people with disabilities, give priority to welfare enterprises for persons with disabilities to work on such businesses and determine which products are to be produced exclusively by such enterprises on the basis of their special features [...] The government in procurement shall give priority to products and services made by welfare enterprises for persons with disabilities, when other conditions are the same [...] Competent authorities shall, in verifying and issuing business licenses, give priority to persons with disabilities who apply for such licenses for self-employment [...] Departments concerned shall provide assistance for persons with disabilities engaged in various kinds of labour in rural areas by ways of production services, technical guidance, supply of farm materials, purchasing and marketing of farm and sideline products and credit issuance, etc.

The *Law of the People's Republic of China on the Protection of Persons with Disabilities* also provided for a series of legal liabilities for discriminatory behaviour towards persons with disability. Based on the degree of discrimination, offenders shall be subject to administrative, civil or criminal liabilities.

3. Regulations on the Employment of Persons with Disabilities

The *Regulations on the Employment of the Persons with Disabilities* is formulated on the basis of the *Law of the People's Republic of China on the Protection of Persons with Disabilities*. Therefore, it contains the relevant provisions of the *Law*, and includes more specific provisions on the discrimination against the employment of the disabled based on the principles of the *Law* and practical socio-economic needs. In many respect, the *Regulations* is a breakthrough and shows creativity.

Article 4 of the *Regulations* provides that

the State encourages social organizations and individuals to help and support disabled persons to obtain employment through multiple channels and various forms, and disabled persons are encouraged to obtain employment by themselves through various forms such as job interview. No discrimination shall be practiced against disabled persons in their employment.

Article 13 provides that

Employing units shall provide disabled employees with working conditions and labour protection suitable for their physical conditions. No discrimination shall be practiced against disabled persons in promotion, determining technical or professional titles, payment, labour insurance, welfare or in other aspects.

In terms of actual protection, the *Regulations on the Employment of Persons with Disabilities* has made greater progress than the *Law of the People's Republic of China on the Protection of Persons with Disabilities*. For example, in terms of the ratio of persons with disability to be employed in every organization, Article 8 clearly sets forth that "The proportion of disabled employees shall not be lower than 1.5 percent of the overall employees." Employers that fail to meet the target proportion shall pay into the employment security fund for disabled persons. The *Regulations on the Employment of Persons with Disabilities* expanded on the scope by which enterprises benefit from employing disabled persons through tax incentives. Previously restricted only to welfare enterprises for the disabled, tax reduction and exemption benefits are now extended to all entities that organize mass employment for persons with disability. In addition, the ratio of disabled persons has also been specified. Article 11 provides that "In employing units with concentrative employment of disabled persons, disabled employees engaged in all-day work shall account for more than 25 percent of the overall current employees."

4. Regulations on the Education of Persons with Disabilities

Formulated based on the *Law of the People's Republic of China on the Protection of Persons with Disabilities*, the *Regulations* elaborates and supplements the provisions concerning education contained in the *Law*. The *Regulations on the Education of Persons with Disabilities* places a heavy focus on the protection of the education rights of disabled persons, and prohibits any enrolment discrimination. Article 26 of the *Regulations* provides that "Ordinary schools of vocational education must enrol persons with disabilities who meet the State's admission requirements, while ordinary institutions of vocational training shall make efforts to enrol persons with disabilities." Article 29 provides that "Ordinary senior middle schools, institutions of tertiary education and institutions of adult education must enrol students with disabilities who meet the State's admission requirements and shall not deny them enrolment on account of their disabilities." For those who refuse to recruit persons with disabilities according to the relevant State regulations, the same Article has set forth the legal liabilities; persons responsible for the violation shall be subject to administrative penalties imposed by the relevant authorities.

Chinese authorities are commencing the legislative process on the *Regulations on the Rehabilitation of Persons with Disabilities* and the *Regulations on Accessible Facilities*. The regulations aim to progressively build a sound legal system that govern the protection of the rights of disabled persons to eliminate completely the different discriminations against persons with disability and facilitate the full integration and equal participation of such persons in the society and in life.

(II) Chinese Organizations that Inhibit Discrimination against Persons with Disability

(1) Disabled Persons' Work Committee

In September 1993, building on China's organizing committee for the United Nations Decade of Disabled Persons (1983-1992), the Chinese government established the Disabled Persons' Work Coordination Committee of the State Council. Later renamed the Disabled Persons' Work Committee of the State Council on 6 April 2006, it is an advisory and coordination organ of the State Council. The director is the Deputy Prime Minister of the State Council, and it has involvement from 36 entities and ministries, including the Ministry of Education, Ministry of Civil Affairs, Ministry of Manpower and Resources and Social Security, Ministry of Health and the China Disabled Persons' Federation. The key functions of the State Council's Disabled Persons' Work Coordination Committee are to coordinate the planning and implementation of the guiding principles, policies, laws and regulations pertaining to persons with disabilities, and to organize and coordinate major activities of the United Nations concerning persons with disabilities. County-level and higher governments have established disabled persons' work committees, which are standing advisory and coordination organs of governments of the same level. Disabled persons' work committees do not deal directly with cases concerning the discrimination of persons with disability. However, as the government's advisory and coordination organ, the committee is responsible for coordinating major issues relating to disabled. The committee may coordinate the various aspects of work concerning persons with disabilities carried out by many departments, and the formulation and implementation of guidelines, policies, laws and regulations, plans and programs relating to the same. Hence, these committees play an important role in the enforcement of laws and the formulation of policies that eliminate and inhibit discrimination on the basis of disability.

(2) Administrative Organs

Because discrimination affects different aspects of the life of disabled persons, administrative organs have responsibilities and duties for discrimination on the basis of disability within their functional responsibilities. According to Article 60 of the *Law of the People's Republic of China on the Protection of Persons with Disabilities*, "Where the lawful rights and interests of persons with disabilities are violated, the offended shall have the right to ask competent departments to deal with the case in accordance with law." Article 61 provides that

> Whoever, in violation of this law, rejects, delays or holds back the complaint, appeal or report relating to the violation of the rights and interests of persons with disabilities, or retaliates against the one who launches the complaint, appeal or report, shall be ordered to rectify their wrong doing by the organization to which they belong or higher level authorities. Disciplinary measures shall be taken against the people in charge and others directly responsible. [...] Where, not in compliance with his public duties, a civil servant fails to stop actions which violate the rights and interests of persons with disabilities or fail to offer necessary help to the harmed, which leads to serious consequences, the organization to which he belongs or higher level authorities shall take disciplinary measures against the people in charge or others directly responsible.

According to Article 50 of the *Regulations on the Education of Persons with Disabilities*, in the event that schools discriminate against disabled persons and refuse to enrol any person with a disability who should be enrolled according to the relevant provisions of the State, the concerned administrative department of education shall order the school in question to enrol the person with a disability in school. The department shall also impose administrative sanctions on the persons who are held directly responsible. Administrative departments responsible for manpower and resources and social security, health, buildings and civil affairs have corresponding responsibilities in employment, rehabilitation, health, accessibility, livelihood security, etc. When they are discriminated against, persons with disabilities may, depending on the nature of the discrimination, seek relief and assistance from the relevant administrative department.

(3) Disabled Persons' Federation

According to the *Law of the Peoples Republic of China on the Protection of Persons with Disabilities*, the China Disabled Persons' Federation and other local organizations represent the collective interests of persons with disabilities, protects the legitimate interests of persons with disabilities, and unite to serve these persons. Also, the China Disabled Persons' Federation works for the benefit of disabled persons by facilitating equal opportunities and full participation by disabled persons through mobilization of social powers, as provided by law, regulations, the Federation's constitution, or by government mandate. The results of a study of persons with disabilities reveal that the Federation is the first relief channel to which persons with disability turn when they face educational discrimination; the next channel is the local education administration department; after this they institute legal proceedings. When faced with employment discrimination, the Federation is also the first relief channel for disapled persons, followed by suing in court and seeking assistance from the labour department.[19] Hence, the Disabled Persons' Federation is an important agency in inhibiting and eliminating discrimination against disability that represents persons with different disabilities.

(4) The Courts and Arbitration Organs

As the State's adjudication organs, the People's Courts of various levels may hear and assess the liabilities of the parties to discrimination against persons with disability. Article 60 of the *Law of the People's Republic of China on the Protection of Persons with Disabilities* provides that "Where the lawful rights and interests of persons with disabilities are violated, the offended shall have the right to ask competent departments to deal with the case in accordance with law, or submit application to arbitration institutions, or appeal to people's courts in conformity with law." If the discrimination against disabled persons is within the scope of labour disputes, the disabled persons may request that the labour arbitration agency conduct labour arbitration. If it is a civil matter, application to an arbitration agency for arbitration may be submitted upon consent by the parties concerned.

VIII. LEGISLATIVE INHIBITION OF DISCRIMINATION AGAINST DISABILITY: A RECOMMENDATION

1. Establish a Sound Legal System to Prohibit Discrimination against the Disabled

Legislation is an important and effective avenue to inhibit and eliminate discrimination against disability. Although more than 40 countries have enacted laws that oppose discrimination against disability, most have not formulated special laws against discrimination on the basis of disability. Hence, driving countries to enact laws that inhibit discrimination against disability will be an important task for the international community. Article 4 of the *Convention of the Rights of Persons with Disabilities* provides that State Parties shall "take all appropriate measures, including legislation, to modify or abolish existing laws, regulations, customs and practices that constitute discrimination against persons with disabilities."

Although we recommend enacting special legislation for discrimination against disability, our greatest wish is to establish a holistic inhibitive legislative system, instead of a single set of laws. The State's Constitution and civil, criminal, administrative, procedure, labour and education legislation should incorporate the basic principles of non-discrimination on the basis of disability, providing for the inhibition and elimination of discrimination against disability. They should cohere with specific anti-discrimination laws to form a legislative system that is improved and fine-tuned, along with greater economic and social development. This is the only way to ensure the rights of people with disabilities are protected by a solid legal system to ensure effective legislative inhibition of discrimination against disability, and to provide equal opportunities for persons with disability.

2. Clear Definition of what Behaviour Constitutes Discrimination on the Basis of Disability

A clear definition is required for the inhibition and elimination of discrimination on the basis of disability.

We need to draw a clear line between discrimination on the basis of disability and other types of discrimination. There are many types of discrimination, such as racial discrimination, geographical discrimination or discrimination against qualifications, etc.; hence, not all discriminations that may be suffered by persons with disabilities are necessarily on the basis of their disabilities. Discrimination on the basis of disability must be discrimination against disabled persons solely on the basis of their disabilities. This delineation is important, for the relevant provisions under the disability discrimination law may be applied and the relief and protection obtained only if it is truly discrimination on the basis of disability. Other types of discrimination are governed by their corresponding laws and regulations.

We must also clearly define direct discrimination and indirect discrimination, for they hold important theoretical and practical significance. Because indirect discrimination is comparatively more shrouded, the determination of indirect discrimination must be based on more stringent criteria, and the legislation must provide clear interpretation of what is entailed. Particularly for employment, the State must find a balance between its employees who are disabled persons and their employers; over-protection will dampen the willingness of employers to hire disabled persons. It would, therefore, end up being detrimental for the employment prospects of persons with disability.

We must also differentiate between discrimination, harassment and vilification of disabled persons. Although these are all done on the basis of disability, and prejudice the rights of persons with disabilities, they have different constitutive requirements and inflict different harms on disabled persons and society. Thus, measures taken against the three behaviours differ. A clear definition helps identify the behaviours in practice; it also prevents arbitrary definition of what constitutes discrimination against disability, and helps achieve due, reasonable and regulated protection of the rights of persons with disabilities.

3. Establish a Special Agency for the Inhibition of Discrimination on the Basis of Disability

Due to different country specificities, agencies established for the inhibition of discrimination against disability differ. Based on general jurisprudence, persons with disabilities may seek judicial protection by the State – especially relief through court litigation – for all discriminatory behaviours. Many countries permit local human rights agencies to accept complaints about discrimination on the basis of disability and to take relevant relief action. However, the fact that most countries do not have special agencies that inhibit discrimination against disabilities does not favour the inhibition of discrimination against disabilities in practice. Should special organizations for the inhibition of discrimination against disability be established? The answer is obvious. However, a standard model on the specific form of this organization applicable for all countries is not available; differences in administrative systems, history and tradition, religion and beliefs, and level of development will affect the form of the organization. The fundamental principles and ultimate objective of setting up such a special organization is that it must ensure the realization of the provisions of international conventions. At the same time, it must take into full consideration the national specificities in order to safeguard the best interests of persons with disabilities.

4. Establish a Multi-Channelled Dispute Resolution Mechanism for Discrimination on the Basis of Disability

Many countries advocate for the use of alternative dispute resolution by encouraging the disabled to settle disputes through negotiation, conciliation, facilitation, mediation, fact-finding and mediation, mini-trial, arbitration, and a range of other measures. Any disabled person whose right has been infringed upon may request the relevant authorities deal with the infringement according to law, or apply to the arbitration centre for arbitration according to law, or institute legal proceedings with the People's Court. Hong Kong also encourages the settlement of disputes regarding discrimination against disability through mediation. The wide array of dispute resolution mechanisms provides multiple channels and avenues for the resolution of disputes about discrimination against disabled persons. Many countries have seen good dispute resolution results from the outcomes of their judicial practice. Hence, we recommend the establishment of a special agency to enforce the inhibition of discrimination on the basis of disability.

However, our greater hope is that all countries will establish multi-channel dispute resolution mechanisms that offer flexible and case-specific settlement in cases of discrimination on the basis of disability.

ENDNOTES

1   Office of Dictionary Editing, Language Research Institute, China Academy of Social Sciences, *Modern Dictionary of Chinese* (*xian dai han yu ci dian*), Commercial Press, 2005, 5th Edition, p. 1071.

2   *Webster's Dictionary of the English Language Unabridged*, Encyclopaedic Edition, Publishers International Press, 1979, p. 523.

3   Bonnie Poitras Tucker and Adam A. Milani, *Federal Disability Law*, 2004, West, p. 2.

4   *Ibid.*, p. 3.

5   *Protecting the Rights of Persons with Disabilities – International and Comparative Law and Practice*, Huaxia Publishing Co., 2003, Preface.

6   Michael Stein, *Americans with Disabilities Act: Empirical Perspectives*, Studies on the Legal Protection Mechanisms of the Disabled (*can ji ren fa lü bao zhang ji zhi yan jiu*). Huaxia Publication Co., 2008, p. 20.

7   See http://www.eoc.org.hk/cc/home.com.

8   *Protecting the Rights of Persons with Disabilities – International and Comparative Law and Practice*, Huaxia Publishing Co., 2003, 1st Edition, p. 45.

9   *Ibid.*, p. 45.

10   Bonnie Poitras Tucker and Adam A. Milani, *Federal Disability Law*, 2004, West, p. 3.

11   *Protecting the Rights of Persons with Disabilities – International and Comparative Law and Practice*, Huaxia Publishing Co., 2003, 1st Edition, Preface.

12   *Ibid.*

13   Deng Bufang. *The Call for Humanitarianism* (*ren dao zhu yi de hu huan*), 3rd collection, Huaxia Publishing, Co., 2006, 1st Edition, p. 283.

14   *Protecting the Rights of Persons with Disabilities – International and Comparative Law and Practice*, Huaxia Publishing Co., 2003, 1st Edition, Preface.

15   Bonnie Poitras Tucker and Adam A. Milani, *Federal Disability Law*, 2004, West, p. 1.

16   See Wang Zhijiang. *Protection of the Rights of Persons with Disability – The Chinese and International Society* (*can ji ren quan li bao zhang: zhong guo he guo ji she hui*), Rights-Based Development (*yi quan li wei ji chu cu jin fa zhan*), Peking University Press, 2005, p. 197–199.

17   See http://www.un.org/chinese/esa/social/disabled/.

18   Bonnie Poitras Tucker and Adam A. Milani, *Federal Disability Law*, 2004, West, p. 6.

19   Wang Zhijiang *et al.*, "Project Report on Anti-Education and Anti-Employment Discrimination towards Persons with Disability" (*fan dui dui can ji ren jiao yu qi shi, jiu ye qi shi xiang mu bao gao*), The Research Centre for Human Rights, Peking University Law School – University of Ottawa Law School, Canada Project on Promoting Anti-Discrimination in China.

PART FOUR

Discrimination Against Those Living with HIV/AIDS

The Application of International and Regional Instruments to HIV-Related Discrimination in China and Southeast Asia

David Patterson

The purpose of this study is to examine selected international and regional instruments endorsed by China and ASEAN member countries[1] relevant to HIV-related discrimination.[2] Recommendations are then made as to how to strengthen the role of international and regional instruments in national responses to HIV-related discrimination.

HIV-related discrimination is defined broadly as any discrimination which contributes to the spread of HIV and the impact of AIDS. HIV-related discrimination, including gender-based discrimination, has long been recognized as a co-factor in HIV vulnerability. In 1989 the (then) UN Centre for Human Rights and the World Health Organization (WHO) convened an international consultation on AIDS and human rights which identified this link.[3] In 2007, Piot and colleagues described the interaction of gender, discrimination and HIV thus:

> Gender inequality is one of many injustices fuelling the epidemic. The spread of HIV is disproportionately high among many groups that experience discrimination and suffer from a lack of human rights protection. This includes groups that have been marginalized socially, culturally, and often economically, such as injection drug users, sex workers, migrants, and men who have sex with men. Women's susceptibility to HIV is further enhanced in members of marginalized or migrant populations: research in Viet Nam, for example, revealed that women migrant workers were twice as likely as other women to become HIV positive.[4]

More than other infectious diseases, discrimination determines who gets infected with HIV, who is diagnosed as HIV-positive, and what care, treatment and support people receive after diagnosis. HIV-related discrimination also leads to, and is itself a consequence of, socio-economic vulnerability. For example, in sub-Saharan Africa, countries with greater income inequality have higher HIV prevalence. This observation should be of particular concern to countries with significant or increasing levels of inequality.[5]

HIV-related discrimination is a central obstacle to the augmentaion of prevention, treatment, care and support programs. It is therefore an entirely appropriate subject for international scrutiny and for the exchange of experience and best practices. By encouraging countries to address HIV-related discrimination, international and regional instruments contribute to the national and global response to HIV.

This study addresses the following questions:

1. What has been the contribution of international and regional instruments to national responses to HIV-related discrimination, as evidenced by law and policy reform?
2. How can the role of international and regional instruments be strengthened in support of national responses to HIV-related discrimination?

Millions of dollars have been spent on international and regional intergovernmental meetings on HIV, where the resulting declarations and resolutions are regarded as key outputs.[6] Yet some governments pay little attention to the commitments they make at these events. To ensure the maximum return on this investment, we need to examine how national compliance with international commitments can be improved. It is also possible that, rather than creating more instruments, human and financial resources could be more usefully directed to national-level activities to address HIV-related discrimination, and to the implementation and monitoring of existing commitments.

I. INTERNATIONAL INSTRUMENTS

In this article, the term "international instruments" refers to both binding instruments (e.g. treaties) and non-binding instruments (such as declarations of the UN General Assembly and regional intergovernmental bodies).

1. Paris AIDS Summit 1 December 1994

In December 1994, at a meeting convened jointly by France and the WHO, heads of government met for the first time to discuss AIDS. Representatives from the countries in this study came from China, Indonesia, Philippines, Thailand and Viet Nam. In the statement of the meeting (the "Paris Declaration") representatives declared their "determination to fight against poverty, stigmatization and discrimination" and "to provide leadership, advocacy and guidance in order to ensure that non-discrimination, human rights and ethical principles form an integral part of the response to the pandemic."[7] They also undertook to "fully involve non-governmental and community-based organizations as well as people living with HIV/AIDS in the formulation and implementation of public policies…"

One outcome of the Paris AIDS Summit was the GIPA Principle – the "greater involvement of people living with HIV/AIDS."[8] This principle is expressed at the national level by the inclusion of people living with HIV in national strategy development bodies and the country coordinating mechanism (CCM) established to develop proposals for, and monitor the implementation of, grants from the Global Fund to Fight AIDS, Tuberculosis and Malaria (Global Fund). At the international level this principle is expressed through the designation of seats for representatives of people living with HIV (PLHIV)[9] on the governing bodies of the Joint United Nations Program on HIV/AIDS (UNAIDS) and the Global Fund, and a special accreditation process to allow for the participation of PLHIV representatives in UN meetings on HIV, such as the General Assembly sessions noted below.

2. United Nations human rights treaties

Although no UN human rights treaty refers explicitly to HIV, prohibitions of discrimination include "other status" to indicate that the listed grounds of discrimination are not limited. For example, the International Covenant on Economic, Social and Cultural Rights states:

> The States Parties to the present Covenant undertake to guarantee that the rights enunciated in the present Covenant will be exercised without discrimination of any kind as to race, colour, sex, language, religion, political or other opinion, national or social origin, property, birth or other status.[10]

The UN Commission on Human Rights repeatedly affirmed that the term "other status" in international human rights treaties should be interpreted to include HIV status.[11]

In 1996 UNAIDS and the Office of the High Commissioner for Human Rights (OHCHR) convened an expert consultation to explore states' obligations in responding to the HIV epidemic under the UN human rights treaties. The report of the consultation contains 12 principles, now known as the "International Guidelines on HIV/AIDS and Human Rights." The report was included as an annex to the corresponding report of the Secretary-General to the Commission on Human Rights in 1997 (E/CN.4/1997/37). The Guidelines were subsequently annexed to a Commission resolution on HIV/AIDS (1997/33). At that time members of the Commission included China, Indonesia, Malaysia, and Philippines.

The report of the consultation was then edited and published by UNAIDS and OHCHR in 1998 as *HIV/AIDS and Human Rights: International Guidelines.*[12] In 2002 the Guidelines were updated to reflect developments in prevention, treatment, care and support. A consolidated version of the International Guidelines was published in 2006, as *International Guidelines on HIV/AIDS and Human Rights*.[13]

The Guidelines note the wide range of rights implicated in the response to HIV, including the right to non-discrimination.[14] Most importantly, the Guidelines refer to the circumstances in which international law permits the imposition of restrictions and limitations on certain human rights in the context of HIV and AIDS.[15]

In 1998, the Inter-Parliamentary Union (IPU) adopted a broad resolution on HIV at the 99th Conference in Windhoek, Nambia. In 1999 the IPU and UNAIDS published the *Handbook for Legislators on HIV/AIDS, Law and Human Rights*. This publication examines national experience in implementing the Guidelines, and includes a chapter on HIV-related discrimination.[16] In 2007 the IPU, the United Nations Development Program (UNDP) and UNAIDS published a revised and expanded edition, *Taking Action Against HIV*.[17] Of the countries in this study, only Brunei and Myanmar are not IPU members.

All of the countries in this study have ratified at least one human rights treaty relevant to HIV, the Convention on the Rights of the Child, and most countries have ratified several such treaties. Some human rights treaty monitoring bodies have provided specific guidance in the application of the respective treaties to HIV. In 2003, the Committee on the Rights of the Child issued a General Comment on HIV/AIDS and the rights of the child.[18] References to HIV in the country periodic reports to the treaty monitoring bodies give further indication of states' recognition of their binding obligations to take action on HIV under international law. For example, the second periodic report of China under the Convention on the Rights of the Child makes reference to the national response to HIV and AIDS.[19]

Over the period 1997-2005 the Commission on Human Rights requested that governments report on the steps they had taken to promote and implement, where applicable, programs to address the urgent HIV-related human rights of women, children and vulnerable groups, as described in the International Guidelines.[20] In 2005, fifteen governments responded, including Thailand from among the countries in this study.[21] The country reports are available on the website of the Office of the High Commissioner for Human Rights.[22]

Finally, the Convention on the Rights of Persons with Disabilities came into force on 3 May 2008. As of 30 January 2008, all of the countries in this study except Brunei, Malaysia and Myanmar have signed the Convention. Although the Convention does not refer explicitly to HIV, UNAIDS has long urged that the definition of disability include HIV infection,[23] reflecting the interpretation of national disability law in Canada and many other countries.[24]

3. Instruments of the International Labour Organization

All the countries in this study except Brunei Darussalam are members of the International Labour Organization (ILO). In 2001, the ILO published the *Code of*

Practice on HIV/AIDS and the World of Work (the Code of Practice) which includes non-discrimination as a key principle.[25] The Code of Practice was developed through a tripartite process and was issued with the agreement of all ILO members. In 2002 ILO published *Implementing the Code of Practice on HIV/AIDS and the World of Work: an Education and Training Manual.* This manual gives specific guidance on legislation concerning HIV in the workplace, including the prohibition of discrimination relating to HIV status.[26]

In 2005 the ILO published a report on the implementation of the Code of Practice in ASEAN countries.[27] In 2008, the ILO published a further study on the implementation of the Code, including a review of national HIV/AIDS laws and policies.[28] In 2009, the International Labour Conference will consider adopting a "Recommendation" on HIV/AIDS. Although the Recommendation will not be binding, the Governing Body can request that ILO member governments report on the implementation of the Recommendation, thus imposing further obligations to address HIV-related discrimination.[29]

4. Resolutions of the World Health Assembly

All of the countries in this study are WHO members. In 1988 the WHO governing body, the World Health Assembly (WHA), called on members to avoid discrimination on the grounds of HIV status in the provision of services, employment and travel.[30] As of January 2008, China,[31] Malaysia,[32] and Singapore[33] all exclude foreign visitors with HIV, contrary to the WHA resolution and other international guidance.[34]

5. Resolutions of the General Assembly

Under the UN Charter, the General Assembly may meet in special session to consider a wide range of issues of international importance.[35] Resolutions of the UN General Assembly at such special sessions have the status of non-binding recommendations for member states.[36] In November 2000 the UN General Assembly decided to convene a UN General Assembly special session (UNGASS) on HIV/AIDS in New York in June 2001.[37] In addition to the over 1,000 ECOSOC-accredited non-governmental organizations (NGOs) which can participate in such UN meetings, the General Assembly approved arrangements for the accreditation and participation of hundreds of non-ECOSOC accredited NGOs working on HIV-related issues. Preparations for the UNGASS on HIV/AIDS thus occupied the attention of many staff working on HIV in government departments, international agencies, and civil society organization for the following seven months.

In June 2001 the UN General Assembly adopted by acclamation the "Declaration of Commitment on HIV/AIDS," which includes time-bound targets for national action in key areas, including HIV-related discrimination. Countries are requested to report on progress made at subsequent General Assembly sessions, using a standard monitoring framework. Country reports are posted on the UNAIDS website.

In the Declaration of Commitment, all UN members recognized the links between human rights and HIV (para. 16). They also pledged to "ensure the development and implementation of multi-sectoral national strategies and financing plans for combating HIV/AIDS that "eliminate discrimination and marginalization" by 2003 (para. 37). The member states also pledged to address discrimination against women and children, and (para. 58):

> By 2003, enact, strengthen or enforce as appropriate legislation, regulations and other measures to eliminate all forms of discrimination against, and to ensure the full enjoyment of all human rights and fundamental freedoms by people living with HIV/AIDS and members of vulnerable groups.

In 2006 the General Assembly held a major review of progress in implementing the Declaration of Commitment, and adopted a further resolution, the "Political Declaration on HIV/AIDS."[38] In this instrument the General Assembly committed (para.29):

> …to intensifying efforts to enact, strengthen or enforce, as appropriate, legislation, regulations and other measures to eliminate all forms of discrimination against and to ensure the full enjoyment of all human rights and fundamental freedoms by people living with HIV and members of vulnerable groups, in particular to ensure their access to, inter alia, education, inheritance, employment, health care, social and health services, prevention, support and treatment, information and legal protection, while respecting their privacy and confidentiality; and developing strategies to combat stigma and social exclusion connected with the epidemic.

Members also pledged to address gender inequalities, and to adopt measures to address all forms of discrimination against women. Further comprehensive reviews will take place in General Assembly special sessions during 2008 and 2011.

In 2006 the International Council of AIDS Service Organizations (ICASO) undertook a study which considered the implementation of the Declaration of Commitment in 14 countries, including Indonesia. The ICASO study found that there was "a huge gap between what exists on paper in terms of anti-discrimination policies and what happens in reality. Stigma and discrimination are commonplace, and they constitute the major obstacle to the successful implementation of prevention, care, treatment and support services.'[39] The study found that

- Governments have not done enough to create a culture based on rights.
- Governments fail to educate the population concerning the laws and policies.

- The fight against discrimination is not part of the government's agenda.
- There is no formal system for monitoring the implementation of the laws and policies, especially among vulnerable groups.
- Most people do not understand that they have rights and do not know about the legal mechanisms available to protect those rights.
- Most people do not have the skills to fight for their rights.
- Where governments do take action, it tends to be reactive rather than prevention.

The reporting framework developed to monitor states' compliance with the Declaration of Commitment contains a "National Composite Policy Index," which proposes that data on stigma and discrimination be collected every two years through a desk review and key informant interviews.[40] The Policy Index for the 2008 country reports has been updated and now requires information on many of the issues addressed in the ICASO study. The 2008 Policy Index contains two parts: one to be completed by governments (Part A) and another to be "administered to representatives from non-governmental organizations, bilateral agencies, and UN organizations" (Part B).

Regarding HIV-related discrimination, Part A of the reporting framework requests governments to report

- Whether the multisectoral strategy / action framework addresses stigma and discrimination.
- Whether the country has integrated HIV and AIDS into its general development plans (such as National Development Plans, Common Country Assessments/ United Nations Development Assistance Framework, Poverty Reduction Strategy Papers, Sector Wide Approach) and if so, whether the reduction of stigma and discrimination is one of the policy areas addressed in these plans.
- Whether the country has a policy or strategy to promote information, education and communication (IEC) and other preventive health interventions for vulnerable sub-populations and, if so, whether reduction of stigma and discrimination is included for injecting drug users (IDU), men who have sex with men (MSM), sex workers, clients of sex workers, prison inmates, and other sub-populations.
- Whether the country has identified geographical areas in need of HIV prevention programs and, if so, whether IEC on stigma and discrimination reduction is available.

Similarly, Part B of the reporting framework asks

- Whether the country has laws and regulations that protect people living with HIV from discrimination.

- Whether the country has laws or regulations which specify protections for vulnerable sub-populations (women, young people, IDU, MSM, sex workers, prison inmates, migrants/mobile populations) and others.
- If such laws and regulations exist, what mechanisms are in place to ensure that these laws are implemented, and what systems of redress are in place to ensure these laws are having their desired effect.
- Whether there is a mechanism to record, document and address cases of discrimination experienced by people living with HIV and/or most at risk populations.
- Whether the country has human rights monitoring and enforcement mechanisms, including "focal points within governmental health and other departments to monitor HIV-related human rights abuses and HIV-related discrimination in areas such as housing and employment," and performance indicators or benchmarks for the reduction of HIV-related stigma and discrimination.

Part B also asks about geographic distribution of HIV prevention programs, including IEC on stigma and discrimination reduction, allowing a comparison with the government response to the same question in Part A.

The completion of the monitoring framework may be beyond the human resources and financial capacity of smaller or poorer countries without external help. Technical assistance is available from UNAIDS.

II. Regional Instruments

In the region covered by the countries in this study, at least three intergovernmental bodies – Asia-Pacific Economic Cooperation (APEC), ASEAN, and the UN Regional Task Force on Mobility and HIV Vulnerability Reduction (UNRTF) – have considered HIV and issued or endorsed instruments describing international best practices in responding to HIV. In addition, six countries of the Greater Mekong Sub-region (GMS) have signed a Memorandum of Understanding to reduce HIV vulnerability related to population movement.

1. Asia-Pacific Economic Cooperation (APEC)

Of the eleven countries in this study, all except Cambodia, Lao PDR and Myanmar are members of APEC. In 2000 APEC Economic Leaders committed to "fighting HIV/AIDS and other infectious diseases" and called for a report on a "strategy which can be used in APEC to more effectively meet these disease challenges." In 2001 APEC leaders endorsed the strategy, entitled "Infectious Diseases in the Asia Pacific Region: A Reason to Act and Acting with Reason," and called for its implementation.

At the 2004 summit APEC Economic Leaders endorsed an initiative, proposed by China, Philippines and Thailand, titled "Fighting against AIDS in APEC."[41] Although this statement made no direct reference to stigma and discrimination, it acknowledged that gender inequalities drive the epidemic and that "high risk populations and vulnerable groups need protection from HIV infection."

In 2005, the (then) APEC Health Task Force hosted meetings on "Best Practices on HIV/AIDS Management in the Workplace"[42] and on "HIV/AIDS and Migrant-Mobile Workers."[43] The reports of both meetings noted the importance of addressing HIV-related discrimination. The former meeting also suggested that "member economies should consider developing an Agreement on 'No Compulsory HIV Testing for Sending and Receiving Economies' in relation to overseas labour employment contracts." The latter meeting carried this theme forward: recommendations included, "Ensure a rights-based testing and treatment policy for migrant workers that includes the principles of: equal access without discrimination; no mandatory testing; access to care; and, no deportation on the basis of HIV positive status."[44]

In 2006 the APEC Health Task Force approved a proposal by Canada, cosponsored by Thailand and New Zealand, to develop guidelines for creating an enabling environment for employers to implement effective workplace practices for people living with HIV. Draft guidelines were developed through a consultative process involving member economies and other stakeholders. In September 2007, APEC Economic Leaders endorsed "Guidelines for Creating an Enabling Environment for Employers to Implement Effective Workplace Practices for People Living with HIV/AIDS."[45]

The Guidelines reference the ILO Code of Practice on HIV/AIDS and the World of Work. They also address issues not covered in the Code such as gender, children who work, and migrants and mobile populations. The Guidelines are intended for the governments of APEC member economies, public and private employers, business associations, workers, trade unions and other worker organizations, organizations of people living with HIV, and all other groups with responsibilities and activities related to HIV and AIDS in workplace settings.[46] Also in 2007, APEC member economies identified "HIV as an episodic disability" as an area in which exchange of responses and good practices could be of assistance.[47] In February 2008, the APEC Health Working Group agreed to review the experiences of member economies and to make recommendations on addressing HIV as an episodic disability, as well as promoting and implementing the Guidelines.

2. Association of Southeast Asian Nations

ASEAN has addressed HIV and AIDS in numerous ways, including through the creation of the ASEAN Task Force on AIDS (ATFAO); the publication of regional workplans (currently the Third ASEAN Work Program (AWPIII) 2006-2010); and the holding of two special summits on HIV/AIDS, the first held in Brunei in 2001 ans the second held in Cuba in 2007, with accompanying declarations. The Cebu summit Declaration tasked ATFOA with regular reporting on the implementation of the AWPIII. However, unlike the process to monitor the UN Declaration of Commitment, there is no civil society membership of ATFOA, meetings are closed to observers except by invitation, and country progress reports are not routinely posted on the ASEAN website.

3. United Nations Regional Task Force on Mobility and HIV Vulnerability Reduction (UNRTF)

UNRTF membership comprises the countries of Southeast Asia and China (provinces of Guangxi and Yunnan), as well as interested agencies, and national and regional NGOs by invitation. Two regional strategies on mobility and HIV vulnerability reduction have been endorsed by the member countries (2002-2004 and 2006-2008).[48]

The overarching theme of the 2006-2008 Regional Strategy is "to strengthen stakeholders' multi-sectoral response to the heightened HIV vulnerability of migrants and mobile populations in the region." Discrimination is addressed in the Strategy's fourth guiding principle.[49]

4. Memorandum of Understanding for Joint Action to Reduce HIV Vulnerability Related to Population Movement

This instrument was an initiative of the UNDP, WHO and ASEAN and opened for signature in 2004. Six countries have signed the Memorandum: Cambodia, China, Lao PDR, Myanmar, Thailand and Vietnam. Although the Memorandum does not mention discrimination explicitly, signatories nonetheless agreed to "promote development strategies that reduce HIV vulnerabilities" and implement the accompanying workplan, which includes "the establishment and expansion of migrant friendly health facilities."[50] The Memorandum has a five year term and includes a mid-term review. The Memorandum proposes a program coordination committee, coordinated by Cambodia, which is to report to ATFOA and meet one day before regular ATFOA meetings. Unfortunately, this committee has never been convened.

III. Discussion

1. What has been the contribution of international and regional instruments to national responses to HIV-related discrimination, as evidenced by law and policy reform?

Although compliance with international human rights treaties is binding under international law, the treaties contain only weak enforcement mechanisms. Compliance is encouraged through an open process of examination of periodic country reports. There is a backlog in the review of country reports, which has increased as more treaties are created and ratified. Although the application of the treaties to HIV is now accepted, the periodic country reporting process has only started to address HIV-related discrimination more comprehensively in recent years. There are very few references to HIV in the treaty reports from the countries in this study. Therefore, it does not appear that the UN human rights treaties have significantly influenced national law and policy on HIV-related discrimination in the countries in this study.

Of the non-binding instruments noted above, the most comprehensive and closely monitored is the Declaration of Commitment. In 2008, all of the countries in this study except Brunei, Myanmar and Singapore submitted country reports on progress in implementing the Declaration up to 2007.[51] Since 2001, several countries in the region have introduced laws or other legal measures to address HIV-related discrimination, including Cambodia (2002),[52] China (2006),[53] Indonesia (2004),[54] and Vietnam (2006).[55] Philippines has comprehensive legislation which pre-dates the Declaration.[56] Only some of these laws provide clear remedies with enforceable penalties, however. In 2005, the China report on the implementation of the Declaration made specific reference to actions taken to strengthen policy measures.[57] In 2007, the China report notes the introduction in 2006 of the Regulation on AIDS Prevention and Treatment (Decree No. 457).[58] This is evidence of China's intention to implement the commitments in the Declaration.

The preface to the Implementing Guidelines for the Cambodian *Law on the Prevention and Control of HIV/AIDS* notes that "(t)he law follows internationally recognized best practice for responding effectively to HIV/AIDS."[59] This indicates that in drafting the Guidelines the Cambodian authorities took into account international best practices, however there is no specific reference to the sources of such guidance.

In Indonesia, the 2004 Ministerial Decree on HIV/AIDS Prevention and Control in the Workplace[60] addressed discrimination against PLHIV in the workplace, and follows the 2003 Tripartite Declaration to Combat HIV/AIDS in the World of Work.[61] The Tripartite Declaration reflects the principles in the ILO Code of Practice on HIV/AIDS and the World of Work. The ILO and other agencies, including the United States Department of Labor, have provided technical and financial assistance to Indonesia to address HIV in the workplace.

In 2005, the governments of Cambodia and three other GMS countries undertook a national policy audit to assess compliance with selected international instruments in the context of HIV and population mobility, including the UNRTF Regional Strategy, the Declaration of Commitment, and the Memorandum of Understanding.[62] The audit was conducted by government representatives themselves, and in some cases officials became aware of their government's position on issues relating to HIV and mobility for the first time.

In 2006 the Cambodian Minister of Public Works and Transport issued four policies to promote HIV prevention in the public works and transport sector. In his introduction to the policies, the Minister noted that the policies were developed, in part, pursuant to the Memorandum of Understanding (noted above). Policy 4 is titled "Support the

Memorandum of Understanding of the Joint Action to Reduce HIV Vulnerability Related to Mobile Populations (2004-2009) among countries in the Greater Mekong Sub-region (GMS) to obtain a favourable result as requested by the signatories." The policies are published in both Khmer and English, and the Memorandum is attached as an annex. Canada, through the Canada South East Asia Regional HIV/AIDS Program, and other donors have provided intensive technical and financial support to Cambodia to address HIV/AIDS, including in the context of population movements.[63]

Of the six countries that signed the Memorandum however, only Cambodia refers to the instrument as influential in national policy reform. One challenge is that the Memorandum may have been signed in some countries without any or adequate discussion at Cabinet level. Another challenge is that the annexed workplan was not costed, nor were funds identified to implement the obligations in the Memorandum. Perhaps as a result, the proposed program coordination committee has never been convened. Aside from Cambodia, it appears the Memorandum had no impact in influencing HIV-related law and policy in the signatory countries in the period 2005-2007.

2. How can the role of international and regional instruments be strengthened in support of national responses to HIV-related discrimination?
The binding or non-binding nature of the instrument does not appear to determine the level of government response, at least in reporting compliance. It appears that the following strategies may increase the likelihood that an international instrument will have an impact on national responses to HIV-related discrimination:

1. Involve all stakeholders in the development of the instrument. This includes all government departments which may be affected by the instrument, as well as the private sector and civil society organizations.
2. Ensure the instrument is endorsed by an official with recognized signing authority to represent and bind the whole of government, not just one ministry.
3. Ensure all documentation is accessible and disseminated promptly to all national stakeholders in the national language(s). Documentation should be posted on the internet in the national language(s) and in English with scanned copies of the original signed instruments.
4. Ensure that the endorsement of the instrument is a part of a process leading to implementation, not an isolated event. Costs of implementation should be established, a budget attached and financial support identified.
5. Ensure the human resources to implement the commitments have been identified, and that technical support is available where necessary.

6. Conduct periodic policy audits to remind governments of their commitments and assess compliance. Ensure these audits and periodic country reports are published in national language(s) and in English, and widely disseminated, including on the internet.

7. Disseminate the instrument among affected communities and their representatives, national human rights institutions, lawyers, academics, and students.

8. Improve communications between government representatives at international meetings and relevant ministries regarding international commitments.

9. Encourage governments to make reference to their international commitments when drafting national instruments on HIV-related discrimination. Technical assistance should also emphasize this aspect.

10. Explore new opportunities to secure government action on HIV-related discrimination, including through influencing the policies of major donors, and the interpretation and implementation of the UN *Convention on the Rights of Persons with Disabilities.*

IV. CONCLUSION

There is more likelihood that international instruments will impact on national responses to HIV-related discrimination if an adequate monitoring and reporting process is included, and financial and technical assistance to undertake both implementation and monitoring is available. Not every intergovernmental meeting on HIV needs a new commitment or declaration. There may be more value in emphasizing the implementation of existing commitments.

Further research is needed to establish how international instruments influence legal and other responses to HIV-related discrimination. This could be done by examining the preparatory documents, interviews with legal drafters who prepared the bills, and a comparative analysis of the relevant texts.

China should now examine its international and regional commitments to address HIV-related discrimination, and take the necessary steps to comply with these commitments. This includes law and policy reform at the national, provincial and local levels. It also includes educating and training legislators and policy makers, judiciary, police, legal service providers and para-legals at all levels in the purpose and application of the law.[64] Mass organizations of women and youth should also be made aware of the importance of non-discrimination in the context of HIV, not only to promote a harmonious society, but because HIV-related discrimination discourages PLHIV and people most vulnerable to HIV from accessing prevention education and care, treatment and support services. China should also use international and regional forums to share its initiatives as best practice examples for other countries to consider, adapt and apply.

ENDNOTES

[1] Association of Southeast Asian Nations (ASEAN). In 2007 ASEAN member countries were Brunei Darussalam, Cambodia, Indonesia, Lao PDR, Malaysia, Myanmar, Philippines, Singapore, Thailand and Viet Nam. www.aseansec.org (home page).

[2] See Patterson D. and London L. (2002), "International law, human rights and HIV/AIDS," in Bulletin of the World Health Organization. 80:12.

[3] Centre for Human Rights. (1990), Report of an International Consultation on AIDS and Human Rights, Geneva, 26 to 28 July 1989 (HR/PUB/90/2).

[4] Piot P. *et al.* (2007), "Squaring the Circle : AIDS, Poverty and Human Development," PLOS Medicine 4 :10, 1571-5, 1572. www.plosmedicine.org (home page).

[5] See Gillespie S. *et al.* (2007), "Is poverty or wealth driving HIV transmission?" *AIDS.* 2007 Nov; 21 Suppl 7:S5-S16.

[6] References in this article are to United States dollars. See "History of the recognition of the importance of human rights in the context of HIV," in UNAIDS and OHCHR. (2006) International Guidelines on HIV/AIDS and Human Rights. Annex 1. 105-111.

[7] The Paris Declaration. Paris AIDS Summit. 1 December 1994, data.unaids.org/pub/ ExternalDocument/2007/theparisdeclaration_en.pdf.

[8] See UNAIDS. From Principles to Practice : the Greater Involvement of People Living with HIV/AIDS (GIPA), 1999.

[9] "People living with HIV" or "HIV-positive people" (PLHIV) is the preferred terminology to refer to people infected with the human immunodeficiency virus. UNAIDS, (2007), *UNAIDS' Terminology Guidelines.*

[10] International Covenant on Economic, Social and Cultural Rights. Article 2(2). www.ohchr. org (home page).

[11] See e.g., Commission on Human Rights resolution 2005/84, 21 April 2005.

[12] Available on the UNAIDS website in official UN languages, http://www.unaids.org/en/.

[13] Available on the UNAIDS website, http://www.unaids.org/DocOrder/OrderForm.aspx. Subsequent references to the International Guidelines in this study refer to this version.

[14] International Guidelines, paras 104-153.

[15] International Guidelines, paras 104-105. See also "The Siracusa Principles on the Limitation and Derogation Provisions in the International Covenant on Civil and Political Rights," *Human Rights Quarterly*, vol. 7, no. 1 (February 1985) 3-13.

[16] UNAIDS and Inter-Parliamentary Union.,(1999), *Handbook for Legislators on HIV/AIDS, Law and Human Rights.* Chapter 5 addresses HIV-related discrimination. The Handbook is available from the UNAIDS website in English, French and Russian. An unofficial version is available in Chinese.

[17] UNAIDS, UNDP and Inter-Parliamentary Union, (2007), Taking Action Against HIV. Handbook for Parliamentarians No. 15. Chapter 6 addresses stigma and discrimination. The Handbook is available from the IPU website http://www.ipu.org/english/handbks. htm.

[18] Committee on the Rights of the Child, General Comment No. 3 (2003), HIV/AIDS and the rights of the child.

[19] Committee on the Rights of the Child, Second Periodic Report of States Parties due in 1997, CRC/C/83/Add.9, 15 July 2005. All treaty body reports are available through the search engine of the website of the Office of the High Commissioner for Human Rights, http://tb.ohchr.org/default.aspx.

[20] See for example, Commission on Human Rights resolution 2005/84.

[21] Report of the Secretary-General on the protection of human rights in the context of AIDS, A/HRC/4/110.

[22] http://www2.ohchr.org/english/issues/hiv/contributions.htm.

[23] UNAIDS, (1996), HIV/AIDS and Disability. Statement to the UN Sub-Commission on the Prevention of Discrimination and Protection of Minorities, 48th session, August 1996.

[24] R. Elliott and J. Gould, (2005), "Protection against discrimination based on HIV/AIDS status in Canada: the legal framework." *Canadian HIV/AIDS Policy and Law Review*, 10(1), www.aidslaw.ca (home page).

[25] ILO, (2001), An ILO Code of Practice on HIV/AIDS and the World of Work. The Code is also available Chinese, Khmer, Lao, Thai, and Vietnamese. http://www.ilo.org/public/english/protection/trav/aids/index.htm.

[26] ILO, (2002), Implementing the Code of Practice on HIV/AIDS and the world of work: an education and training manual. Module 4.

[27] ILO, (2005), HIV/AIDS and the World of Work in ASEAN.

[28] ILO, (2008), HIV/AIDS and the World of Work. Report for International Labour Conference, 2009. First edition. Appendix III National HIV/AIDS Laws and Policies.

[29] ILO, (2007) Strengthening the ILO's capacity to assist its Members' efforts to reach its objectives in the context of globalization. ILC. 96th Session, Geneva, para. 163.

[30] World Health Assembly. (1988), "Avoidance of discrimination in relation to HIV-infected people and people with AIDS" WHA41.24.

[31] Rules for Implementation of the Control of the Entry and Exit of Foreigners, 1994. http://www.asianlii.org/cn/legis/cen/laws/rfiotcoteaeoa1994666/.

[32] Immigration Act 1959. First Schedule (Part II).

[33] Immigration Act. Section 8(3)(ba) defines as a prohibited immigrant "any person suffering from Acquired Immune Deficiency Syndrome or infected with the Human Immunodeficiency Virus."

[34] UNAIDS and International Organization for Migration. (2004), UNAIDS/IOM Statement on HIV/AIDS-related travel restrictions. See also International AIDS Society. (2007), "Banning entry of people living with HIV/AIDS. Policy Paper' http://www.iasociety.org/ (home page).

[35] United Nations Organization. (1945), Charter of the United Nations, Chapter IV.

[36] Hillgenberg H. (1999), A fresh look at soft law. *European Journal of International Law* 1999 10(3):499-515, 515.

[37] UN General Assembly. (2000), Review of the problem of human immunodeficiency syndrome / acquired immunodeficiency syndrome in all its aspects. A/Res/55/13 (3 November 2000).

[38] UN General Assembly. (2006), Political Declaration on HIV/AIDS. A/Res/60/262. (2 June 2006).

[39] International Council of AIDS Service Organizations. (2006), Implementation of the UNGASS Declaration of Commitment on HIV/AIDS, (Toronto: ICASO), 2.

[40] UNAIDS (2007), Guidelines on the Construction of Core Indicators.

[41] APEC. Fighting against AIDS in APEC (2004), http://www.apec.org (home page).

[42] APEC. Best Practices on HIV/AIDS Management in the Workplace, 2005/SOM3/HTF/002.

[43] APEC. Report of the APEC Workshop on: "HIV/AIDS and Migrant/Mobile Workers," 2006/SOM1/HTF/ 006.

[44] These reports were not available from the APEC web site www.apec.org on 8 February 2008. The reports (obtained previously by the author) do not include a list of meeting participants

and it is not possible from the reports to determine which APEC member economies were represented at the meetings.

45 APEC. "Guidelines for Creating an Enabling Environment for Employers to Implement Effective Workplace Practices for People Living with HIV/AIDS" http://www.apec.org (home page).

46 Patterson, D. (2007) "Use of soft law to influence government policy and reduce HIV vulnerability of construction workers in the Greater Mekong Subregion of Southeast Asia," HIV/AIDS Policy and Law Review 12 (2/3). www.aidslaw.ca (homepage).

47 An "episodic disability" is a disability which can result in periods of impairment and time away from the workplace, followed by periods of relative good health and capacity to work.

48 UNDP (2006). Report of the joint meeting of the UN Regional Task Force on Mobility and HIV Vulnerability Reduction and Kunming Medical College. 10-13 October 2006. www. hivmobilitysea.org.

49 UN Regional Task Force on Mobility and HIV Vulnerability Reduction. (2006). UN Regional Strategy on Mobility and HIV Vulnerability Reduction in South-East Asia and Southern China 2006-2008, p. 22.

50 Memorandum of Understanding for Joint Action to Reduce HIV Vulnerability Related to Population Movement. www.hivmobilitysea.org.

51 See UNAIDS. Monitoring the Declaration of Commitment on HIV/AIDS. 2008 progress reports submitted by countries. www.unaids.org.

52 Law on the Prevention and Control of HIV/AIDS, 2002.

53 Regulations on AIDS Prevention and Treatment. Decree of the State Council No. 457, effective 1 March 2006.

54 Decree of the Minister of Manpower and Transmigration (KEP.68/MEN/2004) on HIV/AIDS Prevention and Control in the Workplace, 28 April 2004.

55 Law on HIV/AIDS Prevention and Control, 2006.

56 Philippines AIDS Prevention and Control Act, 1998.

57 Office of the State Council Working Committee on AIDS. (2005). Progress on Implementing UNGASS Declaration of Commitment in China 2005.

58 UNGASS Country Report PR China (Reporting Period January 2006-December 2007). www.unaids.org.

59 National AIDS Authority of Cambodia. (2005). Implementing Guidelines of the Law on the Prevention and Control of HIV/AIDS.

60 Minister of Manpower and Transmigration (Indonesia). (2004). Decree on HIV/AIDS Prevention and Control in the Workplace. KEP.68/MEN/2004. 28 April 2004.

61 (2003), Tripartite Declaration to Combat HIV/AIDS in the World of Work. 25 February 2003.

62 Canada South East Asia Regional HIV/AIDS Program. (2006). Consolidated National Policy Self Audits. Available at www.csearhap.org. Also available at www.hivmobilitysea.org. Another audit will be undertaken in 2008 to establish progress made since 2005.

63 Available at www.csearhap.org. Also available at www.hivmobilitysea.org.

64 In Kunming, Yunnan, in December 2007 the Righteous Law Firm and the Daytop Drug Abuse Treatment and Rehabilitation Center held a workshop for lawyers on HIV in order to improve the provision of legal services to PLHIV and vulnerable groups. The workshop was supported by the Asia Pacific Council of AIDS Service Organizations (APCASO) and the International Development Law Organization (IDLO). After the workshop a network of lawyers was established to address HIV issues and a guide to HIV and the law was written.

CHAPTER TWELVE

Gender and HIV/AIDS
Understanding and Addressing Stigma and Discrimination Among Women and Girls

Barbara Clow and Linda Snyder

> In my view, ...the most vexing and intolerable dimension of the pandemic is what
> is happening to women. ... Gender inequality is driving the pandemic, and we
> will never subdue the gruesome force of AIDS until the rights of women become
> paramount in the struggle. ... I challenge you, [therefore] to enter the fray against
> gender inequality. There is no more honourable and productive calling. There
> is nothing of greater import in this world. All roads lead from women to social
> change, and that includes subduing the pandemic.
>
> Stephen Lewis,
> United Nations Special Envoy for HIV/AIDS in Africa[1]

INTRODUCTION

Stephen Lewis has been among the most prominent and impassioned personalities in
the campaign to raise awareness of the role of gender in the HIV/AIDS pandemic,
particularly in the latter half of his tenure as UN Special Envoy for HIV/AIDS in Africa.
His efforts complement the work of researchers, decision makers, advocates, and service
providers from around the world who have laboured for more than a decade to explicate
the ways in which women and girls are differentially infected and affected by HIV and
AIDS-related illnesses. His words, therefore, provide an appropriate and powerful point
of departure for this discussion of gender, HIV/AIDS and discrimination.

The paper begins with an overview of the ways in which sex and gender work
together to put women and girls at risk of HIV infection. While both men and women
are contracting HIV and dying of AIDS-related illnesses, gender inequity throughout
the world is deepening the suffering of women and girls as well as contributing to the
spread of HIV. Moreover, gender roles and expectations contribute to stigmatization of
women and girls, particularly those from marginalized populations.

The second part of the discussion provides a gender-based analysis of the HIV/AIDS
epidemic in Canada, followed by a brief comparison with South Africa's experience

with HIV. Although the two countries are vastly different – in terms of infrastructure, culture, history and the scope and impact of HIV – nonetheless, the trajectory of the pandemic is disturbingly similar, at least with respect to the vulnerability of women and girls. Disadvantaged groups of women and girls in both Canada and South Africa have been hardest hit by HIV and AIDS-related illnesses.

The last section of the paper addresses international recommendations for responding to the HIV pandemic, specifically the implications of United Nations (UN) and World Health Organization (WHO) guidelines for countries with a low incidence of HIV infection. By comparing the management of HIV in South Africa and Canada, the argument will be made that international guidelines, by ignoring gender and the plight of women and girls, contribute to the spread of HIV. Moreover, because the guidelines recommend focusing on those at highest risk of HIV infection, they may serve to deepen the stigma associated with positive sero-status and encourage discrimination and marginalization of women and girls infected and affected by HIV/AIDS. Low incidence countries, including Canada and China, may be in a position to learn from this analysis and to fashion more effective responses to the pandemic.

SEX, GENDER AND HIV

Since the end of the Second World War, there has been an increasing tendency in western societies to distinguish between the words "sex" and "gender." Although these terms share common linguistic and historical roots, feminist researchers, activists and social commentators have sought to associate the word "sex" with biological structures and physiological processes that differentiate the male from the female body while defining "gender" as the array of roles, relationships, personality traits, attitudes, behaviours, values and relative power that society ascribes to females and males on a differential basis. [2] "Sex" is, therefore, innate to the physical body, while "gender" is a product of socially constructed norms and expectations. For example, babies are usually born with external genitalia that identify them as male or female, but girls and boys acquire beliefs and behaviours, such as how to dress or express emotion, that are defined socially as either feminine or masculine.

Feminists and other social activists adopted the strategy of distinguishing between sex and gender in order to expose and challenge stereotypes that were being used to deny women access to labour markets, educational and political institutions, and the full range of political, economic and social benefits enjoyed by men in their communities. For example, stereotypes that characterized women as more emotional and less logical in their thinking than men were used to exclude women from high-paying and prestigious jobs in the natural and applied sciences. While much progress has been made in breaking down barriers to women's rights and well-being, at least in some parts of the world, the HIV/AIDS pandemic has demonstrated how much more needs to be done – and urgently – in the area of gender equity.

Women and girls are almost always at greater risk than men and boys of exposure to and infection by HIV. Physiological factors, or *sex differences*, are partly responsible for increased vulnerability among women. Delicate tissues in the female reproductive tract are more receptive to viral transmission, especially if these tissues sustain injury or are immature, as among younger women.[3] Moreover, the larger area of the female reproductive tract creates increased opportunities for transmission of the virus, particular in comparison with the single point of entry in the penis.[4] In addition, women and girls are exposed to greater concentrations of HIV during heterosexual intercourse than are their male partners because semen tends to carry a higher viral load than vaginal secretions. As a result, women and girls are far more likely to be infected by HIV-positive male partners than they are to pass on the virus to their male partners. According to one report, teenaged girls in sub-Saharan Africa were infected at rates five to six times greater than teenaged boys.[5]

Gender differences, especially those that contribute to social, political, and economic inequity, are also responsible for the heightened vulnerability of women and girls. In many parts of the world, women and girls have less power and fewer resources than do men and boys. Economic dependency as well as violence and coercion make it difficult for women to negotiate safe sex practices, such as condom use, to refuse sex or to leave a relationship that puts them at risk. Gendered customs and social values also contribute both to the spread of HIV and greater vulnerability among women and girls. For example, ubiquitous social norms that encourage multiple sexual partners for men but frown on this practice among women, not only increase the likelihood of women being exposed to HIV, but also contribute to stigmatization and marginalization of women who contract the disease, regardless of whether they have had one or many sexual partners. Similarly, in some cultures women who are widowed not only lose their rights to family property and land, but they themselves may be "inherited" by a male relative. These types of customs leave women economically dependent and, when the husband had died of AIDS, they contribute directly to the spread of HIV.[6]

Stigma, discrimination and marginalization of all kinds – as well as the threat of HIV/AIDS – follow women and girls. When women and girls test positive for HIV, they may be ostracized, abandoned, abused, or even killed. While any woman or girl diagnosed with HIV is liable to face discrimination, the situation of women and girls who are already marginalized or are living with the burden of intersecting inequities is more dire still. Tolson and Kellington, for example, noted that "it is the people who are the bottom of the social and political hierarchy in their society whose risk for HIV/AIDS is greatest. For a woman in Vancouver, living on welfare in a dangerous area, using valium or heroin or alcohol to cope, her risks are determined not by the right personal selection of a healthy option, but instead by a socially-determined lack of options."[7] In Canada, women who engage in commercial sex work, use injecting drugs or come from racialized populations are among those at greatest risk of stigma and discrimination, particularly when a diagnosis of HIV is added to their burdens.[8] In a study of Aboriginal women in Canada, for example, Ship and Norton observed that "many HIV-positive First Nations women live in secrecy because of the multiple forms of stigma associated with the disease, including being branded 'promiscuous,' 'a bad mother,' and 'deserving of HIV/AIDS'."[9] Jackson likewise notes that female sex trade workers, rather than their male clients, have been blamed for the spread of HIV, thereby deepening the stigma and discrimination they experience.[10] In such situations, women and girls fall deeper into poverty, social isolation and various forms of dependency. They may enter into sex trade work or selling blood simply to support themselves and their children, they may begin to utilize substances of various kinds to escape the realities of their lives, but these activities all increase their risks of exposure as well as the spread of HIV.[11]

All of this is not to suggest that sex and gender do not contribute to HIV vulnerability among men. While women and girls are generally more at risk physiologically, the exception to this rule is men who have sex with men, specifically a man who is a "bottom" and assumes the receptive role in anal intercourse. Like vaginal and cervical tissue, the tissues of the intestinal tract are highly fragile and injury makes them more susceptible to HIV infection. And like the female reproductive tract, the intestinal tract offers a large expanse of tissue for infection to take hold.[12] Gender norms also create risks for men. The most obvious example is the tremendous stigma attached to homosexuality in many countries around the world. Men who have sex with men may feel compelled to conceal their sexual preferences, thereby putting their partners – female and male – at increased risk of HIV infection.[13] At the same time, gender stereotypes of masculinity affect both straight and gay men. Societal norms that assume males are knowledgeable about sex may leave everyone in the dark; men and boys feel unable to ask for information while women, girls and "bottoms" may assume that they do not need to ask for information. Gender norms for men also encourage multiple sexual partners and, in some cases, sexual aggression, both of which contribute to the spread of HIV.[14] Male sex trade workers seem to be equally vulnerable to violence, coercion and dependency as their female counterparts.

While both women and men are suffering the effects of the pandemic, it is also true that more women and girls are living with HIV and AIDS-related illnesses – more than men and boys and more than ever before. According to the lastest statistical report released by UNAIDS, women accounted for half of the adult population living with HIV around the world, but in sub-Saharan Africa – the epicentre of the pandemic – women accounted for nearly 61 percent of adults living with HIV and the proportion of women affected in other parts of the world is continuing to climb steadily.[15] It is also the case that gender norms and roles create an unequal balance of power between women and men, with women and girls having "fewer legal rights and less access to education, health services, training, income-generating activities and property."[16] And finally, women and girls are taking up the work of caring for those living and dying with HIV and AIDS-related illnesses: girls are kept home from school and social activities to provide care for their younger siblings or ill parents, grandmothers step in to provide care for millions of children orphaned by HIV/AIDS. In the process, their ability to protect and provide for themselves and their families is eroded. It is critical, therefore, to place in the foreground the role of gender in the pandemic. To paraphrase Stephen Lewis and many others, "the face of AIDS is the face of a woman."[17]

SEX, GENDER AND HIV/AIDS IN CANADA

Canada has always been, and continues to be, a country with a low incidence of HIV/AIDS. As compared with other nations around the world, only a tiny percentage of the Canadian population is infected or affected. According to current estimates from UNAIDS, approximately 60,000 Canadians, or 0.3 percent of the population, are living with HIV.[18] China, with a much larger population, has many more people living with HIV, but the prevalence rate, at 0.1 percent, is even smaller than in Canada.[19] It is also deemed a low-incidence country.

At the same time, the epidemic in Canada seems to be "confined" to specific populations. Men who have sex with men (MSM) and injecting drug users (IDU) accounted for close to 70 percent of those living with HIV at the end of 2005.[20]

The fact that rates of new infections among MSM and IDUs have dropped dramatically, particularly from the early days of the epidemic, is routinely cited as a good news story, a sign of the successful management of HIV in Canada.

Figure 1: Distribution (percent) of estimated new HIV infections among MSM, by time period

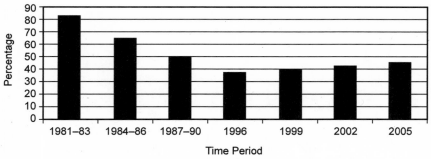

Source: Public Health Agency of Canada, (2007) *HIV/AIDS Epi Updates,* Ottawa: Public Health Agency of Canada.

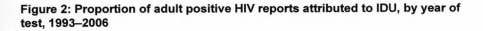

Figure 2: Proportion of adult positive HIV reports attributed to IDU, by year of test, 1993–2006

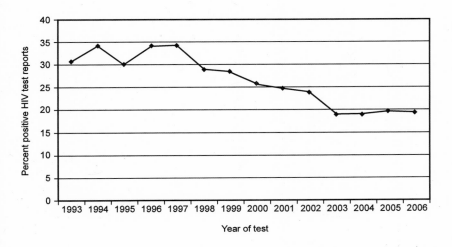

Year of test

Source: Public Health Agency of Canada, (2007) *HIV/AIDS Epi Updates*, Ottawa: Public Health Agency of Canada.

But there are other significant changes in patterns of HIV infection that demand our attention. Between 1995 and 2006, HIV infections attributable to heterosexual contact – alone or in combination with other factors – have increased alarmingly, from 7.5 percent to 37 percent.[21] Similarly, AIDS diagnoses attributable to heterosexual contact in the same period have risen from 7 percent to approximately 26 percent.[22]

While these trends in transmission of HIV affect both men and women in every age category, they have profound implications for women. In 2000, approximately half of women diagnosed with HIV had contracted the virus through heterosexual contact. In 2006, this proportion had reached 76 percent. Thus, while people living with HIV and AIDS in Canada are still most likely to be men who have sex with men and/or injecting drug users, those newly infected with HIV are increasingly likely to be heterosexual women.

Infection rates among women of all ages in Canada are increasing. Between 1997 and 2006, the proportion of adult females diagnosed with HIV has risen from 12 percent to nearly 28 percent. Moreover, the proportion of adult women living with diagnosed AIDS has increased from 6.1 percent in 1994 to 24.2 percent in 2006.[23] But the biggest change has been for young women, between the ages of 15 and 29 years. Females accounted for 12 percent of all new infections in this age group in the early 1990s, but the proportion has increased almost four fold by 2006.[24]

Figure 3: Estimated exposure category distributions (percent) of new HIV infections in Canada, by time period

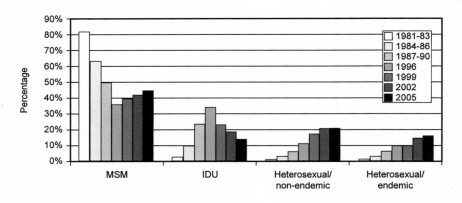

Source: Public Health Agency of Canada, (2007) *HIV/AIDS Epi Updates*, Ottawa: Public Health Agency of Canada.

Figure 4: Percent of all positive HIV test reports accounted for by women by age group and year of test, 1985–2005

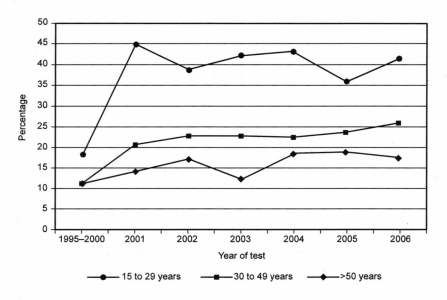

Source: Public Health Agency of Canada, (2007) *HIV/AIDS Epi Updates*, Ottawa: Public Health Agency of Canada.

Not only are women and girls in Canada experiencing heightened risks of HIV infection, particularly through heterosexual contact, but also when they are infected with HIV, they are more likely to have poorer health outcomes than men and boys. According to Health Canada, women tend to "... have a lower survival rate than men... [as a result of] late diagnosis and delay of treatment because of misdiagnosis of early symptoms; exclusion from drug trials and lack of access to antiviral treatment; lack of research into the natural history of HIV in women; higher rates of poverty among women and lack of access to adequate health care; and the tendency of many women to make self-care a lower priority than the care of children and family."[25] In a study of AIDS-related deaths in Vancouver between 1995 and 2001, women were found disproportionately to have died without having received any treatment.[26] The stigma associated with a diagnosis of HIV makes it challenging for women to seek and get the care they need. One woman, after learning that she was HIV-positive, learned that her doctor "didn't want me in his office. He said I would infect his staff."[27]

HIV poses a growing threat for all women and girls in Canada, but some populations are much more vulnerable to infection than others. While the rates of infection among white Canadians have been dropping steadily in recent years, black Canadians and Aboriginal persons have experienced disproportionate increases. Aboriginals, for example, represent approximately 3 percent of the total population of Canada, but in 2006, 23 percent of all new HIV infections were found among Aboriginal people.[28]

Figure 5: Comparison of reported AIDS cases and positive HIV reports among Aboriginal and non-Aboriginal females

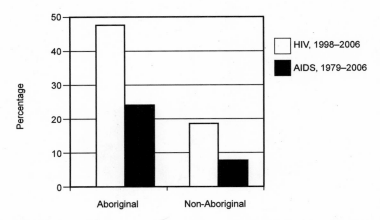

Source: Public Health Agency of Canada, (2007) *HIV/AIDS Epi Updates*, Ottawa: Public Health Agency of Canada.

There are also stark differences between Aboriginal and non-Aboriginal women and girls when it comes to age at diagnosis and modes of transmission: Aboriginal females are generally diagnosed at a much younger age than non-Aboriginal females and are more likely to be infected through injection drug use rather than heterosexual contact.

Figure 6: Comparison of age at time of diagnosis for reported AIDS cases and positive HIV tests among Aboriginal and non-Aboriginal women and girls

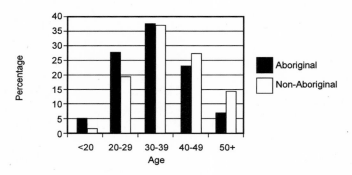

Source: Public Health Agency of Canada, (2007) *HIV/AIDS Epi Updates,* Ottawa: Public Health Agency of Canada.

Figure 7: Distribution of exposure categories among positive HIV test reports of Aboriginal females (n = 672), January 1998–December 31, 2006

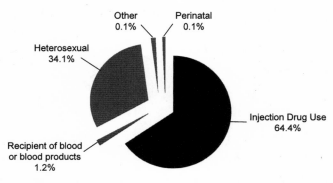

Source: Public Health Agency of Canada, (2007) *HIV/AIDS Epi Updates,* Ottawa: Public Health Agency of Canada.

It is also important to bear in mind that the "Aboriginal" category, like the "non-Aboriginal" category, includes many different populations and communities, each with its own culture, history, legal status, geographic location, etc. The latest Canadian report on HIV/AIDS reveals significant variation among Aboriginal women and girls in Canada, particularly with respect to age of diagnosis and method of exposure. First Nations and Inuit women, for instance, are much more likely to be diagnosed with AIDS in their twenties and thirties, as compared with Métis women and women of unspecified Aboriginal descent, who are diagnosed later, in their thirties and forties. Injection drug use is the most common method of exposure for First Nations peoples while heterosexual transmission accounts for the largest proportion of HIV infections among Inuit peoples.[29]

While it is clear that women and girls of Aboriginal descent are much more vulnerable to HIV infection, the statistics themselves do not explain why. In part, the differences can be attributed to the fact that Aboriginal people are over-represented in high risk groups, such as injecting drug users, sex trade workers, and prison inmates. For example, a First Nations male is 24 times more likely to be incarcerated in a provincial jail than a non-Native male and a First Nations female is 131 times more likely to be incarcerated than a non-Native woman. Similarly, in some cities, up to 75 percent of those using needle exchanges are Aboriginal and a large proportion of those engaged in commercial sex work.[30] But Aboriginal people *are* over-represented in high-risk groups because of their histories as well as the social, political and economic realities of their lives.

Figure 8: Reported AIDS cases among women of First Nations, Inuit, Métis and unspecified Aboriginal descent in Canada, 1979–2006

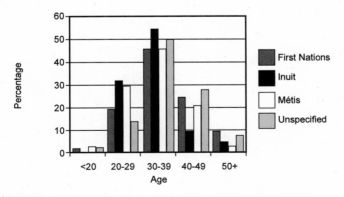

Source: Public Health Agency of Canada, (2007) *HIV/AIDS Epi Updates*, Ottawa: Public Health Agency of Canada.

Aboriginal people in Canada have suffered from the ongoing effects of cultural denigration, racism and colonialism. The legacy of this experience is apparent: on average, Aboriginal people have higher rates of incarceration, higher rates of suicide, drug and alcohol use, more poverty, and poorer health than the non-Aboriginal population of Canada. These are risk factors for HIV.[31]

Aboriginal women and girls often face even greater challenges than either Aboriginal men or non-Aboriginal women and men. For example, 48 percent of Inuit females do not complete high school, as compared with 47 percent of Inuit males, 22 percent of Canadian females and 23 percent of Canadian males. Similarly, Métis people earn about $7,500 less per year on average than non-Aboriginal Canadians, but Métis women earn $11,000 less per year than Métis men.[32] According to the Canadian Aboriginal AIDS Network, Aboriginal women are more than twice as likely to be living in poverty as their non-Aboriginal counterparts and they are more likely to be exposed to substance use and domestic violence on a daily basis. Ship and Norton likewise report that many of the Inuit women they interviewed had experienced abuse as children and then again later in life at the hands of men. Several of these women recognized that they used drugs and alcohol as a mechanism to cope with the abuse.[33] Aboriginal women also experience discrimination, both within their own communities and in dealing with non-Aboriginal health services. Because they fear being judged or spurned, because they fear having their children taken away from them, Aboriginal women are less likely to reveal their HIV status or to access services before it is too late.

In many ways, the experiences of women and girls in Canada, particularly those from marginalized populations, mirror those of women and girls around the world, in developing and developed countries. Women and girls in Canada typically face greater risks of exposure to HIV than do men and boys, both because of physiological differences between the sexes and as a result of gender inequity. Vulnerability and risk increase further for women and girls from marginalized populations. As researcher Joanne Csete concludes:

> [W]hile women in Canada may not suffer the extremes of subordination faced by many of their counterparts in other parts of the world, inequality and violations of women's human rights still contribute to their vulnerability and to the challenges they face in seeking treatment for HIV/AIDS. As in other parts of world, women living in poverty, women who inject drugs, Aboriginal women, women in the sex trade, and many women who come from countries where HIV is endemic are particularly vulnerable to HIV/AIDS.[34]

Stigma and discrimination can affect anyone and everyone diagnosed with HIV in Canada, but the experiences of women and girls are generally worse. For example, both women and men who are HIV positive have been charged with aggravated assault for failing to disclose their HIV status to a sexual partner. But a woman charged in 2005 was "portrayed in the press as a sexual predator and wantonly promiscuous." Moreover, as the charges involved a member of the Canadian Armed Forces, officials in the military chose to disclose the woman's identity and HIV status across Canada and to the world, "though it is unclear that they did anything to emphasize to soldiers their own responsibility for safer sex."[35] Similarly, pregnant women who test positive for HIV are regularly condemned for exposing an unborn child to the risk of infection and a woman who breastfeeds an infant in Canada could face prosecution. As with risk of exposure, women and girls from marginalized populations are more likely to suffer negative or more deeply negative consequences as a result of HIV. For example, women injecting drug users may be reluctant to seek medical help because they routinely experience discriminatory exclusion from health and social services, including women's shelters and emergency services.[36] Similarly, African Canadian women living in Toronto discuss the discrimination that surfaces within their cultural communities and in the dominant culture. As one woman concluded, "We live with it every day. It's not just HIV ... I'm black ... I'm a woman ... I was a single mom ... on social assistance. Right there I cover all the grounds for you."[37] Thus, while a recent survey suggests that Canadians are increasingly accepting of people living with HIV, stigma and discrimination continue to mark and mar the experiences of women and girls who test positive for HIV.[38]

ENGENDERING THE RESPONSE TO HIV/AIDS

Given the challenges that women and girls face in protecting themselves against HIV exposure and infection, it might seem reasonable to expect that national governments and international agencies would already have devised gender-appropriate strategies and interventions for prevention, care, treatment and support. Many efforts have been and are being made to develop prevention methods for women and girls, including the female condom and microbicides. Educational and informational programs for women and men, girls and boys are also common in many countries around the world, including Canada and China. Increasingly, there is high-level acknowledgement of the role of sex and gender in the pandemic. Notwithstanding the efforts being made to control and eradicate HIV, the numbers of people – the numbers of women and girls – who are living with and dying from HIV continue to rise. Perhaps the time has come to revisit and re-evaluate national policies and international guidelines using a gender lens.

The United Nations and the World Health Organization have been in the vanguard of international responses to the HIV pandemic and the guidelines for dealing with HIV established by these organizations have been highly influential with national governments around the world, including that of Canada. In recent years, both UNAIDS and the WHO have developed greater awareness of the role of gender in the pandemic as well as the plight of women and girls infected and affected by HIV. Increasingly, their publications and recommendations include attention to gender as well as to women and girls. A significant exception, at least in our opinion, is the advice for effective HIV prevention in low incidence countries. UNAIDS and the WHO differentiate between the responses needed in low-incidence countries, also labelled "low-level epidemic states," and those needed in high-incidence countries or "generalized epidemic states." According to a recent UNAIDS report on HIV prevention,

> An understanding of the nature, dynamics and characteristics of local epidemics is needed to ensure that HIV prevention strategies can be reviewed and adapted to fit local conditions. In low and concentrated HIV prevalence settings where the epidemic is nascent, attention needs to be given to prioritizing HIV prevention among those at highest risk, identified after epidemiological and social mapping. In generalized HIV epidemics, strategies for such populations combined with broader strategies to reach all segments of society at sufficient scale.[39]

On the surface, this seems like a reasonable approach, based on the assumption that intensive intervention with those most likely to contract HIV will serve to contain the epidemic. It also seems like an eminently realistic approach to HIV, ensuring that amounts of money will be used to greatest effect. While targeted responses are excellent in theory, the history of HIV suggests that focused efforts have not only failed to stem the tide of the pandemic, but have also contributed to the spread of HIV among those already at greatest risk – women and girls. A comparison of the history of the epidemic in Canada and South Africa underscores the hazards of adopting a targeted approach to HIV/AIDS.

In many respects, Canada's experience with HIV has been dramatically different than that of South Africa. Canada, with an HIV prevalence rate below one percent of the population, has always been defined as a low incidence country while South Africa, with a prevalence rate of 20 percent or more, has long been among the countries with the highest incidence rates in the world. Yet what is often missed in analysis of the pandemic – and in international guidelines for prevention – is an appreciation that the early trajectory in many high incidence countries is identical to that of the trajectory in low-incidence countries. In South Africa, for example, the first case of HIV was diagnosed in 1982 – the same year as in Canada. And for the first years of the epidemic in South Africa, HIV was found predominantly in gay white men – the same as in Canada. Even as late as 1990, the incidence of HIV among women in South Africa was relatively low – 0.8 percent of pregnant women tested through antenatal clinics. The incidence of HIV among pregnant women in Canada in 2000 included an estimate of 0.3 percent among Aboriginal women in British Columbia.

Through the 1990s in South Africa, the prevalence of HIV increased steadily, from 1.4 percent of the adult population in 1992 to 24.5 percent in 2000. But equally significant was the shift in modes of transmission: by 1991 in South Africa the number of HIV infections attributable to heterosexual contact was on par with the number attributable to men having sex with men. Canada's prevalence rate also rose through the 1990s, though not as much or as quickly as in South Africa. At the same time, Canada began to experience a shift in exposure categories similar to that of South Africa. Between 1995 and 2006, HIV infections attributable to heterosexual contact – alone or in combination with other factors – increased in Canada, from 7.5 percent to 37 percent.[40] Infections among women and girls are overwhelmingly the result of heterosexual contact, at a rate of 76 percent.[41] Moreover, by 2004, the Canadian government noted significant increases in HIV infection, particularly within specific populations: "Every day, approximately eleven Canadians become infected with HIV. There have been disturbing increases among those who are often socially and economically vulnerable. Injection drug users, women living in poverty, Aboriginal peoples, young gay men and prison inmates are increasingly threatened by the disease."[42]

The HIV epidemic raged in South Africa during the 1990s, in part because of political and social upheaval associated with the end of apartheid. While the country focused on eliminating racially-based oppression and establishing democracy, "the spread of the virus was not given the attention it deserved, and the impact of the epidemic was not acknowledged."[43] At the same time, the challenges of fighting HIV in a resource-limited setting contributed to the escalation of the pandemic in South Africa. Canada, by comparison, has enjoyed both wealth and freedom from major social and political change in the last two decades, with the result that the epidemic has developed much more slowly here.

Nonetheless, the national responses to HIV/AIDS in Canada and South Africa – particularly in the early years of the epidemic – also have some striking similarities. Both countries followed the guidelines established by UNAIDS and the WHO, targeting specific "high-risk" groups. According to Olive Shisana, Chief Executive Officer of the Human Sciences Research Council of South Africa, it was the wrong strategy.[44] By focusing on the risks facing specific groups within the population, rather than alerting everyone to the threat of HIV/AIDS, the government and civil society gave the epidemic time to become firmly established in a group that no one thought was especially vulnerable – women and girls. By 1993, it was clear that HIV in South Africa had been transformed from a low level to a generalized epidemic, as evidenced by a prevalence rate of more than one percent in pregnant women. In the post-apartheid era, the South African government has developed and adopted intervention strategies that address the impact of HIV/AIDS on all of society, including women and girls. At a recent meeting of the Southern African Development Community in 2006, which includes South Africa, the evolution and innovation in thinking about the role of gender in the HIV pandemic was apparent.

Figure 9: Drivers of the HIV Epidemic in SADC

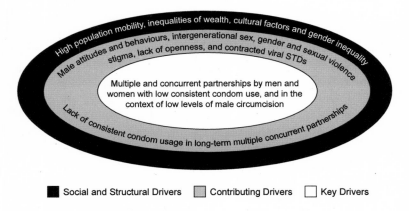

Social and Structural Drivers   Contributing Drivers   Key Drivers

Source: Expert Think Tank Meeting on HIV Prevention in High Incidence Countries in Southern Africa: Report, Maseru, Lesotho, 10-12 May 2006.

Recommendations from the Think Tank also focused on the continuing need to address gender inequity across the spectrum of social, political and economic factors driving the epidemic.

Meanwhile, Canada has continued to pursue a targeted approach to HIV/AIDS. The *Federal Initiative to Address HIV/AIDS* identifies eight populations requiring discrete and intensive intervention: people living with HIV/AIDS, gay men, injection drug users, Aboriginal people, prison inmates, youth at risk, women at risk and people from countries where HIV is endemic. According to the Canadian government, a "populations-specific approach results in evidence-based, culturally appropriate responses that are better able to address the realities that contribute to infection and poor health outcomes for the target groups."[45] While it is undoubtedly important to invest in helping those at greatest risk and in greatest need as a result of HIV, it is an approach that has failed to halt the pandemic because it ignores the role of gender. Women and girls do not comprise a sub-population of Canadian society; at 51 percent they are the majority of people living in Canada. Furthermore, women and girls are found in six of the seven other priority populations – among people living with HIV, people from HIV endemic countries, youth, injection drug users, Aboriginal people, and prison inmates. The seventh population, gay men, obviously does not include females, but not all men who have sex with men identify themselves as gay or confine their sexual activity to male partners, with the result that women and girls are also associated with this "target group."

Despite the fact that women and girls appear in or connected to every priority population, "the range of government-supported programs meant to address HIV prevention among women in Canada appears not to be the result of a coherent national strategy for addressing HIV/AIDS among women."[46]

At the same time, though the *Federal Initiative to Address HIV/AIDS* is ostensibly "grounded in the concepts of social justice and the determinants of health," there is no mention of gender or gender-based analysis.[47] Yet just as women and girls are represented in every priority population, so too is gender a cross-cutting theme – and this applies to society in general as well as the HIV pandemic. Gender norms or stereotypes contribute to the attitudes and behaviours of males and females in every society: they also put both males and females at risk of exposure to HIV. But because gender roles and expectations are differential and relational, they increase the vulnerability of women and girls to a greater degree. As a result, programs that help women prisoners to avoid contracting HIV are incomplete if they focus only on the period of incarceration because women's vulnerability does not stop at the prison gates. Similarly, policies to address the alarming increase of HIV among young people in Canada have to move beyond encouraging safe sex practices to deal with the social, economic and political disadvantages facing women and girls. Focusing on target populations encourages neglect of broader social forces driving the epidemic, including gender. As Csete observes, "HIV/AIDS programs that explicitly address the subordination that puts all women at risk of HIV appear to be rare in Canada."[48]

Targeted responses to the pandemic also contribute to stigma and discrimination by singling out certain groups for intervention and thereby fuelling fear and/or censure of everyone associated with these groups. The Canadian HIV/AIDS Legal network made the point that,

> In spite of all that is known about the science of HIV/AIDS and about combating the epidemic, people living with HIV/AIDS still face stigmatization and discrimination every day. [...] [And] people living with HIV/AIDS are not the only ones who suffer from stigma and discrimination. Groups of people linked with HIV/AIDS in the public mind – like intravenous drug users, gay men, sex workers, and people who come from countries where HIV/AIDS is widespread – also face stigma and discrimination.[49]

Although attitudes towards people living with HIV/AIDS have been improving in Canada, a great deal of stigma and discrimination still exists. As recently as 2006, close to 30 percent of Canadians said they would not be comfortable working in an office with someone with HIV and 43 percent of parents reported that they would not be comfortable having their child attend school with an HIV positive student. One in ten Canadians surveyed felt that those who contracted HIV got what they deserved.[50]

In other words, targeted approaches to HIV prevention allow those in mainstream society to distance themselves from "others" in high risk groups, to believe that bad behaviour rather than systemic factors are responsible for the spread of HIV. The discrimination associated with this distancing creates barriers to testing and treatment and deepens the suffering of people living with HIV or assumed to be at risk of exposure, including women and girls. Interestingly, the HIV/AIDS Attitudinal Tracking Survey, a component of the Canadian *Federal Initiative to Address HIV/AIDS*, identified the sex of participants but did not investigate participants' attitudes towards HIV positive women versus HIV positive men. As a result, no data on gender-based attitudes to HIV is available from this survey. But other research underscores the vulnerability of women and girls to negative interpretations, particularly if they belong to targeted groups such as commercial sex workers and women coming from HIV-endemic countries.

CONCLUSION

An analysis of HIV/AIDS in Canada, including a comparison with the epidemic in South Africa, leads to three main conclusions. First, one of the principal drivers of the epidemic, in Canada and around the world, is gender. Women and girls are rendered vulnerable to infection as a result of widespread and diverse forms of gender inequity. Second, high-incidence countries have become sensitive to the role of gender in the pandemic, but in low-incidence countries such as Canada and China, policies and programs often remain gender-blind.[51] Third, HIV/AIDS strategies should be generalized rather than targeted – because the epidemic is everyone's problem and because gender affects everyone.

ENDNOTES

[1]   Stephen Lewis. (2006). *Keynote address* at the closing session of the XVI International AIDS Conference. Toronto, Canada. Retrieved from Stephen Lewis Foundation Website, 31 March 2008. http://www.stephenlewisfoundation.org/news_speech_item. cfm?news=1382&year=2006.

[2]   Commonwealth Secretariat and Maritime Centre of Excellence for Women's Health. (2002). *Gender Mainstreaming in HIV/AIDS: Taking a Multisectoral Approach.* London, UK: Commonwealth Secretariat; Health Canada. (2003). *Exploring Concepts of Gender and Health.* Ottawa: Minister of Health.

[3]   Interagency Coalition on AIDS and Development. (2002). *HIV/AIDS and Prevention Options for Women.* Ottawa: ICAD; Nikki Kumar, June Larkin and Claudia Mitchell. (2001). "Gender, Youth and HIV Risk." *Canadian Women's Studies.* Vol. 21. Summer/Fall.

[4]   Nikki Kumar, June Larkin and Claudia Mitchell. (2001). "Gender, Youth and HIV Risk." *Canadian Women's Studies.* Vol. 21. Summer/Fall.

[5]   Commission on the Status of Women. (2001). "Agreed conclusions on women, the girl child and HIV/AIDS." 45th Session of the UN Commission on the Status of Women. New York: United Nations.

[6]   Commonwealth Secretariat and Maritime Centre of Excellence for Women's Health. (2001) *Gender Mainstreaming in HIV/AIDS.*

[7]   Margreth Tolson and Stephanie Kellington, "Changing the Balance of Power: The Listen Up! Project and Participatory Research with Marginalized Communities," in Carol Amaratunga and Jacqueline Gahagan., eds. (2002). *Striking to the Heart of the Matter: Selected Readings on Gender and HIV.* Halifax: Atlantic Centre of Excellence for Women's Health.

[8]   Peggy Millson, Alexandra Moses, Naushaba Degani, Chere Chapman, Carol Majro and Evelyn Wallace, "Gender, Injection Drug Use and HIV Risk in Ontario, Canada," and Lois Jackson, "HIV Prevention Programmes and Female Prostitutes: The Canadian Context," in Carol Amaratunga and Jacqueline Gahagan, eds. (2002). *Striking to the Heart of the Matter: Selected Readings on Gender and HIV.* Halifax: Atlantic Centre of Excellence for Women's Health.

[9]   Susan Judith Ship and Laura Norton, "HIV/AIDS and Aboriginal Women in Canada," in Carol Amaratunga and Jacqueline Gahagan., eds. (2002). *Striking to the Heart of the Matter: Selected Readings on Gender and HIV.* Halifax: Atlantic Centre of Excellence for Women's Health.

[10]   Lois Jackson, "HIV Prevention Programmes and Female Prostitutes: The Canadian Context," in Carol Amaratunga and Jacqueline Gahagan, eds. (2002). *Striking to the Heart of the Matter: Selected Readings on Gender and HIV.* Halifax: Atlantic Centre of Excellence for Women's Health.

[11]   Claire Higgins-Dickson. (2006). "Discrimination and HIV in China." International Conference on HIV and HBV Carriers. Beijing, China; Commonwealth Secretariat and Maritime Centre of Excellence for Women's Health. (2001) *Gender Mainstreaming in HIV/ AIDS.*

[12]   Nikki Kumar, June Larkin and Claudia Mitchell. (2001). "Gender, Youth and HIV Risk." *Canadian Women's Studies.* Vol. 21. Summer/Fall.

[13]   Family Health International. (2001). "HIV Interventions with Men who have Sex with MEN." State of the Art Briefs on HIV/AIDS, quoted in Commonwealth Secretariat and Maritime Centre of Excellence for Women's Health, *Gender Mainstreaming in HIV/AIDS;* Interagency Coalition on AIDS and Development, (2004) "Fact Sheet: HIV/AIDS and Homophobia" and (2006) "Fact Sheet: HIV/AIDS and Gender Issues," Retrieved 30 March 2008, http://www.icad-cisd.com/content/pub_details.cfm?id=194&CAT=9&lang=e.

[14]   Commonwealth Secretariat and Maritime Centre of Excellence for Women's Health. (2001). *Gender Mainstreaming in HIV/AIDS;* Interagency Coalition on AIDS and Development, (2004) "Fact Sheet: HIV/AIDS and Homophobia" and (2006) "Fact Sheet: HIV/AIDS and Gender Issues," http://www.icad-cisd.com/content/pub_details. cfm?id=194&CAT=9&lang=e.

[15]   UNAIDS, (2007) *AIDS Epidemic Update,* http://data.unaids.org/pub/EPISlides/2007/2007_ epiupdate_en.pdf

[16]   Commonwealth Secretariat and Maritime Centre of Excellence for Women's Health. (2001). *Gender Mainstreaming in HIV/AIDS.*

[17]   Stephen Lewis, quoted in "Globalization Failing Victims of Global HIV/AIDS Pandemic," 27 June 2004, National Union of General and Public Employees, http://www.nupge.ca/ news_2004/n27jn04a.htm.

[18]   UNAIDS. (2007). *Country Responses: Canada.* www.unaids.org/en/Country Responses/ Countries/canada.asp.

[19]   UNAIDS. (2007). *Country Responses: Canada.* www.unaids.org/en/Country Responses/ Countries/china.asp.

[20]   Public Health Agency of Canada. (2007) *HIV/AIDS Epi Updates*. Ottawa: Public Health
       Agency of Canada.
[21]   Public Health Agency of Canada. (2004). *HIV and AIDS in Canada, Surveillance Report to
       June 30, 2004*. Ottawa: Public Health Agency of Canada; Public Health Agency of Canada.
       (2007) *HIV/AIDS Epi Updates*. Ottawa: Public Health Agency of Canada.
[22]   Public Health Agency of Canada. (2004). *HIV and AIDS in Canada, Surveillance Report to
       June 30, 2004*. Ottawa: Public Health Agency of Canada; Public Health Agency of Canada.
       (2007) *HIV/AIDS Epi Updates*. Ottawa: Public Health Agency of Canada; *Canada Statistics
       Summary*. (2007). www.avert.org/canstatg.htm.
[23]   Public Health Agency of Canada. (2004). *HIV and AIDS in Canada, Surveillance Report to
       June 30, 2004*. Ottawa: Public Health Agency of Canada; Public Health Agency of Canada.
       (2007) *HIV/AIDS Epi Updates*. Ottawa: Public Health Agency of Canada; *Canada Statistics
       Summary*. (2007). www.avert.org/canstatg.htm.
[24]   Public Health Agency of Canada. (2004). *HIV and AIDS in Canada, Surveillance Report to
       June 30, 2004*. Ottawa: Public Health Agency of Canada; Public Health Agency of Canada.
       (2007) *HIV/AIDS Epi Updates*. Ottawa: Public Health Agency of Canada; *Canada Statistics
       Summary*. (2007). www.avert.org/canstatg.htm.
[25]   Women's Health Bureau. (1999) Women and HIV/AIDS Factsheet. Ottawa: Health
       Canada.
[26]   Joanne Csete. (2005). *Vectors and Vessels: HIV/AIDS and Women's Rights in Canada*. Toronto:
       Canadian HIV/AIDS Legal Network.
[27]   Study participant, quoted in Margreth Tolson and Stephanie Kellington, "Changing the
       Balance of Power: The Listen Up! Project and Participatory Research with Marginalized
       Communities," in Carol Amaratunga and Jacqueline Gahagan, eds. (2002). *Striking to
       the Heart of the Matter: Selected Readings on Gender and HIV*. Halifax: Atlantic Centre of
       Excellence for Women's Health.
[28]   Public Health Agency of Canada. (2007) *HIV/AIDS Epi Updates*. Ottawa: Public Health
       Agency of Canada.
[29]   Public Health Agency of Canada. (2007) *HIV/AIDS Epi Updates*. Ottawa: Public Health
       Agency of Canada.
[30]   Canadian HIV/AIDS Legal Network, *Aboriginal Prisoners and HIV/AIDS: Legal Issues*,
       2004-2005.
[31]   Canadian HIV/AIDS Legal Network, *Aboriginal Prisoners and HIV/AIDS: Legal Issues*,
       2004-2005.
[32]   National Aboriginal Health Organization, "Presentation: Broader Determinants of Health
       in Aboriginal Context," http://www.naho.ca/english/pub_determinants.php.
[33]   Canadian Aboriginal AIDS Network, and Ship and Norton, cited in Joanne Csete. (2005).
       Vectors and Vessels: HIV/AIDS and Women's Rights in Canada. Toronto: Canadian HIV/AIDS
       Legal Network.
[34]   Joanne Csete. (2005). *Vectors and Vessels: HIV/AIDS and Women's Rights in Canada*. Toronto:
       Canadian HIV/AIDS Legal Network.
[35]   Joanne Csete. (2005). *Vectors and Vessels: HIV/AIDS and Women's Rights in Canada*. Toronto:
       Canadian HIV/AIDS Legal Network.
[36]   S. Boyd and K Faith. (1999). "Women, illegal drugs and prison: views from Canada."
       International Journal of Drug Policy, Vol 10.
[37]   E. Lawson, F. Gardezi, L. Clzavara, W. Husbands, T. Myers, W. Tharao and the Stigma
       Study Team. "How African and Caribbean people in Toronto experience and respond to

HIV stigma, denial, fear and discrimination," www.accho.ca/pdf/Stigma%20Fact%20Shee t%20ENGLISH.pdf

[38] Public Health Agency of Canada. (2006) *HIV/AIDS Attudinal Tracking Survey Final Report.* www.phac-aspc.gc.ca/aids-sida/publication/por/2006/exsum_e.html

[39] UNAIDS. (2005). *Intensifying HIV prevention: UNAIDS policy position paper.* Geneva: UNAIDS.

[40] Public Health Agency of Canada. (2004*). HIV and AIDS in Canada, Surveillance Report to June 30, 2004.* Ottawa: Public Health Agency of Canada; Public Health Agency of Canada. (2007) *HIV/AIDS Epi Updates.* Ottawa: Public Health Agency of Canada.

[41] Public Health Agency of Canada. (2007) *HIV/AIDS Epi Updates.* Ottawa: Public Health Agency of Canada.

[42] Public Health Agency of Canada. (2004). *Moving Forward Together.* Ottawa: Public Health Agency of Canada.

[43] HIV/AIDS in South Africa, www.avert.org/aidssouthafrica.htm.

[44] Olive Shisana, CEO, Human Sciences Research Council, to Barbara Clow, Executive Director, Atlantic Centre of Excellence for Women's Health. (2004). Personal communication.

[45] Public Health Agency of Canada. "Populations at risk." www.phac-aspc.gc.ca/aids-sida/ populations_e.html

[46] Joanne Csete. (2005). *Vectors and Vessels: HIV/AIDS and Women's Rights in Canada.* Toronto: Canadian HIV/AIDS Legal Network.

[47] Public Health Agency of Canada. "Populations at risk," Retrieved 8 April 2008 from www. phac-aspc.gc.ca/aids-sida/populations_e.html.

[48] Joanne Csete. (2005). *Vectors and Vessels: HIV/AIDS and Women's Rights in Canada.* Toronto: Canadian HIV/AIDS Legal Network.

[49] Canadian HIV/AIDS Legal Network. (2005). Press Release: Stigma and Discrimination are Fuelling the HIV/AIDS Epidemic In Canada. www.aidslaw.ca/publications/ interfaces/ downloadDocumentFile.php?ref=497.

[50] "The Current State of the Epidemic: Why We Need to Step Up Our Efforts," Leading Together: Canada Takes Action on HIV/AIDS. www.leadingtogether.ca/304_cur.html; Public Health Agency of Canada. (2006) *HIV/AIDS Attudinal Tracking Survey Final Report.* www.phac-aspc.gc.ca/aids-sida/publication/por/2006/exsum_e.html.

[51] UNAIDS. (2007). *Country Responses: Canada.* Retrieved 30 March 2008 from www.unaids. org/en/Country Responses/Countries/china.asp; Sunyou Wu, Seena G. Sullivan, Yu Wang, Mary Jane Rotheram-Borus, Roger Detels, "Evolution of China's response to HIV/AIDS," *The Lancet,* Vol. 369, 24 February 2007-2 March 2007.

CHAPTER THIRTEEN

Promoting the Right to Education for AIDS Orphans and Vulnerable Children (OVC)
A Study on Anti-Discrimination

Ma Yinghua, Ding Suqin, Wang Chao, and Yuan Mengyao

According to the *Protocol for the Identification of Discrimination against People Living with HIV* (2000) by UNAIDS,[1] "HIV/AIDS related discrimination" is defined as "[a]ny measure entailing an arbitrary distinction among persons depending on their confirmed or suspected HIV serostatus or state of health." The study included three categories of AIDS-afflicted children: HIV-infected children, children orphaned by AIDS (refers to children under the age of eighteen who have lost one or both parents due to AIDS), and children made vulnerable by AIDS (refers to children with one or both parents infected with AIDS, and living in a household with one or more chronically ill adults). Discrimination may result in the neglect or infringement of such children's right to education. According to sources, discrimination relating to the right to education may be divided into institutional discrimination and public discrimination. Institutional discrimination originates mainly from a legal and policy perspective. Public discrimination occurs in schools, and from parents and existing students. In addition, orphans and vulnerable children (OVC) stigmatization and discrimination may impair their right to education. This study was conducted between March 2006 and March 2008 to determine if OVCs are denied access to education due to discrimination, as well as the causes of such discrimination. Solutions are also proposed to ensure access to education, to create a caring and non-discriminatory education environment, and to promote anti-discrimination in China.

DESIGN AND METHOD

I. Policy Review
Policy reviewed is carried out throughout the entire study. Prior to the field research, we collated AIDS and education-related laws and policies to see if there was any direct

or indirect discrimination. After the field research, we compared our research findings with the earlier analysis, and examined the state of implementation and operability of such laws and policies.

II. On-Site Research

(I) Study Site and Study Subject

1. Study Site
Heilongjiang, Beijing and Henan were selected using stratified sampling in order to have representation from areas with different AIDS situations (according to UNAIDS, there were 241 cases of HIV infections in Heilongjiang, 2,580 in Beijing, and 30,820 in Henan as of the end of December 2005[2]).

2. Study Subject
    (1)   The public, including students, parents, teachers and the general public
    (2)   HIV-infected children and OVCs

(II) Measurement Tools and Parameters
Both quantitative and qualitative analyses were used. We developed the outlines for the questionnaires and interviews with assistance from university and secondary school students. Further studies were carried out before the final questionnaire and interview designs were improved and finalized.

1. Quantitative Analysis
Two types of self-administered questionnaires were used:
    (1) Knowledge, Attitude and Practice (KAP) Questionnaire: Includes questionnaires for students, parents, teachers and the general public. Measurement parameters include the basic understanding of the general situation and of AIDS, attitude towards HIV/AIDS-infected persons, view and attitude towards the education of OVCs, AIDS-related discriminatory behaviour, and knowledge of the relevant policies and rights.
    (2) Stigma Questionnaire: Includes questionnaires for OVCs, students and parents based on the HIV Stigma Scale[3] and questionnaires designed by relevant local and foreign journals. By using the projective technique and situation analysis, we designed self-administered questionnaires, based on the attributes of the study subjects. Measurement parameters include general situation, basic knowledge of AIDS, stigma, and the general public's perception of OVC stigma.

2. Qualitative Analysis
Open-ended questions and small group interviews were used for self-administered questionnaires. Interview outlines include outlines for students, teachers, and OVCs.

(III) Data Analysis

1. Quantitative Analysis
After all questionnaires were reviewed for completeness, logic and consistency, the data from the study was entered into EpiData 3.0 to establish a database. Data analysis was performed using SPSS 12.0. Appropriate statistical methods were selected based on data characteristics, and test was defined at $\alpha=0.05$.

2. Qualitative Analysis
Interview results from the recordings and notes taken during the on-site interviews were collated. Keywords were identified from the original information, and coded and classified. Additionally, based on the frequency of occurrence of such keywords, we established primary and secondary viewpoints. Analyses and interpretation were carried out based on these viewpoints.

(IV) Ethical Issues
This study is in strict compliance with general principles of ethics in medical research.

1. Respect for the children's right of participation. Questionnaire and interview outlines were designed with students' participation.
2. Respect for the subjects' right to informed consent. The subjects were informed of the purpose and details of the study prior to completing the questionnaire and participating in the interviews. Participation was voluntary.
3. Respect for the subjects' right to privacy. Investigation was carried out anonymously, and information provided by the subject was kept strictly confidential. Such information will not be used for purposes other than this study, to protect the subjects' privacy.
4. Guarantee of adolescent rights. The study will provide for the students who were interviewed with the relevant knowledge and information on AIDS, as well as guidance on the relevant issues.

RESULTS AND ANALYSIS

Part 1. Outcome of Policy Analysis

I. Provisions in Documents on International Human Rights on Non-Discrimination and the Right to Education
According to Paragraph 1 of Article 2 of the *Convention on the Rights of the Child* by the United Nations Committee on the Rights of the Child, "State Parties shall respect and ensure the rights set forth in the present Convention to each child within their jurisdiction without discrimination of any kind, irrespective of the child's or his or

her parent's or legal guardian's race, colour, sex, language, religion, political or other opinion, national, ethnic or social origin, property, disability, birth or other status." Paragraph 2 of the same Article provides that "State Parties shall take all appropriate measures to ensure that the child is protected against all forms of discrimination or punishment on the basis of the status, activities, expressed opinions, or beliefs of the child's parents, legal guardians, or family members." Paragraph 2 of Article 28 provides, "State Parties recognize the right of the child to education, and with a view to achieving this right progressively and on the basis of equal opportunity."

The provisions under Paragraph 3, Article 10 of the *International Covenant on Economic, Social and Cultural Rights* of the Committee on Economic, Social and Cultural Rights states, "[s]pecial measures of protection and assistance should be taken on behalf of all children and young persons without any discrimination for reasons of parentage or other conditions," and according to Paragraph 1 of Article 13, "[t]he State Parties to the present Covenant recognize the right of everyone to education."

Article 7 of the United Nations *Universal Declaration of Human Rights* provides that "[a]ll are equal before the law and are entitled without any discrimination to equal protection of the law. All are entitled to equal protection against any discrimination in violation of this *Declaration* and against any incitement to such discrimination." Under Paragraph 1 of Article 26, "[e]veryone has the right to education. Education shall be free, at least in the elementary and fundamental stages. Elementary education shall be compulsory. Technical and professional education shall be made generally available and higher education shall be equally accessible to all on the basis of merit."

According to Guideline 5 of the *International Guidelines on HIV/AIDS and Human Rights* by the Economic and Social Council of the United Nations,

> States should enact or strengthen anti-discrimination and other protective laws that protect vulnerable groups, people living with HIV and people with disabilities from discrimination in both the public and private sectors, ensure privacy and confidentiality and ethics in research involving human subjects, emphasize education and conciliation, and provide for speedy and effective administrative and civil remedies.

II. Legislation and Enforcement of Non-Discrimination and the Right to Education in China

(I) Relevant Domestic Legislation

1. Article 33 of the Constitution of the People's Republic of China provides that "[a]ll persons holding the nationality of the People's Republic of China are citizens of the People's Republic of China. All citizens of the People's Republic of China are equal before the law. Every citizen enjoys the rights and at the same time must perform the

duties prescribed by the Constitution and the law." And Paragraph 1 of Article 46 provides that "[c]itizens of the People's Republic of China have the duty as well as the right to receive education."

2. According to Paragraph 3, Article 3 of the *Law of the People's Republic of China on the Protection of Minors* (effective 1 June 2007), minors shall be accorded equal rights under the law, regardless of gender, ethnic group, race, family financial situation, or religious belief. Paragraph 2 of the same Article provides that minors shall be entitled to the right to education, and the State, society, school and family shall respect and guarantee the right of minors to be educated. Under Article 13, parents or other guardians shall respect minors' right to receive education, enable minors of school age to attend school and receive compulsory education according to the law, and shall not cause minors receiving compulsory education to drop out of school. Article 18 provides that the school shall respect the right of minors to be educated, show care and consideration for these students, and provide patient education and assistance for students with character and behavioural flaws, or who have difficulties learning. The laws and State regulations shall be observed and students who are minors shall not be expelled. According to Article 28, the various levels of the people's government shall guarantee the right of minors to be educated, and shall take measures to ensure that minors from financially deprived families, from the floating population, and whose parent(s) have a disability receive compulsory education.

3. Article 9 of the *Education Law of the People's Republic of China* provides that "[t]he Citizens of the People's Republic of China shall have the right and duty to receive education. All citizens, regardless of ethnic group, race, sex, occupation, property status or religious belief, shall enjoy equal opportunities for education under the law."

4. Article 4 of the *Compulsory Education Law of the People's Republic of China* stipulates that "[t]he state, community, schools and families shall ensure school-age children's and adolescents' right to receive compulsory education, regardless of sex, ethnic group, race, family property status and religious belief, as provided by law."

The above laws provide general protection for non-discrimination and the right to education. China has also enacted laws relating to communicable diseases and AIDS.

5. According to Article 16 of the *Law of the People's Republic of China on the Prevention and Treatment of Infectious Diseases*, no entity or individual shall discriminate against patients suffering from infectious diseases, carriers or suspected patients of infectious diseases.

6. Article 3 of the *Regulations on the Prevention and Treatment of HIV/AIDS* (effective 1 March 2006) provides that "[n]o entity or individual may discriminate against people infected with HIV, AIDS patients, and their family members. The legitimate rights of such persons in marriage, employment, medical treatment, and education shall be protected by law." Under Article 45, "AIDS orphans and HIV-infected minors with livelihood difficulties receiving compulsory education shall be exempted from paying

miscellaneous fees and for books. Such persons receiving pre-school education and high school education shall receive reduction or exemption of school fees and other similar fees."

7. The *Action Plan for Containing and for the Prevention and Treatment of the HIV/ AIDS Epidemic (2006-2010)* proposes, under the heading "Prevention and Treatment Strategy and Action Plan," to develop extensive outreach education programs; to disseminate information on the prevention and treatment of AIDS and on free blood donation; and to create a social environment that cares for HIV/AIDS patients, and that supports the prevention and treatment of AIDS.

8. In 2003, the State promulgated the "Four Frees and One Care" (*si mian yi guanhuai*) policy that is aimed at the prevention and treatment of AIDS. The *Regulations on the Prevention and Treatment of HIV/AIDS*, implemented on 1 March 2006, provided a regulatory foundation for the "Four Frees and One Care" policy. The policy provides that AIDS orphans and HIV-infected minors, who have livelihood difficulties and are receiving compulsory education, shall be exempt from paying miscellaneous fees and for books. Such persons receiving pre-school and high school education shall receive a reduction of or exemption from their school and other fees. The county-level and higher level of government will provide relief for persons living with HIV/AIDS and their family members.

9. In March 2006, fifteen ministries, including the Ministry of Civil Affairs, published the *Opinions on Improving Relief for Orphans*. The *Opinions* provided preferential policies for orphans, including children orphaned by AIDS. These preferential policies concerned nine areas, including living, education, medical, rehabilitation, housing, and employment. The *Opinions* also provided that the Ministry of Education shall exempt orphans at the age of compulsory education from miscellaneous fees, shall provide them with money for textbooks, and shall give subsidies for living expenses to boarding students. Orphans accepted by ordinary high schools, secondary vocational schools and tertiary schools shall be included in the current system of education bursaries.

10. The "Two Frees and One Subsidy" (*liang mian yi bu*) policy asserts that the State shall provide students receiving compulsory education (at the primary and secondary level) and who are from poor families with free textbooks. The State shall also exempt these students from miscellaneous fees, and shall provide boarding students with subsidies for living expenses.

The above legal policies ensure non-discrimination and the right to education of persons living with HIV/AIDS, and provide OVCs with preferential and supportive policies. UNAIDS's *Protocol for the Identification of Discrimination against People Living with HIV* identified 10 major areas in the social lives of HIV/AIDS infected persons in which distinctions, exclusions or restrictions, actual or presumed, may occur. Discrimination in education is determined by whether there is denial of access to education, and if there are restrictions imposed in an educational setting (e.g., segregation). Local laws and policies do not impose restrictions in an educational setting.

(II) Enforcement of Laws and Policies
This study identifies problems with the enforcement of laws and policies by referring to relevant journals and other sources of information, as well as to questionnaires and interviews with the public, persons living with HIV and OVCs.

1. Although there are laws in China protecting the right to education of OVCs and persons living with HIV, these people continue to face discrimination in various forms.

According to OVCs and persons living with HIV, discrimination against them is manifested in various ways. For example, people give them peculiar looks, refuse to eat at the same table as them, and refuse to play with their children. Some people have even moved away from infected persons, transferred their children to other schools or discriminated against people who bear the same family name as the infected person. Furthermore, some family members have abandoned infected relatives. Schools refuse to allow OVCs to attend on other grounds. Discrimination from classmates, their parents and teachers may occur in school. For example, classmates will stay away from or ostracize OVCs; parents of classmates may tell their children not to play with them; and teachers who do not understand these children may treat them unfavourably in class. Despite the presence of relevant laws and regulations, discrimination still exists in various forms. The outcome of this study is in line with those of other studies.[4]

2. To some extent, the laws and regulations have been successful in guaranteeing the right of OVCs to education. However, implementation is inconsistent in different areas, and not all OVCs benefit from these laws and regulations. Policies such as the *Regulations on the Prevention and Treatment of HIV/AIDS* and the *Action Plan for Containing and for the Prevention and Treatment of the HIV/AIDS Epidemic (2006-2010)* protect the rights of persons living with HIV/AIDS. The "Four Frees and One Care" policy was especially successful at addressing the living and educational difficulties of children orphaned by AIDS. According to China's report on the *Declaration of Commitment on HIV/AIDS 2005*, various regions were aggressively implementing the "Four Frees and One Care" policy that provide free schooling and living subsidies for children orphaned by AIDS. There are 4,385 children of school age attending school for free, and this accounts for 92.71 percent of AIDS orphans of that age group.[5] According to the *Joint Assessment of HIV/AIDS Prevention, Treatment and Care in China (2007)*, as of the end of March 2007, there were 277 Care Centres (e.g. "Sweet Home" (*wenxin jiayuan*) and "Sunny Home" (*yangguang jiayuan*)) in 127 demonstration zones, providing aid for 3,167 orphans (93 percent of all school-age children) under the "Two Frees and One Subsidy" program.[6] However, implementation was inconsistent, and not all children benefited from the program. The "Four Frees and One Care" policy is better implemented in

AIDS endemic areas; those living in non-endemic areas are neglected, since living subsidies and free schooling for children orphaned by AIDS are not guaranteed.[6,7]

3. Inadequate Support Measures and Regulatory Enforcement of Laws and Policies

The "Four Frees and One Care" and "Two Frees and One Subsidy" policies provide schooling assistance for OVCs living in poverty. However, OVCs often do not wish to expose their identities because of their unusual circumstances. The result is that they do not benefit from these policies. In fact, they will be further discriminated against if their status is disclosed.

Results of our qualitative interviews reveal that OVCs applying for aid must do so through their school. In some areas, students receiving aid get books labelled with words, such as "Provided Free by the State." During our policy review, we also found that the way in which certain provinces provide aid jeopardizes the privacy of OVCs. For example, the *"Two Frees and One Subsidy" Implementation Measures for Compulsory Education in the Rural Areas of Henan Province* provides that, "[u]pon determining the students to receive aid, the school shall exempt such students from paying for text books, and shall indicate on the title page 'This book is provided free by the State'," and, "to receive aid, the student shall personally submit the application, and a public announcement shall be made by the school and the village committee where such student's family is located."[8] The *Provisional Implementation Measures for the "Two Frees and One Subsidy" Program* for a region in Chongqing also provides:

> [t]he student or his/her guardian shall complete the application form for "Two Frees and One Subsidy." The school and the village committee (town or sub-district office) shall conduct a preliminary review of such an application. The review comments shall be endorsed and published, and the schools shall collate the relevant information to be submitted to the district education committee, education committee and district finance committee for centralized review and approval. The names of students who qualify for aid will be given to the schools, and the schools and village committees (town or sub-district offices) shall again publish such names on their notice boards, in order that they will be monitored by the local public and public opinions.[9]

The regulations in other provinces and cities are similar. Thus, many children would rather forego the subsidy than reveal that they are infected persons or persons from a family with an infected person.

Regulatory enforcement in certain areas is weak. For example, instead of giving subsidies to families of HIV-infected persons, such subsidies found their way into the pockets of relatives and friends of cadre members.

· 4. Lack of Adequate Awareness of the Laws and Regulations among the Public.

Despite the presence of laws and policies, on-site investigation showed that there is little awareness of the laws and policies on this issue.

18.6 percent of students, 33.0 percent of parents, 35.0 percent of teachers, and 18.2 percent of the general public know about the *Convention on the Rights of the Child* and the provision on the right of children to education. The percentage of those who have only heard of the *Convention* is 24.3 percent, 21.9 percent, 32.0 percent and 22.4 percent respectively.

26.3 percent of students, 36.3 percent of parents, 42.3 percent of teachers, and 35.8 percent of the general public have heard of the "Four Frees and One Care" policy. Those who have knowledge of the details of the policy are 37.0 percent, 42.5 percent, 46.5 percent and 32.4 percent respectively. Ignorance of the laws and policies may lead to disregard or even infringement of those rights. Therefore, there is a need to augment public knowledge of the laws and policies in order to instil a more rational attitude towards infected persons and OVCs, and a greater respect for their rights. Enforcement of the laws would keep discriminatory behaviour in check.

5. Disparity in Definition between the Law and Reality

The *Regulations on the Prevention and Treatment of HIV/AIDS* provides that "no entity or individual shall discriminate against persons living with HIV/AIDS and their family members" and that "the legitimate rights of persons with AIDS and their family members to marriage, employment, medical treatment and school education are protected under the law." In reality, most discrimination is emotional experiences, whether it is discrimination as determined by the public, or discrimination that persons with HIV personally found intolerable. The public ranks the top five most common discriminatory behaviours as: "use of abusive language towards infected persons and their family members," "refusal to shake hands with infected persons," "refusal to allow infected persons or their children to be put in childcare centres or to attend school," "refusal to participate in group activities with infected persons," and "staying away from infected persons to avoid being infected." We need to explore the ways in which such discriminatory behaviours can be contained, and how to build a caring and non-discriminatory environment.

Part 2. On-Site Investigation

I. Outcome of Quantitative Research

(I) Results of the Analysis of the KAP Questionnaire

1. Basic Information of Study Subjects

(1) Students
1,775 student responses were received. 1,664 were valid, and the valid response rate was 94.81 percent. Among them, 594 or 35.7 percent were students from Heilongjiang,

502 or 30.2 percent were from Beijing, and 568 or 34.1 percent were from Henan. 865 or 52.0 percent were male, and 799 or 48.0 percent were female. 446 or 26.8 percent were primary students, 423 or 25.4 percent were secondary students, 483 or 29.0 percent were high school students, and 312 or 18.8 percent were university students. The average age was 15.36 ±3.079 years.

93.4 percent of the students had heard of AIDS a year ago; 5.9 percent had heard of AIDS within the last year. Only responses from those who had heard of AIDS were used, which comprised 1,645 questionnaires in total. 51.1 percent among those surveyed had received AIDS-prevention education (including seminars) in school, 48.9 percent had not.

(2) Parents

582 parents were surveyed. 123 or 21.1 percent were from Heilongjiang, 230 or 39.5 percent were from Beijing, and 229 or 39.3 percent were from Henan. 242 or 41.6 percent were parents of primary students, 194 or 33.3 percent of secondary students, and 146 or 25.1 percent of high school students. Most parents had high school or secondary vocational education (30.2 percent), and vocational or university education (40 percent). Those with secondary, post-graduate and below primary education account for 17.2 percent, 10.9 percent and 1.8 percent respectively. 541 or 94.6 percent of the parents had heard of AIDS a year ago, and 25 or 4.4 percent learned about AIDS within the last year. Only the 566 questionnaires of respondents who had heard of AIDS were used in our analysis.

(3) Teachers

219 responses were received. 205 or 93.61 percent were valid responses. Teachers from 23 provinces were surveyed; 60 or 29.3 percent were from Hielongjiang, 21 or 10.2 percent were from Beijing, and 94 or 45.9 percent were from Henan. Teachers from the remaining provinces constituted 14.6 percent of the total number surveyed. Of the teachers surveyed, 62 or 30.2 percent were male, 143 or 69.8 percent were female. The youngest teacher surveyed was 21 years old, and the oldest was 62. Mean age was 35.77 ±9.340 years. Among those surveyed, 8 or 3.9 percent had high school or secondary vocation education, 180 or 87.8 percent had vocational or university education, and 17 or 8.3 percent received post-graduate education. The mean value of teaching years was 13.24 ±11.38 years.

(4) General Public

158 responses were received. 152 or 96.2 percent were valid responses. 46 or 30.3 percent had families located in Heilong Jiang, 39 or 25.7 percent in Beijing, 19 or 12.5 percent in Henan, 11 or 7.2 percent in Hebei, 10 or 6.6 percent in Shandong, and the remaining 17.7 percent were from 12 other provinces, including Liaoning, Tianjin and Zhejiang, from each of which between one and four responses were received. Males

accounted for 61 or 40.1 percent, and female accounted for 91 or 59.9 percent. The youngest was nine years old, and the oldest was 66. The mean age was 30.03±10.120 years. In terms of education level, eight or 5.3 percent had secondary education, 35 or 23 percent had secondary vocation or high school education, 90 or 59.2 percent had vocation or university education, and 18 or 11.8 percent had postgraduate education. One person or 0.7 percent did not respond.

Among those surveyed, 143 or 94.1 percent had heard of AIDS a year ago, and 7 or 4.6 percent learned of it within the last year. Only the 150 respondents who had heard of AIDS were used in our analysis.

2. Public Attitude towards AIDS
(1) Public Understanding of the Relation between AIDS and Morality; and the Lives of Infected Persons

In response to the question, "Do you agree that AIDS is caused by immorality (drug abuse, casual sex, etc.)?", the percentage of students, parents, teachers and the general public who expressed disagreement was 30.3 percent, 28.7 percent, 44.2 percent and 49.0 percent respectively.

Table 1: Public Understanding of the Relation between AIDS and Morality, and the Lives of Infected Persons

	Students		Parents		Teachers		General Public	
	n	%	n	%	n	%	n	%
Do you agree that AIDS is caused by immorality (drug abuse, casual sex, etc.)?								
Agree	818	50.3	335	59.0	94	47.3	54	36.2
Disagree	492	30.3	158	28.7	88	44.2	73	49.0
No comments	315	19.4	68	12.3	17	8.5	22	14.8
An HIV-infected person can remain positive and maintain a healthy way of living and can live normally for many years.								
Agree	1,236	76.1	407	73.6	100	79.2	106	71.1
Disagree	161	9.9	47	8.5	30	14.4	28	18.8
No comments	228	14.0	99	17.9	13	6.4	15	10.1

(2) Public Compassion towards Persons Infected with AIDS through Different Channels
Refer to Table 2 for the public's ranking of compassion pertaining to the different channels of infection and the respective breakdown in percentages. We see that the

public's ranking is consistent with the general view that infection through "Blood Transfusion or Surgery" and "From Mother's Pregnancy or Breast-Feeding" is worthy of sympathy, while infection through "Sharing of the Same Injection Needle during Drug-Taking" and "Casual Sex" is not. This is an indication that people generally treat infected persons differently based on the way in which they were infected.

Table 2: Public Compassion towards Persons Living with AIDS infected through Different Transmission Routes

Ranking	People Infected with AIDS through Different Channels	Students		Parents		Teachers		External Public	
		n	%	n	%	n	%	n	%
1	Blood Transfustion or Surgery	1,479	90.3	521	93.0	195	95.1	142	94.7
2	From Mother's Pregnancy or Breast-Feeding	1,477	90.0	505	89.7	194	94.6	140	94.6
3	Selling of Blood	1,092	66.6	375	67.3	149	72.7	100	68.0
4	Sex between Husband and Wife	825	50.4	283	51.5	141	69.5	101	67.3
5	Sharing of the Same Injection Needle during Drug-Taking	324	19.9	97	17.7	50	24.6	20	13.6
6	Casual Sex	144	8.8	49	8.9	25	12.3	10	6.8

(3) Public's Behaviour towards School Education for OVCs
The percentages of students, teachers, parents and the general public who believe that students living with HIV should continue with their education are 60.7 percent, 62.8 percent, 77.6 percent and 7.2 percent respectively. The percentages for the same groups who agree that they themselves (or their children) should attend the same class as children who have parent(s) living with AIDS are 58.9 percent, 40.3 percent, 79.0

percent and 28.9 percent respectively. The percentages for the same groups who agree that they themselves (or their children) should attend the same class as students living with AIDS are 49.7 percent, 32.6 percent, 62.0 percent and 27.0 percent respectively.

Refer to Table 4 for the public's behaviour towards a hypothetical AIDS-infected child. We see that most of the public do not discriminate against infected persons and

Table 3: Public's Attitude towards School Education for OVCs

	Students		Parents		Teachers		General Public	
	n	%	n	%	n	%	n	%
Do you think that students living with HIV should be allowed to continue with their education?								
Yes	988	60.7	348	62.8	156	77.6	115	77.3
No	229	14.1	46	8.3	15	7.5	4	2.7
Depending on how the student was infected	257	15.8	102	18.4	22	10.9	26	17.4
No comments	154	8.5	58	10.5	8	4.0	4	2.7
If the parent(s) of a student in class is (are) infected with AIDS, are you willing to allow your child to attend the same class as this child?								
Yes	959	58.9	221	40.3	158	79.0	43	28.9
No	131	8.1	72	13.1	9	4.5	44	29.5
Depending in how the student was infected	256	15.7	135	24.6	22	11.0	37	24.8
No comments	281	17.3	120	21.9	11	5.5	25	16.8
If a student in class is infected with AIDS, are you willing to allow your child to attend the same class as this child?								
Yes	805	49.7	181	32.0	131	62.0	40	27.0
No	203	13.5	141	25.4	21	10.5	53	35.8
Depending in how the student was infected	323	19.9	129	23.2	41	20.5	36	24.3
No comments	289	17.8	105	18.9	14	7.0	19	12.8

Table 4: Public's Attitude towards Hypothetical OVCs

Choice	Students n	%	Parents n	%	Teachers n	%	General Public n	%
Demand that infected persons transfer to another school or class to avoid infecting other persons.	110	6.7	75	13.6	5	2.5	11	7.4
Request to transfer to another school or class to avoid being infected.	92	5.6	30	5.4	–	–	1	0.7
A separate seat away from the rest of the class should be arranged at the last row of the class for infected persons.	167	10.2	64	11.6	8	4.0	18	12.1
No demand, but will avoid contact with the infected person as much as possible.	503	36.3	239	43.4	16	7.9	63	43.0
It's OK. Will treat the person normally.	766	46.0	168	30.5	49	24.3	61	40.9
If help is required, I or my child will help the infected person.	1,143	70.0	295	53.5	151	74.8	119	79.9
Must sympathize with the infected person and give him/her extra care.	536	32.9	151	27.9	47	23.3	58	38.9

are willing to provide assistance. However, a small proportion displays discriminatory behaviour, such as "demand infected persons transfer to another school."

3. Public Awareness of Rights and Policies

(1) Right to Education
Table 5 indicates that more than 90 percent of the public agree that OVCs should have the right to education.

Table 5: Public Attitude on the Right to Education

Relevant Statements	Students		Parents		Teachers		Greneral Public	
	n	%	n	%	n	%	n	%
Everyone has the right to education	1,591	97.0	530	98.1	203	99.5	149	99.3
Disabled children have the right to education	1,594	97.3	531	98.7	205	100.0	150	100.0
Children whose parents are infected with HIV or who have died of AIDS have the right of education	1,527	93.1	518	96.1	204	99.5	145	96.7
Students living with HIV have the right to education	1,488	90.7	513	95.0	200	97.6	143	95.3

(2) Privacy
Refer to Table 6 for the public's attitude towards the right to privacy and the right to know the identity of those living with HIV around them. The information indicates that the public tends to believe in the right to know the identity of persons living with HIV around them, whereas they tend to believe in the protection of privacy if they were the infected persons.

Table 6: Public Attitude towards the Privacy of Persons Living with HIV

	Students		Parents		Teachers		General Public	
	n	%	n	%	n	%	n	%
Do you think you have the right to know who the persons living with HIV around you are?								
Yes	798	48.8	325	60.9	123	61.2	85	57.0
No	462	28.2	111	20.8	46	22.9	43	28.9
No comments	376	23.0	98	18.4	32	15.9	21	14.1
If you or your parents were infected with AIDS, are you willing to disclose to others?								
Yes	442	27.5	137	25.3	30	14.9	17	11.6
No	701	43.5	202	37.3	115	57.2	95	65.1
Depending on how I/they were infected	172	10.7	94	17.4	22	10.9	18	12.3
No comments	295	18.3	108	20.0	34	16.9	16	11.0

4. Public Understanding and Ranking of the Unjustifiability of the Different Behaviours Towards Persons Living with HIV

Refer to Table 7 for the ranking and percentages of different groups on the unjustifiability of different behaviours towards persons living with HIV.

5. Analysis of Factors Affecting Anti-Discriminatory Attitude

Anti-discriminatory attitude is analyzed as follows: first, values are assigned to anti-discriminatory attitudes. Positive attitudes are assigned positive values, and negative attitudes are assigned negative values. A full mark is -13 – 14 points for students, -14 – 13 points for parents, -12 – 15 points for teachers, and -14 – 13 points for the general public. A higher mark indicates a more positive attitude. Statistical analysis for the differences between the groups was carried out using ANOVA or t-test. Upon determining that the data is statistically significant after ANOVA, multiple comparisons were carried out using LSD. Second, values were assigned for "relation between AIDS and morality," "knowledge of the lives of infected persons," "right to education," "right to privacy," and "policy," and the Spearman Rank Correlation with students' anti-discriminatory attitude was performed. Third, the total anti-discriminatory attitude value as a dependent variable was used, and all variables were included in a multiple linear regression analysis.

Table 7: Understanding and Ranking of the Unjustifiability of the Various Attitudes towards Persons Living with HIV

Attitude	Students		Parents		Teachers		General Public	
	%	Ranking	%	Ranking	%	Ranking	%	Ranking
Use of abusive language and behaviour towards infected persons and their family members	93.3	1	93.5	1	99.5	1	100.0	1
Refuse to shake hands with infected persons	80.5	2	72.1	4	86.2	5	87.3	5
Refuse to allow infected persons or their children to be put in childcare centres or attend school	79.7	3	75.7	3	90.6	3	91.3	2
Refuse to participate in group activities with infected persons	77.9	4	71.5	5	91.1	2	88.0	4
Stay far away from them to avoid being infected	77.5	5	78.9	2	88.7	4	91.3	3
Forced segregation of infected persons to avoid infecting other persons	72.9	6	69.9	6	82.1	7	87.2	6
Refuse to have meals with infected persons	68.0	7	52.6	7	82.2	6	77.3	7
Inform the infected person's colleagues or schoolmates of his/her illness	40.6	8	39.5	8	67.0	8	63.3	8
Prohibit infected persons from marrying or giving birth	30.6	9	17.1	9	32.0	9	32.9	9
Doctor informs the infected person's spouse of his/her illness	13.5	10	8.0	10	6.4	10	7.3	10
Prohibit HIV-carriers from donating blood	6.6	11	3.4	11	2.5	11	5.4	11

(1) Analysis of Factors Affecting Anti-Discriminatory Attitude among Students

The results show that total anti-discrimination points for students was 4.85 ±3.990 points. No statistical significance was found for the differences between students of different regions and different genders. The differences in scores between students of different levels are statistically significant. Primary students scored 3.26 ±4.105 points, secondary students scored 4.80 ±4.121 points, high school students scored 5.40±3.385 points and university students scored 6.19 ±3.845 points. Thus, students with a higher level of education tend to have a more positive attitude towards persons living with HIV. Scores for students who received education (5.53 ±3.951 points) are higher than scores for students who did not have education (4.12 ±3.905 points), and the difference is statistically significant.

Analysis of the relevant results indicate that the overall anti-discrimination score is positively correlated with the total score for knowledge of AIDS, and the scores for knowledge of non-transmission route, prevention knowledge, knowledge of diagnosis and treatment, relation between AIDS and morality, knowledge of the lives of infected persons, right to education, and policy; the correlation coefficients for each of these categories being 0.387, 0.417, 0.295, 0.290, 0.175, 0.199, 0.413 and 0.114. Thus, an anti-discriminatory attitude is highly correlated with scores for knowledge (especially "knowledge of non-transmission route" and "knowledge of diagnosis and treatment") and the right to education. An anti-discriminatory attitude has no correlation with transmission route or privacy.

Regression analysis shows that, compared to mothers with secondary education or lower, the attitudes of mothers with university or vocational or higher education tend to be more negative. The overall score for anti-discriminatory attitude does not correlate positively with the scores for non-transmission route, relation between AIDS and morality, knowledge of the lives of infected persons, right to education and right of privacy.

(2) Analysis of Factors Affecting Anti-Discriminatory Attitude among Parents

Overall the anti-discriminatory attitude among parents was 2.47 ±3.998 points. There is no correlation between parents' attitude and a child's sex, school level, parents' status, educational level and occupation. Results of the relevant analysis indicate that the anti-discriminatory attitude of parents is positively correlated with the scores for knowledge (non-transmission route, prevention, and diagnosis and treatment), relation between AIDS and morality, knowledge of the lives of infected persons, right to education, right to privacy and policy. The results of regression analysis show that the overall score for parents' anti-discriminatory attitudes positively correlates with the scores for the knowledge of non-transmission route, relation between AIDS and morality, knowledge of the lives of infected persons, right to education, right to privacy and policy. Compared to parents in Heilongjiang, parents in Henan have a greater positive tendency.

(3) Analysis of Factors Affecting Anti-Discriminatory Attitude among Teachers
The overall score for the anti-discriminatory attitude of teachers was 7.02 ±3.328 points. The differences in the anti-discriminatory attitudes between teachers of different groups were statistically insignificant. The relevant analysis results indicated that the overall score for teachers' anti-discriminatory attitude is positively correlated with knowledge (of non-transmission route, prevention, and diagnosis and treatment), relation between AIDS and morality, right to education, right of privacy, and policy. The results of regression analysis show that, compared to Heilongjiang, teachers of Beijing, Henan and other regions tended towards greater positivity. There is no statistical significance with other variables.

(4) Analysis of Factors Affecting Anti-Discriminatory Attitude among the General Public
The overall score for anti-discrimination among the general public was 3.67 ±3.767 points. The difference in scores between the general public with different education levels showed statistical significance. Further analysis showed that the general public with high school or secondary vocation level education or lower scored lower than those with vocation, university or post-graduation education. This indicates that discrimination is more apparent among the portion of the general public with a lower level of education. Relevant analysis results showed that an anti-discriminatory attitude in the general public is positively correlated with the scores of knowledge (of transmission route, non-transmission route, and prevention), relation between AIDS and morality, and knowledge of the lives of infected persons. Correlation with knowledge of non-transmission route, knowledge of prevention, and the relation between AIDS and morality is high. Regression analysis results showed that the anti-discriminatory attitude of the general public is not correlated with non-transmission route, relation between AIDS and morality, and policy. The anti-discriminatory attitude among the general public tends to be more positive with higher scores for non-transmission route, relation between AIDS and morality, and policy.

(II) Results of Analysis of the Stigma Questionnaire

1. Basic Information of Study Subjects
(1) Students
215 students were surveyed. All were from Beijing. 78 or 36.3 percent were male, and 135 or 62.8 percent were female. 2 or 0.9 percent did not respond. 100 or 46.5 percent were secondary school students, 69 or 32.1 percent were high school students, and 46 or 21.4 percent were university students. Students surveyed were between the ages of 12 and 22, and the mean age was 15.55 ±2.786 years. 199 or 92.6 percent of students have received training on the prevention of AIDS in school, and 16 or 7.4 percent have not received any training.

(2) Parents
50 parents were surveyed. All were from Beijing. 19 or 38.0 percent were female, and 31 or 62.0 percent were male. Parents' ages were between 33 and 68, and the mean age was 41.44 ±5.379 years. 1 parent or 2 percent had a primary or lower level of education, 10 or 20 percent had secondary education, 18 or 36 percent had high school or secondary vocation education, 17 or 34 percent had vocational or university education, 3 or 6 percent had post-graduate education; 1 parent or 2 percent did not respond.

(3) OVCs
18 OVCs were surveyed. All were from Henan. 9 or 50 percent were male, and 8 or 44.4 percent were female. 1 student or 5.6 percent did not respond. All 18 students are currently attending a special primary school for OVCs. Among them, 4 or 22.2 percent were in primary 3, 4 or 22.2 percent in primary 4, 5 or 27.8 percent in primary 5, and 5 or 27.8 percent in primary 6.

2. HIV Stigma Comparison
Situational analysis is used, and case studies were prepared to compare HIV stigma among students, parents and OVCs.

Case 1
"Xiaoli, a high school student, has good grades, and has been a 'Triple "A" Student' every year. Her dream is to study in a top university in the country. Lately, she has not been feeling well, and has been feeling lethargic. She has been suffering from serious flu with increasing frequency. Once, she was down with mild pneumonia. She also discovered that she had skin ulcers that took a long time to heal.

She visited the doctor, who suggested that she take an AIDS test. The test results were positive. She told her parents and family members, and her parents refused to accept the fact that their daughter is infected with AIDS. Zhu Xu, her boyfriend, saw that she was depressed and asked her what was bothering her. Xiaoli was very confused, as she did not know if she should tell him the truth."

Xiaoli, the key character in the case, is a person living with HIV. We used this case to explore HIV stigma among students, parents and OVCs. The projective technique is used for students and parents: respondents subconsciously project their own attributes, attitudes and subjective processes onto other people. It is generally believed that the attitude of the majority reflects the true attitude of the group in question to some extent. The attitude of OVCs towards the character Xiaoli will reflect their own stigmas to some extent because they share similar experiences with her. What OVCs believe to be the attitude of the majority reflects the stigma and discrimination that they have experienced. 35 variables were set for the above case, and values were attributed to them. Each variable is assigned a score of between -2 and 2, the higher the score, the greater the tendency towards a more positive attitude.

Table 8 indicates the average score for each variable among the various groups. The box plots in Figures 1, 2, 3 and 4 describe the distribution of the scores of variables within different benchmarks for the different groups. "– Other" refers to what was believed to be the majority's view.

From Table 8 and Figure 1, in terms of intention, we see that the overall behaviours of students, parents and OVCs are positive. In terms of the variables dealing with intention, OVCs display the highest scores, followed by students, then parents. Some of the differences between variables showed statistical significance. Students, parents and OVCs reported that the behaviour scores of the majority were lower than those of their own behaviour. Certain variables are statistically significant, which implies that the scores for the actual behaviour intention of students and parents were even lower. There is no statistical significance between the difference between the perception of the majority's behaviour by OVCs and those of students and parents. This shows that there is no difference between the discrimination felt by OVCs and actual discrimination.

Table 8 and Figure 2 show that, in terms of emotional response, the behaviours of students, parents and OVCs were positive. OVCs scored the lowest, whereas students scored higher, implying that OVCs have a stronger stigma. Some of the differences observed between the variables of students and those of OVCs are statistically significant. However, the differences between parents and OVCs were statistically insignificant. Students and parents reported lower scores for the attitudes of the majority compared to their own, which showed that the true emotional responses of students and parents were even lower. The scores for emotional responses of OVCs were lower than those of their own behaviour, which implies that the scores of the true emotional responses for students and parents should be even lower.

Table 3 and Figure 3 show that in terms of behaviour response, the behaviours of students, parents and OVCs were generally positive. Behaviour response scores of students and parents were lower than those of OVCs. Differences between certain variables were statistically significant. The scores on the behaviour response of the majority as reported by students, parents and OVCs are close to their own scores. Only the differences for specific variables of students were statistically significant. The behaviour response scores experienced by OVCs are higher than the scores for true behaviour responses for students and parents.

Table 8 and Figure 4 show that in terms of disclosure of illness, the scores for students, parents and OVCs were negative, which imply that they support disclosing the illness. Parents scored slightly higher. Students, parents and OVCs reported that the majority's scores are not very different from their own. Only differences for specific variables for students were statistically significant.

Table 8: Stigma of Students, Parents and OVCs towards Persons Living with HIV

	Student (1)		Student-Other (2)		Parent (3)		Parent-Other (4)		OVC (5)		OVC-Other (6)	
	n	Ave	n	Ave	n	Ave	n	Ave	n	Ave	n	Ave
Behaviour Intention												
1. It is safe for the child to play with Xiaoli	212	0.71	195	0.62	50	0.92	48	0.35	15	-0.20	15	0.07
2. Xiaoli's freedom should be restricted	211	0.87	196	0.81	50	0.76	48	0.71	18	0.44	16	1.20
3. I feel uncomfortable playing with Xiaoli	214	0.26	196	0.06	50	0.16	48	0.02	18	0.67	16	0.38
4. Xiaoli is no different from other people	213	-0.13	195	0.28	48	0.29	48	0.62	17	0.18	16	0.19
5. I am willing to talk to Xiaoli	214	0.91	213	0.29	48	0.38	50	0.18	16	1.38	16	0.25
6. I will participate in activities in which Xiaoli participates	214	0.83	211	0.21	48	0.42	49	0.04	16	0.75	16	0.31
7. I will eat the food that Xiaoli has prepared for dinner	214	0.34	212	0.07	48	-0.15	50	-0.24	16	0.94	13	0.15
8. If Xiaoli needs help, I will help	214	1.09	209	0.73	48	0.90	49	0.51	16	1.13	15	0.53
9. I am willing to maintain my friendship with Xiaoli at this time	215	1.04	212	0.68	50	0.58	50	0.20	17	1.18	17	0.65
10. Agree (for my child) to study in the same class as Xiaoli	215	0.88	209	0.52	50	0.64	50	0.28	17	1.24	17	0.35
11. Agree (for my child) to eat at the same table as Xiaoli	213	0.41	212	0.16	50	.20	50	-0.12	17	.94	17	0.18

Emotional Response

12. Xiaoli deserves sympathy and understanding	212	1.35	210	1.22	49	0.98	49	1.06	16	0.63	18	0.94
13. Xiaoli deserves it	211	1.17	199	1.07	46	0.72	48	0.83	18	0.50	17	0.76
14. Xiaoli deserves to lose her "Triple A" award	213	1.28	196	1.07	49	0.43	48	0.65	17	0.41	16	0.50
15. Xiaoli is filthy	211	1.41	193	1.30	50	1.02	48	0.90	18	0.89	16	1.13
16. Xiaoli has lost all meaning in life	212	1.29	196	1.14	49	0.86	47	0.87	18	0.44	15	1.13
17. Xiaoli does not deserve to be trusted	212	1.34	196	1.09	50	0.82	46	0.78	16	0.37	15	1.13
18. Xiaoli should feel ashamed	211	1.14	195	1.07	49	0.90	47	0.77	16	0.69	14	0.14
19. Xiaoli is not guilty	213	1.24	194	0.96	48	0.94	47	0.87	15	1.20	13	0.77
20. Xiaoli is repugnant	212	1.32	195	1.20	50	1.10	48	0.79	17	1.12	16	1.50
21. Xiaoli will be abandoned by the test of the world, and will live a live of solitude	214	1.10	196	1.01	50	0.84	48	0.77	17	0.82	15	1.13

Figure 1: Behaviour Intention Box Plot of Different groups towards Persons Living with HIV

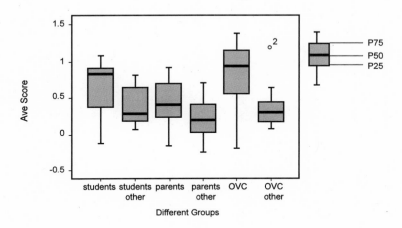

Figure 2: Emotional Response Box Plot of Different Groups towards Persons Living with HIV

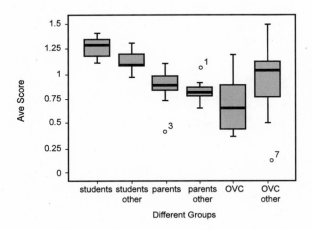

Figure 3: Behaviour Response Box Plot of Different Groups towards Persons Living with HIV

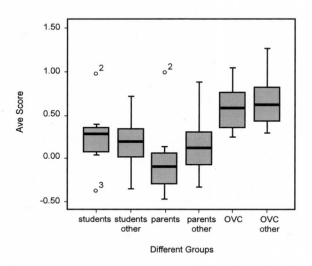

Different Groups

Figure 4: Disclosure of Illness Box Plot of Different Groups towards Persons Living with HIV

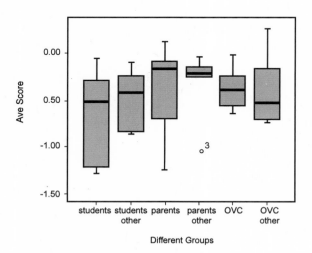

Different Groups

3. Comparison of Stigma of Children Orphaned by AIDS

Case 2

"Xiaolang, age twelve, is a primary five student and is a member of the class's sports committee. He is vivacious and performs well in his studies; hence, he is a favourite among teachers and classmates. However, some time ago, Xiaolang started missing classes frequently, and did not appear as happy as he used to be. When his friends asked him what the matter was, he denied that there was anything wrong. Finally, when the form teacher asked him what happened, he said his father was ill, seriously ill. He has to help take care of his father, and missed classes as a result.

After some time, Xiaolang was able to attend class again. However, his enthusiasm had clearly waned. Friends heard from unidentified sources that his father had died from AIDS. Since then, they started staying away from him. Xiaolang used to be surrounded by friends during physical education lessons. Now, classmates would disperse as soon as he appears, even keeping hundreds of metres away. Some would make signs behind his back. The teacher started to stop marking his homework, and his seat was moved to the back of the classroom. Not long after, the principal requested a meeting with his mother, and told her in a regretful tone that many parents had demanded that Xiaolang transfer to another school. If Xiaolang does not transfer, they would transfer their own children to another school. The principal hoped that Xiaolang and his mother would give the matter due consideration."

Xiaolang, the character in the case, is a child orphaned by AIDS. We used this case to examine the stigma of students, parents and OVCs toward children orphaned by AIDS. Based on the above case, 19 variables were set. The procedures employed were the same as those in Case 1.

Table 9 and Figure 5 showed that in terms of emotional response, the scores for the different variables were positive for students, parents and OVCs. Students scored the highest, followed by parents; OVCs scored the lowest. The differences for some of the variables were statistically significant. This reveals that OVCs have a stronger stigma. The scores for the emotional response of the majority as reported by students are lower than their own. Results from the same reports by parents and OVCs are consistent. Comparing OVC stigma and the actual attitude of students, there are more variables with statistically significant differences. However, when compared to parents, only the difference for one variable is statistically significant. This shows that OVC stigma is stronger than the actual stigma of students and parents.

Table 9 and Figure 6 show that the scores of students, parents and OVCs for "rights awareness" are positive. This indicates that students and parents respect non-discrimination and the right to education of children orphaned by AIDS. OVCs are also aware of their rights. The difference between students' scores for "Schoolmates should give Xiaolang more love" and the scores for parents and OVCs are statistically significant; students' scores are higher. The score for rights awareness of the majority as reported by OVCs is lower than the scores for the actual rights awareness of students and parents. These differences are statistically significant.

Table 9 and Figure 7 show that in terms of education, the scores for students and OVCs for the variable, "Hopefully, a special school will be built, so that Xiaolang can go to school with children of similar circumstances" are negative. Although parents' score was positive, they believed that the score for the majority was also negative. This indicates that all three groups of people hope that a special school will be built for OVCs. Also, the score for "Xiaolang will threaten the health of other students if he remains in school" for OVCs is negative, which implies that they believe that children orphaned by AIDS will threaten the health of other students. This could be the reason for their wish to have special schools built. However, this survey was conducted only in a school where OVCs congregate, which means that investigation results of OVCs are not representative.

Figure 7 indicates that there are quite a number of outliers and extreme values. The score of OVCs for their own attitude is lower. They also believe that the majority will hope for a special school to be built, and that demanding children orphaned by AIDS transfer to another school is reasonable. Thus, the stigma experienced by the OVCs surveyed is stronger. They hope that special schools could be built, so that children orphaned by AIDS can attend together.

II. Results of Qualitative Analysis

(I) Summary of Open-Ended Questions in KAP Questionnaire

1. Do you think students living with HIV should be allowed to remain in school?
(1) Those who replied in the affirmative gave reasons that fall within the following categories: 1) from a rights perspective: everyone has the right to education, everyone is equal, and AIDS infection does not deprive them of such right; 2) from a medical perspective: AIDS is not contagious, and studying in the same class as the infected person is not threatening to one's health; 3) from an emotional perspective: people should sympathize with persons living with HIV, and not ostracize them; 4) from a non-discrimination perspective: people should not discriminate against persons living with HIV, and should exercise the spirit of humanity; 5) from a learning perspective: even infected persons have to learn in order to pursue their dreams and a good future; 6) being infected with AIDS is not their fault; 7) from the country's perspective: the country requires talent.

(2) Those who replied in the negative gave the following reasons: 1) worry that they will be infected (this is the main reason); 2) treatment of the disease should be the focus; 3)

Table 9: Sense of Humiliation of Students, Parents and AIDS-affect Children toward Children Orphaned by AIDS

	Student (1)		Student-Other (2)		Parent (3)		Parent-Other (4)		OVC (5)		OVC-Other (6)	
	n	Ave	n	Ave	n	Ave	n	Ave	n	Ave	n	Ave
Emotional Response												
1. Xialoang deserves sympathy and understanding	213	1.58	211	1.47	50	1.32	50	1.06	18	1.50	17	0.94
2. To schoolmates and teachers, Xialoang is a hazard	213	1.05	211	0.93	50	0.82	49	0.63	18	0.44	15	0.73
3. Xialoang does not deserve trust	215	1.32	211	1.13	50	0.96	49	0.65	16	0.63	16	0.44
4. Xialoang should feel ashamed	213	1.30	210	1.14	49	0.90	48	0.98	16	0.75	16	0.63
5. Xialoang has committed no mistake	214	1.40	210	1.30	50	1.10	49	1.10	17	1.24	15	0.80
6. It is safe for Xialoang to attend school with his classmates	212	1.19	209	1.04	49	1.08	49	1.02	17	0.76	15	0.80
7. Xialoang is repugnant	215	1.45	210	1.15	50	1.14	48	0.98	18	0.94	17	0.47
8. Xialoang is a plague; a walking disaster	215	1.36	206	1.24	49	1.12	49	1.08	18	1.06	16	1.00
9. Xialoang transferring to another school is a matter of course	213	1.18	209	1.01	50	0.60	49	0.65	18	0.17	16	0.19
10. Xialoang's freedom should be restricted	213	1.12	211	0.89	50	0.98	48	0.81	18	0.17	17	0.41

Rights Awareness

11. Schoolmates should give Xiaolang more love	211	1.54	205	1.40	50	1.18	49	1.08	16	1.00	16	0.75
12. Xiaolang should not be subject to differential treatment	214	1.19	210	0.98	50	0.98	48	0.98	15	0.60	16	0.18
13. Xiaolang should see legal assistance to protect his right to school education	215	1.19	211	1.04	49	1.06	49	1.06	17	1.00	15	0.33
14. The government authorities are responsible for providing Xiaolang with free compulsory education	213	1.02	211	0.91	50	0.84	49	0.88	18	1.39	17	0.59

Receiving Education

15. Xiaolang will threaten the health of other students if he remains in the school	212	0.83	211	0.78	49	0.73	49	0.78	18	-0.22	16	0.94
16. Hopefully a special school will be built, so that Xiaolang can go to school with children in similar circumstances	214	-0.25	211	-0.30	50	0.02	49	-0.20	18	-0.78	17	-1.65
17. It is reasonable of parents of schoolmates to demand that Xiaolang transfers to another school	215	1.02	210	1.02	50	0.84	49	0.73	18	0.56	16	0.25
18. Students should stay far away from him	211	1.16	211	1.00	48	0.85	49	0.90	17	0.24	16	1.13
19. Xiaolang has no right to go to school	215	1.40	208	1.31	49	1.12	49	1.10	18	1.00	16	1.13

Figure 5: Emotional Response Box Plot of Different Groups towards Children Orphaned by AIDS

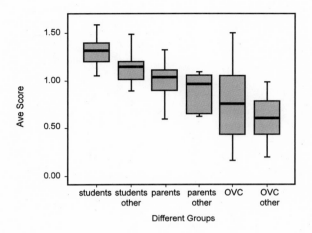

Figure 6: Rights Awareness Box Plot of Different Groups towards Children Orphaned by AIDS

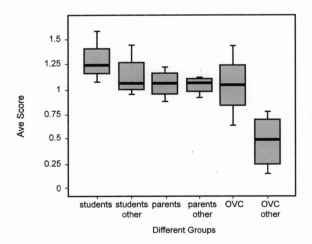

Figure 7: Attitude to Education Box Plot of Different Groups towards Children Orphaned by AIDS

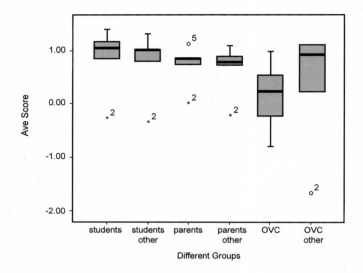

infected persons will be discriminated against; 4) students living with HIV should learn with other children who are infected as well.

(3) Those who gave responses that are dependent on the transmission route, or who had no comments gave the following reasons: 1) not sure if others can be infected; 2) relate transmission route to morality; 3) depends on the seriousness of the illness; 4) conflict between awareness of self-protection and morality.

2. Are you agreeable to you or your child attending the same class as a student who has a parent or who is a person living with AIDS?
(1) Those who agreed with this statement gave the following reasons: 1) AIDS is transmitted via blood and sexual activity and not via normal study activities; 2) we should care for and help this student; 3) we should not discriminate; 4) if only the parent of a child is infected, it does not imply that the child is infected as well. The fault of parents cannot be attributed to the child; 5) we should treasure friendship, and think that "because he is my friend, I can be closer to him."

(2) Those who do not agree gave the following reasons. Most were afraid of being infected and did not feel safe. Parents felt that "children may scratch their skins during

play and get infected," and that "the children are young and do not know how to take precautions. This has nothing to do with a loving heart."

(3) Those who gave responses that are dependent on the transmission route or who did not have comments gave the following reasons: 1) one cannot be sure that a student is infected just because their parents are infected with AIDS; 2) it depends on the parent's or the child's route of infection; 3) it depends on the seriousness of the illness; 4) caught between fear for the disease and a sense of morality; 5) parents believe that children have inadequate awareness and ability to protect themselves.

3. Do you think you have the right to know if there is anyone living with HIV around you?
(1) Those who replied in the affirmative gave the following reasons: 1) the public has the right to health. Knowledge enables them to take effective precautionary measures to prevent themselves or other people from being infected; 2) people can better help the infected person after knowing about the infection; 3) people have the right to know; 4) yes, if information is obtained from "legitimate channels."

(2) Those who replied in the negative gave the following reasons: 1) it is a private matter, other people do not have the right to know; 2) that knowledge will cause harm to persons living with HIV, even discrimination; 3) do not want to know because they believe they will not be infected.

4. In your view, what kind of behaviour towards children orphaned by AIDS and children living with HIV is considered discriminatory behaviour?
Answers included language, such as insult, ridicule, sarcasm, etc.; avoidance, such as staying away; refusal to join any activity where the infected person is present; aggressive behaviour; infringement of rights, such as restrictions on employment, medical treatment, etc. Excessive care may be a disguised form of discrimination.

(II) Results of Interviews with Students

1. Overview of Students Interviewed
One university, high school, secondary school and primary school from each of Heilongjiang, Beijing and Henan were selected. Interviews with one or two groups were carried out in each school. 17 groups, or 136 students, were interviewed in total. 65 or 47.8 percent were male, 71 or 52.2 percent were female. 58 or 42.6 percent were from Heilongjiang; 36 or 26.5 percent were from Beijing, 42 or 30.9 percent were from Henan. 28 or 20.6 percent were primary students, 49 or 36.0 percent were secondary students, 33 or 24.3 percent were high school students, and 26 or 19.1 percent were university students.

2. Results of Interviews with Students

(1) Students' knowledge of AIDS

All students interviewed had heard of AIDS. The main channels from which they learned of AIDS were mass media, such as television, newspaper and radio, and school-conducted courses, display boards and posters. A small number had heard from their parents.

When AIDS was mentioned, most students would think of issues relating to the disease and the emotional experience of persons living with HIV. A small number thought of AIDS-related social problems. The things that came to the minds of most of them were "death," "transmission," "incurable" and "how to prevent the disease." In terms of emotional experience toward persons living with HIV, most would think of "discrimination," "fright," "care," "pitiful," "terrifying," "scary," "the infected person will feel lonely," and "pain." When it came to AIDS-related social problems, most students thought of "orphans," "drug abuse," etc.

Most students are aware of the three transmission routes of AIDS (blood, sex and mother-to-child), and were able to identify if various daily activities would facilitate transmission. However, there were some misconceptions about transmission routes; some students thought that HIV can be transmitted through saliva, air, the sharing of a cup, etc.

(2) Attitude towards Persons Living with HIV/AIDS

Most students were caring and non-discriminatory towards persons living with HIV/AIDS, and respected the rights of such persons. There were students who felt that HIV is terrifying, and would discriminate against or avoid HIV-infected persons.

The majority of the students believe that their attitude should depend on the transmission route. Some students feel that "if a person was infected due to an innocent cause, then that person deserves sympathy; if infection was due to drug-taking, then the infected person deserves it." There were students who did not share this belief. They were of the opinion that "even drug abusers do not wish to be infected" and should not be punished with a disease. These students felt that HIV infected persons should be treated equally, regardless of whether infection was via drugs or mother-to-child transmission.

(3) Attitude towards OVCs

Although there are controversial attitudes towards persons living with HIV/AIDS, the attitude that students expressed toward OVCS is that they were "innocent," "deserve sympathy," "we should care for them," "we should not discriminate against them," "we should treat them equally," "they should have the same right to education as children of the same age," and "we should help them through our own efforts and those of the State and school."

Most students believe that OVCs have the right to education and that they should be able to attend school. However, many students suggested that special schools should be built for OVCs, and that infected students, especially children living with AIDS, should be segregated from the others. There were also many students who were against this idea, and believed that it constitutes discriminatory behaviour.

Some students believe that if they are careful about protecting themselves, attending school with OVCs will not threaten their health. Other students thought that their health would be threatened, and that they cannot face OVCs with calm or free of reservation. These students felt that they would remain friends with OVCs if they were friends before, but that the relationship would not be as close as before the child became an OVC. A minority of students made it explicit that they were unwilling to attend school with OVCs.

(4) Discrimination against OVCs

Students believe that discrimination against OVCs could manifest itself in the following ways: deliberately staying away from or ostracizing OVCs, such as not sitting at the same table as them; verbal attacks, such as ridicule and insult; refusal to allow OVCs to attend school; parents demanding OVCs transfer schools or have their own children stay away from OVCs; building a separate school for OVCs and segregating them from the other students; behaviours that infringe on their privacy; and excessive concern: students believe that what OVCs need is equality, and excessive concern may make OVCs feel special and inferior. As a result, OVCs with a strong sense of pride will be hurt.

(5) Reasons for Discrimination

The students interviewed believe that the main reasons for discrimination against persons living with HIV and OVCs are:

- Lack of knowledge; knowledge of AIDS is incomplete and unsystematically acquired; lack of understanding regarding transmission routes; and the belief that AIDS is transmitted through daily contact.
- Fear of AIDS because "AIDS is a communicable disease and incurable till now. Fear of being infected."
- Connecting AIDS with bad behaviour and morals, because "AIDS comes together with many bad behaviours; hence, many people will think of hideous things at the mention of AIDS, and feel that infected persons are guilty."
- Many students believe that discrimination originates more from the care and love that parents have for their children. Some students think that such protective behaviour from parents is not restricted to AIDS. For example, one student told of "a classmate who shared the same table with me had tonsillitis.

My parents refused to let me share a table with him when they knew of it."
- Lack of publicity, inappropriate advertising methods, and lack of depth in advertising content. Some students stated: "Inadequate publicity. We had opportunities to attend seminars, but most know little"; "Care is not knowledge. We should organize talks in communities to increase the level of understanding among parents and residents." There were students who proposed, "Current ads focus on the nature of AIDS as a disease. This exaggerates the outcome of the disease and produces fear. On the other hand, very little on the prevention of AIDS has been mentioned, and people's fear cannot be alleviated." Others said, "Some publicity focused on the wrong message and create too much fear. Fear is exaggerated, but prevention is neglected."
- A minority of students think that discrimination depends on personal disposition, or on the inability to empathize with others.

(6) Recommendations for Eliminating Discrimination
To eliminate discrimination, students are of the opinion that there should be greater public knowledge about the disease. Some felt that a publicity campaign must start with the general public, and that the content and format of current forms of publicity on the issue must change. For content, students recommend, "intimidating language should be avoided. Instead, focus should be on prevention and the message of love in order to help people to confront the disease objectively." In terms of format, one suggestion was that publicity methods should be more audience friendly, and fun. Most students think that the school should organize seminars and health classes, instead of being limited to distributing publicity materials only. On the matter of discrimination from parents, most students believe that parents have good intentions – that their discrimination is caused by love for their children – but that parents' views are nevertheless wrong. Students recommend that the school should send the message through students, or organize classes for parents to promote understanding and support.

(III) Results of Interviews with Teachers

1. Overview of Teachers Interviewed
Interviews with teachers were carried out in two groups. One group consisted of four interviewees, while another group consisted of six interviewees. Two were male, and eight were female. Most teachers had undergraduate qualifications; there was one Chinese language teacher, one mathematics teacher, four English teachers, two geography teachers, one tourism major teacher, and one head of political education. The average age of the teachers was 31.1 ±2.807 years.

2. Results of Interview with Teachers
(1) Teachers' Knowledge of AIDS

All teachers interviewed had heard of AIDS. They relate AIDS to: sex, drug-abuse, blood donation, blood transfusion, death, terrifying, frightful, affecting the next generation, expensive medical fees, and affecting the next few generations, etc.

Teachers said that they are aware of the three transmission routes, and that AIDS is not communicated through daily work and learning. Their knowledge of AIDS is mainly derived from television. The school has also distributed CDs and student readings.

(2) Behaviour towards Persons Living with HIV/AIDS
Some teachers believed that persons living with HIV must be given benevolence and care because they are victims as well as patients. These teachers also did not relate the illness to the transmission route because they believe that infection may have been caused by a one time mistake.

Some teachers related the disease to the route of infection. They believe that certain people were infected as a result of a moral flaw, but that some infected persons, such as children who were victims of mother-to-child transmission, are innocent.

(3) Attitude towards the Right of Children Orphaned by AIDS to Education
Even though the teachers surveyed had not come into contact with children orphaned by AIDS, they believed that these children have the right to education. The teachers also believe that teachers are responsible for and have a duty to help and protect these children.

(4) Acceptance by the School of the Difficulties of OVCs
Teachers believe that schools have difficulty accepting OVCs mainly because of parents. Many parents simply refuse to accept an OVC into the same class as their children. The school has little choice if parents will not yield. Protection of the rights of OVCs requires the joint efforts of every member in society.

The teachers revealed that if parents demand that OVCs be transferred to another school, they would talk directly with parents to try to convince them to change their minds. Teachers also try to explain to parents that giving OVCs the right to education does not cause any hazard to other students.

(5) Teachers' Responses and Difficulties if an Infected Student is in their Class
Teachers said that the identities of OVCs should be kept confidential if they have not been disclosed. There is no need to disclose a child's circumstances to other students and parents if the child is not infected. If an OVC's status has already been disclosed, then mitigating measures must be taken.

Some teachers also believe that the presence of an OVC in their class will put huge pressure on them, and it may make it difficult to communicate with other teachers or parents. Some parents may accept working alongside infected persons, but may not tolerate their children to be in contact with infected children. The teachers are of the opinion that parents' discrimination is closely related to their educational level.

Some teachers think that even though they can accept infected children, acceptance by other students is just as important. They made some suggestions on how the school should convince other students to accept and respect an OVC: the school and its teachers must do a good job at imparting knowledge of the disease, and conduct lessons to encourage scientific knowledge of HIV/AIDS. Teachers should also respect OVCs, so that other children will treat them normally. Teachers must lead by example. If teachers respect OVCs, the attitude of the other students will gradually improve.

(6) Opinions of teachers if the parent(s) of a student is (are) found to have been infected with AIDS, and the school requires that such student provide a blood test report every six months.
Teachers think that this measure is excessive, and will be a blow to OVCs. However, this measure is understandable, since it is for the benefit of the larger student population. Teachers believe that discrimination is also a form of mental isolation.

(7) Teachers' Recommendation on the Elimination of Discrimination in School
Most teachers believe that setting a good example on their part is critical in eliminating discrimination, and has an enormous impact on students and parents. Instead of discriminating against OVCs, teachers should respect OVCs' right to education, and should care for, sympathize with and help OVCs, as well as live and eat with them. This will inspire people to abandon their discrimination. That said, teachers should also take precautions to protect their own well-being. Thus, AIDS education for teachers must be clear and systematic, and should include measures like emergency tactics.

For the school, teachers suggested increasing primary and secondary AIDS education. Activities may be organized to promote understanding or educate students about the issue from a human rights perspective.

In terms of parents, teachers recommend that details about the disease should be more specific, and public coverage must reach the communities to create a caring atmosphere and to inspire society's acceptance of OVCs.

(IV) Results of Interviews with Persons Living with HIV

1. Overview of Infected Persons Interviewed
Two groups and a total of six people living with AIDS were interviewed. Each group consisted of three persons. All interviewees were from Henan. Two were male, four female. One was infected through blood transfusion, two through sexual activity, and the mechanism of transmission of the other three was unknown. Also, three were from non-governmental organizations (NGOs) working with AIDS victims, and the other three were "loving mothers" (*aixin mama*) – special volunteers who take care of

children – at a school for OVCs. The four females interviewed have children. One has four children, two of whom were studying in universities in other cities; one has three children, all of whom were attending an OVC school; one has two children, one of whom was in secondary school and the other in high school; one has children but no details were provided. One of the male interviewees was already a grandfather, and the other one lived alone. Interviews with HIV-infected persons reveal how their children were discriminated against.

2. Results of Interviews

(1) OVCs may face different forms of discrimination in school. For example, parents of schoolmates may forbid their children to play with them. Teachers may fail to understand these children, or even arrange for them to sit at the back of the class. Classmates stayed away and refused to play with them. Discrimination against persons living with HIV exists in different degrees and in different forms. Most forms of discrimination manifest themselves in the following ways: peculiar eye expressions; refusal to eat at the same table with the infected person; refusal to play with children of the infected person; some infected persons and their families moved away after their identities were exposed; children transferred to another school; discrimination of people within the same village who bear the same family name as the infected person; and infected persons were even abandoned by family members. Discrimination is a barrier that prevents many infected persons from taking medical examinations or from revealing their identities.

(2) Policy enforcement lacks support mechanisms to guarantee the rights of OVCs. The "Four Frees and One Care" and "Two Frees and One Subsidy" policies provide subsidies for OVCs in difficulty. However, application for such subsidies must be submitted through the school, and certain regions provide textbooks printed with the words "This book is provided free by the State." Procedures such as these will expose the identities of OVCs, and many of these children would rather forego their subsidies than reveal that they are HIV-positive or are from families with persons living with HIV.

(3) OVCs are usually unwilling to remain in the same school once their identities are exposed. Despite the availability of subsidies if they remain in the same place, many choose to transfer to another school.

(4) Schools will refuse to accept OVCs on other grounds. The new school may reject the student's transfer if it comes to know that the transferee or his/her parent is a person living with HIV.

(5) Parents of OVCs are usually reluctant to reveal the truth of their AIDS infection to their children. However, children will come to know of their parents' illness as they

grow older, and as the family receives frequent telephone calls and visits from officers of relevant government departments. Some know that their parents are sick but do not know what the illness is; others know that their parents are suffering from AIDS, but know little about the disease.

(6) Impact on the children. Parents of OVCs are worried that their children may not be understood if they attend public schools. Therefore, parents living with HIV send their children to schools for OVCs. Having HIV-infected parents affects the courtships and marriages of the children.

(V) Results of Interviews with OVCs

1. Overview of OVCs Interviewed
Nine OVCs were interviewed. Five were infected, four were children orphaned by AIDS. Of the five infected children, four were victims of mother-to-child transmission and one was infected through blood transfusion. The children were between the ages of 10 and 15, the mean age being 12.89 ±1.69 years. Six of the interviewees were males and three were females. All were studying at a school for OVCs in Shangshui County, Henan, at levels between primary 3 and 6.

2. Summary of Results of Interviews
(1) OVCs have a certain understanding of AIDS.

(2) OVCs are discriminated against in their original schools (public schools) by teachers, classmates and the parents of classmates. Some gave examples of discrimination: "I was put at the back of the class. I could not see the board"; "Classmates do not play with us. They ignored us"; "Classmates were cold to us"; "Classmates' parents told them not to play with us"; "The teachers will not be nice (to us) if they know (that we were from a family with persons living with AIDS). They will ignore us, and their facial expressions will change." OVCs were depressed, but had no one to confide in. Hence, they did not wish to return to their original school.

(3) Children said that they liked their current school (for OVCs) because "(they) are happy there, and no one discriminates against them," "the teachers are more caring," and "they feel better after going (to the school)."

(4) They believe that "discrimination means no one bothers with them or plays with them, people talk behind their backs and bully them, and boys fight with them."

(5) The reason for discrimination is that "people are afraid of being infected."

(6) OVCs hope that society and schools can provide assistance, that the school, their schoolmates and relatives will not discriminate against them but will treat them correctly, and that they will receive everybody's understanding, concern and love.

DISCUSSION

I. Policies

1. There are laws against discrimination based on HIV/AIDS and laws governing the protection of the right of children to education in China. To some extent, these laws and regulations have been successful in guaranteeing the right of OVCs to education.
2. Implementation of policy is inconsistent in different areas.
3. Inadequate support measures and regulatory enforcement of laws and policies.
4. Low awareness of the laws and regulations among the public. Therefore, greater effort is required in terms of promoting the laws and policies.
5. Disparity in definition between the law and reality.

II. The Public

Building a discrimination-free environment in schools depends on the concerted efforts of the government, society, schools and the public (principals, teachers, students and students' parents). Hence, this study looks at the attitudes of students, parents and teachers, and explores the possibility of creating a caring and discrimination-free environment for OVCs.

1. Positive attitude, such as sympathy and care, of the public (including students, parents, teachers and the general public) towards OVCs.
Our study revealed that the majority of the public is sympathetic to and care for OVCs, and believe that they have the right to education. Between 60.7 percent and 77.6 percent of the public believe that children living with HIV should continue with their studies; between 27.0 percent and 79.0 percent are willing (or allow their children) to attend the same class as OVCs. If an HIV carrier was studying in the same class, most people chose not to discriminate against the person, but to help him/her instead. This indicates that most of the public respect the rights of an infected person, had positive intentions toward infected persons, and are willing to help when they are in need. The attitude and positive intention of this group are essential to the creation of a discrimination-free environment. Thus, people belonging to this group should be given guidance and encouragement.

2. Despite a positive attitude towards OVCs, some members of the public still display attitudes of avoidance and rejection if there is an OVC near them.

The results of our study also indicate that 2.7 percent to 35.8 percent of the public have clearly expressed that students living with HIV should not be allowed to go to school, or that they will not (or will not allow their children to) attend the same class as an OVC. Assuming there is an OVC in the same class as their children, 2.5 percent to 13.6 percent of the public exhibit discriminatory behaviour such as demanding that the infected person transfer to another school or class. Hence, in the event of an OVC in the same class, students, parents and teachers will tend to avoid and reject the OVC. Discrimination from various sources remains unavoidable. Our study results are consistent with other local and foreign research results.[10]

Common reasons for public discrimination against persons living with HIV and against OVCs.
By analyzing a single or multiple reasons for discrimination against different groups, and by reading the results of the analysis in tandem with qualitative analyses, we have derived the following key reasons for discrimination:

(1) Lack of a complete and logical understanding of AIDS.
It is important to accurately identify the transmission route of AIDS and differentiate what is right from wrong. For example, believing that AIDS is transmitted by eating at the same table as infected persons will aggravate discrimination against persons with AIDS.[11] Results from regression and correlation analyses show that members of the public who received high scores for knowledge (especially non-transmission routes and prevention) tend to have a more positive attitude. This shows that better knowledge can somewhat alter attitudes. When compiling and analyzing the answers to the open-ended questions, we discovered that most of the public was afraid that they (or their children) would be infected. This is revealed by their responses to the statement, "persons living with AIDS should not be allowed to go to school." Thus, the public's knowledge of AIDS is insufficient to provide them with enough confidence to prevent the transmission of AIDS. Investigations by Herek *et al.*[12] discovered that despite the respondents being very clear about how AIDS is transmitted, very few know of the non-transmission routes. Those who think that AIDS is transmitted through normal daily contact tend to be even more fearful of coming into contact with infected persons. They will also support punitive policies and infringements of the rights of infected persons.

(2) Fear of AIDS.
AIDS is a communicable disease with no vaccine at the moment, and has a high mortality rate. Compared to diseases that do not pose apparent threats, AIDS patients tend to face greater discrimination. Study results indicate that most will associate words, such as "death," "incurable," "terrifying," "fear" and "frightful" at the mention of AIDS. The public is worried of getting infected by going to school with OVCs. Despite knowing that the probability of getting infected is small, people do not wish to

take the chance. The theory of accusation[13,14] interprets the stigma and discrimination faced by AIDS victims as the public's accusation and fear of AIDS patients. The theory proposes that when people are threatened by AIDS and are situated in a society with a highly dangerous communicable disease, they often direct accusations at other social groups instead of censuring the inner group to which they belong. AIDS stigma and discrimination is a natural emotional response by the public. People try to control risk and to ensure their own safety by accusing the stigmatized group.

(3) Discrimination against AIDS is, to some extent, discrimination against the perceived wrongful behaviour and morals of the infected party.
This study reveals that certain members of the public believe that AIDS is caused by immorality, such as drug taking and casual sex. The majority think that infection due to blood transfusion and mother-to-child transmission deserves sympathy, and infection due to drug abuse and casual sex does not. Therefore, we can conclude that people are sympathetic towards the infected persons, and discrimination may be directed at their wrongful behaviour. Such discrimination may spill over to AIDS patients infected through other transmission routes.

Through regression theory and judgment of responsibility, Weiner et al.[15,16] explored cause ascription, judgment of responsibility, and emotional response to events that trigger stigma and repulsion, and the relevant strategies in response to such behaviours. Research by Zhou Fanglian et al.[17] has also proved that the public tends to think that public attitudes toward persons living with HIV is related to the cause of a person's infection. Compared to uncontrollable causes (such as contaminated blood), controllable causes (such as sex and drugs) produce a stronger judgment of fault, more negative emotions, less sympathy, and less willingness to help the infected person.[18,19]

(4) Limited knowledge of rights and policies.
This study shows that the degree of public understanding of rights and policies will also affect the attitude of people towards infected persons and OVCs. Hartell et al. state that the lack of knowledge of AIDS-related laws and policies will not support or protect the rights of infected persons, and discrimination will continue.[20] Studies have discovered that the public has little knowledge of the policies on this issue. Therefore, despite the presence of relevant laws, the rights of OVCs may continue to be ignored or even infringed upon. Furthermore, an infected person or patient who has inadequate knowledge of his rights and policies will not be able to take timely advantage of the law in order to protect her own rights.

(5) Inadequate, inappropriate, and superficial AIDS publicity and education.
From the feedback through interviews with the public, many felt that the dissemination of knowledge about AIDS is inadequate, that the slogan kind of publicity will not do the

job, and that systematic education is necessary. Current publicity focuses on describing AIDS as a disease. For example, telling the public it is a fatal disease exaggerates the outcome of the disease and leads to fear. Very little has been mentioned about the prevention of AIDS, and people do not know how to alleviate their fear. The public also suggested that the content of publicity campaigns should "include more information on prevention, concern and helping people to look at the disease more positively." The format of the public ads should be more audience-friendly and fun.

(6) Discrimination may arise from improper media reporting.
AIDS-related reporting by the media should avoid using descriptions that may lead to discrimination, such as differentiating between "not innocent" infected persons from "innocent" persons, or using words such as "high risk group" or "AIDS orphan." The media should also refrain from disclosing the identities of OVCs or any information that may lead to speculation of an OVC's identity. An OVC's right to education may be prejudiced, or there may be greater discrimination, if his/her privacy cannot be guaranteed.

3. Anti-discrimination characteristics of students, parents and teachers.
(1) Students' positive attitude increases with their level of study. Compared to students who have not been educated, those who have been educated tend to be more positive. AIDS-prevention education for primary students should be stepped up.

Results of our study show that anti-discriminatory behaviours amongst students are related to their education status. A higher education level is correlated with a greater tendency towards anti-discriminatory behaviour. As such, discriminatory behaviour is more apparent among lower level students. Also, our qualitative analysis has found that discrimination among primary students stem from their ignorance of AIDS. Their discrimination is not directed only at AIDS victims, but any student who is different, such as one who gets poor grades or has unusual looks, etc., will be treated differently. This could be related to their lack of rational thinking and the lack of understanding of the concept of equality. This is why OVCs may face a certain degree of discrimination in primary school.

Additionally, educated students scoring higher in anti-discriminatory behaviour indicate that education produces significant results in establishing anti-discriminatory behaviour. Thus, this study reveals that it is necessary to provide elementary education on AIDS prevention. The content may be simpler, since the aim is to allow elementary school students to have a basic understanding of AIDS, so that they will not fear or discriminate against AIDS victims. Education will also teach them self-protection skills, and will instil in them the spirit of humanity, and respect for people and for equality. Teachers who were interviewed also believed that AIDS education for primary and secondary students should be augmented. The *Outline for AIDS Prevention Education for*

Primary and Secondary Students, issued by the Ministry of Education in 2003, provided that secondary schools should organize six periods of AIDS prevention education lessons, and four periods in high school. There is no specific requirement for primary school. Anti-discrimination education is required for high schools, but no provision for the same is set forth for secondary schools. Therefore, we recommend that AIDS education should commence at the primary level, and anti-discrimination education should be included at the secondary level.

(2) In relative terms, discrimination among parents is greater; parents have to balance their children's safety and morality.

Our study has found that parents who are agreeable to having their children study in the same class as children whose parents are living with AIDS account for only 40.3 percent. This percentage is lower than those of children (58.9 percent) and teachers (79.0 percent). The percentage of parents who will allow their children to study in the same class as students living with AIDS is only 32.6 percent, which is also lower than that of students (49.7 percent) and teachers (62.0 percent). 13.6 percent of parents selected the option, "demand that the infected person transfer to another school or class." This is a higher percentage than that of students (6.7 percent) and teachers (2.5 percent).

Some students believe that the main source of discrimination comes from parents, because of their concern and care for their children. Teachers interviewed also believed that schools have difficulty accepting OVCs mainly because of parents. Many parents simply cannot accept an OVC studying in the same class as their child. Interviews with persons living with AIDS and OVCs also indicate that other parents will tell their children not to play with the children of persons with AIDS.

From responses to open-ended questions in the questionnaire, parents revealed that many of them were in a dilemma, and are caught between their children's safety and their own sense of morality. Parents are worried that their children lack the ability to protect themselves, and that they will be infected with AIDS. Thus, despite the low risk of infection, parents are not willing to take the risk.

(3) Discrimination by teachers against OVCs is relatively less, and most teachers are aware that they should set an example in the creation of an anti-discriminatory education environment. However, teachers think that the school's acceptance of OVCs will generate tremendous pressure.

Based on the study results, teachers' discrimination is comparatively less than the other groups. Results of interviews with teachers also indicate that they believe that OVCs have the right to education, and that teachers have the responsibility and duty to help and protect these children. Teachers realize that their own behaviour is an important example for students and parents. However, teachers also believe that they will be under tremendous pressure if there is really an OVC in class, and that it is necessary to communicate with other teachers and parents. Students may not accept an OVC in class. From our quantitative analysis, we also found that 10.5 percent of the teachers have made it explicit that they did not wish to have an AIDS-infected student in their class. A small number have also selected the discriminatory option, "demand the infected person to transfer to another school or class." Interviews with infected persons and OVCs indicate that some teachers exhibit discriminatory attitudes. Such discriminatory attitudes may be more prominent in rural areas. Therefore, one of the things we must do is improve AIDS and anti-discrimination education for teachers to create a caring and discrimination-free environment. On the other hand, teachers hope that their education can be more systematic and clear, such as teaching them how to deal with situations involving OVC students.

III. OVCs

1. OVCs face different degrees of discrimination in school.
During interviews with infected persons and OVCs, we discovered that OVCs face varying degrees of discrimination from teachers, classmates and parents of classmates. Discrimination manifests itself in different forms, such as having to sit in the last row in class, being ostracized and rejected by classmates, having classmates' parents tell their children to not play with them, etc. OVCs usually prefer not to continue their education in the same school as soon as their identities are revealed, even though they will receive subsidies if they stay in that school. Most prefer to transfer to another school, or even move out of the community. However, in the process of their transfer, the new school may find other reasons to reject them if it comes to know that the child is an infected person or comes from a family with an infected person. Furthermore, State subsidies may not benefit them, since they will need to apply for such subsidies through the school, and the village committee at the school; the applicant's family's domicile will also assess the application, and put up in the public notice before the subsidy can be disbursed. In certain areas, subsidized students would receive books printed with the words, "This book is provided free by the State." This makes it difficult to protect the privacy of OVCs, and they face discrimination in school. Discrimination is traumatic to OVCs, and will result in anxiety, fear and a sense of hopelessness. Their grades will deteriorate, they will begin to detest school, refuse to socialize with people or will socialize only with people who have had similar experiences (other OVCs), or even drop out of school.[21]

2. The stigma experienced by OVCs is stronger than the stigma perceived by the public. Hence, OVCs choose to stay away from the school environment to avoid or reduce discrimination.

According to studies by Berger *et al.*,[22] the stigma felt by OVCs is the perception by persons with HIV of the actual or possible social deprivation (incomplete acceptance by society, or rejection by society); of limitation or deprivation of opportunities (e.g. housing, employment or medical treatment); and of negative changes in social identity (how they are perceived by others). The stigma felt by OVCs is affected by two factors: the infected person's perception of social attitudes, and his personal knowledge. Perceived stigma can lead to different outcomes, such as change in self-image, emotional response toward the discriminator, concealment of illness or escaping from society to avoid or reduce discrimination. In our study's stigma questionnaire, the attitude scores of OVCs in aspects such as emotional response and education are lower than those of students and parents. Hence, it indicates that OVCs have stronger stigma. For variables such as "It is safe for the child to play with Xiaoli" in Case 1 and "Xiaolang will threaten the health of other students if he remains in the school," all reveal negative scores for OVCs. This indicates that they (infected persons' personal knowledge) also believe that it is unsafe to be with HIV-infected persons and children orphaned by AIDS. At the same time, the scores for attitudes, such as emotional response, awareness of rights, and education, that they experience were lower than the actual attitudes of parents (infected persons' perception of social attitudes). This may be the initial feeling. OVCs may opt to escape from their present school to avoid or reduce discrimination because of the presence of stigma. For the question, "Hopefully, a special school will be built, so that Xiaolang can go to school with children of similar circumstances" in the stigma questionnaire, OVCs obtained negative scores. This indicates that they agree to the building of a special school. This could be a means of escapism for them, and a means for them to avoid or reduce discrimination.

3. The public and OVCs hope to see special schools for OVCs built.
During group interviews with students, some students said that a special school should be built, so that all OVCs can be put in the same school. The same findings were obtained in the analyses of the responses from students, parents and OVCs in the stigma questionnaire and through interviews with OVCs. Restrictions imposed in an educational setting (e.g., segregation), is one of the indicators that determine if discrimination exists in the education sector under the *Protocol for the Identification of Discrimination against People Living with HIV* by UNAIDS. Many students in the groups interviewed think that building a special school is discrimination against OVCs. However, at this stage, when social discrimination is not eliminated, children studying in public schools will have to deal with different forms of discrimination. This discrimination is extremely detrimental to the physical and mental development of OVCs. They may develop various psychological problems, such as lacking a sense of security, solitude, unwillingness to study, feelings of inferiority, depression, anxiety, anger, and the feeling of being insignificant. As such, it may be a better option to build

a special school at this point. The problem is that, in the special school, the students' standard of education is much lower than children of the same age due to the lack of education resources, poor teaching facilities, as well as insufficient teachers and their limited abilities. On the one hand, special care centres and schools must be established; on the other hand, more has to be done to enable public schools to create a caring and discrimination-free environment for OVCs, so that all students are able to return to society, be respected, and will not be discriminated against, marginalized or ostracized.

RECOMMENDATIONS

1. Improve support measures for enforcement of laws and policies, and increase regulatory enforcement. Implementation of care policies depends on contact with persons living with HIV/AIDS. If protection of the privacy of infected persons and their family members is neglected during policy implementation, the benefits of care and support policies will not be enjoyed by their intended recipients, and may even lead to discrimination. Therefore, putting in place the necessary support measures for law and policy enforcement will better protect the rights of infected persons and their family members. Furthermore, issuing of relief materials and resources should be subject to more stringent regulatory management in order to ensure that all relief materials are given to the infected persons and their family members.
2. Where possible, discrimination should be defined and discriminatory behaviour prohibited under the law. This will better protect the rights of persons living with HIV/ AIDS and of OVCs, and will be conducive to the creation of a discrimination-free environment.
3. Government authorities should increase publicity surrounding laws and policies, and on HIV/AIDS and anti-discrimination education. Insufficient awareness of AIDS-related laws and regulations will undermine anti-discrimination efforts. The government has announced a series of policies, such as the "Four Frees and One Care" policy, which were, to a certain extent, effective at ensuring the rights of OVCs to education. However, our study has shown that public awareness of these policies is low. Therefore, the focus must be on building awareness of laws and policies. Knowledge of HIV/AIDS is required for anti-discrimination. The government is responsible for disseminating educational information on HIV/AIDS and anti-discrimination.
4. Recommend to the Ministry of Education to include HIV/AIDS education at the primary level and anti-discrimination education at the secondary level. Specifically, to revise the *Outline for AIDS Prevention Education for Primary and Secondary Students* to include clear provisions that include AIDS-prevention education in primary schools, and anti-discrimination education in secondary schools. Although there is anti-discrimination education in secondary schools in some areas, the *Outline* should provide the authority to this requirement binding. This way, secondary students will have a definite understanding of the significance of anti-discrimination in AIDS prevention.

5. Regulate media reports to ensure that reporting is scientific and objective, and that the opinions contain healthy guidelines for the public. Most students, parents, teachers and the general public obtain their knowledge of HIV/AIDS from mass media. Thus, the media's perspective will affect the attitude of the public towards HIV/AIDS. Besides ensuring scientific and objective reporting, media reports should be positive and audience-friendly. This will help eradicate fear and inspire an anti-discrimination attitude.

6. The school and the community should target HIV/AIDS and anti-discrimination education and publicity at parents and teachers. The attitudes of parents and teachers cannot be neglected if discrimination against OVCs is to be discouraged, and if the right of OVCs to education is to be protected. Even if schools have accepted these children, parents may apply pressure on the school and demand that OVCs transfer to another school. Teachers may also refuse to teach OVCs. Therefore, schools must encourage publicity and education on HIV/AIDS, and aim anti-discrimination programs at teachers and parents. For example, the "Hand in Hand" (*xiao shou la da shou*) initiative, where pertinent information is disseminated to parents by the school or through the parents' group at an opportune time, should be encouraged. There must be different forms of publicity, such as inviting expert speakers to give special talks, field visits to institutions where AIDS patients and OVCs congregate, or invite persons living with AIDS to talk about their own experiences. This will allow parents and teachers to truly understand the experiences of persons living with HIV/AIDS, and to improve empathy so that their fear of AIDS will be eliminated over time.

7. Use teachers as living examples to create a discrimination-free education environment. During our interviews with teachers, many of them realized that their behaviour is critical. Teachers must serve as role models in the elimination of discrimination against OVCs and to promote their right to education. Teachers' behaviour directly affects the students and their parents. Teachers who respect and care for OVCs will provide positive and constructive guidance for students. Teachers must communicate with parents who fail to understand the reasoning behind this behaviour.

8. Increase psychological care for OVCs, help them to get to know themselves, and encourage them to express their own emotions. To achieve this, there must be intensive research into the type of psychological care suitable for the Chinese socio-cultural tradition, and to ensure that OVCs will have good psychological health and sound character development.[23]

ENDNOTES

[1]   Joint United Nations Program on HIV/AIDS (UNAIDS). *Protocol for the Identification of Discrimination Against People Living with HIV*, 2000.
[2]   http://www.unchina.org/unaids/document percent20link.htm.

3   B. E. Berger, C. E. Ferrans, and F. R. Lashley. "Measuring Stigma in People with HIV: Psychometric Assessment of the HIV Stigma Scale," *Research in Nursing and Health*, 2001, 24, 518-529.

4   Y. Yang, K. L. Zhang, K. Y. Chan, *et al.*, "Institutional and structural forms of HIV-related discrimination in health care: a study set in Beijing," *AIDS Care*, 2005, 17 (supplement 2): S129-S140.

5   State Council Working Committee to Combat AIDS, *Report on the 2005 Declaration of Commitment on HIV/AIDS*, 2005.

6   State Council Working Committee to Combat AIDS, the UN Theme Group on HIV/AIDS in China, *Joint Assessment of HIV/AIDS Prevention, Treatment and Care in China (2007)*, 2007.

7   China Ministry of Health, UNAIDS, World Health Organization, *China AIDS Epidemic and Prevention Progress 2005*, 2006.

8   http://www.ha.xinhuanet.com/add/zfzx/2007-09/10/content_11102468.htm.

9   http://www.cqjlp.gov.cn/zwgk/3884.htm.

10 Gregory M. Herek, John P. Capitanio, "Public Rections to AIDS in the United States: A Second Decade of Stigma," American Journal of Public Health, 1993, 83, p. 574-577; Ma Yinghua, Hu Peijin, Chen Yichen, "A Study on the Needs for Education in AIDS-Related Knowledge, Attitude, Behaviour and Health of Secondary Students and Teachers in Yunnan Province" (*"Yunnan sheng zhong xue sheng yu jiao shi dui ai zi bing xiang guan zhi shi, tai du, xing wei he jian kang jiao yu xu qiu de yan jiu"*), *Chinese Journal of Public Health*, 1999, 15 (6), p. 541-544; Yan Jingyi, Xu Liuchen, Yang Yulin, "Behavioural Analysis on the Knowledge of and Attitude towards AIDS for 5870 Secondary and University Students in Shandong Province" (*"5870 ming da zhong xue sheng ai zi bing zhi shi tai du xing wei fen xi"*), *Chinese Journal of School Health*, 2006, 27(2), p. 163-165; Li Guiyin, Chu Tianxin, He Xiong *et al.*, "Investigation on the AIDS Knowledge, Attitude and Behaviour of Parents of Secondary and High School Students," *Chinese Journal of Public Health*, 2006, 22 (8), p. 899-900.

11 Joint United Nations Program on HIV/AIDS (UNAIDS), *Monitoring the Declaration of Commitment on HIV/AID*, Guidelines on Construction of Core Indications. Geneva, Switzerland, 2005, 7.

12 G. M. Herek, J. P. Capitanio, and K. F. Widaman, "HIV-related stigma and knowledge in the United States: Prevalence and Trends, 1991-1999," *American Journal of Public Health*, 2002, 92 (1), p. 371-377.

13 Helene Joffe, *Risk and "The Other,"* Cambridge: Cambridge University Press, 1999.

14 Yang Ling, Zhu Yawen, Li Jiansheng, "A Review of Research on AIDS Stigma" (*"ai zi bing wu ming ya jiu ping shu"*), *Journal of Northwest Normal University (Social Sciences)*, 2007, 44 (4), p. 59-63.

15 B. Weiner, "Intrapersonal and Interpersonal Theories of Motivation from an Attributional Perspective," *Educational Psychology Review*, 2000, 12 (1), p. 1-14.

16 B. Weiner, "A native psychologist examines bad luck and the concept of responsibility," *The moist*, 2003, 86 (1), p. 996-1010.

17 Zhou Fanglian, Zhang Aiqin, Fang Lainyi *et al.*, "Responsibility Attribution and Punitive Behavioural Response of University Students towards Person Living with AIDS" (*"da xue sheng dui ai zi bing huan zhe de ze ren gui yin ji cheng jie xing wei fan ying"*), *Psychological Science*, 2005; 28(5), p. 1216-1219.

18 Udo, Rudolph, Scott C. Roesch, Tobias Greitemeyer, *et al.*, "A meta-analysis review of helping giving and aggression from an attributional perspective: Contributions to a general theory of motivation," *Cognition and Emotion*, 2004 18(6), p. 815-848.

19   Gisela Steins and Bernard Weiner, "The Influence of Perceived Responsibility and Personality Characteristics on the Emotional and Behavioral Reactions to People with AIDS," *Journal of Social Psychology*, 1999, 139(4), p. 487-495.

20   C. G. Hartell and S. Maile, "HIV/AIDS and Education: A study on how a selection of school governing bodies in Mpumalanga understand, respond to and implement legislation and policies on HIV/AIDS," *International Journal of Education Development*, 24(2004), p. 183-199.

21   UNICEF China HIV/AIDS Program, Booklet on the *Psychosocial Care of AIDS Orphans and Vulnerable Children*, Beijing: Peking University Medical Press, 2005, p. 20-27.

22   B. E. Berger, C. E. Ferrans, F. R. Lashley, "Measuring stigma in people with HIV: Psychometric assessment of the HIV stigma scale," *Research in Nursing and Health*, 2001, 24, p. 518-529.

23   Liu Jitong, "Policy Recommendations for the Welfare Building of AIDS Orphans and Vulnerable Children," *China Social Welfare*, 2007 (9), p. 19-21.

CHAPTER FOURTEEN

The State of Life and Survival Strategies of AIDS-Infected Rural Women

An Analysis Based on Field Investigations in Selected Areas of Henan

Qin Mingrui and Lai Xiaole

I. PROPOSITION OF QUESTIONS

There is a special group of persons living with AIDS in China. They are farmers in Henan Province who contracted AIDS from selling blood. They are special because: firstly, nearly all of them are farmers; secondly, their infection is connected with government behaviour; thirdly, a blood-borne AIDS infection of such a large scale is rare anywhere in the world. There is yet another neglected group within this special group: the women. Females are often in a more difficult situation than males. As infected persons or family members of infected persons, the survival tactics they employ to manage the predicament brought forth by AIDS and their state of life are the key areas of concern of this paper. Although there have been relevant reports on the situation of infected females, there are few comparative studies on gender structure and gender behaviour. Reports or studies of such events normally focus on either their official political context or a government omission, discrimination suffered by the victim, and descriptions of tragic circumstances. The gender issue usually gets lost within the larger context. Those that have addressed the gender issue have usually considered AIDS-infected females as a unitary entity, neglecting the intrinsic differences within this larger group. As of today, no detailed study from a social gender perspective on the daily lives and behaviour of females who contracted AIDS by selling blood has ever been conducted.

On this basis, the authors attempt to answer the following important questions:

1. What are the survival tactics chosen by the females or their family members prior to contracting AIDS?
2. What are the bases of the choices of survival tactics of females living in the AIDS village? How are these bases related to the various roles played by the females?

3. What is the relationship between the outcome of the survival tactic chosen by females in the AIDS Village and the motives for their subsequent choices?

4. What are the changes in the females' motives and bases for choosing survival tactics under the extreme circumstances after having contracted AIDS?

II. RESEARCH METHODOLOGY AND RESEARCH MATERIALS

This analysis is based mainly on experience materials, including those obtained through field research in a county in Henan, conducted by the project team for the "Study on the Survival State of Females Living with AIDS," to which the authors are a party.[1] Our analysis is mainly qualitative. This is a method commonly used for feminist studies. Its aim is to discover the experience of the subject of the study, and to understand the subject's world from his/her experience and perspective. It avoids using social or academic prejudices or stereotypes to understand or judge a social phenomenon or an event (Xiong Bingchun, 2001). Because of inherent limitations, case studies are often regarded as unrepresentative or inferential. However, case studies often allow us to see structural problems, as well as understand interpersonal relationships, and the relationship between people and their society. It provides us with a window to observe how the society works. In this paper, by conducting in-depth interviews with females living in the AIDS village and analyzing such interviews, we discern the cultural and social perceptions hidden in the females' survival methods, as well as the compromise and tug-of-war between females' choice of survival methods and the social structure.

1. Selection of Interviewees

In June 2006, our project team conducted field research in a particular county in Kaifeng City, Henan Province. The area is a well-know "AIDS County" in Henan because of its high prevalence of AIDS. There are two reason for choosing this "special" group of persons who were infected from selling blood as our study subjects: (1) Since the discovery of the *xuehuo* ("blood disaster") in Henan in 1999, this much talked-about incident was gradually forgotten. Reports relating to the incident are rarely seen nowadays. The state of the lives of persons living with AIDS in the Henan villages is one of our main concerns; (2) Our understanding of this "special" group of persons is derived mainly from papers and writings by the media and the general public. They have, without exception, reflected the sorry state of the AIDS village. We do not deny the truth of the descriptions. But from a sociological perspective, we are more concerned with the response of the individuals after their infection, especially the different responses of the different genders concerned. Before carrying out our investigation in the village, our research focused on the state of discrimination of infected females. But during our interviews, we discovered that females encounter extremely complex situations after they or their relatives have been infected with HIV. The simple belief that the female victims are discriminated against does not reveal the entire picture. We therefore began paying more attention to the daily lives of these females, and saw their tears and laughter, as well as their struggle and diligence, under the devastation of AIDS.

2. Interview Method

We employed in-depth interviews for two of the villages we investigated. We conducted interviews directly in the subjects' homes. In the other two villages, we combined small-group interviews and in-depth interviews. The interview materials were documented using voice recording and manual records, based on which text materials were prepared after the interview. The interviews were semi-structured. An interview outline was designed before the interviews, during which the outline was later amended. This was especially true for the small-group interviews, as we basically allowed the interviewees to speak freely. We merely listened to their narration. Where necessary, we reminded the interviewee to refrain from digressing too far from the topic. This method of research allowed us to collate a lot of materials. In-depth interviews are usually constrained by the subjective intents and behaviour motives of the interviewer and interviewee. Indeed, this happened during our investigation. We often met with the following difficulty during our investigation: the interviewee failed to recall the date of a certain event. However, by using certain questioning methods and changing tactics, we were able to elicit the interviewee's recollection of the relevant date. For example, the first time some interviewees sold blood was a long time ago (more than twenty years for some), and they could not recall the specific time-frame. However, the villagers have a special way of remembering time: they usually recall an incident by connecting it with another event that has greater significance to them. For example, some were able to derive the first time when they sold blood by basing it on when they were married or the ages of their children. We also employed cross-verification to determine the reliability of certain information. As the time of occurrence has long passed, recollection based on individual memory may be wrong. Fortunately, as there were common experiences, the authenticity in the information which we received was evaluated through the cross-verification of the experiences of different interviewees. We tried to approach the original situation as closely as possible. This method was of particular importance for certain major events.

3. Interview Materials

22 cases and 46 parties from 5 villages (*cun*) were involved in our interviews: 13 from Kongjiacun, 14 from Ruanjiacun, 11 from Wangxiangcun, 7 from Hanji, and one from Xigangcun. 30 were females and 16 were males. Among the persons living with AIDS, 5 were male and 20 were female. 18 were family members of persons living with AIDS; 3 included a village doctor, a village head and a member of a non-governmental organization. Among the 30 females interviewed, 20 were infected with AIDS; the

remaining 10 were family members of infected persons. All infected persons interviewed were married with one or more children. For the infected females, 3 were more than 55 years of age, 3 were between 40 and 54, and the remaining 14 were between 28 and 39 years. All had primary education or lower. Except for one, who was infected by her husband, the rest were infected through selling blood. Having lower education than the males, most females had only primary or lower education (90 percent of the female interviewees).

The age of most of the females fell within the range of between 28 and 39 years. Due to the small number of male interviewees, we were unable to reach any conclusion as to their age categories. In terms of education distribution, the education level of females was clearly lower than that of males.

III. SOCIAL GENDER STRUCTURE AND SURVIVAL TACTICS OF FEMALES IN CHINESE RURAL FAMILIES

"The society in the countryside is one that differentiates the male from the female. It is also a stable society." (Jai Xiaotong, 1998: 47). To the village women, the gender structure in this stable society is the basis of their survival. Home is the place where their mode of survival is best evinced. This paper discusses the influence of the family's social gender structure on their mode of survival, i.e. family power, family finances, division of labour and customs. In essence, these four aspects are closely interrelated, therefore inalienable from each other.

1. Social Gender and Family Power

Without doubt, families in the countryside in present-day China are male-centred. Male-centredness differs from "patriarchy" to some extent. Patriarchy refers to a gender system passed down from history. But the "male-centredness" we refer to is a specific reference, a description of a specific phenomenon. What reflects the family power structure most directly in our interview materials is that local women address their husbands as "our boss at home" (*an dangjia de*) or "our shopkeeper" (*an zhanggui de*). This power structure is exhibited through the division of family roles and different activities. Engels attributes the unequal power relations and systems in the family to the emergence and development of the private ownership system. Before the emergence of the private ownership system, both production labour provided by males and domestic labour provided by females offered the same social significance, i.e. both genders participated in the production of survival necessities. However, when production for exchange activities emerged outside of the family, the work females did became family labour that served the purpose of maintaining the family. Karen Sacks (1998) corrected the historical hypothesis proposed by Engels. She believes that the appearance of the private ownership system and status on the scene is not necessarily the foundation of gender repression. She proposed the concept of "social adults," and believed that the social and family status of males and females relates to the non-social adult identity of women. To Sacks, participation in social labour activities is the only way to become a social adult.

The Chinese traditional society is a family-centred society. In relation to individual-centredness, family-centredness emphasizes that individual behaviours and social relationships must revolve around the family or the family clan. Any individual or social conduct must be based on interests of the family or the family clan. However, the "individual" of this view differs in that the power and status of a female as an individual in a patriarchical family is essentially different from that of a male. From a social gender standpoint, the culture of "family centredness" normally requires the female to sacrifice her personal power and status to protect the same for the male in the family. The reason is because the status of the male represents the status of the family (Tan Lin, Chen Weimin, 2001: 145).

This tradition of family-centredness in the Henan villages in which we conducted our interviews remains deeply rooted. However, the intrinsic qualities of family-centredness have experienced some changes. Our interview materials clearly indicate that "family" refers to the small family formed by husband and wife and children below the age of majority, instead of the traditional large family. Females continue to make the protection of the family's interests their first priority; they do not regard it as a "sacrifice" of individual power. In their hearts, the husband is no longer the family's only representative; instead, both husband and wife are protectors of the family's interests.

Family power relations in rural areas are mainly embodied in husband-and-wife relationships and mother-daughter-in-law relationships. Also, the power of decision-making in important family matters fully demonstrates the power relation in the family. The following section describes three aspects of family power relations.

(1) Husband and Wife Relations

Wives in the rural areas of Henan address their husbands as "our boss at home" (*an dangjia de*) or "our shopkeeper" (*an zhanggui de*). Instead of being mere appellations, these titles contain a string of power relations. Where we conducted our study, most married couples stay with the husband's family (*congfuju zhidu*). Wherever the hometown of the bride or the groom may be, the bride marries into the groom's family. This post-marriage mode of residency reflects, on the one hand, that the family member network is built upon social gender. Under the *congfuju* system, the bride enters the groom's existing relative network after marrying into the family; she gradually distances herself from her parents' relative network. Under this system, the male's relatives are "their own people" (*zijiren*), whereas the female's relatives are "outsiders" (*wairen*). In terms of rights and duties, such differentiation gives rise to many relationships and expectations of the female, the most important being the mother-daughter-in-law relationship and childbearing expectation. After marriage, it is the duty of the daughter-in-law to care for her husband's parents. On the other hand, caring for her own parents takes on more of an assistance nature. Even parents who are recipients of care believe that the persons who are immediately responsible for caring for them are their sons, daughters-in-law and unmarried daughters. Most do not wish to depend on their married daughters to take care of them during old age (Tan Lin, Chen Weimin, 2001: 71). There is a Chinese saying: "having a filial daughter-in-law beats having a filial son." Thus, the ever-present preference for sons will no longer be regarded as unusual. As females distance themselves from the living environment with which they are familiar to re-adapt to a new group with whom they make frequent social contacts, married women have less family-endowed social resources compared to their husbands. Women are now subordinated to their husbands and their husbands' families (Tan Lin, Chen Weimin, 2001: 72); "*an dangjia de*" becomes someone whom every married woman relies on.

Among the groups of persons who were infected with AIDS from selling blood, women account for the largest percentage. However, males have a higher frequency of selling blood (Jin Wei, ed., 2004). This is closely related to local family powers and the gender structure. Given that the local economy is mainly agricultural, the natural division of labour between the male and female prevails. Quoting what the women say, the men are the pillars. When the man falls ill, the family collapses. That is the reason why most women voluntarily undertake the risk of hurting their health, or perhaps even of getting infected, in order to sell blood for money. The following female interviewee's words are evidence:

A (interviewer): Has your *zhanggui* (husband) ever sold blood?
RU (reference number of interviewee; determined by the surname's first or first two letters of the alphabet): No. I don't allow him to. This is bad for health. The family relies entirely on him. The women's chores are not as physically strenuous as the men's. The children were young then. We could not afford to have both of us going out.

The choice of selling or not selling blood depends on whether the sale will benefit the family. And this seems to be the common understanding between all married women. In the aforesaid case, the wife believed that selling blood was detrimental to one's health, yet she herself sold blood and insisted on forbidding her husband to sell blood because the family depended on him to work. However, during our interviews, we found that this interviewee's husband said that his wife's forbidding it was not the main reason for his not selling blood. The main reason was because he is timid, and faints at the sight of blood.

There was a female who was very knowledgeable among those whom we interviewed. She was previously the women's leader in the village, and her husband contracted AIDS after selling blood only once. She felt that selling blood for money was not worth the risk. While she thought that "the man of the household falling sick is the collapse of half the sky," she remained very strong. This is what she said: "there is still six *mu* of land, and another four or five *mu* of contracted land. I've never allowed him to work in the fields. Not even the spraying of pesticides." There were many such women among those whom we interviewed, even including those who have contracted AIDS themselves. The amount of labour undertaken by such women has far exceeded the traditional division of labour between the genders. But in their minds, the husband is still the "head of family."

A local NGO officer once told us that in the rural areas, a woman usually remarries as soon as her husband dies. The children are abandoned. But when a woman falls ill, the man will take care of her (He added that he had only heard of one incident of a husband divorcing his wife when she contracted AIDS during his two years in the area). Generally, the women interviewed were relatively satisfied with the care that their husbands gave them. The following dialogue is a case in point:

A: The work in the fields is all done by your husband?

G: I follow him to do some light labour. He is really good to me. I didn't prepare a meal during the entire winter. He also didn't go out to do jobs...stayed at home.

A: He usually went out to do jobs?

G: Yes. Didn't go anymore after the physical examination. Was so good to me. I, too, followed him to work. But it was only some light work.

A: Is your normal nutrition good?

G: I like snacks (laughed). He always buys for me.

Another female interviewed described the changes in her husband after she fell ill:

I fell (ill) for an entire winter. Could't cook. *Zhangui* (husband) did. Took care of me the entire winter... The two kids were young. I did little household chores. He did more. When I got a bit better, he got a bit freer. The entire winter's chores... did nothing. Did only the lighter ones. My husband did no work last time. Now that I am sick, he can cook. And did household chores....[sigh] and when I made noodles, he'd help me roll (the house has a noodle machine). Earlier, he'd care for nothing. Now anyway, he's afraid I....(am exhausted).

Most infected females in our interviews believed that it was natural for the husbands to care for their wives if the wives became ill. Does this imply that gender power relations are increasingly equal? In fact, under such circumstances, the power relation between husband and wife is more skewed towards the husband. In traditional custom, the wife plays a role more like a caregiver. Now, as the one being cared for, she loses even more of her right to participate in the family decision-making process. During our interviews, we discovered that many women were totally immersed in household chores, and depended entirely on their husbands for a living.

(2) Mother-Daughter-In-Law Relationships

In the traditional society, one of the most important functions of a mother-in-law and daughter-in-law relationship is to "pass on the social gender rules of family gender roles and power relations." At the same time, the role of the mother-in-law "lies more in the inheritance and dissemination of the social gender rules in community family culture, especially on family life, roles and power relations." The traditional mother-daughter-in-law conflicts often manifest themselves in the form of different ways of performing household chores. However, the deeper reason is "the emergence of certain obstacles in the dissemination of such social rules, such as the mother-in-law having a different comprehension of the social rules disseminated by the daughter-in-law" (Tan Lin, Chen Weiming, 2001: 171-172).

The greatest difference between the current mother-daughter-in-law relationships in the rural areas and these relationships traditionally is that the mother-in-law's power has been greatly reduced. In some cases, the power relation between the two parties has even reversed. In some areas in which we conducted our research, most young couples would have to go through the process of *fenjia* (household division and inheritance). After *fenjia*, the mother and daughter-in-law would live separately, which meant that there would be less interaction between them during their daily chores. Many mothers-in-law voluntarily relinquished the right to "control and teach (*guanjiao*) their daughters-in-law," and many daughters-in-law no longer believe that it is only right and proper for their mother-in-law to control and teach them. One of our interviewees was already a mother-in-law, and she said, "Anyway, a daughter-in-law who marries into the family is here to do the chores. It's good as long as we have food. That's how I think anyway." Also, as the old mother-in-law will need her daughter-in-law to take care of her, the daughter-in-law will hold the controlling powers to contain her mother-in-law's activities.

The conflict between mothers-in-law and daughters-in-law may appear to be the "struggle" between two women, but, at another level, it reveals the social effects of gender. Earlier we mentioned the power-reversal between mothers-in-law and daughters-in-law, and how the younger daughters-in-law often have greater autonomy. However, "this increasing autonomy originates from the inter-generation power conversion to a large extent, and not mainly because of changes in the social gender relationships" (Zhu Ailan, 2004: 184). To mothers and daughters-in-law, there will always be a *zhanggui de* (husband), i.e. the mother-in-law's husband and the daughter-in-law's husband. Given that the husbands are the power centres of the household, both the mother-in-law's and daughter-in-law's behaviour will revolve around their wishes. During our interviews, we discovered that both mothers and daughters-in-law sold blood. There were also families in which the mother sold blood to raise money for her son's marriage.

Based on these circumstances, we believe that an analysis of the power relations between mothers-in-law and daughters-in-law does not lie in finding out who is the one with more power. It is about analyzing the social gender relationship behind their relationship. Based on our interview materials, the principles and motives behind the mothers-in-law and daughters-in-law selling blood were similar. Both did it for their families, and for both it was in order to stay within the limits of basic survival.

(3) Decision-Making Power for Family Affairs

Household matters are divided into daily matters and major events. In the investigated areas, daily matters included mainly decisions for daily household expenses, division of household chores, etc. Major family events included: planting, harvesting, house-building, purchasing important agricultural machinery, investing, getting married and conceiving male children. Other important matters included external issues involving finances, such as family planning fines, payment of agricultural taxes, etc.

In our opinion, the decision-making power for major family events clearly reflects the power relations within the family. We did not raise this issue separately during our interviews. However, our investigations reveal that the husband clearly holds the decisive power for major matters. When we interviewed a couple, the husband animatedly talked about crop-planting and was extremely excited when the crops which he had chosen to plant fetched a good price. The wife, on the other hand, only supplemented her husband's description as and when necessary. While interviewing an old couple, we were surprised to discover that the father had no knowledge of his daughter's age. He said, "I don't know too. I don't get involved in these matters." Clearly, the daughter's age was a "small matter" that did not warrant attention in her father's eyes. In this case, the daughter's husband's family was financially well off. Her mother said, "Her husband's family is really well off. The number one family in Zhujia (village). Her father-in-law makes more than a thousand every month. Did business, too, and contracted other people's land. Had their own land too. Huge income, they have." However, her daughter was infected with AIDS when she sold blood before her marriage. Her husband insisted on divorcing her and had his father's support. After the divorce, she was relegated to total poverty. She worked in the county town despite her illness, earning only RMB 300 every month. She had to leave her daughter with her sister's family. This shows that this woman had no power to control the family finances. During our interviews, we discovered that if it was the wife who was infected with AIDS, she would basically withdraw from participating in any of the decisions on any major matter. If it were the husband who was infected, both husband and wife would make these decisions, so long as the husband was not entirely bed-ridden. If both were infected, the original power relation would basically stay the same.

Under such a family power relation configuration, it becomes natural for the women to sell blood. And when the women become infected with AIDS, the family power relation skews even more towards the male.

2. Social Gender and Family Finances

E. Boserup compared and studied the effect of the different production methods in the agricultural society on women's family status. Under shifting agriculture, women undertook most of the agricultural labour, and played the central role in traditional market trading. A woman's roles as mother and producer were equally important, and she had greater power and a more important position within the family and in society. Under ploughing agriculture, because the nature of the job had a higher demand physically, most agricultural labour was undertaken by males. Women assumed only supplementary roles. As the women were progressively left idle at home, such that women became dependent on their husbands financially, women's family and social status decreased (Tan Lin, 2001: 175). Henan's rural setup is not the pure agricultural society as defined by Boserup. Although wives generally regarded their husbands as the head of the household, women were definitely not "left idle at home," and did not "assume only supplementary roles."

During our interviews, the women unanimously believed that the men were the financial pillars of the family, and the main creators of economic income. They failed to mention their own economic income. In the eyes of the wives, husbands were people who earn "flexible money" (*huoqian*). This concept has not changed since the mid 1990s. Now, when farmers no longer have problems feeding and clothing themselves, they still have little money in hand. According to the interviewees, their main source of income was from selling crops and from the men working in non-agricultural sectors such as construction sites (mainly constructing private homes). The women can hardly earn anything. Most women who go away to work in another city are usually single. Married women hardly go away to work.

During our interview, a wife told us that she insisted that the husband not sell blood because of his important contribution to family finances. Later, the wife contracted AIDS from selling blood. Instead of going to work in jobs, her husband stayed at home to care for her. Their only income was from selling crops:

A: Has your husband ever sold (blood)?

RU: No. I didn't let him. Bad for health. The family depends on him. The kids were young. We cannot both go out.

In another case, the wife also contracted AIDS from selling blood:

A: Are you running any business now?

RA: (Husband) followed the construction team. Had left again.
A: Does he always do that?
RA: Always.
A: He came home everyday?
RA: Everyday. He's busy these two days, so cannot come home. 20 (RMB) a day. Sometimes 25.
A: Do you work much in the fields?
RA: He always works in construction. I work in the fields. Want to earn some money.

Wives believe that their husbands are able to earn "flexible money." Daily necessities, fertilizers and children's education need "flexible money." Such "flexible money" is important to the family. To the women, selling blood is also an avenue to earn "flexible money," except that it is not a long-term solution. This is why they wanted their husbands to retain their physical strength, in order to ensure that their family income would continue.

Even though both men and women agree that the men are the financial pillars of the home, their actual behaviours tell us that there is a rather big disparity in their perception. This is exemplified in the change of a woman's daily behaviour when the man of the house has contracted AIDS. An interviewee (former women's leader in the village) told us: "(the family has) six *mu* of land. Contracted four or five *mu* of land too. I never allowed him to work in the fields. Not even spray pesticide."

Another interview, Z, was a very strong lady. She met her husband at the blood station. Her husband was found to have contracted AIDS as early as 2002. She, too, found out that she had AIDS in 2004. But her husband is still unaware that his wife is an HIV-infected person. She told us, "Some still don't know now. But it's hard to keep a secret. What is there to hide? I don't hide. No matter who I meet, no one dares say I am sick. I am well, healthy. I do all the work myself."

A: But have you told him (husband) of your illness?
Z: No. Never mentioned.
A: He doesn't know now?
Z: No. Did not tell him. Only told him I am sick. But not this illness. The children are (still) young. What is there to say? The kids even cried at times.

Clearly, the above two women had become the financial pillars of their families. Although they still addressed their husbands as *an zhanggui de*, they had already taken on a heavy family burden. Also, their family financial situation was extremely bad, and poverty loomed over them. Some agricultural activities that cannot be done single-handedly, especially some cash crops (e.g. watermelon, cotton, etc.) that fetch good money, were nearly impossible for them. It was also not possible for them to disregard their sick husbands and young children to go out and find jobs, not even construction work in the nearby areas. They said no woman does that, because women cannot do it. On the other hand, if the woman is sick, even though the husband cannot leave for somewhere far away, he can do construction work, or some small business. Despite being ill, the wife can still do some work at home and take care of the kids. But most women did not realize their contribution to the family finances, especially those who were ill. They thought they were the ones being cared for. Women who were family members of AIDS-infected females thought that a woman earning income for the family was only a stop-gap solution.

3. Social Gender and the Division of Labour

Talcott Parsons regarded the family as a social system. He believed that cooperative interaction is linked to mutual dependence, and that the husband, wife and children together constitute one unit. According to Parsons, family roles are classified according to age and gender, and into four basic roles and positions: instrumental leadership role, assumed by the husband (father); expressive leadership role, assumed by the wife (mother); instrumental follower's role, assumed by sons (brothers); expressive follower's role, assumed by daughters (sisters). An instrumental role provides a material guarantee to the family; it is that of the breadwinner of the family. An expressive role protects the family's inner relationships and sentiments between family members. Hence, the Parsons's family theorem is premised on the social gender division of labour. Such gendered division of labour under the male-centred patriarchal system is the foundation of family stability and continuance. On the surface, both roles serve their own purposes. However, such a division of labour is in fact a manifestation of gender inequality. Parsons' later followers maintain that the differences between the unique male and female qualities are biological and natural, as opposed to cultural or artificial. Women must be subordinate to men; this is nature's law (Rosemarie, 2002: 75).

Kate Millet, a representative of radical feminism, wrote in her 1970 book *Sexual Politics* that "sex is politics." This is because, first of all, the male-female relationship is the paradigm of power relations. The male's control of the public and private domains constitutes a patriarchy. The ideology of a patriarchy exaggerates the biological differences between men and women, and clearly specifies the permanent role of male dominance or male qualities, while the female will always assume a role of subordination or female qualities. The male acts through academic, religious and family institutions, each of which justifies and strengthens the submission of women to men (Rosemarie, 2002: 73). As such, the inequality in family gender roles is an extension of the inequality in gender roles in society. The gendered division of labour in the family is an extension of the gendered division of labour in society. We may use this Chinese saying to summarize the status of the gender division of labour in China: "men are breadwinners; women are homemakers" (*nan zhuwai, nü zhunei*, which literally means: the men take care of the outside, the women take care of the inside).

In the rural areas, the division of labour is mainly based on the biological characteristics of men and women. Here, social gender seems to have lost its function. A detailed study will uncover that social gender has not lost its role, but is in fact hidden behind the veil of apparent physical appearance (e.g. men have greater strength than women). This can be seen in their various daily activities of the two genders.

Ordinarily, besides taking care of the family's daily living and performing household chores, women also work in the fields – planting and processing grains for family consumption, picking firewood and feeding livestock – and receive no compensation for their labour. The men usually produce and sell economic crops, both of which are paid forms of labour. During our initial interviews, we asked questions that separated "household chores" (housework) from "work in the fields" (planting). But the women who were interviewed looked baffled. Clearly, to them, both "household chores" and "work in the fields" needed to be performed. Before the interview, we misunderstood what was meant by "men are breadwinners; women are homemakers" (*nan zhuwai, nü zhunei*). We had thought that household chores were "inside"-related, and work in the fields was "outside." From the interviews, we discovered that our understanding of what is "inside" and "outside" differed greatly from the understanding of our interviewees. To them, both "household chores" and "work in the fields" were "inside"; to go out and work in jobs or earn "flexible money" was "outside." Thus, *nan zhuwai, nü zhunei* means men going to work to earn "flexible money," and the women staying back to work in the fields.

However, it is difficult to determine if selling blood is an "inside" or "outside" activity. As the interviews progressed, we gradually discovered that even selling blood is divided into "inside" and "outside." The locations where the women sold blood were usually blood stations near home. Women whose children were very young when they sold blood especially preferred blood stations near home. To quote their words, "It's convenient if it is near home. Don't need to go out. Can go at night." The places where the men frequented to sell blood were further afield, such as in Zhengzhou and Kaifeng, where the blood stations are comparatively more properly operated. Blood stations that are near home are usually illegal, and blood-taking procedures extremely improper. Hence, the probability of women contracting AIDS was much greater than that of the men.

The division of labour is closely related to the status of the women in the family. The women had no doubt that their husbands were the head of their households, even after the women themselves had become the family "pillars." Without realizing it, they had denied their own roles. Although the division of labour between men and women has become increasingly blurred, the practice of regarding the man as the centre of the household has, in principal, remained unchanged.

4. Social Gender and Traditional Customs

Pierre Bourdieu's *Theory of Practice* (1977) focuses on the practical strategies used by people in their everyday lives. As the basic principle of practice dictates, a strategy is not the actor's creation from nowhere; it is gradually nurtured and formed by the material environment reared by his or her life and family.

Bourdieu calls it habitus. Habitus is a generative structure. It is also a product of history, and an externalized internalization. Individual actors can only produce different kinds of rational generally-known behaviour through the effect of habitus (Li Meng, 2001: 279-280). Zhu Ailan (1989) is of the opinion that customs may be regarded in the same vein as habitus. She also believes that "it differs from similar concepts outlined in Bourdieu's theory of practice, in that the concept of custom receives a clearer, more specific and intuitive systematic description than (unconscious) habitus or pre-law" (Zhu Ailan, 2004: 200). Customs possess the flexibility to allow and facilitate the disconnection between the official structural model and practice. Through customs, people create and recreate strategic and adaptation methods, and adjust the way they handle people relationships using the breaking off of customs from social order (Zhu Ailan, 2004). Within the vast rural areas exists a large number of specific social gender customs. These customs have been internalized by the individual, and become a natural basis for action. For example, "women's blood is immoral" is a custom that has long existed in the central plains. Women therefore believe that they can sell more blood than the men. A female interviewee's words expressed this philosophy:

> Women can sell twice a day. Women give birth, and menstruate. Isn't that blood? (She repeated this sentence six to seven times). Men can't. If we fall sick, the women will definitely be less serious. The amount of blood lost during child birth is far more than the amount sold. Some sold blood without knowing that they were pregnant. When it was diagnosed, the child was fine; so was the adult. Women's blood is immoral. Sell when we menstruate, don't give it a thought. Didn't feel uncomfortable then. Anyway, had some transfusion.

The women found a justifiable reason for their selling blood. They found some kind of mental and physiological balance. Custom gave the women's sale of blood a legitimate outer coat.

The preference for boys is a common custom in Henan rural areas. A family that does not produce a son is despised by the village folks. The status of women in their husband's home is often related to whether she bears a son. And especially when this is linked to property inheritance, status is often converted to a material interest relationship. According to many rural women, to receive benefits by bearing a son is the way of life. In a case cited by Professor Gui Xi'en, a village woman who was infected with AIDS took the risk of getting pregnant just to bear a son. This clearly illustrates one fact: to them, the stress and suffering that result from the lack of a son is greater than the risks and pain brought forth by AIDS (Jin Wei, 2004: 101). In rural areas, where social security is unreliable, the notion of bearing a son as a guarantee of care during one's old age is entrenched in the minds of the people. Although such faith has been restricted by many practical changes, it is still believed and practiced by many farmers. After family planning was implemented, bearing sons became a real goal in life. But exceeding the birth quota is punishable by a fine, and the fine amount is outside the means of farmers. Quite a number of people therefore sell blood to pay the fines, or to make up the financial void created by such fines. Many women were distressed and guilt-ridden as they were no longer able to bear a son because of AIDS. A seriously ill woman whom we interviewed not only suffered physically, but also mentally, because she no longer could bear her husband a son.

Among our contacts with our interviewees, the only factor that led to an AIDS-related divorce was that the wife could no longer bear a son. As this woman held a job in the county town, we interviewed her parents. X's mother told us that X had married into Zhujia Village. Her husband's financial situation was good; her father-in-law was a State teacher, and X and her husband opened a shoe store in Kaifeng. They had a close relationship, and had a daughter. X sold blood twice when she was fifteen or sixteen; it was then that she became infected with AIDS. Her plans were foiled. Being extremely unhappy, her parents-in-law encouraged their son to divorce her, and even collaborated with other family members to torture X. Although the court subsequently ruled against the divorce, X's husband had already cohabited with another woman and had a son. Her only option was to leave her daughter with her sister and work in a linen yarn factory in the county town, relying on a meagre RMB 300 to live.

X's mother cried as she told us that:

> they tortured X as soon as she was diagnosed with the illness in 2004. Didn't allow to eat, and didn't eat together. Had to work in the peanut fields in the mornings, and didn't allow her home at noon. Only allowed her to use cold water. Couldn't use hot water. Didn't allow her to drink tea or talk. No one talked to her. The village folks pitied her. (Son-in-law's) family members didn't care for her. Didn't let her touch anything. Didn't give her money too. Was diagnosed in July. Filed for divorce in September. X was angry because of the suit. Both of them had never gotten angry with each other. So angry that she's a bit mentally unstable. I saw her all the time. Had to inject liquid. Four or five bottles a day. We spend on her. I cannot sleep all the time...(sobs).

The following are the two dialogues we had with X's mother:

A: When did X leave her husband's family?

XM: Since July, when the test results were out, she had not gone back. When there was work, she would go home to do it. She'd cry each time when she went back. Then, they still allowed her to go back. By September, when the suit started, she had never gone back. He did not allow her to enter the house. Say, when she went home during the Lunar New Year, he'd even beat her four times during the twelfth lunar month (an auspicious month in which no violence is normally allowed). Refused to allow her home. He would beat her a few times, kick her a few times, or slap her. I told him to send her to the hospital for treatment, he'd agree. But overnight, he'd go to the Ruan family to discuss with his parents, and he would disallow again, afraid that I...

A: Does X wish to go back?

XM: She wants to go back, but she could not.

A: And X does not wish to divorce?

XM: At first she didn't, but now she cannot go back. She has livelihood problems. X said that she would agree to a divorce if they met her conditions.

A: What are X's conditions?

XM: Xiaoniu's (daughter) custody, he (husband) pays alimony. But he disagrees, refuses to discuss.

......

A: Is it because she cannot bear him a son because of this illness?

XM: (Sigh) That is how they think. Want them to divorce. Many in other families had this illness. They continued when they had to. He is wicked. Didn't want her anymore.

A: They were rather loving previously. Did the father-in-law instigate?

XM: (Sigh) That father-in-law insisted on not having her. He went for the hearing. Was afraid that the son didn't know how to say. The court didn't rule for divorce. X was thinking, if no divorce, he can still marry another one. As long as they allow her in the house.

This case shows the disadvantaged position of women in traditional customs. X's tragedy is not only a matter of her AIDS infection. More importantly, AIDS infection prevented her from bearing a son. And because she could not bear her husband a son, she felt guilty, and was even prepared to tolerate her husband's finding another woman, as long as he did not divorce her. The gender inequality in traditional customs is a time-bomb that can be set off at any time. As soon as AIDS ignites the fuse, the bomb's mighty power will be set off. In this case, X eventually agreed to a divorce, and hoped to protect her rights and her daughter's rights through legal means. From the court's decision (divorce rejected), X seemed to have won the case. But she and her daughter did not manage to improve their livelihood. Her husband had not fulfilled his duty to support his daughter, and even committed bigamy openly.

IV. Analysis of the State of Life and Survival Tactics Before and After Blood-Selling
More than a decade ago, many rural females chose to sell blood for a livelihood. The practicalities of their situations did not leave many females with any better choice than to sell blood to improve their livelihoods. Earlier, we analyzed the rural social gender structure. Now, we would like to explore the daily living conditions of females and their direct relationship with blood-selling. We would also like to look at the following question: after being infected with AIDS, what were the changes to the situation of life and choice of survival tactic of the females?

1. The Reality
(1) Household Division and Inheritance
Fenjia (household division and inheritance) is a common phenomenon in rural areas. In places where we conducted our investigations, whether or not the families had brothers, when a new bride joined a family, the newly married couple would have to leave the man's family and set up their own home. What they received as property would depend on the ability of the new bride, the son's position at home, and the current financial situation of the husband's family. Under normal circumstances, the *fenjia* would be witnessed by a well-respected elder in the clan. But despite that, dispute is inevitable; mainly between the husband's mother and the bride. The son normally had to keep within a certain distance of this parents and siblings. Therefore, the amount of property they received depended on the daughter-in-law's ability. An aggressive daughter-in-law would normally receive more. This of course depended on how much there was in total for distribution.

The amount received from household distribution was very important, as it was the capital for the new family and determined the family's future. Such distribution allowed the young and married son a part of the family resources, so that the couple would have a foundation on which to lead an independent life. We discovered during our interviews that the sale of blood by females between the ages of 28 and 39 years after marriage occurred after *fenjia*. These women received nothing during *fenjia*; not even necessities for daily living. The following interview explains the relationship between *fenjia* and individual blood sales:

> Earlier, we mentioned that when the former women's leader spoke of the reason for her husband selling blood, she said that "everybody cared for themselves (i.e. the brothers were unable to help). When the man of the household falls ill, half the world collapses. It'd be good when little ones grow to sixteen or seventeen and can do work. Am angry nothing was received during *fenjia*. If it weren't because of that, there would have been no need to sell blood to build a house. The little money I brought from my *niangjia* (woman's parents' home) was used to contract land. You can't chase the oldies out (of the house). One wrong step, and you

cannot reverse it with another hundred steps." She regretfully said, "Six months (after *fenjia*). If only it had been later. Then would not have to sell blood that time.

When we asked another female W why she sold blood, she also replied that

99 was the year we just *fenjia*. Had to build a house and had no money. Took a loan of 3500 yuan. My parents helped a little. But it wasn't enough, so had to sell. Then, we couldn't even bear to drink soup when we ate rice. People were poor. Some sold blood everyday. Their arms and legs were all swollen.

On the same question, another female S said,

if it were now, I wouldn't have sold (blood) even for 1,000 every time. The money I received the first time I sold blood was used to buy an aluminium pot. Didn't even get an aluminium pot during *fenjia*. Received four rooms. Was hot as hell during summer, and was leaking everywhere. When it rained outside, it rained inside. Couldn't afford to build. And the children still had to go to school.

Because the finances of their husband's family were not too good, the property received during *fenjia* was limited. It was challenging for a young couple to earn an income. In fact, many small families were caught in a crisis of survival after *fenjia*. The above mentioned Mrs. S bought an aluminium pot after she sold blood for the first time. At a time when the blood business was so buzzing with activity, selling blood became a natural thing to do. Also, selling blood is something that one can control. There is no external skill required, and it can be carried out according to one's physical condition. Although there are State regulations restricting the minimum time interval between each blood sale, it is a rule to be bent for the individual. Especially when the structure of the entire blood station and the taking of blood is not properly regulated, any individual may continue to sell blood, so long as he/she does not feel uncomfortable after selling.

In the investigated areas, one of the most important aspects of *fenjia* is land distribution. To a young couple, the amount of land they receive is critical to the well-being of their family finances. To many small families, the land remains the foundation of survival. The local per capita arable land is a very small area – not more than one *mu*. Contracted land for a three member family is less than three *mu* (there was a village with a higher per capita arable land of 1.6 *mu*). The following situation was very common: After the new bride married into her husband's family, if it was not a time for adjusting land distribution in the village, or if there was no land for adjustment (generally, land is adjusted when a village woman marries into another village, or upon the natural death of the village population), she will not receive any land even after having married into the family for many years. The same will happen to her children. We discovered numerous such examples during our interviews. Here is one of them:

The earlier mentioned interviewee, Z, started selling blood even before marriage. Neither of her sisters-in-law at her parents' home in Shangqiu had land:

> My sisters-in-law had no *hukou*, no land. The earlier one (eldest brother's wife) went earlier, (now) already in her forties. She has land. The other two have no land.

> There was less land at that time. I had more allocated. Was allocated nine parts (of land), some were allocated seven parts, land was little. Half a *mu*, seven parts.

Sun Liping once described the Chinese rural areas in the 1990s in this way: "A family is a production unit, planting a very small piece of land, receiving agricultural by-products, having to consume a substantial part of it itself, and having very limited products to sell" (Sun Liping, 2003: 15). Then, in the village, it was impossible to maintain a decent life by only planting grains. Farmers with little land often faced a survival crisis during the end of the 1990s. To the local village women, going away to work was a far-fetched dream. They did not even think of finding a job. As what Z has said:

> Living, oh, my seven sisters (brothers and sisters), I am the youngest. My father is handicapped, also paralyzed.

> As early as I had memories, my father was already ill. Couldn't even fill our stomachs. I was afraid that my mother would suffer, so I went to contribute blood. How else, would I have contributed? My father has passed away. Passed away for five years.

Z got to know her husband when she went to sell blood. There are altogether four of them in the family. Last year they had four and a half *mu* of land. But this land is equivalent to the size of land for three people. Her younger daughter is already five years old, and received land only in 2006. For this, Z was very happy. She said, "Last year was four and a half *mu* of land. Here (one person) was distributed more. Had more than one *mu*"; "Have land. Now more than five *mu* of land. Only this year we have land for four. This daughter of mine now has land. (The children's) Grandfather is also paralysed, cannot do any work. I feed the whole family. I alone." But because she has exceeded the birth quota with the birth of her younger daughter, she has to pay RMB 1,000 to the village for getting land. "Her uncle took out the money. We needed 1,000 yuan. Gave the production brigade. Gave the branch secretary. Here we have to pay money to be given land. Both my children had to pay (for land distribution)." Now, the survival of Z's entire family of four depends entirely on this five *mu* of land. Land, in Z's eyes, is the lifeline of their entire family.

(2) Mother-Daughter-in-Law Relationship and *Niangjia* Support

In the rural areas, women generally leave their parents' home after marriage to live with their husband's family, an unknown social territory. However, where we conducted our investigation, it was uncommon to marry far; the most common form of marriage was to marry someone living nearby. Most people chose their spouses within the same township, which meant that the bride's home was not far from the groom's home, and it was convenient for the bride to visit her parents. During our interviews, we only came across three trans-regional "foreign" brides who came from Shangqiu, Nanyang and Guizhou. Basically, these foreign brides did not return home. There were many reasons, but all could be summarized in one sentence: too poor, do not feel like returning. Although a "married daughter is thrown water," *niangjia* support is important to a woman's life in her husband's family. The mother-daughter-in-law relationship is directly related to *niangjia* support. If the mother-daughter-in-law relationship is strained, then *niangjia* support is even more important, because it will help to alleviate the husband's family's suppression of their daughter-in-law.

All along, the relationship between mother-in-law and daughter-in-law has been an important relationship in the family. Earlier we introduced the gender structure embodied in mother-daughter-in-law relationships. Here, we would like to focus on analyzing the practical significance of mother-daughter-in-law relationships vis-à-vis the females' choice of survival tactic. There is no retirement age (retirement here refers to no longer working) in the rural areas. Retirement is determined by the health condition of the aged person. The aged female believes that even if she has "retired," she must continue performing the household chores (including feeding the livestock) that she can handle. The mother-in-law believes that her relationship with her daughter-in-law will directly affect how soon she "retires." An amicable relationship will mean that the mother-in-law will help her daughter-in-law to take care of the children and do housework; also, that her son and daughter-in-law will cultivate the land. If the mother-in-law loses her ability to perform manual labour, it becomes more necessary for her to maintain a good relationship with her daughter-in-law, because under normal circumstances, the daughter-in-law is the person who is directly in charge of caring for her, and the quality of the mother-in-law's life will depend on the quality of her daughter-in-law's care.

In the locations where we conducted our interviews, the typical family consisted of a few brothers, and the older members of the family were cared for on a rotating basis: When they lost their ability to perform manual labour, they would rotate their stay among their sons' homes. The son with whom they would stay would be responsible for their day-to-day living, but their daughter-in-law, his wife, would take care of them.

In the rural areas, the criteria for a good mother-in-law are varied. But the criteria for a good daughter-in-law are clearly specified: respect the in-laws, be diligent and capable, and be able to produce sons. However, these criteria – especially the one on respecting the in-laws – are gradually losing their effectiveness. A mother-in-law usually has no alterative but to accept her daughter-in-law's determination to fight for her own rights. Zhu Ailan (2004: 148) believes that the reason "these aged women could accept such change with certain rationality is because their own lives became easier at a time earlier than they had anticipated." However, this reasoning appears too simplistic. Based on the author's understanding of the actual situation, the main reason is that the daughter-in-law's dependence on her mother-in-law has been greatly reduced, such that she does not need to receive more survival "tools" from her mother-in-law. On the contrary, the mother-in-law has to rely on her daughter-in-law to care for her; therefore, the power relation between mother and daughter-in-law has become more skewed towards the daughter-in-law. Most relationships between daughters-in-law and mothers-in-law are fair: on one hand, because they are not connected by blood, it is difficult for the two women to maintain a close relationship; on the other hand, because of the moral standard requirements in rural areas, daughters-in-law do not want to be known as "bad" daughters-in-law.

Besides the son, grandchildren also help to bridge the mother-daughter-in-law relationship. Whether or not the mother-in-law helps to take care of her grandchildren has a huge effect on the relationship. Based on custom, the grandmother is the first choice of persons to care for her grandchildren. This has nothing to do with *fenjia*. It is the grandmother's duty to take care of her grandchildren, at least in the eyes of her daughter-in-law. This is also one of the criteria for judging a good mother-in-law – especially in the eyes of her daughter-in-law. A mother-in-law does not need to interact with her daughter-in-law after *fenjia*. However, she cannot absolve herself of the responsibility of taking care of her grandchildren. For example, RU (mentioned earlier) said that she had never had a good relationship with her mother-in-law. She said, "I was angry from the day I came (married) here. I was angry in his family even before I had the young (children). Don't know why she cannot stand the sight of me. I was young, and didn't know how to do a lot of things. Had many sisters at home, and never did anything. Found me useless." "(Grandmother) didn't allow me to see the two children. Doesn't it make me angry?" She also thought that her mother-in-law had no knowledge at all of her AIDS infection:

A: Did she (mother-in-law) know you were ill?
RU: Why would she know? She didn't know.
A: Does she know now?
RU: I don't know. I don't know if she knows. She has never come here to ask me.

There is always some kind of bickering between mother-in-law and daughter-in-law, but what pained some daughters-in-law most was that their in-laws had cut off all communications with them after they had contracted AIDS.

H, a female interviewee, and her husband were both infected. But their greatest suffering was not the torment of illness; rather, it was their relatives' severing of all relationships with them. H said, "All relatives had cut off relationships with us. No one would connect with us. Relatives don't socialize with us anymore." During the interview, L, an NGO representative, added, "there were more serious cases. They do not socialize with you. They'd go to your house, stand at the main door, throw the stuff through the doorway, and leave." During the interview, H cried, and said, "They ousted us. We have no more relatives. They looked down on us. There is only one brother and he is sick. Only my parents came and visited us. We have no more relatives (she repeated 'no more relatives' many times, as tears continued to fall)."

We asked, "What about your husband's relatives?" H was choking with sobs, and said, "They despised us. His mother also looked down on me." Z, who was present, said, "then that is not good, when even the parents despise you."

We felt that the interviewees' situations had gone beyond plain discrimination. Infected persons who were forced to cut off any further contact with their relatives had to tolerate greater torment than plain discrimination. In villages where family relations are one's basic support system, being cut off from all family relations is a grave matter. However, the family members that H mentioned were those of her husband's relations. Under these circumstances, support from her parents' family (*niangjia*) became unusually important.

During our investigation, we found that *niangjia* support was mainly in the form of financial support. Apart from support from parents, siblings also provided support. Such support was usually retained for major projects or emergencies, such as the building of a house. When the *niangjia* had contributed substantially for major financial expenditures, the daughter-in-law ended up with a louder "voice" in the family. She could be very proud, and the husband would be somewhat humbled. To some extent, the status of a daughter-in-law in her little family depends on her *niangjia*'s support, including both her dowry and postnuptial support. If the daughter-in-law has a few brothers, her husband's family will be wary, and her opinions will be given consideration. Thus, when the women interviewed met with major problems, *niangjia*'s support was their first consideration.

Among those whom we interviewed, nearly every female was able to obtain support from her *niangjia*. However, the degree of such support was limited to her *niangjia*'s financial situation. If her *niangjia* was threatened, then the amount of support she received would be minimal. But between "having sincerity" and "having ability," people place greater value on "having sincerity," because "ability" is based on objective circumstances, while "sincerity" is a subjective willingness. The women believed that they could depend more on the members of their *niangjias* than their husbands' siblings who were only interested in caring for themselves, and therefore, undependable. The husbands' families in which women sold blood before they were married queried directly how their *niangjias* "had disciplined the daughter." The mother-in-law of R, a female interviewee, gave her opinion on the daughter-in-law's sale of blood before her marriage:

> I also didn't know (that the daughter-in-law sold blood). If I had known, I'd say, she is so young, I would look for her mother. I will tell her, her (father-in-law) said that three feet within the door and three feet outside the door, she has not reached our door, we cannot control. I don't have enough people to help. If she enters our door and has not energy to work, what should we do?

We previously mentioned a woman X who was abused because of her illness. After she was thrown out of her husband's family, she had to rely almost entirely on her parents and sisters' financial support to stay alive.

But most parents forbid their daughters to sell blood before they marry. Most girls do so regardless, without their parents' knowledge.

X's father said: "I wasn't aware (X selling blood). If I had known, I'd rather starve to death than to allow her to sell blood. She sold only twice. Sold at Wangxiao Village. She didn't go to school at that time. She didn't complete her primary school education. She didn't tell the family. No one at home knew."

W, a female who was interviewed, said, "who would have known that selling blood would bring harm. At that time, few people sold blood at where my parents' home was. Not like the east side. I have five sisters. No one sold. There were people at my hometown who did sell, but our family doesn't. We won't sell, no matter how difficult life is."

The mother of another interviewee, AH, beat her because she sold blood. Her mother forbade her to sell blood. But she said, "(mum) said not to go, not to go and sell blood. But when I get married, no one will bother at my husband's family."

Although most parents forbid their daughters from selling blood, many sell secretly, just to buy some sundry goods, such as a new outfit or a new bottle of shampoo. Except in the case of Z, who sold blood before her marriage to help her mother with the household expenses, parents did not think that an unmarried daughter had a duty to care for the family. At the same time, an unmarried daughter had no part in her family's household division and inheritance, even as an adult. However, before a daughter was married, parents did their best to provide a dowry, because this would affect the daughter's status in her husband's family.

(3) The Impact of *Gongjia* and Blood Sales

Many females mentioned *gongjia* (public or government-owned) during our interviews; such as blood stations owned by *gongjia*, medicine distributed by *gongjia*, *gongjia* family planning fines, etc. In the eyes of the women, the concept of *gongjia* was very ambiguous.

Gongjia can be as small as the village committee, and as big as the central government. To them, *gongjia* was a mysterious yet authoritative entity, which means that although *gongjia* is an abstract entity, its authority is definitely irresistible. It pervaded their daily lives, was an important reference for their daily decision-making, and played a decisive role in their behavioural choices. Their trust in *gongjia* played an important role when they decided that selling blood was a survival tactic. When they were diagnosed with AIDS, they felt unfortunate, but did not blame *gongjia*. They believed that they had sold blood according to their own will, as they were not forced by *gongjia*. Recipients of the "Four Frees and One Care" policy (*si mian yi guanhuai*) were often full of gratitude, saying: "If not for *gongjia*'s care, all would have died." They also felt that it was correct for *gongjia* to undertake their medical expenses, since they had contracted AIDS at the *gongjia*-operated blood stations.

A common phenomenon occurred in rural reform, i.e. the female's role was minimized or played down in official communications (Zhu Ailan, 2004). Except for policies related to childbearing, the government rarely pays attention to the condition of women. By doing so, the government has created a false impression, such that women feel like they have no connection with *gongjia*. And, in fact, the family planning policy, which mainly targets women, does not provide adequate attention to and sufficient guarantees of women's interests. As the family planning policy is being implemented in rural areas, women's rights are frequently infringed upon. In reality, the enforcement of the family planning policy has resulted in a certain portion of women having to sell blood. The following interview explains the author's conclusion:

A: Were you fined after giving birth to the second child?

AN: Yes. I was fined more than four thousand (RMB).

A: Could the family afford this amount?

AH: We had to find it, or borrow it.

A: Were you also fined?

AD: (Yes) Five to six thousand (RMB).

A: Why were some fined four thousand, some five or six thousand?

AH: (Family planning) is stringent one year, and relaxed another year.

AG: Mine's even (more) expensive.

AD: They take your things when you have no money.

A: Take the wheat (Taking away the wheat as payment in lieu of fine)?

AD: Yes, take wheat. Things were all taken away.

A: Does the village decide how much to fine?

AH: Doesn't the State decide it?

A: Then, why does it differ every year?

AH: One township is strict, another is easy-going. Follow the town (there is something to do with it), I think. The county, whatever amount they demand, we pay.

AD: I was really tormented at that time. Poor me! Why is it that this child of mine
cannot afford to go to school, and that youngest child of mine goes to school
one year later, (age) older than other children. Other children got in. When he
followed those of the same age to go to school, he could not afford to. Waited
for the following year (went to school with the next batch of children). This
youngest son, I could afford for a while, and could no longer afford after that.
Both my children are quite good in their studies, (people even) said that your
two kids are good in their studies (why don't they go). I said I could do nothing
if I had no money.

The desire to have sons encouraged some villagers to oppose the *gongjia* family
planning policy. They used various means to realize their dreams. The more common
tactic was for the woman to leave and hide in a relative's home as soon as she became
pregnant, returning only after she had given birth – by which time, it was too late
to do anything, and therefore she viewed the government's fine as justifiable. During
her seclusion, the expecting women would usually refrain from appearing in public,
because she would have to go through an induced abortion if she were caught. This
made it difficult for women to have regular check-ups during the risky period of their
pregnancies. The expecting mother's health is highly at risk when neglected. Most
penalties for violation of the family planning regulations consist of the imposition of
fines; the amount of which is huge for rural families, and may mean bankruptcy for
some. If the fines are not paid within the stipulated period, everything of value in the
house (such as wheat or livestock) will be taken away as payment in lieu of cash. Most
families are in utter destitution when the child is born and they cannot afford the most
basic living necessities.

The influence of *gongjia* on the women was implicit and omnipresent. Selling blood
may be viewed as the outcome of *gongjia*'s control over the villagers' fate. However, the
State's power is segmented into detailed symbols affecting individuals in rural activities.
At present, customs begin to coalesce with State power to produce an extremely potent
effect, so much so that it is believed that "custom is a site of privilege at which State
power emerges in rooted and effused forms. Here, State power quietly encounters,
without any coercion, and meshes with the social gender politics of every day life. It
is also here that rooted State power gains its social genderization" (Zhu Ailan, 2004:
201). Probably due to various limitations (such as education level), rural females usually
tried to relate contracting AIDS to specific experiences (e.g. for a son's marriage, for an
infant's milk powder, etc.) when reflecting on the reasons for their selling blood. Rarely
did they explore the social reasons associated with their infection.

2. Female's Responsibility
According to Chinese tradition, the main responsibility of women is to the family. The
same notion applies today, even in modern Chinese agricultural societies, and both

genders identify with the notion. However, this does not exclude the men's responsibility to raise the family. In fact, the general belief is that one of a man's main responsibilities is feeding his family. The only difference between the responsibilities of men and women is that family responsibility is linked to female morality. A perfect family is the main embodiment of a woman's good character and behaviour, whereas feeding the family is but one responsibility of the man. A man seeking personal development is a matter of course.

The female's responsibility is related to her role at home. In the locations where we conducted our investigations, the turning point for the women's change of responsibility was marriage. Here, we would like to identify marriage as the critical turning point of roles, and discuss the female's responsibilities and their changes as she becomes a daughter, wife and mother.

(1) The Secret of Female "Independence of Choice"

The female's responsibility changes with the form of the family in which she lives. In a rural society, the three roles of a female are clearly delineated. However, they have a commonality: the female is a caregiver. But when she sells blood under these three different identities, her behavioural motives are vastly different. As a daughter, she sells blood to fulfil her personal desires. As a wife and mother, she does it for the survival of the family. After her transformation from wife to mother, she accepts her change of social identity very quickly, and is able to accept and perform such a woman's duties (i.e. taking care of the family, self-sacrifice, following through with "the woman cares for the 'inside' and the man cares for the 'outside'," etc.), derived from rules of tradition, custom and society. Their behaviour motives and specific behaviours also undergo a huge transformation during this process.

In rural areas, parents do not rely on their daughters to take care of them in their old age. However, this does not imply that daughters have no responsibility towards their parents; it only means that they have a different responsibility from their brothers. Compared to their brothers, daughters are in a more disadvantaged position within the family power relation structure; the environment in which they live and their opportunity for development is unequal. Under normal circumstances, daughters receive a shorter education than their brothers (our interviews showed that most females received primary education and below). Daughters who have dropped out of school must help their parents to take care of their younger siblings and old people at home. Most women in the interview locations married young (first marriages usually took place when they were below twenty years). Among the AIDS-infected females, few were able to go out and work in non-agricultural sectors. Most would stay at home to care for their parents. The fact that parents do not rely on their daughters to care for them in their old age is exemplified by their attitude towards selling blood: they do not encourage their daughters to sell blood. Yet most young girls sold blood secretly, to satisfy some of their needs and desires, such as to buy a new dress, a bottle of shampoo, etc. Few did it for their family's livelihood.

After marriage, few females consider their own needs. Their individual needs gradually disappear in the family, and their individuality is masked by their roles as wife and mother. The family survival tactic replaces the individual survival tactic. Family-centred choices become the choice of survival tactic. This is in fact an extension of female responsibilities; that is, that females should be the caregivers of the family and should sacrifice themselves for the family. This can be clearly seen in their motive for selling blood and behaviour after realizing of their illness.

A: Why did you sell blood then?

RU: Didn't have milk then. My daughter takes milk powder. Had to buy milk powder. One packet for 9 yuan. I can't even remember how many yuan.

A: Then, in 1995, did you know that taking blood will make you ill?

CH: They said. The doctor told me in 1989 and 1992, when I went to Kaifeng. 10 and 20 years later, you know. It's bad for your health. That doctor said. The doctor whose surname was Wang told me, you are so thin, you need blood transfusion. And you still sell blood. Don't anymore. 10 and 20 years later you know yourself. Didn't wait till then to discover that many died. Thought of this when someone dies.

A: That was 1992 when the doctor told you. Was it the time when you gave blood?

CH: At first she said there was no illness. Just said bad for health. 15 and 25 years later, you know, she said. That lady with the Wang surname said this. She said you are so skinny you should not sell. Go do some business somewhere to earn 45 yuan. I said I didn't know how to do business.

A: What did you think after listening to her?

CH: Didn't care how I thought, didn't care about my health. Had to get the money first. Take care of one step at a time.

A: You wanted money.

CH: Wanted money. No money for fertilizer, no money for my younger son's fine. If you don't pay the fine, they don't give you land. You can't ask for land.

A: How much were you fined?

CH: Fined for 2,400. Was fined when I had my second child.

The interviewed women were most worried about their children after learning the results of their check-up. This seemed to be the worry of all infected females. She said:

(Most worrying) is the child. Afraid that the child got it too. I am not afraid for me (illness). Am old (the author interrupted that she said she was old when she was so young). Adults can suffer anything. Pity the children.

Zhu Fengli interrupted: Without the adult, that happens to the child? Other people (raising) is not as good as the real (parents raising).

No matter what the specific reasons were for selling blood, it would appear that such behaviour was a voluntary choice by the women. But if we were to remove this so-called "autonomous veil," we would discover that an unequal social gender construct naturally produces unequal female-male responsibilities. Although both husband and wife may choose to sell blood, and the specific reasons between the two sexes for doing so do not differ much, the driving forces behind their decisions are different. The male behavioural expression is also vastly different. Generally, females are more concerned with the family's future state of life.

(2) Gender Disparity in Blood Selling Behaviour from the Perspective of Different Family Responsibilities of the Male and Female

As mentioned above, our investigation showed there was little difference between men and women's specific reasons for selling blood. Most did so to build a house, raise the children, purchase agricultural materials, etc. According to statistics by Jin Wei (2004), although a greater number of females sell blood, the average frequency of males is greater than females. Our interviews did not reveal this situation. However, even if the average frequency for females was lower, this does not mean that women have received special care and concern. In reality, they have not. We mentioned earlier that this phenomenon is closely related to gender and family roles. Men know that they will automatically become the head of their own household, which also implies that they are to provide the family's financial support. Hence, it is understandable that mature males would sell blood more frequently. We also discovered this during our investigation: during courtship or in the early phase of marriage, couples sold blood together. After marriage and once a child was born, many of the women stopped selling blood because they had to raise the child, care for the elderly, do the household chores, feed the livestock, and work in the field. When the blood-selling frenzy had just started, one would travel a distance to sell blood at a proper city blood station; this conflicted with the daily routine of the village's women, who had to stay home to care for the family; hence more men sold blood. Later, when many private blood stations were opened just at the women's doorstep, selling blood became convenient, and no longer took time away from the women who had to take care for their families. This is when more women began selling blood. The following excerpt from an interview explains this:

A: There were many in the village already selling blood before you did.
GQ: There were many selling blood.
A: And you did not think of selling?
GQ: No.

A: Then why did you sell later?

GQ: If was just outside my house. I didn't need to go out. I went at night.

A: Were there many people selling blood?

R: Many, (because) they were just at the doorstep (in front).

A: Oh, they (blood stations) were just at the doorstep, and the head of the blood station came to the house to collect blood?

R: (Sigh). The young one was really young (children too young). We needed money.

Thus, the traditional gender division of labour has led to a gender-differentiated blood-selling behaviour. Such behaviour cannot be judged simply by the frequency and quantity of blood sold by the two genders. The mushrooming of private blood stations has provided married women with an avenue to sell blood, and has resulted in a huge increase in the number of blood-contributing females. And this avenue (near and time-saving) is a representation of social gender differentiation. During our interviews, we also discovered that even though both husband and wife sold blood for money, the wife would tend to believe that she earned merely pocket money and that her husband was the family's true financial pillar. Differences in gender responsibilities resulted in the women's continued negation of their contribution to the family.

3. Transmission Channels Accentuate Gender Disparity

Having witnessed the spread of AIDS from selling blood, the villagers were most concerned with the problems of sexual transmission between husband and wife, and mother-to-child transmission. What was interesting – and different from what we had imagined – was that the villagers were neither concerned with how these channels facilitated transmission, nor how to take precautions. Instead, they were most concerned with the fact that the achievement of their dream of having a son would be seriously impaired by these two transmission channels.

(1) Sexual Transmission

Among those interviewed, almost no one complained of their sex lives being affected by AIDS. In fact, many felt that it is disgraceful to be infected from sexual activity. The following dialogue taken from an interview exemplifies this finding:

A: So, does your husband know how this disease is transmitted?

Z: Who knows? I have never asked him. He only knows that it is caused by selling blood. He has never visited prostitutes.

A: You know that visiting prostitutes can lead to AIDS infection?

Z: Some say that they contracted AIDS from "that." It's better to get AIDS other ways.

A: Who did you hear that from, that prostitution gets you this illness?

Z: I heard that from other people. Visiting prostitutes is easy to get this illness. And there is virus in the blood for this illness. Poisonous gas. Said there's medicine?

A: Did you tell your family after your husband became ill? Was your sex life normal?

Z: Normal. But we slept on separate beds since then.

A: Why separate beds?

Z: He is ill. Afraid of getting it. Suspect I may get.

A: You suspect and you have no sex life with him?

Z: No. Have been sleeping separately for many years.

A: Since he became ill?

Z: Slept on separate beds since he came back from Guangzhou.

A: So no sex life since then?

Z: No.

A: No one distributed condoms?

Z: Distributed. Our clinic (distributed). Came with this medicine. I didn't want it.

A: Didn't want it? Why?

Z: We were just not together. (Since he) returned from Guangzhou, was like no (longer) husband and wife. Became strangers. He had this illness, he was afraid. Was afraid that something will happen to the three of us. There's the two children, and me. He said it was for the children's good. Anyway, we had no sex life. Separated. Still eat together. But no longer sleep together.

The above case indicates that the villagers knew that AIDS could be transmitted through sexual activity. Also, AIDS reduced the couple's sexual activity, despite the distribution of free condoms; not only because of the torment of the illness, but also because of the tremendous mental torture (such as fear, shame, etc.) that had led to reduced or even suspended sexual activity. By studying the cases in detail, we discover that this change is also gender-differentiated: if the husband is infected with AIDS, then sexual activity will stop almost entirely, whether or not the wife is infected. Z is a case in point. If the infected party is the wife, then sexual activity will only be reduced.

Regarding the channels of transmission, there were many myths among people interviewed. A male interviewee believed that the chance of women passing the disease to men was smaller than if it were the other way around; hence, he felt lucky and concluded that there was no need for him to wear a condom. Z thought that AIDS transmitted through prostitution was more serious than AIDS transmitted from selling blood. Hidden within her belief was a moral judgment: sexual transmission is disgraceful. The women's leader (mentioned earlier) said,

the first time I heard of AIDS) could have been in 1994 when I was in school. At that time, Gao Yaojie came to train us. She mentioned AIDS. Said that transmission can occur even when a piece of paper is put with a dollar note. Maybe Dr. Gao did not know of the transmission channels at that time. I didn't dare mention anything when I came back. Because I heard it was sexual transmission.

(2) Mother-to-Child Transmission

We discovered during our interviews that most were not concerned with how exactly mother-to-child transmission occurred. People were more concerned by the mere existence of such a channel, that their hopes of having a son would be difficult to fulfil. Many husbands felt sorry, and wives felt pain. Also, the existence of such a channel worried the infected mothers. They were afraid that their disease would pass to their child. Nearly every family with an infected person will send their children for repeated medical checks. The following interview details such worry of the infected party:

A (asked AM's husband): Your wife seems down?

AMZ: We have a daughter. Now I have this disease. Cannot have another child. There are four of us in my family. Three are sisters. I am the only son.

AHZ: (Unwilling to send the daughter for AIDS test) "What do you say, the heart...is not happy. Let her (daughter's) life be. If she is sick, let her. If she does not have (AIDS), she is lucky. We can't help it. This is not like other illness, which can be cured.

AHP: Hope to adopt an AIDS orphan (boy).

A: (asked X's mother): How long has Xiuying been working in the county city?

M: More than half a year....At first her father-in-law didn't know. His sister knew, and told his father. Said to his son, Qingfeng, divorce her. If you don't I won't let you off. Cannot have a second one. We have the means. Why have her. Find another one. QF then proposed a divorce to X. X asked him where she could go. He said you can go wherever you want. XX (X's daughter) you can let me have her if you don't want. If you don't divorce me, my father will not let you off. At first he was secretive, called X when taking a meal. Later, he hardened. On the sixth day of the ninth month, he found another girl. Even met his family. Didn't admit. But after new year, he didn't allow X to go home.

This case shows that the interviewed family was most concerned about having a son. Because mother-to-child transmission could prevent the wife from having a son, women who had not given birth to sons were in a more disadvantaged position. AHZ was unwilling to allow his daughter to be tested. He preferred to leave the question to fate. The mother-in-law hoped to adopt a grandson because the daughter-in-law could no longer bear a son. AMZ and QF were troubled because their wives were infected and could not have sons. For the same reason, Xiuying allowed her husband to marry a second wife. The situation surrounding mother-to-child transmission highlights the issue of gender inequality. This is something that we failed to anticipate before our field investigation.

V. CONCLUSION

From the above analysis, we may conclude following:

1. Survival tactics of females in the AIDS Village are closely related to the world of their daily lives. After contracting AIDS, their choice of survival tactic is always to put the immediate family's interest above all else. The presence of the traditional gender division of labour prevents the female's survival tactic from surmounting the boundaries of her immediate family. At the same time, although local governments have implemented the "Four Frees and One Care" policy, support for the infected women continues to come from their families instead of society. The possibility of her achieving self-actualization is closely intertwined with her family's fate.

2. The motive for selling blood before and after marriage differs between the male and female. Before marriage, the women sell blood to improve their personal lives and the men do so to improve their family's survival situation. After marriage, the motive behind women's decision to sell blood experiences a marked change: they sell blood solely for the survival of their immediate family; and to ensure the family's viability, females often forbid their spouses to sell blood. After they or/and their spouse are infected with AIDS, some women will assume all duties of the home – such as rearing and educating the children, tending to agricultural activities, and caring for the old folks at home – to enable the men to go out and perform economic activities.

3. In China's rural areas, *fenjia* has given rise to an increasing number of small families. However, the man is still the centre of the small family. Women try to work at home and maintain the family, and we see that they recognize the male-centred family structure. Such small families replicate and disseminate a traditional and unequal social gender structure, and become the invisible hand that controls the behaviour of women.

4. Although the effects of the gender factor – among the determining factors of the female's choice of survival tactic – incorporated in the State's public policies are obscured by the significance of the family to women, gender is the other invisible hand that controls the female's choice of survival tactic.

5. With two invisible hands working together, what appears to be the outcome of "independent choice" of survival tactic by women in the AIDS village is in fact permeated with social gender effects of every dimension. Also, social gender is "invisible" in their daily lives, and is intertwined with the different events of livelihood (such as the gender effects incorporated in the State's public policies). They are blinded by the multiplicity and complexity of daily living, so much so that they fail to see the presence of social gender.

6. Even if women in the AIDS village fail to realize the impetus of the social gender structure, it does not imply that their behaviour is entirely shaped by the social gender factor. Truth is, the specific behaviour in choice of survival tactic by women in the AIDS village has long broken the traditional division of labour. When a family member (usually the husband) is infected with HIV, the female shoulders the responsibilities previously divided between the couple. However, these women fail to realize the significance of such an initiative. Often, they neglect and negate their daily roles in life. Without knowing the significance of social gender, the various initiatives taken by females for survival under very limited resources may be a kind of struggle for survival of its own. However, it is a struggle of great importance.

ENDNOTE

[1]   The project is part of the collaborative research project on "Promoting Anti-Discrimination in China" between the The Research Centre for Human Rights of Peking University Law School and the University of Ottawa, Canada, between 2005 and 2008.

PART FIVE

Discrimination Against Minorities

CHAPTER FIFTEEN

The Canadian Constitution and Charter of Rights and Freedoms
A Global Template for Minority Rights?

Errol P. Mendes

INTRODUCTION

The rights of minorities are an arena that is becoming perhaps the principal battle ground for human rights in the 21st century.

Recent history would seem to offer a stunning paradox: that the federal state may not be the best form of human governance for societies with multi-ethnic populations. The former Soviet Bloc had nine states, six of which were unitary states while three were federal in structure. With the unification of Germany, the six unitary states are now five, but the three federal states, Yugoslavia, the Soviet Union, and Czechoslovakia are now 22 independent states, perhaps 23 if we include Kosovo.[1] Most of these newly independent states were forged by minorities who did not feel that their rights were sufficiently protected by the federal structures in which they previously existed.

At first sight, facts such as these do not bode well for the notion that federations are particularly good structures for the protection of minority rights. Yet, the orthodox thesis is that it is federations rather than unitary states that can best protect minorities across diverse populations or across large territories.

Perhaps this view is outdated and should be replaced with the thesis that it is only multi-ethnic societies, whether federations or not, that develop the appropriate constitutional and legal frameworks on the substantive equality rights of minorities, together with an appropriate method of balancing individual and collective rights, that can hope to remain united and avoid the human rights catastrophes that we see today in so many multi-ethnic societies.

More controversially, I suggest that the protection of such minority rights is even more important than instituting the procedural elements of democracy in a multi-ethnic society, as the tragedy unfolding in Iraq demonstrates. In another tragic example, Sri Lanka, a democratic multi-ethnic state, has stood accused of violating the human rights and equality rights of its Tamil and other minorities and found itself in a seemingly intractable civil war that has left more than 64,000 dead.[2] Similarly, other formally democratic multi-ethnic states, such as Indonesia and Russia,[3] are, in practice, refusing to go down the road of an effective constitutional and legal framework that respects the substantive equality of their minorities – with similar disastrous human rights consequences.

The future for authoritarian non-democratic multi-ethnic states is even bleaker. We only have to look at the genocidal carnage in Sudan to understand this horrible future.

WHAT DOES SUBSTANTIVE EQUALITY MEAN IN THE CONTEXT OF MINORITY RIGHTS?

I suggest that the core of what substantive equality means for minority groups is the recognition that identical treatment of minorities[4] with the treatment of the dominant population can lead to a sense of oppression that can fuel civil conflict. Substantive equality, I suggest, would involve treating all groups in a multiethnic society with equal concern and respect, which often requires differential treatment to respect their human dignity; formal equality would promote identical treatment of all minorities, regions, and citizens.[5]

Canada could provide a global template, albeit one that is not perfect, of an appropriate striving to attain the foundational value of substantive equality for its minorities and indigenous populations within a multi-ethnic federation. This being said, it must also be accepted that Canada has been far from perfect in treating its minorities and indigenous populations with substantive equality during the course of its history.

Canada is both a very new country, less than 200 years old, and also a very old country, since its first inhabitants, the Aboriginal peoples of Canada, have lived here from time immemorial. We have, in comparison to many European nations, a very diverse population. Over one-third of Canadians can trace their origins from France and they are concentrated in the province of Quebec, where they form a powerful majority. However, over a million francophones live outside Quebec in minority linguistic communities spread across the country. Increasingly, Canadian society is becoming a mirror of the global society as we welcome immigration from all over the world. Our major cities – Toronto, Montreal and Vancouver – in the near future will have a majority non-European population in origin, creating calls by racial and ethnic minorities for collective rights to non-discrimination and equality.[6]

The foundational Act of the Canadian state, the *British North America Act*, is replete with provisions related to diversity. However, what is particularly interesting about the evolution of the Canadian Constitution is that it contains critical provisions that sometimes allow differential treatment (asymmetrical) and sometimes identical treatment (symmetrical) for minorities, intended to allow differences to flourish.

Examples include the guarantee of 75 seats for Quebec in the Canadian Parliament (Section 37), a critical asymmetrical provision; the entrenchment of the provinces symmetrical jurisdiction over property and civil rights in Section 92(13), a critical symmetrical provision that allows differences between the provinces to flourish; the protection of denominational schools in Ontario and Quebec (Section 93), and the official use of English and French in the Canadian and Quebec legislatures (Section 133), both important asymmetrical provisions. Likewise the maintenance of the civil law system in Quebec is another example of asymmetrical federalism entrenched in the constitutional history of the country. The genius of the founding architects of Canadian nationhood was to entrench asymmetry up to the limits of the politically possible, but then to permit differences to flourish under other symmetrical provisions.[7]

Leading American federalism theorists such as the late William H. Riker[8] have argued that it is only symmetrical federalism that is truly compatible with democratic federalism. However, where multi-ethnic nations have large and historically settled national ethnic, linguistic, or religious minorities, an insistence on symmetrical federalism or constitutional frameworks would be a denial of the substantial equality of these minorities. Absolute symmetrical federalism and formal equality can often lead to the assumption of uniformity where it does not exist, and could lead to the coercive institutions of the federal state imposing uniformity and assimilation, an imposition national minorities will naturally resist. The result can be disastrous, as we have seen in the case of the former Yugoslavia.

Asymmetrical constitutional provisions in multi-ethnic federations are especially important in order to promote the essential features of cultural self-determination of such minorities; these features can include language, education, culture, religion and, as in the case of Canada, the legal traditions and systems. Assymmetrical provisions are essential in order to protect against the "nationalizing" tendencies of the dominant population in a multi-ethnic federation through effective participation by national minorities in decision making at the central level and at the highest political levels; these may be asymmetrical in proportion to the minorities' percentage of the federation's population.[9] This is the chief rationale of providing a permanent 75 seats to Quebec, regardless of what percentage of the Canadian population the Quebec population comprises. It also accounts for the fact that three of our Supreme Court of Canada judges must be from Quebec, as well as the tradition of ensuring regional and national minority representation in the governing party's federal cabinet.

To reiterate, substantive equality differs from formal equality in that it recognizes that identical treatment can lead to discriminatory treatment of minorities and impose uniformity and coercive assimilation that would threaten their existence.[10] Democratic multi-ethnic federal states such as India[11] and Canada, and some would add Spain,[12] have learned that asymmetrical federalism has been critical to the survival of their countries.

The dilemma of how to fit minority rights within a constitutional framework that respects both individual and collective rights is being confronted in theory and practice by Canadians and within the Canadian constitutional framework. Will Kymlicka argues that "group specific" rights are compatible with liberal tenets that uphold the supremacy of individual rights. The fundamental premise of these theorists (and I include myself in this group) is that it is because the rights and liberties of individual citizens include the right to associate that most such rights have a group related or specific dimension; thus, belonging to a minority based on common cultural, linguistic, or religious heritage is indeed an important factor of identity and indeed of human dignity for most of its members. Where individuals thus freely associate, no central or state government or majority, however large, may deny the right of such groups to cultural self-determination, within the limits of the supremacy of individual and universal rights and the rule of law.[13]

Some of the collective rights of the growing diversity of Canadian society have been guaranteed in the *Canadian Charter of Rights and Freedoms,* entrenched in the Constitution in 1982.[14] In the Constitution, Canada recognizes the collective rights of Aboriginal people. Through court decisions and provisions of the original Constitution and the *Charter of Rights*, it recognizes the collective rights of linguistic minorities and, in the case of Quebec, of a linguistic majority in one province that wishes to preserve its language within a predominantly English-speaking continent.

The wording of some of the provisions in the Canadian Constitution and *Charter*, which recognize collective rights, pose some interesting dilemmas to those steeped in the classical liberalism of the American legal tradition. In what follows I shall briefly discuss one example, section 23(3) of the *Charter.*

Section 23(3) of the *Canadian Charter of Rights and Freedoms* entrenches minority linguistic education rights of French-speaking minorities outside Quebec and English-speaking minorities within Quebec where numbers warrant. The Section states:

> The right of citizens of Canada under subsections (1) and (2) to have their children
> receive primary and secondary school instruction in the language of the English or
> French linguistic minority population of a province
>> (a) applies wherever in the province the number of children of citizens who have
>> such a right is sufficient to warrant the provision of them out of public funds of
>> minority language instruction; and
>> (b) includes, where the number of those children so warrants the right to
>> have them receive that instruction in minority language educational facilities
>> provided out of public funds.

This is a curious type of right to be found in a constitutional document in a western liberal democracy, where the exercise of the right is contingent on the number of people who wish to exercise it! Imagine a similarly contingent right related to freedom of speech. This entrenchment of linguistic rights in Canada points to the fact that collective rights require an examination of the sociological, economic and cultural backgrounds from which they arise.[15] The Supreme Court of Canada demonstrated this necessity in *Arsenault-Cameron v. P.E.I.*,[16] handing down an excellent example of the need for a socio-economic context of the human rights framework for protection of minority rights.

In this case, the individual francophone parents entitled to have their children schooled in French under Section 23 of the *Charter* sought to have their children schooled at the primary level in a school located in their local community of Summerside, Prince Edward Island. The provincial Minister of Education insisted that such minority language education could be provided at an existing French language school, approximately 57 minutes away by school transportation services. The Supreme Court ruled, in a judgment delivered by Mr. Justice Bastarache, a former academic expert on linguistic rights, and Mr. Justice Major, that Section 23 was not meant to uphold the status quo by adopting a formal vision of equality where the majority and minority language groups were treated alike. The Court held that the purpose of Section 23 was to remedy past injustices and provide minority language communities with equal access to high quality education in circumstances where community development is enhanced. The reference to "where numbers warrant" in the section must take into account community development, even where the numbers in the Summerside area were between 49 and 155.

In a clear expression of the fact that Canada has taken a different liberal democratic route from the United States, the Court held that focusing on the individual right to instruction at the expense of the linguistic and collective rights of the minority community effectively restricts the collective rights of the minority community.

Protection of minorities has been confirmed as one of four foundational principles of Canadian federalism by the Supreme Court in its landmark ruling on the right of Quebec to unilaterally secede from Canada, in the *Reference re. Secession of Quebec*[17] decision. But the *Charter* and Canadian society also recognize the equal value of civil and political rights based on the dignity of the individual human being. I suggest that through Section 1 of the *Charter* a mandate was given by the Parliament of Canada to the judiciary, in particular the Supreme Court, to work out a legal framework for the adjudication between collective and individual rights. Section 1 of the Charter allows governments in Canada to sometimes infringe rights if they can demonstrate that such infringements are reasonable limits demonstrably justified in a free and democratic society.

During the relatively brief period of the existence of the Canadian *Charter*, there have been cases where, I suggest, the Supreme Court met well the challenge of creating this uniquely Canadian framework of collective and individual rights adjudication. The landmark decision of the Canadian Supreme Court in *Ford v. Quebec (A.G.)*[18] is, I suggest, one such example. In this case, five businesses operated by English-speaking Quebeckers sought a declaration that sections 58 and 69 of the Quebec Charter of the French Language infringed the individual right of free expression as they required exclusive use of French on exterior commercial signs. The Court held that this was too heavy an infringement of the individual right of free expression and so struck down the law. The Court even suggested a different legislative scheme that would be constitutionally acceptable. The Court suggested that requiring the predominant display of the French language, even its marked predominance, would be proportional to the legitimate goal of promoting and maintaining a French "*visage linguistique*" in Quebec. Ultimately, even a subsequently elected separatist government in Quebec accepted this suggestion by the Court to be a just way to deal with cultural self-determination while respecting the human rights of all the province's citizens.[19]

In the rather complex interpretations of Section 1, it should never be forgotten that one of the most pre-eminent jurists in Canadian history, Chief Justice Dickson, in *R. v. Oakes,* focused upon the final words of Section 1 as they were seen to be "the ultimate standard against which a limit on a right or freedom must be shown, despite its effect [...]."[20] Chief Justice Dickson argued that because Canada is a free and democratic society, the courts must be guided in interpreting Section 1 by the values inherent in concepts such as,

> respect for the inherent dignity of the human person, commitment to social justice and equality, accommodation of a wide variety of beliefs, respect for cultural and group identity, and faith in social and political institutions which enhance the participation of individuals and groups in society.[21]

There can be no better conclusion as to what constitutes the fundamental values that must underpin multi-ethnic states if minority rights are to be protected.

What is the relevant knowledge that China could learn from this Canadian experience?

First, while minorities are only approximately nine percent of China's population, that accounts for over 110 million people and the numbers are growing. The territories where most minorities live contain most of China's natural resources. While official China often talks of the grim struggle with separatist or "splittist" forces, in the long run the strength of China's territorial integrity will, in my view, depend in large measure upon how the PRC government enhances ethnic relations and minority rights.

While many in China would argue that the constitutional and legal structure of minority rights in China, including the provisions for limited autonomy and ethnic self-rule, together with the proliferation of preferential policies, do benefit minorities, some experts within and outside China point out three critical weaknesses[22]:

First, the law and Constitution of China have yet to provide unquestionable genuine autonomy to minority areas. Such autonomy involves fewer powers than are minimally required to ensure cultural self-determination. The PRC Constitution refers to regional autonomy for minorities living in compact communities who are free to "preserve or reform their own ways and customs" (Article 4). The *Law on Regional Autonomy* (LRA) that implements the Constitution both sets out and also restricts such autonomy. Such autonomy must be "under unified state leadership" and under the principle of "democratic centralism"; in other words, under CPC discipline. In addition, all self-governing organs of minorities must implement the laws and policies of the state (Article 4). Under Article 118 of the Constitution and Article 19 of the LRA, autonomous area laws and regulations that govern the exercise of autonomy must be approved by higher bodies. Those of the five autonomous regions, Inner Mongolia, Xinjiang, Guaggxi, Ningxia and Tibet, must be approved by the National People's Congress of China (NPCSC).[23]

Second, the policies and laws do not allow for sufficient economic autonomy to meet the challenge of bridging the gap between the Han majority and the various minorities. There is a large and growing income disparity between minorities and the Han majority population. There is a twenty to one wealth gap between the rapidly developing coastal areas and the minority northwestern provinces and within the minority areas there is a wage gap between the minority group peasants and the majority Han peasants. Some call this an "ethnic psychological imbalance" which can threaten the unity of the country.[24]

Third, there is insufficient protection against encroachment of cultural self-determination by the Han majority. In particular, minority leaders accepted by the Chinese government as legitimate representatives, such as a Xinjiang Governor, Adbulahat Abdurixit and an NPC Vice-Chair, Tomur Dawarnat, have argued strenuously against unlimited migration of those from the Han majority to minority areas. These leaders have voiced opposition to the plan to move 100,000 people, mostly from the Han majority, from the Three Gorges Dam site area to Xinjiang. Such cultural encroachment is also worsened by what some leading Chinese scholars call the affront to the dignity of minority peoples by the discriminatory attitudes of the Han majority (and Han minorities in autonomous areas), who regard many minorities as backwards and uncivilized in culture and education.[25]

In conclusion, both Canada and China have struggled with the evolution of minority rights in their multi-ethnic societies. In Canada, our constitutional, legal and societal evolution has come to recognize that minority rights constitute a central part of Canadian identity, unity and our competitive advantage in a global economy. In China, I suggest that much of the constitutional, legal and societal evolution of minority rights that occurred in the 1980s was premised on a planned economy, in which minority rights and preferences were regarded as part of the centrally-organized development of the state. Today, with globalization making non-minority areas of China such as the Special Economic Zones (SEZs) more autonomous than the autonomous regions themselves, with all of the attendant economic and social development benefits, some have suggested that it may be time to contemplate offering the minority autonomous regions the status of special cultural zones (SCZs), in which there could be permissible divergence from the unified leadership of the Party.[26] This could, in time, be the solution not only to the problem of separatist movements, but also generate a competitive advantage to China in the global economy as demonstated by the example of Canada.

ENDNOTES

1. See A. Stephan, "Federalism and Democracy: Beyond the U.S. Model," (1999) 10 *Journal of Democracy* 4, p. 19-34. For an excellent analysis of how federal structures in the Former Republic of Yugoslavia (FRY) did or did not contribute to its breakup, see S. Malesevic, "Ethnicity and Federalism in Communist Yugoslavia and its Successor States" in Yash Ghai, ed., *Autonomy and Ethnicity, Negotiating Competing Claims in Multi-Ethnic States* (Cambridge: Cambridge University Press, 2000), p. 147. The author's thesis is that regarding the value of federal arrangements for the maintenance of multi-ethnic societies, "A great deal depends on the historical, political and social conditions of the particular society. What is crucial is the way in which the agreement between the constituent units is reached."

2. See Neelan Tiruchelvam, "The Politics of Federalism and Diversity in Sri Lanka," in *Yash Ghai, op. cit.,* p. 198. The author, a friend and colleague, was a moderate Tamil scholar and jurist who paid with his life for his belief that constitutional reform in the direction of regional autonomy could resolve Sri Lanka's ethnic conflict. He was killed by a suicide bomber on 29 July 1999.

3. The annual reports of Amnesty International and Human Rights Watch continue to condemn the gross human rights violations and lack of effective democratic institutions in both countries, see online: Amnesty International <http://www.amnesty.org>, Human Rights Watch <http://www.hrw.org>.

4. For a discussion of equality and the accommodation of differences between minority groups and majorities, see W. Kymlicka, *Multicultural Citizenship* (Oxford: Oxford University Press, 1995), p. 108-116.

5. For further discussion of this hotly contested view, see D. Milne, "Equality or Asymmetry: Why Choose?" in R. L. Watts and D. M. Brown, eds., *Options for a New Canada* (Toronto: University of Toronto Press, 1991), p. 285-307.

6. For details of Canada's demographics, see Census, 1996, online: Statistics Canada http://www.statcan.ca/Daily/English/050322/d050322b.htm. Eventually demands for equality by these groups may lead to a push for representation in elected bodies as an extension of the principle of federalism that regions should be represented in national institutions, see Kymlicka, *op. cit.,* p. 137.

7. For the landmark text which discusses and analyzes how the division of powers under the *Constitution Act, 1867* allows for asymmetry, even while symmetry predominates, see G-A. Beaudoin, *La Constitution du Canada : institutions, partage des pouvoirs, droits et libertés* (Montreal: Wilson & Lafleur, 1990).

8. See William H. Riker, "Federalism," in F. Greenstein and N. W. Posby, eds., *Handbook of Political Science* (Boston: Addison-Wesley, 1975), vol. 5, p. 93-172.

9   See Kymlicka, ed., *The Rights of Minority Cultures* (Oxford: Oxford University Press, 1995) for a collection of essays by some of the leading experts in the world on this theme.

10   See Kymlicka, *Multicultural Citizenship, op. cit.*, p. 10-130.

11   See A. Stephan, *op. cit.*, p. 53.

12   While not a classic federal state, Spain, through its autonomous communities, demonstrates some of the features of asymmetrical federalism, see Conversi, *op. cit.*, 122.

13   See Kymlicka, *Multicultural Citizenship, op. cit.*, p. 75-106.

14   Canadian Charter of Rights and Freedoms, Part 1 of the *Constitution Act, 1982*, Schedule B of the *Canada Act*, 1982 (U.K.) C.11 [*Charter*]. For one of the most comprehensive analyses of the provisions of the *Charter*, see, G.-A. Beaudoin and E. Mendes, eds., *The Canadian Charter of Rights and Freedoms, 3rd ed.* (Butterworths, 2005).

15   See M. Bastarche, ed., *Les droits linguistique au Canada* (Montreal: Yvon Blais, 1986).

16   [2000] 1 S.C.R. 3.

17   [1998] 2 S.C.R. 217.

18   [1988] 2 S.C.R. 712.

19   For a detailed discussion of this case, see E. P. Mendes, "Two Solitudes, Freedom of Expression and Collective Linguistic Rights in Canada: A Case Study of the Ford Decision," (1991-92) 1, *National Journal of Constitutional Law*, 283.

20   [1986] 1 S.C.R. 103 at 136.

21   *Ibid.*

22   Barry Sautman, "Legal Reform and Minority Rights in China," Hong Kong University of Science and Technology, Working Paper in the Social Sciences, No. 11, 9 May 1997.

23   *Ibid.*, p. 22-23.

24   *Ibid.*, p. 5.

25   *Ibid.*, p. 6, 15-21.

26   *Ibid.*, p. 39.

CHAPTER SIXTEEN

Indigenous Peoples and Hunting Rights

Scott Simon

INDIGENOUS PEOPLES AND HUNTING RIGHTS

The incorporation of indigenous hunter-gatherer peoples and their territories into modern nation-states, historically without their informed consent, has long provided human rights challenges to states and local communities. In the evolving international human rights regime, it has been slowly recognized that indigenous peoples have inherent rights due to their presence on and use of their traditional territories prior to the arrival of the modern nation-state. The United Nations (UN) *Declaration on the Rights of Indigenous Peoples*, passed by the General Assembly on 13 September 2007, is only the most recent addition to international customary law on indigenous issues.[1]

Hunting and fishing practices, which sometimes conflict with other uses of territory conceived by state administrators and other actors, may seem unrelated to human rights. Yet, they are emotionally salient to indigenous people as part of their culture and identity; and they are central to issues of autonomy. These traditional practices, relevant to indigenous peoples in Canada and Taiwan, are important issues in the process by which states have recognized the legitimacy of indigenous ways of life. They have become central to indigenous political and legal demands.

This paper looks at the issue of indigenous rights to traditional means of subsistence and resource utilization, referring to the experience of the Cree Nation of Eeyou Istchee[2] and the Taroko Nation on Taiwan.[3] In Quebec and Canada, the legal recognition of hunting rights has been among the main demands of indigenous peoples and has historically been written into nation-to-nation treaties with the Crown. In Taiwan, hunting rights are considered by many indigenous people to be central to their demands and are sometimes the centre of emotionally charged protests against national parks. These rights have also been included in legislation for indigenous rights.

It is important for scholars of indigenous rights to understand how indigenous peoples in different legal contexts have negotiated and continue to negotiate these rights. This paper does so through a comparison of the Cree of Quebec and the Taroko of Taiwan. There are a number of reasons to compare these two indigenous nations from these two particular jurisdictions. First, the indigenous peoples of both places are egalitarian hunting-gathering peoples who perceive nature as a sacred land regulated by the ancestors and based on relations of respect with animals. Second, they both face a positivist legal regime of civil law that would seemingly deny the existence of indigenous legal orders before the arrival of law-based state regimes.[4] Third, they both have been negotiating new relations with the State in recent years within the evolving framework of indigenous rights. Finally, both of these indigenous peoples are political actors in democratic societies with similar contexts of struggle over nationalism and sovereignty. These similarities make it possible to make meaningful comparisons and for the communities in both places to learn from each other's experiences.

This paper focuses on the following questions. How has hunting come to be perceived as an indigenous right in international law, as well as in these two jurisdictions? How do hunting rights articulate with other rights, such as environmental and development rights? What makes it possible for indigenous peoples in some contexts to demand the recognition of these rights; whereas it is more difficult in other places? In order to begin to address these questions, it shall be necessary to summarize the concepts of indigenous peoples and subsistence rights in the evolving norms of international law.

INDIGENOUS RIGHTS AND TRADITIONAL ECONOMIC PRACTICES

Many Asian countries have either been reluctant to recognize the existence of indigenous peoples in their territories (e.g. Japan) or have claimed that, with the exception of immigrants, all of their people are indigenous (e.g. Malaysia). In Asia, only the Philippines and Taiwan have legally recognized the existence of indigenous peoples within their jurisdictions. This legal recognition conforms with the so-called "Cobo Definition" proposed by José Martinez Cobo to the UN.[5] This definition consists of four characteristics: 1) historical continuity with societies preceding colonialism or invasive settlement from outside the territory under consideration; 2) self-definition as distinct from other sectors of societies; 3) a position of non-dominance; and 4) a determination to continue to exist as peoples.

The Austronesian peoples on Taiwan, including the Taroko, clearly fit into this definition. First, they have historical continuity with societies existing on the island before Chinese settlement in the 17th century. Those in the mountains and parts of the East Coast of the island were known as "raw barbarians" (*shengfan*) because they were not assimilated into Chinese culture or submissive to Qing administrative control. They were incorporated into the administration apparatus of the modern nation-state only after military conquest by the Japanese and the 1895 Treaty of Shimonoseki that ceded sovereignty over Taiwan to Japan. They self-identify as indigenous peoples, form non-dominant sectors of society, and are determined to develop and transmit their existence as peoples in accordance with their own cultures and institutions. The Cree also possess all four characteristics of the Cobo Definition.

Historically, states have been reluctant to recognize the existence of indigenous *peoples* with collective rights within their national territories, preferring to deal with the individual rights of indigenous *people*. Considering that Article 1 of the UN Charter calls for "self-determination of peoples" and Article 73 gives provisions to "non-self-governing territories" to achieve self-government,[6] many states have feared that recognition of indigenous rights could lead to separatist claims and fragmentation of their national territory. In fact, however, indigenous claims have been less ambitious, calling for new relations within existing states rather than for judicial independence. Those peoples, such as the Palestinians and East Timorese, who seek the establishment of independent states, have historically done so outside of the judicial framework of indigenous rights. Customary international legal practice, therefore, would add a fifth characteristic to a definition of indigenous peoples: they seek self-government *within* established nation-states rather than statehood of their own. *Indigenous rights should not be confused with separatist movements.*

Indigenous rights, like other forms of collective rights, have gradually entered the international human rights regime. The 1948 *Universal Declaration of Human Rights* concerns principally individual rights and says nothing about the collective rights of indigenous peoples.[7] The first international legal instrument to specifically address the rights of indigenous and tribal peoples was the 1957 International Labour Organization Convention No. 107 (ILO 107), concerning the "Protection and Integration of Indigenous and Other Tribal and Semi-Tribal Populations in Independent Countries."[8] Governments at the time thought that the best way to advance the health and well-being of indigenous peoples was through integration and assimilation into mainstream societies. There was no mention of rights to subsistence and traditional use of natural resources.

ILO 107 was signed by 28 countries. It was not ratified by Canada; nor was it possible for the People's Republic of China (PRC) to sign it as they were not members of the UN in 1957. Chiang Kai-shek's Republic of China, however, did sign ILO 107 in 1962 when they were still China's representative in the UN and other international organizations.[9] They did this partly with the intent to demonstrate to the world that they treated their tribal populations better than did the People's Republic, which had put down an uprising in Tibet in 1959.

IOL 107 was broadly rejected by indigenous peoples who called for recognition as separate and distinct peoples. It was revised and replaced by ILO 169, which was drafted in 1988 and 1989 with the participation of indigenous representatives as well as states. This new way of drafting international conventions, which provided the precedent for the UN *Declaration*, was possible in the ILO because they traditionally operated on the principle of union representation as well as state involvement. The guiding principle of

ILO 169 is that indigenous and tribal peoples have the inherent right to continue their existence with their own culture and identities, as well as to determine their own way and pace of development.

In terms of traditional economic activities, the Convention highlights the importance of traditional economies for culture and economic self-reliance, the value of traditional knowledge and technology, the need to promote traditional economies, the need to provide enough land for such economies, and the responsibility of states to provide the financial and technical assistance needed to continue traditional economic practices in a sustainable way.[10] Article 23 is quite clear in regard to hunting rights:

Article 23
1. Handicrafts, rural and community-based industries, and subsistence economy and traditional activities of the peoples concerned, such as hunting, fishing, trapping and gathering, shall be recognized as important factors in the maintenance of their cultures and in their economic self-reliance and development. Governments shall, with the participation of these peoples and whenever appropriate, ensure that these activities are strengthened and promoted.
2. Upon the request of the peoples concerned, appropriate technical and financial assistance shall be provided wherever possible, taking into account the traditional technologies and cultural characteristics of these peoples, as well as the importance of sustainable and equitable development.[11]

Parallel with ILO work on this issue, the UN Economic and Social Council established the Working Group on Indigenous Populations (WGIP) in 1982 with a mandate to determine minimum standards of human rights for indigenous peoples. During the drafting of the UN *Declaration*, 1995 to 2004 was recognized as the International Decade of the World's Indigenous People and 2005 to 2015 as the Second International Decade of the World's Indigenous Peoples.[12] In June 2006, the Draft Declaration was adopted by the UN Human Rights Council. On 13 September 2007, the UN *Declaration on the Rights of Indigenous Peoples* was adopted by the UN General Assembly with 143 votes in favour, four against, and eleven abstentions. China voted in favour, whereas Canada voted against. In the spirit of ILO 169, Article 20 protects the right of indigenous peoples to engage freely in traditional economic activities:

Article 20
1. Indigenous peoples have the right to maintain and develop their political, economic and social systems or institutions, to be secure in the enjoyment of their own means of subsistence and development, and to engage freely in all their traditional and other economic activities.
2. Indigenous peoples deprived of their means of subsistence and development are entitled to just and fair redress.[13]

For cultural and economic reasons, therefore, indigenous peoples have the right to pursue lifestyles that include hunting, fishing, trapping and gathering. States are encouraged to strengthen and promote these activities, giving financial and technical assistance when possible and compensating those groups who have been deprived of these resources. These practices, however, do not only involve human beings; they also affect wildlife in a global context of broader environmental destruction, loss of habitat, and extinction of animal species. Unsustainable hunting and trapping affect not only wildlife, but also plants dependent on wildlife for pollination and seed dispersal.[14] It is thus important to consider environmental rights at a wider level when setting policies on this issue.

ENVIRONMENTAL CONCERNS AND INDIGENOUS HUNTING

More than two decades of international cooperation on sustainable development and environmental protection has led to a consensus that indigenous peoples, due to their traditional knowledge of the wilderness, have an important role to play in the future of our planet. Principle 22 of Agenda 21, written in Rio de Janeiro at the UN Conference on Environment and Development, states clearly that:

> Indigenous people and their communities and other local communities have a vital role in environmental management and development because of their knowledge and traditional practices. States should recognize and duly support their identity, culture and interests and enable their effective participation in the achievement of sustainable development.[15]

The *Convention on Biological Diversity*, born at that meeting, has 188 parties and has become the main international platform for promoting sustainable development and poverty alleviation. Canada and China immediately signed the *Convention*, Canada ratifying it in 1992 and China in 1993. The Convention Secretariat is located on Mohawk territory in Montreal. Indigenous traditional knowledge and practices are integral to the *Convention*, as stated in its preamble:

> Recognizing the close and traditional dependence of many indigenous and local communities embodying traditional lifestyles on biological resources, and the desirability of sharing equitably benefits arising from the use of traditional knowledge, innovations and practices relevant to the conservation of biological diversity and the sustainable use of its components...[16]

Article 8 (j), the most important section for indigenous peoples, is considered central to the *Convention* and has a working group dedicated to the implementation of its principles and related provisions. Indigenous people are involved in all aspects of this group, including decision making. According to Article 8 (j),

> Each contracting Party shall, as far as possible and as appropriate:
> Subject to national legislation, respect, preserve and maintain knowledge, innovations and practices of indigenous and local communities embodying traditional lifestyles relevant for the conservation and sustainable use of biological diversity and promote their wider application with the approval and involvement of the holders of such knowledge, innovations and practices and encourage the equitable sharing of the benefits arising from the utilization of such knowledge innovations and practices.[17]

The main goals of Article 8 (j) are benefit-sharing, prior informed consent to development, the regulation and protection of sacred space, and protection of traditional knowledge. Voluntary policy guidelines negotiated in the Mohawk community of Kahnawake underscore the need for baseline studies of proposed development projects to include identification of traditional hunting and social impact assessment studies taking traditional economic activities such as hunting into consideration.[18] Acknowledging the value of indigenous knowledge about wildlife and related practices of hunting and trapping are thus integral to both indigenous rights and sustainable development. There is hope that indigenous knowledge can provide important guidelines for sustainable development and environmental protection worldwide.

Considering that wildlife populations continue to thrive in the traditional hunting territories of indigenous peoples, it is logical to assume that their practices have historically been sustainable. Research around the world does indeed show that hunting can be sustainable even if the meat is supplied to markets. In Ghana, for example, where bushmeat markets have existed for centuries, ecological research has demonstrated that they can be sustainable. Vulnerable taxa (slow reproducers) have been depleted rapidly in the past and are scarce, whereas robust taxa (fast reproducers) are still traded. The policy suggestion is thus to protect vulnerable species and permit trade in robust species.[19]

Indigenous traditional knowledge has long been concerned with sustainability and the reproductive capacity of animals. It is thus increasingly accepted that community wildlife management with full participation of local people can best contribute to sustainability.[20] At the same time, however, their territory is increasingly encroached upon by the activities of outsiders for such activities as forestry, mining, hydroelectric development, agriculture, and the creation of national parks or conservation areas without prior consultation. These activities, more dangerous to the habitat and to wildlife than hunting or gathering, make the job of wildlife management more difficult than ever. In this context, it is important to examine how indigenous peoples in different jurisdictions have gained hunting rights and the right to participate in regimes of environmental conservation and resource use. There are important lessons to learn from both the Cree and the Taroko.

THE CREE OF EEYOU ISTCHEE

The Cree of Eeyou Istchee constitute approximately 14,000 people on some 350,000 square kilometres in northern Quebec.[21] Since time immemorial, they have been a hunting people for whom the land is both a source of subsistence and a connection with their ancestors.[22] In the past, they were dispersed nomadic groups of egalitarian communities who moved frequently in search of wildlife, but eventually settled around the trading posts of the Hudson's Bay Company (HBC) in eight communities known as bands.[23] Early anthropological studies focused on the conflicts between these communities and the difficulties of dispersed hunting communities in establishing higher order political organizations.[24] In a relatively short period of time, however, the Cree proved them wrong not only by successfully challenging Quebec in court, but also emerging as international leaders in the assertion of indigenous rights. McGill University anthropologist Richard Salisbury described these changes as "an evolution from a village-band society to a regional society" and the creation of a Cree homeland.[25]

Eeyou Istchee was not included in early treaties between the Crown and indigenous nations of Canada. The HBC, which conducted the fur trade in the territory, "ceded" northern Quebec to Canada in 1871. The *Quebec Boundary Extension Acts* of 1898 and 1912 transferred the lands to Quebec jurisdiction with the proviso that Quebec must negotiate treaties settling indigenous land claims on that territory, just as Canada had long done.[26] Until 1971, the Cree had been largely left alone by Quebec, receiving some services from Ottawa but generally left to continue their hunting and trapping lifestyle.

In 1971, without consulting the Cree, Quebec Premier Robert Bourassa announced the James Bay Hydro Project which would flood major Cree hunting territories. The Cree, who had never ceded an inch of their territory nor negotiated a treaty with Quebec, perceived this as an invasion of their lands and took action. They withdrew from the Indians of Quebec Association, which had previously represented their interests in Quebec, and formed the Grand Council of the Crees of Quebec (GCC) in August 1974.[27] After intense negotiation and constant referral of each clause back to villages for discussion and approval by the Cree, the *James Bay and Northern Quebec Agreement* (JBNQA) was signed on 11 November 1975. This agreement, to which the Inuit were also signatories, is known as the first "modern" treaty concerning relations between indigenous nations and the State.

The JBNQA, in addition to financial compensation for flooded territory, created a land regime on the remaining territory in which different categories of rights would apply.[28] On Category I land, about 1.3 percent of the traditional territory, the Cree and Inuit would have permanent settlements in collective form. On Category II lands, about fifteen percent of the territory, the Cree and Inuit would have exclusive rights to wildlife for subsistence but no surface rights. Category III lands, about 83 percent of the territory, would be open to indigenous and non-indigenous people, but indigenous subsistence would take priority. Quebec maintained a "right to develop" Category II and III lands, subject to environmental assessment.[29]

The JBNQA institutionalized the organizations of Cree governance and service delivery. The GCC was the political body of the Cree,[30] with the Cree Regional Authority (CRA) established to deliver services. Each band would govern its reserve land as "municipal corporations." Provisions were made for autonomous boards in health and education, albeit under the jurisdiction of Quebec ministries and partially funded from Ottawa.[31]

The JBNQA established the organizations that would enforce Cree hunting rights. The Quebec-Cree Hunting Trapping and Fishing Coordinating Committee (HTFCC) was established to give the Cree and Quebec equal participation in policy decisions regarding wildlife use and conservation. Formally, the HTFCC only made recommendations to the relevant ministers, but any change from those recommendations required public justification.[32] An Income Security Program (ISP) for Hunters and Trappers was established to guarantee full-time hunters a minimum cash income fixed according to family size and a per diem allowance for each day spent in the bush. A Cree Trappers Association was also formed.[33] Through these institutions, the Cree were able to make decisions on wildlife, but Quebec still continued to introduce new projects including mines, roads, forestry, and hydro-electric projects.

These institutions were largely successful at meeting the needs of hunters, maintaining culture, and facilitating mutual aid in terms of meat sharing. The ISP led to an increase in the number of hunters in a viable subsistence economy, incorporating men and women, old and young.[34] Strengthening of the hunting economy further affirmed Cree autonomy and insured that its benefits would be widely spread, thus legitimizing the GCC and the CRA as representatives of the Cree. Problems continued to exist, largely because the HTFCC did not give the Cree adequate control over forestry[35] and because of conflict with non-indigenous sports hunters.[36]

Negotiating with Quebec, the Cree have defended their autonomy within a wider political context marked by debates about nationalism and sovereignty. In general, the pro-independence Parti Québécois (PQ) has been more favorable to indigenous autonomy than the Parti Libéral du Québec (PLQ).[37] In 1985, when the PQ was in government, the National Assembly passed a motion recognizing collective indigenous rights, including rights of harvesting, fishing, hunting, trapping, and participating in drafting wildlife policy.[38] Like most First Nations, however, the Cree nonetheless seemed to place more trust in Canada, which had incorporated Aboriginal and treaty rights in the *Constitution Act* of 1982 and its Charter of Rights and Freedoms.[39]

The Cree have done well in this context. After the Quebec government proposed the Great Whale River Project in 1988, the Cree and the Inuit lobbied against the project. They even mobilized international support by canoeing to New York City in protest. In a subsequent speech in Washington, Grand Chief Matthew Coon Come denounced the Quebec government as racist. In 1995, the Cree held their own referendum at the same time as the Quebec referendum, clearly showing their own preference to remain in Canada. These actions gave political clout to the Cree, as both Canada and Quebec hoped to gain and keep their support.[40] Most importantly, Quebec nationalists became aware that their posture toward First Nations would impact the international legitimacy of their own nationalist aspirations.

In 2002, Cree hunting and resource management rights were strengthened with the signing of the nation-to-nation *Agreement Concerning a New Relationship between the Cree Nation and the Government of Quebec*. In an improvement over the JBNQA, it increased revenue sharing with the indigenous peoples, involved the Cree more actively in economic development, recognized Cree traditional knowledge and authority at the level of kin-based hunting territories, and raised the status of those territories as management units. In order to better adapt forestry practices to Cree activities, a Cree-Quebec Forestry Board was established with five members appointed by the Cree, five by Quebec, and a chair acceptable to both. At the local level, joint working groups were also established with equal representation from the affected communities and the *Ministère des Ressources naturelles* (MRN). Cree hunting territory leaders were given greater management powers over certain areas, including one percent of each hunting territory that would be off-limits to forestry and 25 percent designated as under their direct responsibility.[41] These new measures were designed to increase hunters' rights, deepen Cree autonomy, and manage natural resources more sustainably with the incorporation of traditional knowledge. Even without Canada's support of the UN *Declaration*, the Cree have managed to assert their autonomy and implement much of its content in Quebec.[42]

THE TAROKO NATION OF TAIWAN

The Taroko of northeastern Taiwan, first classified as part of the Atayal tribe by Japanese anthropologists at the beginning of the last century, were legally recognized by the ROC Executive Yuan Council of Indigenous Peoples as an independent tribe in 2004.[43] They consist of some 23,383 people officially registered under that tribal affiliation.[44] Like the Cree, the Taroko have since time immemorial been a hunting people for whom the land is both a source of subsistence and a connection with the ancestors, or *utux rudan*.[45] In the past, they were also dispersed nomadic groups of egalitarian communities who moved frequently in search of wildlife. Although hunting is now restricted (see below), the men base their personal identity on hunting skills and take pride in their ability to return to the villages with such delicacies as flying squirrel, wild boar, and muntjac.

Like all indigenous nations in Taiwan and the Cree until 1975, the Taroko have never concluded a comprehensive land claim agreement or treaty with a state. If the Taroko were to get a land claim for all townships with a significant Taroko population, however, the land area would add up to at most 4,556 square kilometres including Xiulin, Wanrong, and Zhuoxi Townships of Hualian County and Renai Township in Nantou.[46] They thus have a larger population than the Cree, but a much smaller territory. The Taroko territory is rough mountainous terrain mostly covered with subtropical rainforest.

The Qing Dynasty had never administered the area claimed by the Taroko, who became subject to state control only after the Japanese conquest of their communities, particularly after Governor-General Sakuma Samata launched the "Five Year Plan to Subdue the Barbarians" in 1910. They thus had less early contact with modern states than the Cree, who had contact with the Hudson's Bay Company for generations and were regulated by the *Indian Act* since 1876.

Because of their lack of set territory or leadership roles, Japanese anthropologists considered the Taroko (as part of the Atayal) to be an "incomplete society."[47] Under Japanese administration (1895-1945), they were settled in the lowlands and encouraged to take up agriculture.[48] After the 1930 Wushe Incident, in which indigenous villagers rose up against the Japanese, all but two Taroko communities were forcibly relocated to the plains. Like the Cree, they were settled into bands and required to elect chiefs and village councils. The true power in the villages remained with the Japanese police officers, and even the institution of the chief was eliminated in 1939. The village council remained as a communication channel from the Japanese government to local communities.[49] The similarity with North American policies of establishing chiefdoms and band councils is not just fortuitous. Shortly after the Japanese had arrived on Formosa, American consul J.W. Davidson observed the problems Japan faced with the indigenous peoples there and provided them with materials on US Indian policy.[50]

Once the Japanese left Taiwan after the conclusion of the Second World War, administration of the island was given to the Republic of China under Chiang Kai-shek. In 1945, the new state created thirty "mountain townships" with different levels of government including the township with a township office, the village with a village office, and neighborhoods. In 1950, under the principle of "local autonomy" for indigenous communities, they established an electoral system for the township magistrate, the members of the township council, and village heads. In mountain townships, only aborigines were eligible to run for office. In effect, this policy established indigenous municipalities charged with implementing policies decided by others. It was a form of indirect rule that preserved indigenous communities as well as the social distinction between indigenous and non-indigenous peoples.

In spite of the existence of local democratic elections, it is important to remember that opposition parties were illegal in Taiwan until the lifting of martial law in 1987.

Until the liberalization towards the end of the martial law period, it was impossible for indigenous people to create their own organizations or launch protests like the Cree. Some individuals certainly learned important governance skills in the township governments. These institutions, along with the property rights regime of reserve land, also kept their ethnic identities alive. Yet they were unable to respond like the Cree when the ROC state imposed on them infrastructure projects including mines, hydroelectric projects, forestry, and the creation of national parks. Most of these projects restricted the land available to hunting and endangered the habitat of fauna.

In the 1980s, an indigenous social movement began to form, especially in urban areas. The movement began formally with the establishment of the *Mountain Greenery* (*Gaoshan Qing*) newspaper in 1983 and the foundation of the Alliance of Taiwan Aborigines (ATA) in 1984. One of the main objectives of the ATA was the creation of autonomous regions with corresponding legal recognition of resource rights. Throughout the 1990s, the Taroko of Hsiulin Township were active in the "Return our Land" movement, notably through protests against Asia Cement and the Taroko National Park. Another important social movement in Hualien was the Taroko Name Rectification Movement (*zhengming yundong*) based largely in the Taroko Synod of the Presbyterian Church and composed of some of the same cadres as the other movements. These social movements had international contacts with foreign missionaries, including Urban-Rural Mission (URM) trainers Dr. Ed File of York University and his Mohawk wife Donna Loft. Their work was influential in bringing ideas to Taiwan from the Canadian First Nations experience.[51] Throughout the social movement period, however, activists found that hunting and land were the *only issues* that could consistently mobilize large numbers of indigenous protesters.[52]

Like the Cree, the Taroko benefitted from a larger context in which nationalism and sovereignty were debated at a wider level. In 1999, delegates of all tribes including the Taroko and Sediq signed the "New Partnership between Indigenous Peoples and the Taiwan Government" with pro-independence Democratic Progressive Party (DPP) candidate Chen Shui-bian on Orchid Island. That document included the legal term natural rights (*ziran zhuquan*) to recognize that indigenous peoples were the original owners of Taiwan and have rights that precede the arrival of the state on Formosa. These include the right to high level autonomy. These electoral promises were further refined and discussed in the 2000 DPP White Paper on Aboriginal Policy; much of it to be subsequently adopted in the Kuomintang (KMT) White Paper on the same subject.[53] After legal recognition of the Taroko in 2004, the Taroko Nation Autonomous Region Promotion Team (*Tailugezhu Zizhiqu Tuidong Gongzho Xiaozu*) was created and began lobbying for the creation of an autonomous region, promising as well that autonomy would lead to hunting, trapping and fishing rights. They are now lobbying for co-management with the Taroko National Park, and have been successful in preventing a hotel project on that territory.

The most important legal change to come out of this two decade process of protest, lobbying, and negotiation was the *Basic Law on Indigenous Peoples* (*yuanzhuminzu jibenfa*), passed on 21 January 2005. Although as a basic law it still required all relevant laws and regulations to be redrafted and implemented, it did offer hope to indigenous peoples, including on the issue of hunting rights. Article 19 stipulated that:

> Indigenous persons may undertake the following non-profit seeking activities in indigenous peoples' regions: 1) Hunting wild animals; 2) Collecting wild plants and fungus; 3) Collecting minerals, rocks and soils; 4) Utilizing water resources. The above activities can only be conducted for traditional culture, ritual or self-consumption.[54]

In the absence of any substantive legal revisions, some township governments took it upon themselves to begin taking registrations and giving permits for limited catches for cultural and ritual purposes. These were generally defined as festivals or rituals when local people might need two to three wild boars. They did not consider other cultural reasons such as courtship, nor did they give permission to individuals to hunt for subsistence purposes. Police, however, continued to arrest hunters. The arrests angered the hunters even though the charges were consistently dropped in the courts.

In April 2007, hunters protested at the Taroko National Park, leading to a public apology by the Chief of the National Park Police. KMT legislator Kung Wen-chi (Yusi Dagun) subsequently held a public hearing at the Legislative Yuan encouraging revision of all relevant laws and suggesting that the DPP was not sincere about indigenous rights. Icyang Parod, DPP-appointed Minister of the CIP, said in November that it is the responsibility of the Legislative Yuan to pass relevant legislation, including that which will resolve the hunting problem. Just months before the 2008 presidential election these issues had not yet been resolved. It is important, however, that both the KMT and the DPP now feel a need to prove that they can best protect indigenous rights. The indigenous social movement on Taiwan has not had the same success as that in Canada, but it has managed to put indigenous rights, including hunting rights, on the political agenda.

CONCLUSIONS

In conclusion, there are a few lessons to learn from Quebec and Taiwan about indigenous human rights, including the rights to hunt, trap, and fish. The importance of these practices to indigenous peoples cannot be underestimated. As one study for the Canadian government found:

> A number of intangible and unquantifiable factors such as taste preferences, traditional food preparation and eating practices, the esteem in which a successful

hunter is held in a community, and the simple satisfaction of being in control of one's means of livelihood, combine to make any dollar estimate of the value of the Native renewable resource harvest totally inadequate from a Native person's perspective. Its loss or diminishment cannot be compensated for because there are no real substitutes.[55]

A number of points need to be made in conclusion to understand how hunting has become recognized as an indigenous right; and what the exercise of this right means for the Cree, the Taroko and other First Nations worldwide. First of all, the actions of indigenous peoples themselves have put hunting rights and indigenous autonomy on the international human rights agenda and on domestic political agendas. Even in Quebec, where the Canadian government had forced Quebec to recognize aboriginal title, the Cree were only able to claim and enforce their rights because they formed their own organizations, lobbied the government, pursued them in courts, and sought international allies. In Taiwan, the Taroko and other indigenous peoples were similarly able to form their own social movement and assert their rights, but only after a process of liberalization began in the 1980s and martial law was lifted. Indigenous rights thus need a democratic context including freedom of assembly and freedom of speech. Without these, even the most enlightened government cannot understand what issues are important to indigenous communities.

Second, both the Cree and the Taroko have been able to negotiate new relations with states on their respective territories within a wider political context in which national identity and sovereignty are already being questioned. In Quebec, the PQ has recognized that the international legitimacy of their own nationalist project depends very much on how well they respect indigenous rights. In Taiwan, the DPP has used indigenous peoples as a symbol of Taiwan's distinct identity, but has been slower than Quebec to make concrete change. It took Quebec four and a half years, from the announcement of the James Bay Project in April 1971 to the signing of the JBNQA, to recognize the inherent rights of the Cree and to negotiate a mutually acceptable agreement with them.

The Cree remain suspicious of both Quebec nationalism and Canadian federalism, but have become skilled at playing these two agendas off of each other in the promotion of their own rights. Chen Shui-bian recognized the natural rights (*ziran zhuquan*) of Taiwan's indigenous peoples in 1999. Yet, after eight years in office, the promised "new partnership" was not realized. It is not surprising that Taiwanese indigenous activists are disappointed, yet committed to pursuing these issues with a new government.

Finally, this research also shows that hunting rights and political autonomy are mutually reinforcing. On the one hand, formal political autonomy without control over subsistence or local industry risks creating conditions of dependency in which indigenous leaders have no way to exercise power without controlling and exploiting the people themselves.[56] On the other hand, the formalization of hunting rights including the creation of appropriate governing bodies is one of the most potent assertions of local sovereignty. The Cree have managed to increasingly assert sovereignty through the growing power of their HTFCC in forest management. On paper at least, the indigenous peoples of Taiwan are also gaining recognition of these rights. The Taroko have made important progress by creating the Taroko Nation Autonomous Region Promotion Team. Their next step will surely be forest co-management with the Taroko National Park and other authorities; steps that will of necessity include the creation of a hunters' organization like the Cree HTFCC.

Indigenous rights, including the rights to hunt, fish, trap and participate in other traditional economic activities, have become a part of the international human rights regime. These rights are still contested in many parts of the world, including Taiwan and Quebec. Progress has been made, but largely when indigenous communities have enjoyed democratic rights to association and expression. The result is increasing indigenous stewardship of natural resources, widely recognized as the best hope for sustainable development and poverty reduction. If the world really is committed to social justice and environmental sustainability, therefore, the struggle for indigenous rights is part of the struggle for a better world for all.

ACKNOWLEDGEMENTS

The author thankfully acknowledges the Social Sciences and Humanities Research Council of Canada for funding the research in Taiwan that made this paper possible, the Canadian International Development Agency for funding this symposium, as well as colleagues at the University of Ottawa and Peking University for their support.

ENDNOTES

1   Canada, along with the United States, Australia, and New Zealand, voted against the *Declaration*. Canada was concerned about issues of consent, access to natural resources, and the possibility that acceptance of the *Declaration* would open up the possibility of lawsuits regarding previously negotiated treaties with First Nations.

2   Eeyou Istchee means "people's land" in Cree. They call themselves Eeyouch. Although the Cree live across the subarctic areas of Canada, this paper focuses on the James Bay Cree of Northern Quebec.

3   Discussion of the Taroko is based on eighteen months of field research conducted by the author in Taiwan from 2004 to 2007. Discussion of the Cree is based on the relevant scientific literature.

4   Lajoie *et al.*, 2000, p. 172. Canada, by contrast, has common law, which is perceived as more likely to recognize actual practices in local communities as guides for emerging legal practice.

5   Indigenous communities, peoples and nations are those which have a historical continuity with pre-invasion and pre-colonial societies that developed on their territories, consider

themselves distinct from other sectors of societies now prevailing in those territories, or parts of them. They form at present non-dominant sectors of society and are determined to preserve, develop, and transmit to future generations their ancestral territories, and their ethnic identity, as the basis of their continued existence as peoples, in accordance with their own cultural patterns, social institutions and legal systems (Cobo, 1986, cited in Hodgson, 2002, p. 1039).

6   UN Charter, http://www.un.org/aboutun/charter/.

7   UN Universal Declaration of Human Rights. http://www.un.org/Overview/rights.html.

8   http://www.ilo.org/ilolex/cgi-lex/convde.pl?C107.

9   Iwan, 2005, p. 33.

10 The ILO provides assistance to state and indigenous groups, usually through NGO-based projects, to promote and implement ILO 169, including in countries that have not yet ratified it. As of December 2007, 19 countries had ratified it, the most recent being Nepal on 14 September 2007. Neither Canada nor China has ratified the *Convention*. Even in countries that have not ratified ILO 169, however, it is still recognized and used in many places as a guide to lobbying and policy making on indigenous issues.

11 http://www.ilo.org/ilolex/cgi-lex/convde.pl?C169.

12 The addition of the "*s*" in the second decade reflects a consensus that indigenous rights are collective rights that they share as peoples.

13 http://daccessdds.un.org/doc/UNDOC/GEN/N06/512/07/PDF/N0651207. pdf?OpenElement; this document is also available in Chinese at: http://daccessdds.un.org/ doc/UNDOC/GEN/N06/512/06/PDF/N0651206.pdf?OpenElement.

It should be noted that the Chinese term *tuzhu renmin* is considered pejorative because it has connotations of being attached to the soil, primitiveness, and savagery. On Taiwan, there has been considerable controversy about which term to use in Chinese. Due to the success of the indigenous social movement, the ROC state accepted in 1994 the term *yuanzhumin* (indigenous people) and incorporated it into the constitutional revisions of that year (Rudolph, 2003). *Yuanzhu minzu* (indigenous peoples) has become accepted usage in subsequent legislation.

14 Cowlishaw, Mendelson and Rowcliffe, 2005, p. 460.

15 United Nations General Assembly, "Report on the UN Conference on Environment and Development A/CONF.151/26 (Vol. 1)." http://www.un.org/documents/ga/conf151/ aconf15126-1annex1.htm.

16 http://www.cbd.int/doc/legal/cbd-un-en.pdf. The Chinese version is available at: http:// www.cbd.int/doc/legal/cbd-un-zh.pdf.

17 http://www.cbd.int/doc/legal/cbd-un-en.pdf. The Chinese version is available at: http:// www.cbd.int/doc/legal/cbd-un-zh.pdf.

18 Secretariat of the CBD, 2004, p. 17, 19.

19 Cowlishaw, Mendelson and Rowcliffe, 2005.

20 Bennett and Robinson, 2000; Noss *et al.*, 2004; Smith, 2003.

21 The total land area of Taiwan, for comparison, is only about 32,260 square kilometres.

22 Niezen, 2003, p. 66. The spiritual practices and values of Cree hunting and trapping have been well documented in the anthropological literature (Brightman, 2002; Tanner, 1979). These practices are important to both indigenous livelihoods and environmental sustainability, but remain outside of the scope of this paper.

23 Salisbury argues that year-round village life began only after 1947 when schools and medical clinics were established at these posts. He notes that the "band" refers to groupings that did not exist before contact with Europeans and are thus "administrative bands" created by the

Department of Indian and Northern Affairs (DINA) after the 1876 *Indian Act*. The smaller hunting groups of around twenty people might be called "micro-bands." Even in groups that previously had no chiefs, DINA required them to vote for a formal chief (Salisbury, 1986, p. 8-9).

24   Chance, 1968.

25   Salisbury, 1986, p. 12.

26   Salisbury, 1986, p. 54.

27   This entire process, which included long legal battles and social impact studies by anthropologists at McGill University, is chronicled by Salisbury, p. 53-60.

28   Excluded from this treaty were waterways, including the seashore, beds and shores of principal lakes and rivers, and a 200-foot strip on the shores. These exclusions were thus "held by the Crown in the right of Quebec" (Scott, 2001, p. 9).

29   Mulrennen and Scott, 2001, p. 80-81.

30   The National Office was located in Nemaska, with an additional office in Montreal and an Embassy in Ottawa. Interested readers are encouraged to consult the website of the GCC at: http://www.gcc.ca/.

31   Salisbury, 1986, p. 57.

32   Salisbury, 1986, p. 81.

33   Salisbury, 1986, p. 57.

34   Scott and Feit, 1992. Further, 45 percent of the beneficiaries were women (Scott and Feit, 1992, p. 80).

35   Feit and Beaulieu, 2001.

36   Scott and Weber, 2001.

37   Lajoie *et al.*, 2000, p. 178.

38   Lajoie *et al.*, 2000, p. 180.

39   Lindau and Cook, 2000, p. 14. Quebec did not sign the 1982 Constitution.

40   Morantz, 2002, p. 256.

41   Scott, 2005.

42   In October 2007, the Cree and Canada settled another set of legal issues in the *Agreement Concerning a New Relationship between the Government of Canada and the Crees of Eeyou Istchee*.

43   They are known officially as the Truku tribe in English translation. For information, see the website of the Executive Yuan Council of Indigenous Peoples: http://www.apc.gov.tw/english/docDetail/detail_ethnic.jsp?cateID=A000205&linkParent=151&linkSelf=151&linkRoot=101.

44   There are also more than 6,000 people in Nantou County who are eligible to register as Truku, but (with 81 exceptions as of October 2007) the vast majority of them have retained Atayal legal identity. Some of them prefer to be called members of the Sediq Nation, which was legally recognized by the ROC on 23 April 2008. Whether they call themselves Taroko or Sediq, all agree that they belong to one distinct ethnic group composed of speakers of three dialects: Truku, Teuda, and Tkedaya. For a history of the Taroko and Sediq name rectification movements, see Hara, 2003, 2004, 2005.

45   There is a nascent literature on this subject, including a study by Taroko hunter Huang Chang-hsing (2000) and an M.A. thesis (Liang 1996).

46   There are, however, other ethnic groups in those townships. The main problems would be that the Bunun are prevalent in Zuoxi and might prefer their own autonomous region, whereas the Sediq in Nantou do not wish to be part of the Taroko Nation. Of course, the presence of non-indigenous people does not preclude autonomy. In James Bay, for example,

there are over 100,000 non-indigenous Quebecers. For examples of Taroko nationalist literature outlining their plans for autonomy, see Siyat, 2004 and Tera, 2003.

[47] Wang, 2006, p. 30.

[48] By far the most detailed study of the resettlement history is the two-part article by Masaw (1977, 1978).

[49] Masaw, 1998, p. 48-49.

[50] Fujii, 1997, p. 151.

[51] For the role of the Presbyterian Church and foreign missionaries in Taiwan's indigenous social movement, see Rudolph, 2003; Simon, 2004; and Stainton, 1995.

[52] Rudolph, 2003, p. 401.

[53] See Simon, 2007.

[54] Resource Management Consultants, 1980, cited in Asch, 1990, p. 25.

[55] Niezen, 2003, p. 90.

Composed by Brad Horning in Adobe Garamond Pro 10 on 13

The paper used in this publication is Roland Opaque Natural 60 lb

PRINTED AND BOUND IN CANADA

Marquis Book Printing Inc.

Québec, Canada
2009

Sáenz Díaz, Manuel, 56
Sala Serra, F., 180
Sánchez de Toca, Joaquin, 154
Sánchez-Albornoz, Nicolás, 15, 56, 58, 64,
    83, 98, 100, 108, 111, 129–30, 207,
    253
Sandberg, L. G., 119
Sanz, Jésus, 247
Sardá, Juan, 152
Say, Jean Baptiste, 181
Senador, Julio, 243
Simón Segura, Francisco, 47
Simpson, James, 48–49, 56
Singer, H. W., 128, 207
Söderland, E. F., 202
Sotilla, Eduardo de la, 50
Spanish-American trade, 253–54
State intervention, in foreign trade, 155–58
Sudriá, Carles, 56

Tallada Paulí, J. M., 108
Tariff protection, in foreign trade, 155–58
Tartiere, José, 217
Tedde de Lorca, Pedro, 100, 103, 108, 113,
    114, 116, 122, 142, 143
Terms of trade, 131–34, 144–45
Torres, Manuel, 275
Tortella, Gabriel, 45, 56, 57, 58, 83, 96, 97,
    98, 100, 103, 108, 109, 110, 113, 122,
    142, 244
Transportation
    overland, 93–94
    railroad construction, 97–99
Trevilock, Clive, 199

Urbanization
    demographic trends and, 30–34
    regional variations in, 32–33

Valencia
    banking industry, 277
    citrus industry, 272–77
    manufacturing industry, 280–81
    viticulture, 269–72
Van Neck, Anne, 172
Velarde Fuertes, Juan, 160, 161
Vicens Vives, Jaume, 129, 152
Victoria de Lecea, Federico, 215
Villares Paz, Ramón, 223, 229, 233
Viticulture
    in Castile, 246–47
    in Valencia, 269–72

Wool manufacturing, in Castile, 245–46